Dedication

To my parents,
Helmien, Ellen and Jeroen

Economics and Management of Organizations
Co-ordination, Motivation and Strategy

George Hendrikse

The **McGraw·Hill** *Companies*

London	Boston	Burr Ridge, IL	Dubuque, IA	Madison, WI	New York
San Francisco	St. Louis	Bangkok	Bogotá	Caracas	Kuala Lumpur
Lisbon	Madrid	Mexico City	Milan	Montreal	New Delhi
Santiago	Seoul	Singapore	Sydney	Taipei	Toronto

George Hendrikse
Economics and Management of Organizations: Co-ordination, Motivation and Strategy
ISBN 0-07-709992-3

Published by McGraw-Hill Education
Shoppenhangers Road
Maidenhead
Berkshire
SL6 2QL
Telephone: 44 (0) 1628 502 500
Fax: 44 (0) 1628 770 224
Website: www.mcgraw-hill.co.uk

British Library Cataloguing in Publication Data
A catalogue record for this book is available from the British Library

Library of Congress Cataloguing in Publication Data
The Library of Congress data for this book has been applied for from the Library of Congress

Acquisitions Editor: Julian Partridge
Senior Development Editor: Caroline Howell
Editorial Assistant: Deborah Newcombe
Senior Marketing Manager: Petra Skytte
Production Editor: Eleanor Hayes

Cover design by Ego Creative
Text design by InPerspective
Page make-up by Northern Phototypesetting Co. Ltd, Bolton

Printed and bound in Spain by Mateu Cromo Artes Graficas SA, Madrid

ISBN: 0-07-709992-3

Brief
Table of Contents

Detailed
Table of Contents

Contents

Contents

Contents

Contents

Contents

Contents

Contents

Preface

This book is inspired by the exiting developments at the frontiers of the economics and management of organizations which have taken place since the end of the 1970s, and by the demand for a textbook which makes these insights accessible to students at the undergraduate and beginning-graduate levels. In the last three decades major shifts have taken place in how organizations are perceived and analysed. For example, the production technological perspective has been replaced by the contractual, while the analytical tool of real analysis has been superseded by game theory. The result has been many insights concerning situations with conflicting interests, the availability of information, authority, strategic interactions, bounded rationality and alignment. What is attractive about these developments is that they not only have reduced the tensions between the theory and practice of organizations, but also have diminished the differences between various fields like accounting, finance, logistics, organization and technology in areas such as business, economics, law, psychology and sociology. The hope is that students will get a sense of excitement about the new approaches to solving the economic and management problems of organizations. In attempting to avoid being overwhelmed by the wide array of theories and approaches which have been developed, it is helpful to observe that two main themes have emerged where the economics and management of organizations are concerned: the *co-ordination* and the *motivation* of strategically interacting persons. Moreover, the massive amount of material on these is organized round just two behavioural aspects: the degree of self-interest and the range of cognitive capacity of human decision-makers.

The book consists of seven parts. Part I introduces the themes of co-ordination and motivation by the law of comparative advantage. A framework of analysis and a classification scheme are presented for the systematic treatment of these themes in various settings. Part II formulates two classic results. They concern a society that starts out in a primitive state of nature (lacking any institutional details except property rights). These results serve henceforth as benchmarks in the sense that assumptions are specified in such a way that the choice of organization does not matter. Many organizational phenomena are explained in the next five parts by relaxing the assumptions of these benchmarks. Thus, throughout the book, organizations progressively develop modern characteristics. This gradual approach facilitates the explanation of what drives various organizational choices. Part III highlights various forms of asymmetric information in situations with conflicting interests, while authority in organizations is the focus of attention in Part IV. Part V formulates a typology for the strategic interactions between organizations. Limited cognition in organizations features in Part VI. Finally, Part VII brings the previous parts together by focusing on alignment. The organization of the material in each chapter is such that each insight is explained as much as possible in words, easy mathematics and figures, and is subsequently illustrated with various applications and exercises.

Acknowledgements

Many colleagues, secretaries and students have contributed to the structure and quality of the various successful Dutch editions of this book during the last decade. I would like to thank especially Rudi Wielers and Michael Rauh for their many valuable comments on the current revised and updated edition.

I have dedicated this book to my parents, Helmien, Ellen and Jeroen. They not only confirm, each in his or her own way, the breadth of the ideas and concepts presented but also indicate repeatedly, intentionally or otherwise, the limitations of the starting positions adopted and the method of analysis employed.

George Hendrikse
Rotterdam, November 2002

The publishers would like to thank the following reviewers for their helpful advice and comments on the book as it progressed through its draft chapters to the final text:

Svetlana Andrianova, University of Loughborough
Thankom Arun, University of Ulster
John Chard, University of Exeter
Clive Lewis, Buckinghamshire Chilterns University College
Catherine Liston-Heyes, Royal Holloway, University of London
John Lucas, University of Salford
Jester Norus, Copenhagen Business School, Denmark
Claudio Piga, University of Nottingham
Indra Ray, University of York
Michael Rauh, University of Liverpool
Pierre Regibeau, University of Essex
Andrew Robinson, University of Leeds
John Scouller, University of Strathclyde
Annabel Sels, University of Tilburg, The Netherlands
William Sjostrom, University College, Cork, Ireland
Louis Slangen, Wageningen University, The Netherlands
Steve Thompson, University of Leicester
Hans Van Ees, University of Groningen, The Netherlands
Dirk Willenbockel, University of Middlesex
Ulrich Woitek, University of Glasgow

The publishers would also like to thank the following organizations for their permission to reproduce material from their publications in this textbook:

Administrative Science Quarterly
Cambridge University Press
Joel Demski – permission to use Figure from *Information Analysis*, Wesley, 1980
Journal of Agricultural Economics
Journal of Law and Economics
RAND Journal of Economics
Pearson Education Limited
Simon & Schuster
The Economic Journal
The University of Chicago Press

Every effort has been made to trace and acknowledge copyright and to clear permission for material produced in this book. The publishers will be pleased to make suitable arrangements to clear permission with any copyright holders whom it has not been possible to contact.

Guided Tour

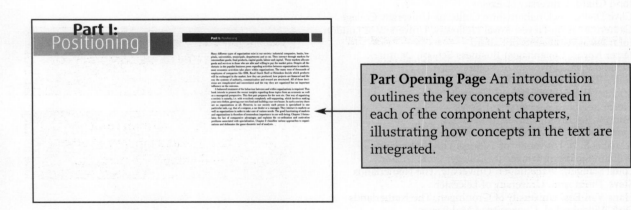

Part Opening Page An introductiion outlines the key concepts covered in each of the component chapters, illustrating how concepts in the text are integrated.

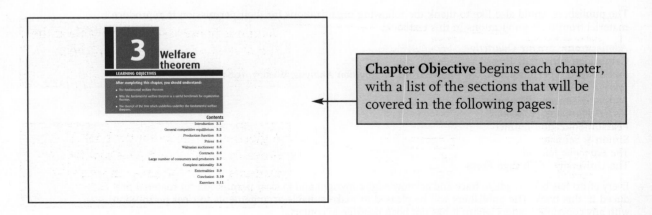

Chapter Objective begins each chapter, with a list of the sections that will be covered in the following pages.

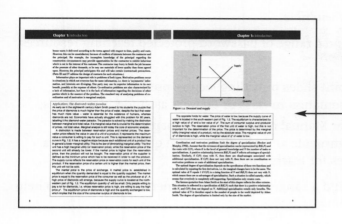

Application boxes provide examples that apply the ideas and theories presented within the chapter.

Clear figures and graphs also help to illustrate the theory described in the text.

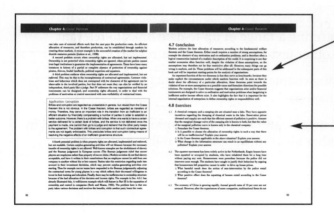

End of chapter conclusions sum up the ideas that have been discussed in each chapter.

Exercises provide questions and problems for students to test whether they have understood the material.

Solutions to exercises are available at the end of the text so students can check their progress.

A glossary at the end of the book provides a useful reference tool for students as they progress through the material.

Teaching and Learning Resources

A variety of teaching resources for lecturers and learning materials for students can be found at the Online Learning Centre website for this book, at:

www.mcgraw-hill.co.uk/textbook/hendrikse

Lecturers visiting the site will find a range of password-protected teaching resources, including:

- Chapter-by-chapter PowerPoint slides providing lecture presentations of the material in the book for presentation in class or delivery as student handouts;
- A chapter-by-chapter Lecturer Manual offering a brief chapter synopsis and suggestions for further assignments and exercises, exam questions and extra sources, reading and websites for teaching purposes.

Students visiting the site will find a range of extra supplementary materials to help them with their module, including:

- A Glossary of Key Terms providing the opportunity to revise and test comprehension of new concepts;

- Suggested Further Reading offering a range of up-to-date links to relevant websites and suggestions for other text-based sources for research;

- Student Test Questions offering chapter-by-chapter quick tests to recap and revise the key ideas in each chapter;

- Case Examples featuring real organizations, supplementing the applications in the textbook and pulling together ideas into applied, real-life case studies.

Part I:
Positioning

Many different types of organization exist in our society: industrial companies, banks, hospitals, universities, municipalities, departments and so on. They interact through markets for intermediate goods, final products, capital goods, labour and capital. These markets allocate goods and services to those who are able and willing to pay the market price. Despite all the rhetoric in the popular business press regarding activities between organizations in markets, most economic activities take place within organizations. The many tens of thousands of employees of companies like IBM, Royal Dutch Shell or Heineken decide which products will be exchanged in the market, how they are produced, how projects are financed and the way the systems of authority, communication and reward are structured. All of these decisions are complicated and interrelated and the way they are organized has an important influence on the outcome.

A balanced treatment of the behaviour between and within organizations is required. This book intends to present the recent insights regarding these topics from an economic as well as a managerial perspective. This first part prepares for the next six. One way of organizing a society is autarky, i.e. with everybody completely self-supporting, which involves making your own clothes, growing your own food and building your own house. In such a society there are no organizations at all. However, in our society each person is specialized in one particular task, e.g. that of a surgeon, a car dealer or a manager. They interact in markets as well as organizations in order to take care of various needs. The good functioning of markets and organizations is therefore of tremendous importance to our well-being. Chapter 1 formulates the law of comparative advantages and explains the co-ordination and motivation problems associated with specialization. Chapter 2 classifies various approaches to organizations and delineates the game-theoretic tool of analysis.

1 Introduction

After completing this chapter, you should understand:

- Why specialization is desirable.

- Which problems are associated with additional specialization.

- Why organizatiional efficiency is at least as important as maket efficiency.

- Which levels of institutional analysis can be distinguished.

Contents

Specialization and exchange can generate tremendous benefits (Sec. 1.1), but the associated coordination and motivation problems require efficient organizations (Sec. 1.2). Section 1.3 claims that the efficient design of organizations is at least as important as the good functioning of markets in order to establish the desired level of specialization and smooth exchange. Section 1.4 concludes.

1.1 Specialization and exchange

The available resources (time, money, capacities) of a person are limited, which implies that choices have to be made. A person, company or country can try to be completely self-supporting, but this section will show that the output of an organization, a society or a number of countries will increase when everyone specializes and the resulting goods and services are exchanged.

Hardly anyone is completely self-supporting in a modern economy. Labour is offered to perform specific productive tasks in exchange for money. The income earned is used to buy goods and services. *Specialization and exchange* make it possible for people to produce many more goods and services together than if everyone was completely self-supporting with respect to food, clothes, transportation and housing. Adam Smith observed more than 200 years ago that specialization, and the implied division of labour, can result in tremendous increases in productivity. He identified as the three important causes for the attractiveness of specialization the increased level of skill, the greater possibilities of mechanization and the shorter time wasted in switching from one task to the next. A famous quote from the *Wealth of Nations* (1776) illustrates this:

> To take an example, therefore, from a very trifling manufacture; but one in which the division of labour has been very often taken notice of, the trade of the pin-maker; a workman not educated to this business (which the division of labour has rendered a distinct trade), nor acquainted with the use of the machinery employed in it (to the invention of which the same division of labour has probably given occasion), could scarce, perhaps, with his utmost industry, make one pin in a day, and certainly could not make twenty. But in the way in which this business is now carried on, not only the whole work is a peculiar trade, but it is divided into a number of branches, of which the greater part are likewise peculiar trades. One man draws out the wire, another straights it, a third cuts it, a fourth points it, a fifth grinds it at the top for receiving the head; to make the head requires two or three distinct operations; to put it on, is a peculiar business, to withen the pins is another; it is even a trade by itself to put them into the paper; and the important business of making a pin is, in this manner, divided into about eighteen distinct operations, which, in some manufactories, are all performed by distinct hands, though in others the same man will sometimes perform two or three of them. I have seen a small manufactory of this kind where ten men only were employed, and where some of them consequently performed two or three distinct operations. But though they were very poor, and therefore but indifferently accommodated with the necessary machinery, they could, when they exerted themselves, make among them about twelve pounds of pins in a day. There are in a pound upwards of four thousand pins of a middling size. Those ten persons, could make among them upwards of forty-eight thousand pins in a day. Each person, therefore, making a tenth part of forty-eight thousand pins, might be considered as making four thousand eight hundred pins in a day. But if they had all

wrought separately and independently, and without any of them having been educated to this particular business, they certainly could not each of them have made twenty, perhaps not one pin in a day; that is certainly, not the two hundred and fortieth, perhaps not the four thousand eight hundredth part of what they are at present capable of performing, in consequence of a proper division and combination of their different operations.

An explanation for this specialization and the exchange of goods and services is the *law of comparative advantages*. This states that individuals, companies or countries benefit together from specializing in the activities they are relatively good at. Specialization will be advantageous to society. This insight will be illustrated with an example and will then subsequently be formulated more precisely.

Different people possess different capacities and skills. These differences can blossom when people specialize. Specialization implies a *division of labour*. It entails that the production process is divided into a number of simple steps, so that a person (or a machine) can dedicate himself completely to one step in the production process. People are more productive when they specialize. The optimal division of tasks is determined by one person's ability relative to the ability of others. The concepts of 'absolute advantage' and 'comparative advantage' are used in this respect.

Someone has an *absolute advantage* when he can produce a good or service in less time or with less resources than another person. If everyone has an absolute advantage in a different task then it is clear that specialization is attractive. The production of this book required the drawing of figures and research of the scientific literature. My secretary and I could each have taken care of half of both activities. The absolute advantage of my secretary compared with me in processing figures, and my own absolute advantage compared with my secretary in the research of the scientific literature, make it clear that each person should carry out the task he or she has an absolute advantage in. This results in the highest level of production.

It can also occur that a person is better in both activities than the other, i.e. has an absolute benefit in both activities. Assume that Jones and Williams take care of the production of pins in the above passage from Adam Smith, in which the production of pins consists of making points and heads. Jones can make 100 points, 100 heads or a combination of both, for instance 80 points and 20 heads, in one day. Williams is less productive in both activities. His capabilities enable him to make a maximum of 30 points, 60 heads or a combination of both in one day. Figure 1.1 shows the production possibilities lines of Jones and Williams. Jones has an absolute benefit in both activities compared with Williams, because his production possibilities line lies entirely above that of Williams.

Jones is able to produce 70 points and 30 heads during a day. This is shown by point A in Fig. 1.1. Williams can choose B, which means a production of 20 points and 20 heads during a day. The question arises whether another allocation of the time of Jones and Williams can result in a higher production for Jones and Williams together. If Jones concentrates on the production of points (C) and Williams on the production of heads (D), then the output of points increases from $70 + 20 = 90$ to $100 + 0 = 100$, and the output of heads from $30 + 20 = 50$ to $0 + 60 = 60$! The explanation for this surprising result is that the production of heads by Jones is taken over by the person who is *relatively* most productive in

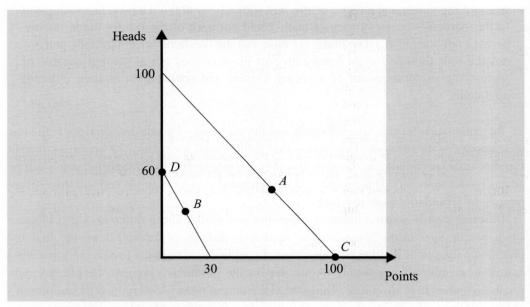

Figure 1.1: Production possiblities lines

this task, i.e. Williams, while the production of points is completely taken care of by Jones. Jones is less efficient in producing heads than Williams.

This result can be explained further by the notion of *opportunity cost*. The opportunity cost of a certain choice is defined as the value of the best alternative choice available. For example, Jones can do two things during a day: make points or make heads. The time he needs to produce a point can also be used to produce a head. Both activities are equally time-consuming for Jones. The opportunity costs of the production of one point are therefore equal to one head for Jones. To produce one point, he needs to give up the production of one head.

For Williams, the opportunity costs of producing one point are higher than they are for Jones. For Williams, each additional point produced comes at a cost of two heads. Jones has the lowest opportunity costs and therefore a *comparative advantage* in the production of points. A person has a comparative advantage in the production of a good (or service), compared with the production of another good, when he performs the task relatively better than someone else. Williams has a comparative advantage in producing heads compared with Jones, because the slope of his production possibilities line is steeper. Notice that Jones has an absolute advantage in both activities – but this does not tell us who specializes in doing what. The thing that decides who specializes in what is the difference in opportunity costs. The comparative advantage determines who should specialize in which activity in order to generate the highest level of production of all persons together. This result is known as the *law of comparative advantages* (Ricardo, 1821).

Law of comparative advantages. The total output (production) of a group (persons, companies, countries) is largest when each good or service is produced by the person with the lowest opportunity costs (the comparative advantage).

1.2 Co-ordination and motivation

The law of comparative advantages demonstrates that specialization can be very beneficial. However, there are costs involved, because all kinds of interdependencies are created. Tasks are divided between various people, so that everyone needs others for parts of their work. Each has become *dependent* on the other. Motorists need gasoline from oil companies, oil companies need employees, employees need housing and so on. Another example of interdependency is the effects of a payrise. If a successful salary demand of employees cannot be included in the prices then it will result in a decrease in the firm's profits. However, if the increase of costs can be included in the price of the good or service then customers may go to another supplier. As a result, employees may be fired, which is likely to be unpleasant for all concerned.

Bilateral and multilateral dependencies and differences are everywhere in organizations, and March and Simon (1993) highlight this in their characterization of organizations as

> systems of coordinated action among individuals and groups whose preferences, information, interests, or knowledge differ.

This definition implies a focus in the research that is conducted into organizations:

> Organization theories describe the delicate conversion of conflict into cooperation, the mobilization of resources, and the coordination of effort that facilitate the joint survival of an organization and its members.
>
> These contributions to survival are accomplished primarily through control over information, identities, stories and incentives. Organizations process and channel information. They shape the goals and loyalty of their participants. They create shared stories – an organization ethos that includes common beliefs and standard practices. They offer incentives for appropriate behaviors.
>
> Effective control over organizational processes is limited, however, by the uncertainties or ambiguities of life, by the limited cognitive and affective capabilities of human actors, by the complexities of balancing trade-offs across time and space, and by threats of competition.
>
> As organizational actors deal with each other, seeking cooperative and competitive advantage, they cope with these limitations by calculation, planning, and analysis, by learning from their experience and the experience and knowledge of others, and by creating and using systems of rules, procedures, and interpretations that store understandings in easily retrievable form. They weave supportive cultures, agreements, structures, and beliefs around their activities . . . We try to understand how collections of individuals and groups coordinate themselves in relatively systematic ways.

Two important topics for the study of organizations can be extracted from this description: co-ordination problems and motivation problems. These are a direct result of specialization. (Part VI is dedicated to co-ordination problems.) Building a house asks for – among other things – a certain amount of stones, wood and pipelines which have to be processed by masons, carpenters and plumbers in a specific time order. Co-ordination between these parties is required, even though they have joint interests. Motivation problems are addressed by designing incentives in order to reduce conflicts of interests. The principal in the building of a house wants it delivered according to the terms agreed with respect to time, quality and costs. However, this can be unsatisfactory because of conflicts of interests between the contractor and the principal. For example, the incomplete knowledge of the principal regarding the construction circumstances may provide opportunities for the contractor to exhibit behaviour which is not in the interest of his customer. The contractor may hurry to finish the job because of the pressure of other demands, or he may use materials of lower quality than those agreed upon. However, the principal anticipates this and will take certain (contractual) precautions. (Parts III and IV address the design of contracts for such situations.)

Information plays an important role in problems of both types. Motivation problems occur in situations in which not everyone has the same information, i.e. there is 'asymmetric' information, and interests are diverging. One party may use its superior information to its own benefit, possibly at the expense of others. Co-ordination problems are also characterized by a lack of information, but here it is the lack of information regarding the decisions of other parties which is the essence of the problem. The standard way of analysing problems of co-ordination and of motivation is *marginal analysis*.

Application: The diamond–water paradox

As early as in the eighteenth century Adam Smith posed to his students the puzzle that the price of diamonds is much higher than the price of water, despite the fact that water has much more value – water is essential for the existence of humans, whereas diamonds are not. Economists have actually struggled with this problem for 80 years, labelling it the *diamond–water paradox*. The paradox is solved by making the distinction between marginal and total value. It is marginal value that is crucial for the determination of prices, not total value. *Marginal analysis* is still today the core of economic analysis.

A distinction is made between reservation prices and market prices. The *reservation price* reflects the value in use of a unit of a product. It represents the maximum value a consumer is willing to pay for such a unit. This is represented on the demand curve in Fig. 1.2. It has a negative slope because each additional unit of a product has in general a lower marginal utility. This is the *law of diminishing marginal utility*. The first unit has a high marginal utility (or reservation price), while the reservation price of the second unit will already be lower. If the market price is higher than the reservation price, then the product will not be bought. The reservation price of the supplier is defined as the minimum price which has to be received in order to sell the product. The supply curve reflects the reservation price or reservation costs for each unit of the product. If the reservation price of a certain unit is higher than the market price, then this unit will not be sold.

The *market price* is the price of exchange. A market price is established in equilibrium when the quantity demanded is equal to the quantity supplied. The market price is equal to the reservation price of the consumer as well as the producer at q^*. A high price of diamonds will emerge, because the supply curve is located at the north-western part of Fig. 1.2. The equilibrium quantity q^* will be small. Only people willing to pay a lot for diamonds, i.e. whose reservation price is high, are willing to pay the high price p^*. The equilibrium price of diamonds is high and the quantity exchanged is low, which implies that the size of the consumer surplus of diamonds is low.

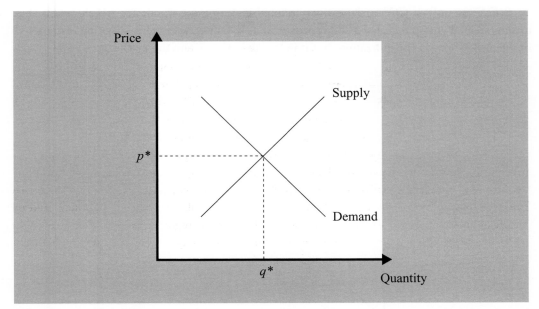

Figure 1.2: Demand and supply

The opposite holds for water. The price of water is low, because the supply curve of water is located in the south-eastern part of Fig. 1.2. The equilibrium is characterized by a high value of q^* and a low value of p^*. The sum of consumer surplus and producer surplus is high. The reservation price of the first unit of water is high, but this is not important for the determination of the price. The price is determined by the marginal utility (marginal value) of a product, not by the absolute value. The marginal value of unit q^* of diamonds is high, while the marginal value of q^* of water is low.

Co-ordination and motivation problems limit the *degree of specialization* (Becker and Murphy, 1992). Assume that the revenues of specialization can be represented by $B(K,N)$ and the costs with $C(N)$, where K is the level of general knowledge and N the number of tasks or specializations. A positive relationship between $B(K,N)$ and N reflects advantages of specialization. Similarly, if $C(N)$ rises with N, then there are disadvantages associated with additional specialization. If $C(N)$ does not vary with N, then there are no co-ordination or motivation problems or costs of additional specialization.

The optimal degree of specialization depends on the specification of these two functions and is calculated by equating the first derivatives, i.e. the marginal changes have to be the same. The optimal value of N equals 1 if $C(N)$ is a rising function of N and $B(K,N)$ does not vary with N, which means there are no advantages of specialization. Such a situation is called *autarky*, which means that everybody is completely self-supporting. Specialization only creates costs.

The famous quotation from Adam Smith at the start of this chapter reflects the other extreme. This situation is reflected in a specification of $B(K,N)$ such that there is a positive relationship with N, and $C(N)$ does not depend on N. Additional specialization entails only benefits. The optimal value of N is therefore equal to the number of people in the world depicted by Adam Smith. The degree of specialization is limited only by the size of the market.

$B(K,N)$ as well as $C(N)$ are positively related to N in most situations, which means that further specialization entails advantages as well as disadvantages. This situation is depicted in Fig. 1.3. There is specialization, but it is less than the size of the market.

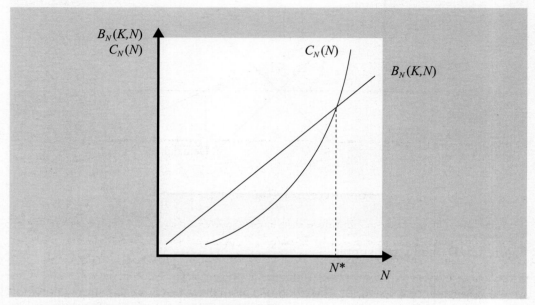

Figure 1.3: Optimal degree of specialization

The optimal degree of specialization is also determined by the level of general knowledge K. Assume that the direct effect of K on $B(K,N)$ is positive, i.e. general knowledge raises the productivity of everyone. Assume also that the indirect effect of K on $B(K,N)$ through N is also positive, i.e. that more general knowledge raises the productivity of larger teams. A consequence of these assumptions is that more general knowledge raises the optimal level of specialization. Exercise 1.2 addresses a number of other cases.

1.3 The importance of organizations compared with markets

Economic analyses have been concerned mainly with firms competing in markets, while the internal functioning of companies has received relatively little attention. The firm was treated as a 'black box', its nature and origin left unexplained. This emphasis on markets is curious, because most economic activities occur within organizations. Most people spend only a small part of the day buying and selling goods and services – and even if they spend more time it is usually because they are on company business. The efficiency of an economic system depends therefore to a large part on the organization of activities outside markets.

Figure 1.4 illustrates that an efficient organization is at least as important as a well-functioning system of markets (Williamson, 1994). Suppose product q is sold at price p and that the costs, including the costs of slack, equal p. The amount of slack is the result of unnecessary bureaucracy, negligence, conflicts and misunderstandings and is equal to the difference $p-c$. The costs per unit are only c when the organization is able to eliminate the waste.

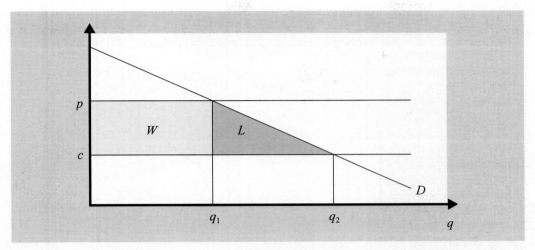

Figure 1.4: Organization versus competition (Williamson, 1994, p. 368)

An efficient organization is therefore able to generate a considerable amount of additional surplus, which is shown in Fig. 1.4 by rectangle W. Assume with respect to the functioning of markets that the organization, after eliminating the slack, initially is able to establish a price p. After a while, competitors enter the market, resulting in a drop in the price level and an increase in production. This generates an additional surplus to society, represented by triangle L. The area of rectangle W is much larger than that of triangle L, which implies that an efficient organization can generate more value than a well-functioning market system.

Prices usually allocate resources in markets, while administrative procedures play a prominent role in organizations. The systematic analysis of this organizational realm is an important theme of this book. Organizations generate co-ordination and motivation problems quite different from those generated by the market. So while in economics the emphasis used to be on the price mechanism, and the subject used to be characterized as the science that studied the allocation of resources, the subject today encompasses also the study of co-ordination and motivation problems in organizations.

A distinction is usually made between institutions and organizations. Institutions are the broad, overarching framework of rules and constraints, formal and informal, that govern interactions between individuals, e.g. constitutions and general or social norms. North (2001, p. 97) provides the following characterization:

Institutions are the humanly devised constraints that structure political, economic and social interaction. They consist of both informal constraints (sanctions, taboos, customs, traditions, and codes of conduct), and formal rules (constitutions, laws, property rights).

Organizations are about groups of individuals, interacting under specific rules that operate within the general framework of institutions, in pursuit of some common purpose. Examples of organizations are firms, co-operatives, political parties and universities. Organizations are the implementers or carriers of the general rules. The different levels at which institutions and organizations are studied are presented in Fig. 1.5 (Williamson 2000, p. 597). The different levels are distinguished by the frequency, i.e. the pace, of change in the institution.

Level	Theory	Frequency (years)	Purpose
Embeddedness: informal institutions, customs, traditions, norms, religion	Social theory	100 to 1000	Often non-calculative; spontaneous
Institutional environment: formal rules of the game – esp. property (polity, judiciary, bureaucracy)	Economics of property rights / positive political theory	10 to 100	Get the institutional environment right.
Governance: play of the game – esp. contract (aligning governance structures with transactions)	Transaction cost economics	1 to 10	Get the governance structures right.
Resource allocation and employment (prices and quantities; incentive alignment)	Neoclassical economics/ agency theory	Continuous	Get the marginal conditions right.

Figure 1.5: Institutional and organizational analyses (Williamson, 2000, p. 597)

1.4 Conclusion

Specialization and exchange may result in the best possible outcome for all parties involved. However, they also entail bilateral or multilateral dependencies, which usually creates co-ordination and motivation problems. An important role of organizations is to deal with these potential problems in an effective way. This book offers insights from various organization theories regarding these themes.

1.5 Exercises

1.1   A Explain the difference between market price and opportunity costs.
      B What is the relationship between level of education and opportunity costs (reservation salary)?

1.2   Use the model of Becker and Murphy (1992) to determine how the degree of specialization changes because of
      A Improved communication devices;
      B A higher level of education;
      C Lower transportation costs due to European unification;
      D Improved market exchange.

2 Primer: Economic concepts for organization

LEARNING OBJECTIVES

After completing this chapter, you should understand:

- Which two ontological criteria will be used for classifying organizational theories.

- The five ingredients of a non-cooperative game.

- Nash equilibrium.

- How non-cooperative game theory can be used to organize the managerial implicatons of oganization theories.

Contents

This chapter consists of four sections. Section 2.1 outlines the scheme of thought which will be used to address a variety of problems in organization and strategy. Sections 2.2 and 2.3 present game theory as a method in line with this scheme of thought. A conclusion is provided in Sec. 2.4.

2.1 Economic analysis

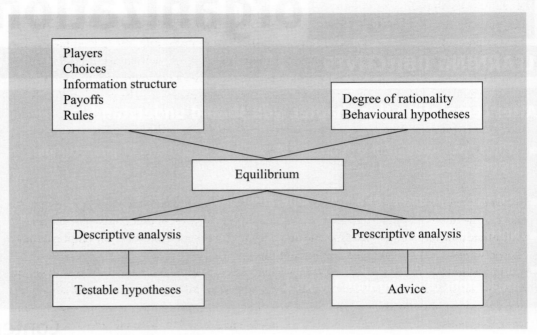

Figure 2.1: Scheme of thought

Figure 2.1 presents the basic scheme of thought of this book (Panzar and Rosse, 1984). The structure is simple: a theory consists of the specification of the problem and the behavioural assumptions. The problem specifies what we want to analyse and which variables are considered relevant. Important aspects are which persons take decisions, the choice possibilities available to them, the level of costs and benefits, the availability of information and the institutional rules or setting. Behavioural assumptions say something about the nature of the theory: the cognitive capacities of the decision-makers and the driving force behind their behaviour. The solution of the model is called equilibrium. It determines how the behaviour of individuals at the micro level, based on the interactions between individuals, will result in an organizational outcome. The individual will be the basis for the definition of equilibrium. Two types of equilibrium analyses can be performed: descriptive and prescriptive. The next three subsections will go into more detail with respect to the characterization of the problem, the behavioural assumptions and equilibrium. The point is ultimately whether we are able to gain insight in the behaviour of organizations with this scheme of thought. This can be done only by putting meat on the bones, which will be done in Sec. 2.1.2 by distinguishing organization theories according to their assumptions regarding the cognitive capabilities of the decision-makers and the behavioural hypothesis.

2.1.1 Problem description
The five parts of the problem description will now be elaborated upon.

2.1.1.1 Players
Players are decision-makers like employees, employers, consumers, producers, banks, accountants, universities, unions, political parties, countries and the government. The number of players, their positions and also their cognitive capacities are important. It is obvious that the number of players is important. For example, a company with five employees has an organizational structure different from that of a multinational. The position of a player can to a large extent determine his or her behaviour. For example, employer and employee view their company in different ways. Finally, the cognitive capacities of the players may have an effect on the number of tasks assigned to a person.

2.1.1.2 Choice possibilities
Choices specify the possibilities from which the player can choose. A company, for example, chooses the number of players which will be employed, the level of debt, the degree of decentralization and the salaries assigned to the various functions. Likewise, an employee may choose whether to go for an early retirement plan.

Agreements between parties with diverging interests are important, because they can result in surplus-generating transactions which otherwise will not materialize. Promises and threats will be formulated in order to sustain these agreements but these are not very credible when they consist only of words – if circumstances change and the attractiveness of promises or threats has decreased, then the incentive to adhere to the agreement is reduced. Either party can formulate this line of reasoning and therefore hardly take the contract seriously, so an agreement will mean something only when it is accompanied by some sort of mechanism which translates words, by way of promises or threats, into actions.

The irreversible implementation of choices by way of promises or threats is called commitment, the idea being that it can be profitable to limit the number of choice possibilities available to you (Schelling, 1960). It is usually not attractive to limit your choice possibilities, but it may pay to do so in strategic situations when it moulds the behaviour of the other party in a desirable way. A commitment entails a choice made in such a way that the other party has to take it for granted.

Only credible promises and threats count. However, credibility is often hard to establish. Sometimes it is impossible because the law forbids certain actions. Slavery is an example. It means that an employee can never promise to his employer in a credible way that he will stay with the company for the rest of his life. If the employee decides to leave after all, then the employer cannot force the employee to stay by judicial means because slavery is forbidden. However, there are a number of ways in which agreements can be made more credible. Dixit and Nalebuff (1991) distinguish three ways in order to establish credibility: changing the players, changing the possible choices and changing the payoffs. Section 2.4 will explain what this entails.

2.1.1.3 Payoffs

Payoffs reflect the costs and benefits for the players involved. For example, the payoffs of a firm include its profits, which depend on market demand on the benefit side and the production technology and input prices on the costs side. Market demand summarizes the preferences of the consumers and the impact of competitors, and the costs reflect fixed and variable costs. Many things are therefore hidden behind profits. How much detail is presented of the composition of profits will depend on the specific problem. Another example of a payoff is the salary of a manager. A large company is usually supervised by a manager or managers who do not own it. Investment decisions by managers may therefore be guided not only by company objectives but also by personal ones, like status, power and future employment possibilities. The payoff for a political party is the number of votes it receives.

The specification of a problem always entails that relationships are specified between the dependent and the independent variables. This is reflected in the payoffs. For example, a higher income will result in more consumption, while lower costs will result in higher profits, and unattractive behaviour will more likely be discovered when there is more inspection. Decisions of players can be focused on a common goal, but quite often there are diverging or conflicting interests. Both an employer and an employee will probably benefit from a higher profit, but they also have conflicting interests, e.g. in the employee's salary and the number of hours he or she works. Individual decisions therefore have consequences for others.

One of the main interests in this book is in how individual decisions are influenced by the decisions of others and how this may be anticipated. Thus, an employer determining the terms of the contract for an employee will think about the response of the employee when it is offered. Again, the decentralization of activities may create not only additional possibilities for dealing with new information, but also opportunities for the exertion of political influence. The dichotomy between the common and the individual interest will feature regularly. It is the systematic analysis of these interactions which is the focus of analysis in this book.

2.1.1.4 Information structure

The information structure specifies who knows what and when. It is sometimes possible that everybody has all the relevant information. However, this is exceptional. Usually imperfect information prevails. For example, firms do not tell each other about progress made in developing new products, while employees often know more about specific production circumstances than top management.

Application: Card games
The impact of information on behaviour can be illustrated by a card game (Milgrom and Roberts, 1987, pp. 184–185).

> To get an idea of the role of informational asymmetries in strategic behavior, consider three simple card games. In the first, each player is dealt five cards face up, the players make any bets they want and the best hand wins. In the second, each player receives five cards, some of which are dealt face up and the rest face down. Without looking at their

---

hole cards, the players make their bets, then the cards are turned face up and the best hand wins. Finally, the third game is like the second except that players can look at their hole cards. Again there is betting, the hidden cards are revealed and the best hand wins.

The first is one of complete (and perfect) information. Everyone knows everything, and as long as we assume that people prefer more money to less, it is fairly trivial to figure out what will happen: there will certainly be no betting, and probably no one will bother to play! Clearly not all games of complete information are either so uninteresting (witness chess) or so lacking in explanatory power – especially if we consider nonzero sum games and, even more, games with an explicit dynamic structure. However, in its informational structure, this game typifies both the sort of game theory which is discussed in intermediate micro texts and, indeed, most of standard microeconomic theory itself.

The second game has uncertainty/informational incompleteness, but no informational asymmetries. Its informational structure puts it in the domain of decision theory and the economics of uncertainty. Games of this sort are useful models for studying such issues as insurance, risky investments and learning (especially if we revise the game to have the hole cards revealed one at a time with betting after each is shown). However its play would not generate any interesting forms of strategic behavior.

The third game involves informational asymmetries: while there is some publicly available information, each player is privately informed about his or her hole cards. (In fact, the informational structure of this game, in which the probability distribution over what the particular private information over the various players could be is common knowledge, corresponds very closely to that in the asymmetric information game models used in most applications to industrial organization. The existence of this private information can obviously lead to interesting strategic play: bluffing, signaling, reputation building, etc. It is also the reason why poker is of enduring popularity.

As the above application is meant to suggest, recognition of informational asymmetries and the strategic possibilities they engender can yield models which begin to capture the richness of behavior which marks the real world. This is the great advantage of these methods: they permit us to model, and thereby start to understand, phenomena which made no sense in terms of complete information analyses or ones based on incomplete but symmetric information (uncertainty).

2.1.1.5 Rules

Rules specify the way in which people interact. They can be informal – like certain habits or customs – or formal – like statutes or laws. Many examples can be given of rules. The impact of the offside rule on the attractiveness of the game of soccer has been debated fiercely. Organizational examples of rules are a rigid or flexible salary and promotion policy, the agenda for policy meetings, the organization structure, protective measures like poison pills regarding hostile takeovers and exchange via market, contract or hierarchy. The decisions made are channelled and determined within these institutional rules.

The sequence of decisions of the players can have a large impact on the choices made. The player who decides first may have an advantage in being able to structure the problem to a certain extent, whereas deciding second may be advantageous when the choice of the person deciding first reveals important information. The institutional setting may also place restrictions on the choices available. For example, environmental regulations by the government limit the production technologies which can be adopted, anti-trust policy forbids anti-competitive decisions by firms and labour laws formulate certain rules regarding the relationship between employer and employee. Rules or institutions may affect costs and benefits. It matters for the players involved whether rationing, queues or markets are used for the allocation of resources (Sah, 1987; Elster, 1991). A firm will choose rules so as to structure its enterprise in a favourable way.

2.1.2 Behavioural assumptions

Theories can be developed on the basis of empirical, social or ontological criteria (Maki, 2001).

Empirical criteria can be static or dynamic, inductive or deductive, focus on the nature of empirical evidence and so on. The common element in all of these is that the resulting theories have to be confronted with empirical evidence.

Social criteria may reflect the interests of the scientist(s) or group(s) they are affiliated to, current or traditional theories, social or moral norms and so on. The common denominator is that scientific theories have social aspects and that they play a role in the choice and development of a scientific theory.

Finally, ontological criteria are the third class of criteria for the choice and development of scientific theories. They involve fundamental notions about human nature which cannot be directly tested empirically. Examples are concepts regarding the cognitive capacities of decision-makers, the driving force behind behaviour (idealistic versus opportunistic), social causation (individual versus environment) and social patterns (individualistic versus collectivistic). The common element is that concepts regarding the way the world works serve as criteria for the choice and development of theory. This book adopts two ontological criteria for classifying and explaining organization theories: cognitive capacities and behavioural hypotheses.

2.1.2.1 Cognitive capacities and behavioural hypotheses

Decision-makers differ in the way they are able to respond to their environment. These differences can be captured by the degree of rationality. This is defined as the ratio between the cognitive capacities of the decision-maker and the complexity of the problem he or she faces (Heiner, 1983). This ratio can be increased either by increasing the cognitive capacities of the decision-maker or by decreasing the complexity of the problem. An example of increasing the cognitive capacities of a player is education. Examples of reducing the complexity of a problem are using support from for a computer; splitting a complex production process into a number of parallel processes (De Sitter, 1994); the modular construction of learning processes in 'total quality management' (Wruck and Jensen, 1994); and using additional time in order to solve the problem.

There is complete rationality when the ratio of the cognitive capacities of the decision-maker to the complexity of the problem is 1. The decision-maker grasps and solves a problem immediately and without problems. This is possible only with simple problems and in situations where adjustments are quick. Complete rationality will be used in Parts II and III because it turns out to be a fruitful starting-point for the formulation of theories regarding organizations.

Limited rationality ('bounded rationality') is relevant when the cognitive capacities of the decision-maker are insufficient to grasp the whole complexity of a problem. The ratio of the cognitive capacities of the decision-maker to the complexity of the problem is smaller than 1. It is not possible to take all relevant aspects of a problem into account when a decision has to be made, because behaviour is 'intendedly rational, but only limitedly so' (Simon, 1961), or when perhaps while efforts are made to take the best decision it is actually too costly to do so. Limited time and means often prevent all the relevant information being extracted from the data.

Limited rationality does not mean that people behave inconsistently. The way in which behaviour is 'intendedly rational, but only limitedly so' is interpreted is that behaviour is consistent within the limitations which confront the decision-maker. Thus for example it is amazing that humans are able to create order from the chaos of signals each of us receives every day. There are many more signals received than ever can be processed. This is dealt with by ignoring, one way or another, many of the signals received and processing only the remaining information.

Psychologists and economists differ drastically in their development of theories regarding human cognitive capacities (Rabin, 1998). Psychologists start with limited rationality and allow the specific situation to play a role. This creates possibilities for analysing reference points, biases in decision-making, status, envy and conformity. These topics are hardly addressed in traditional economic models, in which decision-makers know everything, grasp difficult situations immediately and make the optimal choice.

Procedural rationality is relevant when the complexity of a problem is many times larger than the cognitive capacities of the decision-maker. The ratio of the cognitive capacities of the decision-maker to the complexity of the problem is close to zero: the behaviour of people in an extremely complicated environment is typically governed by rule of thumb, rather than by trying to figure things out. Procedural rationality is relevant in environments where the speed of adjustment is low.

The second ontological criterion we will use for classifying and developing organizational theories is the behavioural hypothesis. There are three kinds of these. The first is self-interested behaviour. It reflects people who care about their own interest and are honest and reliable. They keep promises, do not misrepresent information in order to gain something and stick to the rules. The second behavioural hypothesis is opportunistic behavior. People characterized by this assumption strive for their own self-interest without guile. All means are advanced in order to gain benefits, like lying, stealing and treason, but also more subtle forms of dishonesty are considered, like telling only part of the truth or presenting an over-optimistic view of a new product. Finally, the third behavioural hypothesis is idealistic behaviour. People behaving according to this assumption strive for the common interest and take decisions in the interest of the whole organization.

It is necessary for the development of new theories to be clear what the main assumptions regarding the players are and also that these assumptions are maintained throughout the analysis. Only thus can scientific progress be made. This will clarify both the breadth and the limitations of the approach adopted. The limitations are at least as important as the breadth of the approach, because they are often the engine for new developments. It is therefore undesirable that different behavioural assumptions are used for the explanation of the different choices made. The sociologist Coleman (1990) puts it thus:

> The eclecticism – or, one might say, the intellectual disarray – of the microfoundation of sociological theory is evident from a comparison of the received wisdom about bureaucratic authority and the received wisdom about collective behavior (that is, phenomena such as riots, mobs, panics, crowd behavior, fads, and fashions). The ideal type of bureaucracy is envisioned as having a single purposive actor at the top of the hierarchical structure, with the remainder of the structure occupied by entities that differ little from the parts of a machine. Their purposes or interests never play a role in the classical theory of organizational functioning . . . Max Weber's plaintive cry about bureaucratic man . . . is not really about modern man but about Weber's conception of modern man – a robot in the employ of the bureaucracy. Yet these 'robots' are the same persons concerning whom observers of collective behavior have a wholly different conception. They are described as 'excitable', 'emotional', or 'suggestive'; their behavior exhibits 'contagion'; they are subject to 'hypnotic effects of the crowd'. That is, they are irrational, disorderly, unpredictable, and spontaneous, close to the opposite pole from the bureaucratic man Weber envisioned as the typical man of the future.
>
> Such an intellectual disarray is one that sociologists have learned to live with. Social theory has too often taken the easy path of creating, conceptually, exactly the kind of creature at the micro level that by simple aggregation will produce the observed systemic behavior – whether that systemic behavior is the orderly and mundane functioning of a bureaucracy or the spontaneous and emotional outbursts of a crowd. The correct path for social theory is a more difficult one: to maintain a single conception of what individuals are like and to generate the varying systemic functioning not from different kinds of creatures, but from different structures of relations within which these creatures find themselves.

There are various ways of being consistent. For example, sociologists and economists vary drastically in their formulation of theories with respect to social behaviour (Baron and Hannan, 1994). Traditional sociologists start from the assumption that the behaviour, and even the tastes or preferences, of people are determined by social structures, reference groups, organizational procedures, rituals and conventions. Economists usually start from the other end. The behaviour of people in organizations is, according to economists, determined mainly by exogenously given tastes and preferences which are not amenable to change, i.e. people are born with certain characteristics which are to a large extent fixed for life. A similar distinction can be formulated regarding the choice possibilities which are selected or are perceived as able to be selected. A sociologist assumes that the choices of people or organizations are determined largely by the environment or reference group in which one operates and by past events. It is the individual who forms the point of departure for economists. Choices are guided mainly, in their view, by the individual person's own tastes and preferences and the available, possible choices and information.

2.1.2.2 Classifying organization theories

Two organizational problems are at the centre of attention in this book: motivation problems and co-ordination problems. Motivation problems feature conflicting or diverging interests between players in an organization. They often occur in situations where something has to be divided. The classic example is dividing a pie. One person gains at the expense of another. Co-ordination problems are characterized by common or joint interests of the players. The issue is how to enlarge the pie for the players. It matters for the solution of these problems which approach or theory is adopted.

Organization theories will be classified by the degree of rationality and a behavioural hypothesis. Three degrees of rationality and three behavioural assumptions are distinguished in Fig. 2.2 (Kreps, 1990a).

		Behavioural hypothesis		
		Opportunistic	Self-interested	Idealistic
Rationality	Complete	Complete contracts	General equilibrium	System of attributes Team theory
	Limited	Incomplete contracts		
	Procedural	Evolutionary approaches		

Figure 2.2: Behavioural assumptions and organization theories (Kreps, 1990a, p. 747)
A Course in Microeconomic Theory © Reprinted by permission of Pearson Education Limited

Completely rational, self-interested individuals are the starting-point in general equilibrium theory. The main question is under which circumstances an optimal allocation of resources is established by markets. The classic result is the formulation of the circumstances in which markets work perfectly (the 'invisible hand'). Arrow and Debreu (1954) have provided the mathematical formulation of this result. Part II is dedicated to these matters.

Completely rational, opportunistic individuals are analysed in contract theory. The subject for investigation is whether or not it is attractive for somebody to withhold or distort information, and the impact of this on the (contractual) relations between the involved parties. Notice that the assumption of opportunistic behaviour does not automatically imply that players will behave in a bad way. Good behaviour too may be opportunistic. The creation of a good reputation requires good behaviour, which may be used or abused later. The assumption of complete rationality entails that everything relevant will be taken into account. This will show itself in the writing of complete contracts, which may as a result be very complicated. These topics are addressed in Part III.

Part IV explains theories which assume that players are boundedly rational and behave in an opportunistic way. The assumption of complete rationality precludes the possibility that complete contracts can be written. Only incomplete contracts are possible. Contracts are incomplete in the sense that they have gaps when they are written (ex ante), which implies that later (ex post) new agreements have to be made when events occur which are not covered by the contract. The attention is, just as in Part III, geared towards problems with conflicting interests for which the proper incentives have to be formulated.

Part V is dedicated to decision-making characterized by procedural rationality. Evolutionary approaches are important examples in this class of theories. Organizational development can according to this view be compared to biological processes as described by Darwin. Darwinian fitness is the key concept, and selection occurs by an evolutionary process. Firms are still viewed as purposeful, but their behaviour can be characterized by a number of routines and rules of thumb. Routines and possibilities of organizations develop slowly by frequent repetition and application. Experiences are summarized in routines, without those who use them understanding why they work. Evolutionary approaches put a lot of emphasis on the process aspects of production and distribution, and on the learning capabilities of creating, developing and transforming these processes. Scarcity plays only a limited role in the allocation of resources. Routines are limited in number, because it takes a lot of time and money to develop new ones. No one company is identical to any other, because the current capabilities are determined to a large extent by the specific history of the company. It is therefore impossible to imitate the practices of another company. Skills have to be developed again and again. Routines badly adapted to the local environment die out in a process of natural selection, whereas the number of firms or individuals with good, i.e. Darwinian, fitness increases.

Team theory (Marschak and Radner, 1972) and the system of attributes perspective (Milgrom and Roberts, 1990c) focus on co-ordination problems. Local decision-makers try to make choices which are in the interest of the whole organization, but a lack of information or limited cognitive capacities may make this difficult. The results of these approaches address on the one hand the minimal amount of information which is necessary (the 'sufficient statistic') for achieving the best match between the activities of the separate players and on the other hand the effectiveness of various ways to establish co-ordination. Part VI focuses on the possibilities of solving co-ordination problems.

Each theory provides its own definition of the enterprise in order to be compatible with the assumptions made. No theory will therefore ever be completely satisfactory (Monks and Minow, 1995), because each assumption entails certain limitations. The choice of definition also often reflects to a certain extent the perspective of the researcher. The well-known parable of the blind Hindus and the elephant illustrates what is involved. Anyone formulating a definition of the enterprise or firm puts himself in the position of one of the blind Hindus trying to describe an elephant. The first one wiggles the tail and calls it a snake, the second walks into a leg and is convinced that it is a tree, the third one rubs the belly and calls it a cave, the fourth one encounters an ear and describes it as a rug and so on. This book will treat several different definitions and theories of the firm. The reason is that varying types of problems require different types of theories in order to describe them and to propose solutions. Like each Hindu in the parable, each part of the book will take a different standpoint. The picture of an elephant occurs in each of the following parts of this book, then a certain part of the elephant is pointed at and labelled, with the definition of the firm used in that part. This provides a focus on a certain aspect of the organization and will result in many insights, derived from the definition employed. Inevitably it introduces certain biases, which will be compensated for subsequently in the next part by taking the perspective of another Hindu, i.e. another definition of the firm. This way makes clear the limitations of any particular approach and ensures the domain of the theory is clearly delineated.

2.1.3 Equilibrium

A model consists of the specification of the problem and the behavioural assumptions made. Variables in a model are exogenous or endogenous. The values of exogenous variables are determined outside the model, while the values of endogenous variables are determined within the model in equilibrium. The endogenous variables are expressed in terms of the exogenous variables. The notion of equilibrium is used in order to gain insight and to predict what will happen. It is common to formulate the requirements regarding behaviour which have to be satisfied in order be equilibrium behaviour. For example, a requirement may be that everybody takes decisions such that their own interest is served best. This book will use an equilibrium concept in keeping with the general approach throughout that the individual is the starting-point for our analysis of firms. A Nash equilibrium is a situation in which nobody can change his or her decision such that his or her well-being is improved. Sections 2.2 and 2.3 will go into this in much more detail.

The attractiveness of a certain decision will always be viewed from the perspective of the individual as well as from that of the organization. The starting-point will be the individual decision-maker, because all social interactions are after all interactions among individuals. However, this does not imply that we can do without social categories (Arrow, 1994). Social variables, not attached to particular individuals, are also essential for analysing organizations and institutions. The perspective of larger entities like organizations is important, but it has to be complemented or else added to the considerations of the various players, like employers, consumers and firms. Individual choices have a large impact on the outcome of organizations. For example, decisions of the management as well as those of the employees determine the outcome of the enterprise. Jensen and Meckling (1976) formulate it as follows:

> The firm is not an individual. It is a legal fiction which serves as a focus for a complex process in which the conflicting objectives of individuals (some of whom may 'represent' other organizations) are brought into equilibrium within a framework of contractual relations. In this sense the 'behavior' of the firm is like the behavior of a market; i.e., the outcome of a complex equilibrium process. We seldom fall into the trap of characterizing the wheat or stock market as an individual, but we often make this error by thinking about organizations as if they were persons with motivations and intentions.

The notion of equilibrium is geared towards predicting what will happen. The counter side is that it automatically says something about what will not happen. Certain types of behaviour are excluded as equilibrium behaviour. Excluding certain types of behaviour is especially useful when the equilibrium is not unique. A two-tier analysis is advised in such situations.

First, several types of behaviour are excluded. A large class of equilibrium behaviour may remain. Second, additional information is collected, e.g. by in-depth case-studies, in order to narrow down the class of equilibria (Sutton, 1991). Notice that there is a difference between behaviour which is not equilibrium behaviour and behaviour which is impossible. If certain behaviour is excluded by a theory, then this does not imply that this behaviour is impossible. The theory might be wrong. This has to be resolved by empirical evidence.

The notion of equilibrium is used in two types of analyses: descriptive and prescriptive. Descriptive analysis can be summarized as investigations focused on questions regarding 'what is'. Testable hypotheses are formulated such that the effect of the change of an exogenous variable on the endogenous variable can be investigated. This is called comparative statics analysis. For example, an increase in the costs of a firm will shift the supply curve. The intersection of supply and demand results in a higher price and a lower quantity in equilibrium.

Prescriptive analysis can be summarized by investigations focused on questions regarding 'what should be'. Statements are formulated regarding the desirability of a particular equilibrium. The term efficiency is used for this purpose. One role for a social scientist is to give advice and formulate institutional frameworks (rules of the game, organizational structures, bargaining protocols, contracts) in order to facilitate efficient choices. Frequently used notions of efficiency are the sum of consumer and producer surplus and Pareto efficiency. Consumer surplus is defined as the difference between the reservation price of the consumer, i.e. value in use, and the price of exchange. Producer surplus is defined as the difference between the price of exchange and the reservation price of the producer. An allocation is efficient when the sum of consumer and producer surplus is maximized. An equilibrium is Pareto-efficient when there is no other allocation available which improves the well-being of one player without decreasing the well-being of others.

Organizations like to establish an attractive outcome. The decisions involved are based on the available information and require proper incentives for the individual decision-makers. An important responsibility of organizations is therefore to generate and channel the required information and to design the appropriate decisions. The available information determines what can be achieved, and a definition of efficiency has to take this into account. An equilibrium with asymmetric information often differs from the first-best equilibrium in a situation with complete information. If certain information is not available, then this results almost always in a loss of efficiency. Efficiency criteria are therefore usually formulated with respect to the available information, taking into account the costs associated with acquiring the information. An equilibrium is efficient when there is no better outcome possible from the choices of the various players, given the available information. If the available information is characterized by asymmetric information, then the most attractive outcome is called second-best efficient. An important topic in this book is to determine rules, contracts, or institutions which are second-best efficient. Another topic is to determine the impact of a change in the information structure on the equilibrium outcome. Sometimes the equilibrium does not change when the information structure changes, but usually it does.

An equilibrium is not necessarily efficient. One reason for an inefficient equilibrium may be that each player takes decisions which are in their own interest but not in the common interest. A well-known example is the prisoners dilemma, which will be discussed extensively in Sec. 2.3. A prescriptive analysis usually results in policy advice. The efficient outcome is compared with the actual equilibrium in prescriptive analysis. If the result of the analysis indicates that the efficient outcome is the same as the observed behaviour, then the advice is to change nothing. However, it is also possible that the current decisions do not match with the efficient choices. This implies that decisions can be changed in such a way that the overall outcome can be improved. Change is therefore advised. The formulation of advice depends of course on the party asking for advice. For example, society usually likes some competition in markets, whereas firms do not like it. The same applies to efficiency. Efficiency always concerns a certain set of players. It is possible that a certain outcome is efficient from the perspective of a small group of players, but equally possible that it is not efficient when a larger set of players is taken into account. For example, a cartel is attractive from the perspective of the firms involved, but the consumers suffer.

Efficiency has been used as a prescriptive concept in order to evaluate decisions. However, if efficiency is an important consideration in the decisions players make, then it is also a descriptive concept with explanatory and predictive power. This makes good sense, because somebody can propose, in an inefficient situation, an alternative everyone prefers. Inefficient decisions are therefore always vulnerable to better alternatives. (Efficient decisions are less likely to be changed, because there will always be somebody who will oppose the change.) Inefficient proposals have the tendency to be winnowed out in the course of time, while efficient ones tend to stay when the circumstances are favourable. Some caution is necessary, however. First, decisions in organizations are sometimes driven by considerations of fairness, which implies that Pareto efficiency as a descriptive concept may result in bad predictions regarding behaviour. Second, an equilibrium is a stable configuration, and therefore an inefficient equilibrium is also stable. However, the inefficient equilibrium may result in actions which change the situation drastically, which may result in the inefficient outcome being an equilibrium no longer.

The above notions of efficiency are geared towards total value created by the players involved, but say nothing about the equity aspects of a certain equilibrium. Considerations like small or large, or poor or rich, are not taken into account. Efficiency therefore does not necessarily go together with a fair allocation of resources. The cartoon by Mankoff (Frank, 1985) in Fig. 2.3 illustrates the lack of the aspect of equity in the definition of Pareto efficiency.

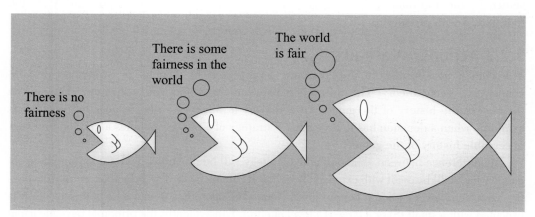

Figure 2.3: Pareto efficiency is not necessarily fair (Frank, 1985, p. 109)

2.2 Game theory

Game theory is a method to describe and analyse situations in which multiple parties take decisions. The interactions between the parties are central, i.e. each party takes the behaviour of the other parties into account when a decision is made. This method is especially suitable for the theme of this book: the co-ordination and motivation problems within and between organizations. Situations with joint as well as opposing interests can be described and addressed with this method. Myerson (1999, p. 1068) writes: 'Game theory is a unified analytical structure for studying all situations of conflict and co-operation.' The next section is dedicated to the management implications of game theory.

A non-cooperative game consists of five ingredients:

- Players;
- Actions/strategies;
- Payoffs;
- Information structure;
- Rules.

These five ingredients and the most common equilibrium concepts in non-cooperative game theory will feature in the next six subsections. We finish this section with a conclusion.

2.2.1 Players

The ingredient 'players' includes anyone who can take a decision. Examples are employers, employees, political parties, countries, firms and so on. This ingredient seems straightforward, but in application it is sometimes difficult to determine who the players are. If you forget to take an important player into account, then your analysis is doomed to fail. For example, it is important to know who a real estate agent is representing when you bargain with him. This will have an effect both on when an agreement is reached and on the price agreed upon.

The players mentioned are all real players. It will turn out that it sometimes convenient to introduce an artificial player. For example, exogenous uncertainty will be represented by the artificial player 'Nature'. The uncertainty regarding good (G) or bad (B) weather is represented by the additional player Nature, choosing G with, for example, probability .6 and therefore B with probability .4.

2.2.2 Actions/strategies

The choice possibilities of a player are represented by actions or strategies in non-cooperative game theory. The difference between an action and a strategy depends on the observable history of the game. An action by a player is a choice possibility which is available when a decision has to be made. A strategy of a player specifies an action for every observable history of the game.

The difference between an action and a strategy will be illustrated with the principal–agent game, which will be dealt with extensively in Part III of this book. The principal (employer) pays the agent (employee) when a certain job is done. The agent has to choose whether the task is executed with a small (S) or a large (L) level of effort. Subsequently, the principal pays the agent a medium (M) or a top (T) salary. Figure 2.4 shows the situation.

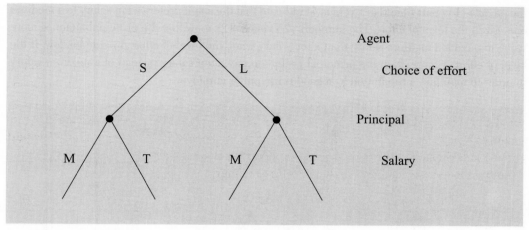

Figure 2.4: Players and actions in the principal–agent game

Each node in this tree diagram indicates where a player has to make a choice, whereas the branches specify the possible actions. The agent and the principal each have two actions in this game. The possible actions of the agent are S and L, those of the principal M and T.

A strategy of a player specifies an action for every possible node a player can be in. The possible strategies of the agent are easy to determine, because the agent is not confronted with a history of the game when he has to decide. The agent decides first. The possible strategies of the agent are therefore identical to his actions: S and L. A strategy of the principal has also to specify an action for every possible history of the game. This is a little more difficult because there are two possible histories of the game the principal may face. The agent may have chosen S, or he may have chosen L. A strategy of the principal has to specify an answer for each situation. It consists therefore of two components. This can be represented by the vector (X,Y), where X is the response of the principal to the action S of the agent and Y the response of the principal to the action L of the agent. In the principal–agent game X as well as Y can be the action M or T. An example of a strategy of the principal is (T,M). This strategy entails that a top (T) salary will be paid when a small (S) level of effort is provided, while a medium (M) salary will be paid when a large (L) level of effort is put forward. The principal has four possible strategies: (M,M), (M,T), (T,M) and (T,T). Notice that the strategy (T,M) does not look like a reasonable strategy for the principal. However, this is not relevant in our example with regard to a possible strategy. It only conveys what a possible strategy is, not its attractiveness. Payoffs are needed in order to determine the attractiveness of a certain strategy.

2.2.3 Payoffs

Payoffs summarize the costs and benefits of a strategy. They are, like players and choice possibilities, represented in the tree diagram. Figure 2.5 illustrates this with the principal–agent game. The first row of numbers at the bottom of the tree diagram represents the payoffs of the agent for each possible history of the game. The second row does the same for the principal. The numbers represent the costs and benefits for the players in the different situations. For example, the payoffs (1 versus 5) and (–1 versus 4) indicate that the agent prefers a top salary to a medium one, given the level of effort. The numbers (25 versus 12) show that the principal attaches more value to paying a medium salary than a top salary when the level of effort provided is low. If the level of effort is large, then the principal prefers to pay a top salary instead of a medium salary in order to maintain a reputation as a good principal or employer.

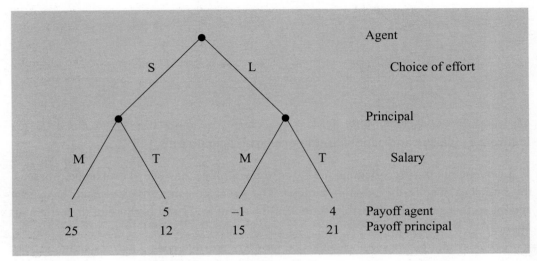

Figure 2.5: Players, choice possibilities and payoffs in the principal–agent game

An important aspect of the payoffs in Fig. 2.5 is that the payoff of a player, the agent or the principal, depends not only on his own choice, but also on the choice of the other player. Game theory is decision theory for situations with multiple persons, where a choice of a player influences the well-being of not only this player but also the others.

Game-theoretic situations can be represented in two ways. The tree diagram in the Figs 2.4 and 2.5 is called the extensive form. A game can also be represented with a matrix. The strategies of the players are the entries in the matrix. The matrix representation is therefore called the strategic form. Figure 2.6 presents the strategic form of the principal–agent game. The first number in brackets is the payoff of the agent, the second number that of the principal.

Nothing has yet been said about the actual choice of a strategy by a player. The next subsection specifies certain requirements which a strategy has to satisfy in order to be chosen. These requirements will be reflected in the definition of Nash equilibrium and subgame perfect equilibrium.

Principal Agent	(M, M)	(M, T)	(T, M)	(T, T)
S	(1, 25)	(1, 25)	(5, 12)	(5, 12)
L	(–1, 15)	(4, 21)	(–1, 15)	(4, 21)

Figure 2.6: Strategic form of the principal–agent game

2.2.4 Equilibrium

The prediction of the outcome of a game is called equilibrium. This can be a complicated affair, because each player takes the actions and reactions of the other players into account. There are many possible actions and reactions. An equilibrium concept formulates certain requirements which a strategy has to satisfy in order to be an equilibrium strategy.

A general, simple requirement which equilibrium choices have to satisfy is the Nash criterion: a player's choices should not harm his or her own interest. Such behaviour is called rational behaviour (Sen, 1987). It entails consistent behaviour, i.e. the choices exhibit a certain pattern, which (possibly) belongs to an underlying goal, like utility- or profit-maximization. A Nash equilibrium specifies a payoff-maximizing strategy for each player, given the choice of strategy of the other players.

Thinking in terms of equilibrium behaviour provides insight into the decisions of others and the behaviour of organizations. The consequent application of this equilibrium concept provides regularly surprising insights regarding the relationship between individual motives (of players) and aggregate or collective behaviour (of the organization). The most famous example is the prisoners dilemma, highlighted in the next section.

Nash equilibrium can be most easy determined by using the strategic form. Figure 2.7 presents the strategic form of Fig. 2.6 again. The difference is that arrows are added. These point to a change in strategy which increases the payoff of the player, given the strategy of the other player. An arrow departing from a certain cell indicates that the associated pair of strategies cannot be a Nash equilibrium. (Only one horizontal arrow is drawn for each cell to avoid cluttering the figure.)

Principal / Agent	(M, M)	(M, T)	(T, M)	(T, T)
S	(1, 25)	(1, 25)	(5, 12)	(5, 12)
L	(−1, 15)	(4, 21)	(−1, 15)	(4, 21)

Figure 2.7: Nash equilibrium in the principal–agent problem

Each vertical arrow indicates a change in strategy of the agent which results in an improvement in the payoff of the agent, given the strategy of the principal. The horizontal arrows are changes in strategy of the principal which increase the payoff of the principal, given the strategy of the agent. The strategies associated with a cell from which no arrows are departing are Nash equilibrium strategies. There are two Nash equilibria in the principal–agent game:

Agent: S;
Principal: (M,M);

and

Agent: L;
Principal: (M,T).

It will now be shown that the first Nash equilibrium satisfies all requirements of a Nash equilibrium. If the principal chooses (M,M), then the agent can choose strategy S with payoff 1 or strategy L with payoff −1. The agent maximizes his payoff by choosing S. Similarly, if the agent chooses S, then the principal cannot increase his payoff by choosing a strategy other than (M,M). The strategy (T,M) generates a payoff of only 12 for the principal, whereas (M,M) results in a payoff of 25. The conclusion is therefore that the strategy L of the agent, together with the strategy (M,M) of the principal, is a Nash equilibrium.

Dynamic games consist of multiple periods. The principal–agent game with complete information is an example of one. An important aspect of a dynamic game is that the decisions in early periods are observable or known in later periods. A problem with dynamic games is that there are often many Nash equilibria, as for example in the above principal–agent game. The existence of several Nash equilibria entails that the predictive power of the concept of Nash equilibrium diminishes. This problem can be at least partly eliminated by introducing additional requirements that an equilibrium strategy has to satisfy. The notion of subgame perfect equilibrium will serve this role and will be introduced with the principal–agent game.

We require that the subgame perfect equilibrium strategies of the players consist of actions which maximize the payoffs of the player after each node of the tree diagram. This requirement will be incorporated in the definition of subgame perfect equilibrium by the notion of a subgame. A subgame of a game starts with a node of a game and consists of everything which follows this node. Figure 2.5 has three subgames: the whole game, the game starting with the node after the S-branch and the game which starts with the node after the L-branch. Notice that each subgame consists of the five ingredients of a non-cooperative game.

A pair of strategies forms a subgame perfect equilibrium (Selten, 1965) when the strategies are a Nash equilibrium in every subgame. Each subgame perfect equilibrium is by definition also a Nash equilibrium. The requirements which strategies have to satisfy in order to be subgame perfect equilibrium strategies are more demanding than the requirements which have to be satisfied in order to be Nash equilibrium strategies, which will therefore definitely result in not more, and, most likely, fewer subgame perfect equilibria than Nash equilibria.

The strategic form is most convenient in order to determine the Nash equilibria. However, this does not hold for a subgame perfect equilibrium. It turns out that the subgame perfect equilibria can be best determined by using the extensive form because the various subgames have to checked. The method of backward induction is used for this purpose. This involves you starting at the bottom of the tree diagram by determining the Nash equilibrium in every subgame. Subsequently you move to the next-to-last period and determine the Nash equilibria in the subgames starting in this period, taking into account the Nash equilibrium responses in the final period. This procedure has to be repeated all the way to the first period. The subgame perfect equilibrium consists of the resulting strategies in all periods.

The method of backward induction will be illustrated with the principal–agent game. Figure 2.8 has circled the subgame which starts after the agent has chosen S. The principal will choose M because 25 > 12. The Nash equilibrium in this subgame is therefore M. This is represented in this subgame by adding a line along the M-branch. We know now already the following of the subgame perfect equilibrium:

Agent: ?
Principal: (M, ?).

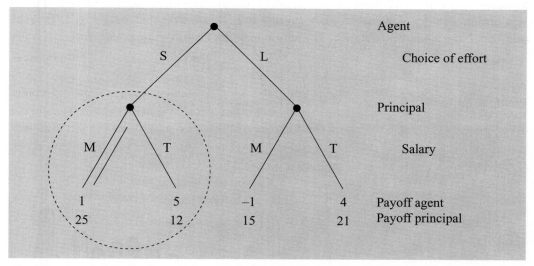

Figure 2.8: Nash equilibrium in the subgame after the S-branch

Figure 2.9 has circled the subgame which starts after the agent has chosen L. The principal will choose T in this subgame, because 21 > 15. The Nash equilibrium in this subgame is T. This is again illustrated in the extensive form by adding a line along the T-branch. We know now the following of the subgame perfect equilibrium:

Agent: ?
Principal: (M,T).

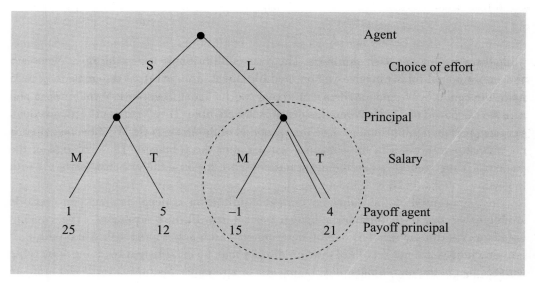

Figure 2.9: Nash equilibrium in the subgame after the L-branch

The subgame perfect equilibrium strategy of the principal is therefore (M,T).

Finally, the payoff-maximizing strategy of the agent has to be determined, given the subgame perfect equilibrium strategy (M,T) of the principal. The subgame perfect equilibrium strategy of the agent is L because 4 > 1. This is indicated in the Fig. 2.10 by the additional line along the L-branch. The subgame perfect equilibrium is therefore:

Agent: L;
Principal: (M,T).

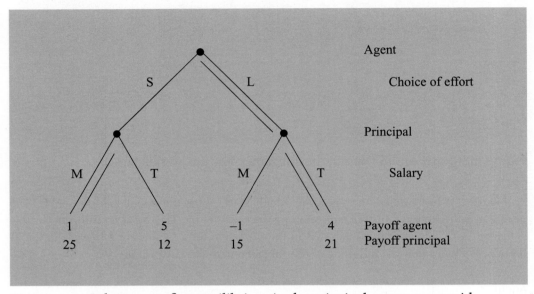

Figure 2.10: Subgame perfect equilibrium in the principal–agent game with complete information

Notice that there is only one subgame perfect equilibrium in the principal–agent game, while there are several Nash equilibria. The Nash equilibrium in which the agent chooses S and the principal (M,M) involves a non-credible threat. The principal threatens to play M following L in order to induce the agent to play S. The agent then plays M following S and gets the big payoff of 25. However, this threat is not credible. This Nash equilibrium is not a subgame perfect equilibrium because the second M of the strategy (M,M) of the principal is not a Nash equilibrium in the subgame starting after the L-branch. The choice M of the principal is not credible when the agent has chosen L because the principal earns 21 with the action T and only 15 with the action M.

The importance of the subgame perfect equilibrium concept is that non-credible strategies or threats cannot be subgame perfect equilibrium strategies. The concept entails a criterion by which it can be determined which policy proposals are credible. If certain choices are not credible, then credibility may be established by doing something with respect to the ingredients players, payoffs or strategies. Section 2.3 will elaborate on credibility.

2.2.5 Information structure

The principal–agent game has been presented as a game with complete information. A more realistic situation is of course that the principal does not know which effort the agent has chosen when he has to decide as to the payment. This information structure is presented in Fig. 2.11 with an oval. The oval contains both decision nodes of the principal. It shows that the principal does not know which choice the agent has made, action S or action L, when he has to decide.

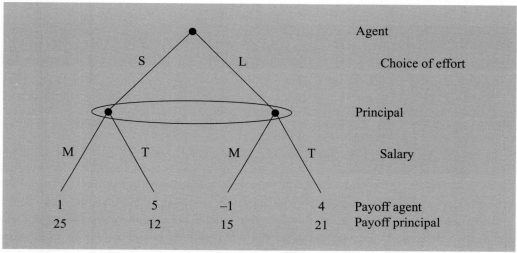

Figure 2.11: Principal–agent game with inperfect information

The oval consisting of two decision nodes is called the 'information' set of the principal. An information set is a collection of decision nodes that the decision-maker cannot distinguish. For example, the principal does not know whether he has to respond to the action S or the action L of the agent. He knows only that the agent has taken a decision, but he does not know which decision.

The above game has two information sets: the information set of the agent, which consists of one decision node, and the information set of the principal, which consists of two decision nodes. The information structure specifies the way in which the collection of decision nodes is partitioned. A specific case is the situation in which every information set consists of one decision node. This is the situation of complete information.

The specification of a strategy depends on the information structure. A different, more precise, definition of a strategy can now be formulated because information sets are defined: a strategy of a player assigns an action to every information set of the player, i.e. it is a specification of an action for every possible observable history (information set) of the game. A strategy is therefore a plan of action for the whole game which specifies an action for every information set. For example, the agent has two strategies, S and L, in the game with imperfect information. The principal has also two strategies in this game, M and T.

A change in the information structure can have a considerable impact on the equilibrium of the game. This can be illustrated with the principal–agent game. Figure 2.12 presents the strategic form of Fig. 2.11. The arrows illustrate that the Nash equilibrium is:

Agent: S;
Principal: M.

The behaviour in equilibrium differs drastically because of the change in the information structure. The agent chooses the effort L and the principal pays T in the game with complete information, whereas the agent chooses S and the principal pays M in the game with imperfect information. Notice also that both players earn less in equilibrium in the game with imperfect information than in the game with complete information.

Agent \ Principal	M	T
S	(1, 25)	(5,12)
L	(−1, 15)	(4,21)

Figure 2.12: Nash equilibrium in the principal–agent game with inperfect information

The definition of a subgame can now be made precise because the notion of information set has been defined. A subgame is a game in which the first decision node is an information set. Notice that in a game with complete information each decision node is an information set. This definition of a subgame implies that the principal–agent game with imperfect information has only one subgame, i.e. the whole game. The subgame perfect equilibrium is therefore the same as the Nash equilibrium.

2.2.6 Rules

Decisions of people are directed and determined in equilibrium by the rules of the game, as e.g. contained in a contract. The next application shows the impact of the order of decisions on what will happen.

Application: Agenda manipulation (McKelvey theorem)

Usually, several persons participate in a decision-making process. Examples are voting in parliament, the approval of the policy of a company by its shareholders and the decision of union members to continue a strike. A collective decision is made by means of some procedure. Many procedures are possible. Electoral systems are a good example. The Netherlands has a proportional electoral system, the United Kingdom a district system and Germany a proportional system with an electoral threshold level. It is easy to aggregate the preferences of all participants in the decision process in one decision when everyone agrees. However, in most situations not everyone does agree.

The decision-making procedure (rules of the game) can have a large impact on the outcome or equilibrium. The election of President Bush in the United States showed this

---

dramatically in 2000. The role of the decision-making procedure or agenda can be illustrated with a trial in which three judges have to decide on the involvement of the suspect in a crime and the degree of the punishment (Dixit and Nalebuff, 1991). The three judges have very different opinions. Judge A is convinced that the suspect is guilty. The death penalty (D) is his first choice. If that is not possible, life imprisonment (L) is his second option. Acquittal (A) should be avoided. Judge B is convinced of the involvement of the suspect as well. Punishment is desired, but judge B is opposed radically to the death penalty. Judge C thinks the suspect is innocent. He prefers A. If a punishment has to be given, then he prefers the death penalty above life imprisonment, because life imprisonment is considered inhuman. The preferences of the three judges are summarized in Fig. 2.13.

Judge Preference	A	B	C
1	D	L	A
2	L	A	D
3	A	D	L

Figure 2.13: Preferences of the judges

The order in which the three judges decide on the involvement and the penalty determine the sentence of the suspect. Three judicial systems will be considered: the American judicial system, the punishment-first system and the Roman judicial system. Decisions are taken by simple, i.e. 50 per cent, majority voting.

American judicial system
The American judicial system entails that the first decision addresses the question of guilt. The penalty is determined subsequently. So, the judges decide first whether the suspect is guilty (Y) or not (N). If Y is chosen, then the judges decide subsequently between D and L. If the majority of the judges decide in favour of N, then the suspect is acquitted (A). Figure 2.14 presents the American judicial system.

The prediction regarding the penalty for the suspect is determined by the method of backward induction (in order to calculate the subgame perfect Nash equilibrium). This entails that the second decision is determined for every possible outcome of the first decision. Subsequently, the first decision is determined, anticipating the outcome of the second decision. If the first decision is Y, then the majority of the judges vote for D, because judges A and C prefer penalty D to L. Only judge B prefers L to D. So, the choice Y in the first stage will result in D and the choice N in A. The choice in the first stage is therefore between D and A. Judges B and C prefer A to D, whereas only judge A prefers D to A. The prediction is therefore that the suspect will be acquitted in the American judicial system.

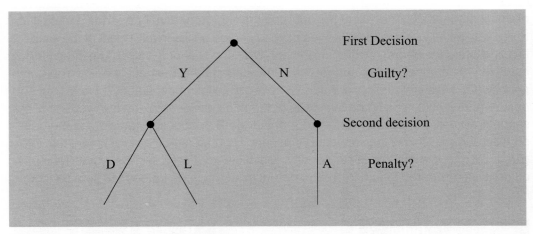

Figure 2.14: American judicial system

Mandatory sentencing
In the mandatory sentencing system, the first decision determines the sentence for the crime. Subsequently the judges vote regarding guilty or not guilty. Figure 2.15 presents the sequence of decisions.

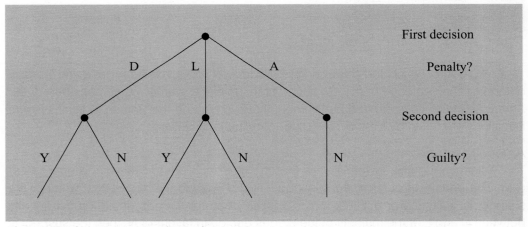

Figure 2.15: Mandatory sentencing system

Judges B and C vote for N, and therefore A, when the penalty is D. Only judge A will vote Y. Judges A and B will vote for life imprisonment when the penalty for the crime is L. Judge C thinks L is inhumane and will vote N, but he is the only one. If there is no penalty for the crime, the result is automatically N. So, the majority of the judges will vote not guilty (N) when the penalty is either D or A, i.e. the suspect will be acquitted. If the penalty is L, then the judges will send the suspect to jail for life. The choice for the three judges in the first stage boils therefore down to L or A. Judges A and B prefer L to A. Life imprisonment will be the fate of the suspect in the mandatory sentencing system.

Roman tradition

The judges take first a decision regarding the death penalty D in the Roman tradition. If this decision is regarded as too severe, they decide whether the suspect deserves L. Acquittal results if there is no majority for L either. Figure 2.16 illustrates the sequence of decisions.

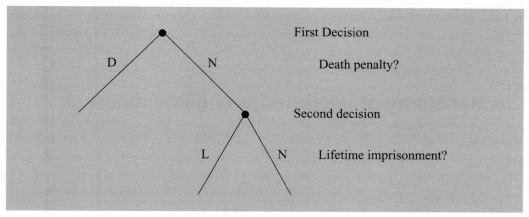

D   N   First Decision

          Death penalty?

          Second decision

L   N   Lifetime imprisonment?

Figure 2.16: Roman judicial system

The judges choose between L and A when there is no majority for D. L will result for the suspect, because judges A and B prefer penalty L above A. When deciding on D, the judges know that rejection will result subsequently in L. Judges A and C prefer D to L. In the Roman tradition, the suspect will face the death penalty.

McKelvey (1976) has shown that the above is not an exception. The McKelvey theorem indicates that almost every possible outcome can be realized through democratic decision-making, by smartly choosing the order or agenda in which decisions are taken. The desired result is established by ensuring that in each stage another composition of the majority determines the outcome of that part of the decision-making procedure. The person who designs the decision-making procedure needs to know the preferences of the participants to achieve his or her most desirable outcome by shifting majorities. It will be clear that the position of chairperson is attractive when he or she has the right to determine the agenda, because it has just been shown that the person controlling the agenda can in principle implement his or her most favoured choice. The expectation is therefore that there will be quite a bit of haggling to obtain this position.

The institutional framework not only specifies the order of decisions, but also the restrictions on the possibilities of choice. Environmental laws of the government restrict the production methods allowed, competition policy prohibits decisions of companies which do too much to hinder the functioning of the market and labour laws specify rules concerning the relationship between employer and employee. Rules or agreements can have consequences for costs and results. Alternative methods of comparing the allocation of means have been researched, like rationing rules, waiting lines and markets (Sah, 1987; Elster, 1991).

Companies make agreements (or choose rules) to structure the competition process (or the organization) in a favourable way.

2.2.7 Conclusion

Game theory is developed for the social sciences in order to analyse situations with multiple parties in a systematic way. It is so far the only method consistent with the assumption that players strive for their own interests and anticipate the behaviour of the other players. This not only characterizes social situations but also formulates predictions regarding behaviour in social situations and offers tools in order to manage social situations. Finally, while this section has treated non-cooperative game theory, there is also co-operative game theory, which will be treated in the appendix to Chapter 9.

2.3 Management implications of game theory

The importance of non-cooperative game theory is twofold. First, it provides insight into situations with multiple parties. A prediction regarding behaviour can be formulated with the notion of Nash equilibrium or subgame perfect equilibrium once the five ingredients of the game have been specified. Second, a number of possibilities are offered in order to establish a more desirable equilibrium in a credible way. This section develops the possibilities regarding establishing a more desirable equilibrium by formulating the management implications of non-cooperative game theory. They entail changing one or more of the five ingredients of a non-cooperative game in order to change the current situation or equilibrium.

The management applications of non-cooperative game theory will be illustrated with the prisoners dilemma in the next five subsections The prisoners dilemma consists of a situation with two persons who are arrested regarding a crime. The police have sufficient evidence to have the two suspects put in jail for some time, but insufficient evidence in order to put them there for a long time. Information from the suspects themselves is needed. The police consider offering a deal to the suspects. They tell each suspect his sentence will be reduced when he confesses and that his confession will imply that the other suspect is guilty. The suspects will be interrogated separately. Figure 2.17 depicts the situation, where S stands for silent and T for talk. The Nash equilibrium is:

Player 1: T;
Player 2: T.

Player 1 / Player 2	S	T
S	(2, 2)	(−1, 3)
T	(3, −1)	(0, 0)

Figure 2.17: Prisoners dilemma

The prisoners dilemma shows that equilibrium does not have to be efficient. A payoff of 2 is possible for each player, but each player earns only 0 in equilibrium. The problem is that each player strives for his own well-being, but this is not necessarily in the common interest. The prisoners dilemma is ubiquitous in the real world. Examples are the disappearance of whales due to hunting by individual whale hunters, the pollution of the environment by individual persons and firms and the advertising and price wars in many industries caused by competition between firms. The next five subsections will investigate the effect of changing each of the five ingredients on the equilibrium in the prisoners dilemma.

2.3.1 Change the players

Changing the players means the number of players is decreased or increased. In the prisoners dilemma reducing the number of players is an obvious option because the action T is very damaging for the other player. Figure 2.18 presents the situation. The Nash equilibrium is:

Player 1 : S.

The equilibrium payoff of player 1 is 2.

Player 1	Payoff
S	2
T	0

Figure 2.18: Prisoners dilemma with only one player

Reducing the number of players can be interpreted in a number of ways. First, a player can be eliminated literally, which sometimes happens between or within criminal organizations. Eliminating a player is an example of a commitment (Dixit and Nalebuff, 1991). A commitment entails an irreversible change of the game by a player so that it will be in the player's self-interest to carry out a threatened (or promised) action. The purpose of a commitment is to establish a more attractive equilibrium for one or more players. Commitments and related strategies, like threats and promises, will be treated extensively in this book.

Second, two parties may merge in order to reduce the intensity of the competitive process. The prisoners dilemma indicates that there can be too much competition. Third, a reorganization may entail reducing the number of decision-makers on a board of directors. The number of parties can also be increased. An example is splitting up a certain department in a reorganization or the departure of a group of enterprising employees setting up their own organization. Another possibility of increasing the number of players is the introduction of a third party. This may establish trust or confidence, or end deadlock, which is often needed in order to resolve labour disputes. Finally, it is obvious that increasing the number of players can have a large impact on the equilibrium when a monopolistic market is opened up by antitrust authorities for other companies.

2.3.2 Change the choice possibilities

Changing the choice possibilities means that the collection of actions, and therefore the number of strategies, is changed. For example, the number of choice possibilities can be reduced from two to one in the prisoners dilemma by eliminating the action T. Figure 2.19 represents this. The Nash equilibrium in this new game is:

Player 1: S;
Player 2: S.

Player 1 / Player 2	S
S	(2, 2)

Figure 2.19: Prisoners dilemma with reduced choice possibilities

An important cause of the unattractive Nash equilibrium is therefore that the players have too many choices available. Organizations are able to influence the number of choice possibilities in many ways. Examples are task assignments, job descriptions, the assignment of responsibilities, open versus closed communication channels and so on. A classic example from military history regarding too much choice is the invasion by Cortes of Mexico. Faced with combat, his soldiers had the option of either fighting or running away. By literally burning the ships, and thereby closing the avenue of retreat, Cortes ensured that they would fight hard. The absence of the option of retreat was likely to give them a strong incentive to fight.

The decrease or increase of the number of choice possibilities is an extreme way of making agreements credible. It is sometimes desirable that the punishment for choosing an unattractive action should not be heavy. However, this can be a problem when the punishment is indivisible, like dropping an atomic bomb. You cannot drop half an atomic bomb (Dixit and Nalebuff, 1991). A punishment can however be reduced by not executing it with certainty, i.e. by allowing uncertain circumstances or randomness to play a role. On average, the introduction of uncertainty makes the punishment smaller. Examples are the uncertainties about the precise motives of an arbitration committee in a labour dispute, uncertainty about decision-making when a problem is moved to a higher level in an organization and uncertainty about the decision of a judge.

These examples show that the introduction of uncertainty entails a number of issues. First, the uncertainty regarding the outcome will be resolved by somebody after some time. Giving control to somebody else introduces a number of disadvantages. A potential threat is that this person can tilt the randomness in a certain direction. This can be prevented by using a mechanism which cannot be manipulated or by employing someone who cares about having a good reputation, like a judge or an arbitrator. Second, the probability of punishment needs to be acceptable to both parties. Third, the uncertainty has to be removed when the desired behaviour has been established. An example is the reorganization of a department in a large organization. Doing nothing is undesirable, whereas abandoning is costly for all concerned. Co-operation can often be obtained by offering the department the choice between reorganization and going private, as privatization would force the department to compete with others in the market. Another example is the possibility of making a deal with the department of justice in order to prevent a costly trial. Judges often offer the possibility of arbitration in a conflict, and many people accept the arbitration offer, even though they are convinced they are right. A deal with the department of justice is often accepted in order to prevent negative publicity or to eliminate the uncertainty regarding the outcome.

The attractiveness of introducing uncertainty in the choice possibilities can be illustrated with a numerical example in the prisoners dilemma. Suppose player 1 chooses the action S with probability 2/3 and the action T with probability 1/3, while player 2 chooses action S with probability 1/4 and the action T with probability 3/4. Player 1 earns $2/3(1/4 \times 2 + 3/4 \times 3) + 1/3(1/4 \times -1 + 3/4 \times 0) = 21/12$ and player 2 earns $1/4(2/3 \times 2 + 1/3 \times 3) + 3/4(2/3 \times -1 + 1/3 \times 0) = 1/12$. Both players benefit. Notice that the elimination of choice possibilities in the prisoners dilemma in Fig. 2.19 can also be formulated in terms of a probability distribution, where players 1 and 2 choose action S with probability 1 and action T with probability 0.

2.3.3 Change the payoffs

Changing the payoffs occurs frequently in organizations. Examples are the restructuring of budgeting systems, reward structures and the required level of return on investment. A change in payoffs can be interpreted in two ways. First, one player can be replaced by another with different preferences, e.g. an easygoing manager by a more exacting one. Second, the payoffs of a player can be changed, e.g. when an output-based salary is replaced with a fixed one. The second possibility will now be illustrated with the prisoners dilemma. Assume that a player who chooses T has to pay 4 to the other player. Figure 2.20 presents the new situation. The Nash equilibrium is:

Player 1: S;
Player 2: S.

Agent \ Principal	S	T
S	(2, 2)	(3, −1)
T	(−1, 3)	(0, 0)

Figure 2.20: Prisoners dilemma with different payoffs

After players and choice possibilities, payoffs are an important third way of establishing credibility. Payoffs can be changed in such a way that it becomes unattractive to withhold a promise or threat. Contracts or reputations can be valuable in this context. Credibility can be established relatively easily by specifying the penalty which has to be paid when certain promises or threats are withheld. Contracts specify these aspects in a formal way. A contract serves two important roles. First, it is a mechanism for establishing credibility. This is important not only for executing current agreements, but also in offering guidance for further activities and making plans for the future. Second, the payoffs have to be structured in such a way that it is in the interest of both parties to honour the contract. A conflict of interest between the parties can be reduced by the structure of payoffs in the contract. An example is the relationship between an employer and an employee. The employer likes to see a high level of production and the employee on a low salary in order to secure a large profit. An employee, on the other hand, may well prefer to take things easy, which tends to reduce the level of production, and prefers a high salary to a low one. The conflict of interest is reduced to a certain extent by making the salary of the employee dependent on the amount produced.

Contracts are not without problems, however. A frequent source of these is the credibility of contractual clauses and agreements, i.e. doubt as to whether or not the contract is completely binding. One of the parties to a contract can decide to renege on it – for example, a customer may refuse to pay for services rendered, or a supplier may not deliver the quantity agreed. It is often difficult in these situations to enforce the penalty agreed upon. Thus an effective contract regularly requires an unbiased party to take an interest in its execution, for example a judge or an intermediator who has an interest in maintaining a reputation for independence.

A second problem may arise when new information becomes available. Rewriting the contract can be attractive to both parties. However, adjusting the contractual terms because of new information becoming available is not without problems. If the parties anticipate that the contract will be adjusted later on, then they may decide not to sign it in the first place. An example is the policy of some companies of providing their managers with incentives in the form of option packages, giving them the right to buy shares in the company in the future at a price determined today. Since a rise in share price is likely to be related to the effort and dedication of the manager, the option package gives the manager an extra incentive to do well. However, such a policy has no effect when the share price decreases. The writing of new options at a lower price becomes attractive for both parties. If managers take these adjustments into account, then they need not really worry about a decrease in the share price.

2.3.4 Change the information structure

A change in the information structure means the number and size of some information sets will be adjusted. Figure 2.5 showed the principal–agent game with complete information, the information structure being composed of three information sets, each consisting of a decision node. Figure 2.11 showed the principal–agent game with imperfect information, the information structure comprising two information sets, one consisting of one decision node and the other of two decision nodes. That change in information structure can have a large impact on behaviour in equilibrium has already been shown in Figs 2.10 and 2.12.

However, this is not necessarily always true. A change in the information structure of the prisoners dilemma can illustrate this; Fig. 2.21 presents the prisoners dilemma with complete information.

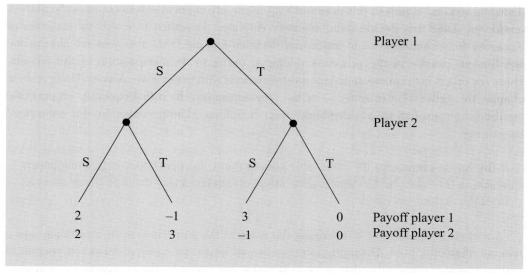

Figure 2.21: Prisoners dilemma with complete information

The Nash equilibrium in the prisoners dilemma with complete information is easiest to determine with the method of backward induction in the extensive form. The Nash equilibrium is:

Player 1: T;
Player 2: (T,T).

More information has therefore no impact on the equilibrium payoffs. The equilibrium outcome remains inefficient, despite the change in information structure.

The strategic form of the prisoners dilemma with complete information is presented in Fig. 2.22. It is intended as a contrast to Fig. 2.17, in order to illustrate the impact of the information structure on the number of possible strategies.

Player 1 \ Player 2	(S,S)	(S,T)	(T,S)	(T,T)
S	(2, 2)	(2, 2)	(−1, 3)	(−1, 3)
T	(3, −1)	(0, 0)	(3, −1)	(0, 0)

Figure 2.22: Prisoners dilemma with complete information in strategic form

2.3.5 Change the rules

Changing the rules of the game is the final possibility which can be considered in order to do something about the unattractive Nash equilibrium in the prisoners dilemma. The first and most obvious possibility of changing the rules of the game is to reverse the sequence of decision-making. However, this does not help in the prisoners dilemma because the players are identical and they decide simultaneously. A related possibility is to alter the structure of decisions from simultaneous to sequential decision-making. This also does not change the equilibrium payoffs in the prisoners dilemma, owing to the composition of the payoffs. However, this is not representative for most situations with two or more parties. Being able to change the order of decisions is often very attractive. It will frequently change the equilibrium (payoffs) in a substantial way. Schelling (1960) writes in the context of bargaining:

> if the buyer can accept an irrevocable commitment, in a way that is unambiguously visible to the seller, he can squeeze the range of indeterminacy down to the point most favorable to him.

A second possible way of changing the rules of the game is to split a problem into a number of smaller ones. Diverging interests are an important cause of a healthy amount of mutual distrust, especially when a lot is at stake. For example, the two parties involved in building a new house, the constructor and the buyer, do not have unlimited trust in each other. The buyer is not willing to pay all the money involved in advance because the possibility exists that the constructor may run away with it. On the other hand, the constructor is worried that the buyer will not pay when the house is completed. A solution to these worries is that regular payments are done for work which is completed, so that both parties run the risk of losing only a small amount. This step-by-step procedure creates trust and establishes credibility for both parties in such a way that the project is completed (Admati and Perry, 1991).

The prisoners dilemma cannot be split into smaller problems, but repetition provides possibilities for establishing an attractive equilibrium outcome. This possibility will receive considerable attention in Chapter 10. It will turn out that bad behaviour today cannot be punished tomorrow when the prisoners dilemma is played only once, whereas repeated interactions provide this possibility. This provides various possibilities for establishing an efficient outcome in the prisoners dilemma.

2.4 Conclusion

The scheme of thought in this book consists of specifying the problem and setting out the behavioural hypotheses. A problem is characterized by five aspects and game theory is presented as a unified method incorporating these. The two ontological criteria of degree of rationality and behavioural hypothesis will be used throughout to classify, develop and compare various approaches to organization and strategy.

2.5 Exercises

2.1 The board of a major bank has to decide where 1 billion euros will be invested. There are three possibilities: Asian markets, biotechnological industries or postpone the decision. The board consists of a chief executive officer and two directors. Decisions are made by majority voting.

The CEO believes strongly in the emerging Asian markets, with biotechnology the second choice. The first director favours the biotechnological industries, but if that is not possible, then postponement is preferred above investing in Asian markets. Finally, the second director prefers the emerging Asian markets above the biotechnological industries. However, postponement is the first choice of the second director because the current stock prices are viewed as too high.

A Define the McKelvey theorem.

B Will the CEO choose the decision procedure in which the board decides first which possibility to consider and decides subsequently about approval? Explain your answer with a tree diagram.

2.2 An agent has to decide regarding the acceptance of a task offered by a principal. If the agent does not accept the task, then each player earns 20. If the task is accepted, then the principal decides about the division of the surplus generated by the project, which is equal to 100. Assume that the principal can choose between a 50–50 division of the surplus and taking the whole surplus.

A Present the extensive form.

B Determine the subgame perfect equilibrium.

C Is the subgame perfect equilibrium efficient?

Part II:
Two benchmarks

Co-ordination and motivation problems can be solved in many ways: by explicit or implicit agreements, by orders or by prices. Each possibility has advantages as well as disadvantages, which makes the optimal choice hard. This part formulates the advantages and disadvantages of the price mechanism. Circumstances will be determined in which the price mechanism has only advantages, and are summarized in the welfare theorem in Chapter 3. This is an important theoretical result, because it on the one hand delineates what can be achieved at most and on the other hand shows how co-ordination and motivation problems can be dealt with in order to reach this result. The Coase theorem extends this result in Chapter 4. Figure II.1 shows which behavioural assumptions are made to formulate these results.

		Behavioural hypothesis		
		Opportunistic	Self-interested	Idealistic
Degree of rationality	Complete rationality		General equilibrium	
	Limited rationality			
	Procedural rationality			

Figure II.1: Positioning of Part II

The parable of the blind Hindus and the elephant (Sec. 2.1.2.2)will be taken literally at the beginning of each part in order to highlight the perspective of the firm which is taken. The firm is conceptualized as a production function in the theory of general equilibrium. Figure II.2 illustrates the view of the firm taken in this part.

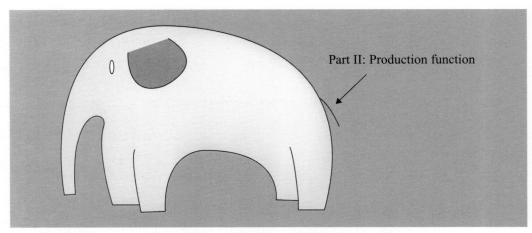

Part II: Production function

Figure II.2: View of the firm in the theory of general equilibrium

3 Welfare theorem

LEARNING OBJECTIVES

After completing this chapter, you should understand:

- The fundamental welfare theorem.

- Why the fundamental welfare theorem is a useful benchmark for organization theories.

- The concept of the firm which underlies the fundamental welfare theorem.

Contents

3.1 Introduction

Since the eighteenth century, economic analysis has been directed towards social interactions between people who on the one hand aim to advance their self-interest and on the other have diverging interests. Adam Smith (1776) made it clear that it may actually be beneficial for society when everybody is self-interested:

> He intends only his own gain, and he is in this, as in many other cases, led by an invisible hand to promote an end which was no part of his intention.

Individuals pursuing their own self-interest can, according to Smith, unintentionally accomplish something which is in the interest of all:

> By pursuing his own interest he frequently promotes that of the society more effectually then when he really intends to promote it.

Another important contribution to economic analysis is formulated by Marx (1863). He acknowledged the early successes of capitalism, but predicted its downfall as a result of the concentration of property (capital) in the hands of a few capitalists. Walras (1874) provided a mathematical foundation for the advancement of self-interest by people which explains the relative value of goods and services. Pareto (1909) gave content and meaning to the concept 'efficient use of means'. Finally, the theory of general equilibrium established the relationship between individual behaviour characterized by self-interest and the efficiency of the aggregate outcome. Arrow and Debreu (1954, 1959) are main contributors to the theory of general equilibrium.

This chapter highlights the *fundamental welfare theorem* as the most important result in the theory of general equilibrium. In the model of general equilibrium all economic activities occur via markets and prices play a crucial role in order to establish an attractive outcome.

3.2 General competitive equilibrium

In Chapter 1 we discussed the law of comparative advantages. The highest total level of production is established when people specialize in the activities in which they have a comparative advantage. Production is usually followed by (voluntary) exchange between the various parties in order to establish Pareto improvements. This can be illustrated by the Edgeworth box, which is also a nice stepping stone to the fundamental welfare theorem.

Suppose there is a two-person economy, where Tim and Nancy are the two agents (Schotter, 1997). Every morning they gather fruit which grows on the trees. Assume that Tim picks 8 pounds of apples and 1 pound of oranges every day, while Nancy picks 2 pounds of apples and 7 pounds of oranges every day. This economy consists therefore of 10 pounds of apples and 8 pounds of oranges at the end of the morning. Tim and Nancy will trade apples and oranges when they can both benefit from the exchange. The possibilities for (mutually) beneficial exchange are presented by the Edgeworth box in Fig. 3.1.

The Edgeworth box presents Tim and Nancy as the two parties to the trading process, the two goods, their endowment or wealth, and their preferences. The horizontal axis presents the total amount of 8 oranges, while the vertical axis depicts the total amount of 10 apples. Each

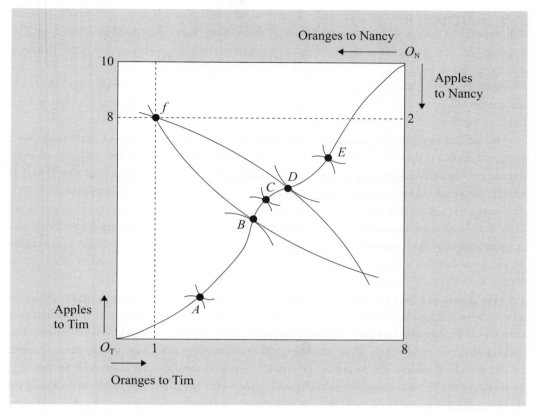

Figure 3.1: The benefits of trade

point in the Edgeworth box reflects a possible allocation of the two goods to Tim and Nancy. Point f reflects the endowment or wealth of the two parties at the end of the morning, i.e. the amount of oranges and apples possessed by Tim and Nancy. The preferences of the two parties are presented by the indifference curves. The curve bowed towards the south-west is an indifference curve for Tim, i.e. all combinations of apples and oranges on this curve have the same level of utility for him. The curvature reflects the law of diminishing marginal rate of substitution, i.e. reducing the number of apples requires more and more oranges in order to maintain the same level of utility. Indifference curves to the north-east of the depicted curve represent higher utility levels for Tim. Similarly, the curve bowed towards the north-east is an indifference curve for Nancy.

The above Edgeworth box shows that there are many opportunities for Pareto-improving trade at the end of the morning. Each allocation inside the lens entails a strict Pareto improvement for Tim as well as Nancy compared with the endowment allocation f. We define the *contract curve* as the set of Pareto-efficient allocations, i.e. the set of points (x,y) for which the two indifference curves touch. No party can increase his or her level of utility without decreasing the level of utility of the other party. Efficient bargaining results in a point on the contract curve. $O_TABCDEO_N$ is the contract curve.

All points between B and D on the contract curve are efficient and entail a Pareto improvement for Tim as well as Nancy. However, Tim and Nancy are not indifferent between

B and *D*. The actual point on the contract curve at which Tim and Nancy agree finally to trade will depend on how well they bargain. Point *B* shows that Nancy is a good bargainer, i.e. she receives all the gains from trade. Similarly, point *D* reflects a situation where Tim is a relatively good bargainer compared with Nancy. Notice that the allocations on O_TB are efficient. However, they will be blocked by Tim, i.e. Tim prefers the (inefficient) no-trade allocation *f* to every allocation on O_TB. Similarly, points on DO_N are efficient, but they will be blocked by Nancy.

One of the reasons the range of possible equilibrium trades cannot be narrowed down further than *BD* is that there are only two persons in this simple society. The addition of other agents reduces the bargaining power of any single agent. Extreme allocations like *B* and *D* will be eliminated by the addition of other agents by a process of blocking (Schotter, 1997). The range *BD* will shrink ultimately to one point *C* when the number of agents becomes large. This is the *unique competitive equilibrium* allocation, where the price of apples and oranges is determined by the tangency of the two indifference curves. Each agent will be a *price taker* because each agent separately will have no bargaining power when the number of agents is large.

This result can be extended to a society consisting of many consumers and producers, where there is a market for each possible good and service. Equilibrium prices are such that consumers buy products which satisfy their needs best, given their budget restrictions. The same holds for producers. They choose profit-maximizing activities, given the available production technology. There are no possibilities left in equilibrium such that somehow a more attractive outcome can be established. This result is called the *fundamental welfare theorem*. Milgrom and Roberts (1992, p. 62) state this result as follows:

If
1   each firm maximizes its profits, knowing the prices and its own production technology;
2   each consumer maximizes utility, knowing the prices and his or her own preferences;
3   income and prices are such that demand equals supply for every good and service
then
     the resulting allocation of goods and services is Pareto-efficient.

The price mechanism equals the quantity demanded and the quantity supplied in *every* market. The equilibrium is Pareto-optimal because the maximum value of the sum of consumer and producer surplus is realized in every market. It is remarkable that this decentralized system – without any explicit planning and exchange of information – solves all *co-ordination* and *motivation problems*, where all the relevant information is transferred by prices. Only local information and prices are necessary to accomplish the co-ordination of decisions. Entrepreneurs, motivated by profit, make decisions based on purchase and sale prices, while utility-maximizing consumers are led by prices in buying products. The assumption that everyone is self-interested provides the stimulus (motivation) to take good decisions, which eventually results in a Pareto-optimal allocation for society as a whole. The market system solves co-ordination and motivation problems perfectly when certain circumstances are satisfied.

The range and scope of the fundamental welfare theorem should not be underestimated. It is *general*, rather than partial, equilibrium because it is assumed that there is a market and a price for all goods and services and the quantity demanded is equal to the quantity supplied in every market. A broad interpretation of the notions of goods and services makes it possible to accommodate time, uncertainty and location in the analysis. *Time* can be incorporated in the analysis by making a distinction between, for instance, oil today and oil next month. Companies which are going to produce 'oil next month' will use the inputs 'oil today' and 'inventory space today'. Both 'oil today' and 'oil next month' have different markets – the spot market and the futures market – and a price is determined in each market. Another example is the rental of skis. Skis in summer differ from skis in winter. Therefore the prices for these products will differ. *Location* of goods and services is processed in the same way in the analysis. Ice-cream in Spain is a different product from ice-cream in Norway; each has its own market and a price. *Uncertainty* is incorporated in the analysis by distinguishing the circumstances as a characteristic of the product: a bicycling holiday in a rainy summer is a different product from a bicycling holiday in a sunny one. Similarly, the effect of technologies yet unknown, like for instance the impact of the use of nuclear fusion on that of a product like oil, can be dealt with in the same way.

The model of general equilibrium is based on the two concepts of the individual and the market. The behaviour of *individuals* is the outcome of profit maximization or utility maximization under certain constraints. Exchange conditions adjust until the quantity demanded equals the quantity supplied in the *market*. The local behaviour of innumerable individuals results in an attractive outcome for the whole system. The welfare theorem is a remarkable result, because the price system, together with self-interested behaviour, is sufficient to establish an efficient allocation. Central planning is not needed. Enthusiasm about this impressive result is expressed in the following quote regarding desk lamps (Evans and Gross-man, 1983):

The production and distribution of any commodity entails many stages and much coordination. Perhaps your desk is illuminated by a lamp. Your lamp is designed to fit on your desk by a special attachment; has a plug which fits into an electrical socket on the wall of your office; has a frame coloured to match your rug; was sold to you in a lamp store which enabled you to choose a lamp to match your tastes and which you were able to reach by car. The lamp manufacturer produced neither your wall socket nor your lamp's electrical parts. He simply thought of the lamp's design and supervised its assembly. Many things could have gone wrong but did not. The electrical plug is compatible with the same electrical socket you plug your radio and calculator into. The bulb socket is compatible with bulbs sold by several manufacturers at numerous convenient locations. A retail store, located in a shopping mall where you purchase many other goods, stocked the lamp you wanted. Yet the lamp manufacturer owns neither the shopping mall, the retail store, the companies that manufacture the wires and sockets, the electrical cables that deliver the electricity to light the lamp, the electricity generating plants, nor the roads you drove upon.

You purchase light for your desk at home by purchasing a lamp from a manufacturer who, in turn, probably purchased the parts for the lamp from several other manufacturers; by purchasing a house, with electrical sockets and wires made by a number of companies; by buying electricity from your local utility; and by buying a lightbulb from one of several manufacturers. You do not have to install a different type of wall socket for every appliance you use. You do not have to find separate power sources or buy expensive adaptors to operate your appliances. If you move, your new home will have wall sockets that accommodate your old appliances and receive the same voltage of electricity as your old home. You do not have to travel far from home to purchase a light-bulb that fits your lamp. You are able to light your desk because numerous businesses found it in their self-interest to produce commodities that are mutually compatible and interconnective.

This quotation contrasts strongly with the many anecdotes which are around regarding the central planning system in the former Soviet Union. Well known is the cartoon showing an enormous nail hanging in a large workshop: 'The month's plan fulfilled,' says the director, pointing to the nail. In tonnes, of course. However, black markets and queues illustrate the flexibility and power of the market mechanism as a simple social system with an unambiguous result even when its functioning is frustrated – by fixing prices and removing stimuli for taking good decisions – by a system of centralized planning.

General equilibrium theory has been the standard model in economics for a long time. It is an important result because everybody is perfectly happy, given the preferences and constraints. However, daily life may be different according to the general equilibrium perspective because one or more of the assumptions of the welfare theorem are not met. Causes for the *failure of the market system* are incomplete information, asymmetric information, market power, limited cognition and externalities. In these cases the market is not necessarily the most appropriate institutional structure to accomplish an attractive exchange of goods and services. This opens the door for exchange outside markets – for instance through contracts or within organizations. It is therefore important to know what the causes of the failure of market functioning are – and to formulate solutions. Violations of explicit or implicit assumptions of the welfare theorem which are responsible for failure of the market system will feature in the following sections, while Parts III to VII will formulate possible solutions for these problems.

3.3 Production function

The firm is conceptualized as a production function in the theory of general equilibrium. Labour (l) and capital (c) are transformed somehow (f) into output (y) in the production function view of the firm. This is represented as

$$y = f(l,c).$$

Specifications of the function f, e.g. Cobb Douglas, Translog and CES (Varian, 1978), have been used to deduce input demand and supply relationships. Such relationships are established by determining the cost-minimizing combination of inputs which can produce a certain level of output. The firm is viewed as a cost-minimizing entity, in which scale and scope advantages play an important role.

This approach has turned out to be useful in the analysis of a large number of problems at the market level of analysis. One example concerns determining the influence of changes in the environment (exchange rates, taxes, wages) on changes in production decisions in companies (Varian, 1978) and determining the consequences of strategic interactions in oligopolistic markets (Tirole, 1989). At a lower level of aggregation than the market, the view of the firm as a production function has some weak points. In the neoclassical approach, the *size of the firm* is not explained, because the production function is assumed to be given. A larger company is created by combining two production functions. The number of possible input–output combinations can increase only because of a merger, which means that production can be done more efficiently. This results in the prediction that companies will merge as much as possible. When eventually a single vast organization comes about, which is very unlikely in reality, this process will stop. The main objection against this technological view of the firm is that it is viewed as a 'black box', in which inputs are plugged in and production comes out. Figure 3.2 illustrates this.

Figure 3.2: The firm as a production function

In the production view of the firm, the way in which this transformation occurs and the problems which arise are left open. Interesting co-ordination and motivation problems can hardly be addressed, although they are important in the daily affairs of enterprises. *Co-ordination problems* receive hardly any attention, because in this perception one decision-maker chooses the optimal combination of inputs and outputs. This decision-maker considers all possibilities and simply takes the decision which maximizes profit (or minimizes costs). Co-ordination problems do not occur, because there is no interaction between different persons. In real organizations, however, many people continuously take decisions which need to be co-ordinated.

Motivation problems do not play a role in the production function view either, because no conflicts of interests between the parties are recognized. There is only one party taking decisions regarding inputs and outputs. In the production function view the factor 'labour' is presented by a number which summarizes how many people are employed in the organization. There is no explicit role for management tasks like formulating, implementing and supervising the policy of the company; co-ordinating different divisions or working units; balancing the differing interests of employees, owners, customers, suppliers and providers of capital; or giving performance stimuli. Individualized labour contracts and the organization of tasks and functions at the level of the smallest production unit can be approached better by a view of the firm other than that of the production function. Less aggregated conceptualizations of the firm will feature in the following parts, which will make it possible to analyse problems of motivation and co-ordination between the different parties within and between firms.

Information is valuable for at least two reasons: to support the decision-making process and to control the activities of others. Information from a firm's accounts gives the opportunity to pursue better control. Such information can also be used in designing contracts. The *availability* of information will turn out to be important in the explanation of several organizational practices. Asymmetric information will feature prominently in several organizational theories, i.e. one party has information which others have not. This simple starting-point provides insights regarding the incentive aspects of reward systems, financial structures, accounting techniques and organizational structures.

The distinction between technological perceptions of the firm and approaches which emphasize co-ordination and motivation problems can also be found in classic organizational theories. A famous author in organizational theory is Taylor (1911). His name is associated with technological aspects of labour and organization. In his view, technical efficiency is the dominant consideration in order to determine the 'one best way' of organizing. Organizations to which Taylor's insights can be applied are characterized by known objectives, constantly repeated tasks, outputs which are sold easily and inputs which are available at constant quality. Fayol (1916) emphasizes other aspects of organizations. He distinguishes five management tasks: 'To manage is to forecast and plan, to organize, to command, to coordinate and to control.'The problems which come with these activities are highlighted in this book, separately as well as in an integrated fashion. Attention will focus on people and their motives, and not so much on the technological aspects of organizations. This book follows Marshall (1890) and Schumpeter (1942) in considering organization, next to labour and capital, as an important factor of production.

3.4 Prices

The interactions within and between markets and the role of prices in transferring information are the focus of attention in general equilibrium theory. A *price* is a number in currency units, which indicates that it is attractive to start a project or to buy a product when the value is higher than its price – and not to do so when it is lower. Many aspects are associated with prices, like information and motivation (3.4.1), the law of one price (3.4.2), price formation (3.4.3), information structure (3.4.4) and robustness (3.4.5).

3.4.1 Information and motivation

'Information' and 'motivation' are expressed in prices. The *information aspect* of the price is expressed by the fact that a low (high) price means that less (more) activities are desired. The *motivation aspect* is reflected in the incentive, by the level of the price, to develop the desired activities. People are inclined to produce less (more) goods or services when the price is low (high).

3.4.2 Law of one price

The level of the price in a market economy is usually interpreted as the result of the interaction between demand and supply. The equilibrium price 'clears' the market, in the sense that demand is equal to supply. Possible shortages disappear by price increases, while surpluses do so by price decreases. Those willing to pay the price for the product receive it from those wanting to sell it for that price. This is the *law of demand and supply*. A price is determined for each product and each service.

One price is established on all markets according to the fundamental welfare theorem, for which the quantity supplied is equal to the quantity demanded. This result is called the *law of one price*. However, the law of one price does not hold always. First, there are situations where the demand curve and the supply curve do not intersect, for example markets with increasing returns to scale. Increasing returns to scale can be caused by a production technology with high fixed costs and almost constant marginal costs. In this situation, the supply curve shows a discontinuity ('gap'), because the company does not produce below a certain price level, while above this level the quantity produced is high. The price is not able to equate the quantity demanded and the quantity supplied.

A second reason why the law of one price does not hold always is the restrictive character of the assumption of *anonymity* of consumers and producers in markets. This assumption implies for instance that the name 'Mr Jones' does not have any informative value for a bank issuing a loan, because all characteristics of all customers are perfectly known. The loan can be made fully dependent on the characteristics of the person involved. It will be emphasized in various parts of this book that the anonymous character of markets will disappear in situations with asymmetric information in the form of hidden characteristics, in which reputations of consumers and producers play a role. On top of that, it may be attractive for a bank to offer various loan proposals at the same time, because different customers choose different contracts. So, different prices can be established for the same product, i.e. the law of one price does not hold.

3.4.3 Price formation

Price formation is not explained by the fundamental welfare theorem. An invisible hand (the Walrasian auctioneer) functions as a *deus ex machina* to equate demand and supply. This is reflected by the intersection of demand and supply. The price equates demand and supply, i.e. the price clears the market. The way in which this price is determined is not specified and not necessary, because all relevant information is available when the assumptions are satisfied. The resulting price assures that after the exchange everybody is at least as well off as before it.

However, if what the other person is willing to pay or receive is unknown, i.e. if reservation prices are unknown, then the bargaining process may result in inefficiencies. Bargaining entails costs. Exchange may be delayed, or not occur at all, whereas exchange would happen instantaneously were all information known to everybody. Asymmetric information offers possibilities for misrepresentation, which may mean that a surplus-generating exchange will not occur.

In a sense, demand and supply are too succinct a summary of the underlying characteristics of consumers and producers. Exchange is established in a bargaining process, in which various problems may emerge but are shoved under the rug, as it were, by referring to an invisible hand. Another way to formulate this assumption is the fact that the fundamental welfare theorem assumes implicitly that bargaining is efficient. There is no bargaining process specified in which people formulate offers and bids and may misrepresent their reservation prices. Every profitable exchange is deemed to occur. It has to be said that the same fundamental welfare theorem can be constructed by formulating a bargaining process. This will not be elaborated upon in a context of markets. A lot of attention will be paid to various bargaining problems and their implications for the choice of organization.

3.4.4 Information structure

The results of general equilibrium theory apply mainly to markets without information problems. In markets with low information costs, the law of demand and supply and the law of one price are usually valid. Prices summarize all relevant information. However, such revelations are very sensitive to small changes in the *information structure*. Relationships between individuals are usually more complicated than those of the world created by the assumptions of general equilibrium theory, because, for instance, not all information is available to everyone. One party may have access to superior business information which can be used to his or her own particular benefit. A party can also distribute unfavourable or even wrong information. The other parties in the market may anticipate this and take the appropriate precautionary measures, which may result in market outcomes which are not efficient. Part III will show that this can even result in the disappearance of a market. Alternatives to prices will then be developed in order to transfer or acquire the desired information. Formulating contracts between parties is an example here; the desired information may be acquired or the wrong initiatives prevented by the right choice or design of the contract specifications.

3.4.5 Robustness

Another aspect of the fundamental welfare theorem is the fact that a firm can try to imitate the impressive market result internally by a system of *transfer prices*. Chapter 10 will address the role of transfer prices in a context of incomplete contracts, while Chapter 13 will examine what top management can contribute when only local managers are well informed regarding the production function and each seeks to maximize the profit only of his or her own division. We will see that there are situations in which the price mechanism is less robust towards wrong information than are other co-ordination mechanisms.

3.5 Walrasian auctioneer

Important assumptions of the fundamental welfare theorem are that firms know the prices and their own production technology, that consumers know the prices and their own preferences, and that the prices are such that the quantity demanded is equal to the quantity supplied. The informational needs of consumers and producers are limited, because only local information (own production technology or preferences) and prices are required for decision-making. Information regarding the preferences and production technologies of others is not needed in order to establish co-ordination. According to Adam Smith, all decisions are co-ordinated as if they are guided by an '*invisible hand*'. General equilibrium theory incorporates this invisible hand by introducing the '*Walrasian auctioneer*'. This has implications for the communication structure (3.5.1), decentralization (3.5.2), co-ordination (3.5.3), corruption (3.5.4), honesty (3.5.5) and the order in which decisions are made (3.5.6).

3.5.1 Communication structure

All information flows are directed to, or come from, the Walrasian auctioneer. He *collects* all relevant information (reservation prices) from everyone, and subsequently *calculates* market-clearing prices based on the collected information, which are finally *reported* as information to the persons involved. This Walrasian communication structure is shown in Fig. 3.3. The Walrasian auctioneer is located at the centre. All individuals communicate only with the auctioneer, by reporting information in the form of reservation prices and by receiving information in the form of prices. All (potential) co-ordination and motivation problems between individuals are solved by this communication structure with the auctioneer at its centre.

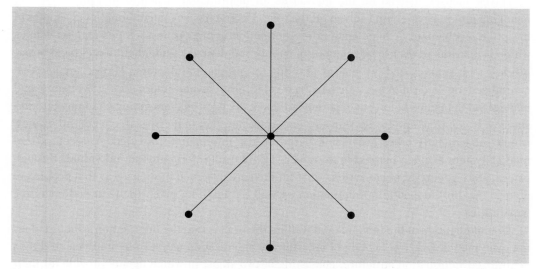

Figure 3.3 Communication structure in the fundamental welfare theorem

Figure 3.3 shows there is communication only between the Walrasian auctioneer and the market parties. The auctioneer collects the relevant information of all persons involved, processes it, and sends back the relevant information through prices. There is no direct communication between market parties. Auctions are an example of such a communication structure. Many other communication structures exist. Employees in companies communicate directly with each other, buyers and sellers negotiate and companies exchange information. The communication structure also plays an important role in the centralization or decentralization of activities in organizations and within many companies will typically have various layers. All this exchange of information between the members of an organization occurs when the right performance incentives for revealing information are formulated. If these incentives were provided, the choice of *information system* would even be irrelevant. In the theory of general equilibrium all these aspects of communication are ignored because of the presence of the Walrasian auctioneer, who of course in reality does not exist.

3.5.2 Decentralization

The fundamental welfare theorem is usually interpreted as characterized by decentralization, because consumers and firms each decide individually about their course of action. Exchange occurs at market-clearing prices. However, the way market-clearing prices are formed is not decentralized at all. All relevant information is collected by the Walrasian auctioneer in order to determine the market-clearing price in every market. Subsequently these equilibrium prices are transmitted to everyone. When all local information can be collected centrally without any problems, there is no reason to decentralize. A central authority can make efficient choices too. However, real decentralization means that decisions are being delegated to those who use the local information most efficiently. Therefore according to

Hayek (1945) it is wrong to interpret the fundamental welfare theorem as decentralized in character. In the theory of general equilibrium it is centralization which seems to characterize the fundamental welfare theorem.

Hayek focuses instead on the market as an institutional structure in which new and changing problems are being solved all the time. He emphasizes the informational aspects of the price mechanism. A huge amount of information is present in societies and economies which is distributed over local relations of supply and demand, embodied in technical possibilities and summarized in the availability of production factors. Hayek argues that centralized decision-making can hardly involve all relevant information. Economic and managerial decisions belong to experienced, local decision-makers facing changing circumstances. It is unrealistic to expect every important new fact to be passed to a central agency, which subsequently takes a decision based on the information provided. A decentralized market system is much more able to transfer all relevant information to individuals through prices. More generally, organizations (institutions) are designed in such a way that people are able to handle the available information as well as possible, given their limited cognitive capabilities.

One implication of the fundamental welfare theorem is that the information structure does not even matter. Every allocation of an arbitrary organization can also be implemented by a centralized information structure, consisting of two steps, in which agents provide all their relevant information to the principal (the center), who subsequently translates this into an allocation. The communication of information from the agents to the principal is supposed to be costless. However, a prime concern in the choice of hierarchical structure (organization) is often the smooth processing and use of information. When as well as only limited possibilities for communication there are also conflicts of interests between parties, the issue arises of performance stimuli in delegation issues (Melumad *et al.*, 1991).

3.5.3 Co-ordination problems

There are no *co-ordination problems* in the model of general equilibrium. The Walrasian auctioneer collects all the relevant information and determines an equilibrium price for every market. This enables every producer and consumer to determine without any problems where the best prices are offered. However, no one can ever examine where trading is most attractive for all products and services, because it involves too much time and money. One has to collect information from various sources, like experience, friends, experts and reports in the media. A lot of useful information can be gathered in this way, but it involves a lot of time and effort. One has at some point to stop gathering information and make a choice, or the costs of searching become too high, though this will inevitably result in missed opportunities. Therefore in such circumstances explicit contracts or organizations may prove superior alternatives to markets. Many co-ordination problems do also occur inside organizations, e.g. between a production and marketing department or between the members of a quality circle. Part VI will deal with co-ordination problems.

3.5.4 Corruption

It is implicitly assumed in the fundamental welfare theorem that the centralized Walrasian auctioneer *cannot be manipulated*. However, someone *can* aim to influence the decision of the auctioneer in a way which serves his or her own interest. This situation is different from the one analysed above, and therefore requires a different approach. Commitment is an important consideration in this context and will be addressed repeatedly.

3.5.5 Honesty

Another aspect of the fundamental welfare theorem is honest reporting. Three assumptions have to be satisfied in order to make honest reporting an attractive strategy for consumers as well as producers. First, the Walrasian auctioneer must be able to bind himself in a credible manner to a mechanism which determines market-clearing prices. Second, agents must be able to transmit all their information. Third, there must be no restrictions regarding the type of contracts which can be used. If these assumptions are satisfied, then there is no role for *organizations* to be served, i.e. they create no value. However, organizations are to be expected in situations where these assumptions are not met. Various organizational practices will be viewed as a response to the violation of one of these three assumptions.

3.5.6 Order of decisions

In the model of general equilibrium all agents report their information *simultaneously* to the Walrasian auctioneer. When there are no restrictions on communication their order is not important. However, this will change in an environment with limited possibilities for communication. Sequential transmission of messages by the agents may be optimal. A hierarchical structure (of contracts) creates extra *flexibility*, because the contract between two agents can be based on better (local) information than a single, all-encompassing contract formulated by the Walrasian auctioneer for all agents. Delegation exploits the possibilities of the flexible handling of local information in decision-making. A disadvantage of delegation however is the *loss of control*, because the agent will use his or her monopoly position regarding information to his or her own benefit. Part III elaborates on this extensively. In choosing an organization structure, the tradeoff between flexibility and loss of control has to be taken into account when an organization structure is chosen.

3.6 Contracts

A contract is a document which specifies the rights and obligations of the players. An effective or meaningful contract specifies an agreement for every observable situation which can occur. Two kinds of agreements can be distinguished. A *specific agreement* is made when the observable situation or information can also be verified by a third party, for instance a judge. A *general agreement*, for instance the allocation of decision rights, is made for all the observable situations in which the circumstances cannot be verified by a third party.

Completely contingent contracts prevail in the theory of general equilibrium. These contracts are specific because the assumption of complete rationality is responsible for the fact that everything can be, and will be, made fully contingent or dependent on every characteristic of every possible situation. There are only goods and services with well-observable characteristics, and the participants can ascertain without costs whether the agreements regarding the exchange are met. Therefore it is possible to draw up comprehensive contracts. These contracts consist only of specific agreements.

Part III abandons the assumption that all relevant information is available to everyone. There is still complete rationality, but all relevant information is no longer available to everyone. (This entails problems with asymmetric information for which, to a certain degree, contractual solutions will be formulated.) The assumption of complete rationality allows the design of a *complete contract*, in which are written only those agreements for which the relevant information is available to *all* persons involved. (Agreements regarding situations in which not all relevant information is observable by everyone cannot be part of a meaningful or effective complete contract.) A complete contract, like a complete contingent contract, consists only of specific agreements.

Part IV will no longer assume that all observable information will be processed in contracts. Bounded rationality precludes the possibility that contracts can incorporate without costs all relevant information regarding every possible circumstance. This results in an *incomplete contract*. Incomplete contracts leave (ex ante) room for unexpected or unanticipated future circumstances (ex post). Specific agreements are part of a meaningful or effective incomplete contract for every situation in which the information is observable as well as verifiable. General agreements cover situations where the relevant information is observable but not verifiable. This creates possibilities for raising questions regarding governance structure, control, authority and leadership, which is not possible in Parts II and III because of the assumption of complete rationality.

3.7 Large number of consumers and producers

The fundamental welfare theorem assumes that a *large number of consumers and producers* is present in all markets. However, often only a limited number of players are active in a certain market, because of the nature of the production technology or the size of the market. A limited number of firms often results in behaviour which is profitable, e.g. monopoly profits, but it is inefficient for society as a whole. The prisoners dilemma in Chapter 2 has illustrated this dramatically. People often claim that the main message of Adam Smith in his *Wealth of Nations* is that greed is good. That is false and the prisoners dilemma shows this. The point of the *Wealth of Nations* is that greed in competitive markets is good. The important question is, when is a market is competitive? In fact, experimental economics (Smith, 1989) shows that three parties on each side of the market are enough to result in efficient outcomes.

Section 3.5.5 has specified the requirements needed for honest reporting. These requirements are not needed when the number of buyers and sellers is large. A large number of buyers and sellers makes it unprofitable for an individual buyer or seller to depart from the rules of perfectly competitive behaviour when everyone else continues to abide by these rules. However, if the number of buyers and sellers is limited, then it pays to misrepresent preferences in order to achieve a higher payoff. Part III will address the extent to which contracts can deal with this problem.

3.8 Complete rationality

Complete rationality is a strong assumption in the theory of general equilibrium. For all goods and services, a price is established which equates demand and supply. All relevant information is available and is taken into account in the determination of the prices. There are as many prices as there are goods and services. These goods and services depend on location, time and uncertainty. However, it is unrealistic to assume that everyone takes all these prices into account when decisions are made. Parts IV to VI relax the assumption of complete rationality.

3.9 Externalities

Markets may have problems with *externalities* and public goods. Externalities and public goods entail collective consumption or production. If these effects are not accounted for in the prices, then prices signal the wrong information. In such situations, costs are not paid for by the party generating the costs (*negative externality*) or the benefits are not received by the person creating the benefits (*positive externality*). An example of a negative externality is pollution. The costs are often charged only partly to the polluter, the remainder being paid for by third parties. The supply function is lower than in the situation in which all costs are paid by the polluter. Therefore, too much pollution is produced in equilibrium. An example of a positive externality is fundamental research. Not only the specific field of research benefits from fundamental research but so also does scientific development in general. The prediction is that the market will generate an inefficient amount of fundamental research. Externalities can be interpreted as the absence of markets – because there are no prices associated with positive or negative effects. The next chapter will examine under which circumstances the market can handle externalities in an efficient way.

3.10 Conclusion

The importance of the theory of general equilibrium is that it specifies under which circumstances fields like accounting, finance, marketing and organization do not matter. All co-ordination and motivation problems are addressed in an efficient way by complete contingent contracts and the all-knowing Walrasian auctioneer. There is no role left for accounting, finance, marketing or organization to provide solutions for problems of co-ordination or motivation.

The fundamental welfare theorem acts as a *benchmark* for the development of theory regarding accounting, finance, marketing and organization. Other benchmarks have been formulated, like the Modigliani–Miller theorem in the field of finance and the Coase theorem, which is highlighted in the next chapter. Parts III to VII will relax the assumptions of the fundamental welfare theorem, which will bring to the surface various co-ordination and motivation problems which markets may not handle well. This provides an important role for accounting systems, financial instruments, marketing instruments and organizations in addressing co-ordination and motivation problems in a way better than markets can.

3.11 Exercises

3.1   There are three buyers. Each wants to buy exactly one unit of a product. The reservation prices are 2, 1 and 0.5 euros. Also three sellers want to sell exactly one unit each. Their reservation prices are 0.25, 0.75 and 1.5 euros.
   A Draw the demand curve.
   B Draw the supply curve.
   C Which price is established in equilibrium in the market?
   D What is the sum of the consumer and producer surplus?

E Is the equilibrium Pareto-optimal?

F Does equity play a role in equilibrium, i.e. is the surplus divided equally over all buyers and sellers?

G Suppose there is a centrally planned economy instead of a market economy. Is there an allocation possible such that three units are exchanged and that prices are determined such that everyone receives the same surplus?

H What is the sum of the consumer and producer surplus?

I Why is the allocation in question G unstable?

J Question C assumed implicitly that an unstructured bargaining process resulted in equilibrium. Do you think that a more specific prediction regarding the price can be formulated when buyers are allowed to propose the final bid?

K Assume that the market consists only of the buyer with a reservation price of 1 euro and the seller with a reservation price of 0.75 euro. Do you think that the availability of information regarding the reservation prices can have an effect on the occurrence of exchange?

3.2 The fundamental welfare theorem states the conditions under which the price mechanism resolves all motivation and co-ordination problems in an efficient way.

A State the fundamental welfare theorem.

B Which communication structure is implicitly assumed in the fundamental welfare theorem? Explain your answer.

C Formulate an example which shows that there are also other communication structures. Explain your answer.

3.3 Suppose a country is faced with waiting lists regarding health services, extensive traffic jams and many people receiving social security benefits.

A What do you advise from the perspective of the fundamental welfare theorem in order to solve these problems?

B Which view of the firm is taken in the fundamental welfare theorem?

C State three causes from the perspective of the fundamental welfare theorem which may have led to at least one of the above problems.

4 Coase theorem

LEARNING OBJECTIVES

After completing this chapter, you should understand:

- The Coase theorem.

- Why the Coase theorem is a useful benchmark for the development of organization theories.

- The effect of bargaining and income constraints on the assignment of property rights.

Contents

4.1 Introduction

Markets seem to have problems with externalities and public goods (Sec. 3.9), but they can be supported in a number of ways. For example, activities with negative externalities can be made more expensive by raising *taxes*, while activities with positive externalities can be *subsidized*. However, taxes and subsidies are not without problems. For example, an efficient tax authority has to be created with the appropriate knowledge regarding activities with externalities.

A second way of dealing with externalities is to *internalize* them. The conflicting interests of the producer and the receiver of the externality evaporate when they are merged. Consider for example a firm and a holiday resort situated near a lake. The pollution of the firm eliminates the possibilities for a successful development of recreational activities. However, a company owning the firm as well as the recreational activities will try to maximize total value. The amount of pollution will decrease when the associated costs are compensated for by the increasing recreational activities. This second solution is also not without problems. The possible benefits of merger or centralization are stressed without taking into account the *costs* of centralization. An important disadvantage of centralization involves the problems regarding the processing of information, which were treated in the previous chapter (Hayek, 1945). Individuals already have difficulties processing a lot of information, let alone a centralized organization.

This chapter offers a third way to solve the problems of markets with externalities (3.9) and small numbers of players on the supply or demand side (3.7). The creation of an additional market is the focus of attention in Sec. 4.2. The main result is formulated and explained in Sec. 4.3. Sections 4.4 to 4.6 provide additional depth regarding the assumptions of the Coase theorem. Section 4.7 concludes.

4.2 Additional market for externalities

A basic problem with externalities is the wrong allocation of *ownership rights*. If a choice is accompanied by the legal responsibility for its effects, then there is no problem with externalities. However, there is often a discrepancy between a range of activities and the legal responsibility for the effects of those activities. This is the cause of too much pollution or too little fundamental research – when the decisions about such activities are left completely to the market. Coase (1960) suggests, as a third way for dealing with externalities, the creation of a *market for externalities*, in which ownership rights have to be traded. These rights cover the gap between the range of activities and the legal responsibility for the results.

The problem with externalities is: who pays for the costs? If a polluting firm near a lake causes costs, either the local residents can pay the firm to give up production or the firm can pay or compensate the local residents for the damage suffered. In the first situation, the ownership rights regarding the lake are possessed by the polluting firm, in the second by the local population. This example will now be elaborated upon in order to explain how equilibrium choices are influenced by the *allocation of ownership rights*.

Assume that *the decision rights regarding pollution have not been determined.* Figure 4.1 presents the value of one marginal unit of pollution of the firm (*VMP*) and the marginal damage for the local residents (*MD*). The *VMP* represents how much the firm is willing to pay to get rid of the garbage, i.e. the reservation price of pollution. The *MD* represents how much the residents are willing to pay to get rid of pollution, i.e. the reservation price of damage. If no pollution rights have been determined, then the firm will dump B units of pollution in the lake. In this situation the costs for the firm of dumping are zero, whereas the profits are represented by *VMP*.

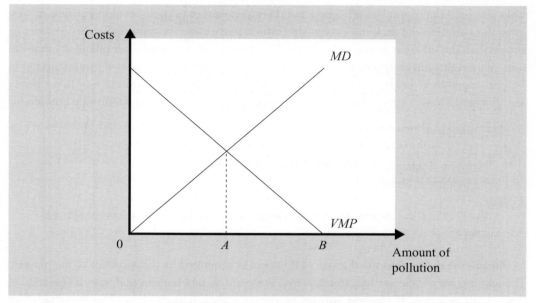

Figure 4.1: Reservation prices of pollution of local population and the firm

Assume that pollution rights have been determined and that there is a market in which the ownership rights can be traded. The pollution rights can be allocated in several ways. Two cases are considered. First, suppose that the firm owns the pollution rights, i.e. the firm has the right to dump B units of pollution in the lake. However, this is not what the firm will do. The local residents are willing to pay the firm for reducing the amount of pollution from B to A units, because for every unit between A and B it holds that $MD > VMP$. Although the firm owns the pollution rights, it will pollute less than B, because the residents are willing to pay more than the *VMP* to stop the production of these marginal pollution units. Both parties profit from this outcome. The amount of pollution will not be less than A units, because in these situations $VMP > MD$. The residents are willing to pay at most *MD*, whereas the polluter wants to receive at least *VMP* to decrease its production further. The conclusion is, from the viewpoint of the firm as well as the local population, that an efficient amount of pollution is produced when the pollution rights are owned by the firm. The sum of the consumer and producer surplus is highest when the amount of pollution is A units. This is a first-best situation. Notice that some pollution is desirable (efficient), i.e. the efficient amount of pollution is not equal to zero. The efficient amount of pollution is determined by comparing the costs of pollution with the costs of no pollution.

Second, suppose that the *pollution rights are owned by the local residents*, i.e. they possess all the rights to a clean environment. They can therefore stop all the pollution of the lake. However, the residents will allow some pollution, because $VMP > MD$ holds for all marginal pollution units between 0 and A. The firm can pay the residents an amount between *MD* and *VMP* for the right to pollute. The local population will accept. Both parties gain, i.e. there is a Pareto improvement. Again, the negotiation process regarding the pollution rights stops when A units of pollution have been traded, because no additional surplus can be created. This is again a *first-best situation*.

An important insight yielded by this example is the fact that the amount of pollution is A when the pollution rights are allocated and there is a market to trade them, *regardless* of who owns the pollution rights. It does not matter which party owns the pollution rights in order to accomplish the efficient amount of pollution A. However, it is essential for efficiency that the ownership rights are assigned. In a market economy, a clear determination of ownership rights (a legal framework) is crucial, but it doesn't matter in terms of total welfare how these rights are allocated. Coase (1960) shows that it is important for this result that bargaining is efficient.

> *Coase theorem.*
> If
> 1   property rights are defined, allocated and enforced;
> 2   bargaining is efficient;
> then
> every allocation of property rights in externalities will result in a Pareto-efficient allocation.

Bargaining determines the division of the surplus generated by the activities of the players. The assumption of efficient bargaining means there are no problems in realizing the creation of the maximum value. If efficient bargaining prevails, then bargaining power affects only the *division* of costs and benefits, and not the *size*. Efficient bargaining results in the complete *internalization* of externalities (external pollution costs), regardless of the ownership of these rights. Exchange occurs without transaction costs when bargaining is efficient.

The Coase theorem can be presented graphically (McKelvey and Page, 1999). Assume that x is the amount of pollution produced by the firm, where x is between 0 and 1. Define y as the payment to the residents, where y can be either a positive or a negative number. A negative value of y is interpreted as a payment by the residents to the firm. For example, if the firm has the right to pollute the lake, then the residents are probably willing to pay the firm in order to reduce the amount of pollution.

Suppose that the combination (x,y) is valued at $u(x,y)$ by the firm and valued at $v(x,y)$ by the residents. These (utility) values (or preferences or reservation prices) can be depicted with indifference curves. An indifference curve of the firm is a set of points (x,y) with the property that they all have the same value $u(x,y)$. An indifference, e.g. (x,y) with $u(x,y) = 3$, has a positive slope because a higher value of x results in a higher level of utility for the firm and a higher value of y results in a decrease of the level of utility. Indifference curves of the firm have a higher value when they are located more to the south-east. Indifference curves of the residents have also a positive slope, and they have a higher value when they are located more to the north-west.

A party has the property rights when it is allowed to choose the value of x when no agreement is reached. The governance structure *firm rights* prevails when the firm has the right to determine x. If there is no bargaining, i.e. the value of y is equal to 0, then the firm pays nothing to the residents ($y = 0$) and chooses the level of x which maximizes $u(x,y)$. The highest level of pollution will be produced, i.e. $x = 1$. The governance structure firm rights results in the status quo point (1,0). The two parties can try to establish an improved (x,y) by bargaining. The allocation which results with the governance structure firm rights when bargaining is efficient is called E.

The governance structure *residents' rights* assigns the right to choose x to the residents. If there is no bargaining, then the residents pay nothing to the firm ($y = 0$) and they choose a value of x which maximizes $v(x,0)$. The lowest level of pollution will be chosen, i.e. $x = 0$. The governance structure residents' rights results therefore in the status quo point (0,0). The two parties can try to improve on the status quo point by bargaining. The allocation which results with the governance structure residents' rights when bargaining is efficient is called E^*.

Figure 4.2 depicts the situation. The status quo points (1,0) when the firm has the rights and (0,0) when the residents have the rights are clear. The indifference curves of the firm and the residents in a situation where there is no bargaining ($y = 0$) and the firm holds the rights are represented by u^1 and v^1, respectively. (Notice that all points enclosed by the indifference curves u^1 and v^1 are Pareto improvements compared with the status quo point (1,0).) Similarly, u^0 and v^0 are the indifference curves of the firm and the residents when the governance structure residents' rights prevails. The line through the points A, E^*, B, C, E and D is the contract curve, where the points on the line segment AB represent an improvement for each party compared with (0,0) and the points on the line segment CD represent an improvement for each party compared with (1,0).

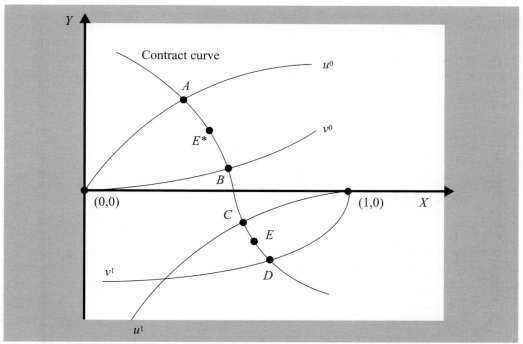

Figure 4.2: Coase theorem

McKelvey and Page, 'Coase Theorem', *Economics and Philosophy*, 1999 © Cambridge University Press

Notice that both allocation E and allocation E^* are efficient because they are on the contract curve. E as well as E^* is a Pareto-efficient outcome, i.e. no player can increase his level of utility (by moving to another indifference curve), without decreasing the level of utility of the other player. However, this does not imply that the firm and the residents are indifferent between E and E^*. The level of pollution of allocation E is higher than the level of pollution of allocation E^*. The firm prefers E above E^*, while the opposite holds for the residents. Ownership is therefore attractive.

The amount of pollution is higher when the firm has the rights than when the residents have them. This result differs from the example at the beginning of this section where the amount of pollution was invariant to the property rights regime. However, this can also be represented in Fig. 4.2 by changing the preferences of the two parties, i.e. by changing the slope of the indifference curves of the two parties. Figure 4.3 reflects this in the vertical contract curve. The accompanying strong version of the Coase theorem is:

Coase theorem (strong version).
If
1 property rights are defined, allocated and enforced;
2 bargaining is efficient;
3 preferences do not exhibit income effects,
then
(a) every allocation of property rights in externalities results in a Pareto-efficient allocation;
(b) and the amount of damage is invariant to the allocation of property rights.

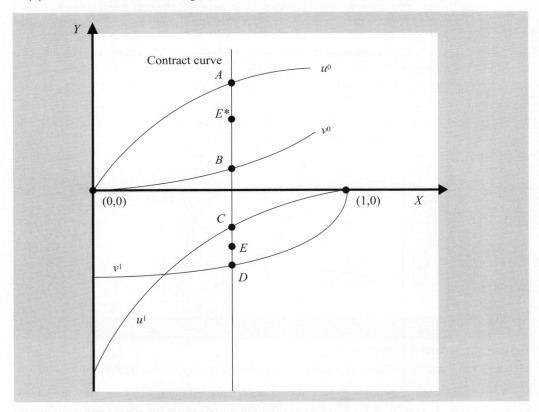

Figure 4.3: Coase theorem (strong version)
McKelvey and Page, 'Coase Theorem' (Strong Version)', *Economics and Philosophy*, 1999
© Cambridge University Press

Income effects occur when decisions depend on the level of wealth of the players. Figure 4.3 represents a situation with no income effects, because the amount of pollution is identical for each point on the contracts curve, regardless of the amount of money transferred. This situation is not typical. If large amounts of money are involved in decision-making, then income effects are likely to occur. For example, the spending behaviour of a person probably changes after an unexpected salary raise. The occurrence of income effects is also affected by the possibilities of insuring oneself against the results of a bad decision. For example, it is not a good idea to hold an air traffic controller completely responsible financially for accidents caused by his decisions. He is simply unable to carry the financial responsibility. Even holding someone partly responsible financially can be undesirable, because this can cause over-cautious behaviour. Income effects have important ramifications for the way organizations motivate their employees financially.

Application: Apples and bees

Apples and bees generate a positive externality for each other (Cheung, 1973). The bees of the beekeeper pollinate the blossom of the trees of the apple-grower. The beekeeper therefore generates a positive externality for the apples in the orchard, in the form of pollination. Likewise, the owner of the orchard provides food for the bees of the beekeeper, in the form of nectar. The apple-grower therefore generates a positive externality in the form of honey for the beekeeper.

If the apple-grower does not take the positive pollination externality into account, less apples are grown than is desirable from the viewpoint of the apple-grower and the beekeeper together. Figure 4.4 shows this situation. The supply curve S represents the costs of growing apples when the positive externality of the beekeeper is not taken into account. The demand curve D represents the demand for apples by consumers and therefore the yield of the apples. The point of intersection of the curves S and D determines the amount of apples the apple-grower will grow.

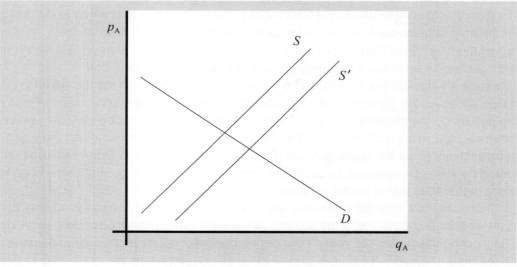

Figure 4.4: The market for apples

If the beekeeper places his hives in the orchard, the costs per apple will decrease. The curve S' reflects this positive externality. The point of intersection of S' and D represents the equilibrium when the positive externality is taken into account. The amount of apples grown will increase.

A similar analysis holds for the honey market. If the beekeeper does not take the positive nectar externality of the apple-grower into account, less honey is produced than is desirable from the viewpoint of the apple-grower and the beekeeper together. Figure 4.4 is therefore also representative of the situation on the honey market. The curve S reflects the production costs of honey when the positive externality is not taken into account. The curve D reflects the consumer demand and thus the yields of honey. The curve S' represents the lower costs as a result of the positive externality of the availability of the orchard for the beekeeper.

The externalities in the production of apples and honey result in a low level of output of both products, because the positive externality is not taken into account. Markets appear to malfunction in situations with externalities. A Pareto improvement is possible, because each party does profit if the other produces more. Coase showed that these inefficiencies can be resolved by markets by creating markets for externalities. It turns out that markets for these externalities or services actually do exist.

Ownership rights are clearly defined and allocated in the above situation. The beekeeper owns the hives and has the right to exploit the pollination services. These rights are in principle tradable. The same applies to the right to place the beehives in the orchard. These rights are owned by the apple-grower. The pollination services are important to the apple-grower, whereas access to the orchard is important to the beekeeper.

The market price of both services depends on the relative size of the two externalities. In spring, the trees are blossoming and pollination is important to the apple-grower. Apple-growers are therefore willing to pay a considerable rent for placing beehives in the orchard. The beekeeper sells the right to use the hives (temporarily) to the apple-grower. The honey yield is quite low during this time of the year. The price that will be established for the right to place the hives in the orchard will therefore be low. The net result, i.e. the rent of the hive minus the price of access to the orchard, is that the apple-growers pay the beekeepers an amount of money in order to place hives on their land.

Figure 4.5 depicts the situation in both markets during spring. In the market for pollination services, the demand of apple-growers for these services (D_f) is high, whereas the supply by the beekeepers (S_b) is normal. In the market for nectar services, which means access to the orchard, the demand of beekeepers (D_b) is low, whereas the supply of these services by the apple-growers (S_f) is normal. In spring, therefore, beehives are rented by the apple-growers, because the price in the market for pollination services is much higher than that of nectar services.

Circumstances change drastically after spring. The honey season is during the summer and the beginning of the autumn, whereas the demand for pollination services is low during this part of the year. In this period beekeepers pay a considerable amount for the right to place hives on the land of the apple-growers, who are not willing to pay

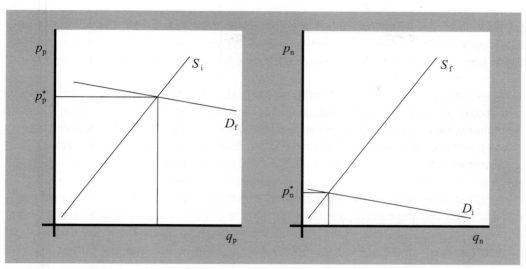

Figure 4.5: The markets for pollination services and nectar during springtime

anything to rent hives. This can be represented in a figure similar to Figure 4.5. D_f has to move downwards in the market for pollination services, whereas D_i has moved upwards in the market for nectar services. In autumn, the beekeepers pay for access to the orchard, because then the price of pollination services is much lower than that of nectar services. In short, according to the Coase theorem, markets can in fact deal with externalities in an efficient way when ownership rights are defined and have been allocated.

Application: The Golden Age/Industrial Revolution

The Netherlands was once, in the Golden Age, the most powerful country in the world, and the West has, thanks to the Industrial Revolution in the nineteenth century, achieved enormous welfare for its citizens during the last two centuries, leaving the Arab and Chinese civilizations far behind. Why are some countries or continents prosperous while others are not? History books point often towards the invention of the steam engine as the beginning or cause of the Industrial Revolution. North and Thomas (1973, p.2) do not agree:

> The factors we have listed (innovation, economies of scale, education, capital accumulation, etc.) are not causes of growth; they are growth. This book focuses on what causes economic growth. Growth will simply not occur unless the existing . . . organization is efficient. Individuals must be lured by incentives to undertake the socially desirable activities. Some mechanism must be devised to bring social and private rates of return into closer parity.

According to North and Thomas, the development of the steam engine is not the cause of the Industrial Revolution, but an expression of growth. Growth is in their view caused by efficient organization, or the efficient assignment of ownership rights. Efficient organization means that institutions and ownership rights are determined in such a way that incentives for individuals match their own interest as well as the common interest. North and Thomas (1973, p. 132) write about the Netherlands in the Golden Age:

> In general the economic interests of these rulers lay in promoting international trade, in reducing guild exclusiveness and monopoly and in preventing the local guilds from imposing their restrictive practices on the development of industry in the country. These were precisely the policies that favored the development of an efficient economic organization.

A higher level of economic development has to be supported by many aspects of a society, like new institutions, the development of capital markets, temporary financial agreements, piece-rate payments, double accounting and so on. The system as a whole is evolving, in which the various elements need to be matched with each other.

4.3 Focus of the Coase theorem

The Coase theorem entails more than the above simple formulation suggests. This section will highlight several implicit and explicit aspects of the Coase theorem. Ownership structure (4.3.1), number of producers and consumers (4.3.2), decentralization (4.3.3), institutions (4.3.4), and negotiations (4.3.5) will be discussed.

4.3.1 Ownership structure

An *ownership structure* specifies who has the ownership rights. The composition of the ownership structure has a large influence on the value that will be created with an asset. Ownership rights are distinguished in decision rights and income rights (Boycko, 1995). *Decision rights* are all rights that involve the use of an asset. *Income rights* are rights to receive the profits and pay the costs associated with the use of an asset. Well-defined ownership rights are crucial for economic success. If the ownership rights are well specified and the person who decides pays the costs and receives the revenues, then the means of production are often used in the most efficient way.

Application: Ownership structures regarding land

A simple numerical example will illustrate the importance of a well-designed ownership structure. Suppose a farmer can use his land in two ways. Growing vegetables himself will yield 100, whereas rental to a third person yields 150. An efficient ownership structure creates the maximum value 150.

Consider three possible ownership structures. The first ownership structure assigns the decision and income rights to the farmer. The farmer will not use the land for growing vegetables, because renting it out will yield more (150 > 100). This ownership structure, in which the farmer owns both rights completely, is therefore an efficient one.

The second ownership structure also assigns the farmer all decision rights. However, the allocation of the income rights now depends on the way the farmer uses his land. He

---

has the full right to the income generated when he cultivates the land, but the income rights of rental are testamentarily divided 50–50 between him and his brother. The farmer will grow vegetables because 100 > 150/2. This is an inefficient ownership structure, because only a value of 100 is realized, whereas 150 is possible.

The third ownership structure assigns the income rights to the farmer, but he shares the decision rights regarding another use with his brother. The brother wants compensation for his approval to a proposal of the farmer to change the use of the land, for instance half of the yield. The farmer will grow vegetables himself with this ownership structure (100 > 150/2). This ownership structure is therefore inefficient as well.

The Coase theorem indicates that the results of an inefficient control structure can be handled best by doing nothing. According to the Coase theorem, there is no problem with an inefficient assignment of ownership rights. The efficient outcome will be established by bargaining about buying or selling decision rights (to invest, to not interfere in future). For the above, this means that the farmer and his brother can solve the inefficiency in the second and third ownership structures.

In the second ownership structure, the farmer and his brother could sign a contract in such a way that the brother would get 20 per cent of the rent instead of the 50 per cent in the testament. This way, the ownership structure will lead to the efficient decision. The farmer will now decide to rent, because this will yield 120 as compared with 100 if he grows vegetables himself. Similarly, the brother now receives 30, whereas a 50–50 division of the rental income would not result in rental and therefore would mean no income for the brother at all. Both players gain.

In the third ownership structure a contractual solution is possible as well. If the farmer pays his brother 30 to abandon his decision or approval right, then the efficient decision will be made. The farmer gains 20 because rental generates 120 for him, whereas the brother gains 30 by selling his decision right.

4.3.2 Number of producers and consumers

The Coase theorem extends the domain of the fundamental welfare theorem considerably. Large numbers of consumers and producers are *not* necessary to establish efficiency. Inefficiencies between one buyer and one seller can be resolved by bargaining. The same applies to externalities. Additional markets for externalities can be created such that markets generate an efficient outcome. Trading ownership rights on an additional market prevents externalities being a problem for the efficient functioning of markets.

4.3.3 Decentralization

The Coase theorem can be interpreted as a *decentralization* result. It specifies circumstances in which decentralization establishes an efficient allocation, without paying attention to possible associated problems. Decisions guided by self-interest alone result in an efficient outcome for all participants together. If efficient bargaining prevails, then there will be no need to study various organizations (institutions). In such circumstances there will be no co-ordination and motivation problems. Many of the subsequent chapters will argue that in fact such circumstances hardly ever occur, which decreases the attractiveness of decentralization. The nature of market imperfections has to be delineated in order to determine which institution can handle inefficiencies best. The Coase theorem focuses attention on the way in which various organizations handle imperfections in bargaining. *Decentralization* can turn out to be optimal, but of course it doesn't have to be; *centralization* may be more attractive in handling co-ordination and motivation problems.

4.3.4 Institutions

An important contribution of the Coase theorem is that *institutional aspects* – like legal status and ownership rights – are given a more prominent role than in the fundamental welfare theorem. As well as the price and quantity aspect of market functioning, the allocation of ownership rights has received attention in Fig. 4.1. The Coase theorem emphasizes that a variety of institutions are necessary to make the market mechanism function well. The allocation of ownership rights, the design of contracts and the choice of the institutional framework are no longer exogenously given, but have become an important object of analysis. The traditional focus of the neoclassical economic approach turns out to be too narrow, because it is geared to production costs. Institutional costs, which are associated with the management of organizations and the design and execution of contracts, are neglected.

The importance of the Coase theorem for the development of organization theory is that it specifies in which circumstances the allocation of ownership rights does not matter. However, these circumstances are very specific, which implies that they are hardly ever met. Perfect market functioning will be the exception rather than the rule, and the allocation of ownership rights will often prove important. Determining the circumstances in which the conditions of the Coase theorem are not met is important, because this is fertile ground for the rise of institutions or organizations other than markets that will reduce the inefficiencies of exchange via markets. Situations in which bargaining is inefficient, and/or where income effects do play a role, form a starting-point for the explanation of organizations.

4.3.5 Bargaining

The Coase theorem assumes that the costs of settling and executing an efficient arrangement are zero. If market exchange is inefficient, one can still achieve an efficient result when bargaining is without problems. An efficient allocation will be established when bargaining is efficient, regardless of the presence of perfectly competitive markets, the allocation of ownership rights, externalities, and the division of bargaining power. Section 4.5 will explore which bargaining problems make it difficult to establish an efficient allocation.

4.4 Income effects

Income effects hardly play a role when the amount of money at stake is just a fraction of the wealth of the players. The absence of income effects implies that the problem of the *division of value* or welfare or surplus between persons can be separated from the problem of the *creation of value* or the size of the surplus. The absence of income effects makes it possible to establish a relationship between the allocation of resources and Pareto optimality. In the absence of income effects, an allocation is Pareto-optimal only when the total value of the parties is being maximized (Milgrom and Roberts, 1992). An increase in the joint surplus can always be established, because the additional surplus can always be divided in such a way that everybody gains.

The Coase theorem does not always hold in reality. This may be due to the theoretical assumptions underlying it. Financial restraints undermine the assumption of no income effects and can prevent the realization of efficient results. For example, a new business idea may not come into existence because of a poor *financial position*. Another aspect of income effects is *income inequality*. It can have several effects on the establishment of the efficient outcome. First, the least-wealthy party may not be able to compensate the other party for altering his or her choice. Second, salary differences between employees may hinder Pareto efficiency within companies. This is the problem of optimal salary inequality in organizations, which will be addressed in Part IV. Such considerations will turn out to have important implications for the possibilities which organizations have of influencing the behaviour of their employees by their decisions regarding reward structure, accountability, task freedom, local autonomy and so on.

4.5 Bargaining problems

The second assumption of the Coase theorem is *efficient bargaining*. The importance of bargaining is often underestimated. Demand and supply analysis is an illustration. The price is determined in some unspecified way ('the invisible hand') by the intersection of the demand and supply curves. From an aggregated level like the market, or even the entire economy, that might be all anyone wants to know, but for the people involved at the micro level, bargaining is of eminent importance. A great many things involve bargaining, for example formulating collective labour agreements and marriage contracts and also purchasing cars and houses.

Important aspects of negotiation are, among others, the number of players involved, the patience of the players, the available alternatives, the importance of the various contributions and the availability of information. For example, a limited number of parties can cause problems because strategic behaviour regarding the real preferences can result in a breakdown of the bargaining process. One party can misrepresent preferences in order to establish a better bargaining result, but this behaviour can also result in no agreement at all. This section will treat in more detail asymmetric information (4.5.1 and 4.5.2) and multiple parties (4.5.3).

4.5.1 One-sided asymmetric information

The effect of one-sided asymmetric information will be illustrated by the governance structure residents' rights. If the firm and the residents are honest about their preferences $u(x,y)$ and $v(x,y)$ in the bargaining process, then equilibrium E^* results in Fig. 4.6. The utility level of the firm is $u(E^*)$. Suppose now that the firm misrepresents its true valuation $u(x,y)$ in the bargaining process by u'. The residents continue to say that their preferences are summarized by v. (Notice that the set of Pareto improvements compared with the status quo point $(0,0)$ has shrunk.) If the residents believe the firm, then the equilibrium will be E'. The firm earns $u(E')$. Notice that the firm prefers E' to E^* because E' is on a lower indifference curve than is E^*. The firm has therefore benefited from misrepresentation.

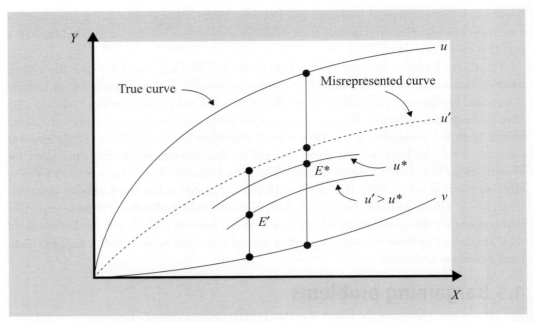

Figure 4.6: Misrepresentation by the firm
McKelvey and Page, 'Misrepresentation by the Firm', *Economics and Philosophy*, 1999
© Cambridge University Press

Many situations in daily life seem to contradict the Coase theorem. Second-best results are, according the Coase theorem, due to violations of one or more assumptions. For example, bargaining may be inefficient, ownership rights allocated in the wrong way or income effects revealed as important. An important aspect of these assumptions is often complete information. Figure 4.6 has already shown that asymmetric information in bargaining makes misrepresentation beneficial.

The Coase theorem indicates that it doesn't matter for efficient outcomes who owns the ownership rights, as long as they are allocated to someone and bargaining is efficient. This result can even be achieved in situations with *one-sided* asymmetric information, but then the identity of the party having the ownership rights is important. The efficient allocation of ownership rights entails that the decision to determine the price is assigned to the party with the superior information.

The party with the superior information should have the decision authority, in order to realize the maximum surplus.

This concentration of bargaining power entails that this party receives the entire surplus, because he or she knows, and will ask, the reservation price of the other party. It is efficient, but not necessarily fair. A more equal division of the surplus can be achieved by transferring a fixed amount of money to the other party.

Application: Allocation of bargaining power in the bidding process for a house

Assume the buyer knows the reservation price 2 of the seller, but the seller does not know the reservation price 5 of the buyer. If the buyer has the power to determine the price, then the price will be 2. The buyer will accept this price. The efficient outcome, with the sum of consumer and producer surplus equal to 5 – 2 = 3, is achieved. The buyer earns 5 – 2 = 3 and the seller 2 – 2 = 0.

If the seller has the power to determine the price, then it not clear which price will be established. The seller should make a guess regarding the reservation price of the buyer. If the seller thinks the buyer is willing to pay 4 for the house, a price of 4 is asked and the outcome is efficient. The buyer earns 5 – 4 = 1 and the seller earns 4 – 2 = 2. However, it is also possible that the seller estimates the reservation price of the buyer as 6. A price of 6 is asked and the efficient outcome, i.e. exchange, is not achieved. Each party earns nothing. The seller will on average gain from having the bargaining power, but this allocation of bargaining power is Pareto-inefficient because once in a while a valuable trade will not occur.

4.5.2 Two-sided asymmetric information

It turns out that the efficient outcome of the situation of full information can sometimes be accomplished even when there is asymmetric information. However, there is usually some inefficiency because it is appealing to each party to always *misrepresent* a little bit in the bidding process (Milgrom and Roberts, 1992). Offers which differ just a little from the real valuation or reservation price are usually attractive. The probability of such offers being accepted is high, whereas the probability of surplus being lost owing to overbidding by the seller or underbidding by the buyer, and therefore no exchange, is low. The strategy which maximizes the payoff therefore entails that the buyer always slightly underbids, while the seller always makes a bid a little bit higher than his real valuation. If the valuations of the two parties do not differ much, then there is a problem. There will be no exchange.

> Exchange in a situation with asymmetric information will occur only when the surplus involved is large enough.

The example of the firm and the local residents can be extended to a situation with two-sided asymmetric information. The residents can, like the firm, also misrepresent their true valuation. Figure 4.7 shows the misrepresented preferences v' of the residents. (Notice that the set of Pareto improvements regarding the status quo point (0,0) has shrunk further.) The equilibrium is E''. E'' is closer to the status quo point (0,0) than the equilibrium E^*.

The property rights regime will in general have an effect on the level of pollution when asymmetric information prevails. The party owning the property rights will benefit. Property rights therefore have value in a situation with asymmetric information.

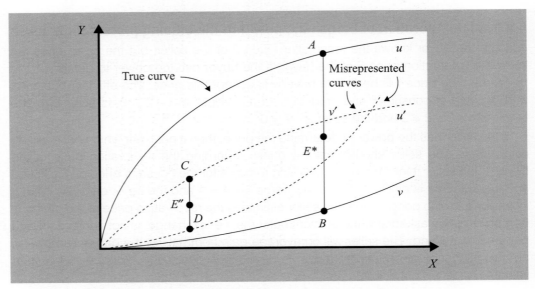

Figure 4.7: Misrepresentation by both parties
McKelvey and Page, 'Misrepresentation by Both Parties', *Economics and Philosophy*, 1999, © Cambridge University press

---

Application: Asymmetric information in the bidding process for a house

Asymmetric information may result in bargaining problems, because a better price may be achieved by *misrepresentation*. A buyer willing to pay 5 for a house can pretend to be willing to pay at most 3 in order to establish a lower price. If the house is worth 2 to the seller, then the seller can try to convince the buyer that at least 4 has to be paid. The behaviour of the buyer as well as the seller may result in no exchange, while the reservation price 2 of the seller is lower than the reservation price 5 of the buyer. However, it can be attractive for the buyer to have no trade because of misrepresentation once in a while when this frequently results in a lower price.

4.5.3 Multiple parties

Besides assuming only two reservation prices, it is also assumed that only two parties bargain, i.e. a buyer and a seller. More parties would further complicate exchange when there is asymmetric information. A small minority can threaten to block an agreement in order to receive a larger share of the pie which is to be created. Such 'free-rider' behaviour makes it hard to establish unanimity.

Application: Public organizations

From the viewpoint of an efficient allocation of ownership rights, public organizations own many characteristics of an inefficient control structure (Boycko, 1995). The decision rights are divided among managers and several politicians, which makes it hard to establish agreements. If it is not possible to establish an agreement, then an attempt may be made to buy the decision rights in such a way that they end up in the hands of a

---

limited number of players. This can be costly, because decision rights are owned by many different parties.

Another aspect of public organizations is that the decision rights are often separated from the income rights, which means that those who take the decisions are not confronted with the revenues and costs of their decisions. This can often result in the wrong decisions from the point of view of efficiency, because the motives of politicians do not need to coincide with those of efficiency.

Finally, not all contracts which are needed to establish efficiency, which may entail paying bribes to politicians to take the efficient decisions, are legally enforceable. The next section will elaborate on this.

4.6 Property rights

The solution of the Coase theorem to solve inefficiencies by means of contractual agreements has several implications. First, ownership rights have to be specified. Second, an institutional structure is needed, with organizations like the judiciary or police or land registry, in order to enable the exchange of ownership rights and make sure they are respected and traded. Third, contracts have to be honoured and enforced (possibly by a third party). In practice, governance structures are usually inefficient, not all ownership rights can be traded and contracts are not always either honoured or enforced.

Problems with property rights arise from the inadequacy of institutions or the inefficiency of the ownership structure. Five problems can be distinguished. First, the failure of institutions can be expressed by the fact that ownership rights are not allocated. Classical examples are the use of water and air, the reduction of the rain forests and too much fishing in the oceans.

Application: Ozone layer

Examples of damaging effects of the absence of ownership rights are the disappearance of the ozone layer as a result of people using sprayers, the extinction of whales as a result of hunting, desert creation by too much felling of trees, excessive advertisements, price wars and the pollution problem. The problem in all of these examples is that ownership rights are not well defined or are difficult to enforce. This results in a non-optimal amount of these activities, because everyone separately chooses actions in his or her own *self-interest*, and this does not coincide with the *general interest*. What is good for one individual is not necessarily good for the rest. There is almost always a tension between the share of the surplus which everyone receives separately and making the total surplus as large as possible. The reason for this is that the decision of one person influences not only their own payments, but also those of the other(s). However, this externality is not taken into account when a decision is made, which decreases the size of the total surplus.

The Coase theorem highlights the importance of ownership rights. The *absence of well-specified* ownership rights can result in inefficient allocations. Coase suggests creating markets for externalities in order to solve the above problems. The main idea is that the introduction of exchangeable pollution rights, like emission rights and fertilizer production rights, can take care of external effects such that the user pays the production costs. An efficient allocation of resources, and therefore production, can be established through markets by creating these markets. A recent example is the successful creation of the market for sulphur dioxide emission permits (Joskow *et al.*, 1998)

A second problem occurs when ownership rights are allocated, but *not implemented*. Ownership is not protected when ownership rights are ignored, when private parties cannot trust legal institutions to guarantee the implementation of agreements. There have been many instances in history of a partial or complete absence of protection of ownership against pirates, thieves, feudal landlords, political superiors and squatters.

A third problem surfaces when ownership rights are allocated and implemented, but *not enforced*. This may be due to the incompleteness of contractual agreements. Contract violations and behaviour which does not correspond with the character of the agreement can be observable to the involved parties, but that does not mean they can also be verified by an independent, third party like a judge. Part IV addresses the way organizations and financial instruments can be designed, and ownership rights allocated, in order to deal with the problems of motivation or control associated with non-verifiability of contractual terms.

Application: Corruption

Bribes and corruption are regarded as undesirable in general, but viewed from the perspective of the Coase theorem this is not obvious. In the Coase theorem, bribes are regarded as transfers of money. Therefore, they serve an important role in the transition from an inefficient to an efficient situation by financially compensating a number of parties in order to establish a better outcome. However, there is a problem with bribes. When one wants to have a certain service delivered for a certain level of bribes, and the service is not delivered once the payment is made, one cannot then go to a judge and demand that the other party keeps to the agreement. The problem with bribes and corruption is that such contractual agreements are not legally enforceable. This precludes bribes and corruption being means of resolving the negative effects of an inefficient governance structure.

A fourth potential problem is when property rights are allocated, implemented and enforced, but not *tradable*. Certain surplus-generating activities will not blossom because the necessary transfer of ownership rights is not allowed. Well-known examples are the abolition of slavery and the Bosman judgement in European soccer. (The Bosman judgement ruled that soccer players are the employees rather than the property of soccer clubs.) Modern societies do not find slavery acceptable, and have it written in their constitutions that an employee cannot be sold from one company to another without his or her consent. Parties take this restriction regarding trade into account in their investment decisions, which may prevent surplus-generating activities ever starting. Thus for example soccer teams have responded to the Bosman judgement by adjusting the contractual terms for young players in a way which reflects their decreased willingness to invest in their training and education. Finally, there may be inefficiencies in ownership structure because of the bad allocation of the decision and income rights. The example in Sec. 4.3.1 has already illustrated this. A well-known example which will feature in Part III is the separation of ownership and control in companies (Berle and Means, 1932). The problem here is that one party takes various decisions and receives the benefits, while another party bears the costs.

4.7 Conclusion

Markets achieve the best allocation of resources according to the fundamental welfare theorem and the Coase theorem. Either result requires a number of strong assumptions, for example the absence of any motivation and co-ordination problems, and is therefore often a logical construction instead of a realistic description of the world. It is surprising to see that market economies often function well, despite the violation of these assumptions, so the assumptions may therefore not be that restrictive after all. However, many things can go wrong in markets, and do. These problems will be addressed in the subsequent parts of this book and will be important starting-points for the analysis of organizations.

An important function of the two theorems is that they serve as benchmarks, because they make explicit the circumstances under which markets function well. As soon as there is doubt about the efficiency of a particular allocation, these theorems point towards the violation of one or more assumptions as a possible cause and formulate directions for possible solutions. For example, the Coase theorem suggests that organizations arise and/or financial instruments are designed to solve co-ordination and motivation problems when bargaining is inefficient and/or income effects exist. It also highlights the fact that it is important for the internal organization of enterprises to define ownership rights or responsibilities well.

4.8 Exercises

4.1 A chemical company and a camping site are situated near a lake. They have opposite incentives regarding the dumping of chemical waste in the lake. Reservation prices (demand and supply) are such that the efficient amount of pollution is positive. Assume that the marginal damage curve of the camping site is known to both, but that the value of the marginal pollution curve is known only to the chemical company.

A Formulate the Coase theorem.

B Is it possible to choose the allocation of ownership rights in such a way that there will be no inefficiencies? Explain your answer.

C Is the Coase theorem applicable to the above situation? Explain your answer.

D What change in the information structure can result in an equilibrium without any pollution? Explain your answer.

4.2 The squatter movement has been widely active in the Netherlands. Empty houses have been squatted or occupied by students, who have inhabited them for a long time without paying any rent. Houseowners were powerless because the police did not intervene soon enough. The students have sought to justify their behaviour by arguing that houseowners left properties vacant in order to drive up house prices.

A What harmful result does the action of non-intervention by the police entail according to the Coase theorem?

B What positive effect does the squatting of houses entail according to the Coase theorem?

4.3 The economy of China is growing rapidly. Annual growth rates of 10 per cent are not unusual. However, after the experiences of some companies, multinational firms do not enter China without various safeguards for their investments. Two cases may illustrate this. China's most renowned state or public concern, China International Trust & Investment Corp. (CITIC), refuses to pay its debt of 40 million dollars to the London Metals Exchange. A spokesperson for CITIC reports that 'the transactions were made by non-authorized persons. The CITIC does not want to take responsibility,' although the approval for currency speculations was given personally and in writing by the highest director.

The American fast-food concern McDonald's has had to leave its world's biggest restaurant near Tiananmen Square in Beijing; in its place will be erected a Li Kashing shopping mall. The fact that McDonald's signed a lease agreement with the local municipality for 20 years is not considered relevant. 'It is our land,' said a spokesperson for the municipality.

A Which (implicit) assumption of the Coase theorem do the cases described here not meet? Explain your answer.

B What harmful effect can be expected in the future according to the Coase theorem?

4.4   The first page of the album *The Edelweiss Motive* by the Belgian comic Kiekeboe shows an agitated Kiekeboe. His lovely Saturday afternoon is being disturbed by the smoke produced when his neighbour van der Neffe burns some rubbish. The relationship between the amount of rubbish burned, the profit for the neighbour van der Neffe and the damage to Kiekeboe is shown in the next table:

Amount of garbage burned	Benefit to van der Neffe	Damage to Kiekeboe
0	0	0
1	15	10
2	30	30
3	45	60
4	60	100

A How much rubbish will payoff-maximizer van der Neffe burn when there are no arrangements about ownership rights or accountability?

B What solution does Coase suggest to peacefully solve the problem described?

C How much rubbish will payoff-maximizer van der Neffe burn when he is not responsible for the damage he produces? Explain your answer.

D How much rubbish will payoff-maximizer van der Neffe burn when he is not responsible for the damage he causes and when ownership rights are enforceable by law? Explain your answer.

E Which two assumptions underlie the Coase theorem?

4.5 The exam for a course is scheduled for 17 May, a date which is also announced in the course manual. Student 1 has a preference for the end of June because of other exams, while student 2 prefers 17 May because of a holiday to Spain booked for June. The Coase theorem suggests that the efficient date for the exam will be established.

A Which three conditions need to be fulfilled to establish a Pareto-efficient date for the exam according to the Coase theorem?

B Are the rights to determine the exam date allocated?

C Are there bargaining inefficiencies?

D Are there financial constraints?

4.6 Suppose there are three buyers interested in buying a house. The reservation prices of the buyers 1, 2 and 3 are respectively 5, 6 and 7. The reservation price of the real-estate agent is 4. The real-estate agent proposes a price, which subsequently the buyer accepts or rejects. Assume there is complete information.

A Present the extensive form. (Hint: Introduce the artificial player Nature in order to make sure that each buyer arrives with equal probability at the office of the estate agent.)

B Determine the subgame perfect equilibrium.

C What is the average payoff of the buyers?

D What is the average payoff of the estate agent?

E How large is the expected level of the sum of consumer and producer surplus?

Assume that the estate agent does not know the reservation the of the buyer entering his office.

F Present the extensive form.

G Determine the subgame perfect equilibrium.

H What is the average payoff of the buyers?

I What is the average payoff of the estate agent?

J How large is the expected level of the sum of consumer and producer surplus?

K Why is the answer to part J lower than the answer to part E?

L How high is the informational rent earned by the buyers?

4.7 Suppose a project is set up at date 0 and all decisions are taken and benefits earned at date 1. Assume that the total value of the project, i.e. its present value, is V. The entrepreneur receives a fraction s of the project cash flows and the investor receives the remaining $(1-s)$. The entrepreneur enjoys a private benefit B of executing the project. The date 1 objective function of the entrepreneur is max $B + sV$ and for the investor max $(1-s)V = $ max V.

Decision and income rights are specified when a governance structure is chosen. Suppose that the only decision to be made concerns whether the project should be terminated or continued (at date 1).

A Assume $s = 0.1$, $B = 100$ and $V = -200$. What is the efficient decision?

B Will the efficient outcome be reached when the investor makes the decision?

C Will the efficient outcome be reached when the entrepreneur makes the decision?

D How much is the investor willing to offer the entrepreneur in return for terminating the project?

E Assume $s = 0.1$, $B = 100$ and $V = -80$. What is the efficient decision?

F Will the efficient outcome be reached when the investor makes the decision?

G Will the efficient outcome be reached when the entrepreneur makes the decision?

H How much is the entrepreneur willing to offer the investor in return for continuing the project?

I Which assumption of the Coase theorem is probably not satisfied?

Part III:
Complete contracts

In the model of general equilibrium complete information prevails regarding the activities and characteristics of buyers and sellers. In this part these assumptions will be relaxed. Conflicts of interests and asymmetric information are the most important ingredients of complete contracting theory. The problems associated with opposing interests and asymmetric information are analysed with the *opportunistic behavioural assumption*. The assumption of *complete rationality* is used to incorporate all the available information in the design of contracts. Figure III.1 positions complete contracting theory in terms of the behavioural assumptions.

		Behavioural hypothesis		
		Opportunistic	**Self-interested**	**Idealistic**
Degree of rationality	**Complete rationality**	Complete contracts		
	Limited rationality			
	Procedural rationality			

Figure III.1: Positioning of Part III

Chapter 5 explains the common structure underlying the various complete contracting models. Chapters 6 and 7 discuss the two most common complete contracting problems: hidden action or moral hazard problems and hidden characteristics or adverse selection problems.

5 Principal–agent models

LEARNING OBJECTIVES

After completing this chapter, you should understand:

- The three ingredients of the principal–agent problem.

- The difference between a complete contingent contract, a complete contract and an incomplete contract.

- The difference between a hidden action problem and a hidden characteristics problem.

- Why sensible contracts take the participation and incentive compatibility constraints into account.

Contents

This chapter starts the analysis of situations characterized by opposing interests and asymmetric information. It explains the common structure which underlies the various complete contracting models. Figure 5.1 shows the various ingredients of a principal–agent problem and its behavioural assumptions.

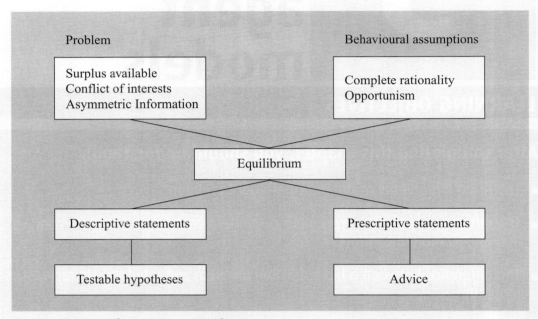

Figure 5.1: Complete contracting theory

The three ingredients of a principal–agent problem are elaborated upon in Sec. 5.1. The two behavioural assumptions are explained in Sec. 5.2. Section 5.3 presents two principal–agent models. They differ regarding the sequence of decisions and the information structure. Several requirements regarding a profit-maximizing contract are explained in Sec. 5.4. The view of the firm in complete contracting theory is outlined in Sec. 5.5. Section 5.6 concludes.

5.1 Ingredients of the principal–agent problem

The standard representation of a situation of conflicting interests and asymmetric information is the *principal–agent model*. The most simple principal–agent relationship consists of two people. One person (the principal) hires the other (the agent) to perform a certain task. The relationship is governed by a contract, which is chosen and designed by the principal. Subsequently, it is the agent who decides whether to accept the contract. Finally, the agent chooses a level of effort or an investment decision. Effort applies to many different things, like the number of hours worked, the dedication of managers to taking unpleasant decisions such as warning, punishing or firing employees, the savings regarding fringe benefits like the size of a company car, the quality of the hotel during a business trip or the size of the office of the CEO.

The delegation of tasks and responsibilities from the principal to the agent is in general not without problems. The principal can observe the result of the effort of the agent, but the agent usually has superior information regarding the effort provided and the circumstances. It is therefore difficult for the principal to observe the activities of the agent, which implies that the principal faces a *loss of control* over the agent.

An interesting principal–agent model has three ingredients:

- An available surplus;
- A conflict of interests;
- Asymmetric information.

The next three subsections will explain these ingredients.

Application: Physician–patient relationship

The classical example of a principal–agent problem is the physician–patient relationship. The physician is the agent, who takes decisions regarding the well-being of the patient (the principal). The superior knowledge of the physician is the basis of the relationship. The patient is not able to control the effort and dedication of the physician because of his or her lack of knowledge. Other examples are the student–professor relationship, the shareholder–manager relationship, the employer–employee relationship, the company–accountant relationship and the landowner–farmer relationship.

5.1.1 Surplus available

An interesting principal–agent problem entails there being a basis for the relationship. This basis exists when the principal is willing to pay more for the execution of a task than it will cost the agent, i.e. a surplus can be generated.

5.1.2 Conflict of interests

Management (by the agent) and ownership (by the principal) are separated in most companies. Managers have to advance the interests of the owners of the company, i.e. the shareholders. They are controlled by a board of directors chosen by the shareholders. The shareholders give this board the power to represent them in making important decisions and to determine the salary structure of managers.

The *separation of ownership and control* does not have to be bad, because the owner is not necessarily a good manager. Specialization is beneficial according to the law of comparative advantages. However, specialization is not without problems. The problem is usually not that the manager does not work hard enough, but that he or she is advancing towards objectives other than maximizing the value of the company. For example, a manager may go for his or her own financial benefit, power, prestige or career development. According to Berle and Means (1932), this has to result in managers using their power to pursue their personal interests at the expense of the shareholders. These observations have already been made by Adam Smith (1776):

'The directors of such [joint-stock] companies, however, being the managers rather of other people's money than of their own, it cannot well be expected, that they should watch over it with the same anxious vigilance with which the partners in a private copartnery frequently watch over their own. Like the stewards of a rich man, they are apt to consider attention to small matters as not for their master's honour, and very easily give themselves a dispensation from having it. Negligence and profusion, therefore, must always prevail, more or less, in the management of the affairs of such a company.'

The problem of the separation of ownership and control is exacerbated by the dispersal of shares over many thousands of shareholders. It is not in the interest of any one shareholder to supervise or control the manager. (Banks and institutional investors are exceptions.) Efficient control of the management of the company is a public good, which gives no single individual sufficient stimuli to develop these activities.

These observations illustrate the importance of the ingredient *conflict of interests* in a principal–agent problem. This conflict of interests can be extreme, in for instance a situation in which the buyer (the principal) wants to receive an expensive, high-quality product for a price agreed in advance, whereas the seller (the agent) will benefit from delivering cheap, low quality. A more sympathetic example is the delegation of the choice of investment project by the employer to the employee. The employee will be guided to some extent by considerations like job satisfaction, developing experience in his or her profession, the feeling of achieving something, curiosity, career development and so on (de Bijl, 1996) at the expense of the employer. A recurring element in these examples is the conflict of interests. The activities of the agent will have opposing effects on the payoffs of the agent and the principal. Providing additional effort, for instance, is usually appreciated by the principal, but not by the agent. The ultimate example of conflicting interests is the distribution of the surplus generated: an increase in the share of one person is automatically at the expense of the other.

5.1.3 Asymmetric information

The separation of ownership and control arises because managers and owners are different people. It usually entails a loss of control of the owners over the managers. Unforeseen and hard-to-observe circumstances often hinder the observation of the effort of the agent by the principal. Examples abound. The recovery of a patient may not be related to the diagnosis and treatment of a doctor. The principal does not know how hard the earth is in which a ditch is being dug. The production in a company depends not only on the decisions of the manager, but also on the availability of raw material, the dedication of the employees and the reliability of the machines. These examples illustrate how impossible it is to make the reward of the agent directly dependent on the effort provided. It is impossible for the principal to determine whether a high level of production is due to the effort of the agent or to favourable circumstances, whereas a low level of production may be caused by a lack of effort or just bad luck.

A manager is usually better informed than the owners about the day-to-day affairs, the business opportunities and the profitability of the company. The possibilities for managers to develop activities other than those in the interests of owners become more attractive when the owners are less informed about the decisions of the manager. Owners can reduce this lack of information by collecting and controlling the information and the decisions of the subordinate. However, this involves costs, so the net effect of these activities may well not be positive.

Asymmetric information characterizes the above situations because the agent has superior information regarding the provision of effort. This is the third ingredient of a principal–agent problem. For example, the physician can judge the specific health situation better than the patient, the teacher is better acquainted with the specific difficulties in the study material than the student, the employee is better informed about the local production factors than the employer and the farmer knows the specific land and weather conditions better than the landowner.

5.2 Behavioural assumptions

This section discusses the behavioural assumptions of complete rationality and opportunism in the principal–agent model.

5.2.1 Complete rationality

Complete rationality implies that a problem can be grasped easily. This will be expressed in the subsequent chapters by the contractual solutions the principal is able to choose in order to structure the behaviour of the agent to a certain extent. Contracts will contain all available information, and the conditions in the contract will reflect all possible observable situations which may occur in the future. Contracts will be complete and may be very complex because the assumption of complete rationality allows every technological restriction and all available information to be incorporated in the contract *for free*.

Meaningful contracts require that agreements are not only observable but also verifiable. If an agreement is not verifiable, then there will be little trust that it will be obeyed. The complete contract theory in this part assumes that breach of a contract by one of the parties will always be discovered and dealt with appropriately. No distinction is made between observing and verifying a breach of contract in the theory of complete contracts. Complete contract theory assumes that every observable agreement is also verifiable.

Notice the difference between the complete contingent contracts in Part II and the complete contracts in this part. The provisions in a meaningful complete contract can be based only on observable variables. This entails that the various unobservable aspects which determine the level of an observable variable cannot be used in the specification of the contractual agreements. For example, the level of production is observable, but its various components like effort and circumstances are not. A high level of production can be the result of a high level of effort by the person involved, or may be due to favourable circumstances.

This is the main difference from the circumstances under which the fundamental welfare theorem is formulated. A complete contingent contract does not need to be based on the level of production, because it can be made directly dependent on the level of effort of the agent and the specific circumstances. These contracts can be made completely dependent on all relevant variables. Complete contracts can be based only on the level of production which is observable by everyone. If a party has information at his or her disposal which the other party has not, this information cannot be taken into account in the design of a contract, despite its relevance.

A distinction will be made between observable and verifiable choices in the theory of incomplete contracts in Part IV. Agreements which are *observable* but *not verifiable* are not included in meaningful (incomplete) contracts. Figure 5.2 summarizes the differences between the various types of contracts of Parts II to IV.

Contract	Is everything observable to everyone	Is the observable information also verifiable?
Complete contingent	Yes	Yes
Complete	No	Yes
Incomplete	No	No

Figure 5.2: Types of contract

5.2.2 Opportunism

The ingredient 'conflict of interests' will be analysed with the opportunistic behavioural assumption. The principal will take into account in the design of contract the fact that the agent will use his or her superior information to his or her own benefit.

5.3 Sequence of decisions and information structure

Three decisions are distinguished in the formulation of the principal–agent problem. First, the principal chooses the *rules of the contract*. These may include, for instance, labour conditions (among them salary structures and promotion policy), the organizational structure and insurance policies. Second, the agent decides regarding *acceptance* of the contract. Finally, the agent chooses an *action*.

Asymmetric information makes the principal–agent relationship interesting (Arrow, 1985a). There is a *hidden action problem* if both parties have the same information during the contract design stage, but the decision of the agent as well as the specific circumstances are known only to the agent (and are not observable to the principal) once the contract has been accepted. The principal is able to observe only the level of output. The hidden action problem entails an *ex-post information asymmetry* because there is symmetric information during the contract design stage, but the agent has superior information once the contract is signed and a level of effort chosen. The principal can observe only the outcome of the decision of the agent, not his or her actual level of effort.

There is a *hidden characteristics problem* when the agent already has more information than the principal during the contract design stage. There is then an *ex-ante information asymmetry*. A certain proposal by the agent to the principal is observable for both parties, but certain characteristics of the agent are not. Therefore, it is not clear what led to the request of the agent. Examples are the creditworthiness of an applicant for a mortgage, the health risk of a person applying for insurance or the suitability of an applicant for a job vacancy. Figure 5.3 summarizes the differences regarding the information asymmetry in the decision order in each principal–agent problem.

The following two sections elaborate on the differences between hidden action and hidden characteristics problems.

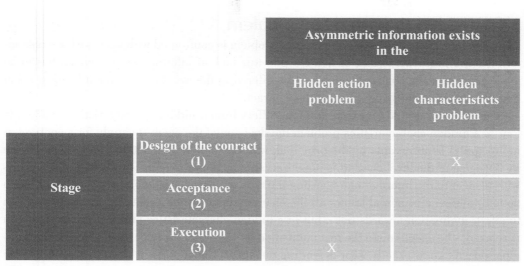

		Asymmetric information exists in the	
		Hidden action problem	Hidden characteristicts problem
Stage	Design of the conract (1)		X
	Acceptance (2)		
	Execution (3)	X	

Figure 5.3: Asymmetric information in complete contracting models

5.3.1 Hidden action problem

A hidden action problem consists of three stages. First, the principal chooses or designs the contract. Subsequently, the agent decides regarding accepting the contract. Finally, the agent chooses the level of effort or investment. The level of output is not necessarily a good measure of the effort provided by the agent, because external circumstances may interfere. This informational asymmetry can be used or misused by the agent in determining his or her investment decision, because the cause of a bad result cannot be discovered exactly by the principal. This use of incomplete information in the execution of an assignment by the agent is called *shirking*.

Hidden action problems are also called *moral hazard* problems. The label 'hidden action' focuses on an important ingredient in the model, whereas the label 'moral hazard' is directed to the behaviour of the agent in equilibrium. Figure 5.4 positions the different labels.

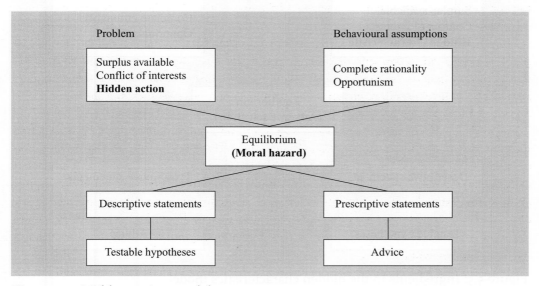

Figure 5.4: Hidden action model

5.3.2 Hidden characteristics problem

The principal in the hidden characteristics problem is confronted with agents whose characteristics are unknown to him or her. Despite this lack of information, a decision has to be made regarding the contract which will be offered to the agents. Subsequently, each agent decides regarding the acceptance of the contract.

The first way a hidden action problem differs from a hidden characteristics problem is that in a hidden characteristics problem the decision of the agent (to apply for a contract or not to apply) is observable by the principal, whereas in a hidden action problem the choice by the agent of the level of effort is not observable by the principal. The second difference is with respect to the information regarding the type or characteristic of the agent: in a hidden action problem a principal knows all the characteristics of the agent (capabilities, aversion to effort, inclination towards risk), but in a hidden characteristics problem this assumption is relaxed; the agent knows the real motivation for his or her own decision, whereas the principal doesn't know exactly what is guiding the agent. Chapter 7 will show that markets may have problems with these situations, which results in various organizational and contractual answers in order to generate a surplus or trade despite the asymmetry in information.

Agents with different characteristics will respond differently to the same contract offered by the principal. Some agents will accept the contract, others reject it. Only agents with certain characteristics will accept the contract offered, i.e. there will be some selection in the types of agents accepting the contract. The contract acceptance behaviour by the various agents is called *adverse selection*. Hidden characteristics problems are therefore also labelled as 'adverse selection' problems. The hidden characteristic label focuses on an important ingredient in the model, while the adverse selection label describes the behaviour of the agents in equilibrium. Figure 5.5 positions the two labels.

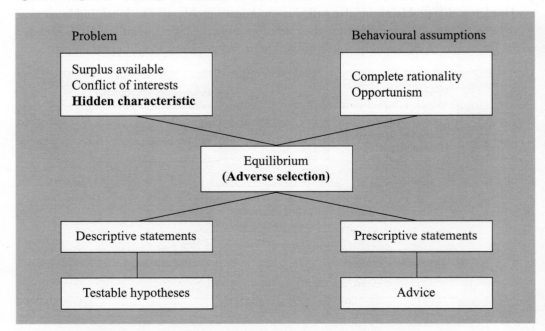

Figure 5.5: Ingredients in the hidden characteristics model

5.4 The profit-maximizing contract

In a principal–agent problem the principal and the agent sign a contract regarding a trans-action. The principal designs the contract on the basis of observable variables in such a way that his or her payment is maximized. A contract can be written regarding such different things as reward structures, information systems, the allocation of ownership rights and the allocation of tasks and functions.

Once a contract has been determined by the principal, the agent decides regarding the acceptance of the contract and the way it will be executed. The divergence of interests, and the fact that the agent has superior information compared with the principal, can be used or misused by the agent in executing the assignment. In designing the contract, the principal takes the considerations of the agent into account. This anticipation by the principal of the response of the agent will now be elaborated upon by the participation constraint and the incentive compatibility constraint. Subsequently the equilibrium behaviour of the principal and the agent will be addressed.

5.4.1 Participation constraint

Section 4.6 has explained that the decision rights regarding people are not tradable. The prohibition of slavery means that people cannot be forced to accept contracts. People cannot be forced into relationships. Chapters 6 and 7 take this condition or restriction of the consti-tution explicitly into account. This requirement of voluntary participation is called the *participation constraint*. It implies that the principal has to design the contract in such a way that the agent earns at least his or her opportunity costs when the contract is accepted. The principal and the agent therefore start a relationship governed by a contract only when both parties do not lose.

5.4.2 Incentive compatibility constraint

The intentions of the principal with regard to a certain contract have to match with the interests of the agent. If the principal wants a high level of production, then the contract should provide incentives for the agent to achieve it. This restriction in the design of meaningful contracts is called the *incentive compatibility* constraint. It means that the behaviour the principal desires of the agent will be chosen by the agent because the rules of the contract are such that it yields the highest payment for the agent. For example, if the principal in a hidden action problem wants the agent to make a substantial effort, then the contract can motivate the agent to do this by paying a higher wage for a high level of output than for a low level of output. This seems obvious, but this condition is not always met in real-life situations. For instance, it is said that social security benefits in many European countries are so large that for many people receiving unemployment benefits is more attractive than participating in the labour force.

5.4.3 Equilibrium

The behaviour of the principal and the agent in equilibrium is not exactly clear. Is the principal at the mercy of the agent, or does he or she have possibilities to influence the behaviour of the agent (in equilibrium)? The next two chapters will show that the principal designs the contract in such a way that the conflict of interests is reduced, taking into account the conditions regarding participation and incentive compatibility. In equilibrium, the principal chooses to incorporate *incentives* in the contract in such a way that the self-interest of the agent is aligned with the self-interest of the principal and/or to gather *additional information*. An example of incorporating incentives is making the agent's salary dependent on the amount produced. Examples of generating information are appointing a controller, using information resulting from an enduring relationship, or comparing different agents in similar situations.

The choice of contract by the principal in the situation of asymmetric information differs substantially from the one in the situation of complete information. The reason is that a meaningful contract can be based only on verifiable information. Usually, the behaviour of the agent will change as a result of a change in the information structure. In the hidden action problem, the agent can show 'shirking' in equilibrium, which means he or she will take an investment decision different from the one which would be taken in the situation of complete information. Similarly, some agents will not accept the contract the principal offers them in the hidden characteristics problem, whereas they will if there is complete information. The reason is that the principal tailors the design of the contract to the available information. If different agents have to be offered the same contract because of the lack of information, then *adverse selection* may occur. For example, if only one type of health insurance contract is offered, then the people with relatively good health may not accept the contract, while the those with relatively poor health will.

5.5 The firm as a nexus of contracts

In economics, the standard representation of the firm is as a *profit-maximizing entity*. Such a concept may have been suitable for companies in the nineteenth century with an owner-manager, but it is not a satisfactory description of modern companies. Berle and Means (1932) disagree strongly with the perception of a firm as a single entity. On the basis of empirical studies, they disagree with the view that in most companies management and ownership are unified in one person. The most important results of their study are that:

- A large company has many shareholders, and no shareholder or group of them owns an important part of the shares (this has moved the actual authority from the shareholders to the professional managers);
- The managers usually own only a small part of the outstanding shares;
- The interests of management and shareholders diverge strongly.

Therefore the firm consists of many parties with diverging interests.

This part focuses on a theory that addresses some weak points in the neoclassical view of the firm as a production function. The holistic view of the firm, the assumption that the company works as an entity towards one joint goal, is abandoned. The *firm* is viewed no longer as an individual, but as an entity that consists of *various parties with different interests*. In this context, Jensen and Meckling (1976) write that 'questions such as "what should be the objective of the firm" . . . are seriously misleading.'

Application: Japanese versus American firms

The different parties or stakeholders associated with a firm have objectives which do not completely coincide. The *objective of a firm* therefore cannot be determined unambiguously and is determined partly by the view on, or the way of, organizing. An agency approach of the firm is characterized by market-oriented contracts, by the maximization of the value of the firm and by many levels of control which are related hierarchically. This last aspect is presented in Fig. 5.6 and entails a strong bargaining position for the highest layers. Therefore, in this view the objective of the firm is maximizing the firm's value. The shareholders come first and the employee is seen as a production factor to be hired when he or she is needed, and fired otherwise. Such a view is common in the United States, where the financial manager is almost always the number two of a company, whereas the head of the personnel department is usually not a member of the board of directors.

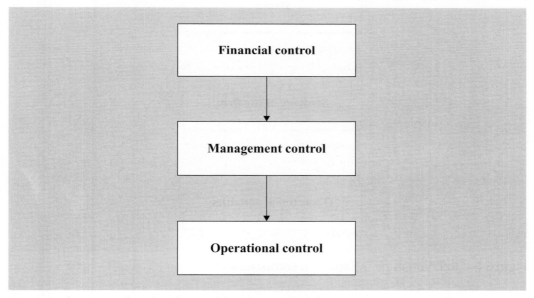

Figure 5.6: Hierarchical order in the agency model

Two important principal–agent problems can be distinguished in organizations. First, the board of directors has to ensure that the top managers (the agent) take decisions that are in the interest of shareholders (the principal). The second problem consists of the motivation of the employees (the agent) by the manager (the principal). The Japanese system is strong in formulating solutions for this conflict of interests.

Employees in Japanese companies have an input in decision-making at the company level, because collectively they possess information that is valuable in operational processes. The possible threat to withdraw co-operation in the future gives them an implicit bargaining position of some importance in the decision-making process. Nevertheless, banks are not powerless, because on the one hand they provide the financial funds, and on the other the employees cannot set up a firm themselves. Figure 5.7 illustrates this situation. Efficient company policy in Japanese companies therefore pays attention to maximizing the value of the company as well as to the interests of the employees, with the weight of the various objectives determined by the bargaining positions. In Japan, the employee is an important stakeholder, followed at some distance by the shareholder. The head of the personnel department is usually number two in the company and the CEO has usually occupied this position before ascending to the top.

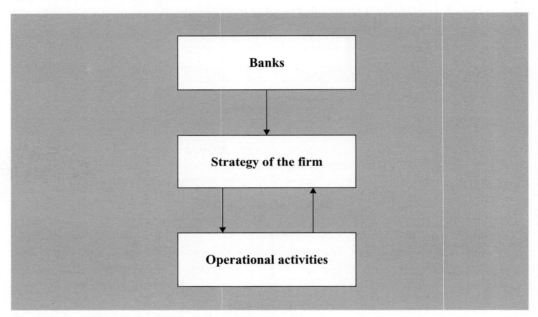

Figure 5.7: Relationships in Japanese companies

Various aspects of the contractual relationship between two parties are analysed in this part. In reality, companies have relationships with many parties, and a definition of the company has to take that into account. The contractual approach to organization takes the variety of stakeholders into account by considering the firm as a *nexus of contracts*, agreements and understandings between several parties (Jensen and Meckling, 1976). Figure 5.8 illustrates this. In this view, the firm is a legal entity which establishes relatively simple, bilateral contracts with external parties like suppliers, investors and customers, and with internal parties like employees and managers. Without this legal construction, which makes it possible to sign contracts with everyone separately, more complex agreements with more parties would have to be written at the same time.

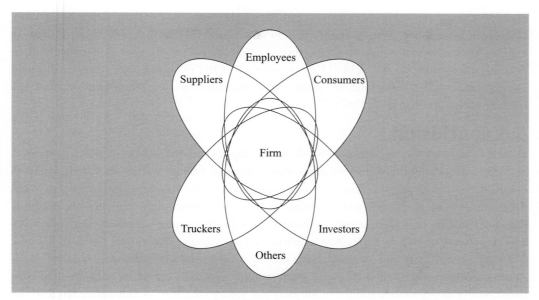

Figure 5.8: The firm as a nexus of contracts

It is in principle possible to design a different contractual structure for each situation which might occur. However, a certain nexus (or network) of contracts is often useful in many situations, which results in the existence in reality of a number of legal standard forms, for instance partnerships, corporations, co-operatives or foundations. They differ in, among other things, accountability, voting rights, continuity, financing and government regulation. Restructuring is always possible, or even liquidating the organization by changing the contractual conditions.

A point of concern regarding the conceptualization of the company as a nexus of complete contracts (Fig. 5.9) has to be mentioned. This conceptualization seems attractive, but it turns out to be incomplete in some aspects. First, the question of what a firm is exactly is being

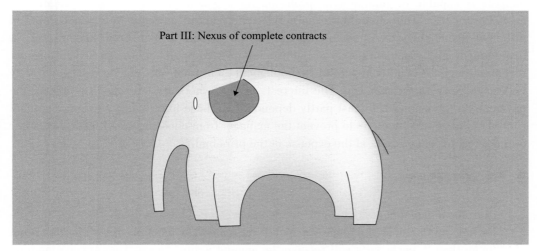

Figure 5.9: View of the firm in complete contracting theory

avoided to some extent. In this view, everything can be seen as a contract. A firm is a fiction, because it is simply a certain standard form of contracts. From this view, it is difficult to explain why companies spend such enormous resources on mergers and restructuring. Second, assets such as the skills of the personnel or the resulting profits are hardly paid attention to. Finally, this definition cannot give an explanation of the boundaries of a firm, i.e. the size of the firm can be unlimited.

5.6 Conclusion

Part III focuses on the separation between ownership and control or management. The *divergence of interests* and asymmetric information between various parties in organizations is emphasized. The separation between ownership and control has some interesting implications in this context. If each party maximizes his or her utility, then management probably does not consider only the interests of the owners. It becomes necessary to design incentives which motivate managers to develop activities in line with the interests of the shareholders. Not only explicit performance incentives can be used in reward structures; indirect disciplining mechanisms like the labour market, capital market and product market can also be used. Such considerations influence not only the salary structure of managers, but also the financial structure of the company and the design of tasks, functions and institutions. All these mechanisms can result in behaviour of the agent which is more in line with the interests of the principal, despite the conflict of interests.

The contribution of Berle and Means (1932) to the theory of the firm has been neglected for a long time, despite the existing dissatisfaction with the standard conceptualization of the firm. Various alternative theories have been developed, for example March and Simon (1958) view firms as 'satisficers', and Baumol (1959) takes a revenue maximization perspective. Such theories have been received with suspicion, because it has not been clear how activities other than profit-maximizing ones can survive in a market. If that doesn't happen, managers can be replaced, company units can be eliminated or companies can be taken over and restructured. Nevertheless, complete contract theory provides the older management theories with a solid basis. It proves that neither the shareholder theory nor the market for mergers is capable of guaranteeing profit-maximizing activities if not all information is available for free. The separation of ownership and control in companies is according to principal–agent theory responsible for behaviour which is not profit-maximizing. A beginning of a management theory of the firm is provided by this approach. It will turn out that for owners it is usually impossible to implement their profit-maximizing strategy directly via a contract with the manager. The interests of the owners are advanced by making the payments to the manager at least partly dependent on these interests, but even an optimal contract is in general not able to prevent the manager from choosing activities in his or her own interest to some extent, at the expense of the principal.

5.7 Exercises

5.1 Assume an amount of 2 has to be divided between two parties. Each party has to write an amount 0, 1 or 2 on a piece of paper. If the sum of the amounts of both parties is not more than 2, each party will receive the amount written down. They receive nothing when the sum is more than 2.

A Present the above with the strategic form.

B Is this situation an example of a conflict of interests? Explain your answer using the matrix of part A.

5.2   A student wants to have a broken bicycle repaired. The costs of repair are unknown, but will be at least 12 for a bike shop. The student is willing to pay at most 10 for the repair of the bicycle.

A Who is the agent?

B Is there surplus to be generated?

C Is there a conflict of interests involved?

D Is there asymmetric information?

E Is this an interesting principal–agent problem?

6 Hidden action problem

LEARNING OBJECTIVES

After completing this chapter, you should understand:

- How a hidden action problem is characterized.

- The difference between hidden action and moral hazard.

- Which four factors determine the intensity of incentives.

- When providing weak incentives is advised above strong incentives.

- The ways in which additional information can reduce the hidden action problem.

Contents

The essence of the hidden action problem is the conflict of interests between the principal and the agent, and an information asymmetry. The agent knows more than the principal and can use this superior information at the expense of the principal. These problems are anticipated by the principal, and this will be reflected in the contractual terms offered to the agent in order to discourage undesirable behaviour by the agent.

Two types of solutions for hidden action problems will be addressed. They are in line with the ingredients of the hidden action problem. The first solution entails changing the payoffs in order to reduce the conflict of interests. Payoffs in the contract will be structured in such a way that the interests of the principal and the agent are better aligned. The second solution concerns changing the information structure. The principal will try to gather additional information in order to reduce the information asymmetry. A third possible solution for the hidden action problem is changing one of the players, i.e. the principal or the agent. This solution will not be treated in a separate section, because it is on the one hand straightforward and on the other has some features which are addressed in Chapter 7.

Section 6.1 explains the effect of the information structure on the nature and design of meaningful contracts. Reducing the conflict of interests by the design of the contract is addressed in Sec. 6.2. Section 6.3 highlights a situation in which the agent performs several tasks. Including additional information in the contract in order to reduce the information asymmetry is the topic of Sec. 6.4. The nature of the firm is addressed from a complete contracting point of view in Sec. 6.5. Section 6.6 concludes.

6.1 Contract design

The use of performance stimuli in contracts in order to reduce the conflict of interests between principal and agent will be introduced with a numeral example. First, the situation of complete information is outlined. Second, the effect of asymmetric information on the design of the contract is examined in the same example. The analysis is based on Milgrom and Roberts (1992).

6.1.1 Complete information

Suppose that the payoff of the agent equals $\sqrt{w} - e$, where $\sqrt{w}$ is the valuation of the salary w by the agent and e the level of effort of the agent. The payoff of the principal is $P(e) - w$, where $P(e)$ is the value of output when the level of effort provided by the agent is e. A higher level of effort will increase the level of output. Assume that the opportunity costs of the principal are 0 and the opportunity costs of the agent are 1. The specification reflects the conflict of interest between the principal and the agent, because a larger effort increases the level of output for the principal, but it reduces the payoff of the agent by the additional costs of providing this higher level of effort.

The payoff $P(e) - w$ of the principal reflects *risk-neutrality*, because the payoff function is linear in w, i.e. a payoff with certainty is valued as high as an uncertain payoff which is on average the same. This is often representative for the principal, because the principal is usually a company or a person who handles many other projects as well. Risks can therefore be spread, i.e. uncertainty regarding specific projects has little influence on the average results of the entire portfolio of projects.

Agents are usually largely dependent on one project for their income. Uncertainty can therefore result in large fluctuations in the salary of the agent, which is usually not appreciated. *Risk aversion* is the term used for this attitude towards risk. The specification of the payment function of the agent exhibits risk aversion. A salary with certainty is valued higher than an uncertain salary which is on average the same. (Mathematically, $\alpha \sqrt{w_1} + (1 - \alpha)\sqrt{w_2}$ $< \sqrt{(\alpha w_1 + (1 - \alpha)w_2)}$, where w_1 and w_2 are two different salary levels and is a number between 0 and 1. The concavity of the payment function of the agent is responsible for this inequality.) Appendix 6.1 provides a graphical presentation of risk aversion.

In choosing e, the agent can influence the level of output directly. However, there are in general other factors outside the control of the agent which have an effect on the level of output. For example, consider the relationship between a landowner (principal) and a farmer (agent). The size of the harvest is determined not only by the effort of the farmer, but also by the weather conditions. These two aspects will be incorporated in the analysis by assuming that a larger level of effort raises the *probability* of a high level of output. Assume an agent can choose only between $e = 0$ and $e = 1$ and that the level of P can be only 10 or 30. An effort $e = 0$ results in $P = 10$ with probability 2/3 and therefore $P = 30$ with probability 1/3. A higher level of effort increases the probability of a good result, which can be represented by '$e = 1$ results in $P = 10$ with probability 1/3' and therefore '$P = 30$ with probability 2/3'.

Complete information prevails when the effort of the agent can be observed directly or when there is a stable relationship between effort and production, so that the effort can be inferred from the amount produced. In a situation of complete information, contractual conditions can be made directly dependent on the effort of the agent. A *complete contingent contract* can be written such that the level of effort can be specified which is required for a certain salary. The contract in the current example consists of two numbers. The complete contingent contract is $\{a,b\}$, where the salary w of the agent is equal to a when an effort $e = 0$ is provided and $w = b$ when the agent chooses $e = 1$. Therefore, in a situation of complete information the effort e determines the salary for the agent completely. There is no uncertainty regarding the salary w of the agent. The wage w is independent of the result which emerges eventually.

The sequence of decisions and the information structure in the hidden action problem with complete information is presented in Fig. 6.1. The principal takes the first decision by choosing the contract. For the sake of simplicity, only two contracts, i.e. $\{a,b\}$ and $\{a_1,b_1\}$, are presented. (There are of course countless possibilities.) A further simplification is made in Fig. 6.1 by presenting only choice possibilities subsequent to the choice of contract $\{a,b\}$. (All other contracts should have the same sequence of subsequent decisions, but this would unnecessarily clutter the figure.) After the choice of contract by the principal, the agent has to decide regarding acceptance. If the agent does not accept (N), then no further decisions are made. The principal does not earn anything, while the agent goes for his or her outside opportunity and earns the reservation wage 1. If the agent accepts (A) the contract, then he or she has to take a second decision. This third decision entails the choice of effort, i.e. $e = 0$ or $e = 1$.

External circumstances as well as the choice of effort of the agent determine the level of output. This is incorporated in Fig. 6.1 as the fourth decision. The artificial player 'Nature' decides whether the result will be 10 or 30, where the level of effort of the agent determines the probability of the final result. If the agent chooses $e = 0$, Nature will choose a bad result with probability 2/3. A high level of effort will result in a bad result with a probability of only

1/3. Finally, a fifth decision moment is incorporated to facilitate the comparison with the situation of asymmetric information. This means that the principal pays the agent according to the contract. There is only one choice possible, because the contract specifies for each possible situation exactly how much the principal has to pay the agent.

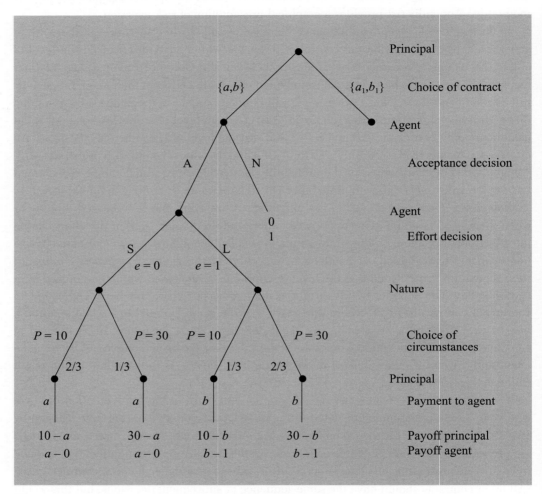

Figure 6.1: Decision order and complete information

The choice of acceptance of the contract and the choice of the level of effort by the agent have to be taken into account in the design of a meaningful contract. Backward induction (Sec. 2.2.4) dictates that we start with the final decision of the agent. The agent chooses an effort level $e = 1$ instead of $e = 0$ when this yields more than making no effort. The payoff of the agent in the right block in Fig. 6.2 has therefore to be higher than in the left block in order to have him or her put forward a high level of effort, i.e. $\sqrt{b} - 1 \geq \sqrt{a} - 0$. This is called the *incentive compatibility constraint*.

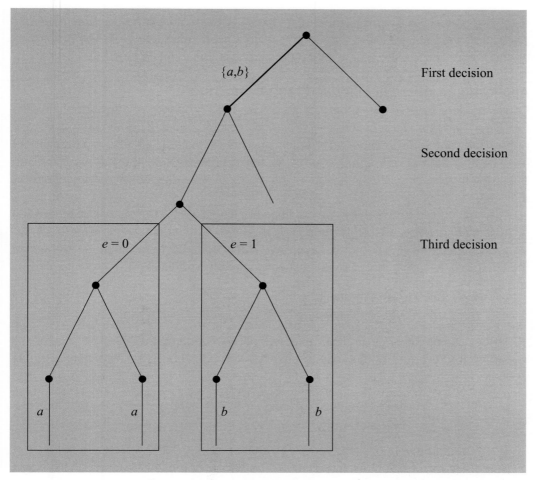

Figure 6.2: Incentive compatibility constraint when there is complete information

Application: Tonsil and open heart surgeries

In a number of countries, a continuing subject of public debate is the organization of the health service. Hot issues are the introduction of new technologies, the influence of the system of legal responsibility for mistakes in the number of tests performed, the extent of medical care in the terminal life phase and the payment system for medical employees. Califano (1986) has collected some remarkable facts regarding the impact of rules and institutions on the costs of the US health service. The focus is here on the impact of the payment system for medical specialists on the number of treatments.

The United States of America is especially suitable for conducting comparative studies in the medical sector, because each state has its own medical policy. It turns out that large geographical variations exist regarding the number of medical treatments. The role of the reward system is remarkable. States where medical specialists (agents) are rewarded on the basis of the number of medical treatments show many more treatments per patient than states where surgeons receive a fixed salary per year. The probability of open heart surgery is twice as high, that of tonsils treatment 15 times.

Application: Limited liability and capital structure

Equity holders receive the profits or losses of the company, whereas debt holders receive a fixed remuneration for making capital available during a certain period. In case of bankruptcy, the debt holders have a claim on the remaining assets. The equity/debt ratio of a company has some impact on the probability that the company will go bankrupt. It determines the behaviour of the manager regarding risky investment opportunities to a certain extent.

The relationship between the way of financing investment projects and the selection of investment projects will be illustrated with a numerical example. Assume there are two investment projects with uncertain revenues. The uncertainty regarding the revenues of the first project is represented by a stochastic variable x, where

$$x = 900, \qquad \text{with probability } .5$$
$$= 1500, \qquad \text{with probability } .5.$$

The expected revenue is 1200 and the variance equals 90 000. The uncertainty regarding the revenues of the second project is represented by the stochastic variable y, where

$$y = 0, \qquad \text{with probability } .9$$
$$= 11\,000, \qquad \text{with probability } .1.$$

The expected revenue is 1100 and the variance 10 980 000.

Both projects require financing of 1000. The choice of project depends on the way it is financed. If the project is completely financed with *equity,* then the first project will be chosen. This project has higher expected revenues and is less risky.

The choice of investment project changes when it is financed with 100 equity and 900 *debt.* The uncertain cash flow of the first project is now

$$y = 0, \qquad \text{with probability } .5$$
$$= 600, \qquad \text{with probability } .5.$$

If the low revenue 900 materializes, then it has to be used completely to pay back the debt holders. The equity holders of 100 have seen their money evaporate, i.e. the investment turned out to be unproductive. If the high revenue 1500 is generated, then it will be used to pay back 900 to the debt holders. The remaining 600 is for the equity holders. The first project therefore has an expected cash flow of 300. The uncertain cash flow of the second project is

$$y = 0, \qquad \text{with probability } .9$$
$$= 10\,100, \qquad \text{with probability } .1.$$

Again, the revenues are used first to pay back the creditors. If the revenues are 0, then the project has generated no money and the debt holders do not get their money back. This is called the *limited liability* aspect of debt. If the outcome 11 000 occurs, then the debt holders are paid 900 and the equity holders receive 10 100. The expected revenue of the second project for the equity holders is therefore 1010. Although this project has a higher variance than the first project, the expected revenue is so much higher that a not-too-risk-averse manager will choose this one. Equity holders have to take the 'downside' of the investment, whereas debt holders see only the 'upside'.

The composition of the financial structure can therefore result in adopting the project with the lowest expected revenues and the highest risk. The driving force behind this result is that the manager faces only limited liability regarding bad results when the company is heavily financed with debt. Financing with debt makes the profit function convex. This encourages risk-taking behaviour. Figure 6.3 illustrates the limited liability aspect when there are many different circumstances possible, where the circumstances are summarized by θ on the horizontal axis. (The above example has only the circumstances good or bad.) It is assumed that a higher value of θ results in a higher revenues, i.e. there is a positive relationship between θ and $R(\theta)$. The level of debt is equal to D. Profits are never negative when there is debt financing. This is due to the limited-liability aspect of debt, i.e. debt is not paid back when the revenues are exhausted. The profit function is therefore

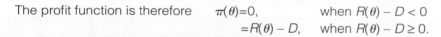

The profit function is therefore
$$\pi(\theta)=0, \qquad \text{when } R(\theta) - D < 0$$
$$=R(\theta) - D, \qquad \text{when } R(\theta) - D \geq 0.$$

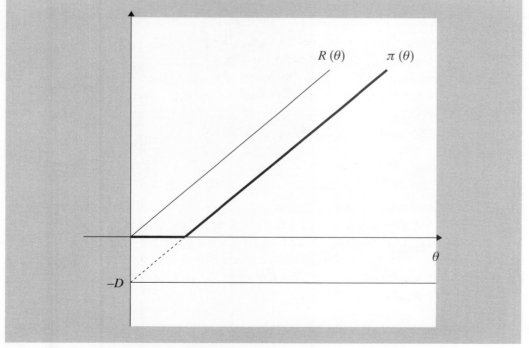

Figure 6.3: Limited liability of debt

A final remark regarding limited liability and investment selection concerns the frequently used criterion of *net present value* for choosing investment projects. The net present value is determined by discounting the expected future cash flows, in which the costs of capital and the risk associated with a project are taken into account. The above numerical example shows that other considerations, which do not necessarily match the interests of the company, play a role in the choice of investment projects. It is therefore to be expected that companies will defend themselves by gathering extensive information about potential projects as well as the person(s) executing them. In practice, various rules and procedures have to be followed in order to get a project accepted.

The principal has, in addition to the incentive compatibility constraint, also to take into account that the agent has opportunities elsewhere. A contract will be accepted by the agent only when he or she earns at least as much with the contract as without it. This second constraint in the design of a meaningful contract is called the *participation constraint*. The payoff of the agent with the contract depends on the level of effort which is put forward, i.e. the incentive compatibility constraint has to be incorporated in the specification of the participation constraint. The agent will choose $e = 1$ once the contract has been accepted when the incentive compatibility constraint is met, i.e. the agent earns $\sqrt{b} - 1$. Contract $\{a,b\}$ will be accepted when $\sqrt{b} - 1 \geq 1$. This inequality is called the participation constraint. The participation constraint requires that the payment for the agent in the left block of Fig. 6.4 should be at least as high as in the right block.

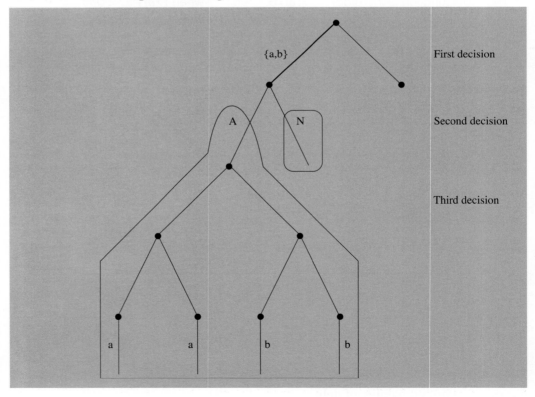

Figure 6.4: Participation constraint when there is complete information

Application: Subcontracting in Japan

One of the characteristics of Japanese industry is the tight relationship between firms and their *suppliers*. Inputs are more often procured from third parties in Japan than in the United States: 69 per cent of the value of output is obtained by a contract with suppliers in Japan, whereas this is 58 per cent in the United States (Kawasaki and McMillan, 1987). Viewed from the perspective of Berle and Means (1932), this is an attractive situation for Japanese companies. There will be less 'corporate plundering' because there is no separation of ownership and control with external procurement through independent suppliers.

It is sometimes suggested that subcontractors are in an undesirable position and can hardly survive. This is reflected in the sequence of decisions in the principal–agent problem. The large company has a strong bargaining position because it formulates the procurement proposal. However, the subcontractor is not powerless. First, he or she can refuse the contract when a more attractive alternative is available. It is important to have alternative sources of demand. Subcontractors are aware of their bad position relative to one large customer. Even the smallest Japanese subcontractors have on average three large companies as customers for their products, and this number increases with the growth of the subcontractor. This is illustrated in Table 6.5 (Kawasaki and McMillan, 1987). Second, the subcontractor still has to choose an action which is important for the success of the project. The subcontractor has superior information regarding local circumstances, which can be used to his or her advantage in the bargaining about the price.

Size of subcontractor	Average number of customers
1–3 employees	3
20–29 employees	6
200–299 employees	11

Figure 6.5: Bargaining position of Japanese subcontractors

The contract $\{a,b\}$ will be accepted by the agent and will result in an effort e $= 1$ when the incentive constraint $\sqrt{b} - 1 \geq \sqrt{a} - 0$ as well as the participation constraint $\sqrt{b} - 1 \geq 1$ are both met. There are many values of a and b which meet both of these constraints, which is illustrated by the shaded area in Fig. 6.6. The principal chooses the contract which maximizes his or her profit. This is the case when $a = 0$ and $b = 4$. The contract $\{0,4\}$ means that the agent receives nothing when $e = 0$ is provided and is paid a wage 4 when an effort $e = 1$ is put forward. The contract $\{0,4\}$ yields the agent $\sqrt{4} - 1 = 1$ and the principal earns $1/3 \times 10 + 2/3 \times 30 - 4 = 58/3$.

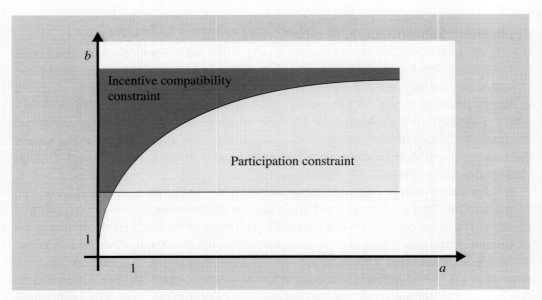

Figure 6.6: Incentive and participation constraints when there is complete information

Notice that the result is still uncertain, but the risk-neutral principal bears all the risk. The agent receives a wage of 4 when $e = 1$ is chosen, while the principal receives the (uncertain) output. The allocation of risk is Pareto-optimal, because the risk-neutral principal is better able to bear the risk than the risk-averse agent.

6.1.2 Incomplete information

Assume that only the agent knows the choice of e and the specific circumstances. The principal observes only the final result. This situation is characterized as a situation with asymmetric information. Figure 6.7 represents the change in the information structure. One information set applies to the situation where the principal observes result $P = 10$, while the other information set is geared towards the observation $P = 30$. A result $P = 10$ is composed of two effects: a choice of effort by the agent and the decision of Nature regarding the circumstances. The principal is not able to distinguish these two effects. Only the result $P = 10$ is observed, not the level of effort. The same applies to $P = 30$.

A meaningful contract can be based only on *observable facts*, and is therefore simple to achieve in a situation of complete information, because all relevant information is available and payments can thus be made fully dependent or contingent on the effort e of the agent. However, it is not possible in a situation with incomplete or asymmetric information. Only the result R is observable to the principal, not the level of effort e. The wage of the agent can therefore be made dependent only on the level of output. Complete contingent contracts are not possible anymore in a situation with asymmetric information. There can only be *complete contracts*.

A complete contract $[y,z]$ consists also of two numbers. However, the interpretation of these numbers is quite different from that in the example above. The two numbers of the complete contingent contract $\{a,b\}$ are geared towards effort levels, whereas the two

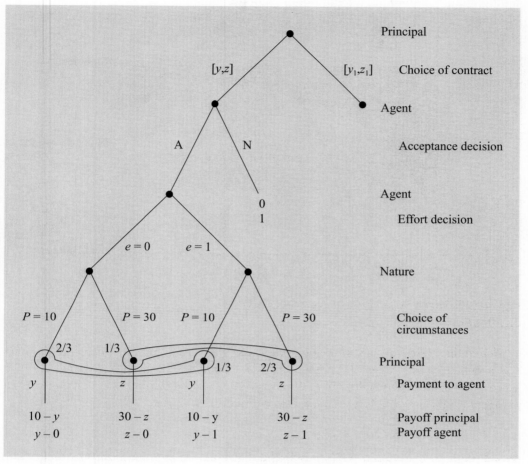

Figure 6.7: Decision order and asymmetric information

numbers of the complete contract [y,z] are geared towards the two levels of output. The agent receives $w = y$ when $P = 10$ and $w = z$ when $P = 30$. (Note that the complete contract is presented with square brackets in order to distinguish it from the complete contingent contract {a,b}.)

Again the payoff-maximizing contract of the principal will be determined, while taking the considerations of the agent into account. The agent chooses effort $e = 1$ when this is more attractive than the choice $e = 0$. Figure 6.8 illustrates this incentive compatibility constraint. It entails that the agent earns more with $e = 1$ than with $e = 0$, i.e. the expected payoff of the agent in the left block has to be lower than the expected payoff in the right block. *Expected* payments have to be compared because there is now some uncertainty regarding the wage of the agent when a choice of effort is made. An effort $e = 0$ may result in $P = 10$ or $P = 30$, each with a certain probability and an associated wage. The agent will choose $e = 1$ instead of $e = 0$ when:

$$1/3(\sqrt{y}-1) + 2/3(\sqrt{z}-1) \geq 2/3(\sqrt{y}-0) + 1/3(\sqrt{z}-0)$$
$$\Leftrightarrow \sqrt{z} \geq \sqrt{y} + 3.$$

This inequality is called the *incentive compatibility constraint*.

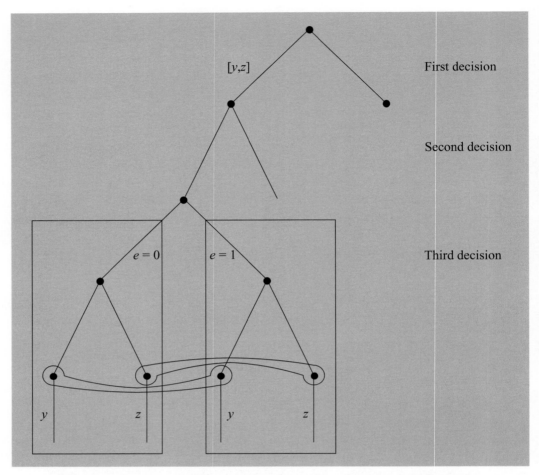

Figure 6.8: Incentive compatibility constraint under asymmetric information

A meaningful contract satisfies also the *participation constraint*. This constraint entails that the agent earns at least as much with the contract as without it, i.e. the reservation wage. Figure 6.9 illustrates this constraint. The payment in the left block has to be at least as large as the payment in the right block in order to get acceptance of the contract by the agent:

$$1/3(\sqrt{y}-1) + 2/3(\sqrt{z}-1) \geq 1$$
$$\Leftrightarrow \sqrt{z} \geq -5\sqrt{y} + 3.$$

The principal chooses y and z such that his or her expected payoff is maximized, while taking the incentive compatibility and the participation constraints into account. The cross-hatched area in Fig. 6.10 consists of all values of y and z satisfying these constraints. The payoff of the principal is maximized when $y = 0$ and $z = 9$. The contract [0,9] is accepted by the agent and results in an effort 1. Notice that the optimal value of y does not equal the optimal value of z. The principal appreciates a high level of effort, but the agent does not. The agent is motivated to provide a high level of effort, which increases the probability of a good result, by paying him or her more for a good result than for a bad result.

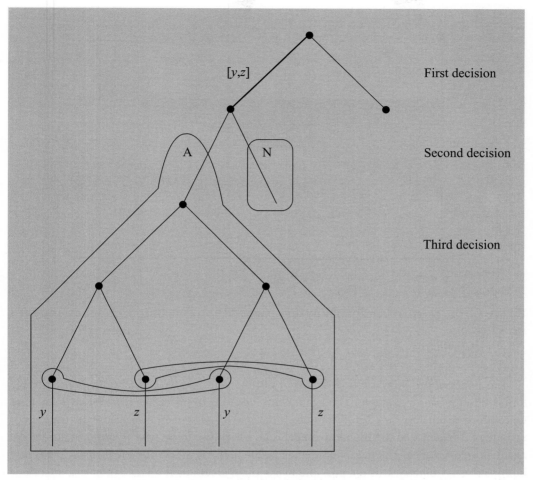

Figure 6.9: Participation constraint under asymmetric information

The agent earns again exactly $1/3(\sqrt{y}-1) + 2/3(\sqrt{z}-1) = 1/3(\sqrt{0}-1) + 2/3(\sqrt{9}-1) = 1$, i.e. his or her opportunity cost. The strong, take-it-or-leave-it *bargaining position* of the principal is responsible for this division of the surplus. The principal designs the contract, i.e. chooses y and z, in such a way which the agent just accepts the contract. However, the payment of the principal has decreased from 58/3 in the situation of complete information, to $52/3 (= 1/3(10-y) + 2/3(30-z) = 10/3 + 42/3)$ in the current situation of asymmetric information.

Uncertainty and risk aversion by the agent is responsible for this decrease of 2. A risk premium of 2 is paid to the agent, i.e. the expected wage paid to the agent has increased from 4 in the situation of complete information to $6 (= y/3 + 2z/3 = 0/3 + 18/3)$ in the situation of asymmetric information. The situation of incomplete information therefore implies that the agent receives part of the surplus (*informational rent*), which is due to the superior information that is at the disposal of the agent. This higher average wage is necessary because the risk-averse agent has to be compensated for bearing the risk. The agent values the uncertain average wage of 6 as high as a wage of 4 with certainty.

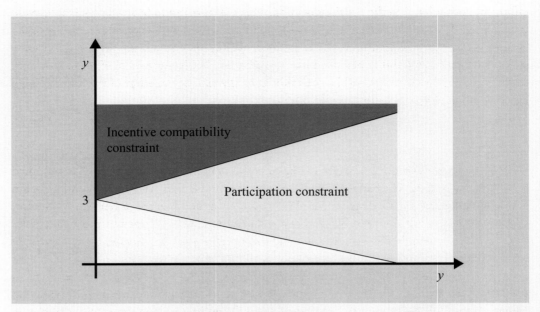

Figure 6.10: Incentive compatibility and participation constraints under asymmetric information

The impossibility of observing the effort of the agent results in a *loss of efficiency*. This loss is 2 in the above example. The agent continues to earn his or her reservation wage (and therefore did not lose anything), but the principal experiences a decrease in (expected) income of 2 because of the higher average wage which has to be paid in order to attract the agent as an employee. The loss of efficiency is due to the conflict of interests and the ex-post information asymmetry. It is not possible to establish an efficient allocation of risk as well as efficient incentives. A compromise in the design of the contract is chosen by the principal between the efficient allocation of risk and efficient performance stimuli. In the situation of complete information, the contract can be made dependent on the effort e. Strong incentives are formulated and the agent does not bear any risk. All uncertainty is ascribed to the principal, which is efficient because the principal is risk-neutral. This is not possible any more in a situation of asymmetric information, because the contract can be based only on observable variables. The optimal contract in the situation of incomplete information is a compromise between risk-spreading and performance stimuli. However, such a compromise always entails a loss of surplus.

6.2 The incentive intensity principle

This section will elaborate on the hidden action problem of the previous section. Aspects like risk-aversion, uncertainty about the environment, discretion of the agent and the impact of the agent's activities on the profit of the project will be explicitly incorporated in the analysis. The presentation of the hidden action problem will be somewhat different than in the previous section, but the underlying ideas remain the same. The first difference is that the effort of the agent will now be treated as a *continuous* variable, whereas only two levels of effort were considered in the previous section. This will turn out to have some advantages in interpreting the results. A second difference is the way in which the non-observability of the effort of the agent is treated. In Sec. 6.1, the level of effort determines the probability of each outcome, e.g. the probability of a good result increases if a higher level of effort is provided. In this section, the result (z) will be determined by the *sum* of the effort of the agent (e) and the realization of a stochastic variable (x), i.e.

$$z = e + x.$$

The stochastic variable x represents the uncertain environment. Its value is determined by the player Nature. The expectation of x is assumed to be zero. The agent therefore again determines the probability distribution of the result or output with his or her choice of effort e. The expected result or output is $e + 0 = e$ and can therefore be chosen by the agent, while the variance of z equals the variance of x and can therefore not be affected by the choice of effort of the agent.

Again it is crucial that the principal cannot observe the level of effort e of the agent. It therefore cannot be used in the design of the contract. The principal can only observe z, and payments can only be based on z. Various values of e and x result in the same level of z. A high level of effort can be neutralized by bad luck, whereas a low one can be disguised by circumstances which are better than expected. However, this is inevitable in situations with asymmetric information.

Suppose that the principal restricts him or herself to *linear payment structures*. These consist of a fixed base salary, α, and a variable part, β, based on the amount of production, z. The parameter β will be interpreted in various applications as a commission, royalty or piece wage percentage. A contract consists therefore of two numbers (α, β), in which α and β are chosen by the principal. The wage or salary of the agent is

$$w = \alpha + \beta z.$$

Expected utility theory treats decision-making under uncertainty in a systematic way. Each possible outcome of a decision is assigned a value and a probability. The expected value of a decision or project is obtained by summing up the value of each possible outcome times its probability. Differences in attitude of individual decision-makers towards uncertainty are formulated in terms of risk aversion. Subsequently, the *risk premium* is defined as the difference in value between receiving a result with certainty and obtaining the same result as an average of a number of uncertain outcomes. Risk aversion prevails when the risk premium is positive, i.e. a *risk-averse agent* values an average income composed of a number of uncertain incomes less than one with certainty. Risk aversion is associated with a concave benefit function, i.e. the marginal utility of additional income is decreasing. Appendix 6.1 provides a graphical illustration of expected utility theory. The opposite holds for a risk-seeking agent: the risk premium is negative and the utility function is convex.

One result of expected utility theory is that someone's valuation of an uncertain income can be summarized by a simple formula. An uncertain income w is valued as $E\{w\} - .5r \, \text{Var}(w)$, which means that the uncertain income w is valued at the difference between the expectation of w and the risk premium $.5r \, \text{Var}(w)$. The amount $E\{w\} - .5r \, \text{Var}(w)$ is called the *certain equivalent of the uncertain income w*. The *risk premium* $.5r \, \text{Var}(w)$ consists of two parts. First, the attitude towards uncertainty of the person receiving the income or wage plays a role. This characteristic is represented by the *coefficient of absolute risk aversion r*. A person is risk-neutral if r equals zero, risk-averse if r is larger than zero, and risk-seeking if r is smaller than zero. Second, the volatility of the income w enters the risk premium by $\text{Var}(w)$. The agent is not willing to pay a risk premium in order to remove all uncertainty when either the income is not uncertain ($\text{Var}(w) = 0$) or the agent is risk-neutral ($r = 0$).

Risk-averse individuals do not like to be exposed to risk. The risk premium indicates that they are willing to pay substantial resources to reduce it. One way to establish this reduction of uncertainty is by risk-sharing or *risk-pooling*. The *law of large numbers* says that this will be realized. This statistical result entails that if an event happens independently with probability p for each of a large number of individuals, then the proportion to whom it happens in a given year will almost always be close to p. Insurance is based on this insight. Suppose that the probability of dying before the age of 40 is 0.03. This poses *a* problem of financial uncertainty for *a* family, but not in a sample of 1 000 000 homes. The number of persons dying before the age of 40 will be very close to 30 000. The payments of an insurance company are therefore very predictable and a stable insurance premium policy can be followed. Risks are spread over the whole population.

Partnerships, joint-stock companies, insurance markets, futures markets, stock market, and speculation have no rationale in a world of certainty. They are based on the same principle. Risks of people are kept to a minimum by investing in numerous independent projects. This insight is summarized in the saying 'Don't put all your eggs in one basket.'

The profit-maximizing contract is designed by the principal in the same way as in Sec. 6.1. It is again assumed that the principal is risk-neutral and the agent risk-averse. $P(e)$ is again the value of output when the level of effort provided by the agent is e, and the cost for the agent of providing a level of effort e is $C(e)$. The incentive intensity of the profit-maximizing contract outcome is called the *incentive intensity principle* (and is derived in Appendix 6.2).

> *Incentive intensity principle.* The optimal incentive intensity is
> $$\beta = P'(e)/[1 + rVC''(e)].$$

The incentive-intensity principle shows that payments of the agent will be based to a larger extent on output, i.e. stronger incentives are provided, when:

1 The agent is less risk-averse;
2 It Is easier to measure the activities of the agent;
3 The effort of the agent has more impact on the level of output;
4 The agent has more discretion regarding the choice of activities.

Each of these four aspects will now be elaborated upon.

6.2.1 Risk aversion

The *degree of risk aversion* of the agent (r) is inversely related to the optimal β. A more risk-averse agent is less able to bear risk, given the risk-neutrality of the principal. More risk aversion entails that a higher risk premium has to be paid to the agent in order to make him or her indifferent between receiving an uncertain income and the same average income for certain. A payoff-maximizing principal will in the design of the contract decrease the variable part of the wage of the agent (β smaller) and therefore increase the fixed part of the wage (α larger) when faced with a more risk-averse agent. The principal therefore bears a larger part of the risk.

The negative relationship between r and β in the optimal contract reflects the opposing effects of incentives and the allocation of risk. From the viewpoint of *incentives*, the principal should choose a β as high as possible. A high β entails that all additional output due to additional effort will go to the agent. This can be interpreted as if the principal lends his or her production technology to the agent. The agent becomes the *residual claimant*, which encourages him or her to choose a high level of e. This is a general solution for hidden action problems and features regularly in this book. Incentives problems disappear when the claim to profit is entirely allocated to the party taking the hidden action.

However, β should be as low as possible when viewed from the perspective of the *efficient allocation of risk*. The principal is risk-neutral and therefore does not care about uncertainty, whereas the agent is risk-averse. A risk-averse agent has to be paid a salary which is independent of the output, i.e. $\beta = 0$, from the perspective of allocation of risk, because the agent is willing to receive a lower risk premium when he or she is confronted with less uncertainty. From this viewpoint, the risk should be borne by the principal. He or she is usually less risk-averse than the agent, because he or she has many other activities. The principal is risk-neutral in this section. It is therefore optimal for him or her to bear the entire risk. The choice $\beta = 0$, however, frustrates all incentive aspects of the contract, because the agent has no reason to provide effort. Additional effort is costly to him or her and it is not rewarded when $\beta = 0$. He or she receives a fixed salary, regardless of the result.

An optimal contract takes the considerations regarding incentives and risk simultaneously into consideration, and therefore does not handle each separate consideration optimally. The optimal contract is a compromise between the aspect of incentives and the aspect of risk-sharing, and is therefore *second-best* in terms of efficiency. The second-best nature of the contract is due to a lack of information. In general, the principal will bear part of the risk, in order to reduce the risk premium. The agent therefore has reduced incentives to perform. This results in a smaller total surplus.

The equilibrium contract in the situation with incomplete information is Pareto-optimal. It is possible to give the agent incentives such that he or she behaves the same as with the optimal contract in the situation with complete information. However, such a contract is not second-best in the situation with the asymmetric information. A high β has as a disadvantage that the agent bears a lot of risk. He or she is willing to accept such a contract only when it goes together with a high risk premium. This is expensive for the principal, so that he or she usually prefers to bear part of the risk him or herself, in order to reduce the risk premium. Although the lower β is associated with less effort of the agent, this loss of production outweighs the lower risk premium paid to the agent.

Notice that a principal prefers to hire the less risk-averse agent when he or she can choose between two agents with different attitudes towards risk. This agent will accept a contract with a higher β (and a lower α), which will result in a higher level of e and a higher level of output. The contract with the less risk-averse agent therefore results in an increase in profit for the principal, because the participation constraint dictates that the average salary of the payoff-maximizing contract offered by the principal equals what can be earned elsewhere by the agent.

6.2.2 Uncertainty regarding the environment

The degree of *uncertainty regarding the environment* is inversely related to the optimal incentive intensity. A low β is desirable when the result of the efforts of the agent is difficult to measure, i.e. V has a high value. Strong incentives are not desirable in such a situation, because a high value of V for the agent entails considerable risk and will translate into a high risk premium. The size of the risk premium is reduced by decreasing β. A high value of β is desirable when the principal is at least to a large extent able to separate the effect of effort and the effect of the circumstances on the level of output.

6.2.3 Profitability of incremental effort

The *sensitivity of the increase in profit to additional effort* ($P'(e)$) is important for the choice of effort by the agent. The incentive intensity β will be higher when the outcome is more sensitive to the activities of the agent. A higher β is therefore not always desirable. An example is the situation in which the agent has to carry out an assignment with a rigid production technology. A higher β makes the agent work faster. However, if the additional production cannot be processed in the next step of the production process, then additional effort by the agent has hardly any effect on the output of the organization. The optimal contract takes this into account, by making payments less dependent on performance.

6.2.4 Discretion regarding the choice of activities

$C''(e)$ can be interpreted as the *discretion* of the agent regarding the choice and execution of activities, like the speed of the production line and the tools and methods used. A high value of $C''(e)$ shows that additional effort by the agent is accompanied by a large increase in personal costs. An example is a bureaucratic organization in which it takes a lot of effort to accomplish additional production. Payments should not be made strongly dependent on the level of output in such a situation according to the incentive intensity principle. In general, $C''(e)$ will be smaller as the size of a company is smaller because employees have more discretion regarding their activities. Output-based wages encourage value-enhancing activities in such environments.

Application: Team production and reward structure

Team production means that the individual contributions of team members cannot be distinguished. There is joint production. An example is moving a piano. The total result can be easily determined, but the effort of each individual team member cannot. Payments to individual team members have therefore to be based on the joint result.

Team production is associated with incentive problems. An *independent entrepreneur,* i.e. a team consisting of one person, knows that he or she will receive all the benefits generated by his or her effort, which will not occur if the team consists of several

---

individuals. Assume there are n team members and the benefits are divided equally. Every team member knows that the benefit of an additional unit of effort has to be shared with all other team members, i.e. input of a team member generates a *positive externality* for all other team members. However, this positive externality is not taken into account when the level of effort is chosen, because the payoff of a team member is determined by the difference between the payment received and the costs of the provided effort. Benefits have to be shared, whereas the costs of providing effort are completely paid for by the provider of effort. The public character of team production results in every team member being a *free rider*. Every team member will provide a lower level of effort than in the situation of independent entrepreneurship.

The problems with team production are due to the unobservability of individual effort levels. Payments have to be based on the joint result, which creates a tension between the desired individual effort and the joint payment. The agent bears the costs of providing effort completely, whereas the results have to be shared with the other team members. One additional unit of effort in a team of n members results in a share of $1/n$ in the additional result. The implication is that every team member will respond separately by providing a smaller level of effort to the project. However, the free rider problem can be solved by raising the share $1/n$ in the additional result. The principal can choose a salary structure that rewards every additional unit of output n-fold. Each additional unity of effort is paid for by the increase in output, which is n times the share of $1/n$ in the extra result (McAfee and McMillan, 1991). This is a way to resolve the free-rider problem, because the optimal choice of effort of each team member now coincides with the optimal effort of the team as a whole. This reward structure eliminates the negative effect of the positive externality on the choice of the level of output. The variable part of the salaries paid by the principal is equal to n times the value of the output. The principal deals with this deficit by adjusting the fixed component of the salary structure in such a way that each agent earns his or her opportunity costs or reservation wage.

Application: Seniority and mandatory retirement

Incentive contracts often specify a punishment or a prize. An example is the threat of dismissal when the employee performs poorly for a long time. Another example of a reward structure with a punishment is the withdrawal of the right to be the main supplier when the firm has delivered insufficient quality. Examples of prizes are promotion to a more attractive job or the premium salesmen receive when they realize sales above a certain target.

Prices and punishments are examples of discontinuous reward structures. This seems hard to match with the continuous reward structure of this section. However, McMillan (1992) has shown that it is possible that each continuous reward system can be formulated as an all-or-nothing, discontinuous contract. A *discontinuous or discrete contract* implies that the agent receives a high reward when the performance is above a certain level, and a low reward otherwise. The level of the two payments should be such that for the agent the value of this contract equals what can be earned elsewhere, i.e. the participation constraint has to be satisfied.

Lazear (1979) approaches salary structures based on *seniority* from this perspective. The employer (principal) is often unable to examine precisely the activities of the employee (agent). Employees can take advantage of this information asymmetry by developing activities which are in their own interest, but not in the interest of their employer. Employers are aware of these considerations of the agent and take them into account in the design of the salary structure. One way of preventing unproductive behaviour by employees is the policy of making them pay a considerable amount of money at the beginning of their career. This will be returned at the end of the relationship if behaviour has been good, but not if the employer has observed shirking. If this penalty or bond is large enough, then it will keep the employee from any unproductive activities.

A problem with such a salary structure is that the financial position of the employee is often too low to pay a sizeable amount of money at the beginning of his or her career, i.e. there is an income effect (Sec. 4.4). However, the same effect can be brought about using seniority wages, while circumventing the financial constraint. Seniority wages entail that a wage lower than the marginal productivity is paid at the beginning of a career. A condition for later receiving a salary which is higher than the marginal productivity is that the employee will not be caught behaving dishonestly or shirking. The effect of seniority wages is therefore the same as paying a considerable amount of money at the beginning of a relationship. Another advantage of seniority wages is that considerations of reputation need not play a role. This is attractive, because there are often problems with a reputation mechanism at the end of a relationship. Old employees do not value a good reputation as much as young employees, because there is less time left for them to benefit from it.

Employees paid according to their marginal productivity will retire voluntarily when the effects of ageing no longer offset the salary received. However, this does not apply with seniority wages. A policy of seniority wages means that at the end of their career employees

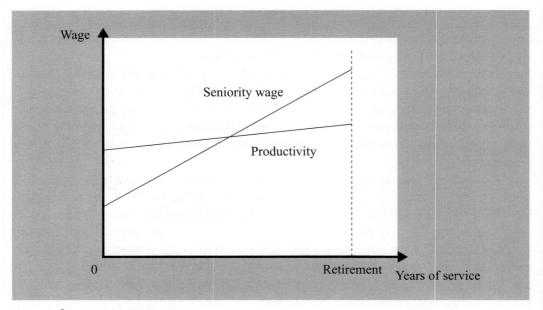

Figure 6.11: Seniority wages

earn more than their marginal productivity. Some employees may therefore decide to work longer than is desirable from the perspective of productivity. In order to solve this problem *mandatory retirement* is therefore usually included in seniority wage contracts. Employees are willing to accept the mandatory retirement clause in the contract, because it does not matter from an income perspective over the entire length of the relationship whether the wages received are seniority wages or wages based on marginal productivity. The employer may want to renegotiate the seniority wage when retirement is approaching because productivity is lower than the wage, but the employee will of course be unwilling to do that. Figure 6.11 presents the seniority wage structure with mandatory retirement.

Application: Capital structure

Part II formulated two important benchmarks regarding markets and property rights. The field of finance also has an important benchmark: the Modigliani–Miller theorem (1958). This specifies the circumstances in which the value of the firm is independent of its capital structure, which implies that the firm's production plan is independent of its financial structure. Hart (2001, p. 1080) paraphrases this irrelevance result as follows:

Modigliani–Miller theorem. In an ideal world, where there are no taxes, or incentive or information problems, the way a project or firm is financed doesn't matter.

The market-value balance sheet in Fig. 6.12 is used to illustrate this result (Myers, 2001). The market values of the firm's debt and equity, D and E, add up to total firm value V. The Modigliani–Miller theorem says that V is constant regardless of the proportions of D and E, provided that the assets and growth opportunities on the left side of the balance sheet are held constant. The proportion of debt financing, i.e. financial leverage, is therefore irrelevant. Using the metaphor of a pizza, the intuition of this result is equivalent to asserting that in a perfect-market supermarket, the value of a pizza (assets-in-place and growth opportunities of a firm) does not depend on how it is sliced (debt/equity ratio).

Assets-in-place and growth opportunities	Debt	(D)
	Equity	(E)
	Firm value	(V)

Figure 6.12: A market-value balance sheet (Myers, 2001, p. 85)

Another way to understand this result is that total firm value V (of the assets-in-place and growth opportunities of the firm or entrepreneur) is obtained by adding up the current value of all the uncertain, future cash flows of all the projects of the firm (Hart, 2001). Now suppose that the costs of these projects is equal to C, where $V > C$. The financiers have to get their C back. This can be done in various ways. They can be given a share s of future revenues, where $sV = C$. Another possibility is that they get debt which has a present value V. The entrepreneur receives the remainder $V - C$. From the entrepreneur's point of view (and the financiers') the method of financing doesn't matter.

The Modigliani–Miller theorem implies that nothing can be said about the debt/equity ratio of different firms in different countries. Nothing is excluded, i.e. a lot of debt is possible, a lot of equity is possible, or something in between may occur. This is not descriptive of the world. There are systematic factors which determine the debt/equity ratio. Using the pizza metaphor again, the values of pizzas do depend on how they are sliced. Consumers are willing to pay more for the several slices than for the equivalent whole. The Modigliani–Miller theorem has to be viewed as a *theoretical benchmark* for the development of a realistic theory of finance. Various ingredients are missing in the Modigliani–Miller theorem. Subsequent developments in the field of finance address various relationships between the value of the firm and its capital structure by relaxing the assumptions of the above result. Themes focused upon are the tax advantages of debt, costs of bankruptcy, asymmetric information, agency costs, voting rights and oligopolistic interactions. This application will focus on the influence of capital structure, i.e. the composition of the right side of the balance sheet, on the incentives for the manager to create value, i.e. the left side.

In order to determine optimal capital structure, Jensen and Meckling (1976) analyse the advantages and disadvantages of equity as well as debt from the perspective of asymmetric information. They argue that the value of the firm V is not fixed. It depends on the actions of management. The observations of Berle and Means (1932) regarding *the separation of ownership and control in firms* are the starting-point of the analysis. Two principal–agent relationships are distinguished regarding cost minimization and investment selection. Three parties are involved: debt-holders, managers owning equity (internal shareholders) and external equity-holders (external shareholders).

The first principal–agent relationship applies to *equity*. Managers own usually only a small part of equity. Most of it is in the hands of external shareholders. This creates problems regarding cost minimization by the managers. Managers receive only a fraction, corresponding with their percentage of the shares, of the results of their efforts, whereas they bear all the costs. Another way of formulating this problem is that managers know that only a share of the benefits created by their savings on unnecessary expenses, like a fancy office, the purchase of a luxurious business plane or staying in expensive hotels, devolves to them. These non-pecuniary benefits or *perks* result in a corresponding decrease in the value of the firm. The problem is that these costs are shared by all shareholders, while only a minority of the shareholders, i.e. the managers, enjoy all the benefits of these unnecessary outlays.

Too many unnecessary expenses are made in equilibrium, because the choice of effort of the manager cannot be observed by the external shareholders. The marginal costs of the manager are equal to the marginal benefits of the manager in equilibrium, but not to the marginal costs and benefits of the entire firm. Managers transfer part of the costs to the external shareholders. It is therefore not surprising that external shareholders are often worried that too much of these unnecessary expenses occur. This inefficiency decreases when the manager owns more equity. Efficiency is attained when equity is completely in the hands of the managers, i.e. there are no external shareholders. If external capital is needed, then this should consist completely of debt.

Two other considerations are favourable for the use of debt. First, Jensen (1986) emphasizes that debt requires that the firm regularly pays off its debt in cash in the capital market. This reduces the amount of *free cash* for managers to choose and develop non-productive activities. Debt therefore restricts managerial empire-building. Second, Grossman and Hart (1982) stress the relationship between debt and the manager's reputation. Bankruptcy is undesirable for a manager when he or she loses his or her managerial function or it hurts his or her *reputation* in the market. A manager of a firm with a lot of debt will therefore be forced, according to this view, to engage only in productive activities. Debt serves as a voluntary commitment by management to sufficient dynamic efficiency to prevent a takeover from an ever-present raider (Zwiebel, 1996). Managers voluntarily choose debt, using potential bankruptcy as a means to commit credibly to forgo bad investments, therefore preventing a takeover. The potential loss of control which may be associated with bankruptcy is the mechanism of managerial restraint. Managerial entrenchment is reduced by the threat of bankruptcy, which in turn affects the likelihood of managerial *replacement*. Bonding by managers with debt is therefore established by the market for corporate control.

Debt has also some disadvantages. The second principal–agent relationship in the analysis of Jensen and Meckling deals with the debt-holders and equity. Their interests are not aligned with the interests of the managers because of *limited liability*. This problem has been explained in Sec. 6.1. The convexity of the payoffs when investment projects are financed with debt (Fig. 6.3) encourages the adoption of risky projects. This implies that an increase in the level of debt of a firm will result in more risky projects. From the perspective of the creditors, too many risky projects are chosen.

The choice of *optimal capital structure* entails that the total costs of capital are minimized. Each form of finance has its own agency costs. Managers should be given such incentives that they effectively minimize costs and choose investment projects with the best profit and risk characteristics. From the perspective of cost minimization, the manager should receive the entire profit, i.e. the manager should own all the equity and the firm be financed completely by debt. Cost minimization is therefore best served by making the manager the 'residual claimant'. However, the choice of investment projects by the manager will be too risky when the firm is financed entirely by debt. The optimal capital structure is a compromise between these two considerations and will therefore in general consist of equity as well as debt. In equilibrium, the marginal benefit of keeping the manager from taking perks is offset by the marginal cost of causing risky behaviour, i.e. the marginal costs of each form of finance are equal. The equilibrium fraction of equity entails a tradeoff between the various forms of finance and is indicated by E^* in Fig. 6.13.

The non-observability of the choice(s) of the manager results in a loss of efficiency. The value of the firm decreases (*residual loss*) because the manager bears only part of the costs of his or her behaviour. There are two other inefficiencies. The principal will

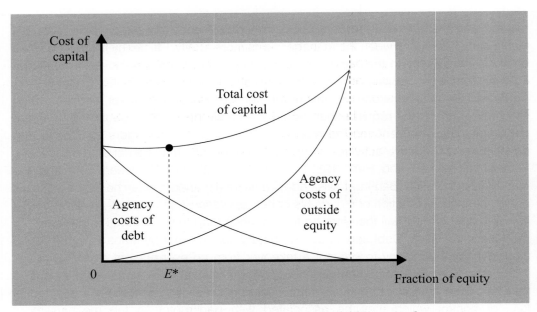

Figure 6.13: Optimal capital structure (Jensen and Meckling, 1976, p. 344)

incur various costs to observe the behaviour of the manager (*monitoring costs*) in order to reduce the information asymmetry. The agent too is confronted with various extra costs. He or she has to convince the providers of capital that he or she will not develop any activities at the expense of the firm (*bonding costs*). An example is the publication of the annual report in order to account for his or her behaviour. These three costs are called *agency costs*. They result in a loss of efficiency as a result of the lack of complete information. The sizes of these agency costs are determined in equilibrium by the behaviour of the principal as well as the behaviour of the agent.

Various predictions can be deduced from the above theory (Harris and Raviv, 1991). First, several *clauses* will be incorporated in contracts in order to deal with the various inefficiencies. Second, companies are financed more heavily with debt when there are fewer possibilities for new, risky projects. Companies in industries with limited growth opportunities are prime candidates. Third, companies in the declining phase of an industry usually require hardly any investment, while they still generate large revenues. This large amount of money (*free cash*) can stimulate managers to choose too many unproductive activities. A high level of debt may prevent this. Industries like steel, chemistry, beer, tobacco, radio and television, wood and paper are examples.

Application: Stockbrokers

Linear contracts were assumed in the derivation of the incentive intensity principle. However, non-linear contracts are sometimes clearly superior. The optimal contract can be very sensitive to the exact specification of uncertainty (Hellwig, 1989). An example of a non-linear contract is the reward structure of some *stockbrokers* on the London stock exchange. Higher profits of a trader are not always considered in a favourable way, i.e.

higher profits are not always rewarded with a higher payment. Very high profits may even result in a lower payment. An optimal payment structure should encourage good behaviour and make bad behaviour unattractive. Extremely high profits for stockbrokers are punished, because they are often the result of bad (risky) behaviour and a lot of luck. A prominent example is the downfall of the Barings Bank in the 1990s because of the investment behaviour of Nick Leeson. Figure 6.13 presents a non-linear salary structure. The employee receives nothing when the results are either very low or very high. Higher intermediate results will be rewarded with a higher payoff.

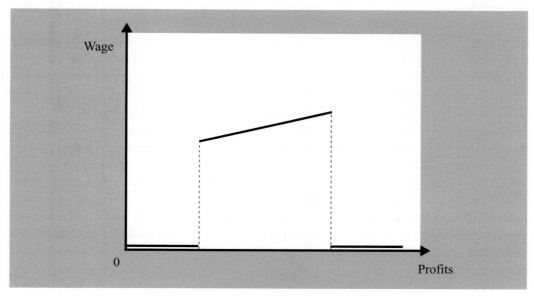

Figure 6.14: A non-linear payment scheme

6.3 Multiple dimensions

Section 6.2 has highlighted the tradeoff between risk or insurance and incentives. Risk-neutral firms insure their employees against random fluctuations in output by reducing the intensity of incentives. Incentives are provided regarding one activity, but agents usually perform many activities. This raises the issue of contractual externalities, which is addressed in this section. Section 6.3.1 addresses the optimal intensity of incentives when multiple activities of the agent are desired, while Sec. 6.3.2 addresses the intensity of incentives when the performance measure deviates from firm value.

6.3.1 Equal compensation principle

It is implicitly assumed in the previous section that the agent performs only one task. However, there are usually many tasks. For example, a secretary makes appointments, writes letters, edits manuscripts, determines which telephone calls are forwarded, responds to unexpected circumstances, anticipates problems and so on. One of the features of this job is the difference in measurability of the various tasks. Writing letters can be measured well, whereas measuring the anticipation of problems is difficult.

Another feature is that the wage of a secretary is usually fixed. The same payment is received each month. This seems remarkable from the viewpoint of the incentive intensity principle. If the different tasks can be distinguished from each other, the incentive intensity principle indicates that the easy-to-measure task will have a large piece-rate component in the wage structure. The reason is that the level of output is a good indicator of the effort provided, and this is exactly what the employer wants to reward. Nevertheless, it often happens that no piece-rate component or just a minimal one is present in the reward system. The difference in measurability of the various tasks of the employee is responsible for this.

Strong incentives may work *too* well, in the sense that the agent concentrates only on those activities for which piece-rate wages are paid. This goes at the expense of other important tasks. An employee paid only for the quantity produced neglects to care for quality. Rewards based on current profits will induce the manager to pay less attention to long-run goals. For example, a piece-rate system will stimulate the dentist to work rather fast. A dentist making a living based on standard treatments therefore earns more than someone who wants to think and experiment. Similarly, someone who applies few critical norms earns more with a piece-rate system than someone who works conscientiously and scrupulously. Quality loses from quantity.

If tasks are hard to separate, then a reward system with a large piece-rate component for all tasks results in outcrowding of tasks which are hard to measure. To make sure that all tasks receive sufficient attention, the payment structure has to be made less dependent on output. A few hard-to-observe tasks will result therefore in payments for all tasks which are based less on piece-rate remunerations than when the tasks are performed separately. A *contractual externality* is involved. This exists when the incentives which influence one decision affect optimal incentives with respect to other decisions. Holmström and Milgrom (1991) have defined this idea formally and labelled the result the *equal compensation principle*.

> *Equal compensation principle.* If an employee's allocation of time or attention between two different activities cannot be monitored by the employer, then either the marginal rate of return to the employee from time or attention spent in each of the two activities must be equal, or the activity with the lower marginal rate of return receives no time or attention.

One implication of the equal compensation principle is that there will be only limited use for contracts with explicit performance stimuli. If a certain activity cannot be measured at all, i.e. if V is large, then this implies that performance stimuli for all other activities are not very effective either. *Fixed salaries* can be understood from this perspective. Sales representatives are directly responsible not only for the amount of sales, but also for giving advice to customers and obtaining information about the competition. Each of these activities is important to sales, but only the first can be measured well. In such a situation the equal compensation principle dictates a salary that is independent of sales, to make sure that effort is spent on every activity. The same often applies to the salary of managers and secretaries. They develop many different, hardly measurable activities. A well-functioning organization requires that all these activities are developed, which is best guaranteed by a fixed salary.

The equal compensation principle implies that it is more costly to allow someone to work on a specific project when he or she has more freedom to develop other activities. The allocation of more *discretion* (i.e. control, authority) should go together with more *financial responsibility*, in the form of rewards being dependent on results. Other activities are made less attractive by assigning a higher marginal revenue to this specific activity for the agent. Other activities can also be made less attractive by subjecting them to rigid, bureaucratic rules. If a high degree of uncertainty concerning important activities makes a high β unattractive, then *reducing the flexibility* of an employee can be a solution. By eliminating his or her marginal tasks, he or she can only dedicate him or herself to the important tasks. Reducing this flexibility will be stronger when the important tasks are harder to measure. (Another way of changing the opportunity costs of effort of the various tasks is function design. This will be addressed in the third application of this section.)

The weak incentives implied by the equal compensation principle can be changed by changing the payoffs (Sinclair-Desgagné, 1999). Suppose there are two tasks. The effort dedicated to task A is easy to determine, while task B requires an audit in order to determine the way it is executed. The equal compensation principle predicts that task B will hardly receive any attention when only task A is measured and the wage is made dependent on this measurement. This problem can be resolved by a payment system in which doing the expensive audit is made dependent on the output of the easy-to-measure task A. Only a good result regarding task A will be responded to by an audit regarding task B. The idea is straightforward. If the result regarding the easy-to-measure task A is good, then not much effort is likely to be spent on task B. The prospect of such an audit increases the incentive to dedicate sufficient effort to task B. This payment system with contingent evaluations transforms the rival or substitute tasks A and B into *complementary tasks*.

This book addresses the way in which organizations – compared with markets – solve coordination and motivation problems. If exchange through markets is inefficient, then alternatives for markets may establish a more efficient allocation. The firm is such an alternative. This is not obvious, because markets provide much stronger performance stimuli than companies, and therefore will result in a higher productivity for certain activities. The equal compensation principle formulates an answer to Coase's question, 'Why is there any organization?' (Coase, 1937, p. 388). In some cases integration is efficient precisely because it eliminates market incentives. The use of low-powered incentives within the firm, although sometimes lamented as one of the major disadvantages of internal organization, is also an important vehicle for co-operation and co-ordination. The effectiveness of low-powered incentives within the firm may be enhanced by simultaneously placing constraints on the employee's freedom to act, e.g. bureaucratic constraints or job design. Proponents of making transactions within firms more market-like often seem to ignore the factors that brought these transactions inside firms in the first place. In such cases, bringing the market inside the firm would clearly be undesirable.

Certain activities may not emerge at all in markets. One reason for the existence of firms is that it offers weak performance stimuli in order to allow important activities to blossom which are hard to observe and hard to verify.Firms may therefore establish results that do not occur in a market relationship between two parties. (Kreps (1997) and Frey and Oberholzer-Gee (1997) bring up similar aspects concerning the relationship between explicit performance stimuli and intrinsic motivation, like autonomy, type of work aversion and norms.)

Application: Reward structure and measurability of quality

Quantity as well as quality of delivered goods and services is important. Quality may be determined by appointing an inspector. However, this entails costs, because the inspector has to be paid and his or her activities are hard to determine. *Piece-rate wages* seem therefore the most appropriate system of performance stimuli. This is attractive in terms of the quantity produced, but it may reduce the level of quality provided. Fixed wages are desirable when quality is hard to measure, whereas piece-rate wages are expected when quality care is no problem at all. The clothing industry is an example. In Hong Kong, employees receive piece-rate wages. The standard of quality control is however more difficult to verify, which explains why quality inspectors receive a fixed salary.

Application: Cost versus profit center

An accounting application of the equal compensation principle concerns the choice between cost and profit centre in the design of an accounting system. A manager in a *cost centre* is responsible only for the costs; revenues are considered outside his or her control. The manager of a cost centre is evaluated on the realizing of the planned activities, given the budget allocated to him or her. A manager in a *profit centre* is evaluated on costs as well as revenues; his or her contract is based on the profits of the division.

Suppose managers are able to control the costs and the generation of revenues. It is important in the choice of an accounting system that the manager is made responsible only for the decisions and results he or she can influence. If the manager can only control the costs, then it is recommended that payments depend only on these costs. However, if the revenues are sensitive to the activities of the manager as well, then the equal compensation principle prescribes that the β used for cost control has also to apply to the performance stimuli regarding revenues (Milgrom and Roberts, 1992).

Notice that non-standard considerations are used in the choice of an accounting system. The role of transfer prices and the allocation of costs are usually analysed without explicitly considering conflicts of interests. Asymmetric information and conflicts of interests are the focus of analysis in this chapter. An accounting system is chosen to handle these problems in an efficient way.

Application: Function design

Suppose there are various tasks that can be measured and evaluated separately. The tasks differ in degree of difficulty, which is represented by a different variance for each task. The question of *function design* is, which tasks should be allocated to whom? Is it desirable to allocate all hard-to-measure tasks to one person, or is it better to give each employee one difficult and one simple task? The equal compensation principle indicates that *similar tasks should be allocated to the same person*. This simplifies the design of an efficient reward structure.

For example, if it is desirable that two tasks should receive equal attention, then the marginal revenue of each task should be equal to the employee. Easy tasks are allocated to one function and provided with a reward structure with strong performance stimuli, i.e. V low and therefore β high, whereas the difficult-to-measure tasks are jointly allocated to another function and are associated with weak performance stimuli in the reward structure, i.e. V high and therefore β low. Another allocation of tasks is not desirable. Allocation of an easy-to-measure as well as a difficult-to-measure task to each employee implies that it is optimal to allocate weak performance stimuli to each function. This excludes the possibility that performance stimuli are being tuned to a specific function (Holström and Milgrom, 1991).

An implication of the above result is the principle of *unity of responsibility*. Two captains on one ship is undesirable. This result follows directly from the above by assuming there are only two tasks. Incentives cannot be geared towards specific tasks when both persons do half of each task. In terms of incentives it is more attractive for the company to allocate one task to each person.

A similar example concerns the success rate in realizing drastic *innovations* being higher in small companies than in large ones (Holström, 1989). Large companies have arisen mainly to realize production and marketing goals. The associated activities are usually surrounded with less uncertainty than are research activities. Both kinds of activities therefore require a different internal organization. This is more difficult to establish in one large organization than in two separate organizations. Small companies do not have such problems, because they can focus completely on innovative activities.

Application: Working at home

The equal compensation principle tells us that the intensity of incentives for a certain task depends largely on the other activities of the agent. If someone is allowed to work at home, he or she can develop personal activities next to his or her professional duties. To prevent this, the professional activities should have strong performance stimuli (high β), which makes it unattractive (i.e. costly) to develop other activities. The theory predicts that people who *work at home* regularly, and have considerable freedom in choosing their activities, generally have stronger performance stimuli than people in comparable positions without such freedom (Holmström and Milgrom, 1991). For example, a freelance journalist is usually paid by the length of an article, whereas employed journalists are not. Suppliers as well as employees should take care of the maintenance of tools and of production. An independent supplier, with his or her own tools, will have stronger performance stimuli than an employee without ownership of the tools, because the first already has strong stimuli (i.e., ownership) to take good care of his or her tools.

Strong incentives are not desirable when certain activities are difficult to measure, because this might result in the neglect of other tasks. In such situations it is desirable to limit the freedom of tasks. An *obligation to be present*, such as a time clock, prevents for example personal activities like watching television, doing the dishes or playing tennis during office hours. Personal activities during office hours can be restricted for example by closing off certain external phone numbers.

Application: Stakeholder organization

Companies are part of a society. They have relationships therefore not only with shareholders like employees, creditors, customers and the government, but also with other stakeholders like the local community and organizations like Greenpeace and Amnesty International which nowadays also claim to be stakeholders. Freeman (1984) defines a stakeholder as a group or person that influences or is influenced by the realization of the goals of the company.

The relationship of each stakeholder with the company can be represented as a principal–agent relationship (Dixit, 1996). The principal-agent relationship is different for each stakeholder. The stakeholders differ regarding the valuation of the output of the organization. Each principal evaluates and values the more dimensional output of the company differently, where the more dimensional output is the result of the various tasks performed by the company or agent. Besides, costs of effort of the agent differ for each principal.

The situation in which various principals co-operate is compared with the one in which they do not, in order to analyse the difference in performance between an organization with a single principal and one with many. The first situation can be associated with an organization that consists of one principal or with more principals of whom only one is taken seriously. The second situation is associated with a stakeholder organization. The main result is that incentives in a stakeholder organization are weaker than in a company with only one stakeholder. This is obvious to a certain extent because co-operating principals can always decide to stop co-operating if that is more attractive.

A stakeholder organization offers weaker incentives than a company with one principal because each principal provides the strongest incentives to tasks that benefit him or her most. Tasks beneficial only to other principals can even be discouraged by the principal in the payment structure of the agent. The other principals are led by comparable considerations in designing the reward structure. More effort in a specific task results in a higher output for one of the principals and therefore a higher payment for the agent. However, part of this higher payment has to be paid to the other principals because they have incorporated a penalty for a high output of tasks which benefit another principal. Stronger incentives for a particular task therefore mean two opposing financial effects for the agent. Developing more tasks for one specific principal results in a higher payoff for this principal. This is accompanied by the payment of a penalty by the agent to the other principals. Therefore, the other principals profit from the stronger performance stimuli, which means that the marginal revenue of the extra performance stimuli decreases. This negative externality of the choice of reward structure of the competing principals results is characterized as a prisoners dilemma. Each principal will choose weaker performance stimuli. In a stakeholder organization the mechanism of free-riding on the performance stimuli of other principals results in weak performance stimuli for all the tasks of the agent.

This can be understood as follows. Assume principals A and B try to direct the agent who performs tasks a and b, where task a is most beneficial to principal A and task b is most beneficial to principal B. The attention the agent gives to each task cannot be observed by either of the principals, but the output of both tasks can. If the agent pays more attention to task *a*, then this goes at the expense of task b. Principal A therefore chooses a reward structure that rewards a-output positively and b-output negatively. (Principal B offers exactly the opposite.) If principal A offers a higher reward for additional a-output, the agent receives a higher payment from principal A, but a higher penalty has to be paid to principal B as well. Part of A's reward therefore flows via the agent to principal B. Principal A is aware of this and will incorporate some performance stimuli in the reward structure (in order to limit the amount of additional money going to the other principal), but definitely not very strong performance stimuli. The same reasoning applies to the other principal, which results eventually in weak performance stimuli in a stakeholder organization.

The conceptualization of the stakeholder organization as a system of principals offers possibilities for *stakeholder management*. Stakeholder management entails maintaining relationships with specific stakeholder groups. Companies with many stakeholders will have to implement adjustments of functions and tasks in their organization in order to be able to survive in the competition with other companies that experience less influence by stakeholders. The uniform compensation principle suggests various possibilities for implementing adjustments of functions and tasks in the structure of a stakeholder organization. Examples are the number of non-cooperative principals with whom the organization is confronted and the set of tasks of the organization.

The negative externality of the choice of a reward structure by a stakeholder for the other stakeholders can be reduced by merging various stakeholders. They maintain their influence, but internalize the negative externality. For example, a company may meet with representatives of the various stakeholders like Greenpeace and Amnesty International together, instead of each stakeholder separately.

Each stakeholder designs a reward structure for the entire set of tasks of the organization. Tasks that benefit the stakeholder will be rewarded and the other tasks discouraged. The organization can prevent the discouragement of tasks by a specific stakeholder by decreasing the set of tasks of the different parts of the organization. Stakeholders will be limited to those parts of the organization which concern them directly. This decreases the negative externality associated with the choice of reward structure. Each stakeholder offers a reward structure with performance stimuli which are stronger than in the situation in which the reward structure applies to a large set of tasks. Restricting the span of the reward structure results in stronger incentives.

Finally, the organization can reduce the impact of each stakeholder, by for instance only informing him or her about, and allowing him or her to influence, those aspects which apply to the stakeholder directly. This establishes also a reduction of the set of tasks which can be influenced by a specific stakeholder, which prevents unnecessary negative externalities for the organization.

6.3.2 Inaccurate performance measurement

Section 6.2 assumed that the value of the activities of the agent for the principal can be measured precisely. However, the measurement of the output of the activities of the agent is usually not perfectly related to the value of these activities for the principal. For example, the value of the activities of teachers can be measured by the number of students passing a test, but this is not necessarily perfectly correlated with providing high-quality education. Similarly, the way in which the activities of employees contribute to firm value is very hard to determine by accounting procedures. The effect of this discrepancy between the performance measure and the value of the firm on the intensity of incentives is addressed in this section.

Baker (1992 and 2000) shows that the distortion between the performance measure used for the worker and firm value requires an adjustment of the incentive intensity principle discussed in the previous section. The optimal incentive intensity has to be multiplied by the correlation between the marginal effect of agent's effort or activities on what can be measured and the marginal effect of agent's effort or activities on what matters for the principal. The optimal incentive intensity will therefore be lower when this correlation is smaller, i.e. it will be lower when the extent to which the performance measure responds to employee actions differs more from how firm value responds to the same actions.

Application: Team production

The incentive package of an employee is based on individual as well as group performance. Each worker in a team engages in tasks which affect his or her own measured performance and also engages in co-operative activities which improve the performance of the entire team. Basing rewards for the worker only on individual performance reduces teamwork and undermines co-operation. Rewarding individuals only for group performance introduces a lot of riskiness because it rewards all of the uncontrollable events and actions of others in the group that affect team output. Baker (2000, p. 418) concludes that the way 'this trade-off gets resolved depends mainly on the value of co-operation (and thus the distortion induced by an individual reward scheme) and the riskiness of group (relative to individual) output.'

Application: Responsibility accounting

The design of reward schemes for plant managers in large multi-unit firms also involves a tradeoff between the risk imposed on the manager and the distortion in the performance measure. The plant manager works for a division manager, who works for the CEO of the company. Costs and revenues are measured at the plant, division and company levels. Figure 6.15 presents five possible performance measures and associated incentive schemes. Each of these schemes can be used for the plant manager's incentive contract. Each of these incentive schemes entails a tradeoff between risk for the plant manager and the distortion associated with the performance measure. Moving down this table represents a reduction in risk because the plant manager has more control over the outcome, but the discrepancy between the performance measure and firm value increases. The choice of performance measure has to be based on additional information. For example, if the amount of interdivisional co-operation or synergy is important, then a performance measure closer to the top of this table, i.e. a less distorted and more risky measure, is advised.

Performance measure	Incentive system
Firm value	Employee stock-ownership
Firm-wide accounting profits	Firm-wide profit-sharing
Divisional profits	Divisional profit-sharing
Plant-level profits	Plant profit centre
Plant-level costs	Plant cost centre

Figure 6.15: Possible performance measures and associated incentive systems (Baker, 2000, p. 419)

6.4 Generating additional information

From a *valuation perspective*, we care only about the output of the agent, i.e. the sum of $e + x$. From a *compensation perspective*, we care about the individual component e. The output of the agent does not therefore necessarily reflect his or her effort, which is shown already in the first two sections. It implies that even when $z = e + x$ is observable there is still a role for additional performance variables in the contract as long as they are incrementally informative about the agent's actions. These additional variables need not be incrementally informative about the outcome, just about the effort. The reason is that a low profit doesn't have to be the result of a small effort by the agent, but can be caused by disappointing demand or unexpected cost increases. A direct implication is therefore that it is attractive for the principal to generate more information about the labour circumstances of the agent and to optimally use the possibilities to control the agent.

This section treats various aspects of generating additional information. Uncertain, external circumstances which influence the performance of the agent can be taken into account to a certain extent by comparing it with the performance of agents in similar situations. Incorporating such information in contracts is analysed in Sec. 6.4.1. Another possibile way to acquire more information about the level of effort of the agent is to increase the control of the agent's activities. This possibility is addressed in Sec. 6.4.2. Additional possibilities and problems that repeated principal–agent relationships offer in the design of contracts are dealt with in Sec. 6.4.3.

6.4.1 The information intensity principle

Sections 6.1 and 6.2 have assumed implicitly that there is only one imperfect indicator of the effort of the agent: the level of output z. However, there is often other information available regarding the performance of the agent, like general economic circumstances and the performance of agents in similar situations. The agent does not have an effect on the external circumstances in his or her choice of e, but these do influence his or her output. General economic circumstances provide some information about the specific circumstances encountered by the agent and are therefore useful to the principal in designing the contract (Holmström, 1979).

Assume that the general economic circumstances are summarized by the stochastic variable y and that the expectation of y equals zero. Bad circumstances result in a negative value of y, good circumstances in a positive one. The relative weight of this information compared with z is represented by γ. An estimate of the non-observable effort e of the agent is $z + \gamma y$. A contract now consists of three numbers (α, β, γ) and the salary of the agent is determined according to $w = \alpha + \beta(z + \gamma y)$.

The profit-maximizing contract is determined in the same way as in Sec. 6.2. This results in $\beta = P'(e)/[1 + r \operatorname{Var}(x + \gamma y)C''(e)]$, where $\gamma = -\operatorname{Cov}(x,y)/\operatorname{Var}(y)$. ($\operatorname{Cov}(x,y)$ is the covariance of x and y.)

The introduction of the variable y is introduced by the principal in order to obtain more information about the uncertain factor x. This may result in a better estimate of the effort e of the agent. However, if y is not related to x, i.e. x and y are independent, then the value of y does not provide any information about x. Formally, the situation in which x and y are independent is summarized by $\operatorname{Cov}(x,y) = 0$ and it is therefore not sensible to allocate any weight to y because it adds only noise. Section 6.2 is the special case $\gamma = 0$ of the above formula.

The parameter γ is equal to 0 when y provides no information about x. Otherwise it is unequal to 0. Suppose there is a *positive relation between x and y*, like a bad situation in the automobile industry being often associated with a decline in the entire economy. According to the above formula, γ is negative in such a situation. The principal observes z ($= e + x$) and y, and uses the value of y in order to infer something about e. Take a certain value of z. If general circumstances are good (y high), then circumstances in a specific market are often also good (x high). This implies that the contribution of e in realizing the value of z has been small. The reward system aims at encouraging effort, so that a high y is not viewed positively when x and y are positively related. The result z (on which the contract is based) is adjusted downward by γy, where γ is negative. Another example of this situation is that a grade of 7 for an exam is not very good when the average is 8. A similar argument applies when general economic circumstances are bad, which means the value of y is negative. This probably entails a setback for the specific circumstances of the agent (x low). The contribution of e must have been relatively high in establishing a particular value of z. The principal rewards this with a higher salary, because the negative value of γ multiplied by the negative value of y is a positive number. For example, a grade 7 for an exam is good compared with an average grade of 6. A similar analysis holds *when x and y are inversely related*. The covariance is negative in this situation, i.e. γ is positive.

The choice of γ that minimizes the variance regarding the estimate of the effort of the agent is an illustration of a more general result called the *informativeness principle* (Milgrom and Roberts, 1992, p. 219). It specifies which information to include in a contract.

Informativeness principle. The total value of a relationship is increased by including (excluding) information in (from) the contract that decreases (increases) the error in the estimation of the effort of the agent.

Application: Yardstick competition

Inefficiencies due to incentive problems can be reduced by generating better information, for instance by comparing the performance of agents with similar tasks. This information can be incorporated in the reward structure by making the wage dependent on the difference between the individual and the average performance, or by allocating a price, premium or promotion to the best performer. If the production of each agent is sensitive to the same uncertainties, then the performance of the group provides the principal with information about these uncertainties. It improves his or her ability to determine which part of the output of the agent is due to his or her effort and which to exogenous circumstances. Reward systems based on relative performance incorporate this information in the design of contracts. This is called *yardstick competition*, because the agents themselves formulate the yardstick for the determination of their wage.

Tournaments or contests are specific cases of such systems. They do not determine the absolute level of performance of everyone, but only the relative position (rank). It is only important who is first, not how large the difference is between the first player and the second. This contrasts sharply with the piece-rate system based on individual production earlier in this chapter. Another aspect of tournaments is that competition is used in a different way: it does not serve the role of stimulating agents to perform better, but to generate additional information about the labour circumstances of the agents.

Notice that the tournament perspective entails a specific definition of the firm. *The firm is viewed as a wage structure.* The composition of the wage structure, i.e. the salary difference between various functions, has an impact on the level of effort that will be provided. The effort of the agent will be higher when the wage differential between functions or positions is larger. An insight that builds on this is that the effect of an increase in uncertainty may be compensated for by a larger wage differential. The reason is that the agent will respond with a lower level of effort when uncertainty rises because the impact of his or her effort on the final result will be less. For example, a tennis player in a hurricane will hardly provide any effort. This effect is diminished by increasing wage differentials.

Application: Relative performance rewards

Section 6.2 showed that the optimal contract entails a compromise between insurance and incentives for a risk-averse agent. The performance stimuli showed up in the contract by basing the wage of the agent to a certain extent on the output of the agent. Lazear and Rosen (1981) consider an alternative way of formulating incentives in organizations. Promotions, also called relative performance rewards, induce employees to put forward effort. This reward structure can be explained by the desire of the principal to reduce the uncertainty regarding the execution of a specific task as much as possible. Uncertain factors faced by an employee apply often also to other employees. This correlation between the productivity of various jobs enables the principal to formulate stronger incentives for the agent and let him or her bear less risk than in situations where this information is ignored.

Green and Stokey (1983) develope this idea further. They show that the degree in which piece-rate wages and relative compensation are used depends on the variance of the uncertainties with which everyone is confronted and the variance of the uncertain component related to the specific effort of the agent. If the variance of the *common risk* is larger than the variance of the *specific risk*, then the principal prefers a tournament (competition element) above individual, independent contracts.

Evaluations in a tournament are based on a standard (the performance of the other agent), which is a stochastic variable. This is sensible, because this standard is highly correlated with the stochastic component of the individual result. In this way, tournaments eliminate the variance to a large extent, while only a little noise is added by the dependence on the results of others. A tournament is not advisable in other circumstances because it increases the uncertainty for each agent and provides little information.

The benefit of filtering away common uncertainties in a reward structure is one important aspect of a tournament. There are three further advantages of a tournament compared with a system of piece-rate wages. First, less detailed information is needed. Only *ordinal information* is necessary in a reward system based on relative performances, whereas cardinal information is needed in a reward structure based on piece-rate wages. The costs of collecting information will therefore in general be less. Another advantage is the *flexibility* of these reward systems. They adjust to the difficulty of a task and are insensitive to a lack of information or agreement regarding the uncertainties in the environment. A third advantage is that they establish a *better commitment* by the principal. The principal can haggle over the delivered performance in a piece-rate wage system in order to pay a lower wage. This is not possible with tournaments because the joint wages are fixed. Competition between the agents determines the division of the joint rewards.

However, payments based on relative performance have also some disadvantages. An example is the possibility to *sabotage*. Agents compete with each other, which makes it attractive to undermine the results of others. This argues for mitigating the differences in the wage structure. Another disadvantage is that the agents can make *collective agreements* to conspire against the principal. A third disadvantage is that relative performance rewards make it attractive to apply for jobs when there are only a *few high-performing colleagues*. Recruiting incompetent co-workers can be seen in the same context. Other factors against relative performance payment systems are the poor *measurability* of the results of others, or the presence of production *externalities* as in team production. Finally, this reward structure can have negative effects on the effort of the agent. Akerlof (1976) has shown that a *rat race* may arise in which agents provide more effort than in the situation with complete information. Notice that this last aspect differs strongly from the result in Sec. 6.2. If the wage structure is based only on information regarding the agent, then the optimal structure will result in a lower effort by the risk-averse agent in a situation with asymmetric information than in the situation with complete information.

Tournaments *use information* in general *inefficiently*. Although they filter the common stochastic component out of the results, they increase the uncertainty by making the reward of the agent dependent on the idiosyncratic uncertainties of the colleagues (competitors). In general, it is inefficient to restrict the design of contracts to individual piece-rate wages and tournaments. Contracts which make the wage of the agent dependent on the individual results of all other agents are usually better (Holmström, 1982).

Application: Cars and electronics

Asanuma (1989) analyses the contracts between suppliers of parts and producers in the Japanese electronics and car industries. These contracts usually specify a particular amount, deadlines and rules for price determination. Prices are based on detailed cost estimations by the supplier and these are subsequently checked by the buyer. Adjustments are based on changes in production costs.

However, the supplier is not compensated for all changes in costs. A distinction is made between costs of labour, materials and energy. The buyer is usually willing to pay only for the rise in price of raw material. All other increases in costs have to be paid by the supplier. This policy provides the right incentives for the supplier to control costs. The supplier is usually not able to have an impact on the costs of material, but he or she is able to control the costs of labour and energy. In the United States, producers of automobiles often do compensate suppliers for the rise in costs of labour, which entails limited incentives to control these costs.

Application: Salaries of top managers

Rewards based on relative performances provide incentives to put forward effort, while the agent is partly insulated from exogenous uncertainty. Indirect disciplining mechanisms, like the labour market, capital market and product market, are therefore obvious sources of information to be used in the design of contracts. However, these advantages of incorporating additional information in the reward structure may also have some disadvantages, which too should be taken into account. The performance of managers elsewhere and the scope of actions at the cost of, or together with, these managers, are important for the design of the reward structure. The costs of measuring the performance of other companies (share prices) have to be low and the possibilities to sabotage or conspire have to be limited in order to make relative performance rewards attractive.

After evaluating these advantages and disadvantages, wages will probably be based partly on relative performances. This will stimulate the manager to manage the company well, because the possibilities for sabotage and collaboration are minimal. The prediction is that the *salaries of top managers* are positively related to the results of the company and display a negative correlation with the results in the industry. A top manager earns more when competitors perform less well, *ceteris paribus*.

Application: Delegation

Delegation of responsibilities and decision authority can generate valuable information (Vickers, 1985). If a company is confronted with uncertainties which are not observable to the board of directors, but are observable to the individual division managers, and if these uncertainties for the various divisions are to some extent correlated, then the relative division results entail a yardstick for the performance of the various managers. Reward systems based on relative performances use this information as a benchmark and result in higher profits for the entire company. These reward systems intensify the internal competition and generate valuable information for the board of directors.

Creating internal competition can be desirable in companies as well as nations. Porter (1990) analyses the success factors of companies. His research shows that local circumstances are important for the success of companies. It turns out that successful companies are often located close to each other. Clusters of supporting and competing companies evolve together and represent a large reservoir of specialized know-how. The strength of a company often derives from intense competition.

Application: Internal labour market

An internal labour market can be approached from the perspective of the fundamental welfare theorem. *Transfer prices* direct the internal allocation of positions according to this view. However, this is usually not a realistic representation of daily organizational practice. The hierarchical structure of an organization often means that individuals on one level compete for a limited number of positions at a higher level. Employees try not only to deliver good work, but also to perform better than their colleagues. Such competition is better presented as a competition, a *race* or a tournament, than by the static form of pure price competition in the fundamental welfare theorem. An implication is that the wage of an individual employee does not usually reflect the value of marginal productivity.

A wage is equal to the value of marginal productivity in every period according to the fundamental welfare theorem. However, Doeringer and Piore (1971) document various characteristics of internal labour markets which differ from this result. First, wages often increase faster than the rise in productivity. Wage increases are often more strongly linked to experience and *seniority* than to rises in productivity. A second characteristic of internal labour markets is that wages are coupled to jobs instead of to persons. *Salary* scales are tied to functions. The differences in rewards between jobs are often determined more by administrative procedures than by the wage developments outside the company. This reduces the possibility of bargaining. Figure 6.16 reflects these two characteristics. The marginal productivity increases in the course of time, but the wage increases faster. Sometimes a salary jump occurs as a result of promotion. A third characteristic is that the *dispersion* of income increases more strongly as the number of years of experience increases. Further, it turns out that the larger part of the better-paid positions in companies are attained through *internal promotion*.

Malcolmson (1984) explains these characteristics of the internal labour market from the perspective of relative performance wages. The essence of his explanation is that employees accept a reward structure in which some of them get promoted. Employees are initially paid less than their marginal productivity in order to discourage the provision of low effort, while they receive more than their marginal productivity close to their retirement. This makes being fired due to unsatisfactory behaviour more costly, and

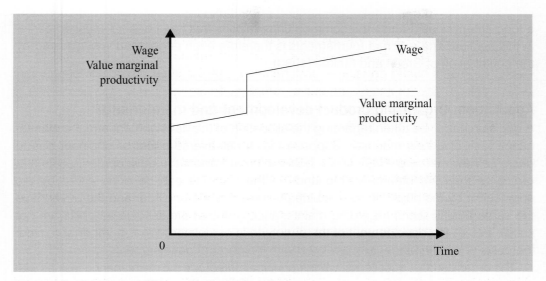

Figure 6.16: Wage and marginal productivity

therefore reduces this kind of behaviour. Notice that employees earn the value of their marginal productivity over their entire career, but the reward for performance is spread over the entire career. Initially one earns less than the marginal productivity, but this is compensated for afterwards. Rewards are paid with some delay with this type of contract. The seniority wage structure discussed in Sec. 6.2 has similar features.

This wage structure makes it attractive for employees to put forward additional effort. Employees with the best results win a prize in the form of *a promotion*. This explains the other three characteristics of the internal labour market. Promotion implies a job with a higher salary. However, promotion is not available to everyone, which implies that employees with similar capacities earn considerably different wages in the course of time. This explains the increase in income dispersion as the years of experience increase. Finally, promotion often occurs internally, because someone has proved to be able to deliver good performances in the tournament (in a competitive relationship).

Some closing remarks remain to be made regarding the structure of the contract. The contracts in this chapter rely on a third party, i.e. the judiciary power, to enforce contracts. Gathering the relevant information is costly. Tournaments have the advantage not only that the necessary information is relatively easy to obtain, but also that the third party is already participating in the tournament. *Employees are a third party for each other.* All other employees together constitute the third party benefiting from bad behaviour by an employee, because this increases their possibilities for promotion. The principal does not have to worry that for the employees the contract is only a fake. Every employee individually does not have to worry that for the employer the contract is not a *commitment*. Breaking the contract either in favour or to the detriment of an individual employee does not benefit the principal, because the total amount of money involved in a tournament is fixed. Agents compete for the available promotions, where the number of promotions is fixed in advance. Finally, the treatment of the internal labour market as a tournament does not use the common uncertainties that have been discussed earlier in this section. The reach of tournaments is therefore even larger than is suggested by the contribution of Green and Stokey (1983).

Application: Organizing product development and maintenance

A decision has to be taken regarding the allocation of the development and the maintenance task of a new machine. Suppose that a risk-averse agent or engineer has to design a new machine. He or she is better informed about the development costs of a prototype than are others. Maintenance of the machine can be done either by the engineer or by the buyer of the machine. Assume that the engineer and the buyer have the same qualifications regarding maintenance and that the associated costs are not known before the development of the prototype is completed. What is important is that the costs of maintenance are correlated with the costs of development.

The organizational question is: will the principal *outsource* the maintenance task as well as the development task to the engineer, or will he or she perform the maintenance task him or herself? The answer depends on the way in which the costs of the two tasks are correlated. If there is a negative correlation, the buyer is better off allocating both tasks to the engineer. The engineer will exaggerate the costs of development when only the development task is allocated to him or her. Exaggeration is less attractive when maintenance is also allocated to him or her. In that situation, the engineer knows that a high claim for development costs will necessarily imply that he or she expects the maintenance costs to be low. The principal can exploit this negative correlation in the design of the contract by relating the compensation for the maintenance task inversely to the claim regarding development costs. Such a contract decreases the incentive to claim excessive costs. An additional benefit is that the risk premium can be reduced, because the negative correlation between the uncertainties reduces the uncertainty facing the agent. If there is a positive correlation between the costs of the two tasks, then the principal is better off doing the maintenance him or herself. Allocating both tasks to the engineer increases his or her incentive to exaggerate the costs of both tasks (Riordan and Sappington, 1987).

Application: Division of tasks

Section 6.3 formulated some ideas regarding the design of a job or function in favour of allocating the responsibility for one task to one person. An attractive aspect of the *division of tasks* is that it offers the possibility of comparing the way different people execute the same task. This can be beneficial in situations where reward systems based on relative performance do well. Another advantage of the division of tasks is that a richer job description is appreciated by employees.

Complementaries between various tasks may exist, i.e. one may become more productive in every task when because of the synergies between various tasks they are all allocated to the same person. An example is the tasks undertaken by scientific staff; allocating research as well as educational functions to the same person helps to incorporate the most recent developments in the lectures (Milgrom and Roberts, 1992).

6.4.2 Monitoring intensity

A second way to use additional information in contracts is to monitor the activities of the agent. Examples are the use of a time clock to control the presence of the employees; reducing the number of employees who report to one manager (so that he or she is able to pay more attention to every individual); executing quality controls; performing time studies on the actions of employees; and audits in accountancy.

The result of these monitoring activities is expressed in the model of Sec. 6.2 by a lower value of the variance V. Supervision not only generates additional information but also entails additional costs. This is incorporated in the analysis by the introduction of a function $M(V)$ for the costs necessary to realize a level V of the variance. The endogenous variable V is determined by the level of β, *ceteris paribus*. It is now possible to show that a higher value of β results in more outlays to accomplish a lower value of V (Milgrom and Roberts, 1992, p. 226). This relationship is called the *monitoring intensity principle*.

> *Monitoring intensity principle.* When the plan is to make the agent's pay very sensitive to performance (β high), it will pay to measure that performance carefully (V low).

The *incentive intensity principle* specifies also a certain relationship between β and V. The variance V is taken as given and determines the value of the endogenous variable β. A lower value of V results in a higher value of β according to the incentive intensity principle, whereas this section has shown that a high β results in activities which result in a lower V. The causal relationship between β and V seems therefore unclear. However, it is not, because an optimal incentive system determines the level of monitoring (V) and the incentive intensity (β) at the same time. Figure 6.17 presents the incentive intensity principle as well as the monitoring intensity principle. The incentive intensity principle line shows the

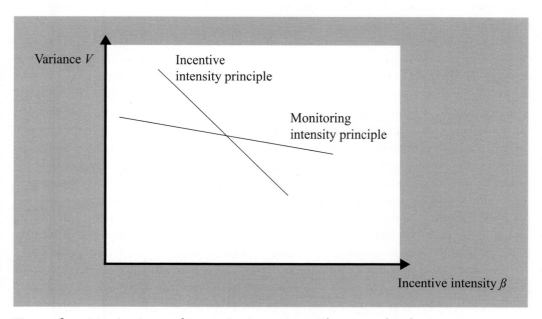

Figure 6.17: Monitoring and incentive intensity (Milgrom and Roberts, 1992, p. 227)

optimal value of β for each possible value of V. The monitoring intensity principle line specifies the optimal value of V for each possible value of β. The value of β and V in the optimal incentive system is determined by the point of intersection of the two lines.

The comparative statics analysis concerns changes in exogenous variables, like P' and C''. According to the incentive intensity principle, a rise of P' or a decline in C'' results in a higher β for each value of V. This entails a shift of the line of the incentive intensity principle to the right in Fig. 6.17. The value of V is lower and the value of β is higher in equilibrium.

Application: Dockworkers and accountants

The costs of monitoring depend strongly on the type of work. In artistic or professional work it is difficult to determine someone's dedication. For example, it is easier to determine the marginal productivity of dock workers or assembly line workers than the marginal productivity of lawyers, public relations agents or accountants. The easy measurability of the level of effort of dock workers and assembly line workers entails that their monitoring intensity principle line in Fig. 6.17 is lower than the one for the other professions. The prediction therefore is that employees on an assembly line or dock workers have contracts with a relatively high β and that their employers spend a lot of money on performance measurement. If observing the inputs is difficult, these performance stimuli contracts are not effective. The expectation is that in such situations other organizational forms will develop which are better capable of solving these problems of asymmetric information.

6.4.3 The ratchet effect

If principal–agent relationships are repeated over time, then additional advantages and disadvantages emerge. A disadvantage will feature in this section, while Chapter 10 highlights several advantages.

In a repeated relationship the principal observes the effort of the agent in period after period. This provides opportunities for the principal to use the current result in the design of the payment structure of the next periods. An example is the way in which the principal may respond to meeting budgets or targets. The principal often formulates a higher future target or allocates a lower future budget if the current goals have been met or even exceeded. The dilemma facing the agent is that a better performance today results in a higher current reward, but is often punished tomorrow by a higher target or tighter budget. For example, by exceeding the current quota, the manager can expect to be 'rewarded' by a higher quota in every subsequent period because output expectations are *ratcheted up* or raised to a higher level. This would be a perverse *dynamic incentive scheme*, where good behaviour today is punished tomorrow, so the agent has no incentive to exceed the target or to be careful with spending the entire budget. Targets then would most likely be barely met and/or budgets exceeded slightly so as to secure a lower target or a larger budget in the following period.

This observation provides a challenge in designing a reward structure which depends on past performance. An employee with a relatively easy task, and who also provides a high level of effort, will probably generate a good result. The principal will infer from a high level of output that the job was easy, and will therefore expect excellent future results as well. The *information intensity principle* implies that such information will have an impact on the design of the optimal reward structure, because the additional information decreases the uncertainty about the contribution of the agent. The reward structure will reflect this by rewarding only excellent results. A higher standard decreases the income of the employee for each level of effort and production. However, basing the target on past results entails dangers. Good results are punished with a higher standard in the future, whereas lower results are rewarded with a lower standard. Employees anticipate this and therefore have an incentive to keep performance low at the beginning of the relationship. The anticipation of the employee that the performance of the first period will be misused in the second period reduces the effective β in the first period. The principal is not naive either, and anticipates that the employees will react in such a way. He or she will therefore try to implement a credible reward structure which is identical in both periods. The total output increases when a commitment to a certain reward structure can be made which does not use the performance of the first period to adjust the contract in the second period.

In conclusion, the principal is not able to design a contract such that the agent provides substantial effort. Agents with simple (productive) tasks will put forward a relatively low level of output in order to hide the productive potential of any one task. This phenomenon is called the *ratchet effect*.

Application: Job rotation

Job rotation is often used in institutions like the church, the diplomatic service, the army and companies, but it is difficult to understand from the perspective of labour productivity. In the course of time, an employee performs a certain task better. Various specific skills are developed, which results in higher labour productivity. Human capital (experience), or a dynamic economy of scale, is therefore destroyed when employees regularly change positions.

Ickes and Samuelson (1987) approach job rotation from the perspective of asymmetric information. Most jobs do have specific productivity characteristics, but the principal does not know them. He or she cannot judge whether good performance is the result of the effort of the agent or of the nature of the job (easy or difficult). The solution formulated in Sec. 6.2 indicates that the principal can design a reward structure such that it induces the agent to put forward the desired level of effort.

A second aspect of the relationship between the employer and the employee is that it is usually long-term. This may entail the additional incentive problem of the *ratchet effect*. This problem is due to the inability of the principal to convince the employees that he or she is committed to the contract. Employees are aware that the employer can change the contract in a way that allows him or her to claim the entire surplus when the exact working conditions become known. The agent will therefore not be inclined to reveal the difficulty of his or her task. The quota will be barely met and the budget will be exceeded slightly.

Job rotation is one way of thwarting the ratchet effect. The problem of too high expectations does not occur when employees are regularly transferred, because good performance in the current position does not reveal anything about productivity in another position. Current circumstances are no longer a good indicator for future performance. Employees therefore have no reason to hide the productivity of activities by performing moderately. The costs of better results, i.e. raising current standards, are no longer borne by the person involved. *Job rotation can therefore be an optimal answer to information problems in long-term relationships.* Another effect of job rotation is that it prevents the development of non-productive (corrupt) team relationships, because employees occupy any one position for too short a time. The disadvantage of job rotation, however, is that human capital is lost.

Sociological and psychological explanations of the value of job rotation often refer to work *satisfaction*. The underlying idea is that varied and diversified work results in greater job satisfaction. Closely related is the economic analysis of task enrichment (Itoh, 1991). Another reason for job rotation may be that a strong corporate culture is created by transferring employees regularly.

6.5 Entrepreneur as monitor

Economic activities in which several persons are involved can be organized in various ways. A well-known organizational form is the company, defined as an organization owned and managed by the same person. The entrepreneur coordinates and controls the activities of the others (employees) and receives the resulting revenues after the payments agreed upon (for example wages and interest) are made. An alternative way of organizing is to co-operate on the basis of equality in a partnership, the adjustment of activities being established by mutual consent.

The question arises of why certain organizational forms occur much more frequently than others. For example, it is a fact that co-operation based on equality hardly exists. Alchian and Demsetz (1972) explain this by pointing to problems with conflicts of interests and asymmetric information in team production. The company is viewed as an institutional solution to team problems.

Team production is attractive in principle, because joint production often allows for more possibilities than individual production. Moving a piano is not possible for one person, but easy when several people combine their efforts. If everyone had to move pianos on his or her own, the productivity would be low or even zero. Other examples of team production are concerts and heart surgery. However, team production entails incentive problems because it is difficult to determine who is responsible for which part of the total output. A contract for an individual employee cannot therefore depend on the individual's contribution. Besides, individual performances are usually not directly observable. A low level of output can be caused either by uncertainties in the environment or else by too small an effort by the team members.

People often face a tradeoff between leisure and work. The former will get more attention when individual contributions to joint output are not measurable. Every team member is inclined to behave in this way and the result is that the level of output is low. This *free-rider problem* is due to the difficulty of measuring of individual performances, which may be due to the indivisibility of the production technology or to increasing returns to scale. This problem was resolved in Sec. 6.2 by raising the financial incentives for the team members.

This section poses *the firm* as an institutional or organizational solution for team and measurement problems.

The information problem in team production therefore has several unpleasant consequences. Result-dependent contracts are out of the question. It is necessary to gather information about the efforts of an agent. Assume that shirking can be discovered by appointing someone who specializes entirely in controlling others. It means that the introduction of this *supervisor* or monitor improves the measurement of individual performances, so that the team will subsequently produce more. The monitor can be appointed of course only when the additional profits of the monitor outweigh the costs.

The design of the salary structure of the supervisor determines how well he or she performs. If the sole reward is to receive only a share of the additional profits, then the supervisor will shirk as well. Alchian and Demsetz solve this problem ('Who monitors the monitor?') by assigning five rights to the supervisor or monitor. The monitor has the right to

- Receive the entire profits (residual income);
- Observe the input behaviour;
- Determine rewards for the inputs;
- Change the composition of the team;
- Sell The previous rights.

The first right entails that the supervisor becomes the *residual claimant*. The additional profits due to the effort of the supervisor go entirely to him or her after the other team members are paid the salary agreed upon. The supervisor has therefore no reason for shirking.

The above structure corresponds with the classical conception of a company. The appointment of the supervisor introduces a hierarchical relationship in the team. He or she or she owns the company, while the others are the employees. This entails that she or he claims the profits, has the right to hire and fire employees, can observe the input behaviour of the employees, can adjust salaries on individual employees and possibly can sell the company. Alchian and Demsetz view the institution 'entrepreneur' therefore as the answer to information problems in teams, with the entrepreneur specialized in monitoring the team members.

6.6 Conclusion

The consequences of asymmetric information in a situation with conflicts of interests have been discussed. The starting-point in the contractual approach of organizations is the voluntary character of participation in a company. Individuals become members of a certain organization when it is in their own interests. An accountant, for instance, is viewed no longer only as someone who collects and distributes information, but also as a party with his or her own goals and alternatives elsewhere. Contractual payments are structured such as to reduce the conflict of interests between the principal and the agent, and extra information is gathered and used to reduce the information asymmetry.

The optimal contract is not able to solve all frictions regarding asymmetric information, risk aversion, the binding character of contracts and measurement problems regarding the effort of the agent. The optimal contract will in general be *second-best*, which indicates the importance of the principal–agent approach for the theory of the firm. The costs of asymmetric information are dealt with by other decision rules, another allocation of tasks and a contractual approach towards organizations. The principal–agent approach does not provide an exhaustive explanation of the structure and functioning of complex organizations. The model is valuable however, because it indicates the causes of and solutions for possible frictions in organizations.

Many extensions of the model discussed in this chapter are possible. First, attention was focused on two parties, namely one principal and one agent. However, organizations often consist of *many layers*, where the same person is a principal in relation to subordinates but at the same time an agent vis-à-vis a superior. This causes new problems, like forming coalitions and delegating tasks (Tirole, 1986). Second, in situations with *two-sided asymmetric information*, the principal owns valuable information too (Maskin and Tirole, 1992). Third, a source of information which has not entered in the design of contracts is the observation of the real circumstances *by the agent*. Making the payments dependent on this observation in the contract is usually attractive for the principal (Demski and Sappington, 1984). Fourth, sometimes it is possible to base the contract only on an imperfect indicator of the objective function of the principal (Baker, 1992). Fifth, situations may arise in which the principal is sensitive to *bribes*; these have not been discussed, either.

6.7 Exercises

6.1 A Which two behavioural assumptions are made in a principal–agent model?
   B Which two aspects does the principal have to take into account in the design of the optimal contract in a hidden action problem?
   C Why is the surplus which the principal receives in the hidden action problem in the situation with incomplete information smaller in general than in the situation with complete information?

6.2 The manager of the soccer team The Flying Boys (TFB) has decided to introduce financial incentives in the contracts of its players. A premium will be paid to the players who score. An attempt to score only succeeds with a certain probability, because the player can miss or because the ball can be stopped.
   A Illustrate in a diagram the financial side of an attempt to score. This diagram has to show the two possible levels of income, the expected income from an attempt to score, the expected utility, the certain equivalent income of the player and the risk premium of a risk-averse player.
   Assume that a bonus of 400 euros is paid for each goal and that the utility function of the extra income equals $U(b) = \sqrt{b}$, where b is the level of the bonus. In the last minute of the game, a TFB player is tackled and is awarded a penalty. The score is still 0–0, which makes the penalty conclusive for a tie or a win by TFB. The manager of the opponents, Polder Prinsen (PP), deviously sends one of his players to the one who is going to take the penalty in order to bribe him.

B What is the minimum payoff which has to be paid to persuade the TFB player to miss? Assume that the players are only moved by financial incentives and that the TFB player scores with a probability of .7 when he or she is not bribed.

At some point during the game Diego de Vries and Jan Romario are free in front of the PP goalkeeper. Diego is in possession of the ball and scores with a probability of .1, while Jan succeeds with a probability of .2. In the current financial system Diego prefers to shoot rather than pass to Jan. The TFB manager wants to avoid this problem in the future by awarding a bonus for a decisive assist.

C What should the bonus be to make Diego pass the ball to Jan in the same situation in the future?

6.3   A Explain the difference between a risk-averse and a risk-seeking agent. Illustrate your answer in words and with a figure.

B Describe the relationship between the behaviour of an agent towards risk and the relationship between the fixed and the variable parts in the salary of an agent for a fixed certainty equivalent income.

6.4   Contracts are used to reduce the divergence of interests between the principal and the agent. They can be very complicated, but assume there are linear contracts, i.e. a contract specifies a fixed component and a variable component based on output.

A Why is the contract based on output?

B In what way does an increase of uncertainty in the environment influence the variable part of the reward structure? Explain your answer.

C Does the profit of the principal increase when a less risk-averse agent is appointed? Explain your answer.

D In what situation is it not recommendable for the principal to use a linear contract for the activities of the agent?

6.5   Assume company A belongs to an industry in which there are many risky opportunities, while company B is in a business in which this is not possible.

A Which company will have the highest equity/debt ratio according to Jensen and Meckling? Explain your answer.

B Do Jensen and Meckling predict that the equity of restaurants will be owned largely by external stockholders?

6.6   Assume a principal has to design an optimal contract $\{m,n\}$. The payments m and n are made to the agent when the observable variable is respectively low and high. The choice of contract by the principal intends to induce the agent to provide a high level of effort. The costs of effort for the agent are 0 (1) when the level of effort is low (high). The agent is allowed to reject the contract of the principal when it is offered. This results in a payoff of 0 for the principal and 1 for the agent.

The effort of the agent together with the external circumstances determine the result R. The outcome is either $R = 5$ or $R = 40$. The effort of the agent influences the probability of favourable circumstances. If the agent does not provide effort, then the probability of a low outcome is 3/4. If the agent does work hard, then the probability of a low level of output is 1/4.

The payment for the principal is equal to R minus the payment to the agent according tot the contract. The payments are valued by the agent as $\sqrt{m}$ and $\sqrt{n}$. The costs of effort are equal to the level of effort and have to be subtracted from this amount.

A Draw the extensive form, while assuming that the principal is not informed about the effort of the agent.

B Which two conditions does the contract $\{m,n\}$ have to satisfy in order to generate a high level of effort? Explain these conditions in words.

C Formulate these two conditions in terms of the expected payments of the agent.

6.7 Suppose there are two players, a principal and an agent. First, the principal designs a contract based on the available information. In the second period the agent decides to accept the contract or not. If the agent does not accept the contract, the relationship ends and each player receives a payment 0. Finally, the agent chooses to provide a low (L) or a high (H) level of effort during the execution of the assignment.

Assume that there is a situation of complete information, which means that the principal can observe the level of effort of the agent. Therefore the principal is able to offer a contract $\{w(L), w(H)\}$, where $w(L)$ is the payment for the agent when effort L is provided and $w(H)$ is the payment for the agent when effort H is put forward. The payment of the principal is $9 - w(L)$ and $w(L) - 1$ for the agent when an effort L is provided. If the level of effort is H, then the principal receives $16 - w(H)$ and the agent $w(H) - 2$.

A Draw the extensive form.

B Which inequality has to hold such that the agent provides a level of effort H once the agent has accepted the contract?

C Which inequality has to be satisfied for the agent to be willing to accept the contract, given that an effort H will be put forward in the final period?

D Determine the payoff-maximizing contract.

Assume the principal can observe only the output of the agent, i.e. 9 or 16, but not any more the level of effort L or H. The probability of output level 9 and 16 is influenced by the effort of the agent. The probability of output 9 (16) is .6 (.4) when an effort level L is provided, while an effort H results in 9 (16) with a probability .4 (.6).

E Draw the extensive form.

F What does a contract in this situation with incomplete information look like?

G Which inequality has to hold for the agent to provide a level of effort H once the agent has accepted the contract?

H Which inequality has to be satisfied for the agent to accept the contract, given that an effort H will be put forward in the final period?

I Determine the payoff-maximizing contract.

6.8 A State and explain the incentive-intensity principle.

Assume that the expected output is a function of the effort of the agent $P(e) = 60 + 40e$. A specific level of output is subject to various uncertain factors, which are summarized by x. The variability of x is Var $(x) = 300$. The costs of effort to the agent are $C(e)$ $= 5e^2$. The coefficient of the absolute risk aversion of the agent is $r = .4$. The agent can work somewhere else for a salary of 60. The principal can realize a return of 22 per cent with another agent.

B What is the optimal marginal incentive of effort provision?

C Compute the risk premium and the fixed part of the linear contract which maximizes the expected profit of the principal, given that the agent can earn 25 somewhere else.

D What is the value for the risk-neutral principal of a decrease of Var (x) from 300 to 200?

6.9 Use $P(e) = Me$, $M > 0$ and $C(e) = e^2$ in the model of Sec. 6.2. The reservation wage of the agent equals A.

A Are the conditions of the model of Sec. 6.2 satisfied?

B Compute the optimal choice of effort by the agent, given a certain contractual structure.

C Why do α and r not occur in the solution of part B?

D Determine the salary of the agent, given a certain contractual structure.

E Which contract will the principal choose?

F Which circumstances of the labour market make it unattractive for the principal to start this project?

G Why is the surplus earned by the principal in the hidden action problem smaller in general in the situation with incomplete information than in the situation with complete information?

6.10 Acme Pin factory has to choose between two methods of production. Each employee executes various tasks or assignments at the same time when the first production technology is adopted, while each employee executes one task or assignment with the second technology. The management can choose between two salary structures for her employees: a system in which the salary depends on the amount produced and a system based on the level of difficulty and the number of different skills obtained by the employees.

A Which advantages and disadvantages are associated with reward structures based on the amount of output?

B Which advantages and disadvantages are associated with reward structures based on skills?

C Relate these advantages and disadvantages to the two production methods.

6.11 The salary of option dealer A of the broker company Coffeng & Co. is set in a way that a higher profit results in a higher salary. Dealer A has to decide between a position of low or high risk. Circumstances have resulted in the investment of a very large amount of money in Coffeng & Co. by dealer A in shares of the Royal Shell Group, which has caused a huge loss.

A Is this a hidden action or a hidden characteristics problem? Explain your answer.

B How has this large loss emerged?

C Why has this loss emerged?

D In which two ways could this loss have been prevented?

Appendix 6.1: **Expected utility theory**

Von Neumann and Morgenstern have formulated the theory of choice between uncertain alternatives. The central premise of *expected utility theory* is that people choose the alternative which has not the highest expected value but the highest expected utility. A numerical value is assigned by the utility function U to the satisfaction associated with different outcomes. The expected utility of an uncertain investment is the expected value of the utility of each of its outcomes z.

Figure 6.18 presents the utility function of outcomes z. A higher level of the outcome z results in a higher level of utility, but the increase in utility is decreasing. The utility function is concave, i.e. it reflects the law of diminishing marginal utility. Define z_a as the average of the two outcomes z_1 and z_2. The average utility of the uncertain outcome z is the average of $U(z_1)$ and $U(z_2)$, which is indicated on the vertical axis by U_a. The *certainty equivalent* of the uncertain outcome is the sure outcome that results in the same expected utility as will be received with the risky outcome, which is indicated by z_c. Finally, the risk premium is defined as $z_a - z_c$.

Section 6.2 defined the risk premium as $.5r\,\mathrm{Var}\,(w)$, where r is the coefficient of absolute risk aversion and $\mathrm{Var}\,(w)$ represents the volatility of the outcome. Therefore a higher level of r as well as a higher level of $\mathrm{Var}\,(w)$ increases the risk premium. Both effects can be illustrated with the above figure. A higher level of r increases the concavity of the utility function, i.e. $z_a - z_c$ increases. (A person is risk-neutral if r equals zero, risk-averse if r is larger than zero, and risk-seeking if r is smaller than zero.) The effect of a higher variance can be illustrated by subtracting an amount y from z_1 and adding y to z_2. This transformation increases the variance without changing z_a. The line through e and f will drop and the distance between g and h will increase.

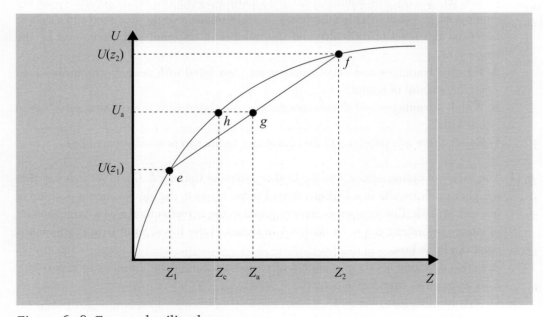

Figure 6.18: Expected utility theory

Appendix 6.2: **The mathematics of the incentive intensity principle**

The wage w consists of a fixed component α and a variable component βz. Each additional unit of z results in an additional payment of β to the agent. The result z is determined by the effort e of the agent and the uncertain circumstances x, i.e.

$$w = \alpha + \beta(e+x).$$

The payment of the principal consists of the difference between revenues and costs. The revenues are equal to the value of the output, which is influenced by the effort e of the agent, a stochastic component x and the production technology. These three aspects are summarized by the expected value of revenue $P(e)$. The costs of production consist of the wage paid to the agent. The expected payment of the risk-neutral principal is therefore

$$
\begin{aligned}
E\{P(e) - w\} &= E\{P(e) - \alpha - \beta\,(e + x)\} \\
&= E\{P(e)\} - E\{\alpha\} - \beta E\{e\} - \beta E\{x\} \\
&= P(e) - \alpha - \beta e,
\end{aligned}
$$

where $E\{.\}$ is the expectation. All expectation symbols disappear from the above expression, because α and β are chosen by the principal and e by the agent, so α, β and e are not stochastic. It was assumed earlier that the expectation of x equals zero.

Revenues and costs can be formulated for the agent as well. The agent provides an effort e and receives for this an uncertain wage w. The uncertain wage is valued at the expectation of the uncertain wage w reduced with the risk premium. The costs associated with an effort e are $C(e)$. It is assumed that these costs increase as e rises and that this increase itself increases. (Mathematically, this means that both the first and the second derivative are positive.) The expected value of the net income of the agent therefore equals

$$
\begin{aligned}
E\{w\} - .5r\,\mathrm{Var}\,(w) - C(e) &= E\{\alpha + \beta(e + x)\} - .5r\,\mathrm{Var}\,(\alpha + \beta(e + x)) - C(e) \\
&= \alpha + \beta e - .5r\,\mathrm{Var}\,(\beta x) - C(e) \\
&= \alpha + \beta e - .5r\beta^2\,\mathrm{Var}\,(x) - C(e).
\end{aligned}
$$

Standard properties of the variance regarding the constants (α and βe) and linear transformation (β) of the stochastic variable (x) are applied to $\mathrm{Var}\,(w)$.

Section 6.1 shows that the principal chooses first and thereby determines the parameters α and β of the contract. Subsequently, the agent decides regarding acceptance of the contract. If it is accepted, then he or she chooses the level of effort. The principal has to take the participation and incentive compatibility constraints of the agent into account when choosing α and β.

The profit-maximizing contract of the principal is determined by backward induction. The choice of effort e is determined by choosing e such that the expression $a + \beta e - 5r\beta^2\,\mathrm{Var}\,(x) - C(e)$ is maximized. Setting the first derivative with respect to effort of this equation equal to 0 results in $\beta = C'(e)$.

This equality is the *incentive compatibility constraint*. It indicates that the agent chooses a level of effort in such a way that the marginal revenue of additional effort (β) equals the marginal costs of additional effort ($C'(e)$). The value of $C'(e)$ increases as e increases, because it is assumed that the second derivative of $C(e)$ is positive. This implies that stronger incentives (higher β) result in more effort by the agent. The fixed component a of the wage does not show up in the expression of the optimal level of effort, because it is independent of the level of effort. It therefore plays no role in the maxizimization problem of the agent. The profit-maximizing principal subsequently chooses α in such a way that the agent earns his or her opportunity costs. This is the *participation constraint*.

There are many values of α and β which result in the same expected payment for the agent as his or her reservation wage. These contracts will be accepted by the agent. The principal will choose out of these contracts the contract which yields him or her most. He or she has all the bargaining power, because he or she chooses first by determining the contract. The contract which yields the principal most is determined by maximizing the total value of the relationship with the agent. It consists of the sum of the expected payment of the principal and the agent. The principal earns $P(e) - w$ and the agent $w - .5r \, \text{Var}\,(w) - C(e)$. The sum of the certainty equivalents is therefore

$$P(e) - w + w - .5r \, \text{Var}\,(w) - C(e) = P(e) - .5r \, \beta^2 \, \text{Var}\,(x) - C(e).$$

Substituting $\beta = C'(e)$ and maximizing with respect to e results in an expression in terms of β. This is the incentive intensity principle. The value of α is subsequently determined by substituting this β in the participation constraint.

The second-best character of the equilibrium can also be illustrated with the above formulas. The incentive intensity principle of the contract is expressed with $\beta = C'(e)$. A higher β results in more effort by the agent. Uncertainty regarding the final payment is not appreciated by the risk-averse agent, which is expressed in a positive risk premium. The height of this premium depends not only on the nature of the agent (r) but also on the degree of uncertainty $(\text{Var}\,(w))$. The parameter β has also an impact $\text{Var}\,(w)$ because $\text{Var}\,(w) = \beta^2 \, \text{Var}\,(x)$. This means that there is one contract parameter (β) that has to solve two problems: providing incentives and insurance. It is therefore usually impossible to handle both problems optimally. The choice of β reflects α compromise between providing incentives and risk-sharing.

7 Hidden characteristics problems

LEARNING OBJECTIVES

- How a hidden characteristics problem is characterized.

- The difference between hidden characteristics and adverse selection.

- How limiting the number of choices may resolve the hidden characteristics problem.

- How increasing the number of choices may resolve the hidden characteristics problem.

- The two ways in which generating additional information may resolve the hidden characteristics problem.

Contents

Transactions occur among anonymous parties in the world of the fundamental welfare theorem. It is not important with whom one does business, because all characteristics of the other party are known. This is the assumption of anonymity (Sec. 3.3). Results like the law of demand and supply and the law of one price are based on this assumption. In equilibrium, markets clear and a single, unique price is established. However, several important characteristics of a trading partner are often not observable to the other party, so that market functioning can be severely frustrated. In such circumstances, the quantity demanded and the quantity supplied are not always equal in equilibrium and several prices may be established in equilibrium.

The most important reason for a piece-rate wage system as in Chapter 6 is that it increases the level of effort of employees. Incentive considerations were the focus of attention. However, it is not obvious that piece-rate wages are the only way to induce a high level of effort. A fixed wage is usually tied to the requirement that a certain level of output is put forward. It is therefore possible that the required level of output of employees receiving a fixed wage is higher than the output produced by employees in a piece-rate system. Fixed wages also therefore provide incentives. Another aspect of fixed wages is that the required output level may be attractive only for the most productive employees, i.e. too demanding for employees of low productivity. These aspects of the wage policy of an organization are also important in order to determine which employees will be attracted.

This chapter analyses the hidden characteristics problem. Conflict of interests and an information asymmetry are again the essential ingredients of the problem. One party knows more about its own characteristics than the other party, and this informational advantage can be used at the other party's expense. These problems are anticipated and (contractual) measures taken to discourage undesirable behaviour.

Three types of solutions will be formulated for the hidden characteristics problem; they are geared towards the ingredients of the problem. The first solution concerns the freedom of choice of the agents. Reducing the freedom to choose by an organizational or institutional decision eliminates the problem. The second solution addresses the conflict of interests. Various contracts will be offered simultaneously, so that everyone can choose the contract which corresponds best with his or her own characteristics. The law of one price is being revoked. The third solution refers to the information asymmetry. Various possibilities will be formulated to generate additional information in order to change the inferior information position of the principal.

The hidden characteristics problem is explained in Sec. 7.1. Hidden characteristics often result in adverse selection and misrepresentation problems. The next three sections discuss solutions to these problems. Section 7.5 addresses the limits and possibilities of exchange in environments characterized by hidden characteristics. Section 7.6 focuses on situations with hidden actions as well as hidden characteristics. The chapter closes with a conclusion.

7.1 Design of the contract

People insure against risky investment projects, storm damage and illness. The advantage of insurance is that risks are shared, so that in principle everyone benefits together. However, there are two aspects that may undermine the realization of this benefit. First, projects to be insured usually differ. Some projects are of low quality, others of high. Second, there is usually an information asymmetry involved. The person asking for insurance has in general more relevant information than the person providing it. The hidden characteristics problem will be introduced with a numerical example. The situation with complete information will be presented first, after which the effect of asymmetric information on the design of the contract will be addressed.

7.1.1 Complete information

Assume that there are only two types of customers: low-risk (L) and high-risk (H). The fraction of projects with low risk is exogenously given. Three decisions are involved. The first decision regards determining the nature of the project or the type of agent. This is represented by the artificial decision-maker Nature. Subsequently, the principal (insurance company) determines the insurance policy that is offered to the agent. Figure 7.1 reflects just two possibilities: deductible clauses (D) or full insurance (F). Finally, the agent decides to accept (A) or reject (R) a certain insurance offer.

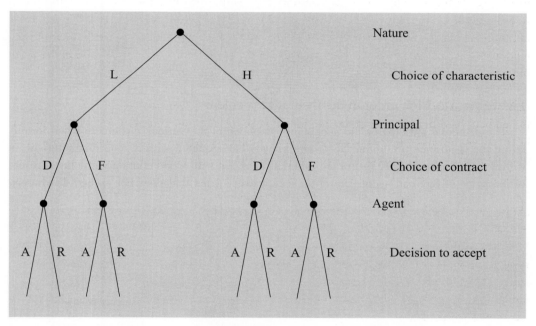

Figure 7.1: Order of decisions in the hidden characteristics problem

Payoffs have to be added in order to complete the extensive form. The expected costs of low-risk customers are assumed to be 3, whereas the high-risk customers have to be paid 7. A low-risk customer has a reservation price of 4 for buying insurance, a high-risk customer one of 8. Assume that the number of good and bad clients is the same.

A contract in the situation with complete information consists of two numbers, because it can be tailored to the type of agent. The first number applies to the low-risk agent, the second to the high-risk agent. The insurance premium can be made completely dependent on the type of agent because of the assumption of complete information. Therefore, the insurance company can formulate a completely contingent contract $\{a,b\}$, in which the number a is the insurance premium for a customer with a good characteristic, b the price for one with a bad one. Figure 7.2 presents four possible values each of a and b.

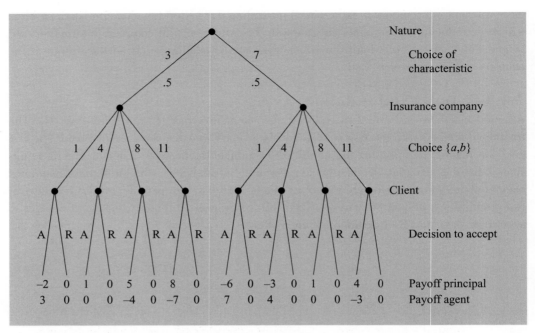

Figure 7.2: Decision order in the insurance problem

The principal anticipates the acceptance decision of the various customers when formulating the insurance premium. He or she knows that an agent with a good characteristic is willing to pay at most 4 for insurance, whereas an agent with a bad characteristic has a reservation price of 8. Good agents therefore accept every price that does not exceed 4, whereas

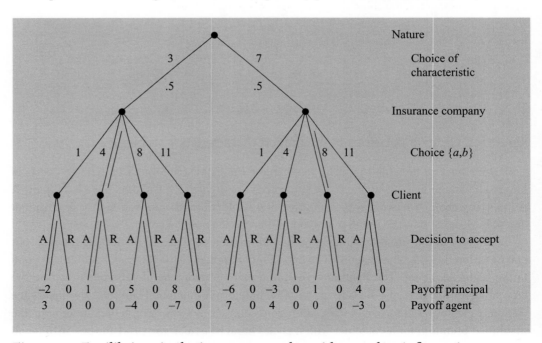

Figure 7.3: Equilibrium in the insurance market with complete information

every insurance premium not exceeding 8 is acceptable to the bad agent. For the insurance company, the profit-maximizing contract is therefore {4,8} and the accompanying profit is .5(4 − 3) + 5(8 − 7) = 1. In equilibrium, an agent with low quality is offered a more expensive premium than a good agent. Both agents buy insurance and the costs are borne completely by the person who causes the costs. The reason is that the policy is made contingent on the nature of the agent. Figure 7.3 depicts the subgame perfect equilibrium choices.

7.1.2 Incomplete information

A more realistic representation of the above problem is that the principal does not know the identity of the player he or she is dealing with. For example, a property developer often knows more about the profit potential of new projects than does the provider of funds, and the somone applying for health insurance knows more about his or her health than the insurance company. The principal has incomplete information regarding the characteristics of the project he or she is confronted with. Although the principal does know the probabilities of good and bad projects, he or she does not know the precise nature of the specific project or the specific agent being dealt with.

Contracts can therefore no longer be made dependent on the type of agent, because the insurance company does not know the characteristic of the applying agent. Complete contingent contracts are no longer possible. Only a complete contract can be formulated. The implication is that everyone should be offered the same contract when characteristics of agents or projects are not known to the principal. An insurance contract consists now of only one number, independent of the type of agent. It is no longer contingent on the type of agent, because this is no longer possible owing to the incompleteness of information. The complete contract is represented by [P], where P is the level of the insurance premium. Figure 7.4 represents the insurance problem with asymmetric information.

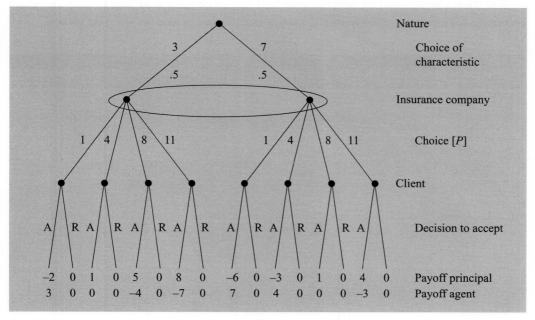

Figure 7.4: Asymmetric information in the insurance problem

A profit-maximizing insurance company will make sure the accepted contracts will not result in a loss on average. A naive insurance company asks an insurance premium of $P = 6$, i.e. the average of 4 and 8. The consideration may be that this will generate on average profit a profit of 1 per agent, because agents with a bad characteristic cause a loss of 1, while agents with the good characteristic result in a profit of 3. However, the low-risk agents are not willing to pay 6 for insurance, because their reservation price is 4. The participation constraint of the low-risk agents is not met. They will decide not to buy insurance when the price is 6. The naive insurance company will after a while notice that the insurance claim will be on average 7, because only the agents with the bad characteristic will accept the offer $= 6$. The naive insurance company will make a loss of 1 on each insurance package sold.

A rational insurance company anticipates these acceptance decisions and should ask a premium of at least 7 in order to prevent losses. Agents with bad characteristics may in a situation with asymmetric information force a rational insurance company to increase the insurance premium to such an extent that the customers with good characteristics do not buy insurance anymore. This is called adverse selection.

Figure 7.5 illustrates, with a number of different insurance premiums, which considerations are important for the profit-maximizing choice of insurance premium by the insurance company. A higher price will increase the level of profits, but some customers may no longer buy insurance. This tradeoff determines the profit-maximizing price of 8. Agents with the good characteristic will not buy insurance at this price. The profit of the insurance company is only .5 and the agents with the good characteristic are not insured. This is a second-best situation.

Some general aspects of markets with hidden characteristics are illustrated by this example. First, fewer goods or services are exchanged in a market with hidden characteristics than in one with complete information. Second, one price emerges in equilibrium, because the price cannot be based on the level of quality. Third, only bad quality is being traded, i.e. adverse selection occurs. This phenomenon of adverse selection has been known in the field of monetary economics for a long time: Gresham's law states that 'Bad money drives out good money.'

Price P	Surplus buyer	Buy?	Expected profit insurance company
3.5	L: $4 - 3.5 > 0$ H: $8 - 3.5 > 0$	Yes Yes	$.5 (3.5 - 3) + .5 (3.5 - 7) = 1.5$
4	L: $4 - 4 = 0$ H: $8 - 4 > 0$	Yes Yes	$.5 (4 - 3) + .5 (4 - 7) = -1$
6.5	L: $4 - 6.5 < 0$ H: $8 - 6.5 > 0$	No Yes	$.5 (6.5 - 7) = -2.5$
8	L: $4 - 8 < 0$ H: $8 - 8 = 0$	No Yes	$.5(8 - 7) = .5$
9	L: $4 - 9 < 0$ H: $8 - 9 < 0$	No No	0

Figure 7.5: Acceptance decisions and payoffs in the insurance problem

Application: Used cars

The classic example of a market with hidden characteristics is in the analysis of the market for used cars (Akerlof, 1970). The problem is that buyer cannot observe the quality of a car perfectly. Often, he or she does not know the previous owner and how this person treated the vehicle.

The buyer is the principal who wants to buy a car with certain characteristics that cannot be communicated credibly by the seller, i.e. the agent. Assume the true level of quality (value) of a used car is represented by θ and that θ is uniformly distributed between 0 and 10, i.e. the quality of a car can be any number between 0 and 10, and each type (θ) is as likely as any other. The average quality of a second-hand car is defined as $E\{\theta\}$ and is therefore 5. Assume that the reservation price of the buyer for a car with quality level θ is equal to θ and that this is also the reservation price of the seller. A buyer is therefore willing to pay a price 2 for a car with quality level $\theta = 2$ and the seller is willing to sell this type of car at a price 2. (Exchange therefore creates no surplus. This assumption is made for reasons of simplicity and still shows the impact of incomplete information on the amount of exchange.)

Nothing has been said yet about the information available to the buyers and sellers. Sellers are assumed to know exactly the quality level of the car they sell. Two situations are distinguished regarding the information available to the buyers. The case in which buyers have *complete information* is treated first. The level of quality θ can be determined before purchase in this situation. Every car (θ) will be sold (at price θ) in equilibrium. An important conclusion is therefore that a different price is established for every type of car in the situation with complete information. A car with quality level θ is traded at price θ.

The situation changes drastically when the buyer cannot determine the quality of a car. *Asymmetric information* prevails, because the buyer does not know the quality of the car, whereas the seller does. One implication is that the price of a car can no longer be based on the true quality of the car, because the level of quality cannot be observed. Only one price will be paid for a car in equilibrium, regardless of the quality of the car. This is illustrated with the demand and supply of cars in Fig. 7.6. The horizontal axis represents the average quality $E\{\theta\}$ of cars, whereas the vertical axis shows the price. The demand function presents the price a client is willing to pay at most for a certain *average* level of quality. This is the 45-degree line. A client does not know the quality of a car, but is willing to pay a price of 4 for a car when the level of quality is uniformly distributed between 0 and 8.

The supply function specifies an average quality level for each price as well. Assume the price is 4. Sellers having a car of quality level 4 or less are willing to sell their car for this price. However, cars with a quality level of more than 4 will not be offered on the market, because a price of only 4 is received, whereas the value (θ) is higher. The cars supplied are of low quality, i.e. the cars of values θ between 0 and 4. The average quality of a car that is offered at a price of 4 is therefore 2. More generally, the corresponding average quality of the cars supplied is only half the price. Another way to interpret the supply function is that it represents the price level that is necessary to get a certain

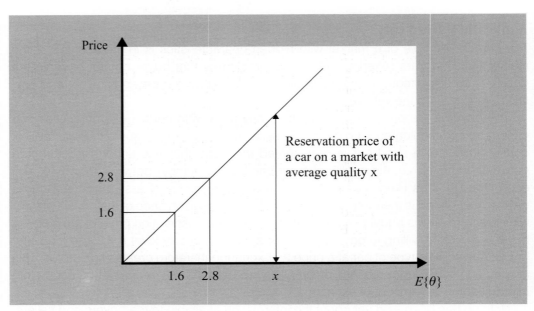

Figure 7.6: Demand curve

average quality level of cars supplied. An average quality level of 2.5 requires a price of 5. For a price of 5, only cars with a quality less than, or equal to 5, are offered. All cars are offered at prices higher than 10. The quality of these cars varies from 0 to 10, so the average offered quality equals 5 for each price higher than 10. This is represented by the vertical part of the supply function in Fig. 7.7.

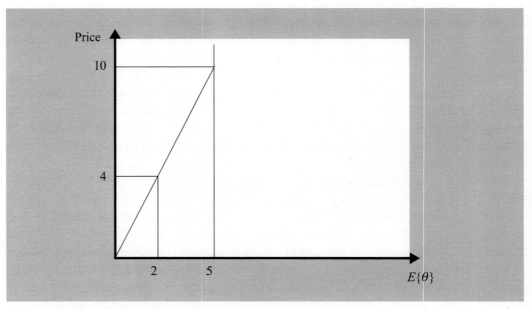

Figure 7.7: Supply curve

The intersection between the demand and supply curves determines the equilibrium in the market. The equilibrium price is 0 and no car is traded in this market with hidden characteristics. The contrast between the situation of complete and incomplete information is dramatic. All used cars are sold in a market with complete information, whereas no cars are traded when asymmetric information prevails.

The *disappearance of the market* is caused by the tension between the average and the actual quality. This can be understood by the following example. Assume the price equals 10. Consumers are willing to pay a price of 10 when the average quality of the cars supplied is at least 10. Although all sellers offer their cars at this price, the average quality of these cars is only 5. This is represented by the arrow from A to B in Fig. 7.8. However, buyers are not stupid. They know that the average quality supplied is only 5 (point B) when the price is 10. Buyers are willing to pay a price 5 only when the average quality is 5 (point C). However, sellers with cars of a quality level higher than 5 no longer offer their car when the price is only 5, because these sellers would receive less than the opportunity cost of their car. The effect from A to B and from C to D is called *adverse selection*. The quality level of the cars supplied decreases. The average quality of the offered cars has decreased to 2,5 (point D). This process continues until the average quality of cars supplied drops to 0 and the market disappears.

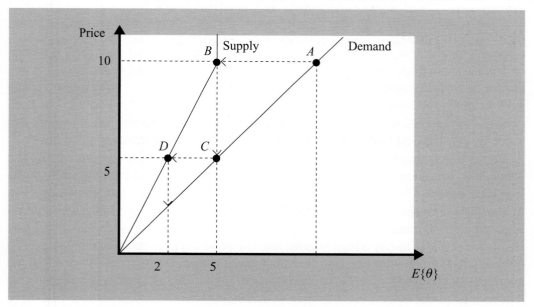

Figure 7.8: Hidden information and disappearance of the market

The complete disappearance of the market is a very drastic outcome. Several aspects of the above model can be amended in order to establish a less drastic result. One way to do this is to incorporate the interaction between the markets for new and used cars (Hendel and Lizzeri, 1999). Another aspect is that it is assumed that all quality levels between 0 to 10 are available. If the assumption of a continuous distribution of quality levels is replaced by a discrete distribution, then some cars will be exchanged in equilibrium. However, they will all be of the lowest quality. This will be illustrated with a numerical example where only two types of cars are supplied. The used cars of low quality are characterized by $\theta = 3$, while the used cars of high quality have a quality level of 7. Assume that half the cars are of bad quality and therefore half of good.

Again the situation with complete and incomplete information will be distinguished. Suppose the buyers have complete information, which means that the quality level of the car supplied can be determined. All cars are sold in equilibrium. The bad cars are sold at a price of 3 and the good cars at a price of 7. If the buyers cannot determine the quality of a car, then they are willing to pay only for the average quality that is being offered. This will result in selection in the cars being offered. For example , the used cars of high quality are not supplied when the price is 5. The cars supplied are therefore all bad ($\theta = 3$) and the average quality is 3. Buyers know the considerations of the sellers regarding their decision to offer the car, and are willing to pay a price of only 3. The owners of the bad cars accept this price. Only half of the cars are traded in equilibrium in the market with hidden characteristics. All these cars are of inferior quality and the price that is established reflects the value of a bad car. The cars traded are 'lemons' and good cars are not traded at all (Akerlof, 1970).

Application: Loans

If you ask for a loan of a million euros at a bank, you will probably not get it. This is hard to understand from the viewpoint of demand and supply. Prices should adjust in such a way that the quantity demanded equals the quantity supplied. Everyone receives what he or she asks for at the resulting equilibrium price. Anyone not willing to pay the equilibrium price does not take a loan, whereas anyone else pays the prevailing interest rate. However, this is not the way the world works. Granting a substantial loan is not based on price alone.

Banks are interested not only in the *interest rate* they receive on a certain loan, but also in the *risk* associated with it. This risk can be represented as the probability that a loan is paid back. This probability differs from person to person, but cannot be observed by the bank. The result is that the level of the interest rate reflects a hidden characteristics problem, because anyone willing to pay a high interest rate is usually a bad risk. He or she is willing to pay a high interest rate because the probability of actually paying back is small. A high interest rate results in the withdrawal of the good risks, so that the average risk of anyone who still wants a loan increases. The profitability of the bank can therefore even decrease when the interest rate increases.

Figure 7.9 illustrates these ideas (Stiglitz and Weiss, 1981). Assume there are two types: bad and good risks. Everyone wants a loan as long as the interest rate is below a certain level (r^*). This is reflected by the part of the profit function with the steepest slope. The average probability of paying back the loan is largest when everybody takes a loan. This occurs when the interest rate is low. However, once the interest rate goes beyond a certain level r^*, the good risks leave the market. The average probability of paying back the loan of the persons still wanting a loan decreases.

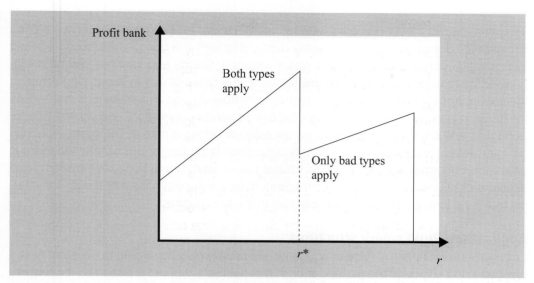

Figure 7.9: Loans, hidden characteristics and two kinds of risk (Stiglitz and Weiss, 1981, p. 397)

Figure 7.9 assumes there are only two types of agents. A large number of different types of agents results in a curve that first increases and then decreases. However, the result that a higher interest rate will eventually lead to lower profits does not change qualitatively, because the good risks will leave the market. Figure 7.10 illustrates this. The *direct effect* of an increase in the interest rate on the profit level of the bank dominates the *adverse selection effect* when the interest rate is low. An increase in the interest rate will result in an increase in the profits of the bank. However, the adverse selection effect dominates the direct effect when the interest rate surpasses r^*.

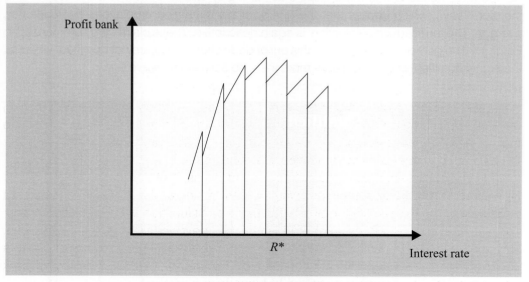

Figure 7.10: Loans, hidden characteristics and many sorts of risk

One aspect of the *fundamental welfare theorem* is that for *each* good or service a price is established that equates the quantity demanded with the quantity supplied. A broad interpretation of goods and services was advocated. Goods and services can be distinguished by location as well as circumstances. Three types of money are distinguished in the current application: money today, money tomorrow in good circumstances and money tomorrow in bad circumstances. When there is complete information, one interest rate for good risks and another rate for bad ones are established in the market. The interest rate can be interpreted as a price. However, this distinction is no longer possible when there is asymmetric information. Then only one interest rate is established, because the information structure precludes making the price dependent on the specific circumstances. The interest rate is no longer a price, but a parameter of the loan contract.

Application: Rigid salary structures

Employees in the health service or education are usually paid according to a system based on scales and seniority. The classification in a certain salary group is based on the requirements of the function, and the age and education of the person involved. Employees are different. Everybody considers salary and job satisfaction important, but some value salary more than others. Assume there are two types of employees. The first type chooses a profession based mainly on the size of salary, whereas the second group is primarily led by the nature of the work. There is also a hidden characteristic regarding the quality of the person. Assume for simplicity that a person is either poorly or highly qualified for the job.

A *rigid salary structure* entails that wages in the government sector differ sometimes from the wages paid for similar positions in the market sector. This is a problem when the wages in the government sector are lower. Employees focused on job satisfaction, low as well as highly qualified, have no reason to look for another job. However, the employees with a focus on the wage will apply somewhere else. This is also a problem from a productivity perspective, because it is more likely that the highly qualified are more successful and therefore leave, which implies that the quality of the remaining employees decreases on average. The term 'adverse selection' is again descriptive. These claims are summarized in Fig. 7.11. The persons staying (+) do this out of dedication and/or are not qualified, whereas the highly qualified who value salary more than job satisfaction leave (−).

Motivation	Qualified	Low	High
Wage		+	0
Job satisfaction		+	+

Figure 7.11: Rigid salary structure and hidden characteristics

7.2 Selection not allowed

The problem with hidden characteristics is that the principal cannot distinguish between low and high quality. Low quality entails higher costs. The contract offered by the principal will reflect these costs of low-quality agents, regardless of the type of agent accepting the contract. The high-quality agents have therefore to pay (to a limited extent) the costs of the low-quality ones. This may be so undesirable for the good agents that they decide not to accept the contract. Only the low-quality agents are willing to accept the contract, or the market may disappear altogether. Solutions to this problem entail somehow keeping the good risks in the market. A drastic solution is reducing the choices available to the agent by prohibiting certain choices by law. For example, the law may *reduce the number of choices to one* by making certain choices mandatory, e.g. contributing to a pension fund. Another way of reducing the number of choices for the agent is that the principal eliminates certain choices of the agent by not offering them at all.

Application: Mandatory insurance

Markets sometimes have difficulties with asymmetric information. Certain surplus-generating transactions will not occur. Some markets show adverse selection, while others disappear completely. Good risks and bad risks require different approaches. However, the principal is not able to distinguish them. Because agents with good characteristics withdraw, the principal is confronted with a group of agents who are on average less desirable. This will be reflected in less favourable contract terms for the agents accepting the contract.

These selection effects may result in such a large loss of surplus that the authorities decide to intervene. The government can decide to make insurance mandatory, as in many European health systems, or management can declare certain choices mandatory for all employees. Individuals are deprived of their freedom of choice in order to secure a desirable exchange which as result of asymmetric information would otherwise not be establisheda.

Application: Rationing

Figures 7.9 and 7.10 illustrated that profit maximization in a loan market with asymmetric information does not imply that the highest possible interest rate should be demanded. A high interest rate will drive the good risks out of the market. However, demand can exceed supply at the profit-maximizing interest rate r^*. A rise in the interest rate is not desirable because this will result in a decrease in profits. Another solution is to maintain r^* and ration the available credits. *Rationing* occurs when some individuals receive a loan and others do not, although the last ones are willing to pay a higher interest rate. The bank does not ask a higher interest rate because this would negatively affect the composition of those who want loans at the higher rate. The bank offers loans only at an interest rate of r^* in order to keep the good risks in the market. This reduces the extent of adverse selection.

7.3 Self-selection

The contracts of Sec. 7.1.2 consist of only one variable, like the insurance premium, the interest rate, the price of a used car, the wage and so on. This implies that all agents rank all contracts in the same way. Low-quality as well as high-quality agents prefer to pay a low rather than a high insurance premium; all agents appreciate a low interest rate; everyone would rather receive a high salary than a low one and so on. However, if contracts consist of two variables, then different agents may differ regarding the ranking of different contracts. The choice of a certain contract may reveal something about the hidden characteristics of the person. This section will consider the implications of increasing the number of choice possibilities by analysing contracts consisting of two variables.

Suppose there is an unattractive ('bad') and an attractive ('good') contract variable for the agent. The first contract variable indicates the amount of the bad aspect, the second that of the good one. Examples of bad contract variables for the agents are the required level of collateral in loan contracts, the extent of non-coverage of insurance contracts and the lack of warranty in car deals. More collateral is harder to deliver for the demander of a loan, less coverage is less appreciated by the buyer of insurance and a low warranty is preferred less than a high warranty in a car deal. Examples of a good contract variable for the agent are the payback status being granted, the interest discount one obtains in loan contracts and the premium discount offered in insurance contracts.

Contracts with a good and a bad variable for the agent offer the possibility to the principal of designing a *menu of contracts*. The agent subsequently chooses a contract from this menu or rejects them all. The idea behind offering various contracts simultaneously to the agent is that everyone can choose the contract to match his or her (hidden) characteristic. This way, costs are borne by the agent making them. *Self-selection* is established.

Graphical illustrations of menu-of-contracts solutions for the hidden characteristics problem use indifference curves. An indifference curve has a positive slope when the analysis is presented with a good and a bad aspect, because less of the good aspect has to be compensated with less of the bad aspect in order to maintain the same level of utility. Agents with differing characteristics are depicted in Fig. 7.12. The bad aspect is on the horizontal axis, the good aspect is on the vertical. The slope of the indifference curve of the agent with the low-quality characteristic (L) is steeper than the slope of the indifference curve of the agent with the high-quality one (H). Type L needs a raise of 3 in the good contract variable to compensate for an increase of 1 in the bad contract variable, whereas a type H needs only an additional compensation of 1. Receiving an additional unit of the bad is more costly for type L than for type H. For example, an L requires a much higher additional loan than an H in order to accept one additional unit of collateral. Notice that indifference curves situated more to the north-west represent a higher level of utility for the agent, because more of a good variable with a fixed level of the bad will result in a higher level of utility for the agent.

The difference between the two types of agents can also be explained in terms of the costs of receiving an additional unit of the good variable. This is shown in Fig. 7.13. Type H is willing to provide more effort $(C + D)$ than an L-type (C) to receive an additional unit of the good contract variable. For example, type H is willing to provide more collateral than type L for an additional loan. It is less costly for type H to increase the attractive contract variable by one unit.

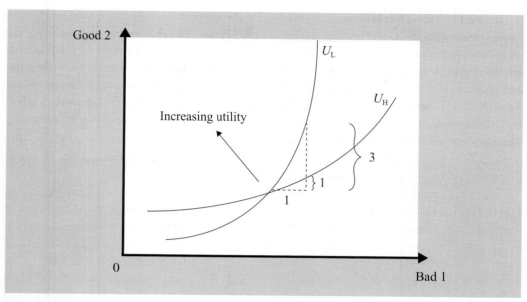

Figure 7.12: Indifference curves of both types of agents

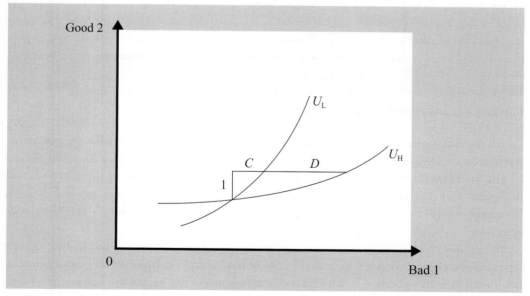

Figure 7.13: Compensation for an additional unit of the good

The choice of the menu of contracts and self-selection by the agents with different hidden characteristics will be explained graphically by using the example of the insurance market. Again, contracts can be based only on observable variables. Both axes have therefore to depict variables that are observable and verifiable, i.e. the hidden characteristic cannot be a contract variable. The variable on the horizontal axis is an indicator of the hidden characteristic, but not the hidden characteristic itself.

The deductible is the bad contract variable for the agent in the insurance market. It is put on the horizontal axis in Fig. 7.14. The other contract variable is the discount on the insurance premium and is put on the vertical axis. Good risks are represented by a flat indifference curve, because they are willing to accept a higher level of the deductible than the bad risks in order to receive an additional unit of reduction in the insurance premium. Assume that insurance companies offer the insurance contracts A and B. Contract A offers almost complete coverage and a high premium (i.e. low reduction of insurance premium), whereas contract B offers the opposite.

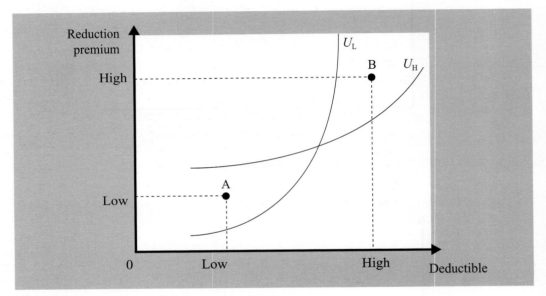

Figure 7.14: Insurance and own contribution

All combinations of the good and the bad contract variable located above a specific indifference curve are preferred to combinations below this indifference curve. An agent of type H will therefore choose contract B instead of contract A, whereas an agent of type L will prefer contract A above contract B. This subgame perfect equilibrium is shown in Fig. 7.15. Insurance contracts have to consist of at least two variables in order to establish self-selection.

Notice that the type of the agent cannot be observed by the principal, but that an agent's type (hidden characteristic) is revealed by his or her behaviour. However, the equilibrium is not identical to the situation in which all characteristics of the agents are known. The high-quality agents have a high deductible. This is a consequence of asymmetric information that is hard to avoid.

No explicit attention has been paid yet to the conditions the principal has to consider in the design of the contracts A and B in order to elicit the desired behaviour. Two familiar conditions have to be taken into account. First, the contract has to yield the agent at least as much as when he or she does not accept it. This is the *participation constraint*. Second, the payments of the various contracts should be designed in such a way that the agent with the desirable characteristics prefers contract B to contract A, whereas the agent of the other type

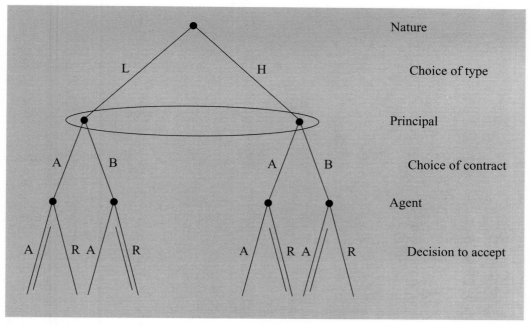

Figure 7.15: Hidden characteristics and self-selection

prefers contract A to B. This is the *incentive compatibility constraint*. These conditions establish that the agents choose the contract intended for them. It implies that they bear their own costs to a certain extent.

Two kinds of equilibria are possible: separating and pooling. A *separating equilibrium* occurs when agents with different characteristics (utility functions, preferences, payoffs) choose different contracts. This equilibrium is also called a self-selection equilibrium. Figure 7.15 therefore represents a separating equilibrium. Note that two prices are established for the same product. The law of one price no longer holds in a market with hidden characteristics.

The different types of agents choose the same contract in a *pooling equilibrium*. Figure 7.16 presents an extensive form with a pooling equilibrium. Type L and type H each make the same choices, i.e. both types accept contract A and both types reject contract B. The principal cannot deduce anything about the nature of the agent from the choice of contract in a pooling equilibrium, because different types of agents choose the same contract.

The type of equilibrium that emerges depends on the type of the agents or payoffs, their alternatives elsewhere and the composition of the population. The nature of the agents is expressed in the incentive compatibility constraints, whereas outside opportunities are expressed in the participation constraints. All applications will present situations where the payoffs are chosen in such a way that a separating equilibrium emerges. It is crucial in applications to define the two contract variables in the right way. The best approach is not to take the perspective of the principal, even though the principal is designing the menu of contract. The perspective of the agent is most useful, because the indifference curves of the various types of agents are depicted in the figures.

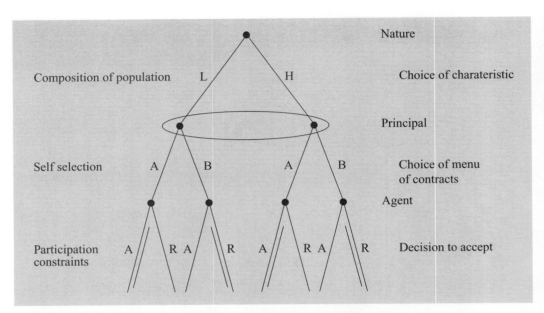

Figure 7.16: Hidden characteristics and pooling equilibrium

Application: Used cars and warranties

Section 7.1 predicted the disappearance of the market for used cars. However, there are many markets for used cars in reality. The prediction of disappearance is due to contracts consisting of only one variable. Not only is there usually bargaining about the price, but other aspects are considered as well. These other aspects will be summarized here by *warranties* (Spence, 1977). Contracts consist therefore of two variables: the warranty and the price. Many contracts are possible. For example, a contract (low, low) entails that the used car is offered with a minimal warranty and a low price.

Figure 7.17 presents the situation with two types of used cars: low-quality and high-quality. The agents with the low-quality cars are depicted with the steepest indifference curve, because they know that their cars will break down regularly. Accepting an additional warranty has therefore to be accompanied by a substantial price increase in order to stay on the same indifference curve. Agents with high-quality used cars also want a higher price as compensation for an extended warranty, but the price increase does not have to be as large in order to stay on the same indifference curve.

The principal (buyer) and the agent (supplier) are willing to exchange a car in equilibrium with either of the contracts, (low, low) or (high, high). The buyer will not offer the contract (low, high), because this will attract the sellers with bad quality as well. Nobody will accept the contract (high, low). The high warranty is no option for the seller with the bad car, whereas the seller with the good car will not accept the low price. The contracts A and B remain. Sellers of bad cars will choose the contract (low, low), while the good cars are sold with the contract (high, high). Self-selection occurs by offering this menu of contracts. Only high-quality cars are traded with contract B, because it is too expensive for the dealers with low-quality cars to accept a high warranty.

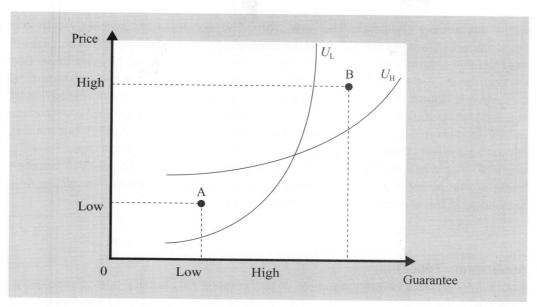

Figure 7.17: Used cars and warranties

Application: Loans and collateral

The first solution to the adverse selection problem in the market for loans involved rationing the loans to match demand with supply (Sec. 7.2). Another solution is the practice of banks of requiring *collateral* in addition to an interest rate (Bester, 1985). This offers the opportunity to design contracts in such a way that the various risks select themselves over the various contracts and that no rationing occurs in equilibrium.

Again the bad and the good aspect have to be formulated from the perspective of the agent in order to use Fig. 7.12. The bad is the level of collateral. The interest rate cannot serve as the good on the vertical axis, because a higher interest rate is of course less appreciated than a lower one. One way to translate the interest rate in a good for the agent is by a variable which represents the opposite, e.g. the reduction in the interest rate. This is put on the vertical axis. Banks offer contracts A and B, where contract A entails a low level of collateral and a low reduction in the interest rate and contract B entails the opposite. Self-selection occurs in equilibrium, because those with a small probability of paying back the loan choose contract A, and the good risks, i.e. those highly likely to pay back the loan choose contract B.

Notice that there is no rationing in equilibrium when contracts are offered that consist of two variables. The bad risks are revealed because they choose the contract with a low collateral and a high interest rate. Collateral can be explained only from the perspective of incomplete information, because it is usually accompanied by costs. These costs arise from its value being derived from providing information on the probability that the loan will be paid back.

Two models regarding loans have been presented. A pooling equilibrium with rationing was established in Sec. 7.2, whereas this application has focused on a model with a separating equilibrium (self-selection). The equilibrium is determined by the *instruments* available in the design of the contract. An additional variable like collateral may result in a separating equilibrium. The *decision order* may also have an impact on the equilibrium. If the agent with the hidden characteristic can take a decision regarding the level of collateral before the principal designs the contract, then this will usually result in a separating equilibrium. This happens because agents with the good characteristics will try to distinguish themselves from the bad ones. (Section 7.4 will focus on this aspect.) However, if the bank offers a menu of contracts before the agent takes a decision, then this will often result in a pooling equilibrium. The competition between banks is often stronger in such circumstances than the efforts by the high-quality agents to distinguish themselves from the low-quality ones.

Application: Education

Figure 7.18 shows indifference curves of two persons. High-ability persons are represented with the flatter indifference curve, because additional effort (E) requires a lower increase in wage (w) in order to stay on the same indifference curve than it does for persons with lower ability. An example is education. Most people don't like to take additional training (bad 1), whereas higher wages (good 2) are appreciated. However, some learn more easily (H-type) than others (L-type). High-ability people want to be compensated by a higher wage, but this raise does not need to be as large as the wage increase the L-types require in order to do the additional training.

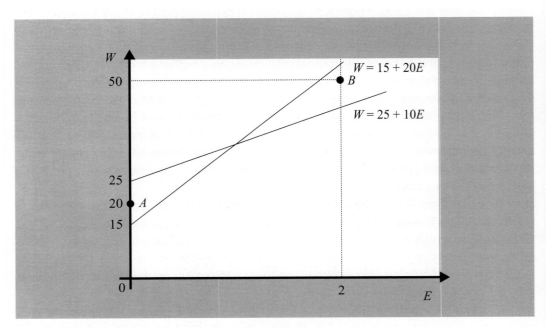

Figure 7.18: Indifference curves in the education example

Application: Piece-rate wages

Products and services are sold by salespeople. However, the quality of the selling efforts varies from person to person and this is difficult for the employer to observe. A highly qualified salesperson knows that his or her activities will result in additional sales, whereas the others cannot be sure of that. The employer may consider offering a menu of contracts to the salespersons: a wage contract with a low fixed-wage component and a high *piece-rate* component, and a contract with a high fixed-wage component and a low piece-rate one. The second contract will result in a lower wage on average. High-quality salesmen will choose the first contract, the others the second.

Application: Seniority wages

Wages are often determined to a certain extent by seniority. There are various explanations for this. More experience results in higher productivity, and more responsibilities are allocated to persons with more years of service. Even if the data are corrected for such factors in empirical studies, a positive relationship remains between age and salary. Salop and Salop (1976) explain salaries based on *seniority* from a hidden characteristics perspective.

Companies invest in their personnel by providing various possibilities for acquiring additional skills, e.g. by additional training. This is costly, especially when an employee resigns immediately after the training. It is therefore important to recruit employees intending to stay with the company for a considerable time. However, the characteristic 'intention to stay' is hard to observe. The appropriate design of labour contracts may provide a solution.

Labour contracts can be designed such that only employees with a small probability of leaving are attracted. The variable on the horizontal axis has to be chosen such that there is a relationship with the hidden characteristic of the employee, e.g. seniority. The wage at the end of the career is put on the vertical axis. An employee with a high probability of staying will choose a company where seniority plays an important part in the composition of the wage structure. Such a wage structure implies that over the course of career the employee earns less than his or her marginal productivity at the beginning, but more than it at the end. This can be interpreted as a *credible commitment* by the employee not to leave the company prematurely. Contract B is accepted only by employees who have no intention to leave prematurely. The others choose a company with a salary structure based only on productivity, so that one of them earns more at the beginning of his or her career than does an employee with contract B. Both contracts result in the same wage over the whole career.

7.4 Generating additional information

The (partial) solutions to the hidden characteristics problem of the previous two sections addressed limiting the number of choices (7.2) and increasing the number of choices (7.3). This section will address changing the decision order through allowing an additional decision by either the agent or the principal to decide twice. This creates the possibility of generating additional information. The high-quality agent will try to make his or her hidden characteristic known to the principal through certain actions (signalling), whereas the principal will try to gather additional information to get a better indication of the hidden characteristics of the agent (screening). Signalling is addressed in Sec. 7.4.1, while screening is dealt with in Sec. 7.4.2.

7.4.1 Signalling

Often it is either not attractive for the individuals with superior information to reveal this information completely ('informational rent'), or else it is impossible for them to provide such information. An individual with good characteristics will have to find ways to convince the other party that his or her characteristics are good. One possible way to do this is by signalling. *Signalling* entails investments by the informed party in order to make it easier for the other party to determine the hidden characteristic. Compared with Fig. 7.4, Fig. 7.19 has an additional decision node: the agent chooses a signal, good (G) or bad (B), before the principal decides regarding the design of the contract, which creates the possibility of incorporating this signal in the design of the menu of contracts.

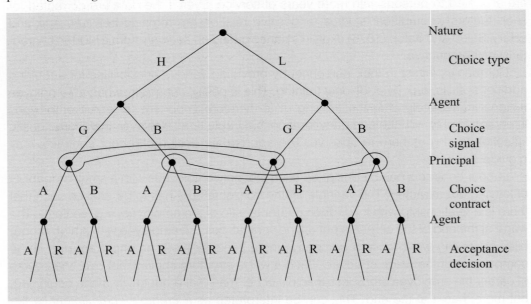

Figure 7.19: Hidden information and signalling

The common element in all applications will be that in order to make the signal credible the high-quality agent has to invest an inefficient high level of resources in it. However, this efficiency is often inevitable in situations with asymmetric information.

Application: Education
Signalling has been analysed in the context of *education* (Spence, 1974). An employer often has limited information regarding the capabilities of an applicant when a hiring decision has to be made. An important source of information is the education of the applicant, because it is an indication of the hidden characteristics of the candidate.

The problem of highly qualified employees is that it is often hard for them to distinguish themselves from others. They can solve this to a certain extent by improving their curriculum vitae by the *choice* of their education, or by developing additional activities *during* it. From this signalling perspective, students anticipate on the evaluation criteria used by employers in their hiring decisions when choosing their education. The crucial assumption is that the effort it takes to complete an education, or to exhibit additional activities, is related to the intrinsic quality of the person. More highly qualified persons have less difficulty developing such activities and will therefore be more inclined to do so. Although costs are involved, they are less than those for the less well qualified. These costs are incurred by the more highly qualified in equilibrium in order to distinguish themselves, whereas those less well qualified are unwilling to put forward this additional effort (and the higher costs).

Application: Dividend policy

Companies paying dividends to shareholders seems curious. Part of the dividend has to be paid directly to the government as tax, while shareholders have to pay income tax in addition. However, dividends can be understood from the hidden characteristics perspective. A dividend is interpreted as a signal regarding the profitability of the company (Bhattacharya, 1979).

Paying dividends is expensive, but it creates an image of a solid company. This can result in more favourable financial terms in the relationship with banks and more attractive relationships with suppliers and customers. The company can be viewed as the agent, whose characteristics are not exactly known to others. It chooses to pay either a low or a high dividend. The principal is the outside world, e.g. a bank, supplier or customer, and has to take a decision regarding the rating of the company. This quality mark is the good contract variable for the company, whereas the size of the dividend is the bad contract variable.

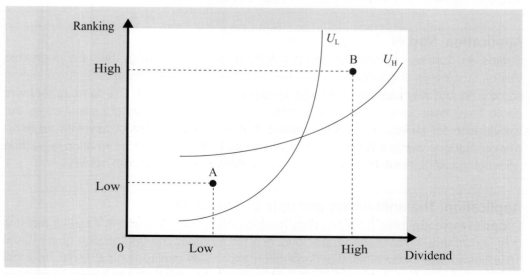

Figure 7.20: Dividend policies and quality of the company

Companies with different characteristics and their choice of *dividend policy* can be illustrated with the same figure as in the previous section. The flat indifference curve in Fig. 7.20 represents the high-quality company. This company has no problem with paying a higher dividend. An increase in the rating will be necessary to remain on the same indifference curve, but the required increase is lower than the increase necessary to compensate a weak company for paying a higher dividend. This dividend is paid when the rating will increase considerably. In equilibrium, a strong company chooses a high dividend, so that a high rating is obtained (point *B*), whereas the weak company will opt for a low dividend and a lower rating (point *A*).

Application: Non-informative advertising

We have all seen commercials on television with a sports or rock star, or page-sized ads with a text that says nothing about the nature of the product. Such lack of information is remarkable, yet high costs have obviously been incurred. One explanation for such advertisements is that they create product loyalty, so that the price elasticity of the demand decreases.

Another explanation for this *non-informative advertising* is that it signals the quality of the product (Nelson, 1974). Only companies with a high-quality product are willing to invest a lot in advertising and will subsequently ask a high price for it (contract B in Fig. 7.14). Repeat sales at high prices justify this investment. The value of this kind of advertisement lies therefore not in information on product characteristics but in its signalling function. It is a mechanism by which companies with high-quality products distinguish themselves from those which produce lower quality. Only companies producing high-quality goods or services are willing to invest substantially in non-informative advertising. Other examples are a firm distributing a product free and a new restaurant offering meals at reduced prices. Such investments can yield returns only when good quality is involved, so that the investment can be seen as signalling it.

Application: Strikes

Strikes are further phenomena which are hard to explain using standard economic theory. Employers and labour unions often establish an agreement after a strike lasting some time, but only after much time and money has been wasted. The same agreement could have been reached without a strike, thus avoiding the unnecessary costs. An explanation for strikes can be formulated from the perspective of asymmetric information. Nobody wants a strike, but they still happen. Strikes reflect information regarding underlying characteristics, for example the credibility of the proposal made.

Application: The unravelling principle of Grossman

Suppose there are three persons. They have quality levels 10, 8 and 6. Assume that it is only known that the average quality level of a person is 8. The person with quality level 10 will try to distinguish himself or herself from those with quality levels 6 and 8, to show that he or she is above average. If this is successful, then the average quality level of the remaining persons drops to 7. The person with quality level 8 will now try to make credible that he or she is not the person with quality level 6. The conclusion is therefore that, if agents with hidden characteristics are able to provide information regarding the hidden characteristic, then all hidden characteristics will be known after a while. This is called *the unravelling principle of Grossman* (Grossman, 1981). Well-known examples are high-quality universities publishing the number of Nobel laureates among their faculty, the most beautiful women wearing a bikini on the beach, and companies showing the results of benchmarking when they come out favourably.

Application: Leadership

Leadership entails the transmission of information. The leader may have valuable information for the followers with respect to redirecting their activities. This valuable information is the hidden characteristic of the principal. Voluntarily taking the directions of the leader is done only when it is in the interest of the followers to do so. Just transmitting information is not enough to make the followers to change their behaviour, because they know the leader has an incentive to exaggerate the value of the activities contributing to joint output, since his or her payoff is determined by the activities of all the team members together. The other team members will contribute to team production only when they believe that this information is valuable, i.e. when they are convinced they are not being misled.

There are two ways for the leader to convince the employees to put more effort into those activities which are truly the most important. One is *leader sacrifice*, when a leader offers gifts to followers (e.g., free coffee or pizza for working in the evening). The other is *leading by example*, when the leader himself or herself puts in long hours on the activity, thereby convincing followers that he or she indeed considers it worthwhile. Leading by sacrifice as well as leading by example are forms of signalling.

Hermalin (1998) analyses this problem with the standard team production problem (Holmström, 1982). Two situations are distinguished. First, the situation is analysed where all relevant information is available for everybody, i.e. there is symmetric information. Each team member has an incentive to free ride. Section 6.2.4 has addressed this situation. Second, the situation with asymmetric information will be analysed. Only the leader knows the revenues of the production by the team. Two signals are available to the leader in this hidden characteristics problem: money and leading by example. The signal 'money' entails giving gifts to the followers, whereas the signal 'leading by example' boils down to working hard. Both signals make it credible that the leader considers the activity important. (Notice that the signal 'money' is inferior to the signal 'leading by example' from a welfare perspective. The reason is that the first signal is a transfer of money from one party to the other party without having a direct impact on the total surplus. Leading by example is a productive action which results in an increase of the surplus.)

It turns out that it is in a situation with asymmetric information rather than in one with symmetric information that leading by example generally results in in a higher level of team production. The reason is that the solution 'leading by example' for the hidden characteristics problem results in such a large increase in production that the (hidden action) free-riding problem in the team is more than compensated for.

Leadership is distinct from authority. Following a leader is a voluntary activity of the followers rather than coerced one. (Authority will be addressed extensively in Part IV.) Leadership is an example of informal authority, because the agent voluntarily accepts directives from the principal.

7.4.2 Screening

In signalling the focus is on the activities of the party with superior information to provide information. This section concentrates on the activities of the party who lacks information. The principal will develop activities geared towards collecting additional information. Such activities are called *screening*. The information generated by screening can be incorporated in the contract.

The worst-informed party (the principal) tries to make the agent voluntarily reveal his or her hidden characteristic by screening. The difference from Fig. 7.4 is that the principal takes two decisions. The principal starts with screening and subsequently designs the contract. Figure 7.21 reflects the decision order and the information structure. Screening is successful when a pooling equilibrium changes into a separating one.

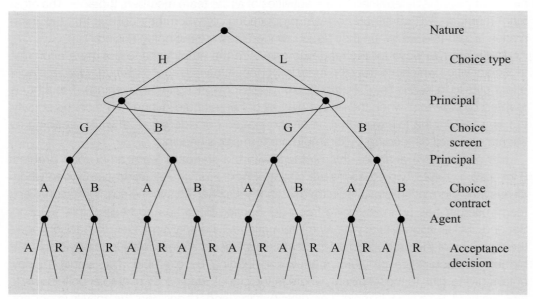

Figure 7.21: Hidden information and screening

Application: Entrance exams

Entrance exams occur in various forms. Schools require students to take tests in order to get a better insight into their capacities, employers use psychological tests and participating in the Olympic Games requires meeting a certain standard. A hidden characteristics problem is present in all these examples, because the agent (student, employee, athlete) knows more of the exact nature of his or her characteristic than the principal. The result of an entrance exam provides some information and is used in the design of the contract.

Application: Credit history

Banks usually collect various kinds of information before they grant a loan. One piece of information is the credit history of the customer in the past. This payback history provides some indication of the hidden characteristics of the agent regarding his or her intentions or possibilities of paying back the loan in the future. Building up a good credit history is difficult for everyone, but is not as difficult for a good risk as it is for a bad risk. By using this information in the design of the contract, it is less difficult for the bank to distinguish the high-quality agents from the low-quality ones. They may self-select themselves over the contracts which are in the menu of contracts offered by the principal.

Repeated interactions offer the possibility of forming a reputation. In the context of this chapter, a reputation is formulated with respect to the impression one has of a certain *characteristic* of an individual. It is impossible to change this characteristic. For example, someone can have an aggressive character by nature. This characteristic does influence the payoffs. Having a good reputation is interesting when the person involved has unique (asymmetric) information about his or her characteristic. How a person or company has behaved in the past provides some information regarding their nature, so the past plays a role in the development of a reputation. The person involved knows this and will take it into account in his or her choices, even though his or her type is determined.

7.5 Revelation principle

In the fundamental welfare theorem, prices equate the quantity demanded with that supplied. Just how the equilibrium price is determined is not specified and need not be, because all relevant information is available. It is therefore appropriate to assume that agreement is reached by negotiations or bargaining. The market-clearing equilibrium price entails that each party receives at least his or her reservation price. However, if the reservation prices are not known, then bargaining may result in inefficient outcomes. Exchange will be established with delay, or will not occur at all, while it will occur immediately when all information is available to everybody. Asymmetric information provides possibilities for misrepresentation, which may prevent surplus-generating exchange from occurring.

Another aspect of the fundamental welfare theorem is that an organization may try to imitate valuable exchange by a system of transfer prices. Section 4.5.2 made it clear that exchange will not always happen in environments with asymmetric information when the reservation price of the buyer is higher than that of the seller. It seemed there that honesty by both parties over their reservation prices in the bargaining process was necessary in order to ensure that valuable exchange always takes place. However, there may exist a radically different set of rules, contracts, procedures or mechanisms such that the involved parties misrepresent their reservation prices, but the misrepresentation is channelled in such a way that exchange will occur always when the reservation price of the seller is lower than the reservation price of the buyer. This section will show that such a procedure cannot in fact exist, i.e. where there is asymmetric information only a second-best result is possible.

Suppose there is a principal facing n agents, each with a hidden characteristic θ_i, where $i = 1, 2, \ldots, n$. The principal chooses the rules of the contract or mechanism. The agents decide subsequently regarding acceptance. Finally, the agents choose independently and simultaneously a *message m_i*, where $i = 1, 2, \ldots, n$. The message may consist of a price, as in an auction, or a report of the annual income to the tax authorities. The contents of the message do not have to be honest. The rules of the mechanism (procedure, contract, institution) specify how these messages are translated in an allocation x_i for each player, where $i = 1, 2, \ldots, n$.

The principal likes to use the information of the agents in the design of the contract. The principal can just ask for this information, but it will only be provided honestly by the agents when the principal provides the right incentives. It is usually not an optimal strategy for the agent to be honest in a *general mechanism G*. A *direct mechanism D* is defined as a contract where agents make claims about their types (rather than claims about something else). A now famous result is that every outcome achievable by a general mechanism can also be established by a direct one (Gibbard, 1973; Myerson, 1979). This result is known as the *revelation principle*.

> *Revelation principle.* Every allocation satisfying the participation and incentive compatibility constraints in a general mechanism can also be established by a direct mechanism in which honest messages satisfy the participation and incentive compatibility constraints.

Figure 7.22 depicts the revelation principle. The general mechanism G elicits the messages $(m_1, m_2, \ldots, m_n)$ of the agents, which are based upon $(\theta_1, \theta_2, \ldots, \theta_n)$. These messages are translated into an allocation $(x_1, x_2, \ldots, x_n)$. The direct mechanism D has the property that $(m_1, m_2, \ldots, m_n) = (\theta_1, \theta_2, \ldots, \theta_n)$. Honesty is established in the direct mechanism by choosing the payoffs in such a way that it is in the interest of each player to report the true value of the hidden characteristic, i.e. the participation and incentive compatibility constraints of the contract are such that each agent maximizes his or her (expected) payoff by reporting the true value of his or her hidden characteristic. Honesty is in that case the best (payoff-maximizing) response in a direct mechanism.

The value of the revelation principle is that it facilitates the computation of the optimal contract. The principal has only to consider those contracts which result in truth-telling by

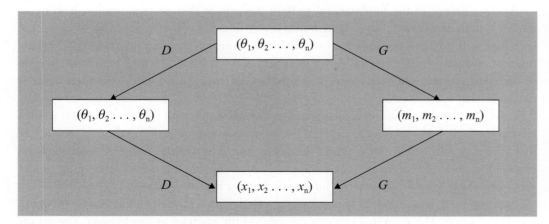

Figure 7.22: Revelation principle

the agent. This makes it possible to determine what can be achieved by an organization in an environment with asymmetric information. The outcome is usually *second-best*, i.e. the efficient equilibrium outcome in a situation with asymmetric information differs from the equilibrium outcome when there is complete information. A mechanism is efficient in a situation with asymmetric information when there exists no other mechanism which is preferred by everybody. The second-best character of the revelation principle seems to be at odds with the Coase theorem. The establishment of the first-best outcome required efficient bargaining, allocated property rights and no income effects. However, an important difference between this section and the Coase theorem is that the latter usually requires complete information. A situation with asymmetric information, e.g. hidden characteristics, often means that the first-best cannot be achieved.

Another difference from the Coase theorem regards *decentralization*. The Coase theorem specifies the circumstances in which decentralization establishes an efficient allocation, without paying attention to the problems associated with decentralization, but here things are the opposite. According to the revelation principle, a fully centralized mechanism is at least as good as delegation. Centralization is attractive when various externalities are involved in decisions and therefore cannot be delegated well. Payoffs are structured such that everybody is compensated for the externalities of a certain outcome. All externalities are internalized by using the reported messages in order to pay exactly the reservation price. Nothing will go wrong because of bargaining. According to Coase this results in decentralization, while the revelation principle states exactly the opposite.

The revelation principle determines what can be established by centralization, without incorporating the costs of centralization in the analysis. Several qualifications regarding this result can be formulated. First, there are several disadvantages of centralized information processing. They have been addressed already in Chapter 3 (Hayek, 1945). People are not good at processing information, least of all within a centralized organization. It is therefore more realistic to incorporate a principal with limited cognitive capacities in the analysis.

Second, it is important to recognize that the revelation principle does not say that truth-telling comes at zero cost. On the contrary, the principal must design the contract to induce the agent to tell the truth. In general, this will force the principal to *pre-commit to 'under-utilizing' information*. That is, the cost of inducing the agent to tell the truth is that the principal cannot use the information as fully as he or she would if the truthful message did not have to be motivated. In fact, in some extreme cases the principal must promise to not use the information at all in order to induce the agent to report honestly. The revelation principle merely states that the cost (broadly defined) of motivating the truth is no greater than the cost of motivating a non-truthful reporting strategy. An implication of the revelation principle is that the resulting allocation is often second-best. One could argue that the principal may change the payoffs in the direct mechanism once the messages by the agents are received. However, if the agents anticipate this, then honest reporting is probably no longer a payoff-maximizing strategy. The pre-commitment assumption is therefore important to the revelation principle, because the principal's promise to 'under-utilize' the information is what gives the agent the incentive to reveal the truth. If the agent believes the information will be used against him or her, it becomes more costly (perhaps too costly) to motivate him or her to reveal the truth. Doubts regarding the pre-commitment as to how the agent's report will be used may account for several organizational practices, like delegation and also independent agencies.

A third implicit assumption is that the principal *cannot be manipulated*. Somebody may consider influencing the decision of the principal. However, this is a different situation from that analysed in this section; it will be addressed in Chapter 8.

A fourth aspect is that honest reporting requires three conditions to be met: the commitment of the principal to the mechanism has to be credible, agents have to be able to transmit all their information, and there must be no limitations regarding the contracts that can be designed. If these conditions are met, then there is no role for *organizations* to create value. In situations where these conditions are not met it is highly likely that agents will not report honestly regarding costs or their income. Several organizational practices can be viewed as a way to handle these problems.

A fifth aspect of the revelation principle is that all information between the members of the organization can be exchanged when the right incentives for the truthful revelation of information are provided. If this holds, then the choice of *information system* becomes irrelevant. An implication of the revelation principle is that the information structure does not even matter. Every allocation of any organization can also be realized with a centralized information structure (consisting of two steps) where agents transmit all their information to the principal (centre) and the principal translates this information subsequently into an allocation. It is assumed that the transmission of information by the agents to the principal is without costs. However, the way information is gathered and transmitted matters when costs are involved. Chapter 3 has addressed this already and Part VI will deal with it more extensively. Hierarchical structures (organizations) are chosen from this perspective in order to enhance the efficiency of the transmission and the processing of information. If, next to the limited communication possibilities, conflicts of interests are also incorporated in the analysis, then also the incentive aspects of delegation can be analysed (Melumadea *et al.*, 1992). Agents may also be limited in their ability to communicate their information.

A sixth aspect is that no restrictions were formulated regarding the structure of the direct mechanism. However, the principal's ability to use the messages may be limited, e.g. by requiring that the principal uses a contract with a pre-specified shape (e.g. piece-wise linear).

A seventh aspect is that all decisions are made ex-ante by the principal or the designer. All conflicts are resolved and all rents allocated ex-ante. This leaves no room for ex-post bargaining. This theme will be addressed in extensively in Part IV.

The revelation principle states that any proposed mechanism involving non-truthful reporting by the agent can be duplicated or beaten in terms of expected utilities by an equilibrium mechanism in which truthful reporting is induced. Similarly, any multi-stage process (the agent submits a tentative message, the principal makes a counter-offer, the agent submits a revised message, etc.) can be duplicated or beaten by a single-stage process in which the agent submits the truth. In the revelation principle agents submit their messages *simultaneously* to the principal. The sequence of messages matters when the possibilities of communication are limited. A hierarchical structure (of contracts) entails additional *flexibility*, because the contract between two agents may be based on better local information than a single, all-encompassing contract of the principal for all agents. Delegation exploits the possibilities of dealing effectively with local information in decision-making processes. A disadvantage of delegation is a loss of control, because the agent will use his or her monopoly position regarding information to his or her own advantage. The tradeoff between flexibility and loss of control has to be addressed in the choice of organizational structure.

In this chapter agents are assumed to be perfectly rational. However, a general mechanism may be so complicated that the agents are not able to determine the optimal strategy. The principal may therefore earn more than can be expected from the perspective of the revelation principle. It is also assumed that the agents participate only once in the mechanism. However, they often meet repeatedly, which may induce co-operation between them. This can be at the expense of the principal. Limited cognitive capabilities on the part of the principal may prevent him or her gathering all relevant information and processing it. Decentralization may be preferred to designing a mechanism in complex environments in order to deal effectively with local information. Parts IV and VI addresses incentive issues in situations characterized by bounded rationality.

Application: Vickrey auction

An *auction* is a market-like institution with a number of explicit rules. These determine whether bids are sealed or oral, the bidding procedure, how the object of the auction is allocated, and the prices to be paid. The decision sequence is such that the auctioneer chooses the type of auction. Subsequently the potential bidders decide regarding participation and about the bid(s) which will be submitted. There are many auctions which are used in many markets, e.g. the English auction with ascending bids in art markets, the Dutch auction with descending bids for flowers, closed-bid auctions for houses, double oral auctions in stock markets, and so on. Auctions are also used for analysing job applications, lobbying for projects and the allocation of a project to one of many departments in an organization.

The auctioneer or principal likes to earn as much as possible, but the number of possible auctions (bidding sequences, allocation rules) is almost unlimited and the reservation prices of the bidders or agents are not known. However, the revelation principle makes it possible to determine what is the payoff-maximizing auction for the principal in this situation with asymmetric information. The same principle indicates that it is sufficient to consider only a limited number of auctions. Only direct mechanisms have to be considered in order to determine the amount of money the auctioneer can earn at most. In this context a mechanism is a process with messages in the form of the bids of the agents as inputs and, as output, the allocation of the object to one of the agents and a price which has to be paid by each agent. Each agent is simply asked to announce his or her reservation price in a direct mechanism.

Vickrey (1961) has proposed the second-price, sealed-bid auction as a direct mechanism. This auction requires simultaneously submitted sealed bids, where the winner is the agent with the highest bid. The winner pays the second-highest bid, while the others pay nothing. The reservation price of each player is private information. This auction is a direct mechanism, because each agent i submits his or her reservation price θ_i as bid. This is the payoff-maximizing strategy, because underbidding entails the unnecessary risk that somebody else will obtain the product at a lower price, while overbidding may result in paying a price higher than the reservation price.

The English auction and the Vickrey auction result in the same revenue for the auctioneer, but the bids by the agents differ between these auctions. Suppose that the reservation prices of the agents are $\theta_1 = 10$, $\theta_2 = 7$ and $\theta_3 = 6$. Agent or bidder 1 will ultimately bid 7 in an English auction and pay this bid to the auctioneer. The auctioneer earns 7. Agent 1 will bid 10 in the Vickrey auction, but pays the second highest bid of 7, i.e. the reservation price of agent 7. The auctioneer again earns 7. This result holds more generally and is called the *revenue-equivalence theorem* (McAfee and McMillan, 1987).

Notice that the English auction is not a direct mechanism. The winner is the player with the highest reservation price, but his or her bid is not equal to his or her reservation price. The agent with the highest reservation price has to pay his or her bid to the auctioneer in an English auction, and therefore has an incentive to underbid. In a Vickrey auction agents bid their reservation price, because they do not have to pay their own bid.

The importance of commitment to the rules of the auction by the auctioneer is illustrated by the Vickrey auction. If the bids have been submitted, then it is attractive for the auctioneer to raise the price to 10 for the winner. However, if the agents anticipate this behaviour, then they will submit different bids or not honour the bids. The principal has to accept that he or she cannot earn more than 7. The result is therefore *second-best* for the principal, but it is inevitable in the situation with asymmetric information. The agent with the highest reservation price earns an '*informational rent*' of $10 - 7 = 3$, because he or she has information at his or her disposal which the auctioneer does not have. The asymmetry of information results in a decrease of the share of the surplus for the auctioneer. Notice that the object of the auctioneer still goes to the agent with the highest reservation price.

It may have seemed unnecessary in the description of the above two auctions to mention that only the winner has to pay. However, this is not always the case. Situations with many agents can often be conceptualized as a competition or race where the winner gains, but all agents incur costs. Examples are applying for a job, the development of a new product in order obtain a patent, or the lobbying for a project. These costs have also to be taken into account in the design of a mechanism. Mechanism can be extended in various ways and applied to more complex problems (Groves, 1973).

7.6 Hidden characteristics and hidden actions

Hidden characteristics and hidden action problems have been dealt with separately, but they can of course occur simultaneously. The principal may lack information regarding the true nature of the agent when the contract is chosen, while afterwards the agent may behave in a way that is unobservable to the principal.

Application: Insurance
Travel insurance entails both a hidden characteristics problem and a hidden action one. Cautious people will take various measures to prevent theft, and are therefore in general less inclined to buy travel insurance than other travellers. The incentive to take preventive

measures weakens when insurance is bought, because it is anticipated that the insurance company will pay for the damage. The information problem is exacerbated. People may decide not to buy insurance when only the hidden characteristics effect is taken into account. However, they will buy it if the hidden action effect is also taken into account.

Application: Loans

Section 7.1.2 demonstrated that the level of the interest rate has implications for which kind of individuals will take a loan. The most desirable clients are scared away from taking one. This adverse selection aspect of ex-ante asymmetric information can also be accompanied by a hidden action problem (Stiglitz and Weiss, 1981). There may be an ex-post information problem once the loan is issued, because the agent may use the loan for excessively risky purposes. Banks have only limited tools for controlling the way the money will be spent. This has a negative impact on the probability that the loan will be paid back.

An increase in the interest rate decreases the profitability of projects for the agent. The response of the agent to such an increase is that projects with a lower probability of success are chosen, but the profitability of a successful project will be higher. Therefore, too many risky projects may be chosen, a possibility also addressed in Sec. 6.1.2. The benefits of a successful project go to the agent, while the principal bears the costs when the project fails. Therefore it can be expected that banks will take both information problems into account in the choice of the conditions of the contract. Agents respond to such contracts with behaviour that is more aligned with the interests of the principal.

Application: Herd behaviour and investment

The relationship between the principal and the agent has been represented by the non-observability of the effort of the agent. The effort provided by managers is important, but other aspects of the behaviour of managers are often more important. Managers often spend many hours working. Therefore it is not the level of effort but rather the direction in which activities are developed that is a major concern for the principal. This application addresses the relationship between career considerations and investment decisions. The familiar starting-point of the analysis is that certain characteristics (of the manager) are surrounded with some uncertainty at the start of a relationship, becoming known only after a while.

It is usually assumed that investment decisions are based on the available information and are efficient as well. However, there are also theories in which group behaviour plays an important role. If the evaluation of others is considered as important, then it may be desirable to work conventionally. Scharfstein and Stein (1990) cite Keynes in this context:

It is the long-term investor, he who most promotes the public interest, who will in practice come in for most criticism, wherever investment funds are managed by committees or boards or banks. For it is in the essence of his behaviour, that he should be eccentric, unconventional, and rash in the eyes of average opinion. If he is successful, that will only confirm the general belief in his rashness; and if in the short-run he is unsuccessful, which is very likely, he will not receive much mercy. Worldly wisdom teaches that it is better for reputation to fail conventionally than to succeed unconventionally.

Scharfstein and Stein analyse the investment behaviour of managers who care about their *reputations* as good decision-makers. It turns out that it is optimal for managers to imitate the investment decisions of others in certain circumstances, despite the fact that a specific manager knows that another decision creates more value. Suppose managers come in two types. Some collect a lot of relevant information and analyse it thoroughly, while others do not. However, this characteristic of the managers is not known. Two sources of information are generated by the investment decisions of the various managers: (*direct*) *specific information* regarding the investment choice of a specific manager, and (*indirect*) *market information* regarding the average success of similar investments by other managers. Both sources of information can be used in order to make a good guess regarding the type of the manager. Private as well as market information is informative.

High-ability managers base their decisions on the information they have collected themselves. The result of the investment project can nevertheless be bad as a result of misleading information or just bad luck. Managers are aware of this possibility, and hence that it is sensible to take the decisions of others into account in the decision-making process. The reason is that the information available will in general not be such that one manager makes the right choice and all the others the wrong one. It is therefore efficient to consider this information. The screening or signalling of the capability of managers strengthens this *group effect*. Deviant behaviour is viewed as being more likely with a bad manager. A bad decision is less bad for a reputation when others do the same. It may imply that a manager does not want to start a project based on his or her own information, but does start it based on the decisions of others. The opposite can also occur, i.e. a project with a positive value does not make it, because others have rejected it before. Such *herd behaviour* in the use of information is *inefficient*.

Chapter 11 will address the aggregation of local decisions into an organization decision when various managers make mistakes independent of each other. The idea behind having a project evaluated by various persons is that each one collects different information. In this section, it has turned out that certain constraints are associated with such group decision-making processes as well. If career considerations play a role in decisions, one can make the decision dependent on the choice of others as well. One can simply copy the choice of the previous person, regardless of their own insights. One way to prevent this loss of valuable information is to make those with the largest career interests choose first. People concerned about their career are usually young managers, because not much is known about their capabilities. They usually do not occupy the highest functions in an organization. It is therefore advisable to have bottom-up instead of top-down information flows in organizations.

Application: Internal labour market

Chapter 6 emphasizes the performance stimuli aspect of promotions in internal labour markets. This certainly plays a role in the decision regarding a promotion, but it is also at least as important that people have a job that suits them well. To use the terminology of Chapter 1, promotions serve the role of assigning a person to the position where his or her comparative advantage is largest. Promotions play an important role in this context, because the performance in the current position provides an indication of the hidden characteristics of the agent (MacLeod and Malcolmson, 1988).

Application: Equilibrium wages above the market clearing wage

All markets clear in the theory of general equilibrium (Chapter 3). Prices adjust (invisible hand) such that the quantity demanded is equal to that supplied. There is no unemployment in the labour market. The theory of complete contracts specifies that the principal, instead of the invisible hand, determines the price. The principal has to cope with a hidden action problem as well as hidden characteristics ones. Hidden action problems result in shirking, because it is hard for the principal to determine the actions of the agent, while hidden characteristics problems are prominent in recruiting.

The principal can deal with these problems by paying a wage *higher* than the market-clearing wage (Shapiro and Stiglitz, 1984). This may resolve the hidden action as well as the hidden characteristics problem. The hidden action problem is resolved because shirking is now more expensive. Being fired for bad behaviour will now decrease the income of the agent, which is not true in the theory of general equilibrium. The hidden characteristics problem is dealt with effectively because only the agents that attract the principal will apply or will remain in the company.

The famous decision of Henry Ford to pay his employees daily a wage of $5 can be understood from this perspective. He reduced the work day from 9 to 8 hours and increased the wage from $2.34 to $5.00 on 12 January 1912. Ford (1922, p. 147) wrote afterwards that this decision 'was one of the finest cost cutting moves we ever made'. Empirical research has shown that the average costs of a car decreased after this decision, the average labour productivity increased and the labour turnover decreased.

Application: Safelite Glass Corporation

Safelite Glass Corporation installs car windshields. It is the largest company in the United States. Until 1994 employees received a fixed hourly wage. There was hardly any relationship between the wage received and the number of windshields installed by the auto glass installers. A piece-rate wage system was introduced in 1994–95. An amount of money was paid for each windshield installed. At the introduction of the new wage system employees were guaranteed that their weekly wage would not drop below a certain level. There was a minimum hourly wage guarantee, so that if the piece-rate wage turned out to be lower than the guaranteed wage the guaranteed wage was paid. This switch in wage structure and its empirical effects will now be addressed (Lazear, 1999).

Define e as the production level of the employee. The employee receives a wage W in the fixed-wage system when at least e_0 is produced and nothing is paid when less than e_0 is produced. Only the level e_0 is produced, because employees like wages, but do not like effort. Employees receive a piece-rate wage b for each unit of output in the piece-rate system when a certain level of production e^*, with $e^* > e_0$, is exceeded and the total wage exceeds W. K is a constant ensuring that the participation constraint is met. The guarantee wage entails that each employee earns at least W. So, should somebody earn less than W in the piece-rate system, then this employee receives a wage W. However, if the piece-rate system results in a higher wage than W, then this higher wage is paid to the employee.

Employees with an aversion to working hard are represented with the steep indifference curve. They are willing to provide additional effort only when a substantial wage increase is offered. The flat indifference curve reflects the attractive employees from the perspective of the employer, because a lower wage increase is necessary in order to make them provide additional effort. Figure 7.23 presents a situation where the employee earns nothing when the level of effort is lower than e_0. Each level of effort higher than e_0 results in a wage W in the fixed hourly wage system. The piece-rate system with the guarantee wage is the same as the fixed hourly wage system, except that the wage will increase when the level of output increases above e^*.

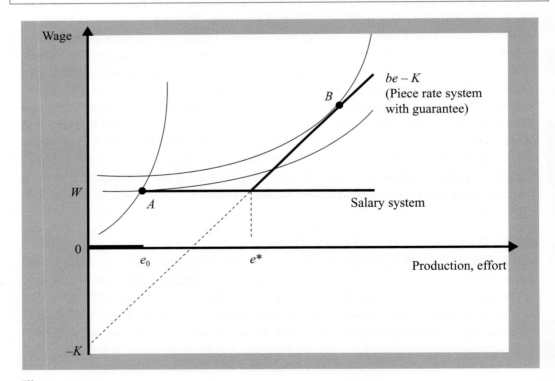

Figure 7.23:

Lazear, E.P. (1999) 'Personnel Economics: Past Lessons and Future Directions', *Journal of Labour Economics*, 17(2) pp. 199–236, University of Chicago

If the employees are offered only the fixed hourly wage system, then everybody will choose point *A*, because additional effort is not rewarded. The productive employees choose *B* instead of *A* when the piece-rate system is introduced. This has at least two effects. First, the average productivity increases, because some employees switch from *A* to *B*. This is the incentive effect. There is also a selection effect. The company will attract more-productive workers, because they can earn more at Safelite.

The actual effect of the introduction of piece-rate wages is remarkable. The total increase in productivity is 44 per cent, where 22 per cent is due to the incentive effect and 22 per cent to the selection effect.

7.7 Conclusion

Models with stable preferences (payoffs), maximizing behaviour and competition often establish a clear relationship between preferences and expected behaviour. The addition of information as a fourth ingredient results frequently in more realistic models, but the accompanying behaviour is sometimes counterintuitive. The reason is that incomplete information has an impact on the relationship between preferences and behaviour. Behaviour that seems curious at first can be understood in environments with asymmetric information because of the transfer of information involved.

This chapter has defined the hidden characteristics problem and characterized adverse selection as equilibrium behaviour. A drastic solution to the problem of adverse selection is to prevent selection from occurring by eliminating certain choices. A second solution entails expanding the choice possibilities by offering a menu of contracts. This may result in self-selection. Finally, additional information can be incorporated in the design of contracts. The agent with the good characteristics will try to distinguish himself from the bad agents by communicating informative signals, while the principal will try to reduce his or her lack of information by screening the agent. Including such information in contracts decreases the hidden characteristics problem, because it provides relevant information regarding the true nature of the agent. Self-selection may emerge again.

Various causes of inefficiency have been addressed, but this has yet to result in a realistic theory of organization. The revelation principle even shows that results which can be established in a decentralized fashion can always be established at least as well in a centralized way. Organizational agreements (organizational structure, contractual agreements, and so on) do not seem to matter. The behavioural assumptions are responsible for this observation. This does not imply that the formulated results are unimportant in problems with other behavioural assumptions. The various kinds of inefficiencies identified occur in such situations as well. The assumption in the next three chapters will be that the organization (or institution) is chosen which handles the various inefficiencies best. The main difference will be that the size of the various inefficiencies is determined by the choice of organization.

7.8 Exercises

7.1 Suppose that the annual dental outlays of a family are 600 euros. The population of families employing a dentist can be divided into five groups of equal size (Fig. 7.24).

Family dental outlay (euros)	Percentage of population
200	20
400	20
600	20
800	20
1000	20

Figure 7.24: Population of families with their dental outlays

    A Suppose a (naive) insurance company asks an insurance premium of 700 euros. How much will this insurance company earn on average?
    B Determine the insurance premium of a profit-maximizing insurance company.
    C Which families will buy insurance?

7.2 A company wants to fulfil a number of vacancies. Employees are characterized by a high productivity, q_h, or a low productivity, q_l. Employees can choose to work for the company or to start their own business at a reservation wage of respectively w_h or w_l. The company does not know the productivity of the applicants, but knows that the probability that an employee will have a high productivity is 2/3 (and therefore the probability of low productivity of 1/3). Assume that $q_h = 10$, $q_l = 4$, $w_h = 10$ and $w_l = 7$.
    A Present the extensive form.
    B Present the supply function of productivity (q) as a function of the wage (w).
    C Assume that the company maximizes q/w. Which salary will the company choose and what will be the resulting productivity level?
    D Which salary structure will the company choose when the productivity characteristics of the employees are known?
    E Who likes the situation of asymmetric information? Explain your answer.

7.3 Managers are interested not only in the well-being of their company but also in the development of their own career. An important aspect of this latter aspect is the reputation of a manager in the market, which is based on the success of decisions made in the past. Assume there are as many competent as incompetent managers. Competent managers obtain valuable information about potential investment projects, while other managers are unable to obtain such information. Besides obtaining this information, managers who are late with their decision can choose to incorporate the decision of early deciders in their decision process.

A On which two sources of information is the reputation of a manager based?

B Is it possible for inefficient investment decisions to be made? Explain your answer.

C Does the presence of considerations regarding reputation in the decision-making process of managers argue for a 'top-down' or a 'bottom-up' organization of information flows in companies? Explain your answer.

7.4   The departure of employees is expensive for a company, especially when it has invested heavily in their education and training. It will therefore try to attract employees who intend to stay. However, it is usually impossible for a company to identify such applicants.

A Is this a hidden action or hidden characteristics problem? Explain your answer.

B It is empirically determined that salaries increase with seniority. Illustrate in a diagram and in words how this salary policy attracts the desired employees.

C How do you explain that a positive relationship between salary and seniority is usually accompanied by mandatory retirement?

7.5   In 1998 the Amsterdam stock exchange was plagued by an extensive fraud scandal. Investors and traders as well as stockbrokers were involved. CEO Möller of the Amsterdam stock exchange announced in his New Year's speech that the integrity and quality of the stock exchange would be increased by setting up an independent institution that would enable traders and bank employees to obtain a quality rating.

A Is this a hidden action or a hidden characteristics problem?

B Who is the principal?

C Who is the agent?

D How is the firm conceptualized in the complete contracting theory?

E Which solution is proposed by Möller?

F Which other solution is possible for this problem?

7.6   The number of transparencies shown on an overhead projector during a lecture and the availability of transparencies before class are two choices a professor has to make. The professor prefers to direct his or her attention to the interested and prepared students, but the heterogeneity of the audience can prevent this.

Students constantly make decisions about the use of their scarce time. Assume there are two types of students. Intrinsically motivated T-students do the readings beforehand, which means they can concentrate on the additional explanations during the lectures. They therefore copy only few sheets. The N-students are not intrinsically motivated and start talking when they have finished copying a sheet. They therefore don't prepare and copy all sheets. The reason is that they cannot make distinction between the additional explanations to the readings and the duplication of the readings.

A Is this a principal–agent problem? Explain your answer.

B Is this a hidden action problem? Explain your answer.

C Present the difference between I- and N-students in a diagram. Explain your diagram.

D Illustrate in a diagram how there are circumstances in which the professor can achieve his or her goal by using a lot of transparencies and by not making them available, which means the I-students receive the attention they desire and the N-students do not talk. Explain your answer.

7.7 The recruitment policy of companies is influenced by national laws. Variations regarding the payment of disability insurance premiums exist between European countries. In the Netherlands a company has to pay additional disability premiums if many employees have left during the last five years with a disability pension, whereas in Germany a company has to pay additional premiums when the percentage of disabled employees falls below a certain level.

A Which two behavioural assumptions underlie the principal–agent model, and which three ingredients are necessary to have an interesting principal–agent problem?

B Are the Dutch and German laws regarding disability insurance premiums focused on solving a hidden action problem or a hidden characteristics one? Explain your answer.

C Does the principal–agent model predict that employers in the Netherlands will discriminate in their recruitment policy more against employees who are old, overweight, smokers and other types with an above-average risk of bad health, than employers in Germany? Explain your answer.

7.8 Suppose there are different types of employees in an industry. The production per employee varies between 0 and 1.

A Determine the average production of an employee when the different types are uniformly distributed.

Suppose the productivity of an employee cannot be determined without costs. Employees choose between employment at company Fixedwage and company Piecerate. Company Fixedwage pays all employees the same wage, where the wage is equal to the average productivity of the company. Company Piecerate pays each employee according to the value of the amount produced minus the cost of measurement θ. The value of one unit of production is equal to 1 euro.

B Is this a hidden action or a hidden characteristics problem?

C Which employee is in equilibrium, indifferent between being employed at Fixedwage and Piecerate? Show your calculation.

D Which employees work at Fixedwage in equilibrium? Explain your answer.

E Which values of θ result in a separating equilibrium?

The above industry consists of two companies. The central bureau of statistics has published the numbers given in Fig. 7.25 about the two companies.

	Company Piecerate	Company Fixedwage
Number of employees	100	100
Production	50	25
Average wage	0.5	0.25
Maximum wage	0.75	0.25
Minimum wage	0.25	0.25

Figure 7.25: Behavioural differences between Piecerate and Fixedwage

F What is the value of θ?

Questions are asked about these numbers in parliament. A member of the conservative party proposes that fixed wages have to be forbidden by law. It is argued that the average productivity of an employee at Piecerate is much higher than the average productivity of an employee at Fixedwage. This is illustrated with the figures published by the central bureau of statistics. A member of the labour party proposes to forbid piece-rate wages. The large salary differences are considered unfair.

G Which proposal creates the highest surplus in the industry?

Part IV:
Incomplete contracts

For the formulation of an interesting organization theory and a theory of capital structure it is necessary that the assumptions of complete (contingent) contracting are relaxed such that results can be formulated regarding the allocation of decision rights, responsibilities, communication channels and evaluation criteria. These topics cannot be dealt with in complete contracting settings because all relevant aspects of exchange are covered by the contract, i.e. decision rights and responsibility are empty concepts in this approach. The theory of incomplete contracts is geared towards determining the boundaries of the firm and the optimal (organizational and financial) governance or institutional structure. The starting-point will be that the design of contracts is costly. These costs result necessarily in incomplete contracts. However, there is a problem when a situation occurs which is not covered by the contract. Contractual clauses have to be formulated regarding who has the right to decide in such circumstances, which determines the type of principal–agent relationship which will prevail. Organizations are perceived as a nexus of incomplete contracts, i.e. a governance structure. The view of the firm in this part is illustrated in Fig. IV.1.

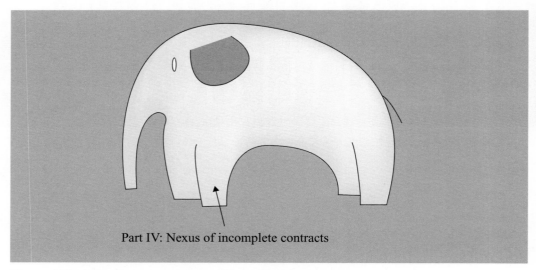

Part IV: Nexus of incomplete contracts

Figure IV.1: The firm as a nexus of incomplete contracts

Organizations start to matter when they determine the type of principal–agent problems which occur, and how these have to be handled in the design of contracts. Certain problems are dealt with explicitly in contracts, while the treatment of other problems is postponed until later. The incompleteness of contracts may result in various forms of renegotiation, like hold-up problems in transaction costs economics and influence activities in the influence costs approach. The attention shifts therefore from the question of the optimal reward structure (in complete contracting theory) to the question of the optimal governance structure (in the incomplete contracting approach). The incomplete contracting perspective places markets and hierarchies or firms at opposite ends of the spectrum of possible institutions to deal with problems of bounded rationality and asymmetric information. Questions of governance are addressed in this part with the assumptions of limited rationality and the opportunistic behavioural assumption. Figure IV.2 presents this with the familiar scheme.

		Behavioural hypothesis		
		Opportunistic	**Self-interested**	**Idealistic**
Degree of rationality	**Complete rationality**			
	Limited rationality	Transaction costs; Influence costs; Property rights; Self-enforcing contracts		
	Procedural rationality			

Figure IV.2: Positioning of Part IV

8

Transaction and influence costs

LEARNING OBJECTIVES

After completing this chapter, you should understand:

- Why valuable specific investments may be not be done.

- How the choice of governance structure may resolve the hold-up problem.

- What influence activities entail.

- When bureaucratic measures are desirable.

Contents

8.1 Introduction

There were attempts to implement the *fundamental welfare theorem* inside organizations in the 1960s. In Part II the theory was that when the right circumstances were created all co-ordination and motivation problems would disappear. Managers would be evaluated on the basis of the profits of their department, competition between departments had to be created and products and services between departments had to be exchanged at marginal costs. However, the viewpoint has now developed that it is not a good idea to approach an organization as a set of markets. The main strength of standard economics is how it shows the price mechanism co-ordinating the use of resources, i.e. how it is focused on supply and demand and on prices and output (Fig. 1.5). However, standard economics is poorly suited to analysing the inner workings of real firms as regards the differences in incentives, control and dispute settlement between alternative modes of governance like markets and firms.

Developments in the 1970s replaced the production function view of the firm with the nexus of complete contracts view discussed in Part III. This latter theory emphasizes the incentive aspects of traditional management questions regarding accounting, finance, marketing and organization. The contract between the principal and the agent is complete, because all available information, regardless of its amount and complexity, is incorporated in the design of the contract. The best possible result is in such circumstances determined with the revelation principle. The equilibrium is second-best. However, an explanation for different organizational forms cannot be formulated, because the assumptions of complete rationality, costless communication and credible commitments make this impossible.

These three assumptions are responsible for the fact that quite different contracts result in the same outcome, which means no unique prediction can be formulated. Two examples from Chapter 6 may illustrate this. First, different reward systems – discrete and continuous – can establish the same result, i.e. there are multiple contractual equilibria. This is unsatisfactory because an unambiguous prediction entails a unique equilibrium. Second, Jensen and Meckling approach the question of the optimal capital structure from the perspective of complete contracting, in which the optimal choice is determined by minimizing the costs associated with various hidden actions. There is another contract which realizes the same behaviour of the manager: a high fixed payment for the manager when the result exceeds a certain level, and a low fixed payment otherwise. Besides this, there is the possibility of achieving results in the short run through discouraging risky projects by making the reward dependent on the long-term share price. These observations indicate that the framework of complete contracts (opportunistic agents with complete rationality) is not always the most appropriate framework for determining the capital structure of a company. It is therefore unclear how changes in the capital structure can be distinguished from changes in the reward structure. Without a satisfactory answer to this question, the incentive aspects of the various capital forms are consistent with the Modigliani–Miller theorem, i.e. the value of the company does not depend on its financial structure. However, the lack of such a relationship was exactly the motivation of complete contracting analysis.

The complete contracting perspective can explain neither the boundaries of the firm, nor capital structure, nor the advantages of different institutional or property rights regimes, because it does not distinguish between contracts in organizations and between organizations. The boundaries of the firm are irrelevant because comprehensive contracts can be designed and there are no problems regarding the interpretation of contracts and the renegotiating of contracts because of the assumptions made. One important assumption is that the principal and the agent have the same information at their disposal when the contract is designed. They agree on the circumstances under which the assignment is being executed, like the probability of favourable working conditions. The implication is that questions regarding the ex-post division of the surplus do not play a role in the design of the contract. A second important assumption is that the principal and the agent are fully committed to an accepted contract. The payments cannot be renegotiated when production has taken place. This chapter relaxes this assumption. The third assumption is that the production of the agent can be verified without costs by an independent third party, like the judiciary power, i.e. there are no problems to enforce the contract. In the complete contracting approach, all observable results are assumed to be verifiable. This chapter will distinguish between observable and verifiable results and circumstances. Sensible incomplete contracts are based only on information which is observable as well as verifiable. Observable information which is not verifiable is left out of a sensible incomplete contract.

The distinction between exchange in the market and exchange in a company seems completely obvious in a market economy with complete information and complete rationality. Companies transform raw materials into goods and services by a production function, while the transition of the ownership of this production is established in the market. However, markets and companies are not always easy to define. First, there is exchange not only in markets but also in the production process inside companies. Second, in fields like logistics and operational activities, two companies in the market may co-operate more closely than two distinct divisions in a company. Third, companies can adopt organizational solutions which resemble markets, like bargaining over transfer prices and judging individual and divisional performances based on profits. Finally, it is not clear from a complete contracting perspective why two production functions cannot be combined into one new production function. Everything which can be realized with two separate production functions should in principle also be possible with an integrated production function as well, and even more so. This implies that the size of the company is in principle unlimited.

Coase (1937) therefore asked the important question, 'What is a company?' His brilliant insight is that the company is not only a part of the market, but is also an alternative to it. To develop this insight he introduced transaction costs, i.e. the costs associated with the price mechanism to establish efficient exchange, examples of which are the costs of bargaining, designing contracts, monitoring, dispute resolution devices and so on (Coase, 1992). In certain circumstances, market exchange is more costly than exchange within a company. Such transaction costs may be reduced by giving one party all the power, within certain limits, to design the contract conditions. Transactions occurring in a company are based on the instructions or orders of superiors, while exchange in markets is negotiated. However, a company is also not without costs. More decision power in the hands of one person increases the probability of mistakes and the abuse of power, and results in more administrative procedures. According to Coase, the size of a firm is determined by the point where the marginal cost of transacting in the market equals the marginal cost of additional mistakes and more administrative rigidity in the company.

Notice that the above costs are almost completely absent in the complete (contingent) contracts approach. Unlimited rationality entails that the structure of a problem can be easily understood. This is expressed in the contractual solutions chosen by the principal in order to structure the behaviour of the agent to a certain extent. The principal incorporates all the available information without costs in the contract for every situation which could possibly occur in the future. These contracts are complete, because every relevant technological restriction and all information are represented in the contract. Complete rationality is not a bad starting-point in simple and easy environments, but in more complex environments it is unrealistic to assume that contracts can be designed without costs and that they anticipate every possibility. These situations are better addressed by an incomplete contract, because then the complexity of the environment is considered in addition to the technological restrictions and the available information. There are various causes of contractual incompleteness. First, it may be too costly to write complex contracts. Second, it may be too difficult to anticipate in all possible contingencies. Third, language is often context-dependent, which allows for different interpretations because of the bounded cognition or opportunism. Finally, the relevant variables may be observable, but not verifiable by a third party.

One way to represent contractual incompleteness is to relax the assumption of the enforceability of a contract. Implicitly, it has been assumed that contracts are enforced by the courts. Observing and punishing a violation of the contract are viewed as identical. However, while it is often the case that many people know when an agreement is violated in the course of business, in fact it is very difficult indeed to prove to a judge that this has happened. In incomplete contracting theory, observable and verifiable contract conditions are distinguished. Agreements observable but not verifiable are not part of a meaningful contract.

These ideas are further developed in this part. Specific investments are treated in Sec. 8.2. Transaction costs economics focuses on the governance solutions for problems with specific investments (Sec. 8.3). Section 8.4 replaces the exogenous variable 'specificity of investments' by either 'measurement problems' or 'bargaining costs' in order to explain the endogenous variable 'governance structure'. The approach via influence on costs addresses organizational solutions to problems on the basis of the transmission of information in organizations (Sec. 8.5). Section 8.6 concludes.

8.2 Specific investments

Williamson (1975, 1985) has developed the questions raised by Coase on the nature of the firm. How do transactions inside a company differ from those between companies? To address this question, the concept of transaction costs is used. Transaction costs in the narrow sense refer to the time and effort necessary to establish a transaction or exchange. These costs can increase considerably when different parties are involved in different locations. Examples are travel costs, making contact, signing agreements and the failure to realize efficient outcomes. A broad conception of transaction costs entails the means required in negotiating the contracts (the costs of gathering information to determine a bargaining strategy), the time needed to enforce contracts and the costs involved with taking precautionary measures. This section is geared towards transaction costs in the broad sense. The central issue is no longer the technological aspects of production, as it was in Part II, but the contractual problems associated with transactions concerning specific investments.

An incomplete contracting approach is put forward to explain various organizational forms. Making explicit all possible contingencies or circumstances – and specifying them in a contract – is almost impossible and very costly. The rights and duties of all parties should also be delineated in all these circumstances, and adequate provisions made for the situation where someone violates the contract. The behavioural assumption of limited rationality precludes such contracts being written.

The incompleteness of contracts results in various transaction costs, which are expressed in co-ordination and motivation problems. Co-ordination problems are related largely to communicating information, and will be treated extensively in Part VII. Motivation problems have been formulated in Part III as hidden action and hidden characteristics problems. Another aspect of motivation problems is incomplete commitment, which means there are problems regarding the credibility of certain promises or threats. Renegotiating contracts may be desirable when circumstances have changed. However, this is problematic when it is difficult to prove that the circumstances did actually change and that changing the contract is not just opportunistic behaviour in order to claim a larger part of the surplus.

A numerical example will now show that lack of commitment or credibility can prevent the occurrence of profitable transactions (Klein *et al.*, 1978). Consider an upstream and a downstream party. The upstream party has spent time and effort to develop new software. The total costs of the inventor are 200, where an amount K of these costs is sunk, i.e. these costs are not recoverable elsewhere because of tailoring to the specific needs of the downstream party or organization. The remaining amount $200 - K$ is recoverable elsewhere, e.g. certain parts of the software can be used for other purposes. The value of the software for the downstream party is 240. Figure 8.1 presents the composition of the revenues.

40	Surplus
K	Sunk costs
$200 - K$	Recoverable costs

Figure 8.1: Composition of the revenues

The development of software is a typical transaction-specific investment. It is developed by the upstream inventor for certain specific downstream purposes, and has therefore much less value in the best alternative use. An investment is said to be specific, i.e. there is asset specificity, when the investment has a higher value inside the specific relationship than outside it. Asset specificity is a measure of non-redeployability. Such investments are called *sunk investments*, because part of the costs are sunk into the relationship, i.e. cannot be recovered elsewhere.

Asset specificity, and therefore the sunk aspect of investments, occurs in so many ways that five types of specific investment are distinguished by Williamson. First, site-specific investments reflect ex-ante decisions to minimize inventory and transportation expenses. It is however costly to move them once they have been made. Examples are the successive stations in a steel company, the construction of a harbour, and equipment to exploit a gas field. Investments in a harbour, e.g. making it accessible for larger ships, are site-specific, because it cannot be somewhere else. Second, human asset specificity concerns knowledge which is very valuable for specific work, like handling a word processing package with mathematical symbols or operating an advanced chemical process. It arises in a learning-by-doing fashion. Third, dedicated assets derive their value from the prospect of selling a significant amount of product to a specific customer. If this customer terminates the contract prematurely, then significant excess capacity results. Fourth, physical asset specificity concerns the design of specific tools required to produce a component of, for example, a car or a computer chip. Finally, a brand name improves the image of a product and therefore the value of the product. However, the investment of building a brand is hard to recoup somewhere else when the other party behaves opportunistically.

The term *quasi-surplus* is used to indicate the size of the possible contractual problems. Quasi-surplus is defined as the value of an investment in its current use minus the value of the investment in its best alternative use. It equals the revenues minus the recoverable costs. The quasi-surplus in the above example equals $240 - (200 - K) = 40 + K$.

The quasi-surplus differs from the notions of consumer surplus and producer surplus introduced in Chapter 2. Surplus is defined as the part of the revenues higher than the minimum amount necessary to recruit an employee or to induce a company to start a new activity. (The surplus in the above example equals $240 - 200 = 40$.) Surplus is therefore defined from the viewpoint of starting a certain activity. Quasi-surplus is formulated with regard to stopping an activity. It is that part of the revenue which is more than the minimum amount necessary to prevent an employee from resigning, or a company withdrawing a certain activity, or that part of the revenue from an investment which is more than the value of the best alternative. Sunk costs are taken into account when an investment decision is taken. However, these costs cannot be recovered once they are made, and therefore play no role in the decision to stop an activity. The difference between surplus and quasi-surplus is the sunk cost. The quasi-surplus is always at least as large as the surplus. Quasi-surplus emerges when specific investments are done.

Incomplete contracts entail possibilities for ex-post opportunistic behaviour, like violating contracts, and renegotiating contracts. The impossibility of making certain agreements credible is especially problematic when transaction-specific investments are involved. Contractual problems occur as a result of what Williamson calls a fundamental transformation. It entails that there are many candidates who can make specific investments, but eventually there is only one investor actually doing it. This party is subsequently (ex post) completely tied to the relationship, because the value of the investment is highest within the relationship. The surplus of this co-operation is allocated partly according to the contractual agreements made. However, the contract did not cover all possible situations ex ante, so that the allocation of the surplus depends to a certain extent also on the ex-post bargaining position. This will now be illustrated using the example already given above.

Assume the bargaining power is such that half of the (quasi-) surplus goes to each party. With this assumption, the contract price can be determined before as well as after the fundamental transformation. The contract between the upstream inventor and the downstream manufacturer is signed before the investment is made. The surplus associated with the transaction amounts to $240 - 200 = 40$. Each party receives half of the surplus, which means that ex ante a contract price of 220 is established. The profit for the upstream inventor (producer surplus) amounts to $220 - 200 = 20$ and the profit for the downstream party (consumer surplus) comes to $240 - 220 = 20$.

Sunk costs are involved after the specific investment in software is made. Some of the costs made by the upstream inventor are specific to the project and cannot therefore be recovered elsewhere. The opportunistic downstream party is aware of this and may claim that there are unforeseen circumstances which make a price decrease desirable, i.e. the downstream party may try to appropriate part of the quasi-surplus by insisting on a price reduction. The upstream inventor cannot defend himself against this appropriation threat, because part of his costs are sunk. Suppose $K = 60$. The upstream inventor can only credibly refuse to deal further with the downstream party when the price drops below 140 once the investment is done. This fundamental transformation in the bargaining positions as a result of specific investments is summarized in Fig. 8.2.

	Ex ante	Ex post
Upstream inventor	200	140
Downstream party	240	240

Figure 8.2: Reservation prices before and after the fundamental transformation

Various unforeseen circumstances can be used by the downstream party as a reason to reduce the price of 220. The incompleteness of contracts creates these opportunities. Bargaining is ex-post about the quasi-surplus, i.e. $40 + K$, instead of the surplus, i.e. 40. The assumption regarding the bargaining power or strength entails that each party receives 50 of the quasi-surplus of 100. The contract price is therefore ex-post 190. Figure 8.3 shows the effect of the fundamental transformation on the contract price.

	Ex ante	Ex post
Contract price	220	190

Figure 8.3: Contract prices before and after the fundamental transformation

Renegotiating the contract by the downstream party is called *hold-up*. The party which has made the relation-specific investments finds itself in a disadvantageous position, because the other party has various possibilities of reducing the price of the contract. Threats to break up the relationship may be used to stipulate better contract conditions than those agreed upon at first. This is possible because contracts are incomplete and there are hardly any other partners available, because of the sunk character of the investments. Unspecified contingencies are the gaps in the contract and can be used by one party to improve its position at the cost of the other party. Williamson uses the term *ex-post haggling* for such activities (in non-verifiable circumstances), where the haggling is about the quasi-surplus. Ex-post haggling is expressed in various bargaining problems.

Hold-up is not necessarily inefficient. If there are no wealth effects and the investment is done anyway, then the surplus of 40 is realized. The only effect of hold-up is a redistribution of the quasi-surplus. However, the prospect of hold-up often results in a hold-up problem. If the investments are made by the upstream inventor, then the downstream party has various possibilities of claiming ex post a larger share of the surplus.

The inventor is not stupid and anticipates these problems, by looking forward and reasoning backward. The result is that he will not invest in developing the valuable software. This is called the hold-up problem. The above project is desirable from a welfare perspective, because it yields a surplus of 40, but the prospect of hold-up results in no investment at all. This is obviously inefficient.

Figure 8.4 presents the hold-up problem. The upstream inventor has first to decide whether to invest. If he decides not to, then each party receives 0. If he does decide to invest, then the downstream party chooses subsequently between no hold-up and hold-up. The downstream party earns 20 in the first situation and $240 - 190 = 50$ in the second situation. It is clear that the downstream party will choose hold-up, given the opportunistic behavioural assumption. The inventor anticipates this behaviour. He anticipates that the hold-up option will be chosen when the investment has been made, which will result in a loss of 10. Not investing will generate a payment of 0. The inventor will therefore not invest. This is a dramatic example of transaction costs.

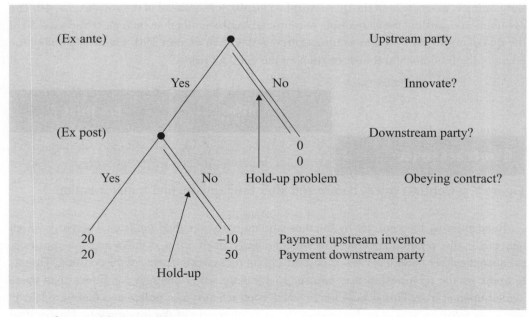

Figure 8.4: Hold-up problem

8.3 **Transaction costs economics**

A starting-point for the analysis of the choice of governance structure is to assume that a governance structure is chosen which minimizes total costs, i.e. the joint transaction and production costs. Transaction costs economics simplifies this analysis by assuming that transaction and production costs, e.g. the presence or absence of economies of scale, are determined separately and can be added together in order to determine the total costs of a certain way of organizing. It implies that production costs can be ignored in determining the most efficient choice of governance, i.e. the choice of governance structure is driven by minimizing transaction costs, according to transaction costs economics.

Transaction-specific investments are the crucial ingredient in transaction costs economics. They are desirable because they generate value; for example, tailoring the investment to the wishes of the customer creates additional surplus. However, according to transaction costs theory, it is not desirable to start a market relationship when significant transaction-specific investments are involved. If the investment is made, then, because of the incompleteness of contracts, various possibilities may arise for ex-post opportunistic behaviour. Examples are ex-post haggling or hold-up. In case such ex-post reneging is not immediately plausible, imagine that the inventor is an employee in the R&D lab of a large pharmaceutical firm, and that the firm has promised to share the profits from inventions 50–50 with the inventor. If the inventor creates a drug worth 10 billion euros, do we expect the firm to keep its promise? Contracts are therefore not the solution to handling the information and incentive problems in such a way that a profitable project is implemented. The person or persons making the specific investment anticipate these problems and may not invest. Governance solutions are necessary to create the circumstances such that valuable specific investments are made. How would the situation regarding ex-post opportunistic behaviour in the above example differ if the inventor had worked in his or her own independent research firm? This is the topic of transaction costs economics.

Transaction costs economics tries to explain the type of organization which will be chosen for transactions. Instead of organization, Williamson (1985) uses the term 'governance structure'. The transaction is the unit of analysis, while governance structures are chosen depending on the characteristics of the transaction. The characteristics of the transaction, i.e. the exogenous variables, are the frequency with which a transaction occurs, the degree of asset specificity and the degree of uncertainty which surrounds the transaction. The endogenous variable is the choice of the governance structure. The behavioural assumptions are opportunism and limited rationality. Figure 8.5 summarizes the structure of the theory.

Many organizational forms or contractual relations can be distinguished, but for sake of simplicity only short-term contracts, long-term contracts and vertical integration are discussed. It will be clear that transactions which occur once in a while do not qualify for long-term contracts or vertical integration. Therefore, we will consider from now on only regularly recurring transactions. For each of the three governance structures the dimensions of the transaction (level of asset specificity, degree of uncertainty, frequency) will be specified in which the particular governance structure is efficient. Transaction costs are used in a broad sense, i.e. the motivation and co-ordination problems associated with a specific organization of activities. Each organizational form has its own advantages and disadvantages.

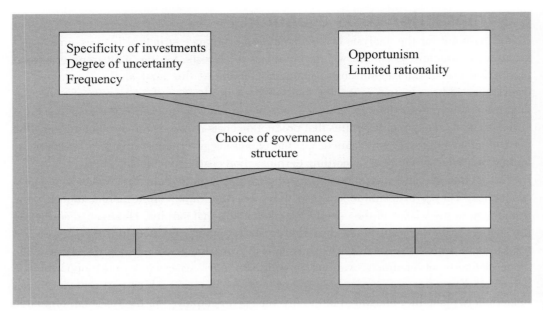

Figure 8.5: Transaction costs economics

Transactions with a low level of asset specificity are governed by market exchange. There are sufficient alternatives available to punish bad behaviour without making high costs. After being deceived, you just deal with someone else. A standard product like grain is offered by many suppliers at the same level of quality, and there are many buyers. The market will ensure an efficient allocation, and authority is not needed. However, transactions requiring a high level of asset specificity are not suited for such short-term contracts, because the ex-post bargaining position regarding the division of the surplus is too poor. The fear will be that the other party will claim the entire surplus. A different governance structure is needed in order to take this fear away.

Figure 8.6 represents this by adding a governance structure stage to Fig. 8.4. An example of governance structure is the market, a long-term contract or vertical integration. A governance structure like vertical integration offers certain safeguards against bad behaviour, while these are not present in the market. With the above payments it is clear that there will be no investment in a market relationship, because hold-up is anticipated once the investment is done. Vertical integration removes the fear of hold-up, and results therefore in valuable investment. Notice that the initial decision node indicates no decision-maker. This is done on purpose, and reflects that transaction costs economics assumes that somehow the efficient governance structure is adopted. This may be a good starting-point for formulating insights regarding governance structure, because very inefficient choices are not likely to survive. (However, there is no guarantee that efficient outcomes will emerge. Strategic considerations may result in an equilibrium governance structure which is inefficient, i.e. the competition between a limited number of firms may drive the choice of various internal organizational decisions. This is the topic of Part V.)

In a situation with a high level of asset specificity, long-term contracts and vertical integration remain as possible efficient forms of governance. The uncertainty which

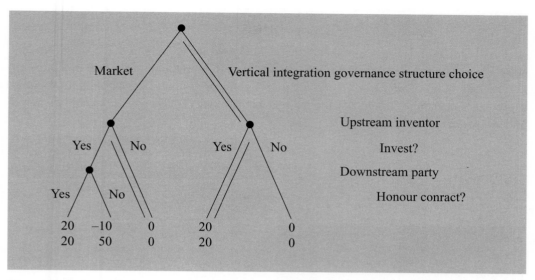

Figure 8.6: Specific investments and governance structure

surrounds a transaction is the exogenous variable which determines which governance structure is efficient. The degree of uncertainty says something about the incompleteness of contracts and the possibilities for ex-post renegotiation in order to claim ex post a larger part of the surplus. A high degree of uncertainty provides many possibilities for ex-post renegotiation, because the causes for a specific outcome are hard to discover and hard to prove. Bringing inside the organization those transactions which require a high level of asset specificity, i.e. vertical integration, changes the ex-post bargaining position in a favourable way, because it aligns previously conflicting interests and eliminates a number of choices. The fear of hold-up may result in the hold-up problem, i.e. surplus-generating investments may not be made when exchange takes place in the market because of the high level of asset specificity. Vertical integration is a way to prevent the hold-up problem, because the conflict of interest between the parties is removed.

Vertical integration is a way to solve certain problems in situations with a high level of asset specificity, but it also introduces a number of internal organizational problems, which do not outweigh the benefits of vertical integration when there is a lot of uncertainty. However, bad behaviour is undesirable in stable markets, because many other parties will find out about it. In the future this will be harmful for the party engaging in it, because , for example, other parties will not be inclined to do business with such a company. A long-term contract is therefore the governance structure which will be chosen in a market with limited uncertainty, because having a good reputation is important in such markets. Bad behaviour is more undesirable when reputation plays an important role in relationships. The value of a reputation depends on how often a transaction occurs, the time span of the relationship, and the profitability of the separate transactions. A reputation is more valuable when transactions occur more often, the relationship lasts longer and the profitability of separate transactions increases. (Chapter 10 will address this more extensively.) The implication is that one usually holds a limited number of contacts. It is not desirable for any party to hold just one or two contacts, because it creates too strong a dependence on one or two other parties. Nor is it desirable to have many contacts, either, because any party wants to be large (important) enough to remain attractive for each of the others.

Finally, if the level of asset specificity is low, then the efficient choice of governance structure is the market. There is no fear of hold-up, and internal organizational problems are absent with this governance structure. Figure 8.7 summarizes the above predictions of transaction costs economics when only the exogenous variables of asset specificity and degree of uncertainty are taken into account.

		Degree of uncertainty	
		Low	High
Asset specificity	Low	Market	Market
	High	Long-term contract	Hierarchy

Figure 8.7: Governance structure choice as a function of asset specificity and the degree of uncertainty

Figure 8.4 assumed a situation in which the upstream and downstream party transacted only once. However, transactions often occur repeatedly. Short-term as well as long-run considerations are important in the decision-making process. It is often advantageous to display bad behaviour in the short run. The prisoners dilemma is a famous example. Bad behaviour is nevertheless costly in the long run, because trust is broken. Once this happens, no one wants to conclude a transaction again with the miscreant. Good behaviour is more likely when future transactions are more important, a situation to be discussed more extensively in Chapter 10.

The hypotheses of transaction costs economics can also be formulated in terms of the level of asset specificity and the frequency with which transactions occur. This is presented in Fig. 8.8. In a unilateral governance structure, of which vertical integration is an example, one party has the power. An example of a bilateral governance structure is a long-term contract; here both parties are independent and have comparable power. Many buyer–seller relationships have this character. Transactions between two parties which are specific and occur infrequently are often established by an external intermediator. One example is the sale of a house. Intermediaries like estate agents may reduce transaction costs like search costs, surveys and dispute resolution. An important incentive for them to do their job well is that they care about their reputation. This is important if they are to be selected as intermediaries in other transactions.

Figure 8.9 summarizes Williamson's hypotheses in terms of the most important exogenous variable in transactions cost economics. The market as governance structure is not suitable for transactions requiring a high level of asset specificity, because the investor is afraid he or she will not get any money back because of the ex-post non-competitive bargaining situation. By internalizing the transaction in the company, the bargaining problems disappear by means of selective intervention. Define the degree of specificity as k. If the degree of specificity of investments is low, i.e. $k \in [0, k_1]$, then the governance structure market has the lowest costs

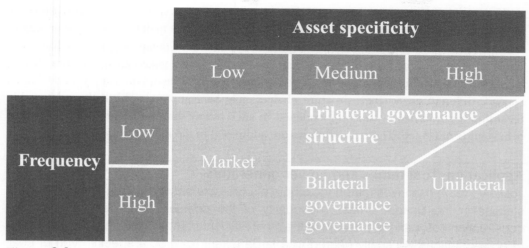

Figure 8.8: Adapted with the permission of The Free Press, a Division of Simon & Schuster Adult Publishing Group, from *The Economic Institutions of Capitalism: Firms, Markets, Rational Contracting,* by Oliver E. Williamson. Copyright © 1985 by Oliver E. Williamson

$M(k)$. For a high level of asset specificity, the hierarchy has the lowest governance costs $H(k)$. In a hierarchical governance structure one party has the residual control rights in all possible unforeseen circumstances. Examples of governance structure hierarchies are stock exchange listed companies, partnerships, labour-managed firms and co-operatives. A hybrid governance structure is chosen to minimize the governance costs when the level of asset specificity is at an intermediate level, i.e. $k \epsilon [k_1, k_2]$. Examples of hybrid governance structures are franchises, joint ventures and co-makership relationships.

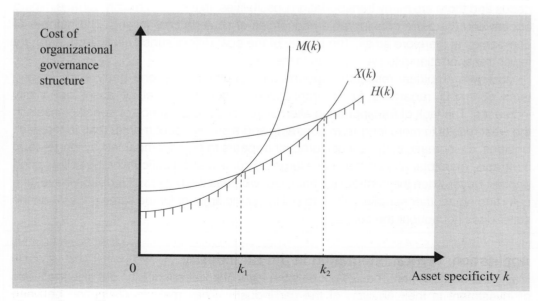

Figure 8.9: Efficient governance structure choice and asset specificity (Williamson, 1991, p. 284) *Administrative Science Quarterly* Volume 36, No. 2

Various empirical studies have used the transaction costs perspective as a starting-point to discover some structure in the data. The aim of such research is to determine whether organizational choices mitigate the negative results of opportunistic behaviour in a credible way. Three types of empirical studies can be distinguished. First, the governance structure characteristics are aligned in such a way that a preliminary ending of the relationship is undesirable. Second, different governance structure choices may be compared. Third, the relationship regarding the transaction can be broadened in such a way that the scope for opportunistic behaviour is mitigated. These possibilities are addressed in the following applications.

Application: Coal mines and power generators

Joskow (1987) has investigated the length of contracts between coal mines and power stations in the United States. The quality of the coal has a large impact on the construction costs and the design of the most efficient combustion oven, i.e. the design of power stations is usually geared to a large extent towards a specific type of coal. Deficiency in the quality of the coal results in bad performance of the oven and possibly costly adjustments. Therefore the power station is tied to a certain type of coal when the design of the oven has been chosen. These specific assets do not necessarily imply that power stations are tied completely to one particular coal supplier. Whether they are in fact so tied depends among other things on variations in the quality of the coal and the available transportation possibilities. If the quality of the coal is relatively homogeneous and the power stations have many alternative sources of supply, then they are not 'locked in' with one specific supplier.

Coal mining is done in the eastern as well as the western part of the USA. The mines in the east are mainly underground and are characterized by limited economies of scale. Many small companies are therefore active. The quality of the coal is relatively homogeneous and there are many transportation possibilities. In the west, mainly surface mining occurs and there are considerable economies of scale in coal mining. The number of companies is therefore small. The quality of the coal differs substantially and there are fewer transportation alternatives than in the east.

Joskow's empirical research supports the hypothesis that one party signs longer-term contracts regarding future transactions when the level of asset specificity increases. The lack of transportation alternatives and the presence of specific assets in the west results in more long-term contracts and a smaller spot market than in the east. Besides, an increase in the annual turnover appears to be accompanied by longer-term contracts. An explanation is that these large amounts make it difficult for the seller to find another buyer when the contract is cancelled, whereas the buyer will probably have difficulty finding another supplier willing to sell the same amount for the same price when the seller does not honour the contract.

Application: Vertical integration in the car industry

Masten *et al.* (1989) emphasize not only the level of asset specificity, but also the types of investment in their analysis of the car industry. They make a distinction between specific investments in physical and human capital.

Specific investments are distinguished regarding ownership and organization. Ownership of specific investments eliminates opportunistic behaviour, because the right to use the machines concerned can be allocated to somebody else. This threat may be sufficient to discourage such behaviour. Vertical integration is a way to organize the production of parts, but this production can also be done outside the company. Car companies often own specific tools with which independent suppliers produce parts. This distinction between ownership and organization cannot be made with specific human capital, because ownership of humans is forbidden by law.

The difference between these two types of specific investment is expressed in the choice of organization. The empirical research indicates that vertical integration can be better explained by investments in specific technological know-how than investments in specific production material. Companies probably expect more problems regarding the exchange of knowledge than with specific tools.

Application: Organization of research in the pharmaceutical industry

The development of new drugs is a complex activity and requires fundamental research. There is a lot of uncertainty involved, as well as various specific investments. Vertical integration seems to be the most attractive way to organize the research, because achievements can probably be evaluated best internally and sensitive information stays within the company.

Pharmaceutical companies use also a number of other possibilities to organize their R&D processes. An important reason is that bureaucratic habits can frustrate the research climate in various ways. This has resulted increasingly in the outsourcing of research to independent laboratories or co-operation with a university. A disadvantage of outsourcing is that there may be problems with the transmission of information regarding the research results.

Independent university researchers have according to Tapon (1989) fewer possibilities for opportunistic behaviour than independent laboratories. The evaluation of scientific articles and proposals by independent peers, the possibilities for duplication of experimental results and also the concern for the academic reputation are all responsible for this. The results are protected by the patent system. These considerations explain the increasing long-term co-operation between universities and pharmaceutical companies.

Application: Granting licences

Developing a new computer chip may create huge advantages. These chips exist in many types and sizes, but a specific chip has very specific characteristics. This is a problem for the inventor when customers have to make specific investments, like educating employees and technical adaptations, in order to use the technology effectively. Customers are willing to do this when the price of chips remains low in the future, but the monopolist cannot promise this in a credible way (Shephard, 1987). It is ex-post, i.e. after the investment of the customers has been made, attractive for the monopolist to raise the price and to deliver less service. Customers anticipate this behaviour, which reduces the demand for these chips.

The inventor can establish credibility by imposing certain limitations on himself. Making the new technology available for competitors is viewed from this perspective (Farrell and Gallini, 1988). The increased competition does no longer allows high prices or bad service, but the reduced possibilities for ex-post opportunistic behaviour result in an increase in demand. Granting licences is a commitment for low prices and good service in the future.

This application illustrates that the choice of organizational form in equilibrium does not entail the minimization of transaction costs, but the minimization of the production and transaction costs jointly, which cannot be treated separately when the organization is chosen. Higher production costs in the form of lost economies of scale and learning effects are accepted by the inventor in granting a licence in order to minimize the transaction costs which would otherwise be incurred in the bilateral monopoly.

Application: Hostages

Contractual agreements are not always honoured and enforced by the courts. Private parties respond to this observation by looking for alternative contractual safeguards. Hostages are used to support exchange when substantial asset specificity is involved, i.e. they provide incentives for honouring contracts. They can have both ex-ante (screening) and ex-post (bonding) effects (Williamson, 1983).

There are various types of hostage constructions, like requiring that the other party also invest in specific assets and recurring future exchange. The willingness of both parties to invest in specific assets indicates that they both value the relationship. This may be necessary in order to start the relationship, given the fear of opportunistic behaviour. The reciprocity of transactions can be interpreted as a credible commitment to reduce the likelihood of opportunistic behaviour. Similarly, both parties have also an interest in a continuation of the relationship once investments are done. A preliminary breakdown of the relationship is not attractive, because the possibilities for alternative use are limited by the specificity of the assets.

Application: Catering and transportation services

Many companies have gone back to their core business activities. Activities like catering and transportation services have been outsourced. This can be understood from a perspective of transaction costs economics. There are various costs associated with the internal organization of these activities. Among the most important additional costs are the higher salaries that have to be paid compared with independent catering and transportation companies. The desire for a balanced or equitable salary structure may be responsible for this. Another aspect is that specific investments are hardly involved. There are many transportation and catering companies. Both considerations argue against vertical integration of these activities.

Application: Flexible production technologies

Several technological developments have resulted in the replacement of very specialized equipment by more general, flexible production technologies. A well-known example is the car industry. In the early twentieth century, Henry Ford rationalized car manufacturing by introducing equipment specifically designed to produce a single standardized product. At the end of the twentieth century, General Motors engineers were able to reset their equipment for the production of another type of car in a few days. Other examples are to be found in the field of electric controls and in the aerospace industry (Milgrom and Roberts, 1990c).

According to transaction costs economics, this switch to flexible production technologies should encourage investments by independent companies, and it decreases the costs of short-term contracts compared with other governance structures, like long-term contracts and vertical integration. Activities are increasingly outsourced, which on the one hand saves on internal co-ordination and motivation costs and on the other requires the establishment of stable relationships with external parties.

Application: Financial governance

Williamson (1988) approaches the choice of financial instruments from the same perspective as the choice of organizational form. In transaction costs economics, debt and equity are financial instruments as well as governance instruments. The characterization of these financial instruments in terms of governance is the core of this application.

Each financial instrument specifies certain control rights and income rights. Debt is characterized by rigid contract rules, like interest payments at fixed intervals in time, liquidity tests and payback requirements at the end of the term. The creditor has claim priority when bankruptcy occurs. The rigidity of the rules governing debt means that they apply to all possible contingencies. The attractiveness of this rigidity is that only a few standard contract rules are considered, which implies that the startup costs of the design of a debt contract are low. The disadvantage of having only a few simple rules is that they are often not well tailored to a particular unforeseen contingency. Their rigidity may prevent efficient adjustment always being made ex post, i.e. debt entails maladaptations to circumstances which are not envisioned in the design of the contract ex ante. This is especially problematic when the hold-up problem looms, i.e. a situation in which efficient investment entails a high level of asset specificity. The implication (of the inability of a few simple rules to respond to all possible contingencies efficiently) is that the risk associated with the transaction rises. Higher risk translates into a higher interest rate, i.e. the cost of debt rises sharply when the level of asset specificity increases.

Equity is a governance structure in which financiers are given rights of control. Outside equity assigns financiers the role of residual claimants in good as well as bad times, there is no payback date and a board of directors is appointed with extensive power to control the management. The variety and flexibility of the control mechanisms available to the board (e.g. power to replace management, access internal performance measures, authorize audits for special follow-up purposes and apprise important investment and operating proposals before they are implemented) allow it to adjust decisions more efficiently to a variety of ex-post circumstances than the rigid financial governance instrument debt. This flexibility of the board to intervene ex post gives financiers confidence that their resources will be used in their interests and will therefore result in lower costs of capital than debt in situations with a high level of asset specificity.

Equity is more complex than debt, because a variety of control mechanisms, like a board, have to be developed. The startup costs of equity are therefore higher than those of debt. The costs of debt as well as those of equity show a positive relationship with the level of asset specificity, but the costs of debt increase faster than the cost of equity. The rigidity (regarding ex-post adjustments) of debt increases the attractiveness of outside equity compared with debt when the level of asset specificity increases.

Only two financial instruments have been distinguished: debt and equity. There are also hybrid forms, which have characteristics of both debt and equity, e.g. warrants and convertible bonds. The costs of these intermediate financial governance structures are also a function of the degree of asset specificity (Williamson, 1988). Figure 8.10 summarizes the above graphically, where $D(k)$, ($Y(k)$, $E(k)$) are the costs of debt (hybrid finance and equity) as a function of the level of asset specificity. The prediction is that debt will be used for projects with a low level of asset specificity ($k < k_3$). Examples are cars and office buildings. Equity will be used when the degree of asset specificity is high ($k > k_4$). Hybrid financial governance structures are expected for intermediate levels of asset specificity ($k_3 < k < k_4$).

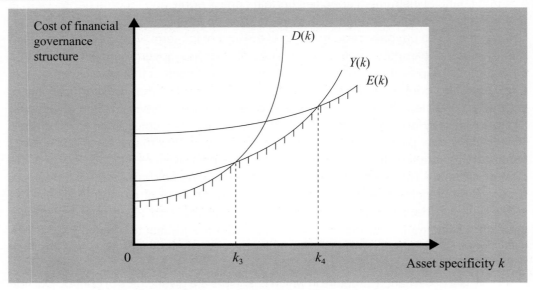

Figure 8.10: Financial governance structure and asset specificity

The above can also illustrate the financial governance differences regarding equity between the USA and continental Europe. Many European countries have only limited rights for shareholders and the market for corporate control is almost non-existent (owing to the extensive use of anti-takeover measures). The providers of equity are the owners of the firm in the USA, whereas all kinds of restrictions are imposed by European law on the rights of outside financiers. Outside equity holders in Europe receive a standard dividend, whereas the remaining part of profits may go to employees and slack. Equity carries limited control rights for the shareholders and therefore does not differ much from debt. This implies that the value of k_4 is larger in Europe than in the USA. Shareholders are aware of this and ask compensation for these reduced control rights. Figure 8.11 reflects this by positioning E_{EU} above E_{USA}.

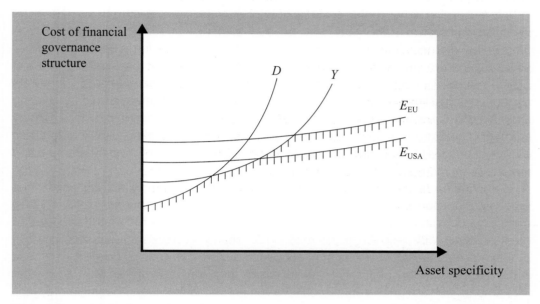

Figure 8.11: Anti-takeover measures, governance structure and asset specificity

Application: Marketing co-operatives

Agricultural and horticultural co-operatives came into existence in the nineteenth century. One aspect of the emergence of co-operatives is the ability of producer-members to achieve economies of size by pooling products and resources. Another aspect is the perishability of the harvest. It puts a small farmer in a weak bargaining position when a price has to be negotiated with a relatively large processor. The fear of the farmer is that there will be hold-up in the negotiation process. Countervailing power is needed to eliminate this fear and is created by downstream or forward integration of many small private farmers into a marketing co-operative (MC). The MC was successful for an extended period. However, at the start of the twent-first century co-operatives seem to face more difficulties than stock exchange listed companies in handling the increasing demand for differentiated products with their investments in specific assets. Farmers as well as external financiers of MCs became dissatisfied.

An MC is not an efficient organizational form when final product markets demand differentiated products, requiring sizeable funds from outside financiers for specific investments at the processing or downstream stage of production (Hendrikse and Veerman, 2001b). The reason is that farmers decide about investments at the downstream stage of production when they are organized in an MC, while the outside financier has no control over how his or her funds are invested. The corporation or investor-owned firm, in which shareholders are the owners of the enterprise, allocates control over investment decisions to shareholders, which gives them confidence that their money will be spent well. We will refer to a corporation or an investor-owned firm as a conventional firm (CF). Farmers have the decision power with respect to processing in an MC, whereas the providers of external equity decide regarding processing in a CF.

Internal and external control systems both play a role in disciplining decision-making in an organization. An MC seems to be a governance structure which has a well-functioning internal control system. First, input suppliers have a large personal financial stake in the downstream firm. This provides a credible signal that they will do their job of policing internal decision-making well. Second, the lack of the market for corporate control enhances the incentives for members in an MC to generate a well-functioning internal control system even further. Shares of an MC are not traded in the stock market. Members therefore face difficulties in trading their financial stakes. Stockholders can easily get out of a CF by selling their stock in the market. Members of an MC cannot, and therefore pay more attention to the way the MC is being run.

Democratic decision-making in an MC encounters some difficulties. First, the process of opinion formation and decision-making regarding important policy shifts is more time-consuming than in other organizational forms. This reduces flexibility and creates inertia with respect to the reaction to changing market circumstances. This problem seems to increasing as markets become more complex. Second, an increase in the degree of asset specificity (k) exacerbates the disadvantages an MC has to face. Investments with a higher k entail less involvement of the members, because they lack the specific knowledge to form an opinion and give their fiat. Higher outlays are therefore required for a well-functioning democratic process of decision-making and the preservation of the 'organized trust'. The process of decision-making will also take more time, because the degree of complexity probably increases with a higher level of asset specificity, especially in a globalizing economy. Third, if k increases without a direct relation with the original activities of the MC (and thereby with the basic activities of the members), members seem to be less informed regarding the corresponding value and risks than are shareholders in a CF. This makes members reluctant to accept that a large part of the surplus will be kept as retained earnings, unless an acceptable rate of profitability on other investments (including their own farm) is realized.

An MC and a CF are two different hierarchical governance structures. Figure 8.12 summarizes the above account of the differences between MCs and CFs with the level of asset specificity at the processing stage of production on the horizontal axis (Hendrikse and Veerman, 2001b). In Fig. 8.9 a hierarchy is a cost-minimizing governance structure when the degree of asset specificity of investments is higher than k_2. MCs and CFs are examples of hierarchies and therefore have to be analysed in this domain. The $H(k)$-curve of an MC is below (above) the $H(k)$-curve of a CF when the advantages of an MC outweigh (are smaller than) the disadvantages. The observations in this section imply that the $H(k)$-curve of an MC is steeper than the $H(k)$-curve of a CF, i.e. the intense monitoring by the farmers of investment decisions is an attractive feature of an MC, but it decreases in effectiveness when the specificity of investments is increasing. Figure 8.12 reflects a situation where an MC is an efficient governance structure for intermediate levels of asset specificity, i.e. $k_2 < k < k_5$. An MC will not emerge or disappear when the costs of its governance structure are higher than those of a CF for every value of k higher than k_2, i.e. $k_2 > k_5$.

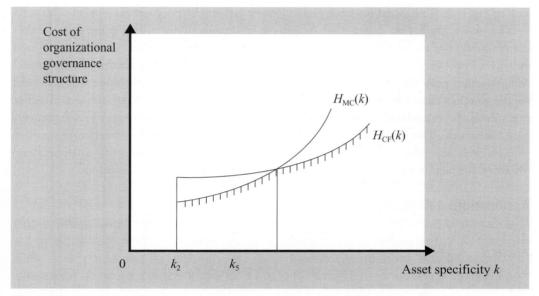

Figure 8.12: Marketing co-operatives versus firms (Hendrikse and Veerman, 2001b, p. 211)

8.4 Measurement problems and bargaining costs

The explanation of transaction costs economics in the previous sections focused on the specificity of investments. Another approach emphasizes the problems associated with the measurement of costs and benefits (Barzel, 1982). The starting-point of the analysis is the observation that often considerable time and energy are spent on measuring individual costs and benefits, while only total costs and benefits are important from the perspective of efficiency. The expectation is therefore that various measures are taken in order to reduce non-productive activities. Predictions are formulated again regarding the choice of governance structure. As in the specific investments approach, a prescriptive concept (efficiency) is used to formulate predictions. It is therefore assumed that the most efficient governance structure is chosen. In the measurement approach the governance structure with the lowest measurement costs is chosen.

An important ingredient in the design of explicit incentives in Chapter 6 was the measurability of the contribution of the agent. Limited measurability problems (V low) result in strong incentives (Sec. 6.2), while hard-to-measure activities argue for weak incentives (Sec. 6.3). Another ingredient in the choice of governance structure is the degree of risk aversion. This may argue against vertical integration, because becoming the owner entails carrying a lot of risk. This is unattractive for a highly risk-averse agent. These considerations result in the prediction that a contract with explicit incentives instead of vertical integration is chosen when measurability is hardly a problem and risks associated with ownership are large. In a contract, risks are shared by both parties. However, if measurability is a problem and ownership entails a limited uncertainty, then vertical integration is the most desirable governance structure. Notice that measurability problems can be an explanation for integration, regardless of the level of asset specificity. Measurement costs have to be on the horizontal axis in Fig. 8.9. (Empirical research has to determine which specification is most relevant.)

The above prediction means that incentives in organizations will in general be weaker than in market relations. Integration concerns activities which are hard to measure. Explicit incentives are therefore hard to implement and are not advised according to the equal compensation principle. It is expected from this perspective that a freelance writer is paid for the number of words in an article, while an employee is paid a fixed amount. Another example is the relationship between the reward structure of store managers and the governance structure. The local store manager with a franchise contract has strong incentives to perform well according to this theory, while the manager of the same store will hardly be rewarded for results when he is an employee of the company owning the outlets.

Application: Salespeople

Anderson and Schmittlein (1984) test the specific investments and measurement cost approaches in the electrical components industry. Specific investments apply to the knowledge of the product assortment and the interests of the customers, while measurement costs concern the impact of the efforts of the salesperson on total sales. The choice of governance structure is between independent salespersons and an own salesperson. The specific investments perspective predicts that vertical integration is more likely when specific investments are more important, while the measurement perspective predicts a positive relationship between the extent of vertical integration and the size of the measurement problems. Their empirical results show that the measurement problems have the largest explanatory power for the choice of governance structure in the electrical components industry.

Application: Sales methods

The choice of sales method by enterprises has been explained from the perspective of market power as well as product differentiation. Kenney and Klein (1983) explain the sales method of diamonds by De Beers from the perspective of measurement costs. The customer specifies the desired diamonds. Subsequently, De Beers composes a package of diamonds and a price about which no bargaining is possible. Refusal of the package and the price implies that the customer will not be invited to submit a specification in the future. This sales method differs strongly from a traditional market where the price of each diamond is negotiated and both parties spend considerable time on determining the precise quality of a stone. The advantage of the De Beers sales method is that bargaining costs are eliminated and the inspection costs of the diamonds reduced.

A similar comparison is formulated for the payment of royalties instead of a fixed payment to authors by publishers. Paying royalties prevents time and energy being spent on estimating market demand in order to determine the right amount. Fruits and vegetables are another example: they are packed in order to prevent unnecessary inspections. Movie studios offer usually various movies at the same time; this limits the number of choices for the movie theatres, which reduces their evaluation costs.

There is a third formulation of transaction costs economics, next to the specific investments approach and the measurement costs approach. This approach focuses on the bargaining costs regarding exchange. Bargaining costs consist of monitoring and executing an agreement, and the costs associated with delay in the negotiations, or their collapse.

Milgrom and Roberts (1990a) distinguish three kinds of bargaining problem. First, there is the co-ordination problem. This argues for bringing the transaction inside the organization, because co-ordination is an important task of management. A second source of bargaining inefficiencies is the costs associated with the collection of information. A lot of time is spent on determining the costs and benefits of a project, because it is known that proposals are submitted by self-interested or opportunistic individuals. Only the total costs and benefits are important from an efficiency perspective, not the individual interests. The third problem is asymmetric information regarding the reservation prices of the involved parties. This offers possibilities for the misrepresentation of preferences, where exchange may not occur even though it is attractive for everybody (this has already been dealt with in Chapter 7).

If bargaining costs are zero, then market exchange is always efficient. Inefficient contracts are replaced costlessly by contracts which result in efficient decisions. (The involved parties have to be risk-neutral and anticipate the future, and there should be no asymmetric information.)

Market exchange is efficient when there are no bargaining costs, regardless of the frequency of transactions, the degree of uncertainty and the level of asset specificity.

There is no reason to doubt the efficiency of market exchange when there are no bargaining costs, because every contract which does not maximize the surplus will be replaced by a contract which induces efficient decisions. The fear of ending up ex post in a disadvantageous bargaining position due to the specificity of investments has no direct influence on efficiency (size of the surplus), but it affects the distribution of the surplus. Circumstances can therefore be specified such that market exchange is strictly preferred above other governance structures.

The bargaining approach replaces specific investments, uncertainty and frequency of transactions with bargaining costs. The horizontal axis in Fig. 8.9 has therefore to be labelled with bargaining costs in order to represent the bargaining costs approach. Markets are efficient when there are no bargaining costs, although this is only rarely the case, especially when there are specific investments.

Efficient bargaining usually requires some competition. However, there is a bilateral monopoly after the fundamental transformation, where each party develops activities in order to receive a larger share of the surplus. (Specific investments can therefore result in bargaining costs, which may be an explanation for the success of the specific investments approach.) The governance structure hierarchy eliminates bargaining problems associated with market exchange. Other problems are associated with developing activities within firms, but these problems may be less important for certain activities than the problems associated with the governance structure market exchange.

8.5 Influence costs

The fundamental welfare theorem indicates that there will be a market for every product and every service, and that in each of these markets the price will equate the quantity demanded with the quantity supplied. This result also extends to internal labour markets and therefore to every position in an organization and all organizational changes, where financial compensations are based on demand and supply, such that nobody experiences any disadvantage. However, the assumptions underlying the fundamental welfare theorem are often not satisfied in internal labour markets. This is due to all kinds of specific characteristics of a job being not included and rewarded in a labour contract.

These imperfections of the labour market are the starting-point of the *influence costs* theory. The effect of these costs on labour contracts and the design of an efficient organization is analysed by Milgrom (1988). Influence costs are defined as the costs of activities aimed at changing organizational decisions to allow interested parties to capture organizational rents. Examples are political activities, lobbying and distorting or manipulating information. One common way performance measures can deviate from the real outcome is that the agent can take actions to increase the reported measure without increasing the real performance. This activity can be thought of as 'performance padding', 'window dressing' or even lobbying supervisors. It can also be considered as a form of earnings management. The (undesirable) aspects in the behaviour of those who inform and advise the decision-maker, and the information flows associated with various organizational forms, will all now receive attention. Organizations respond to influence activities by limiting the access to the decision-making process and by reducing the rents for which the parties compete.

Influence activities are an example of hidden actions, because the employer (principal) cannot determine completely which information is intended for which purposes. Organizational interest cannot be distinguished from self-interest by the employer. It entails three types of costs. First, influence activities may be harmful for the organization, because time and effort could be spent in more productive ways, or just in more leisure. Second, the distortion in the information and advice received by the employer may result in bad decisions for the organization. Third, even if the organization anticipates these activities, there are still costs involved in organizational precautions in order to limit these activities. Notice that these considerations reduce the importance of the contractual solutions offered in Part III. This is a second reason for not using contracts with explicit incentives, besides the equal compensation principle (Sec. 6.3.1).

An employee exhibits influence activities because the incompleteness of contracts prevents all the relevant information being included in a contract. If there are both attractive and unattractive jobs in an organization, and it is too expensive for the employer to design a complete contingent labour contract for each position, then each employee has an interest in influencing the decision-making process such that he obtains the attractive position. A labour contract can be renegotiated if new information arises and this turns out to be advantageous ex post for the parties involved. These limits to the credibility of the binding character of contracts result in inefficiencies. An efficient organization anticipates this kind of behaviour and tries, like a system of prices in a well-functioning market economy, to channel the interest of the employees in such a way that productive actions result.

Transaction costs economics focuses on asset specificity in the analysis of organizational choice, while the influence costs approach highlights bargaining costs and the costs of centralized decision-making (Milgrom and Roberts, 1990d). Market exchange is efficient when the costs of bargaining are zero, i.e. the Coase theorem and the fundamental welfare theorem apply. However, this condition is usually not satisfied, which provides possibilities for other organizational forms to be efficient because they may be able to reduce bargaining inefficiencies, or even eliminate them. This is often easier for an integrated entity, and more possibilities are available for monitoring internal parties than external ones, e.g. accounting checks. An integrated context probably reduces conflicts of interest to a certain extent because of a different atmosphere and feelings of loyalty.

There are two requirements for the occurrence of influence activities. First, somebody has to have the power to take decisions the impact of which for the various organizational members is not yet clear. Second, the interested organizational members have to have access to means in order to influence the decision-maker. A drastic solution with regard to the first requirement, which is almost always fulfilled in organizations, is to abandon the policy of selective intervention by divesting certain departments. However, if this is not desirable then the organization has to take precautions internally in order to reduce influence activities as much as possible.

Notice the difference in emphasis between transaction costs economics and the influence costs approach. Transaction costs economics takes a market failure perspective. The firm is viewed as the governance structure of last resort, i.e. try markets, try hybrids and choose the firm as governance mode for the transaction only when all else fails. The influence costs approach takes the opposing position by taking an organizational failure perspective. The market is viewed as the governance structure of last resort.

8.5.1 Selective intervention

An important aspect of an integrated entity is the authority and autonomy of the top management (Arrow, 1974). Centralized decision-making entails extensive discretion to resolve conflicts and to intervene in the decisions at lower echelons, while these decisions are somewhat insulated from intervention by third parties. This latter aspect corresponds with the judicial practice of forbearance, i.e. courts refuse jurisdiction over internal disputes except where fraud, illegality or conflict of interest is shown. Williamson (2002, p. 441) observes:

> Because the courts forbear, the firm, in effect, becomes its own court of ultimate appeal. Firms therefore have access to fiat, and the coordination benefits that accrue thereto, that markets do not.

The centralization of decisions in organizations provides the employer with the possibility to intervene selectively (Simon, 1951; Arrow, 1974). Selective intervention means the employer can decide to a certain extent what the employee has to do.

Organizations using the power to intervene selectively well could in principle perform as well as the separate organizational parts or even better, and such a company could in theory be limitless in size. However, this is not what we observe. Coase (1937, p. 394) therefore raised the question: 'Why is not all production carried out by one big firm?' Milgrom and Roberts (1990d) analyse the costs associated with centralized decision power. The costs of political activities, i.e. influence costs, are emphasized. They answer the question 'Why cannot a large firm do everything a collection of smaller firms can do, and more?' by systematically delineating the consequences of selective intervention. An increase in the decision power of top management increases the possibilities of intervening selectively, which confers not only a number of advantages but some disadvantages also.

8.5.2 Problems of selective intervention

A problem with the centralization of decisions is that the possibilities of intervening selectively do not always result in an improvement for the whole organization. There are disadvantages associated with bringing transactions within the organization. First, there is always the possibility of the person taking the decisions behaving opportunistically. The management may have an urge to intervene selectively more than is necessary, or may even be open to bribes. Selective intervention creates these possibilities. Organizational provisions limiting such behaviour usually come at a high cost, for example specifying good behaviour and exercising control. It may be desirable to restrict the choice possibilities of the manager, even if opportunistic considerations do not play a role in the manager's decision-making.

The second type of influence costs emerges because employees try to persuade or manipulate the top management into using discretion in the wrong direction. Top management decides regarding salary increases, promotions, allocation of budgets and approval of investment projects. Taking good decisions requires extensive and detailed information, and usually the employees possess this information. They are best informed about the specific situation. Top management determines for example the salaries, but it often lacks the market information regarding the alternatives available to the employees, and this information can be obtained only from these employees. There is thus asymmetric information, where the persons about whom decisions are taken possess valuable information. Participation in the decision-making by these employees is therefore not appreciated.

The problem is that the decision-making has the largest impact on those who have the most relevant information. Decisions which are good for the organization are not necessarily attractive for the people or the department involved. In such circumstances opportunistic employees provide garbled information. Valuable information for the organization will be communicated with information intended only to influence decisions in a favourable way for the person involved. Both types of information are communicated in order to hide from the employer the information which serves only the self-interest of the employee. The conflict between self-interest and common interest results in much time and energy being spent in an attempt to influence decisions of superiors. The associated activities can be valuable for the organization because better performance will be provided at work and valuable information transmitted. However, the available information can also be manipulated entirely in self-interest, for example by distorting the facts, destroying disadvantageous information and repeatedly emphasizing favourable information. Valuable as well as self-serving information will be communicated, where the former hides the latter.

Every organizational change and the associated allocation of decision power generates corresponding information flows and costs. The merger of two firms results in a concentration of decision power. It has the advantage of improving co-ordination between different parts of the organization. However, centralization of planning has the disadvantage that decisions have a larger impact and that the consequent information flows will cause rapidly increasing influence costs. Organizing activities in one organization and the accompanying central-ization of decision power result in costs which increase much faster then revenues. This limits the optimal size of the firm. Figure 8.13 shows that the number of information flows grows rapidly when the organization expands. A company consisting of 5 persons has 10 possible information flows, whereas when there are 6 persons this has grown to 15. Increasing centralization usually generates more disadvantages than advantages. Increasing costs are prevented by a more decentralized way of organizing, which implies that there is an optimal size for the firm. Non-integration is a commitment not to intervene selectively.

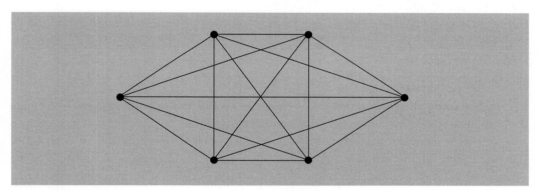

Figure 8.13: Influence costs and the size of the firm

Application: Divestiture

A large part of the restructuring wave around 1990 consisted of divesting product groups, divisions or departments. Usually there was no merger between two companies, only parts of companies being involved. Often in such circumstances the weak parts are divested, the buyer frequently having a strong affinity with these parts. Sometimes a fast-growing, or highly profitable, part is sold, but more often sold are units with bad prospects or low profitability..

Meyer *et al.* (1992) explain these observations from an influence costs perspective. There is according to them a fundamental difference between good and bad times for organizational units. Bad circumstances generate substantial influence activities, whereas this is not true for prosperous times. This asymmetry is due to it being the task of top management to do something about these bad circumstances. A choice has to be made between sackings and divestiture. Firing employees results in sizeable influence activities, because the employees will try to show that the bad situation is only temporary. They will try to capture funds from other departments in order to cover up losses. If these activities are successful, then things will be back as before, which prevents affairs being conducted more efficiently. Next to such departmental efforts, there will be individual efforts to remain unaffected by the reorganization. Divestiture of a department prevents influence activities and is attractive when these activities are substantial. This is more likely when there are fewer alternatives within the organization, and therefore the number of dismissals is higher.

The explanation for the observation that the acquiring party is often active in the same branch is the possibilities of doing similar work. A worsening of the circumstances of a specific unit within a company does not necessarily result in sackings, because the skills of the employees may be used elsewhere. These considerations argue for training and education of employees which is not only specific. A broadly trained employee does not have to fear losing his or her job and will therefore have a weak incentive to develop influence activities in order to keep it.

These considerations regarding divestiture seem applicable also to new circumstances. It is often impossible to start profitable projects within an inert bureaucracy. An organizational solution to these problems is the erection of a new and independent unit or department, where extensive discretion is allocated in order to start something new.

8.5.3 Delegation

In complete contracting theory delegation can never be superior to centralization. Everything that can be arranged by contracts in a decentralized fashion can also be implemented by a comprehensive contract. However, decision-making is often decentralized in companies. Communication of the relevant information entails costs. Information is transmitted by various means, such as budgets, divisional accounting reports and data regarding production costs. It is often impossible to transmit all the relevant information. Some is lost, which opens the door for studying issues regarding delegation.

An advantage of the delegation of decision rights is that each decision is taken by the person or persons involved, who usually possesses the superior local information. However, delegation is not always desirable, despite its greater flexibility. Some control is lost. Determining the optimal degree of delegation in a situation with limited possibilities of communication involves a tradeoff between the better use of local information and the loss of control. In general the efficiency of a relationship increases when the principal does not have all the information and all authority. (This was already shown in the analysis of the ratchet effect in Sec. 6.4. Chapter 10 will address in this context the distinction between formal and real authority.)

Application: Corruption

Corruption is a pervasive phenomenon in enterprises, industries and governments (Klitgaard, 1985; Rose-Ackerman, 1978). It occurs because there are opportunities for two parties to conclude an attractive deal at the expense of a third.   An effective response to corruption often turns out to be the creation of a balance of powers by separating decision authority. A number of examples are illustrative. Hong Kong under British rule experienced hardly any corruption, because an independent corruption agency was endowed with considerable decision authority.

Another example is the independence of the central bank in many countries. Ruling political parties may adopt (temporary) economic policies in order to enhance their prospects of re-election, which may be accompanied by substantial inflation. One way to safeguard price stability against such a threat of inflation is to have a central bank endowed with substantial monetary policy discretion and the accompanying policy instruments. In fact, countries with a less independent central bank do experience a higher rate of inflation.

8.5.4 Delegation and bureaucracy

Organizations like to see that decisions are based on the relevant information, but the possible effect of these decisions may have various undesirable consequences for the people involved. Every organizational choice is accompanied with a change in the costs of the various information flows. Decision processes which are vulnerable for influence activities generate valuable as well as undesirable information, because employees have an interest in providing information and giving advice. Participation of employees in the decision-making generates valuable information (efficiency aspect) as well as influence activities (distribution aspect). An organization will try to choose a decision-making process that balances these two opposing effects.

Organizations try to channel the behaviour of individuals in such a way that activities are geared towards creating value, instead of being focused on getting a larger share of the surplus. These influence activities will increase when more is at stake. Milgrom and Roberts (1990d) show that

> an efficient organisation limits the freedom of choice of (local) decision makers when choices have hardly an impact on the organisation, but are important from the perspective of individual organisation members.

It can therefore be optimal for an organization that, in order to prevent excessive influence activities, managers have to ignore valuable information, which may once in a while lead to the wrong decision..

This result can also be formulated in terms of centralization within an organization. More centralized decisions, or closed decision-making adhering to fixed rules and procedures, means that local information is ignored. An organization has to choose how much decision authority regarding rewarding specific results or circumstances has to be centralized. The advice is that

> decision power has to be centralized, i.e. taken away from local managers, wherever the decisions are of limited importance for the organization, but are important for a local manager.

The reason is that an employee then knows that developing influence activities does not pay, and therefore will not consider them, while no valuable information is lost for the organization. The disadvantage of this policy is that it is difficult or costly to generate valuable signals in bureaucratic organizations, because decision-making goes according to strict procedures. Decentralized or open decision processes are on the other hand desirable when influence activities hardly generate benefits for the individuals, and the information is valuable for the organization. Figure 8.14 Presents this result. Decision processes with an 'open' character are desirable when there is much at stake for the organization compared with the consequences for individuals. The opposite holds for 'closed' decision processes.

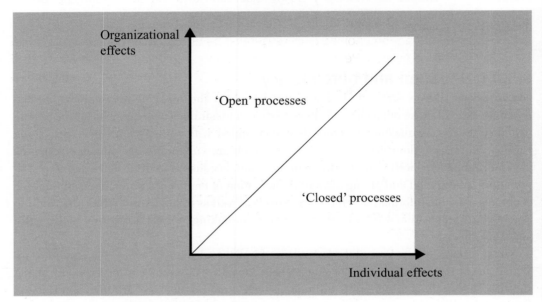

Figure 8.14: Optimal decision processes

A number of less drastic solutions will now be addressed. One way to limit the implications of the decisions of the central authority, with its policy of selective intervention, is to reduce the financial consequences of the parties involved. Reducing the payoff for successful influence activities by a rigid salary system is an example. This may be implemented by salaries based on seniority, or tying salaries to certain positions. A large disadvantage of this policy is that it frustrates incentive and information generation aspects of rewards. The resulting undesirable consequences have been addressed in the treatment of the hidden characteristics problem in Chapter 7. A good illustration is the Peter principle, namely that 'People are promoted to their levels of incompetence' (Peter, 1970). The good people leave, while the less qualified stay.

Abiding by a bureaucratic procedure is another way to discourage influence activities. A certain decision is approved when the requirements are met. Again valuable information is not incorporated in the decision-making process, but unproductive activities do not get an opportunity to become successful.

Open communication channels may generate a lot of information, but also invite inefficient influence activities. The limitation of access to the decision-maker, or the denial or withholding of information by the decision-maker, are methods to deal with this. If the people involved do not have all the relevant information, then the influence activities cannot be as effective. An example is withholding information regarding the salaries of others. This cannot therefore be used in attempts to receive a salary increase by comparing your own achievements with those of others. This is one reason why a personnel department in a company keeps salary information secret. If this information is available, then the lower-paid employees compare their performance with the worst-performing higher-paid ones, and argue for a raise. Bureaucratic inertia, or even refusal to provide answers, is viewed from this perspective as an optimal organizational response to reduce influence activities.

Application: Allocating personnel to aeroplane flights

An example of limiting the choices of managers is the allocation of personnel to airline flights by American Airlines. Personnel are allowed once every month to submit a list of desired flights. Conflicts are resolved by seniority. Management has no discretion regarding the assignment of flights, and that is efficient according to influence costs theory. It does not matter to the airline company who is assigned to which flight, although it is very important for the people involved. Such allocation of flights by American Airlines has to be viewed as a way to prevent non-productive influence activities by employees. The rigidity of this allocation procedure probably means that management will spend less time on employees who invest time and effort in order to realize their most preferred flights. Time spent on such activities is non-productive from the perspective of the firm. The down side of this is that if requests by cabin staff go unmet this may result in less service to the customers.

Application: Rigid salary and promotion systems

Another example of strict rules and bureaucratic inflexibility is the rigid salary and promotion structure in large companies. Rigidity is attractive because it will not leave much leeway for influencing these decisions. The rules, rather than immediate superiors, determine whether a request for a payrise or promotion is granted. Were the manager rather than the personnel department to decide regarding these issues then employees would regularly seek contact with their boss. However, it often occurs that managers tell their employees that they would like to do something for them, but that it is not allowed by the personnel department. The employees anticipate such responses and therefore forgo activities along these lines. The crucial issue is again that it has to be determined whether ignoring information is more valuable (by preventing influence costs) than what it costs (because of lost productivity increasing owing to valuable information not being generated). Similar observations are formulated by Tirole (1986).

Application: Operational and strategic decision processes

We have seen that reducing influence activities sometimes requires that rigid rules and procedures are imposed regarding operational, short-run decisions. Strategic decisions, which deal with the course of action of the enterprise in the next 5 to 10 years, cannot be organized in this way, because they have a much more open character. However, substantial influence activities may be involved in strategic decision-making processes because of the substantial redistributive implications involved. An efficient organization is aware of this and will take precautionary measures.

There are two ways of limiting the extent of influence activities in strategic decision processes. First, the inertia of decision-making in large organizations regarding the strategy of the enterprise and the large effort it takes to come to a substantial change are well known. The advantage of such a slow process is that it becomes harder for the participants to manipulate it in an inefficient direction. It is more likely that hidden agendas in the decision-making process will become known by extensively evaluating proposals for change. Second, another aspect of insulating strategic decision-making processes is that often not much information is revealed in the course of the process, making it difficult for outsiders to focus their influence activities.

8.5.5 Delegation and competition

Hart (1995) signals as the two most important problems of the analysis of government the vagueness of its objective function and the credibility of the promises it makes. Section 6.3 has already addressed the objective function of the government in the application of the stakeholder organization. The commitment problem of the government is stated eloquently by Weingast (1994):

> The fundamental political dilemma of an economic system is this: a government strong enough to protect property rights and enforce contracts is also strong enough to confiscate the wealth of its citizens. Thriving markets require not only the appropriate system of property rights and a law of contracts, but a secure political foundation that limits the ability of the state to confiscate wealth.

He proposes as a possible solution a constitution which limits the freedom of choice of the state in a credible way. This entails the delegation of decision power from the central government to the local governments, i.e. federalism. It establishes in a credible way that there will be no arbitrary interventions in local situations. Another attractive feature of federalism is that it encourages competition between local municipalities. Each municipality will try to bring its local information and conditions as much as possible to value.

8.6 Coase theorem

From the perspective of transaction costs economics, the fundamental welfare theorem and the Coase theorem are viewed as results in an ideal world. In the theory of general equilibrium there is a market for every possible good and service, and it is possible to incorporate every relevant aspect in contracts without problems. However, in transaction costs economics the fundamental transformation means that there is not a market for everything, and the assumption of bounded rationality implies that only incomplete contracts are possible. Similar observations hold regarding the Coase theorem. The Coase theorem (1960) states that every assignment of property rights results in a Pareto-efficient allocation, with no income effects and no bargaining inefficiencies. It highlights the importance of a well-functioning bargaining process as well as the allocation and tradability of property rights. If these requirements are met, then the choice of organization does not matter. Several problems regarding meeting these requirements were discussed in Chapter 4. The implication of the Coase theorem is that a fruitful departure for the explanation of various organizational forms is to identify bargaining problems and financial restrictions. In the circumstances where the assumptions of the Coase theorem are not met, institutional answers emerge. Therefore according to this perspective the purpose of organizations is to deal efficiently with bargaining problems and financial restrictions..

The transaction costs approach starts with the observation that the incompleteness of contracts is problematic in environments with specific investments. The parties involved are tied ex post to each other, because investments are more valuable inside the relationship than outside. The incompleteness of contracts means that it is impossible to specify ex ante how the surplus ex post, i.e. once the investment has been made, will be divided. The division of the surplus will depend on the ex-post bargaining positions. Bargaining positions are determined by the organizational context. Transaction costs economics predicts market exchange in situations with a high level of asset specificity, because the parties involved fear that they will not be able to appropriate the revenues of their investments in a bargaining situation which is ex post not competitive. Bringing the transaction within the firm offers guarantees against opportunistic behaviour and maximizes the size of the surplus.

The Coase theorem applies to a situation where transaction costs are zero according to transaction costs economics, i.e. in that situation it does not matter how property rights are allocated. The transaction costs and property rights approaches focus on bargaining problems by positing that organizational forms or governance structures differ regarding the distribution of bargaining position and/or power. Charting the situations where bargaining inefficiencies occur is interesting, because it is expected that in these situations practices, institutions and organizations will arise to cope with them. Transaction costs are more generally associated with inefficiencies. The role of uncertainty in transaction cost economics is related to the inefficiencies in the bargaining process. Specific investments usually concern one buyer and one seller. The success of such a bilateral monopoly is sensitive to all kinds of uncertainties. The influence activities of each party aimed at capturing a larger share of the surplus often result in bargaining inefficiencies. Specific investments are therefore associated with bargaining costs, which may be an explanation for the predictive power of transaction costs economics. The same remarks apply to measurement costs and bargaining costs specifications.

8.7 Conclusion

This chapter made a start with the comparison of markets with organizations from a perspective of incomplete contracting. Incomplete contracts may result in various forms of renegotiation, like hold-up problems in transaction costs economics and influence activities in the influence costs approach. The organizational or governance response, in order to deal efficiently with investments in specific assets, is central in transaction costs theory, while the efficient channelling of information flows is the main theme of influence costs. However, the respective points of departure for the analysis of these approaches differ substantially.

Transactions costs economics takes the position that markets are replaced by organizations when they are better able to deal with motivation and co-ordination problems, i.e. a market failure perspective is taken. The influence costs approach, on the other hand, starts with organizations and replaces them with markets when they can handle information flows better, i.e. an organizational failure perspective is taken. The next chapter provides a balanced treatment of the choice between markets and organizations by investigating the allocation of residual control. The recurring nature of relations has not received much attention in this chapter; by addressing self-enforcing contracts, Chapter 10 puts it at the centre of analysis.

8.8 Exercises

8.1 Important aspects of transaction costs economics are opportunism and small numbers.
   A Why is the likelihood of opportunistic behaviour larger in a situation with small numbers than where there are large numbers?
   B Explain why the combination of opportunism and small numbers results in high transaction costs.

8.2 A What is the quasi-surplus of an office building in front of a central railway station? (Or: Which number(s) change in Sec. 8.3 when applied to the office building in front of such a station?)
   B What prediction or advice does transaction costs economics formulate regarding the financing of an office building in front of a central station?

8.3 A Which numbers have to change in Fig. 8.4 when a situation of complete contracts would prevail?
   B Explain how the complete contracting perspective cannot be a meaningful starting-point for a theory of organization.

8.4 Company TCE wants to have its annual account checked by an external accountant and chooses the organization KPAA out of 25 accounting organizations available to do this. A year later TCE wants to have its annual account checked again. In the meantime KPAA has gained some experience in checking the annual account, so savings on hours and therefore costs can be achieved. TCE wants to appropriate these savings, which means TCE wants to pay a lower price for the services of KPAA. Is TCE in a better negotiation position to appropriate the savings? In your answer take the transaction costs economics perspective.

8.5 Company Bifi is engaged in collecting rubbish. Bifi is considering whether to vertically integrate forward by buying an existing rubbish incinerator. Nowadays the collection and processing of rubbish is changing substantially, whereas in the past such activities were characterized as static.
   A Can vertical integration by Bifi in this static market be explained by transaction costs economics?

Technological interdependencies exist between collecting and processing garbage, which Bifi puts forward as a reason for a vertical integration.

B Explain why technological interdependency can result in vertical integration.

C Is technological interdependency a good reason to integrate vertically according to transaction costs economics?

Another reason to integrate vertically can be price discrimination.

D Do you think that price discrimination is in general a good reason to integrate vertically?

8.6 The American company Butterfly produces heavy earthmoving machines. In Scandinavian countries these machines are sold by three independent agents. The financial picture of each Scandinavian agent looks as follows:

Yield on Butterflies sales	
(10 machines of $200 000 each)	$2 000 000
Costs:	
Costs of purchase of Butterflies (10 machines at	
$100 000 each)	$1 000 000
Rent of office space	500 000
Investments in specific furniture	
(e.g. desks in the shape of a Butterfly)	100 000
Investments in specific training of the employees	
(to make them capable of repairing the Butterflies)	300 000
Total costs	−1 900 000
Result	$100 000

Butterfly is not satisfied with the Scandinavian agents, but cannot terminate the supply contracts. The company therefore considers whether to increase the price it charges the agents for the machines to stimulate agents to leave the industry voluntarily.

A At which price charged by Butterfly will an agent leave the industry?

B Define quasi-surplus.

C What is the level of the quasi-surplus in the above example?

Butterfly leaves the sale of its products to Ekeveg, a company already selling Butterflies in the Netherlands.

D Do you expect Butterfly to raise the prices it charges the Scandinavian agents in order to stimulate them to leave the industry voluntarily?

Ekeveg decides to take over the Scandinavian agents.

E Will the quasi-surplus mentioned in part C decrease, increase or remain the same as a result of this decision?

8.7 The production of iron produces a by-product which can be used as a raw material for artificial fertilizer. The steel company Ultegra has an installation which the chemical company DSM uses to produce artificial fertilizer. The following figures provide some fictional data on this installation.

Data of the installation

Historical purchase price	€15 000 000
Replacement value	20 000 000
Value in the relationship betwen Ultegra and DSM	8 000 000
Value of selling to chemical company Hydro Agri	5 000 000
Scrap value	€1 000 000

A Define the quasi-surplus.
B What is the level of the quasi-surplus of the installation?
  The quasi-surplus is related to the specificity of the investments.
C What is the degree of specificity of the installation?
  Williamson distinguishes five types of asset specificity.
D Which type applies to this example?
  Assume DSM is the owner of the installation.
E Which party may become the victim of hold-up, Ultegra or DSM?
Ownership can be delineated into decision rights and income rights. The following situation is possible:
Ultegra takes over the installation, i.e. it receives the residual returns; employees of DSM use and maintain the installation to produce goods, i.e. it owns the residual decision rights.
F What can be the result of the separation between residual control and residual returns to the maintenance of the installation?

8.8 A new road haulage company considers whether to penetrate two local markets for the transportation of agricultural products. Suppose that the two markets are identical in all respects, except for the identity of the incumbent firm in each market. The incumbent firm in the first market is a railway company. This company has invested 20 million euros in new tracks and the operational costs per unit of grain by rail are 0.20 euro per kilometre. The incumbent firm in the second market is another road haulage company. This company has also invested 20 million euros in new trucks. The operational costs per unit of grain by railroad are also 0.20 euro per kilometre.

A How are sunk costs measured?
B Which company has the highest sunk costs?
C Does transaction costs economics predict that the governance structure for the transportation of grain will be organized differently in the two markets?
D Which market will be penetrated by the new trucking company?

8.9 A large part of present acquisitions and mergers consists not only of a complete take-over of one company by another, or a full merger between two companies, but also of the splitting off parts of a company, like product groups, divisions or departments. Some companies split off profitable or fast-growing parts, but it is more common to sell low-return parts with bad prospects. Besides, buyers are usually active in fields related to the activities of the company taken over.

A Define influencing activities.

B Which three types of costs of influence do Milgrom and Roberts distinguish?

A company unit is confronted with disappointing market circumstances. The company has to intervene and can choose between firing employees and selling the department.

C Argue from the perspective of influence costs that a fundamental asymmetry exists between growth and decay of a company consisting of various departments.

D Which choice maximizes the profit of a company? Explain your answer.

E Would either a specific or a general education of the employees be valuable in the above situation? Explain your answer.

8.10 Universities consist of various departments and a general board. The general board allocates financial means to the departments. There is always one department which claims that the general board withdraws a lot of financial means from them and allocates it to other departments. To prevent this, this department tries to influence the decisions regarding the allocation of funds by the general board. The resulting influence activities can cause influence costs. The general board could resort to various mechanisms to restrict the influence costs.

A Formulate four ways to restrict the influence costs in a university.

Other decisions as well are made in a university. An example is the decision whether or not to allow a student to take an oral instead of a written exam. This decision can be decentralized (i.e. made by the teacher of the course) or centralized (i.e. made by the student adviser, who applies a set of rigid rules).

B Do you think the decision whether or not to allow a student to take an oral instead of a written exam should be decentralized? Explain your answer.

8.11 The head office in a multidivisional company is responsible for the allocation of means to divisions. Assume that each division wants to receive as many means as possible and that the head office does not know precisely the profit potential of divisions. Additional information regarding the potential profit of a division can be collected by the head office, but the process of collecting information may entail undesirable effects.

Assume that only two parties are involved: the head office and one division. The head office eventually assigns an amount x to the division. This amount is θ when the head office knows the profit potential of the division precisely (Gibbons, 1999). Assume that the available information gives the head office the impression that θ is normally distributed with an average a and variance v. The head office can obtain additional information, summarized with the signal s regarding the value of θ. Higher values of θ result in a higher value of s, but there is also some noise ε, which is independent of θ. This noise has a normal distribution with mean 0 and variance v_ε. A division can display influence activities, represented by $I \geq 0$, which raises the value of s. The head office observes the value of s, but not its separate components θ, L and ε. So, the head office observes

$$s = \theta + L + \varepsilon.$$

The head office prefers x to differ as little as possible from θ and also that the division should put as little effort as possible into unproductive influence activities. This is reflected in the utility function

$$U_h = -(x - \theta)^2 - L.$$

The exact specification of this utility function is not important. What is important is that the most attractive outcome of the head office is $L = 0$ and $x = \theta$. The utility function of the division should show that the division prefers to receive as many means as possible. Besides, influence activities are expensive, despite the fact that they mean a higher value of s, because they take away time from other activities. This is reflected in the utility function

$$U_d = x - \tfrac{1}{2}c^2.$$

Again, the exact specification of the utility function is not important. What is important is that x should be as high as possible and that $L = 0$. The decision order is such that the head office takes the first decision. Means are allocated according to the signal s by the rule

$$x = d + bs,$$

where d and b are parameters which can be chosen by the head office. Subsequently, the division chooses the size of the lobbying activities. Finally, the head office observes the signal s.

A Show that the utility-maximizing level of influence activities of the division equals b.

B Show that the utility-maximizing level of b of the head office equals

$(v - 0.5)/(v + v_\varepsilon)$	when $v > 0.5$,
0	when $v \le 0.5$.

9 Ownership rights

LEARNING OBJECTIVES

After completing this chapter, you should understand:

- The distinction between specific and residual rights.

- The relationship between bargaining power and investing in specific assets.

- The impact of the complexity of the transaction on the choice of governance structure.

- The relationship between the Coase theorem and this chapter.

Contents

9.1 Introduction

This chapter addresses again the specificity of investments, but unlike Chapter 8 uses the *same* behavioural assumption to explain both the costs and the benefits of integration. One problem with the transaction costs economics approach is that *no* explicit *internal organizational theory* is specified which indicates the costs of internalizing transactions. The definition of transaction costs is concerned mainly with the costs associated with the market. These costs are explained extensively, but transaction costs theory is less specific regarding the costs associated with internalizing activities. It is suggested that these costs will decrease because the information structure changes, or because agents will become less *opportunistic*. However, it is unsatisfactory from the perspective of theory development to state simply that information flows change, or agents are less concerned with their own interest because of integration.

Similarly, if integration results always in a decrease of transaction costs, then the size of the company is unlimited. In terms of the *degree of rationality*, this means that the cognitive capacities of people increase because of vertical integration. It is not correct to assume unlimited rationality when vertical integration occurs. The relevant comparison for transactions via markets or transactions within organizations is not between the outcome in a world with incomplete and complete contracts, but between two different incomplete contracts.

A third way to formulate this problem regarding transaction costs economics is by comparing the view of Coase (1937) with the approach in this chapter. Coase claims that there is an important difference between on the one hand two parties who are independent and on the other a relationship between an employer and an employee. In the first situation, one has to convince the other to do something for him by means of *prices* – in which self-interest is the driving force behind the behaviour of the individual parties. In the second situation, the notion of *selective intervention* determines behaviour, which means that the employer can decide what the employee has to do and that he or she subsequently does so. This is not desirable from the perspective of theory development, because the behavioural assumption adopted depends on the situation. In the market, everybody is opportunistic, whereas an employee in a company would follow the orders of the employer without being opportunistic. Similar objections can be formulated regarding the analysis of team production by Alchian and Demsetz (1972). It is not clear why the problems with team production and control can be solved better by integration than in the market. For example, auditing between independent contract parties in markets occurs frequently.

It is more elegant to the use the same behavioural assumption throughout a theory. Similarly, the choice possibilities usually do not change because of a change in governance structure, but a different governance structure may result in different behaviour or choices from the same set of choice possibilities. Integration changes the possibilities for opportunistic behaviour, but does not eliminate them. The same holds for information flows, communication and the cognitive capacities. Grossman and Hart (1986) formulate this as follows: 'Behaviour changes when one of the self-interested owners becomes an equally self-interested employee of the other owner.' This chapter adopts one behavioural assumption in the analysis of various governance structures.

The relationship between governance structure and ownership rights is addressed in Sec. 9.2. Specific and residual decision rights are specified in Sec. 9.3. The consequences of a certain choice of governance structure for the specific investments of the parties involved are analysed in Sections 9.4–9.6. Section 9.7 focuses on the relationship between the complexity of transactions and governance structure. The relationship between the approach in this chapter and the Coase theorem is the topic of Sec. 9.7. Section 9.8 concludes.

9.2 Governance structure

A *governance structure* consists of the rules by which an exchange is administered. Compensating for the incompleteness of contracts, a governance structure is designed to foster efficiency in transacting by deterring one party from appropriating the other, co-ordinating exchange, and resolving disputes due to differences in judgements (motivated partly by differences in objectives). A governance structure is therefore concerned with how firm decisions are made, i.e. the exercise of authority, guidance and control. Examples are the allocation of property rights, the capital structure, the reward system, the board of directors, the pressure of large investors, the competition in the product and labour markets, the organizational structure, the (management) accounting system and so on. This chapter focuses on the collection of rules and constraints structuring the ex-post bargaining process over the quasi-surplus.

The definition of governance structure implies that bargaining over the quasi-surplus is the essence of questions regarding governance structure. The outcome of the bargaining process is determined by:

- Specific contractual agreements (based on observable and verifiable variables);
- General contractual agreements (allocation of property rights with respect to assets);
- Availability of alternatives (i.e. the level of sunk costs of investments);
- Institutional environment (swiftness and effectiveness of the judicial system, professional norms, transparency of the market with respect to the quality of the producer of potential customers, and so on).

Another aspect of this definition is the relationship between generating and distributing the quasi-surplus. The way in which the quasi-surplus is distributed (ex post) has major consequences for the investment behaviour ex ante, which was addressed extensively in the previous chapter.

Complete contingent contracts prevail in the theory of general equilibrium in Chapter 3. They incorporate all relevant information and specify a course of action for every possible contingency which may occur in the future. If complete contingent contracts can be designed without costs, then all decisions are taken ex ante and the complete quasi-surplus is distributed ex ante. A governance structure adds no value, i.e. the choice of governance structure does not matter. If costless complete contracts are possible, then all possible conflicts are resolved ex ante. There is also no role for a governance structure in this situation, because there is no need for ex-post bargaining. The incompleteness of contracts creates a difference between ex-ante decisions (regarding starting a relationship and investing in specific assets) and ex-post ones (when the quasi-surplus is divided). A governance structure is important in an incomplete contracts setting because it allocates decision rights in circumstances for which the contract has made no provisions.

The incompleteness of contracts is crucial for the importance of governance structure. There is a role for a governance structure ex post only when it is costly to design contracts based on observable future variables. If certain aspects are therefore unspecified, then there will be ex post a quasi-surplus which has to be divided and ex-post investment decisions will determine the size of the quasi-surplus. The difference between the value created by the two parties and the best alternative use is the quasi-surplus and it has to be divided ex post. The invisible hand of Adam Smith is thus by definition not helpful in dividing the quasi-surplus. A governance structure adds value for those activities that do not blossom in a market relationship. Figure 9.1 summarizes these observations.

Contract	Is there a role for governance?
Complete contingent	No
Complete	No
Incomplete	Yes

Figure 9.1: Types of contracts and governance

The focus of this chapter is on the choice of governance structure. Little attention is paid to the institutional environment, consisting of the formal and informal rules in society, in which governance structures are embedded.

Application: Customer–grocer relationship

It took a long time before the ideas of Coase (1937) were developed further. This was first because transaction costs are hard to define and to pin down. Second, it seemed that Alchian and Demsetz (1972) formulated a conceptual problem with the view of Coase. They compared an employer–employee relationship in a company with a customer–grocer relationship in the market. An employer has according to Coase some authority over an employee because he or she can tell an employee to do certain tasks. Will an employee execute these directives? Non-obedience by an employee may result in him or her being brought to court for breaking the contract. However, this is unlikely. The worst outcome for the employee is most likely that he or she will be fired. This is exactly what an unsatisfied customer can do. He or she will buy food somewhere else when the grocer does not deliver the desired quality for the desired prices.

Alchian and Demsetz posit that this characterization of authority is not able to distinguish different governance structures like the market and the hierarchy. They argue that there is no fundamental difference according to Coase (1937) and Simon (1951) between firing an unwilling employee and an unsatisfied customer not going back to a grocer. There is according to them no fundamental difference between contracts governing market exchange, as between a customer and a grocer, and contracts between an employer and an employee in a company, because

> I can 'punish' you only by withholding future business or seeking redress in the courts for any failure to honor our exchange agreement. That is exactly all an employer can do. He can fire or sue, just as I can fire my grocer by stopping purchases from him or sue him for delivering faulty products.

Alchian and Demsetz distinguish the employer–employee relationship from the customer–grocer relationship by assigning a number of rights to the employer (monitor), while the customer does not have these rights. These rights were listed and addressed in Sec. 6.5.

The problem with the view of Alchian and Demsetz is that complete contracts are assumed implicitly, whereas the contribution of Coase has to be viewed from the perspective of incomplete contracts. Organizations or governance structures do not add value, i.e. they have no role to play, according to Alchian and Demsetz, because everything regarding the future can be contracted upon. The firm is viewed as a nexus of complete contracts. The criticism by Coase of Alchian and Demsetz applies therefore also to their own contribution. It does not matter according to them whether someone is an independent contractor or an employee, and how contracts are embedded within a certain organizational context. There are no questions regarding the efficient assignment of decision rights in unforeseen contingencies, because all relevant contingencies are already addressed at the beginning of the relationship.

A governance structure adds value only when the following two requirements are met:

- The relationship has to generate a quasi-surplus;
- The quasi-surplus is ex ante not completely allocated.

If no quasi-surplus is generated, then the competitive nature of the market ensures that the price is equal to the costs. There is no use for a governance structure to structure the bargaining, because the quasi-surplus to be bargained about is equal to zero. The second necessary requirement is obvious. If the quasi-surplus would have been allocated completely ex ante, then there is nothing to bargain about.

There are three ways in which the governance structure, determining the ex-post division of the quasi-surplus, affects the size of the surplus which will be generated (Zingales, 1998):

- Ex-ante investment effects;
- Inefficient bargaining;
- Risk-aversion.

There are two ways in which the ex-post division of the quasi-surplus will have an impact on the *ex-ante choice of investments*. First, rational agents will not spend the efficient time or effort or resources on value-generating activities when the governance structure assigns insufficient rewards to them. If hardly any *bargaining power* is assigned, then hardly any activities will be started. Chapter 8 has illustrated this already with the example of the upstream inventor and the downstream party, while a further example will illustrate this again in the next section. Second, rational agents will put forward inefficient activities with the only purpose of changing the *ex-post bargaining position* to their own advantage. A prominent example is influence costs, addressed in Chapter 8. A governance structure may encourage or discourage these activities.

Application: Organizational structure

Chandler (1966) has studied the evolution of the internal organization of large enterprises. In 1920 the most common ways of organizing were the functional organization and the holding. Du Pont (functional organization) and General Motors (holding) were the first to switch to the multi- divisional organization in the 1930s.

Departments in a functional organization are organized around functions like marketing, production and finance. The advantage of such a structure is that scale economies are exploited by the division of labour. The different contributions have to be merged subsequently to a product or service, which entails tremendous co-ordination and motivation problems when the size of the enterprise increases. The limited cognitive capacities of humans are not capable of handling the complexity of these situations. There may also be too much focus by people on the interests of their own department. For example, technicians may underestimate the importance of marketing considerations, while marketing people may have limited understanding of technical aspects. Opportunistic behaviour between departments may also be a concern.

A *holding* is a divisionalized company, without any meaningful strategic role for the head office. The activities are organized around the end products, which means that some economies of scale are sacrificed in order to reduce co-ordination problems. The head office has no discretion regarding strategic decisions. Opportunistic tendencies may emerge, where two-sided favours are granted and cross-subsidization occurs. Revenues are therefore not always allocated to the activities which generate most value.

The *multi-divisional organization* has a head office focusing on the allocation of means to existing and new departments or divisions. The decision-making process is supported and controlled by a staff, and operational decisions are delegated to the separate departments. Figure 9.2 depicts this organizational structure. The separation of decisions not only reduces various problems of limited rationality of the functional organization, but eliminates also the conflicts of interest of the functional organization, because the head office is responsible for the whole organization. The multi-divisional organization therefore combines divisionalization with the possibility of internal control and strategic decision-making (Williamson, 1975).

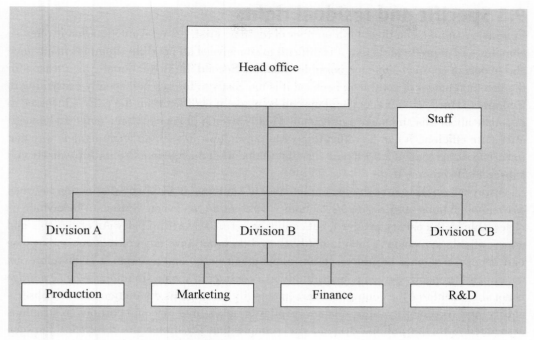

Figure 9.2: Multi-divisional organization

A governance structure has implications for the creation of value, because it determines *the efficiency of the ex-post bargaining process*. There is no role for governance structure in the environment described by the Coase theorem, because bargaining is assumed to be efficient. However, in reality there are often inefficiencies in the bargaining process. A governance structure has an impact on the nature and size of these inefficiencies because it has consequences for:

- The information asymmetries between the parties;
- The co-ordination costs;
- The extent of financial restrictions on the parties;
- The degree of alignment between the parties.

A governance structure has an impact on the value of the total surplus, because it determines *the level and the distribution of risk*. One aspect in the evaluation of the efficiency of a governance structure is the way it allocates risk to the most risk-tolerant party. Chapter 6 addressed this extensively.

The above implies that the purpose of a governance structure is:

- To maximize the incentives to generate value-enhancing investments, while incentives for developing inefficient influence activities have to be minimized;
- To minimize risk, and to allocate the residual risk to the least risk-averse party.

9.3 Specific and residual rights

Contracts can be incomplete for a number of reasons. First, the relevant situation is often so complex and unpredictable that it is difficult to conceive of all possible situations in advance and to design contracts for each possible situation. Second, limited rationality is a reason for the incompleteness of contracts, because it is too costly to foresee and specify everything in a contract. Third, even if specific plans can be made, it is difficult for the parties involved to negotiate about this and make agreements. Finally, even if plans have been made and negotiations are efficient, it can be difficult to write these down in such an unambiguous way that in case of disagreement a third party can determine what the agreement entails precisely and subsequently enforce them.

A way to conceptualize the incompleteness of contracts is making a distinction between *observable* actions and *verifiable* actions. Observable and non-verifiable behaviour is observable by the parties involved, but cannot be verified by a third party. An observable and non-verifiable agreement which is not honoured does not have any consequences, because bad behaviour cannot be proven to an independent party, e.g. a judge. It is therefore not meaningful to specify agreements explicitly in a contract in such a situation, because a judge is not able to enforce the contractual agreements. By making this distinction between observability and verifiability, this chapter explicitly takes into account various restrictions associated with the judicial system. An example that illustrates the difference between observable and verifiable information is an accounting procedure which records the production of a team, but not the individual contributions of its members. A person directly involved will be able to determine the individual contributions, but an outsider (judge) cannot. Only actions which are observable as well as verifiable qualify to be incorporated in a meaningful contract. Only in such circumstances can a third party decide in a meaningful way about conflicts between the parties involved.

The distinction between observable and verifiable actions prevents the design of (meaningful) *complete* contracts. This gives rise to distinguishing two types of contract rights: 'specific' and 'residual' rights (Grossman and Hart, 1986). *Specific rights* delineate the rights and duties in circumstances which are verifiable. *Residual rights* determine who can decide about the use of the means of production in circumstances not described in the contract. (Specific rights are those one has in the contractual relationship, whereas all non-specified rights will be residual ones.)

The contract is incomplete, because not everything is specified ex ante. Ex post, the contract is completed by allocating the decisions, in circumstances not explicitly agreed upon, to the owner of the residual rights. This person decides, according to his own interest, what is most desirable in the prevailing circumstances.

Application: Publisher and author

Assume a publisher and an author reach an agreement about the number of copies that will be printed. However, they do not anticipate a possible additional edition as a result of an unexpectedly large demand. The size of the first edition is the specific right, whereas the right to decide about an additional edition is for the owner of the manuscript. This manuscript can be owned by either the author or the publisher.

Application: Truck ownership

Truck ownership gives drivers a bundle of residual rights (Baker and Hubbard, 2001). An important one of these is the right to decide for which hauls the truck is to be used. There are two types of drivers: employee-drivers and owner-operators. Ownership of the truck has an impact on the actions taken to enhance the value of the truck. All drivers theoretically can refuse hauls proposed by a dispatcher, but only owner-operators have the right to use their trucks for other hauls.

Application: Insurance

Selling insurance entails many non-contractibles, like unforeseen dramatic casualties, opportunities for market development, opportunities for product development, and so on. An important asset in insurance markets is the list of policyholders, which consists of names, addresses and other client information. This list can be owned by either the insurance company or an intermediary. Ownership of this list has implications for the investments by the insurance company and the intermediary insurance agents. These issues will be considered in depth later on.

Figure 9.3 reflects the differences between the contracts in Parts II to IV. In a situation where everything is observable and verifiable to everyone, complete contingent contracts prevail. As in Chapter 6, these contracts are presented in *brace* (curly) brackets. Complete contracts, presented with *square* brackets, are written when not all relevant information is available to everyone, but all observable information is also verifiable. Finally, incomplete contracts, presented with *angle* brackets, specify who has the right to decide in situations where information is observable to the parties involved, but is not verifiable by a third party.

An *organization* is defined as the *collection of (physical) assets with the residual rights in the hands of one party*. The organization is a nexus of incomplete contracts, where the residual rights are concentrated in the hands of a specific party or stakeholder. The value of

	Contract		
	Complete contingent	**Complete**	**Incomplete**
Is *everything* observable for everyone?	Yes	No	No
Is observable information also verifiable?	Yes	Yes	No
Contract based on	True reservation prices	Reported reservation prices	Unforeseen circumstances
Design of contract	$\{a, b, c\}$	$[r, s, t, u]$	$<W>$

Figure 9.3: Types of contracts

the company is according to this view that the concentration of ownership results in investments which are not done when ownership of the assets is dispersed, as in a market. Figure 9.4 distinguishes four governance structures based on the ownership of the residual rights.

Governance structure / Residual rights owned by	Stock listed company	Sales co-operative	Input co-operative	Labour-managed firm
Provider of external equity	X			
Supplier		X		
Buyer			X	
Employees				X

Figure 9.4: Governance structure and allocation of residual rights

The notions of authority and selective intervention are captured by residual rights. They will now be addressed from an incomplete contracting perspective. *Selective intervention* is closely related to the notion of limited rationality. It is too costly to specify all possible circumstances in a contract. However, decisions have also to be taken in unforeseen circumstances. This may occur by bargaining, or by assigning the authority to somebody to take these decisions. A labour contract is viewed from this latter perspective by Simon. A boss, B, exercises authority over a worker, W, when W accepts that his behaviour is determined by the decisions of B. W asks for compensation from B for his willingness to obey his authority. Simon formulates the following two explanations for the employer–employee relationship:

1 W will be willing to enter into an employment contract with B only if it does not matter to him 'very much' which *x* (within the agreed upon area of acceptance) B will choose, or if W is compensated in some way for the possibility that B will choose *x* which is not desired by W (i.e., that B will ask W to perform an unpleasant task);
2 It will be advantageous to B to offer W added compensation for entering into an employment contract if B is unable to predict with certainty, at the time the contract is made, which *x* will be the optimum one, from his standpoint. That is, B will pay for the privilege of postponing, until some time after the contract is made, the selection of *x*.

B has the residual rights, because he or she possesses the relevant information.

The relationship between an employer and an employee is characterized as an *authority* relationship, because of the notion of selective intervention being associated with organizations. The value of the principal or manager, as a derivative of this characterization of the employer–employee relationship, is determined largely by carefully determining and antici-pating unexpected circumstances in order to direct the activities of the employees.

9.4 Efficient allocation of ownership rights when one party invests

Each governance structure entails a certain distribution of bargaining power by the allocation of ex-post decision rights, which implies specific co-ordination and motivation problems. The differences between short-term contracts, long-term contracts, vertical integration and other ways of organizing are viewed in the incomplete contracting perspective as different gover-nance structures for dealing with unforeseen circumstances. This section will examine the relationship between the allocation of residual decision rights and specific investments.

The standard incomplete contracting model consists of three stages. First, the governance structure stage determines the allocation of ownership, i.e. assigns the residual decision rights to a certain person. This determines the distribution of *bargaining power*. Second, the investment stage considers the choice of investment. This determines the *bargaining positions*. Finally, the contract execution stage determines whether or not the contract will be honoured. The difference here from complete contract models is that the first stage has been added. The addition of the governance structure choice decision in the first stage determines the distribution of bargaining power in the third stage when the quasi-surplus, because of the incompleteness of contracts, has to be divided. The allocation of ownership rights is important, because it determines the investment behaviour in the second stage.

The choice and impact of governance structure will again be explained with the example of the upstream inventor and the downstream buyer, i.e. the downstream party can sell the innovation for a price of 240 and the inventor incurs costs of 200. Again, an amount K cannot be contracted upon. The amount K reflects the non-recoverable costs of the investment due to the specificity of the investment. The opportunity costs of the innovation are therefore $200 - K$. The surplus is $240 - 200 = 40$, while the quasi-surplus is $240 - (200 - K) = 40 + K$.

Assume that the distribution of bargaining power in a market relationship is such that the quasi-surplus is divided equally, whereas the owner of the residual rights appropriates the entire quasi-surplus when there is integration. Price formation in the *governance structure market*, <M>, means therefore that each party receives half the quasi-surplus. The price before the fundamental transformation, according to the ex-ante contract, equals the costs plus half the surplus, i.e. $200 + 40/2 = 220$. However, the price after the fundamental trans-formation, because of hold-up as a result of the incompleteness of contracts, equals the sum of the non-recoverable costs and half of the quasi-surplus, i.e. $200 - K + (40 + K)/2 = 220 - K/2$. The payment to the inventor equals the price minus the costs.

Before the fundamental transformation, it is agreed that the inventor earns $220 - 200 = 20$, whereas the inventor earns only $220 - K/2 - 200 = 20 - K/2$ after the fundamental transformation or hold-up. The payoff for the downstream party equals the value minus the price. Before the fundamental transformation, it is agreed that the downstream party earns $240 - 220 = 20$, whereas after the fundamental transformation a payment of $240 - (220 - K/2) = 20 + K/2$ results. Figure 9.5 summarizes the situation.

Notice that the sum of producer and consumer surplus equals the surplus before as well as after the fundamental transformation. The result of hold-up is that a different division of the surplus is established. This different division of the surplus means that the downstream party will always find it attractive to choose hold-up, because $20 + K/2$ is always at least as large as 20. The subgame perfect equilibrium choice of the downstream party is 'not to honour the contract'. If the inventor invests, then the inventor earns $20 - K/2$ and the downstream party $20 + K/2$. Figure 9.5 can therefore be simplified to Fig. 9.6.

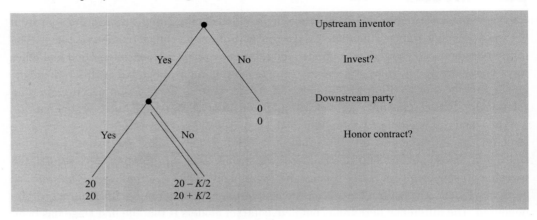

Figure 9.5: Governnance structure 'market'

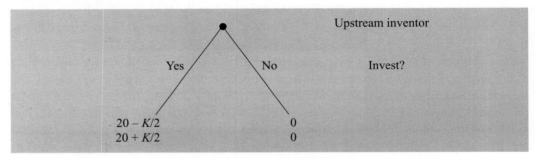

Figure 9.6: Governance structure 'market' in reduced form

The inventor has all bargaining power and appropriates the complete (quasi-) surplus in the governance structure *forward integration* <FI>. The price will be 240. The downstream party does not need to take a decision about honouring the contract, because there is no bargaining relationship. The inventor intervenes selectively and has all the bargaining power. Figure 9.7 summarizes the situation.

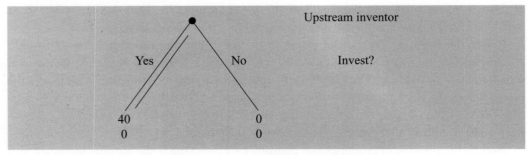

Figure 9.7: Governance structure 'forward integration' in reduced form

The downstream party has all the bargaining power in the governance structure *backward integration* <BI>. He or she appropriates the entire (quasi-) surplus. The price equals $200 - K$ after the fundamental transformation. Figure 9.8 presents this governance structure. Notice that opportunism does not vanish just because of integration, i.e. there is hold-up between the two divisions in the vertically integrated firm.

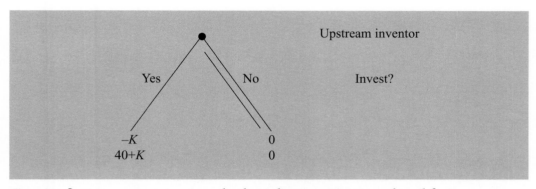

Figure 9.8: Governance structure 'backward integration' in reduced form

Efficiency requires the inventor to invest in the above relationship, because a surplus of 40 can be realized. However, the non-recoverable, or sunk, costs K of the total costs may prevent the inventor investing. The level of the non-recoverable costs K and the choice of the governance structure determine the investment decision of the inventor. The inventor invests when he or she does not have a negative payoff after the fundamental transformation. Three distinct cases will now be described.

First, assume that $K = 0$. If the inventor invests, then he or she earns $20 - K/2 = 20$ in <M>, an amount 40 in <FI> and an amount $-K = 0$ in <BI>. Every governance structure results therefore in an efficient investment decision when $K = 0$. The case $K = 0$ reflects the Coase theorem of Chapter 4. (The next two cases will show that this result is valid only when $K = 0$.) Figure 9.9 presents this situation.

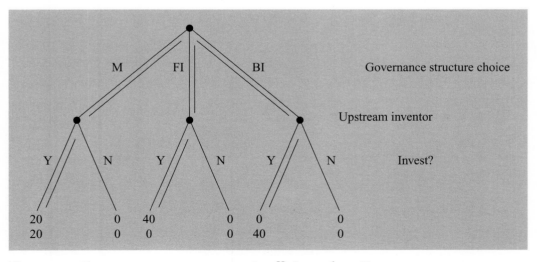

Figure 9.9: Every governance structure is efficient when $K = 0$

Second, assume that $0 < K \le 40$. If the inventor invests, then he or she earns $20 - K/2 \ge 0$ in <M>, an amount 40 in <FI> and an amount $-K < 0$ in <BI>. Only the governance structures <M> and <FI> induce the efficient investment decision when $0 < K \le 40$. Figure 9.10 shows the situation.

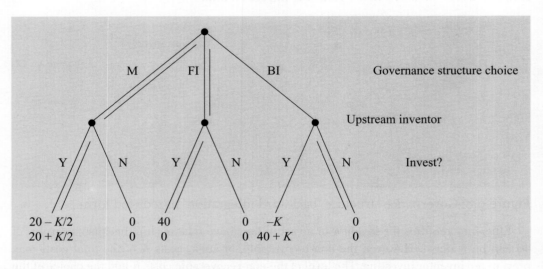

Figure 9.10: Governance structure <BI> is not efficient when $0 < K \le 40$

Third, assume that $40 < K \le 200$. If the inventor invests, he or she earns an amount $20 - K/2 < 0$ in <M>, an amount 40 in <FI> and an amount $-K < 0$ in <BI>. Only the governance structure <FI> results in the efficient investment decision. This shows that the inventor should get more bargaining power in order to induce him to invest when investments become more specific. Figure 9.11 presents the situation.

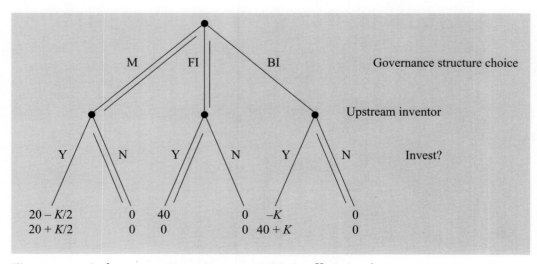

Figure 9.11: Only governance structure <FI> is efficient when $40 < K \le 200$

The following two figures present the importance of the fundamental transformation for the bargaining positions of the two parties in a different way. Before the fundamental transformation the bargaining position of each party is 0. Figure 9.12 shows that before the fundamental transformation every division of the surplus of 40 to the north-east of (0,0) results in an improvement for the upstream as well as the downstream party.

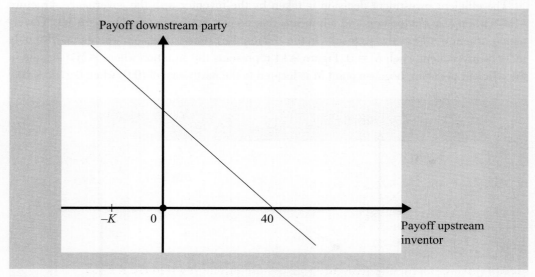

Figure: 9.12: Bargaining positions before the fundamental transformation

After the fundamental transformation, the bargaining position of the upstream inventor deteriorates with an amount K. All divisions of the quasi-surplus of $40 + K$ to the north-east of $(-K,0)$ are possible. However, not all these possibilities are an improvement for the upstream inventor. Only divisions of the quasi-surplus to the north-east of (0,0) are an improvement for both players. Figure 9.13 reflects the situation after the fundamental transformation.

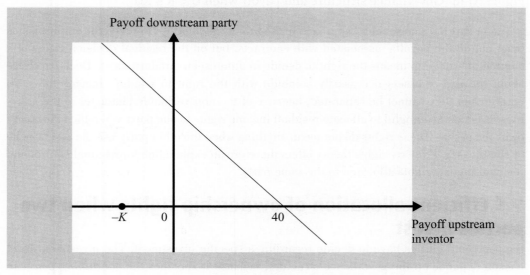

Figure: 9.13: Bargaining positions after the fundamental transformation

The choice of governance structure determines the way in which the quasi-surplus is divided between the upstream inventor and the downstream buyer after the fundamental transformation. The upstream inventor appropriates the entire quasi-surplus in <FI>. Both parties divide the quasi-surplus 50–50 in <M>. Finally, the downstream party obtains the entire quasi-surplus in <BI>.

The efficient investment decision is taken by the inventor with the governance structure <M> when K is not too large, which means that point $(-K,0)$ is not too far to the left. Governance structure <FI> always results in the efficient investment decision, whereas <BI> only induces investment when $K = 0$. Figure 9.14 represents the situation where <M> results in the efficient decision, because point M is located to the north-east of $(0,0)$ when $0 < K \le 40$.

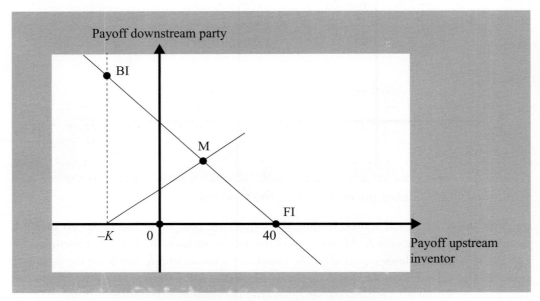

Figure: 9.14: Governance structure and payoff when o < K ≤ 40

As in Part III, a contractual approach to the firm is taken here. However, the emphasis has been not on the payoffs associated with contracts, but on the residual decision rights of a contract. Ownership means the right to decide in unforeseen circumstances. Decision rights about the use of assets necessarily coincide with the right to residual income flows. In equilibrium they cannot be separated, because of the non-verifiable character of the activities. It is not meaningful to allocate residual income rights to one party when the other party owns the assets. These rights do not mean anything when the other party use the assets as he or she pleases. Property rights theory offers therefore an explanation for residual control and residual income rights allocated to the same party.

9.5 Efficient allocation of ownership rights when two parties invest

Suppose both parties have to decide regarding a specific investment. The investment level chosen depends on the governance structure, because it specifies the *bargaining power* in circumstances not covered by the contract. Incomplete contracts entail ex-post opportunistic behaviour, which has consequences for the ex-ante decisions regarding specific investments. A change in the governance structure or ownership rights changes the distribution of bargaining power and therefore affects the ex-ante investment incentives. For example, a switch from market governance to vertical integration changes a situation with two independent employers in a market relationship into a situation with an employer and an employee. This is accompanied by a change in incentives and will result in different opportunistic behaviour. If company I becomes the owner of company J, then I will use its control over residual rights to appropriate a large part of the ex-post surplus, so that it will overinvest and J will underinvest in the relationship. Hart and Moore (1990) formulate this as follows:

> Transferring ownership of an asset from party 2 to party 1 increases 1's freedom of action to use the assets as he or she sees fit and therefore increases 1's share of ex post surplus and ex ante incentive to invest in the relationship; but 2's share of ex post surplus and incentive to invest falls.

Figure 9.15 depicts the three governance structures regarding two assets distinguished in the previous section. Vertical integration is indicated by an oval and the party having the residual rights regarding the assets is indicated by an X. The upstream party has the residual decision rights regarding the assets upstream as well as downstream in the governance structure <FI>, while the downstream party owns these rights in the governance structure <BI>. The governance structure market <M> means that each party has the residual decision rights of the assets he or she or she is working with.

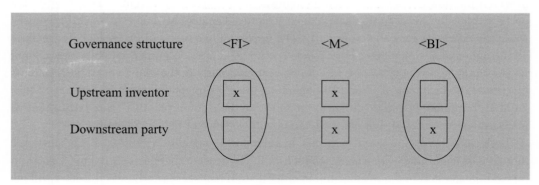

Figure: 9.15: Governance structures and assets

Figure 9.16 shows the consequences of the choice of governance structure for the choice of investment level of each party. The horizontal axis presents the ex-post specific investments of party 1, whereas the vertical axis reflects the level of sunk investment by party 2. Point *FB* shows the first-best investment levels in a situation where complete contracts are possible. The other three points apply to the situation with *incomplete contracts*. There is market governance <M> when the ex-post surplus is divided equally. The governance structure integration, either <FI> or <BI>, implies that one of the two parties has the residual decision rights regarding both assets and therefore appropriates the ex-post surplus.

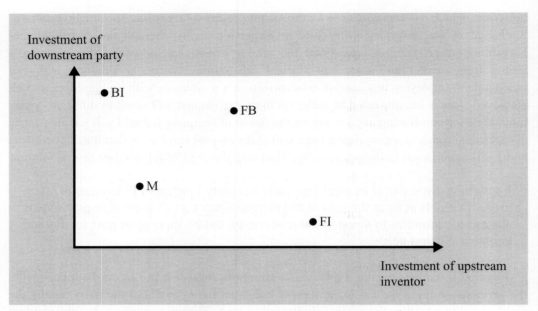

Figure 9.16: Governance structures and ex-ante investments

The investment levels established in a *market relationship* are represented by point M. Both parties invest less than the first-best level, because each party has to incur all the costs of the investment, while only half the revenues are received. Point FI represents the situation in which the downstream party is the employee of the upstream inventor. The downstream party will hardly invest in this governance structure because he or she incurs all the costs, while the revenues go to the other party. The upstream inventor will invest heavily, because all the unforeseen yields this governance structure generates will devolve to him or her. Point BI shows the opposite situation, i.e. the downstream party is the employer of the upstream inventor. (The locations of FI and BI depend on the specific model. Point FI is always below point M, but point FI can be either to the left or to the right of point FB. Similarly, point BI is always to the left of M, but point BI can be either above or below point FB.)

Both parties are supposed to invest in relationship-specific activities. Each party can therefore be confronted with a *hold-up problem*. It will be clear that the owner of the assets will put additional effort in the relationship in order to establish success, whereas the other will not be inclined to do so because he or she has to incur costs without receiving sufficient revenues. If a company decides to take over another company, this has consequences for the activities of the party that is taken over. The self-interest of this party dictates that it behaves differently when it is an independent employer from when it is someone's employee. Every allocation of residual rights therefore entails ex-post investments different from those in the situation with complete contracts. No governance structure, i.e. <FI>, <M>, or <BI>, is able to equal the result obtained when there is complete contracting FB. Efficiency is therefore *second-best*.

The investment levels for the various governance structures have now been determined. Subsequently, the efficient governance structure has to be chosen. The assumption is that the least inefficient governance structure is chosen, because no governance structure is first-best in terms of efficiency as a result of the incompleteness of contracts. The choice of the governance structure is determined by the relative importance of the investments of the various parties. The governance structure *market* is desirable when the investments of both parties are more or less equally important. The ex-post surplus is divided proportionately when there is no vertical integration, which results in a reasonable level of the specific investment by each party. Each obtains the same share in the surplus in <M>. This is important, because the contributions of both are more or less equally important. If both are more or less equally important, then <M> is chosen. There are therefore circumstances in which no integration is strictly preferred to integration.

Integration with I as the owner is desirable when the investments of I are much more important than those of J and the overinvestment by I is a smaller problem than the underinvestment by J. If the investments of the upstream inventor are relatively important, then efficiency requires that integration is chosen and the residual rights are allocated to the upstream inventor. This is reflected by point FI. If however the investments of the downstream party are important (compared with the investments of the upstream inventor) for the success of the relationship, then the surplus is maximized by integration and the residual rights are allocated to the downstream party. This is shown by point BI. These observations imply that *the efficient allocation of ownership rights depends on the relative importance of the specific investments of the various parties*.

> Integration is efficient when the investments of one party are relatively important compared with those of the other party, whereas abstaining from integration is desirable when the investments of both parties are more or less equally important.

Application: Entrepreneur as monitor in team production

The above result corresponds with an earlier result in Sec. 6.2 regarding the effect of the contribution of a person ($P(e)$). Suppose a situation prevails where various people can do a transaction-specific investment, and the ownership rights are allocated to one of them. The above implies that they are allocated to the person whose hard-to-measure activities make the largest contribution to the output of the team. Decision-making authority should be allocated to the person generating the highest value by using his information most efficiently. As in Chapter 6, some qualifications have to be made. The reach of activities and responsibilities of ownership should be taken into account. The equal compensation principle of Sec. 6.3 indicates that vertical integration is not a good idea when it applies only to a small part of the activities and responsibilities, because it would result in a neglect of other tasks.

In the original argument of Alchian and Demsetz (1972) with respect to team production, it is not possible for the contribution of one particular employee to be easier to determine than that of another. Furthermore, it is assumed that the total output is observable. These two assumptions offer the possibility of using the knowledge of some individual contributions together with the total result to determine the contribution of the other team members. In such a situation, knowledge about the marginal productivity of one person's input provides information about the productivity of others. However, assume that the marginal contribution cannot be determined as easily for every employee, so that the individual contributions to the total production cannot be determined with any accuracy (Holmström and Tirole, 1989). It has just been concluded that ownership should be allocated to the input factor the contribution of which is most difficult to determine. A reinterpretation of the theory of Alchian and Demsetz in this context means that the position of the supervisor coincides with the position of the owner, because his or her contribution is important but diffuse. These considerations also correspond to the results of Chapter 6. Reward systems in the form of piecework wages (Sec. 6.2) require that the production of the agent is verifiable at low costs for both parties. However, evaluating performances often includes subjective elements. In such situations piece-rate wages are less suitable, because they do not take sufficient account of various other performance aspects (Sec. 6.3). According to Alchian and Demsetz (Sec. 6.5), this is the reason for the existence of companies.

Application: Definition of vertical integration

Grossman and Hart (1986) characterize the firm by residual control over assets. However, the strict application of this definition can be problematic, because a large company is often associated with many assets and liabilities. Usually, a company does not own all the residual rights. Riordan (1990) illustrates the problem of this definition with *vertical integration*. One way to organize business activities is for a company to buy raw material, hire employees and lease equipment from an independent party based on a contract. Since equipment leased, the residual rights are therefore not owned by the company. According to the definition of Grossman and Hart, the company is not vertically integrated. Another possibility is for this company to rent out specific equipment which is necessary in the production process to an input provider. The company is the owner of the equipment and has the right therefore to decide regarding its use in unforeseen circumstances. This *is* vertical integration according to Grossman and Hart. However, if vertical integration is viewed from the perspective of executing two subsequent stages of production in one company, then the first situation is vertical integration, and the second is not. Figure 9.17 summarizes this example.

Emphasis in integration definition	Assets hired from third party	Assets rented to third party
Ownership assets	No	Yes
Subsequent production processes	Yes	No

Figure 9.17: Vertical integration

This example illustrates that there are situations where the definition of the firm used by Grossman and Hart (the collection of assets over which the company has the residual rights) does not always correspond with the use of terms in daily life. In practical situations, however, this will hardly be a problem. What *is* significant is the importance of specific rights compared with the importance of residual rights. If capital is leased from third parties and the contract contains almost all of the possible contingencies, it does not matter much who owns the residual rights. Although leasing capital implies that the company does not own the residual rights, from a practical viewpoint, leased capital together with an almost complete contract covering almost every possible contingency can be considered as property. The definition of a company by Grossman and Hart can be interpreted in practice as the collection of assets over which the company has the residual rights, where the importance of the residual rights over the assets owned by third parties is small compared with the importance of the specific rights.

A definition of the firm based on ownership of the residual rights regarding *assets* is fundamentally different from a definition of ownership in terms of a claim on *profit*. This latter definition faces problems similar to those faced by the traditional definitions in neo-classical economics and principal–agent literature; in these definitions it is impossible to distinguish between a company and a contract. On the other hand, the example summarized in Fig. 9.17 shows that the residual decision rights do not coincide completely with the residual income rights when several production factors are present. Therefore, residual income rights are also possible as a basis for the definition of the firm.

Application: Insurance industry

Two types of insurance companies can be distinguished: those owning the list of policy-holders and those whose intermediaries own the list. Companies owning the list of policy-holders have the right to offer their clients policies first when the intermediary breaks the relationship with the company. Besides this, the intermediary is not allowed to renew the policies with another insurer. The company whose intermediaries own the list does not have these rights. These intermediaries have the right to do business first with the current clients when the insurance company breaks the relationship with the intermediary. In addition, the independent insurance agent can advise clients to switch to another insurance company.

Contracts are incomplete in this industry because many circumstances cannot be covered contractually between the insurance company and the intermediary, owing to changing market conditions. Specific and residual rights can therefore be distinguished. The allocation of specific rights determines the rights and obligations of both parties, which are based on observable and verifiable circumstances and results. An example of specific rights is the reward structure of the intermediaries, e.g. piece-rate wages or fixed wages are possibilities; Chapter 6 dealt with this topic. The residual rights concern decisions regarding the ownership of the list of policyholders. The allocation of these rights has an effect on two types of non-contractibles: (a) those which may cause damage to the agent when the company owns the list of policyholders and (b) those which may cause damage to the company when the agent owns the list of policyholders. An example of the first is making car insurance less desirable in certain regions by increasing the prices of the policies or decreasing the quality of the service. The incomes of the intermediaries will decrease, because some clients will go elsewhere for insurance. The incentive for the agent to bring in new long-term clients and provide advice will decrease substantially in such situations. The efforts (investments) of the intermediary do not change when the intermediary owns the list, because he or she can advise clients in that case to switch to another company. This can sometimes be good for the client, but can also be inspired by appropriating the profits of the company. The possibility of the agent exhibiting such behaviour influences the ex-post investments of the insurance company. Product development, education of intermediaries, settlement of claims, national advertising campaigns and information provision to clients are examples of such investments. The owner of the list of policyholders has sufficient incentive therefore to build up a list of policyholders, whereas the other has not.

The theory predicts that control over the list of policyholders of company A by company B will be desirable when the ex-post investments of company B are more important than those of company A. The tradeoff is between the advantages of control and its potential costs, because the discretion is taken away from the those who develop productive activities. This implies that the insurance company will be the owner of the list of policyholders of those products for which the continuation of sales is guaranteed and therefore not sensitive to the actions of the agent. Life insurance is a good example. Developing and maintaining a reputation is a specific and costly investment; but once a client is enlisted, he or she will not need a lot of advice and will not switch to another company quickly. However, when sales are not guaranteed and are sensitive to the intermediary's investments the intermediary will be the owner of the list of policyholders. An example is travel insurance, where clients have to be recruited over and over again. This requires a good local reputation, which may be established by providing good service and local advertising. These predictions are empirically supported by data of the American insurance industry (Grossman and Hart, 1986).

Application: Franchise contracts and the product life cycle

A hamburger chain often uses a *franchise contract* to structure the relationship between the company and the local managers. The brand is the asset for which a governance structure has to be chosen. The length of these contracts often varies between 10 and 20 years. The local manager (franchisee) pays the franchiser a fixed amount of money at the start of the relationship, and a percentage of the sales for the right to exploit a standardized outlet with a specific technology and a well-known brand. Besides, many economies of scale can be exploited, like common marketing, bargaining power in input markets and support from the main organization. A certain minimum level of quality has to be maintained and the inputs and equipment have to be bought from a supplier certified by the organization. The franchisee is independent and hires his or her own personnel. The advantages of the relationship for the franchiser are that the other party takes care of a substantial share of the financing of investments and that the flexibility of entrepreneurship is maintained.

Both franchiser and franchisee invest in the development of the market. The valuable brand name and the efforts of the manager are necessary for a successful dissemination of the product. These common efforts are agreed upon and specified in a contract. However, this contract cannot anticipate everything, like for example the growth of market demand. Besides, the efforts of both parties cannot be controlled completely. The franchise contract specifies different aspects regarding the inputs of both parties and the allocation of the *exclusive right* regarding opening new outlets in the area of the local manager. This right can be allocated to either the local manager or the main company. The protection of the local manager by giving him or her the exclusive right provides the right incentive, i.e. potentially high profits, to invest optimally in the development of the local market. However, the disadvantage is that there are few incentives left for the main company to develop supporting activities, like national advertising and maintaining the brand name.

The theory predicts that these exclusive rights are granted to the local manager during the introduction stage of the product, but not any more in the maturity stage. The idea is that during the introduction stage the acceptance of the product by the consumer depends largely on the efforts of the local manager, in for example informing and convincing clients to try the product. The incentive to make these efforts is provided by granting the local manager exclusive (monopoly) rights. In the maturity stage the market is quite different. The product and the availability are known, which implies that the efforts of the manager are therefore relatively less important. Interest is now dependent mainly on the availability of the product and less on the activities of the manager. The analysis of 25 franchise contracts supports these predictions (Mathewson and Winter, 1989).

Application: Franchise fees and royalties

A straightforward implication for franchising of the complete contracting theory discussed in Chapter 6 is that royalties are chosen as a function of risk and incentives and the initial fee extracts rents left downstream by the royalty rate (Lafontaine, 1992). Therefore the principal–agent models imply that the franchise fee as present value of all future profits left downstream should be inversely related to the royalty rate.

The structure of initial fees and royalties depends on the distribution of intangible assets between the franchiser and the franchisee according to the *property rights view* of the firm. 'Intangible assets' are the knowledge and skills (know-how) stored largely in the minds of people which cannot be codified and easily transferred to other agents since they have an important tacit component. The franchisee's intangible assets are the local know-how which results in efficient marketing strategies in combination with the franchiser's system-specific know-how. The franchiser's intangible assets are the system-specific expertise with relation to the brand name. If the franchiser's brand name investments (e.g. national advertising) are crucial to the market success of the product or service, then the franchiser has to be given an important ownership stake to provide the necessary investment incentives. The higher the franchiser's (franchisee's) intangible assets relative to the franchisee's (franchiser's), the more residual income rights should be transferred to him or her and the higher (lower) are the royalties and fees. The property rights view suggests a positive relationship between royalties and initial fees. This view is supported by data from the Austrian franchise sector (Windsperger, 2001).

Application: Capital structure

The way a company is financed influences the behaviour of the parties involved, according to Jensen and Meckling (1976). Financial instruments are often evaluated on the basis of their remuneration aspects. However, the perspective of complete contracts is no theoretical basis for disproving the Modigliani–Miller theorem (1958) that the financial structure of the company does not matter for the value of the firm. It has been shown that reward structures can be designed such that incentives for managers are formulated which generate the same outcome without including financial instruments in the analysis. The complete contracting approach is therefore a theory of optimal incentive schemes rather than a theory of optimal capital structure. Other aspects of financial instruments have to be distinguished in order to establish a relationship between the financial structure of the firm and the firm's value.

Residual rights apply to situations not covered by a contract, which is taken into account in the design of contracts by allocating the decision rights in unforeseen circumstances to one party. This chapter has focused on the importance of residual decision rights for the investment in specific assets. This application focuses on how the allocation of residual decision rights affects the tradeoff between cash flows and private benefits of an investment. Consider a situation with an entrepreneur, an investor and a single project. The project yields cash flows as well as private benefits. The investor is interested only in cash flows, while the entrepreneur is interested in both cash flows and private benefits. Examples of private benefits may be non-pecuniary benefits like psychic value, but also personal satisfaction from working on a pet project, reputation enhancement, appointing relatives or friends even though they are incompetent ('patronage'), the ability to divert money from the project and so on (Hart, 2001).

The existence of private benefits creates a divergence of interest between the entrepreneur and the investor. This conflict of interest is resolved by allocating the residual decision rights. Ownership of these rights determines which decision is taken ex post, e.g. with respect to the continuation of the project. (Exercise 4.7 provided a numerical illustration.) The allocation of income and decision rights to one party or the other will usually depend on the circumstances. *Investor control* is desirable in cases where private benefits, e.g. perks or pet projects, are not very important, because the outcome will be approximately efficient and the participation constraint of the entrepreneur can be met. *Entrepreneur control* is desirable when private benefits are considerable.

Aghion and Bolton (1989, 1992) view specific financial instruments from the property rights perspective, i.e. where every form of capital entails a certain governance structure. Equity as well as debt defines the residual rights implicitly. When the company is financed completely with *equity,* the shareholders determine what will happen in unforeseen circumstances, whereas when it is financed with preferred shares and the manager owns these shares it is the manager who decides. *Preferred stock*s entail more control than ordinary shares. The residual rights belonging to equity as well as preferred stock are allocated to the same party in all possible contingencies. From an incomplete contracting perspective, *debt* comes between these two financial instruments, because it entails contingent control. In a debt-financed company managers decide as long as things go well, whereas the providers of debt obtain control in bad times (bankruptcy). Bankruptcy means therefore that the decision rights change hands. According to this perspective, circumstances which are not bad enough to liquidate the company can give rise to bankruptcy, because the residual rights will switch to another party. This can be desirable when the current management is not the most suitable party to take decisions and manage during hard times. In those circumstances an interim manager can be hired because the allocation of the residual rights allows for this.

Making the allocation of *decision rights outcome-dependent* is an important extension of the theory of Grossman and Hart (in whose analysis residual rights are allocated to one party, regardless of the outcome) Financial instruments are chosen such that the circumstances determine who is the right person to take decisions in the face of the unforeseen. This will relate to the agency costs associated with the different circumstances. Control of the residual rights by the providers of capital results in a strong emphasis on cash flow and takes relatively little account of the private benefits of the entrepreneur or manager. However, if in unforeseen circumstances the manager can decide, then investments will be made in activities which pay more attention to the interest of the manager than to the interests of the providers of capital. A combination of assets and liabilities is efficient if, on the one hand, in the case of bankruptcy the agency costs associated with external financiers are relatively low, and, on the other hand, if when there is no bankruptcy the agency costs associated with control by managers are comparatively small.

There are various examples where the residual decision and income rights are allocated to different parties. Aoki (1989) considers financial contracts between banks and companies in Japan from the above perspective. A large part of the outstanding assets of companies is usually governed by a consortium of banks and the percentage of liabilities is usually high, compared with companies in other countries. Despite this large financial share, banks do not exercise control over the company as long as it performs well. Information is exchanged regularly about the well-being of the company, and banks restrict themselves to the roles of investors. However, if something seems to go wrong, then this is acknowledged in time because of the mutual contacts and the necessary changes. As long as things go well, banks stay aside and the residual rights are owned by the company, whereas during unfavourable times these rights switch to the consortium of banks. Another example is provided by the *venture capital* sector (Kaplan and Stromberg, 2001). Financial contracts in this sector distinguish several rights, like income rights, voting rights, board rights, liquidation rights and other control rights. These rights are usually allocated to different parties, and are often outcome-dependent. For instance, if the firm performs poorly, then the venture capitalists obtain full control. As firm performance improves, the entrepreneur retains or obtains more control rights. Income and decision rights are therefore independent instruments, i.e. they can be allocated to different parties. This entails a substantial deviation from one share, one vote.

Application: Agricultural and horticultural co-operatives

The analysis of agricultural and horticultural co-operatives undertaken in Chapter 8 is now presented in terms of the approach of this chapter. Figure 9.18 is similar to Fig. 9.14. The only difference is that the names of the parties on the axes have been adjusted to reflect the situation in agricultural and horticultural co-operatives and that forward integration (FI) is replaced by marketing co-operative (MC). Figure 9.18 reflects the situation where only the farmers consider investing in specific assets (Hendrikse and Veerman, 2001a). The level of sunk costs K is chosen such that only the governance structure MC is efficient, i.e. BI and M are inefficient governance structures.

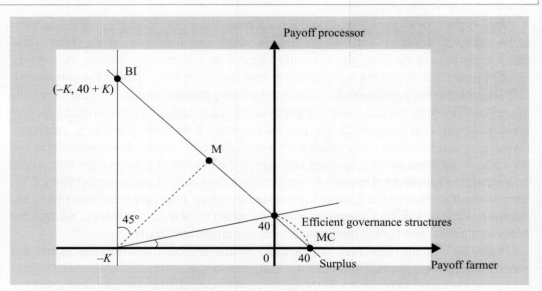

Figure 9.18: Governance structure choice and specific investments (Hendrikse and Veerman, 2001a, p. 59)

Agricultural and horticultural co-operatives are confronted nowadays with two hold-up problems. Current agricultural markets exhibit substantial product differentiation and many specific investments are needed. Farmers fear hold-up regarding the harvest by processors, whereas external suppliers of capital have to be worried about the opportunity costs of providing capital when investments in the production of differentiated products are characterized by substantial asset specificity. Figure 9.19 depicts this situation (Hendrikse and Veerman, 2001a). Farmers as well as external providers of capital have to invest in specific assets, where the sunk costs of the investment by the farmers is depicted by K_f and the sunk costs of the investment by the external financiers by K_e. If both stakeholders have to be given confidence that they will get their money back, then complete control by one party, e.g. the farmers in an agricultural co-operative, is not desirable. Safeguards with respect to opportunistic behaviour have to be provided in the form of (some) control to both parties. The governance structure <MC> therefore seems less suitable for markets where the downstream party has to make substantial specific investments.

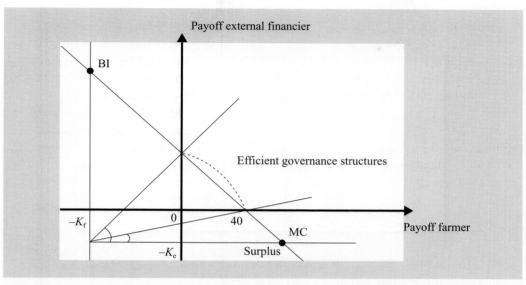

Figure 9.19: Two hold-up problems and efficient governance structure choice (Hendrikse and Veerman, 2001a, p. 61)

Application: Majority decision-making

Hart and Moore (1996) compare the governance structure co-operative with the governance structure outside ownership. In a co-operative, the assets are owned by the members and investment decisions are taken democratically, which means that every member has one vote and that the choice of the majority prevails. Outside ownership means that the profit-maximizing external owner decides.

The outcome of majority decision-making is determined by the composition of the membership. Members have different preferences and will express that in their voting behaviour. The members of a golf club differ with respect to the intensity with which they practice their sport. The most dedicated players are always on the fairway, whereas there are also members who stay mainly at the bar. Figure 9.20 reflects a possible distribution of the preferences of the members. It is important that there are members with different interests. This is reflected in differences between the members regarding the ranking of various investment possibilities.

Assume that there are four possible investment decisions:

A: Invest only in the golfcourse;
B: Invest in the golfcourse as well as the bar;
C: Invest only in the bar;
D: Sell the last nine holes and invest only in the bar.

Three types of golfers are distinguished. Dedicated golfers rank the investment possibilities as A > B > C > D, where > means 'is preferred to'. The members who are mainly interested in the non-golf activities are characterized by the preferences D > C

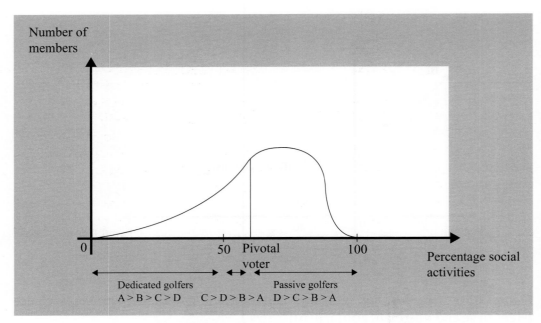

Figure 9.20: Composition of the membership

> B > A. With regard to the dedicated golfers, it is assumed that they are willing to spend at least twice as much for the improvement of the golf course as the members with preferences D > C > B > A are willing to spend for improving the bar. The preferences of the members who value both aspects of golf more or less equally are characterized by C > D > B > A.

The member with an equal number of members to left (in terms of Fig. 9.20) and right is called the *pivotal voter*. It is assumed that this member has preferences C > D > B > A. Finally, assume that for all members together B > C > A > D, which means that choice B is most desirable for all members of the golf club together. (Kim and Parker (1995) discuss aspects of the termination of membership in organizations with democratic decision-making.)

The median voter theorem (Roberts, 1977) specifies in which circumstances the preferences of the pivotal voter are crucial for the outcome of democratic decision-making. In the above situation, the preferences of the pivotal voter are C > D > B > A. The co-operative will therefore choose option C. The golf club with an external owner chooses option A because the dedicated golfers will pay much more, i.e. more than twice as much as the other members, for their first choice. The outside monopolistic owner determines the raise in the contribution by the reservation price of the marginal member in the market niche of dedicated golfers. Both governance structures induce an inefficient investment decision. In the above example, the governance structure co-operative is predicted because it makes the least inefficient investment decision.

The inefficiency in decision-making in a co-operative is due to the feature of democratic decision-making. All decision-making power is in the hands of the pivotal voter. However, the preferences of this member do not coincide with the average opinion of all members, where the average opinion is the weighed average of the preferences of all members. The reason for this difference is that the distribution of the member preferences in Fig. 9.20 is skewed. The majority of the members prefer the social aspect and express this in their voting behaviour, whereas the costs of the investment are paid by all members. Outside ownership also results in an inefficient decision. The reason for the inefficiency in decision-making in a golf club with an outside owner is that the preferences of the social members are not taken into account. The outside owner maximizes his profit by choosing option A and implements a drastic rise in the membership fee. The social members will cancel their membership, but the profit-maximizing outside owner does not care.

The efficiency of a governance structure is determined by the circumstances. Hart and Moore (1996) summarize the circumstances by the degree of skewness in the membership distribution and the degree of competition. The skewness in the membership distribution determines the position of the pivotal voter, whereas the degree of competition indicates the possibilities for raising the contribution. This results in two hypotheses.

First, the governance structure outside ownership becomes relatively more efficient than the governance structure co-operative when the composition of the membership becomes more skewed. This is explained as follows. Assume that a number of dedicated golfers are being injured and start to focus on sitting at the bar. This change in the composition of the preferences of the members can have large consequences for the decision-making of the co-operative, i.e. the pivotal voter can become a member with preferences D > C > B > A. As a result, option D is chosen, which is even less efficient than option C. For the golf club with an external owner, not much changes. Although a number of dedicated golfers are gone, it is assumed that the strategy of a rise in subscription is still the profit-maximizing strategy. External ownership therefore becomes more attractive.

Second, the governance structure outside ownership becomes relatively more efficient than the governance structure co-operative when the competitive pressure increases. Assume that a new golf club is set up in the neighbourhood and that the membership fee is low enough to draw all golfers. The effect on the price policy of the external owner is that he or she is forced to decrease the prices to keep the current members. Option B becomes more attractive for the external owner because it has an attractive aspect for every member. More intense competition results in an increase in efficiency of the governance structure external ownership. For the co-operative, more competition does not result in a change of policy, because it is insulated from competition. The effect of more competition is therefore that the governance structure with an external owner becomes more efficient compared with the governance structure co-operative.

Application: Trucking

Technological developments have made it possible for on-board computers to be introduced in the road haulage industry. These devices provide ex-post verifiable information about how trucks are operated. On-board computers therefore increase the reach of complete contracts. They provide additional possibilities for rewarding good driving, and therefore make it less attractive to explore other opportunities for the use of a truck.

It turns out that the introduction of these devices has 'shifted ownership away from drivers, particularly for hauls where driver ownership would encourage most rent-seeking' (Baker and Hubbard, 2001, p. 192).

9.6 Extensions

A number of extensions of the framework of the previous decisions are presented in this section. Access (9.6.1), multiple decisions (9.6.2) and complementary assets (9.6.3) will be dealt with.

9.6.1 Access

A stylized example (Hart and Moore, 1990) will illustrate the difference in authority between the *customer–grocer* relationship and the *employer–employee* relationship. Assume that there is a luxury yacht in the harbour of a beautiful island in the ocean wide. There is a princess willing to pay 240 for a dinner during a cruise with this yacht. The preparation of the dinner is done by the chef and takes a specific investment by the chef which costs 100. The incompleteness of contracts makes it impossible for something meaningful to be contracted upon regarding the effort by the chef to prepare a good dinner. The skipper takes care of the navigation of the yacht. There is therefore one asset and one specific investment.

The efficient, surplus-maximizing decision of the chef is to prepare the dinner because 240 > 100. The chef is willing to prepare the dinner only when the investment costs of 100 can be recouped. The division of the quasi-surplus of 240 will be determined in the ex-post bargaining process because of the incompleteness of the contract. It is assumed that the quasi-surplus is divided equally between the *essential* parties regarding the transaction.

The crux of the incomplete contracting approach is that the choice of governance structure determines which players are essential for the transaction. Each governance structure is associated with a certain distribution of the ex-post bargaining power between the involved parties. The choice of governance structure determines which share of the quasi-surplus goes to the chef and therefore determines the investment decision of the chef.

Suppose there is only one princess interested in the cruise and that there are many skippers willing to navigate the yacht. This means that the princess is essential, whereas the skipper is not. The choice of governance structure concerns the ownership of the asset, i.e. the yacht. There are three possible governance structures: the yacht is owned by the chef, the princess or the skipper. If the governance structure 'chef owns yacht' prevails, then there are two essential parties: the chef and the princess. The chef is essential for the transaction, because he prepares the dinner and owns the yacht. The princess is essential because she is the only one willing and able to pay for the dinner. The skipper is not essential because there are many skippers available. The governance structure 'chef owns yacht' (and the bargaining assumption) means therefore that the chef and the princess each receive 240/2 = 120 of the quasi-surplus. The chef takes the efficient investment decision because the revenues (120) are larger than his costs (100).

The governance structure 'princess owns yacht' also involves two essential parties. The chef is essential because he has to prepare the dinner, while the princess is essential because she owns the yacht and is the only one interested in the cruise with dinner. The skipper is again easy to replace, i.e. he is inessential. The chef and the princess each receive half of the quasi-surplus and the chef takes the efficient decision. Finally, the governance structure 'skipper owns yacht' makes all three parties essential. The chef is essential because he prepares the dinner, the princess is essential because she is the only one interested in the cruise and the skipper is essential because he owns the yacht. The quasi-surplus of 240 is divided equally between the three parties. The chef does not invest with this governance structure because his revenues $240/3 = 80$ are lower than his costs of 100. This is the well-known hold-up problem due to the incompleteness of contracts. Figure 9.21 summarizes the bargaining positions associated with the various governance structures.

		Governance structure		
		Chef	Skipper	Princess
Bargaining power	Chef	$\frac{1}{2}$	$\frac{1}{3}$	$\frac{1}{2}$
	Skipper	0	$\frac{1}{3}$	0
	Princess	$\frac{1}{2}$	$\frac{1}{3}$	$\frac{1}{2}$

Figure 9.21: Governance structure and bargaining power

The investment decision of the chef is determined for each possible governance structure. It will now be determined which governance structure is chosen. In the incomplete contracting approach the prediction regarding the choice of governance structure is driven by efficiency considerations: the least inefficient, or second-best efficient, governance structure is chosen. This implies in the above example that either the chef or the princess owns the yacht, but not the skipper. The reason is that the first two governance structures entail a bilateral bargaining situation, whereas the third governance structure creates a trilateral bargaining situation. The trilateral bargaining situation dilutes the share of the chef in the quasi-surplus to such an extent that he does not invest. Figure 9.22 presents the subgame perfect equilibrium choices regarding governance structure and investment.

This stylized example clarifies the notion of authority. The employer has in the employer–employee relationship the right to decide, i.e. exercise authority or intervene selectively or be the boss, in unforeseen circumstances. The advantage of selective intervention is that bargaining problems are eliminated. A bilateral bargaining situation, like in a market relationship, transforms in a unilateral bargaining situation, like in a company. In unforeseen circumstances the boss has the right to tell workers what to do.

Hart and Moore (1990) associate authority with ownership over physical assets. In a situation of disagreement authority is established and indirectly exercised by a boss over his or her employee by denying the employee *access* to assets the use of which for the employee is important (Rajan and Zingales, 1998). This aspect of the property rights approach offers

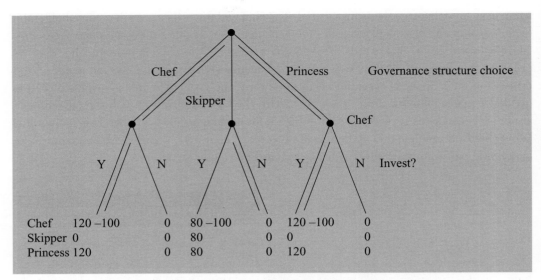

Figure 9.22: Governance structure choice and investment behaviour

the possibility to unite the perspective of Coase (1937) with the criticism of Alchian and Demsetz (1972). Section 9.2 explained that Alchian and Demsetz see no difference between the customer–grocer relationship and the employer–employee relationship. Grossman and Hart (1986) also in principle make no distinction between the available sanctions in the two relationships, but they indicate that the incentives are structured in a different way. These incentives are more aligned in the employer–employee relationship, because the investments of both are important for the success of the relationship. This complies with the reasoning of Coase that the behaviour of the agent in the employer–employee relationship is more in line with the interests of the principal than in the customer–grocer relationship. The reason is that the employee knows that the assets are chosen repeatedly by the principal, which determines the productivity of the employee to a certain extent. This does not hold when they are independent parties. The behaviour of the employee is more in line with the interests of the employer, because the employer makes the assets available.

Every governance structure entails its own degree of authority, because the share of the quasi-surplus, i.e. bargaining power, depends on the governance structure. The behaviour in the customer–grocer relationship differs between the governance structure 'market' and the governance structure 'hierarchy'. If the customer fires the grocer when there is market governance, then the grocer keeps his shop. If the customer is the employer or boss in the governance structure 'hierarchy', then the customer can deny the grocer access to the shop and replace him with somebody else. The grocer will therefore more often satisfy the wants of the customer in the governance structure hierarchy than in the governance structure market.

Ownership over physical assets means that an employee pays more attention to the wishes of the boss than to those of somebody else. Control is exercised indirectly by ownership of physical assets by the boss. More control over physical assets results in more control over human assets. An employee will pay more attention to the goals of the other party when the other party is the boss than when there is a market relationship. The employee will therefore pay more attention to the interests of the employer than will the grocer to those of the customer. The reason is that the employer has more power over the employee than the customer over the grocer. The employer has authority and decides which machines are to be used by the employee and he or she can appoint another employee to use the assets, i.e. the employer controls access. This is important for the employee, because the use of the assets determines his productivity. The customer can only withdraw his demand from the grocer. As long as the customer is small in terms of total sales, then it will not be hard for the grocer to attract new customers. Similarly, ownership of the yacht by the princess results in the preparation of the dinner by chef, i.e. the chef behaves in the interest of the princess. However, if the princess is not the boss of the chef because the skipper owns the yacht, then the chef will not prepare the dinner and therefore does not satisfy the wishes of the princess.

9.6.2 Multiple decisions

Suppose there is *one asset*, e.g. the luxury yacht, and *two specific investments*. The chef has again to take a decision regarding the preparation of the dinner. There is now also a role for the skipper because the princess likes to be told a story about the history of the islands during dinner. The skipper has to decide about spending time and effort in studying the local history. The princess values both items, the dinner and the story at 240 each. The costs of learning the local history are 100 for the skipper. Efficiency means that this investment is made. However, it is not obvious that the efficient decisions 'chef cooks' and 'skipper narrates' are taken. This depends on the choice of governance structure.

Figure 9.23 indicates for each of the three governance structures the share of the quasi-surplus that goes to each player as well as the investment decisions. The first and second columns relate to the investment by the chef and are identical to Figs 9.21 and 9.22. The final two columns are the result of a similar analysis of the investment decision of the skipper. The overall result is that there is only one governance structure where both investment decisions are efficient. The governance structure 'chef owns yacht' is inefficient because it means that only the investment decision of the chef is efficient, while the governance structure 'skipper owns yacht' results in only the skipper investing. Both investors, i.e. the chef and the skipper, take the efficient investment decisions when the governance structure 'princess owns yacht' prevails.

Ownership of yacht		Chef's part of 240	Does the chef cook?	Skipper's part of 240	Does the skipper learn?
	Chef	120	Yes	80	No
	Skipper	80	No	120	Yes
	Princess	120	Yes	120	Yes

Figure 9.23: Investment decisions regarding two assets in different governance structures

This example shows that it can be efficient to assign authority to the party who is essential, i.e. the princess, despite the fact that she does not invest. The reason is that the governance structure 'princess owns yacht' entails two bilateral bargaining situations, i.e. princess–chef and princess–skipper, while the other governance structures create one trilateral bargaining situation, i.e. princess–chef–skipper, and one bilateral bargaining situation, i.e. princess–chef or princess–skipper.

Figure 9.24 shows that the size of the quasi-surplus is maximized with the governance structure 'princess owns yacht'. The share of the quasi-surplus received by each party in each governance structure is also indicated. If the chef owns the yacht, then he is the only one investing and the generated quasi-surplus is divided equally between the chef and the princess. Similarly, if the skipper owns the yacht, then he is the only one investing and the generated quasi-surplus is divided equally between the skipper and the princess. The governance structure 'princess owns yacht' results in investment by the chef as well as the skipper. The princess and the chef each receive half of the quasi-surplus generated by the chef. The princess also receives half of the quasi-surplus generated by the skipper. The other half goes to the skipper.

		Governance structure		
		Chef	**Skipper**	**Princess**
Bargaining power	**Chef**	$\frac{1}{2}$	0	$\frac{1}{4}$
	Skipper	0	$\frac{1}{2}$	$\frac{1}{4}$
	Princess	$\frac{1}{2}$	$\frac{1}{2}$	$\frac{1}{2}$
Size of quasi-surplus		240	240	480

Figure 9.24: Governance structure, size and division surplus

The situation with one asset and two decisions is a second way of undermining the criticism by Alchian and Demsetz of Coase and Simon. Ownership applies usually not to one decision right, but to *multiple decision rights*. An employer has the right to decide regarding the use of assets, to sell the assets and to collect the revenues. Similarly, the owner of a camel in the Sahara has the right to decide regarding a ride on a camel, the right to milk the camel and the right to the meat of the camel after its death. In the same way, a grocer has the right to choose the (quality of) cheese, to determine the price and to decide about quitting. All these rights in all these examples can in principle be assigned to different parties. In the first example, the user of the asset instead of the employer could be assigned all the rights. The tourist interested in a camel ride could be assigned the ownership rights of the camel. The supplier of cheese to the grocer could own the grocery store. These governance structures are theoretically possible, but it is unlikely that they are efficient. All these governance structures involve one bilateral and many trilateral bargaining problems, while the governance structures mentioned earlier are characterized by many bilateral bargaining problems. The example of the cruise with the yacht as asset and two decisions has illustrated that ownership is assigned efficiently to the person who is essential in many decisions.

9.6.3 Complementary assets

A second extension of the luxury yacht example concerns two assets and three investment decisions. The yacht has been conceived of as one asset. Assume now that the yacht consists of two assets: the hull and the galley. All players are assumed to invest. The chef decides regarding the preparation of a specific dinner, the skipper considers studying the history of the islands and the princess considers calling her friends in order to accompany her. Each investment is valued at 240 by the princess, so that a quasi-surplus of 720 can be realized. It is also assumed that nobody is essential, i.e. there are many chefs, many skippers and many princesses. The previous examples have assumed that the cost of each investment is 100 for the investor. This section specifies as the costs of preparing the dinner an amount k_d, the costs k_h of mastering the history of the islands and the costs k_b of calling the friends.

The choice of investment is determined not only by the size of the quasi-surplus and the investment costs, but also by the choice of governance structure. There are $3 \times 3 = 9$ governance structures, because there are two assets and three parties. The essence of this situation can already be illustrated by comparing two governance structures. The governance structure 'integration' means that the chef owns the entire yacht, i.e. the hull as well as the galley, while 'non-integration' is characterized by ownership of the hull by the skipper and ownership of the galley by the chef. Figure 9.25 summarizes the distribution of the quasi-surplus of each investment in each governance structure when all investments are made.

		Non-integration			Integration		
		Investor			Investor		
		Chef	Skipper	Princess	Chef	Skipper	Princess
Part of the surplus for	Chef	120	120	80	240	120	120
	Skipper	120	120	80	0	120	0
	Princess	0	0	80	0	0	120

Figure 9.25: Division of the quasi-surplus in different governance structures

Figure 9.26 indicates for each governance structure the willingness to invest of each party. For example, the princess is willing to invest at most 80 in calling her friends to accompany her on the cruise when the governance structure 'non-integration' prevails. The reason is that the skipper owns the hull and the chef the galley. They each receive one-third of the quasi-surplus generated by the investment by the princess. If the costs of calling her friends is low enough, i.e. $k_b \leq 80$, then the princess takes the efficient investment decision in the governance structure 'non-integration'. If $k_b > 80$, then there is hold-up in this governance structure.

		Governance structure	
		Non-integration	**Integration**
Player	Chef	120	240
	Skipper	120	120
	Princess	80	120

Figure 9.26: Willingness to invest of each party in each governance structure

The investment decision of the chef is always efficient in the governance structure 'integration', regardless of the level of k_d. In this governance structure the chef owns the hull as well as the galley and neither the skipper nor the princess is essential. All the bargaining power regarding the quasi-surplus of the chef's investment is allocated to the chef, and he will therefore appropriate the entire quasi-surplus. If $k_d \leq 240$ then the chef invests, which is efficient. If $k_d > 240$ then the chef does not invest, which is also efficient because the costs of the investment are higher than the value generated by the investment.

Figure 9.26 shows that for a larger set of parameter values k_d, k_h and k_b the governance structure 'integration' results in more efficient investment decisions than the governance structure 'non-integration'. Non-integration results in the efficient investment decision of the chef (skipper, princess) when $k_d \leq 120$ ($k_h \leq 120$, $k_b \leq 80$), while efficient investment decisions in the governance structure 'integration' result when $k_d \leq 240$ ($k_h \leq 120$, $k_b \leq 120$). The conclusion from the perspective of efficiency therefore is that complementary assets, like the hull and the galley, have to be owned by one person. This results in fewer hold-up problems.

This conclusion will be illustrated with a numerical example. Suppose $k_d = 199$, $k_h = 107$ and $k_b = 84$. The governance structure 'non-integration' entails that only the skipper invests with this cost structure. The surplus generated is therefore $240 - 107 = 133$. The chef earns 120, the skipper earns $120 - 107 = 13$ and the princess earns nothing. The governance structure 'integration' entails that all players take the efficient decision. The contribution to the generated surplus of 330 is $240 - 199 = 41$ by the chef, $240 - 107 = 133$ by the skipper and $240 - 84 = 156$ by the princess. The breakdown of the earnings of each party in the governance structure 'integration' is presented in Fig. 9.27.

The costs structure $k_d = 199$, $k_h = 107$, $k_b = 84$ results in two hold-up problems in the governance structure 'non-integration', while there is no hold-up problem in the governance structure 'integration'.

Integration is *second-best* efficient. Integration is less inefficient than non-integration because projects with $120 < k_d \leq 240$ and $80 < k_b \leq 120$ are implemented with the governance

Player	Surplus chef	Surplus skipper	Surplus princess	Total
Chef	240—199	120	120	281
Skipper	0	120 — 107	0	13
Princess	0	0	120 — 84	36

Figure 9.27: Breakdown of the earnings of each party in governance structure 'integration'

structure 'integration', but not with the governance structure 'non-integration'. However, 'integration' is not first-best efficient because projects with either $120 < k_h \leq 240$ or $120 < k_b \leq 240$ are not implemented.

The above examples assumed that each investment could be analysed separately, and that each essential party was allocated an equal share of the quasi-surplus. However, often at least two parties have to invest in order to generate surplus, and the investing parties differ in importance, i.e. one party is somehow more essential than the others. These aspects have to be incorporated in the determination of the bargaining power of each party. The Shapley value is a suitable concept for doing this, and is explained in the appendix 'Cooperative game theory' at the end of this chapter.

9.7 Complexity

The make-or-buy decision has until now been analysed from the perspective of one type of transaction cost: the hold-up problem. The hold-up problem has an effect only on the ex-post investments. There are no ex-post problems because ex-post bargaining is assumed to be efficient. Another important aspect of contractual arrangements is their ability to accommodate adaptation. There are also various ex-post problems when contracts are incomplete, e.g. design failures, unanticipated site and environmental conditions, and changes in regulatory requirements. This section focuses on ex-post problems by considering a different kind of transaction cost: haggling and friction due to ex-post changes and adaptations when contracts are incomplete (Tadelis, 2002).

Ex-post changes and adaptations are relevant when projects are complex because it is not possible to foresee all difficulties in advance. The complexity of a transaction determines the extent of contractual incompleteness. A project is defined as more complex if it is more costly to design a complete contract. More complexity, i.e. a lower level of contractual completeness, entails a higher probability that adaptations are needed ex post, and therefore increases the need to renegotiate changes ex post. The attractiveness of more completeness is therefore that it reduces the probability of ex-post adaptations. The costs of designing a complete contract differ between projects. A simple project is associated with low costs of designing a complete contract, while these costs are high when the project is complex.

There is a negative relationship between the complexity of a project and the intensity of incentives faced by the seller. Stronger incentives mean that the seller bears more of the costs of production. This lowers the costs of production, but make the seller less willing to consider expensive adaptations in unforeseen contingencies. Providing strong cost incentives is therefore good for decreasing the ex-post production cost, but bad for choosing the best ex-post adaptations. Low-powered incentives are advantageous from the perspective of adaptability. If the product becomes more complex, then adaptation becomes more important; it is facilitated by a decrease in the intensity of incentives.

Complexity determines incentive schemes as well as integration decisions. Suppose a seller produces a product for an interested buyer. Integration (or *make*) means that the buyer owns the facilities and assets needed for the seller to produce the product. Non-integration (or *buy*) means that the seller owns these assets. The make-or-buy decision depends on the benefits and costs of integration. The benefits from integration are an increase in the buyer's ex-post value when changes are needed. There are two sources of support for this assumption. First, if the buyer and the seller do not come to an agreement, then it will be less costly to replace the seller because the buyer still has the assets. Ownership of the assets by the buyer entails that the buyer needs only to find another person to do the job when the buyer and the seller do not come to an agreement. Second, ownership of the assets by the buyer gives the buyer more residual rights to have modifications done his way.

The costs of integration are that it is harder to provide cost-reducing incentives to the seller. The equal compensation principle (Fig. 6.3.1) has shown that if the seller uses the assets of the buyer, then when the seller faces incentives to reduce costs he or she will do this at the expense of abusing the assets, reducing the value to the buyer. Another reason it is harder to provide cost-reducing incentives when there is integration is that the owner of the asset has more control over changes. Examples are that the owner of the asset has the responsibility for the accounting rules and has the residual rights of control to change the allocation of assets ex post. These observations imply that the seller will be less responsive to ex-post cost-reducing incentives. These tradeoffs imply that (Tadelis, 2002, p. 435)

[m]ore complex products are more likely to be procured internally (make) and have the upstream unit face low incentives, while more simple products are more likely to be procured through the market (buy) and have the upstream supplier face high incentives.

Application: The aerospace industry

Masten (1984) examines the make-or-buy decision in an aerospace system containing nearly two thousand component specifications, each of which was identified as either a 'make' or a 'buy' item. The entire make-or-buy program is summarized in Fig. 9.28.

Empirical measures for the variables 'design specificity' and 'complexity' are used. Design specificity is based on whether an item is identified as used exclusively by this company (highly specialized), used or easily adaptable for use by other aerospace firms (somewhat specialized) or used in other industries (relatively standard). Complexity captures that more details have to be accounted for and that there are more dimensions in which something can go wrong. An internal, three-way classification scheme is used to determine the relative complexity of the components. It turns out that both specificity and complexity are highly significant, indicating that the probability of internalization is higher for complex and highly specialized inputs.

	Quality	Make	Buy
Top and major assemblies	17	17	—
Components assembly	185	114	71
Structure machining	11	5	6
Structure forgings	8	—	8
Mechanical detail parts	138	53	85
Connectors	180	—	180
Printed circuit wire board assembly	80	80	—
Flexible/hard printed circuit boards	151	147	4
Electrical piece parts	971	11	960
Heat shields	4	—	4
Insulating materials	62	10	52
Harness/coaxial	80	80	—

Figure 9.28: The make-or-buy program (Masten, 1984, p. 408)
Journal of Law and Economics, Scott E. Masten, The University of Chicago

Application: The automobile industry

Monteverde and Teece (1982) obtained a list of 133 automotive components used by General Motors and Ford in 1976. Each of the components was recorded as either produced internally or sourced externally. Again, transaction-specific skills turned out to be an important explanatory variable in the make-or-buy decision, where more specificity was related positively to the probability of vertical integration.

It turns out that the complexity of the transaction is also important. The design, production, testing and modification of an automobile is a complex process, requiring a high degree of co-ordination. For example, engine, transmission, body shell, brakes and other components all have to be aligned. Selective intervention in the governance structure vertical integration provides the power and flexibility to create the conditions for the various components to be in the right place at the right time in the right quantities. Scherer (1980, p. 90) observes:

> The benefits from integration also increase with the complexity of product component interrelationships. It is easier to make the various parts of an automobile fit together when all parties to the coordination effort work for the same boss than when design changes must be processed through a purchasing office.

Monteverde and Teece (1982) show that the greater the complexity of a system (subcomponent), identified by more engineering investment, the greater is the likelihood of internal procurement.

Application: The building construction industry

The vast majority of contracts in the US construction industry are of either fixed-price or cost-plus type (Bajari and Tadelis, 2001). In a fixed-price contract the buyer offers the seller a pre-specified price for completing the project. A cost-plus contract reimburses the seller for costs plus a stipulated fee. The fixed-price contract is viewed as non-integration, whereas integration may be viewed as an extreme extension of cost-plus contracting.

Figure 9.29 presents the conventional wisdom about cost-plus and fixed-price contracting, which is in line with Chapter 6 and the insights of this section (Bajari and Tadelis, 2001, p. 392). For example, the allocation of risk follows immediately from the definitions of the fixed-price and cost-plus contracts. The equal compensation principle of Sec. 6.3 explains how cost-reducing incentives adversely affect quality. A cost-plus contract has more flexibility for change and therefore less-adversarial relationships, but it requires more buyer administration than a fixed-price contract. The fixed-price contract requires the buyer to invest more in design and specification.

	Fixed price	Cost plus
Risk allocation mainly on	Contractor	Buyer
Incentives for quality	Less	More
Buyer administration	Less	More
Good to minimize	Costs	Schedule
Documentation efforts	More	Less
Flexibility for change	Less	More
Adversarial relationship	More	Less

Figure 9.29: Comparing fixed-price with cost-plus contracts in construction (Bajari and Tadelis, 2001, p. 392)

9.8 Coase theorem

The previous sections have shown that the desirability of integration depends on the circumstances. This seems to contradict the result of the Coase theorem in Chapter 4 that every assignment of ownership rights results in the same efficient allocation. However, the difference is caused by the assumptions made.

Incomplete contracts entail costs. Costs of the first type are associated with the relationship between the share of the ex-post surplus that the investor receives and the *ex-ante investments*. A party receiving a small share of the ex-post surplus will not be inclined to make ex-ante investments which are optimal from the viewpoint of all parties together. This ex-ante inefficiency of the relationship depends on the allocation of the residual rights. The impossibility of making agreements about all aspects of the relationship by means of ex-ante bargaining (incomplete contracts) results in an efficiency role for a governance structure. The allocation of ownership rights therefore has efficiency consequences.

Second, there are costs of *ex-post negotiations*. The parties develop non-productive, influence activities in order to receive a larger share of the surplus. Asymmetric information may inhibit the generation of the maximum surplus. It is usually assumed in the property rights approach that the ex-post bargaining process is efficient, i.e. it is assumed that the Coase theorem holds once the contract is concluded. The ex-post bargaining process therefore does not influence the efficiency of the relationship. What is maximally possible is being realized. Chapter 4 has shown that the assumption of efficient bargaining may be problematic. The parties try to appropriate a larger share of the (quasi-) surplus by withholding information. The result is that the surplus is not always generated, i.e. the equilibrium is inefficient. In situations with asymmetric information, the Coase theorem often does not hold. Integration may mitigate these problems, because all bargaining power is allocated to one party. This may induce co-operation. An additional reason for the desirability of integration can be that weak incentives are provided (equal compensation principle). There may be fewer problems in the ex-post bargaining process in that situation, because there is no bargaining. However, Chapter 8 has shown that there may be substantial influence costs. Another advantage of the allocation of the decision rights to one person is that there are no co-ordination problems. The person having the residual rights decides what will happen.

The allocation of control (residual rights) is clear when there is only one party who has unique information. There are no inefficiencies in the bargaining process when control is allocated to the party with superior information (Sec. 4.5.1). This allocation of the residual rights results in the largest possible surplus and is entirely appropriated by this party. A fixed payment can be allocated to the other party in advance in order to realize a more equal division of the surplus. Besides, this allocation of control allows for the practice of rewarding observable, non-verifiable performance. Problems regarding the credibility of the principal do often not play an important role. One does not have to be afraid that the principal will misrepresent the productivity of the agent, because the total reward may be fixed (6.4.1), or having a good reputation may be important for the principal (6.4.3).

9.9 Conclusion

There was no role for organizations (governance structures) in Parts II and III because of the completeness of contracts. Everything is agreed upon in advance, so there is no need for ex-post bargaining when contracts are complete. In such a setting there is no role for ownership, because contractual agreements cover every possible contingency. Nor does the introduction of asymmetric information change this conclusion. The complete contracts of Part III can make provisions for every possible situation. All relevant decisions are made and agreed upon during the design of the contract. This applies also to all rights regarding ownership. There is organizational anonymity, because all parties involved can conclude a contract once and for all. It does not matter who the parties are and how contracts are embedded in an organization. Organizations have a role to play only when they determine partly or completely which incentive problems occur and how these affect the design of contracts.

Every incomplete contract creates its own incentive problems. The *property rights approach* has made this more precise by highlighting not only specific investments, but also bargaining in unforeseen contingencies. In such circumstances governance structures play a role because the execution of contractual agreements depends on the organizational context. Every governance structure entails a certain ex-post bargaining situation, which will be reflected in the ex-ante specific investments of the parties involved. The emphasis is on contractual limitations, while technological aspects of production hardly have any effect. The optimal governance structure is chosen in a way such that specific ex-post investments blossom, or the highest surplus is established, in situations with inefficient bargaining. Ownership is a second-best solution in a world with incomplete contracts in order to protect specific investments against opportunistic behaviour of others.

Incomplete contracts entail a distinction between residual decision rights and specific rights. A governance structure is associated with the allocation of residual decision rights, while contracts consist of specific rights. Residual rights play a role not only with respect to assets like buildings, machinery and cash, but also with respect to patents, brands and reputations. This entails therefore a considerable extension of the traditional view on ownership as having the right to the profit of the company. Residual rights are important when one is confronted with situations not covered by the contract. They determine the division of the surplus and the incentive to invest in specific assets. If an agreement cannot be reached directly, negotiations should be started regarding a solution. Everybody's share of the surplus depends on the distribution of bargaining power, which is determined by the allocation of the residual rights. Residual rights and the choice of the institutional structure therefore play a substantial role in the division of the profits. This ex-post division of the surplus has consequences for the ex-ante investments. The difference between exchange via markets, complex contracts, vertical integration and other ways to establish trade is determined mainly by the institutions (rules) which prevail when unforeseen circumstances occur.

The emphasis has been mainly on the investment incentives associated with a certain governance structure. Residual rights over assets turn out to be a useful starting point for the definition of the firm. The property rights approach associates a company with decision rights in situations not covered by contracts. The value of the allocation of these decision rights is that they protect specific investments. This gives the investor confidence to develop such investments. There are also a number of restrictions or problems associated with the theory of incomplete contracts. First, the optimal allocation of ownership rights is sensitive to the type of incomplete contracts which can be designed. It is not clear which type of incompleteness is most relevant. It depends for example on the level of analysis. If the CEO has discretion to redesign the organization, then, for relationships involving the CEO, the organization chart is informal, i.e. it is backed by promise rather than law. But in analysing the relationship between a middle manager and his or her subordinate, the organization chart can sensibly be viewed as formal, i.e. it cannot be changed without the consent of a higher level in the organization even when the middle manager and the subordinate agree. Second, the development of the theory assumes that every possible future circumstance or contingency is anticipated by the parties involved. Hardly any attention is paid to limited cognition. Although limited rationality doesn't seem to be a crucial ingredient in the theory of incomplete contracts, whereas the behavioral assumption opportunism is, it is probably valuable to take limited cognition more explicitly into account. The allocation of decision rights in incomplete contracts is only a poor substitute for an optimal complete contract because these rights can be abused. Therefore, in practice, decision rights are allocated to various parties and made contingent on the situation or outcome (Aghion and Bolton, 1992; Noldeke and Schmidt, 1995). This is often complemented with external parties to discipline behaviour (Tirole, 1994).

9.10 Exercises

9.1 An important contribution of the Nobel prize laureate Ronald Coase is the article 'The Problem of Social Cost' (Coase, 1960). The Coase theorem is the core of this article.
   A Which two reasons does the Coase theorem formulate for the existence of firms?
   B Describe a policy for each of these reasons which illustrates the superiority of a company as an institutional choice in certain circumstances. Explain your answer.
   C Is efficiency being used as either a positive or a normative concept in the Coase theorem? Explain your answer.

9.2 Company Wreck Ltd dismantles cars. Wreck employs 15 employees to perform these activities. Each of these employees is responsible for a certain part of the production process. One of the most difficult tasks in the process is disassembling the engine. This has to be done almost completely manually. One employee is specialized in this task, and after two months of disassembling has succeeded in decreasing the time needed from two hours to half an hour. What is the danger of idiosyncratic tasks for the employer?

9.3 Use this book with regard to the following statement in order to state
   – What the problem is;
   – Why the statement is wrong;
   – How to formulate the statement well.
   'The Board of Directors has to position itself as the "owner" of all scarce goods in order to strive for horizontal synergy. This entails money, management talent, and unique knowledge and experience.'

9.4 A newspaper reported that 'Heineken extended its interest in the Polish brewer Zywiec from 31.8 per cent to 50 per cent. Heineken will soon extend its interest to 75 per cent.' What explanation does property rights theory formulate regarding the above change in governance structure?

9.5   A Define the hold-up problem.
      B Why does hold-up occur?
      C Which three pieces of information do you have to have in order to determine there is a hold-up problem?

9.6   Which numbers have to change in Fig. 9.21 when the princess is not essential?

9.7   Suppose that there are two players: a farmer and a processor. The farmer considers investing in a knowledge-intensive product, e.g. organic milk. The value of the investment by the farmer is r for the farmer and r for the processor. The knowledge generated by the farmer can be transferred without costs to all players in a coalition with this player, but the knowledge cannot be transferred to players who are not members of the coalition.

The revenues are divided according to the way the two parties are organized, i.e. the choice of governance structure. Two governance structures are distinguished:
- Farmer integration, i.e. the farmer owns his own equipment and the equipment of the processor.
- Market exchange, i.e. each party owns its own equipment.

Assume that the distribution of power in a governance structure is represented by the Shapley value.

A State the definition of the Shapley value.
B Present the characteristic function of each governance structure regarding the investment by the farmer.

Suppose that the processor also considers investing in knowledge-intensive product, e.g. knowledge-intensive processing capacity. The value of the knowledge generated by the processor is s for each player. The knowledge generated by the processor can be transferred without costs to all players in a coalition with this player, but the knowledge cannot be transferred to players who are not members of the coalition.

C Present the characteristic function of each governance structure regarding this investment by the processor.

Assume that the costs of the investment by the farmer are K and will be paid by the farmer. Similarly, the costs of this investment by the processor are L and will be paid by the processor.

D Determine the range of values of K and L such that the governance structure 'farmer integration' is the unique first-best efficient governance structure, i.e. the only governance structure under which both parties invest.

Appendix 9: Co-operative game theory

Game theory is a collection of mathematical methods geared towards situations with multiple players. Examples are non-cooperative game theory, co-operative game theory, and evolutionary game theory. Each branch of game theory has it own focus. Chapter 2 addressed non-cooperative game theory. Five ingredients of a non-cooperative game are distinguished: players, actions, payoffs, information structure and rules. The emphasis in non-cooperative game theory is on the choice of action or strategy by the various players. This is viewed as crucial in order to explain or determine behaviour. However, the five ingredients of a non-cooperative game are often hard to specify in real-life situations. This is considered problematic, because a slight misspecification of the situation may have drastic consequences for equilibrium behaviour. A method is needed to handle situations where the way in which players interact is unstructured. Cooperative game theory is such a method. Aumann (1987) characterizes co-operative game theory as follows:

> Cooperative game theory starts out with a formalization of games . . . that abstracts away altogether from procedures . . . It concentrates instead, on the possibilities for agreement.

A co-operative game consists of two ingredients: players and payoffs. An n-person game in characteristic function form is defined by a pair (N,v), where N is the set of players and v is the characteristic function. The characteristic function assigns a value to every subset of the set of players. This value has to be interpreted as the maximum benefit or maximum cost reduction that can be established when the players within this coalition co-operate.

Co-operative game theory will be illustrated with the two- and three-player shoes game. Suppose person 1 has a left shoe and person 2 a right shoe. (Left and right shoes serve as a metaphor for demand and supply.) The set of players is therefore $N = \{1,2\}$. This set of players has four subsets: ϕ, $\{1\}$, $\{2\}$ and $\{1,2\}$. The empty set ϕ is usually assigned a value 0, i.e. $v(\phi) = 0$. The interpretation is of course that you have nothing valuable when you have no shoes. Having just one shoe also has no value. The value of the subset consisting of player 1 in the two-player shoes game is therefore also 0, i.e. $v(1) = 0$ and $v(2) = 0$. Finally, the subset $\{1,2\}$ of the set of players possesses a complete pair of shoes. A value of 1 is assigned to this coalition, i.e. $v(12) = 1$. Summarizing, the characteristic function form of the two-player shoes game is:

$$
\begin{aligned}
N &= \{1,2\} \\
v(\phi) &= 0 \\
v(1) &= 0 \\
v(2) &= 0 \\
v(12) &= 1.
\end{aligned}
$$

Suppose now that there are three players: person 1 has a left shoe, person 2 a right and person 3 a right. The set of players is $N = \{1,2,3\}$ and the number of subsets is eight. The characteristic function form is:

$$
\begin{aligned}
N &= \{1,2,3\} \\
v(\phi) &= 0 \\
v(1) &= 0 \\
v(2) &= 0 \\
v(3) &= 0 \\
v(12) &= 1 \\
v(13) &= 1 \\
v(23) &= 0 \\
v(123) &= 1.
\end{aligned}
$$

These two- and three-player shoes games have now been described by their characteristic function forms. However, nothing has been said about what will happen. An equilibrium notion has to be defined for this purpose. An equilibrium outcome in co-operative game theory specifies a payoff for every player. Payoffs are equilibrium payoffs when the payoffs satisfy certain requirements. Notice that an equilibrium concept in co-operative game theory cannot be formulated regarding strategies as in non-co-operative game theory because the only ingredients are players and payoffs. Another difference with non-cooperative game theory is that agreements or coalitions are binding in co-operative game theory, whereas agreements in non-cooperative game theory are only binding when they are equilibrium behaviour. Figure 9.30 formulates the main differences between non-cooperative and co-operative game theory.

The two best-known equilibrium concepts in co-operative game theory are the core and the Shapley value. Only the Shapley value will be explained. Shapley (1953) has formulated a number of reasonable requirements that the payoffs have to satisfy in order to be equilibrium ones. It turns out that these requirements boil down to one unique equilibrium payoff for every player. The Shapley value has an attractive interpretation. It is the average value added of a player. It entails two important aspects: value added and every possible emergence of the coalition of all players. This second aspect is needed in order to calculate the average. These aspects will now be illustrated with the two- and three-player shoes game.

Game	Non-cooperative	Cooperative
Presentation	Strategic form Extensive form	Characteristic function form
Ingredients	Players Payoffs Actions Information structure Rules	Players Payoffs
Most important ingredient	Strategies	Payoffs
Binding agreements	No	Yes
Equilibrium concepts	Nash equilibrium Subgame perfect equilibrium	Core Shapley value
Equilibrium in terms of	Strageties	Payoffs

Figure 9.30: Differences between non-cooperative and co-operative game theory

There are two possibilities in which the coalition of all can form: 12 or 21. The sequence 12 denotes that person 1 arrives first and person 2 second. The value added by a player depends on the particular sequence. For example, the value added by player 1 in the sequence 12 is 0 because adding a left shoe to the situation where there is nobody has no value, i.e. the emergence of the coalition {1} by the arrival of person 1 with a left shoe adds no value to the ϕ. The value added by player 2 in the sequence 12 is positive, because the new situation with coalition {1,2} adds value 1 to the old situation {1} because of the completion of a pair of shoes. The reverse holds for the sequence 21. Player 2 adds no value to ϕ, whereas player 1 adds value 1 by completing a pair of shoes when he or she arrives second. It is assumed that every possible emergence of the coalition of all players, i.e. 12 and 21, is equally likely. The average value added of a player in all possible sequences is the Shapley value. The Shapley value is therefore (1/2, 1/2). This is presented in Fig. 9.31.

	Value added player 1	Value added player 2
Sequence 12	$v(1)-v(\phi)=0-0=0$	$v(12)-v(1)=1-0=1$
Sequence 21	$v(12)-v(2)=1-0=1$	$v(2)-v(\phi)=0-0=0$
Sum added values	1	1
Shapley value	1/2	1/2

Figure 9.31: Shapley value in the two-person shoes game

The calculation of the Shapley value in the three-person shoes game is determined in a similar fashion. For example, the value added by person 2 in the sequence 312 is 0. Person 3 arrives first. Adding a right shoe to a situation with no shoes has no value. Person 1 adds value 1 in the sequence 312 because he or she completes a pair of shoes. Finally, person 2 adds no value when he or she arrives with a right shoe because there is already a right shoe. Figure 9.32 presents the value added by each player in all possible sequences and determines the Shapley value as (4/6, 1/6, 1/6) in the three-person shoes game.

The managerial implications of co-operative game theory entail changing the ingredients of the game, i.e. changing the set of players or changing the payoffs. An example of changing the set of players is that two players merge. The above shoes games are illustrative. The players 2 and 3 receive 1/6 + 1/6 = 1/3 in the three-person shoes game, whereas player 2 receives 1/2 in the two-person shoes game. If the players 2 and 3 in the three-person shoe game merge, then they receive collectively 1/2. Agreeing to share the revenues equally results in a Shapley value (1/2, 1/4, 1/4), which is more attractive for the players 2 and 3 than the three-person shoe game with Shapley value (2/3, 1/6, 1/6).

	Value added player 1	Value added player 2	Value added player 3
Sequence 123	$v(1) - v(\phi) = 0$	$v(12) - v(1) = 1$	$v(123) - v(12) = 0$
Sequence 132	0	0	1
Sequence 213	1	0	0
Sequence 231	1	0	0
Sequence 312	$v(13) - (3) = 1$	$v(123) - v(13) = 0$	$v(3) - v(\phi) = 0$
Sequence 321	1	0	0
Sum added values	4	1	1
Shapley value	4/6	1/6	1/6

Figure 9.32: Shapley value in the three-person shoes game

An example of changing the payoffs is the emission of new shares of a company. If one of the players buys all the new shares, then this will change the distribution of power between the various owners of the company. This may have an impact on the projects that will be adopted in the future and is reflected in the payoffs.

10 Self-enforcing contracts

LEARNING OBJECTIVES

After completing this chapter, you should understand:

- Which variables determine the stability of self-enforcing contracts.

- The difference between formal and real authority in organizations.

- The relationship between self-enforcing contracts and asset ownership.

Contents

10.1 Introduction

Part III and Chapters 8 and 9 have two features in common. First, they focus on the formal aspects of relationships. Part III focuses on formal, complete contracts, whereas the incomplete contracts in Chapters 8 and 9 emphasize the formal allocation of decision rights in unforeseen circumstances. However, there are also many silent agreements, informal understandings and historically determined customs inside and between organizations. Implicit or informal contracts may overcome some of the difficulties with formal contracts, i.e. the role of informal contracts is to utilize the parties' detailed knowledge of their situation to adapt to new contingencies as they arise.

Informal agreements and customs may give the impression that parties treat each other less aggressively than one would expect from the perspective of the behavioural assumption of opportunism in this part. However, it turns out that co-operative behaviour between opportunistic individuals emerges when it is in the interest of the involved parties to co-operate. Repeated relationships offer many possibilities for co-operation between opportunistic parties.

Second, it has been assumed that the principal and the agent conclude a contract only once, which results in a lot of inefficiencies. However, relationships in organizations usually have a long-term character. Ongoing relationships within and between firms serve to reduce the transaction costs of short-term relationships: the costs of locating trading partners, of negotiating and monitoring contracts and of enforcing agreements and settling disputes. An illustration of the additional possibilities provided by repeated relationships is the problem of allocating risk. Risk-aversion by the agent can be handled more adequately in a long-term relationship because the salary can be paid as the average of a number of periods, so that the agent is insured indirectly against circumstances out of his control. In this way, the risk of the agent is reduced, without negatively influencing the performance stimuli in the contract.

Informal, repeated relationships are the focus of this chapter. Again the allocation of authority in organizations is analysed when there is a divergence of interests between the various stakeholders, but now the formal as well as the informal allocation of authority is addressed. Knowledge, and its location, are important in analysing the divergence of interests in this setting. Teece (1998, p. 75) echoes this when he writes:

> The essence of the firm is its ability to create, transfer, assemble, integrate, and exploit knowledge assets. Knowledge assets underpin competences, and competences in turn underpin the firm's product and service offerings to the market.

The divergence of interests between different parties becomes nowadays more problematic for two reasons. First, one of the roles of management used to be the transmission of its knowledge about exceptional problems to production employees in the form of directions (Garicano, 2000). However, this becomes problematic when the locus of knowledge shifts from supervisors to employees. Knowledge seems to be residing nowadays more and more at the level of the employee. This renders the notion of direction by managers less valuable for many knowledge creation processes.

Second, the nature of knowledge has changed. In the past, knowledge used to be explicit, or at least codifiable and transmissible in a formal and systematic language. The central challenge was to make manual work more productive. Taylor did this by looking at the task, analysing its constituent motions and adding knowledge, i.e. the way simple, unskilled motions were put together, organized and executed. The employee was programmed by the task. For example, the worker on the automobile assembly line who put on a wheel was programmed by the simultaneous arrival of the car's chassis on one line and the wheel on the other. Nowadays there is a substantial amount of non-manufacturing production, i.e. production work in services, where the task is determined by the worker. Personal, implicit or hard-to-codify information starts to play an important role.

Knowledge which is personal, implicit or hard to codify and to express in the formality of language is called *tacit knowledge*. It is costly to transfer to outside parties and resides usually with a limited number of individuals. The tacitness of information entails that at least somebody has superior information. The tacit component of knowledge is being recognized nowadays as an important feature of knowledge creation processes. It implies that major components of agreements regarding and understandings about these processes between the involved parties are not verifiable by third parties. The complexity of the environment and rapid technological change place a premium on informal forms of organization. Relational forms of organization are most useful in complex environments. *Trust* plays an important role in these situations. The focus in this chapter is on the desirability and feasibility of informal agreements.

Section 10.2 highlights the Folk theorem as the main result in non-cooperative game theory, which serves as the starting-point for the treatment of self-enforcing contracts. Sections 10.3 and 10.4 show that even self-enforcing contracts have their problems, i.e. they are not always efficient. Section 10.5 concludes.

10.2 Folk theorem

The models formulated within the property rights approach are usually limited to one period of interaction. A general feature of short-run interaction problems is the unattractive prisoners dilemma outcome. Underinvestment, due to hold-up, is a prominent example. However, relationships in the real world usually last more than one period. This holds of course not only within enterprises, but also between parties in a market setting. Multi-period interactions between the same parties open the possibility to build a reputation, which might overcome the unattractive prisoners dilemma outcome when there is only one period of interaction. Reputation or trustworthiness is a multi-period notion and can be modelled as a repeated game.

Repetition provides possibilities for establishing an attractive equilibrium outcome in the prisoners dilemma. It will turn out that bad behaviour today cannot be punished tomorrow when the prisoners dilemma is played only once, whereas *repeated interactions* do provide the possibility for punishment. This result is formulated in the *Folk theorem*, which is one of the most important results of non-cooperative game theory. It means that attractive outcomes can be sustained as equilibrium outcomes in the repeated prisoners dilemma, i.e. efficient outcomes can be sustained in a non-cooperative way.

It turns out that many outcomes can be sustained as equilibrium outcomes in the repeated prisoners dilemma. All payoff combinations which are a Pareto improvement to the Nash equilibrium payoffs in the prisoner dilemma game which is played only once can be sustained as a Nash equilibrium in the repeated game. Figure 10.1 illustrates this result. The average payoff per period of players 1 and 2 are on the horizontal and vertical axis. Point (0,0) reflects the equilibrium payoffs when the game is played only once. All the points to the north-east of (0,0) are payoff combinations which can be sustained as equilibrium payoffs in the repeated prisoners dilemma.

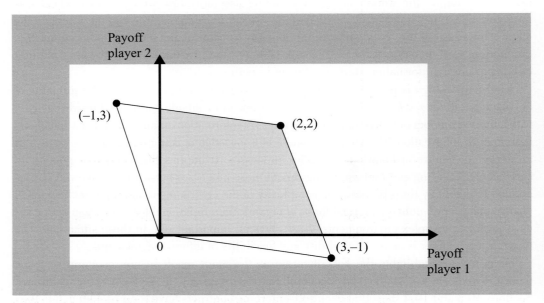

Figure 10.1: Folk theorem

There are several strategies for players 1 and 2 which can be constructed such that a combination of payoffs to the north-east of (0,0) can be sustained as a Nash equilibrium. The idea behind each of these strategies is *reciprocity*. Each party chooses the strategy which sustains the payoff combination as a Nash equilibrium as long as the other player is doing the same. This requirement 'as long as the other player is doing the same' is the stick behind the door. If the other player exhibits unattractive behaviour, then the future choices will be harmful for both players. The perspective of low payoffs in the future when co-operation is withheld will prevent each player from exhibiting such behaviour. It is therefore possible, despite the divergence in interests, to establish an outcome which is attractive for both players. Fudenberg and Maskin (1986) have shown this formally and have labelled this result the Folk theorem, because this idea has existed for such a long time that nobody dares to claim to be the first one to have formulated it.

An example of such a strategy is 'Tit-For-Tat' (Axelrod, 1984). Tit-For-Tat entails that a player starts choosing an action which is nice for the other player, i.e. the action S in the prisoners dilemma. Subsequently the choice of action of the other player in the previous period is imitated. Reciprocity can therefore play an important role in a relationship which lasts more than one period. The payoffs in equilibrium correspond with the payoffs as if the players co-operate. Another example is the 'grim strategy'. This strategy entails that the choice of action in the first period is S. Subsequently S is chosen in all future periods as long as the other player is doing the same. However, if the other player chooses T once, then T will be chosen in all future periods. If each player chooses the grim strategy, then the payoff combination (2,2) is supported as a Nash equilibrium by these grim strategies. Figure 10.2 shows the discounted payoffs per period of this strategy when the discount factor is δ.

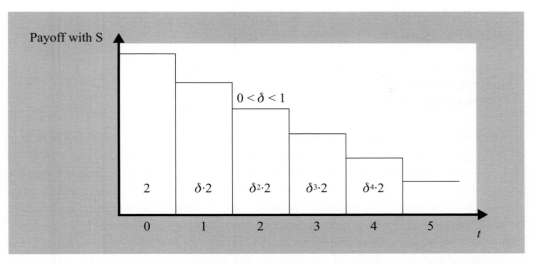

Figure 10.2: Discounted payoffs in the repeated prisoners dilemma for the Tit-For-Tat strategy as well as the grim strategy

Figure 10.3 shows the costs and benefits of the choice T when the other player adopts the grim strategy. The advantage of the choice T is that in the current period an additional payoff of $3 - 2 = 1$ is earned, but the drawback is that a loss of 2 will be suffered in all subsequent periods. If the value of δ is high enough, i.e. the future is important enough, then the action T will not be chosen because the costs of choosing T are higher than the benefits. The prospect of low payoffs in the future, i.e. that the other player will choose T as *retaliation*, establishes that each player will not choose the unattractive action T. Another way of formulating this result is that a *reputation*, of choosing S, is maintained as long as it pays to do so. Notice that the prisoners dilemma that is played only once corresponds with the case $\delta = 0$. If the prisoners dilemma is played only once, then there are no possibilities to punish bad behaviour in the future. This implies that each player will choose T according to the Nash criterium.

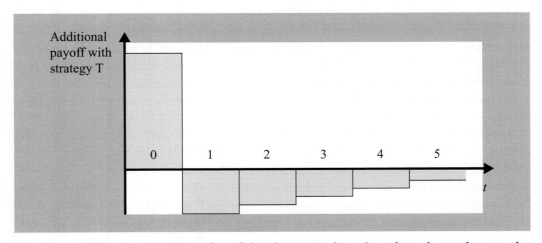

Figure 10.3: The costs and benefits of the choice T when the other player chooses the grim strategy

The Folk theorem is important because it specifies three aspects which determine the stability of attractive long-term relationships:

–   The costs and benefits of finishing a relationship;
–   The history of the relationship;
–   The observability of decisions.

The first aspect is illustrated by the height of the columns in Fig. 10.3. If the benefit of defection by choosing T, i.e. the first column above the horizontal axis, is larger than the costs, i.e. all subsequent columns below the horizontal axis, then it is predicted that the relational contract will fall apart. Second, the natures of the Tit-For-Tat strategy and the grim strategy show the importance of history. A relationship is hard to restore once it is damaged, i.e. recurring relationships are path-dependent. The emergence of relational forms of organization and which ones flourish depend on the history of prior relationships. Finally, the importance of the observability of decisions for the stability of long-term relationships can also be illustrated with Fig. 10.3. If it is hard to detect that an implicit agreement is violated, then two or more columns will be above the horizontal axis. Cheating on implicit agreements becomes more attractive when the observability of decisions decreases.

When the prisoners dilemma is played only once, repeated relationships do not necessarily result in a Pareto improvement compared with the Nash equilibrium. There are various potential problems. First, the future must not be too heavily discounted if co-operation is to be an equilibrium, i.e. the columns below the horizontal axis in Fig. 10.3 have to be large in order to secure the stability of the relational contract. Second, repeated games have multiple equilibria, so the theory does not predict the efficient outcome, but just says that it is possible. In Fig. 10.1 all payoff combinations to the north-east of (0,0), including (0,0), can be sustained as Nash equilibria in the repeated prisoners dilemma. Additional information, for example case-studies, is needed to select a particular equilibrium. Third, whether it is rational to retaliate once a deviation has occurred, rather than renegotiating and starting afresh, is open to question.

The importance of the Folk theorem is that besides allowing several behavioural possibilities it also excludes many types of behaviour as being stable. Below the horizontal axis or to the left of the vertical axis in Fig. 10.3 not every combination of payoffs can be supported as a Nash equilibrium. Pareto improvements are to be formulated with respect to the (threat) point (0,0). This is important from the perspective of organization theory because different institutional arrangements entail different threat points, and therefore exclude different types of behaviour.

Implicit, self-enforcing contracts can be conceptualized with repeated games. This section has shown that the history of a relationship is important for the stability of such contracts. *Reputations* play an important role because they induce adherence to the informal agreement. A link between current behaviour and future payments is created by making future exchange dependent on past behaviour. The future is the stick behind the door disciplining current behaviour. If the costs of breaking the informal agreement, i.e. no future exchange, are higher than the short-run gains of breaking the informal contract, then it is (ex-ante) credible that the contract will be honoured (ex-post). One gains a reputation for 'honesty' in such a situation. In long-run relationships, it is attractive to have a reputation for good behaviour. Good behaviour is responded to by good behaviour, despite the assumption of opportunistic behaviour. It turns out that in a situation with repeated interactions it is in one's own interest not to show bad behaviour. Repeated, informal agreements may therefore be superior to short-run, spot contracts.

Finally, some remarks are due on the relationship between formal and self-enforcing contracts. Formal contracts have at least two opposing effects on implicit, self-enforcing contracts (Hart, 2002). First, if formal contracts cover more contingencies, then there is less surplus remaining for the parties to haggle about. This reduces the incentive to breach a relational contract, because the gains from opportunistic behaviour are less. Second, however, if a relational contract is breached, then the penalty is also lower because many other issues and claims are already covered by the complete contract. This increases the incentive to breach. The net effect of the impact of formal contracts on implicit contracts is therefore not clear.

Application: Trust and the number of suppliers

Most companies maintain relationships with various buyers and suppliers. An explanation for enlarging the number of buyers and suppliers of a company was provided in Sec. 6.1, whereas this section discusses the reduction of the number of relationships. Recurring transactions of the same size cause trust, because both parties know that bad behaviour means the end of the relationship. In situations where the future becomes less important, undesirable behaviour is more likely. Reducing the number of business relationships is a way to make these relationships more effective. In this way, the common interest increases.

The *portfolio of suppliers* of a company reflects this tradeoff by having on the one hand various sources of supply in order to prevent dependency on one party, and on the other hand a limited number of suppliers in order to be sufficiently important for each supplier. The tendencies in industries like automobiles, textile and electronics are examples. Europe and the United States, following Japan, have reduced the number of suppliers drastically. This not only strengthens the basis for trust in a stable and productive relationship, but also decreases the co-ordination problems with suppliers.

Application: Team production

An implicit assumption of the *team production* problem in Sec. 6.2 is that decisions are made only once. This results in free-riding. However, it is more realistic to consider situations in which team production occurs repeatedly (Radner, 1991). A better result is established in each period when each team member delivers the efficient input as long as every colleague does so too, whereas an observed deviance is responded to by permanently choosing the free-riding level of input. These lower future payments when bad behaviour is observed provide sufficient punishment to prevent undesirable behaviour.

Repeated situations play an important role in aligning individual and common interests. For example, if the principal–agent relationship is repeated often enough, the principal can even realize his most preferred outcome. The agent can be stimulated to deliver exactly the preferred effort in each period and, by basing the salary on the average result, bears hardly any risk. An additional advantage of a repeated context is that it makes the binding character of contracts unnecessary. Contracts are not necessary in these situations, because each party has every interest in acting up to the agreement, i.e. the agreement is self-enforcing. In a repeated context opportunistic people behave ethically and unselfishly, because they benefit from adhering to the agreement.

Application: Dispute prevention without courts in Vietnam

Vietnam made a transition from a centrally planned economy to a market economy at the end of the twentieth century. The *de facto* decentralization of economic activity resulted in a bottom-up reform process. In this reform process ongoing relationships among firms played an important role because of the inadequacy of the courts. The reason was that the formal institutions of central planning were not abandoned for a considerable time, and laws were therefore not geared towards the demands of decentralized exchange. These repeated relationships reduce the costs of decentralized exchange in the market: the costs of locating trading partners, of designing contracts, of enforcing agreements and of settling disputes.

The empirical work of McMillan and Woodruff (1999a, 1999b) reveals that if a customer does not repay a debt, then the relationship with the debtor is nevertheless often maintained. Sometimes the reason for the breach is investigated, which may result in delayed payment or in part of the debt being forgiven. Another reason given for continuing the relationship is reluctance to penalize debtors because this may result in a reputation among customers for being difficult to deal with. Punishment for not adhering to an agreement is therefore not as harsh as is indicated by the standard repeated-game story and so not as effective as a sanction. Firms will thus look to other devices to ensure compliance.

The empirical investigation regarding these other devices takes the willingness to grant trade credit as a measure of trust in the ongoing relationships between sellers and buyers. It turns out that the amount of trade credit granted varies with several aspects of the relationship. First, firms which are prospective trading partners are screened before transactions begin by checking their reliability through the business or social network. A second potential device is community sanctioning, where other firms are told of the bad debt and blacklist the debtor. Though it turns out that this device is used infrequently, the empirical work does show that talking with other suppliers regarding customers on a regular basis is positively associated with granting trade credit to customers. This may result in community sanctions. Third, the amount of trade credit granted varies with the buyer's ability to locate alternative trading partners.

The case of Vietnam shows that repeated game incentives, together with governance structures and pre-trade investigation, can support business activity even in the absence of workable laws. Relational contracting depends therefore partly on repeated game incentives and partly on suitably designed governance structures.

Application: Firm as reputation

Reputations become significant when employees have incomplete information about the characteristics of the company, and therefore cannot predict future behaviour accurately. Current and past behaviour of the company is observed and serves to formulate expectations about the future. A reputation offers an implicit promise that processes of adaptation will occur which are reasonable and fair in circumstances in which the contract does not specify anything. Students are willing to accept the authority of a professor when they have some confidence that his or her decision-making power will be used fairly. This trust is based on the professor's reputation. Employees are in a similar position vis-à-vis an employer. The way the professor or the company responds to unforeseen circumstances strengthens or weakens his, her or its reputation, which has consequences for the degree of trust students or employees have in the future. Trans-action costs will be lower, as long as there is more trust in the possibilities and the willingness of the company to solve the incompleteness of a contract in a reasonable way.

Kreps (1990b) conceptualizes the firm as a reputation. The starting-point of the analysis is again formed by the observation that it is impossible, or the costs are too high, to write complete contracts. The previous chapter has shown that the relationship between an employer and an employee is often surrounded by various circumstances which are difficult to write down in a contract. In principle, the employer can intervene selectively in a way which is inappropriate, but the probability that this will happen is not large, because reputations play an important disciplining role in such a context.

Maintaining the reputation is influenced by the allocation of the residual rights. Only those who own the residual rights can form a reputation. The others can do nothing other than simply comply with the arrangements made in the contract. This says nothing regarding their future intentions, so that a reputation cannot be developed. *Residual rights can be allocated best to a party which has invested a large interest in acquiring a reputation*. This is usually the company. The costs of losing a good reputation are higher for the company than the profit from breaking promises in the short term. This provides trust that efficient and fair adaptation processes will occur in unforeseen circumstances. The prediction is therefore that a company which often concludes transactions and is prominently present in the market has the right to complete the incomplete contract. This kind of company has most at stake.

An important ingredient in the conceptualization of the firm as a reputation is a mechanism which transfers reputation capital to the next generation of managers. If there are no further prospects of future transactions with the party owning the residual rights, then bad behaviour becomes more attractive. Such behaviour cannot be punished in the future. *Overlapping generations of managers* are a mechanism which transfers reputation capital. Managers own the residual rights regarding the future yields. These rights can be sold to future managers and they in their turn can sell them to the next generation. In this way, an equilibrium with low transaction costs can be established.

Application: Capital structure and reputation

Reputations may reduce the tendency to choose *over-risky investment projects* of debt. This is called the asset substitution problem. Diamond (1989) analyses the situation in which managers choose relatively safe projects to build up or keep a good reputation. Safe projects lead almost always to a repayment of debts. Choosing safe projects is attractive, because it leads to a lower interest rate on debt.

Creditors are not able to determine the investment behaviour of companies ex post. It is not possible for them to determine whether a bankruptcy is the result of the wrong choices or of bad luck. One can only observe whether a project has been finished successfully. This information offers an indication about the investment behaviour of every arbitrary company. The longer the period in which a company repays its debt, the better is its reputation with the creditors and the lower the interest rate it has to pay for loans. Established companies usually prefer choosing safe projects: the small probability of being successful with a risky project does not outweigh the loss of a good reputation and the accompanying low interest rate. On the other hand, younger companies without a reputation choose risky projects. If such projects succeed for a young company, it will switch to less risky projects in the course of time, and thence become established. Companies with a long history therefore go bankrupt less often and have lower interest costs than younger companies.

Application: Merchant guilds

In the late Middle Ages, trade between different geographical areas took place in centrally located cities, like Bruges in Belgium, Constantinople in Turkey and Genoa in Italy. The possibilities for beneficial long-distance trade (according to the law of comparative advantages) and the presence of an attractive location did not however guarantee that trade actually occurred. Information costs were lowered by the 'development of standardized weights and measures, units of account, a medium of exchange, notaries, consuls' (North, 1991, p. 100). In the Middle Ages, a problem for a potential trade centre was creating credible facilities for foreign traders, to prevent theft, confiscation or tax increases. Merchant law courts were developed to provide incentives for contract fulfilment and trade centres had to offer protection. An institutional environment – for example one with guilds – was desired to ensure the safety of the merchants. Guilds also played a role in reducing the costs of negotiation, registering trade flows and taxes, and creating a strong, common negotiation position.

Greif *et al.* (1994) formulate a contractual explanation for institutions like guilds. The focus is on the role of guilds in providing a contractual solution for ensuring the safety of individual merchants who trade over long distances. A *bilateral reputation mechanism* can prevent either party from behaving badly, in order to avoid danger to future profitable transactions. The reasoning here is that individual merchants who are treated badly by a local ruler will refuse to return in the future. However, this is effective only as long as the trader is important enough to the other party. If the trade flows in the economy develop and the transactions of an individual merchant decrease, his position changes from an important business partner to a marginal trader. Bad behaviour by the local ruler towards a trader is more likely, because there is less at stake for him. The bilateral reputation mechanism is therefore not sufficient to establish the credibility of the ruler as a trustworthy business partner. The punishment for bad behaviour is small and does not have a deterring effect.

A possible way to increase the punishment when one merchant is being treated badly is for all of them to formulate a response together. This restores the balance of power. However, a collective response causes new problems, like examining the causes of a conflict, ensuring that the boycott is carried out by everyone and restoring trust. Therefore, an organization is needed which is able to co-ordinate the activities of the individual traders and to issue effective sanctions against both its own members and others. In the Middle Ages, the merchant guild served this purpose. The guild provided a central mechanism which controlled transactions, evaluated the behaviour of city councils and both gave the signal for a boycott and ensured that members did not break it.

The core of a merchant guild was formed by an administrative unit which co-ordinated the activity of traders from a specific geographical area and to some extent enforced it. It provided the traders with a leadership and a mechanism to issue information about collective action. This ensured co-ordination as well as internal participation. Only an organization such as this, the *multilateral reputation mechanism*, can solve the problem of providing credible punishments. The effectiveness of a guild was based on a system of explicit and implicit contracts between the guild and the city, between the guild and the individual traders, and between guilds. The guild was a nexus of contracts, a legal entity that concluded agreements with individual traders and with trade cities.

In the late Middle Ages, the political power of local rulers was considerable, while trade flows developed because of the rise of the merchant guilds, through which traders acquired a more equal footing with local rulers. This more equal balance of power made it easier to establish a more credible commitment regarding the safety of foreign traders. However, the success of the merchant guild led to its demise. The increasing trade flows resulted in greater political integration of the various city states and the rise of larger political entities (especially nation states) that slowly took over the functions of the merchant guilds.

10.3 Formal and real authority in organizations

An important issue in organizing the enterprise is the allocation of control and authority. The theory of Chapter 9 indicates that the employee should be the owner of the firm when the relationship-specific investments of the employee are most important. However, this seems to be at odds with a basic feature of the firm. Crucial to the notion of the firm is the centralization of decision-making power; i.e. the employer, not the employee, is the owner of the firm. A way out of this problem is to create an additional degree of freedom, e.g. by creating a third party (Bolton and Scharfstein, 1998) or by making a distinction between formal and informal authority (Baker *et al.*, 1999). This section focuses on the distinction between formal and informal or real authority in organizations. Formal authority resides at the top, whereas informal authority can be either centralized or decentralized.

Suppose there are an employer and an employee. The employee evaluates projects and proposes to execute certain ones. The interests of the employer and employee are not completely aligned in the execution of the project. For example, shareholders are probably concerned mainly with the return on investment, whereas employees appreciate working on and choosing pet projects which are not necessarily completely aligned with the interests of the shareholders. Finally, it is assumed that the intensity of searching for new projects by the employee is not known to the employer.

Three governance structures are analysed: centralization, delegation and informal authority. The governance structure *centralization* entails that the employer has to ratify all proposals of the employee. The employee ratifies all proposals when the governance structure *delegation* prevails. A third governance structure is possible in a multi-period setting: contingent delegation or informal authority. *Informal authority* entails delegation as long as the employer does not encounter implemented projects which are bad for him. The informal agreement is terminated when abuse is observed and the employer will switch to either always accepting or always rejecting. This is the standard way of conceptualizing an implicit, self-enforcing contract in a repeated game framework.

Notice that delegation and informal authority differ regarding the identity of the person having a reputation for good behaviour, and therefore having the possibility of abusing a good reputation. The key feature is that one party with authority makes a promise to another party without authority. The employer may renege on the promise to accept all projects when the governance structure delegation prevails, whereas the employee has to maintain a reputation for proposing good projects under informal authority.

Two situations are distinguished. First, suppose the employer is informed about the value of the projects the employee proposes to carry out. The choice between the governance structures centralization and delegation is determined by two opposing incentive effects for the employee. Delegation is attractive because it strengthens the incentives of the employee to search for and develop new projects in every period, but it increases the probability that projects are implemented which are bad for the employer, i.e. the employee may choose projects which are not completely in line with the interests of the employer. Delegation is therefore attractive and feasible when it improves the incentives of the employee substantially and when it is not too important to prevent the implementation of a project which is bad for the employer. Preventing bad projects is not that important for the employer when either the loss associated with a bad project is not too large or the employer is sufficiently patient. Notice that this result is second-best. The employer may be tempted to intervene in the governance structure delegation in order to establish a Pareto improvement when a bad project is proposed. However, this is not desirable from a long-run perspective because it destroys reputation or trust which is needed in subsequent periods in order to induce the employee to search intensely for new projects. The current Pareto improvement may therefore result in a prisoners dilemma in all future periods.

Second, suppose the employer is not informed about the future benefits of the projects when they are proposed, but that this information becomes available when the project is implemented. An example of this lack of information is a situation where investment opportunities arise quickly and do not give the employer sufficient time to evaluate them. In such an environment projects can be rejected or approved by the employer only in a single-period setting. Always rejecting projects results in a payoff of zero for both parties, i.e. there is basically no relationship, whereas always accepting projects boils down to delegating authority.

Notice that delegation of decisions can never be better than centralization. Everything which can be contracted upon in a decentralized way can also be incorporated in a comprehensive, centralized contract. However, employees often have superior local information, which argues for more flexibility in the form of delegation. So, the efficiency of a relationship may be enhanced by giving up some control, i.e. real authority, even though formally control stays at the top (Aghion and Tirole, 1997). Contingent delegation or informal authority may be superior to delegation as well as to centralization. It is superior to delegation because the employee is restrained in proposing projects which are bad for the employer. It is superior to centralization because the search incentives for the employee are stronger.

Informal authority can be sustained as a self-enforcing contract by sharing the rents created. It is a viable governance structure in circumstances where the opportunity cost for the employee of not proposing a bad project is not too high, i.e. when either the employee is not too impatient in capturing private gains or the private gains are not too high. These conditions are not always satisfied. For example, informal authority may be problematic in the software industry. The opportunity costs of not proposing bad projects is probably high for employees in this industry because they enjoy (high) private benefits when they are allowed to work on their pet projects. A way out is to outline projects only in general terms, whereas proposals regarding the details are left to the employees. These broad outlines may make informal authority feasible because they narrow the range of projects with high private gains to such an extent that reasonable alignment with the interests of the employer is achieved.

10.4 Self-enforcing contracts and asset ownership

A governance structure consists of the rules embedding transactions. These rules can be formal as well as informal. The formal are represented by the decision rights of an incomplete contract, while the informal can be conceptualized by an implicit, self-enforcing contract. The performance of formal organizational structures and institutions depends importantly on the informal relationships these structures and institutions facilitate, where the informal rules serve to complete the incomplete contract. An incomplete contract determines to a certain extent which informal agreements will come into existence, and is on the other hand affected by them. Self-enforcing contracts, i.e. credible informal agreements, will be designed such that the reputation of each party is sufficiently important in order to adhere to the informal agreement. (Section 10.2 has shown that maintaining a reputation is determined by the costs and benefits of reneging, the history of the relationship and the observability of decisions.) It may be optimal to choose an organization's formal structure because of its effects on informal relationships within the firm. Similarly, the comparison between firms and markets hinges in part on which of these two governance structures facilitates valuable implicit contracts.

This section highlights the interplay between (formal) asset ownership and (informal) self-enforcing contracts (Baker *et al.*, 2002). The model of vertical integration based on asset ownership (Chapter 9) is combined with the repeated-game model of self-enforcing contracts (Sec. 10.2). Governance structures are therefore distinguished not only by their formal rights, i.e. outsourcing versus employment, or market exchange versus integration, but also by their informal aspect, i.e. spot versus relational contracts, or short-run versus long-run relationships.

The focus is on how asset ownership affects the feasibility of informal agreements, i.e. the question will be how formal aspects of organizations support or constrain informal aspects. Consider an upstream party who works with an asset to produce an input to a downstream party's production process. The owner of the asset decides how it will be used, and in particular what will happen to its output. When the downstream party owns the asset, the upstream party is called the employee (someone who works with the firm's asset and does not own the asset's output), i.e. there is integration. When the upstream party owns the asset, he or she is called an independent contractor (someone who owns their own tools and can sell their output to the downstream party), i.e. the governance structure market prevails. The above distinction between formal and informal aspects of governance structures results in four governance structures: spot employment, relational employment, spot outsourcing and relational outsourcing.

The identity of the party tempted to renege on an informal agreement depends on who owns the asset. As in the previous section, the party with the decision rights makes a promise to the party without such rights. For example, if the downstream party owns the asset, then the upstream party is an internal division rather than an external supplier. The downstream party is interested in receiving high-quality service, and considers providing an incentive for the upstream party to deliver high quality by promising to pay a bonus for it. Unfortunately, this promise is vulnerable to reneging. The downstream party may simply take the intermediate good, paying the upstream party nothing. The implicit contract has therefore to be such that the upstream party trusts the downstream party to pay a bonus for good performance. Similarly, if the upstream party owns the asset, then he or she is tempted to renege by taking actions which increase the value of opportunities elsewhere. The implicit contract must be such that the downstream party must trust the upstream party not to hold up the downstream party by threatening to sell the output of the asset elsewhere.

Not only the identity of the party tempted to renege depends on who owns the asset; so too does the incentive to renege. The temptation to renege on a relational employment contract differs from the temptation to renege on relational outsourcing in a subtle way, depending on who owns the asset. The distribution of bargaining power is identical for both relational governance structures, because of the informal aspect of these arrangements. The reason is that when both parties agree on a certain course of action in an informal, self-enforcing way, then the formal aspect of the relationship does not affect the distribution of bargaining power. Both governance structures therefore produce the same actions and the same surplus. However, the bargaining positions, and therefore the temptation to renege, differ between these two governance structures.

A key difference between relational outsourcing versus relational employment is that the good's value in its alternative use affects the reneging decision under relational outsourcing, but not under relational employment. The choice of governance structure is therefore determined by a tradeoff. Upstream ownership offers the upstream party bargaining power. This increased upstream bargaining power decreases the downstream party's temptation to renege by lowering the payment for the input delivered by the upstream party. However, upstream ownership also encourages the upstream party to consider the interests of other parties, i.e. to improve his or her bargaining position by inefficient actions, and hence may create a temptation for the upstream party to renege. Non-integration is optimal when the first consideration is important, while dominance of the second consideration favours integration.

Vertical integration is according to this perspective an efficient response to widely varying supply prices. Extreme realizations of the supply price undermine the stability of the self-enforcing contract when the governance structure relational outsourcing prevails, whereas the reneging temptation is independent of the supply price when the governance structure relational employment is chosen. Vertical integration therefore reduces the temptation to renege when there is substantial uncertainty regarding the supply price.

The most important insight of this section is that the stability of a self-enforcing contract (informal rules) depends on the allocation of decision rights (formal rights). The allocation of formal rights determines not only the identity of the party developing a reputation but also the costs and benefits of adhering to an informal contract. Chapters 8 and 9 stressed the importance of specific investments in allocating decision rights. This section has in addition shown that this allocation determines to a certain extent the emergence of informal relationships. The allocation of (formal) decision rights to the party doing the specific investments solves his or her fear of hold-up to a considerable extent, but creates also an informal hold-up problem by encouraging (partial) reneging on promises which have been made to the other party.

10.5 Conclusion

The design of governance structures has to take the formal as well as the informal aspects of organizations into account (in order to address all hold-up problems simultaneously). Informal, repeated relationships are highlighted in this chapter, the two previous chapters having focused on the formal aspects of organizations. Informal relationships are important because the tacitness of knowledge regarding an exchange often makes it impossible for major components of, agreements regarding and understandings about the relationship to be verifiable by third parties. The role of implicit contracts is to use this knowledge in an informal way in complex or new situations. This knowledge is repeatedly brought to value by the concern to maintain a reputation for honouring informal agreements. Implicit contracts are self-enforcing when the future is sufficiently important, the environment not too volatile or uncertain and the behaviour of the involved parties observable.

10.6 Exercise

10.1 Describe how the stability of a self-enforcing contract is affected by the following:
   A An increase in the number of participants.
   B An increase in the size of transactions.
   C An increase in the volatility of the environment.
   D An increase in the complexity of the transaction.
   E The availability of new information technologies.

Part V:
Business strategy

This part focuses on the strategic considerations regarding organizational choices. There are several reasons why these considerations have been ignored in the previous parts. First, the emphasis hitherto has been on aspects of the internal organization of firms, the external organization being largely taken for granted. This part focuses on the strategic interactions between firms. Second, Chapter 3 in Part II formulated as a benchmark the perfectly competitive market, where one firm cannot affect the price because there are many other firms in the market, and each firm is a price-taker. However, most markets have only a limited number of competitors. Markets are often oligopolistic rather than perfectly competitive, i.e. firms are price-setters rather than price-takers.

Third, transaction costs economics and incomplete contracting theory (in Part IV) assumed that the efficient governance structure is chosen. Strategic considerations therefore play no role in the choice of governance structure. This may be a good starting-point for formulating insights regarding governance structure, because very inefficient choices are not likely to survive. However, there is no guarantee that efficient outcomes will emerge. Strategic considerations may result in an equilibrium governance structure which is inefficient, i.e. the competition between a limited number of firms may drive the choice of various internal organizational decisions.

Strategic considerations will be analysed with the behavioural assumptions of Part II. Firms are assumed to possess unlimited cognitive capacities and are driven by self-interest. These assumptions are made for convenience in order to highlight the effect of strategic interactions in the choice of various aspects of organizations. Similar strategic insights can be formulated when other behavioural assumptions are used. Figure V.1 positions this part in the familiar way.

		Behavioural hypothesis		
		Opportunistic	Self-interested	Idealistic
Degree of rationality	Complete rationality		Strategic interactions	
	Limited rationality			
	Procedural rationality			

Figure V.1: Positioning of Part V

In this part the focus is on the strategic interactions between firms. This results in a rudimentary characterization of the firm as a production function, as in Part II. However, the ideas presented in this part can be extended easily towards other characterizations of the firm, like those already adopted in Parts III and IV, and those which will be adopted in Parts VI and VII. Figure V.2 presents the familiar picture regarding the concept of the firm used in this part.

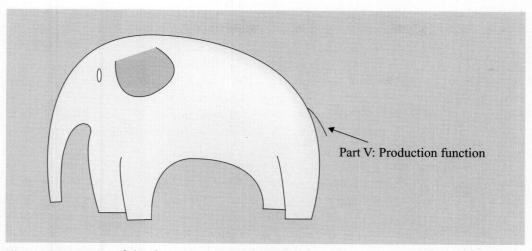

Figure V.2: View of the firm in strategy typology

11 Strategy typology

After completing this chapter, you should understand:

- How a reaction function depicts the nature of competition, various profit levels, the response to aggressive behaviour, increases in costs and increases in demand.

- The distinction between hard and soft investments.

- The impact of the nature of investment, the entry condition and the nature of competition on the profit-maximizing investment strategy.

Contents

11.1 Introduction

This chapter is about the strategic behaviour of firms in markets with a limited number of competitors. Strategic interactions underlie not only market phenomena such as price wars, patent races and advertising campaigns, but also organizational phenomena like delegation, incentive schemes, financial structure and vertical integration. The interactions or interdependencies among the firms can be complicated, but the tool of game theory enables the formulation of a few simple principles regarding the optimal behaviour of a firm in a strategic setting. A strategy typology will be developed which delineates the optimal investment behaviour of the firm in various strategic settings.

Section 11.2 outlines and motivates the decision sequence used in this chapter. Reaction functions in different markets will be determined in Sec. 11.3, while Sec. 11.4 outlines various properties of reaction functions. Section 11.5 develops the strategy typology. Applications related to the topics of this book are formulated in Sec. 11.6. Finally, Sec. 11.7 concludes.

11.2 Decision sequence in the strategy taxonomy

Strategic issues will be illustrated by focusing on the actions or investments of an incumbent firm influencing the entry decision of a rival firm. The incumbent firm is sometimes called the leader and the rival firm the follower. Entry entails a certain sequence of time. The incumbent takes certain investment decisions before the entrant can do something, i.e. the entrant is faced with the investments of the leader when it has to take an action. This provides the opportunity for the incumbent to structure the market in a favourable way, to a certain extent. The three-stage game of this chapter consists of the following:

Stage 1: Investment decision of the incumbent firm;
Stage 2: Entry decision of the entrant;
Stage 3: Competition.

Figure 11.1 depicts the strategic situation considered in this chapter. The incumbent chooses either a small (S) or a large (L) investment. Subsequently, the entrant decides regarding entry into the industry: yes (Y) or no (N). Finally, there will be either price or quantity competition between the firms in the industry.

It turns out that this simple structure can be used for the strategic analysis of many different investments in many different industries. However, various situations have to be distinguished in order to do justice to this huge variety. Eight cases will be considered. These eight cases are the possible combinations which can be formed with two types of investments, two market conditions regarding entry and two types of competitive processes. First, each investment will be classified as either a hard or a soft investment. Second, the market is such that entry is either inevitable or can be deterred by the incumbent. Finally, the market is characterized by either strategic substitutes or strategic complements. So, eight possible games will be considered. Figure 11.2 shows these $2 \times 2 \times 2 = 8$ games. The subgame perfect equilibrium in each of these eight games will be determined in the next sections. The outcome is called the *strategy typology*.

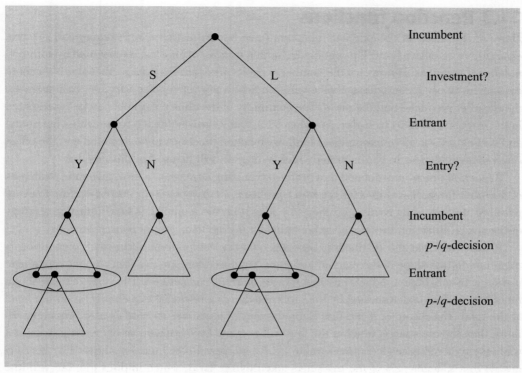

Figure 11.1: Decision sequence in the strategy taxonomy

Type of investment	Entry?	Nature of competition	Profile	SPE investment
Hard	Yes	Strategic substitutes		
		Strategic complements		
	No	Strategic substitutes		
		Strategic complements		
Soft	Yes	Strategic substitutes		
		Strategic complements		
	No	Strategic substitutes		
		Strategic complements		

Figure 11.2: Eight games will be distinguished in the strategy typology

11.3 Reaction functions

Many of the ideas in the previous chapters have been illustrated with numerical, discrete examples in extensive form. This entailed a limited number of choices, represented by a limited number of branches. However, if the number of choice possibilities is large, then it is often more convenient to use a continuous choice variable than a discrete choice variable. Examples are the quantity produced and the price. The continuity of the choice variable can be represented in the extensive form by triangles, as in Fig. 11.1, but it turns out that a figure with a horizontal and vertical axis is more informative. It allows reaction functions to be depicted and the effect of investment choices to be illustrated. Such a diagram will be used in this chapter.

A *reaction function* is defined as a profit-maximizing strategy of a firm, given the strategies of the other firms. It specifies for the firm a profit-maximizing strategy corresponding to every possible strategy of its rivals, and therefore also what the response is to a change in strategy of the rivals. Reaction functions are sometimes referred to as *best response functions*.

It turns out that the distinction between quantity competition and price competition is important for the slope of the reaction function. Suppose there are two firms in an oligopolistic market with substitute products and that there is *quantity competition*. The slope of the reaction function of a firm is determined by the profit-maximizing response to a change in output level of the rival. For example, if the firm is producing 10 units and its rival is also producing 10 units, then the question is whether the firm will respond by increasing or decreasing its output when the rival increases its output level to 15. An increase in the quantity supplied by the rival entails that a larger part of the market is taken by the rival, which implies that the residual demand left for the firm has decreased. The profit-maximizing response for the firm is to decrease its level of output. The slope of the reaction function of the firm is therefore negative when there is quantity competition. Figure 11.3 depicts this situation, where q_1 is the quantity produced by firm 1 and q_2 the quantity produced by firm 2.

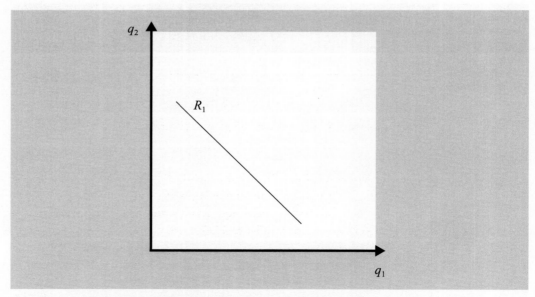

Figure 11.3: The reaction function has a negative slope when there is quantity competition

Notice that there is a quantity level on the horizontal as well as the vertical axis. (The familiar demand function is depicted in a figure with the price on the vertical axis and the quantity on the horizontal.) A reaction function can be depicted in this figure, because a profit-maximizing output level (q_1) of firm 1 is indicated for every possible level of output (q_2) of firm 2.

Suppose now that there is an oligopolistic market with *price competition* and substitute products. The slope of the reaction function of a firm is determined in the same way. For example, if the firm is setting a price of 10 and the rival is also choosing a price of 10, then the question is whether the firm will respond by increasing or decreasing its price when the rival increases its price to 15. The increase in the price of the rival entails that a smaller part of the market is taken by the rival, which implies that the residual demand left for the firm has increased. The profit-maximizing response for the firm is to increase its price. The slope of the reaction function of the firm is therefore positive when there is price competition. Figure 11.4 depicts this situation, where p_1 is the price chosen by firm 1 and p_2 the price chosen by firm 2.

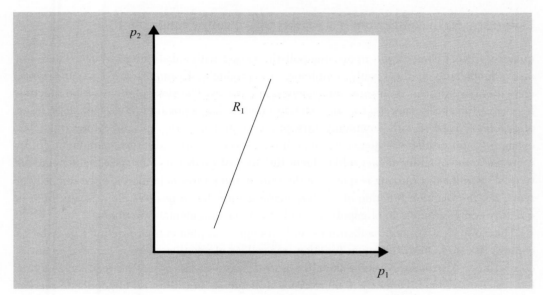

Figure 11.4: The reaction function has a positive slope when there is price competition

A Nash equilibrium is defined as a payoff-maximizing strategy for *each* firm, given the strategies of the rivals. A reaction function is defined as a profit-maximizing strategy of *one* firm, given the strategies of the other firms. These definitions imply that the intersection of the reaction functions is a Nash equilibrium. Figure 11.5 presents the Nash equilibrium in a market with quantity competition. The next section presents various properties of reaction functions.

It will turn out in Sec. 11.4 that the slope of the reaction function is one of the three crucial ingredients in determining the profit-maximizing investment strategy of the firm. This section has shown that the reaction function has a negative (positive) slope when there is

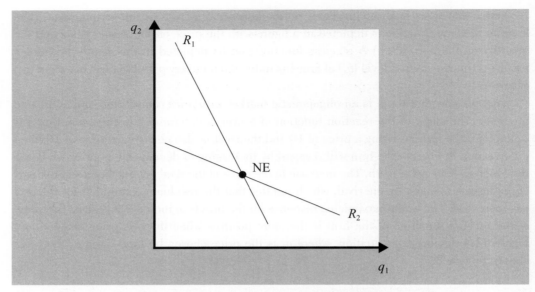

Figure 11.5: Nash equilibrium in a market with quantity competition

quantity (price) competition in an oligopolistic market with substitute products. There are also oligopolistic markets with complementary products. Examples are cars and tyres, computer hardware and software, and cameras and lenses. The slope of the reaction function is reversed in these markets, i.e. the reaction function has a positive (negative) slope in an oligopolistic market with complementary products and quantity (price) competition. For example, suppose there is quantity competition between a car and a tyre manufacturer. An increase in the quantity of cars sold reduces the price of a car. This increases the demand for tyres. The profit-maximizing response of the tyre manufacturer is to increase the quantity of tyres, i.e. the reaction function of the tyre manufacturer has a positive slope when there is quantity competition in an oligopolistic market with complementary products.

The notions of strategic substitutes and strategic complements are defined in order to capture the slope of the reaction function, regardless of whether there is price or quantity competition. A strategic variable is called a *strategic substitute* when the reaction function has a negative slope. Quantity is therefore a strategic substitute in an oligopolistic market with substitute products. Similarly, a strategic variable is called a *strategic complement* when the reaction function has a positive slope. Price is an example of a strategic complement in an oligopolistic market with substitute products.

11.4 Properties of reaction functions

Reaction functions have various properties. Only three properties will be discussed, because they will be used in the strategy typology and the applications. The first property concerns the (profit-maximizing) *response to aggressive behaviour* by the rival firm(s). The response depends on the slope of the reaction function. Suppose that there is quantity competition. An aggressive action by a firm in a market with quantity competition entails that the quantity produced increases, i.e. that a larger share of the market is taken. The residual market demand of the other firm will therefore decrease, and the profit-maximizing response is to decrease the level of output. An aggressive action in a market with quantity competition is responded to in a passive way. Figure 11.6 illustrates this situation, where the reaction function of the responding firm is depicted by R_2. An aggressive action by firm 1, i.e. an increase in the quantity q_1, will be responded to by a decrease in q_2 by firm 2. Notice that R_2 is depicted because the *profit-maximizing* response to aggressive behaviour is determined.

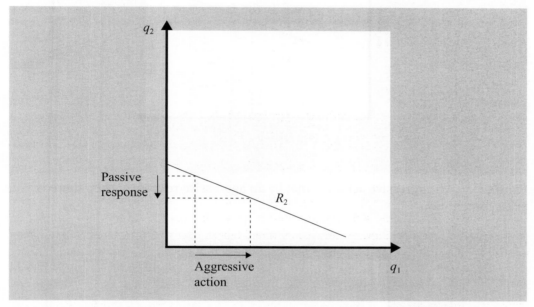

Figure 11.6: An aggressive action is met by a passive response when there is quantity competition

Suppose that there is price competition. An aggressive action by a firm in a market with price competition means that the price will be decreased, i.e. a larger share of the market is taken. The residual market demand of the other firm will decrease, and the profit-maximizing response is to decrease the price as well. An aggressive action in a market with price competition is responded to in an aggressive way. Figure 11.7 presents this situation. An aggressive action by firm 1, i.e. a decrease in the price p_1, will be met by a decrease in p_2 by firm 2.

Each point on the reaction function is associated with a particular *profit level* of the firm. Does the profit level increase when the value of the strategic variable increases? It turns out that the answer to this question does not depend on the slope of the reaction function. Suppose that there is quantity competition. The reaction function of firm 1 is depicted in Fig. 11.8. Moving to the south-east on R_1 implies that the level of output of firm 2 decreases, while the output level of firm 1 increases. The profit level of firm 1 increases therefore to the south-east on its reaction function. (If the level of output of firm 2 has dropped to zero, i.e. $q_2 = 0$, then firm 1 is a monopolist and earns the highest possible profit level. Any increase in q_2 is sure to lower profits.)

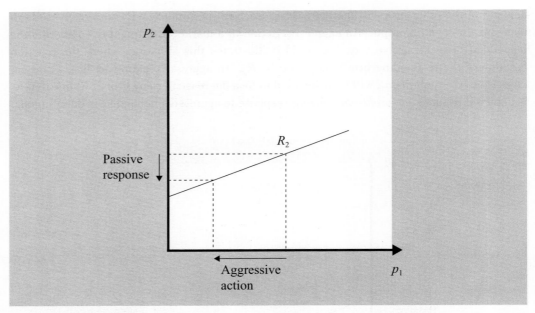

Figure 11.7: An aggressive action is met by an aggressive response when there is price competition

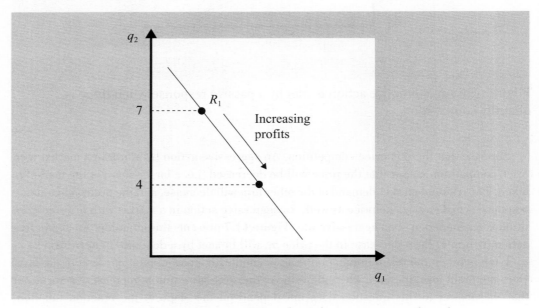

Figure 11.8: Profits of firm 1 increase on R_1 when the quantity produced increases

Suppose that there is price competition. The reaction function of firm 1 is depicted in Fig. 11.9. Moving to the north-east on R_1 implies that the price of firm 2 increases, which implies that a larger share of the market is left for firm 1. Maintaining the same price would therefore already result in a higher profit level for firm 1. However, R_1 implies that firm 1 will even raise its price, which must increase profits even further because R_1 depicts the profit-maximizing choice of firm 1. The profit level of firm 1 increases therefore to the north-east on its reaction function.

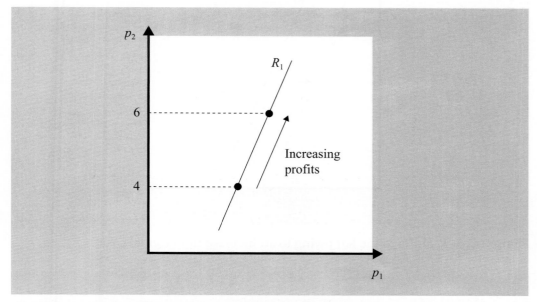

Figure 11.9: Profits of firm 1 increase on R_1 when the price increases

The *location of a reaction function* is determined by the cost structure of the firm and its market demand. A reaction function can therefore move because of a change in either the costs or demand. This will turn out to be crucial in the applications, because the incumbent determines the location of its reaction function by its (strategic) choice of investment. Suppose the market is characterized by strategic substitutes. An increase in the marginal costs, which may be due to replacing the current plant by one with a smaller production capacity, results in a lower profit-maximizing output level for every level of output of the rival. The reaction function therefore shifts to the left in a market with strategic substitutes when the costs increase. Figure 11.10 presents this situation.

The opposite occurs when the market is characterized by strategic complements. Higher marginal costs of firm 1 result in a higher profit-maximizing price of firm 1 for every price level of firm 2. The reaction function of firm 1 shifts to the right. Figure 11.11 depicts the consequences of higher marginal costs of firm 1 for its reaction function when there is price competition.

A reaction function may also shift because of a change in demand. For example, an increase in demand, i.e. an increase in average revenue (AR), results in an increase in the profit-maximizing quantity in a market with quantity competition. The reaction function therefore shifts to the right. Similarly, the profit-maximizing price increases in a market with price competition when the demand for the products of the firm increases. The reaction function shifts to the right. Figure 11.12 summarizes these comparative statics results.

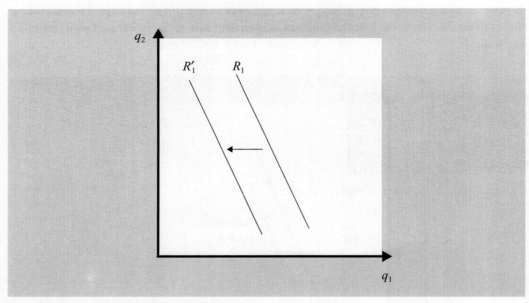

Figure 11.10: R_1 shifts to the left owing to an increase in marginal costs

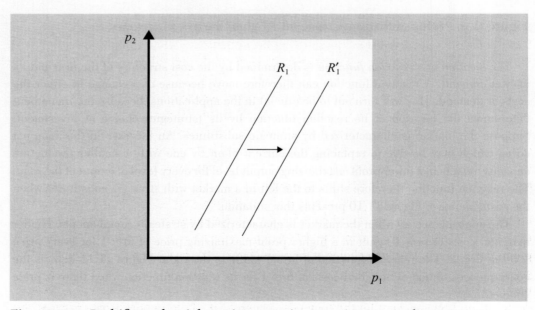

Figure 11.11: R_1 shifts to the right owing to an increase in marginal costs

Increase in		Shift in R_1 in market with	
		q-competition	p-competition
	MC	To left	To right
	AR	To right	To right

Figure 11.12: Comparative statics results

11.5 Strategy typology

The previous two sections have made every preparation to solve the game of Fig. 11.1 in general, and to determine the solution in each of the eight possible games of Fig. 11.2. The profit-maximizing investment behaviour of the incumbent in the first period is determined by three variables: the nature of the investment in the first stage of the game, the entry decision of the rival in the second stage and the nature of the competitive process in the third stage. The decisions in each stage can be phrased in terms of reaction functions, as follows:

Stage 1: Choice of location of the incumbent's reaction function R_1 by the incumbent.
Stage 2: Will there be a reaction function R_2 of the entrant?
Stage 3: Intersection of the reaction function R_1 and R_2 of the incumbent and the entrant.

The subgame perfect equilibrium is again determined by backward induction. So, the profit-maximizing profile of the incumbent in the third stage is determined first. Four cases are distinguished, because the profit-maximizing profile depends on the nature of the competitive process in the third stage, i.e. strategic substitutes or strategic complements, and the profitability of entry for the entrant, i.e. entry is inevitable or it can be deterred by the appropriate choice of investment by the incumbent.

The aim of the incumbent is to choose its profile in such a way that its payoffs are maximized. They are maximized when it faces a passive entrant, or no entrant at all, i.e. an extremely passive entrant. Making the entrant passive is the guiding principle regarding the profit-maximizing investment choice of the incumbent in the four cases which will be distinguished. The effect of investment is distinguished in competition-intensifying and competition-reducing investments. Competition intensifying investments result in more aggressive decisions of the incumbent for the (potential) entrant, like lowering the price or increasing the quantity. This gives the incumbent an aggressive profile. An aggressive profile of the incumbent in the final period establishes a decrease in the profit level of the entrant. The opposite holds for competition-reducing investments. These investments make it attractive for the incumbent to set a high price, or to produce a limited quantity, in the competitive process, which gives the incumbent a passive profile.

Figure 11.13 depicts a market where entry is inevitable and the market is characterized by strategic substitutes. Strategic substitutes are captured by the negative slope of the reaction functions. Two reaction functions are specified for the incumbent: $R_1(A)$ and $R_1(P)$. $R_1(A)$ represents the reaction function corresponding to an investment level which makes the incumbent aggressive, i.e. a high level of output is produced by the incumbent. Similarly, $R_1(P)$ represents an investment level which makes the incumbent passive, i.e. a low level of output is produced. The location of the zero on R_2 indicates that entry is inevitable. The reason is that the intersection of R_2 with $R_1(A)$ as well as $R_1(P)$ determines an output level of the entrant higher than the output level belonging to a zero profit level of the entrant. Another way of formulating this feature is that profits are increasing to the north-west on R_2 for the entrant, which is a straightforward adaptation of Fig. 11.8.

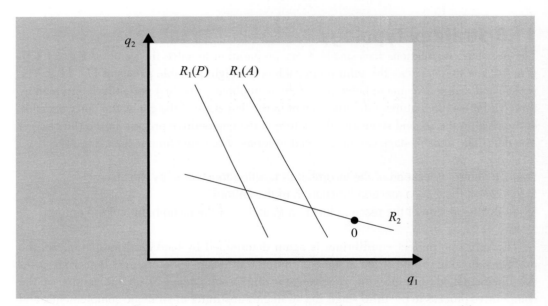

Figure 11.13: A market with strategic substitutes in which entry is inevitable

If entry is inevitable, then the incumbent faces a passive rather than an aggressive entrant. The previous section showed that an aggressive action by the incumbent is responded to in a passive way by the entrant when the competitive process is characterized by strategic substitutes. Therefore in a market with strategic substitutes where entry is inevitable the profit-maximizing profile of the incumbent is to be aggressive. Figure 11.14 summarizes this case.

Figure 11.15 depicts a market where entry is inevitable and the market is characterized by strategic complements. Strategic complements are captured by the positive slope of the reaction functions. Again two reaction functions are specified for the incumbent: $R_1(A)$ and $R_1(P)$. $R_1(A)$ represents the reaction function corresponding to an investment level which makes the incumbent aggressive, i.e. where a low price will be chosen by the incumbent. Similarly, $R_1(P)$ represents an investment level which makes the incumbent passive, i.e. where a high price will be chosen by the incumbent. The location of the zero on R_2 indicates that entry is inevitable, i.e. prices higher than the price belonging to the zero profit level of the entrant will result in equilibrium. The entrant will therefore decide to enter the industry, regardless of the choice of investment of the incumbent.

Entry inevitable?	Nature of competition	Profile
Yes	Strategic substitutes	Aggressive
Yes	Strategic complements	
No	Strategic substitutes	
No	Stratetgic complements	

Figure 11.14: Subgame perfect equilibrium profile in a market with strategic substitutes when entry is inevitable

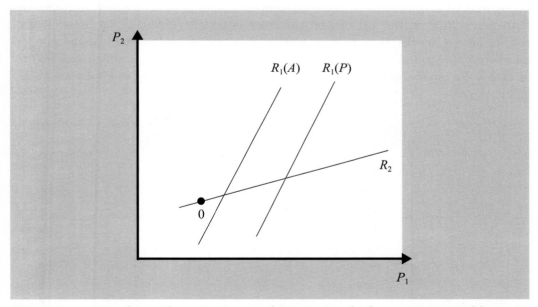

Figure 11.15: A market with strategic complements in which entry is inevitable

The incumbent likes to see a passive entrant. A market with strategic complements elicits a passive response of the entrant when the incumbent chooses a passive action, i.e. a high price. The payoff-maximizing profile of the incumbent in a market with strategic complements where entry is inevitable is therefore to be passive. Figure 11.16 lists this case.

Entry inevitable?	Nature of competition	Profile
Yes	Strategic substitutes	
Yes	Strategic complements	Passive
No	Strategic substitutes	
No	Stratetgic complements	

Figure 11.16: Subgame perfect equilibrium profile in a market with strategic complements when entry is inevitable

The markets where entry can be deterred by the appropriate choice of investment of the incumbent remain to be analysed. The profit-maximizing choice of the incumbent is to invest in such a way that the entrant forgoes entry. This applies to the market with strategic substitutes as well as the market with strategic complements.

Figure 11.17 depicts this market with strategic substitutes. The location of the zero on R_2 between $R_1(P)$ and $R_1(A)$ means that entry is not inevitable. If the investment of the incumbent results in a passive profile, then the incumbent will produce a low quantity. A substantial part of the market will be left for the entrant, which makes entry profitable. Investment behaviour which creates an aggressive profile therefore makes entry unattractive.

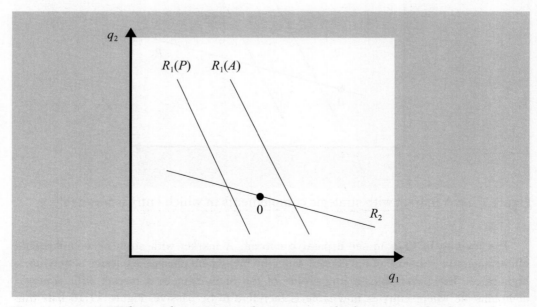

Figure 11.17: A market with strategic substitutes in which entry can be deterred

The profit-maximizing profile of the incumbent in a market with strategic substitutes and the possibility to deter entry is to be aggressive. This deters the entrant, which establishes that the incumbent continues to be a monopolist. Figure 11.18 summarizes this situation.

Entry inevitable?	Nature of competition	Profile
Yes	Strategic substitutes	
Yes	Strategic complements	
No	Strategic substitutes	Aggressive
No	Stratetgic complements	

Figure 11.18: Subgame perfect equilibrium profile in a market with strategic substitutes when entry can be deterred

Figure 11.19 depicts the market with strategic complements and the possibility that entry does not occur. The location of the zero on R_2 between $R_1(P)$ and $R_1(A)$ shows again that entry is not inevitable.

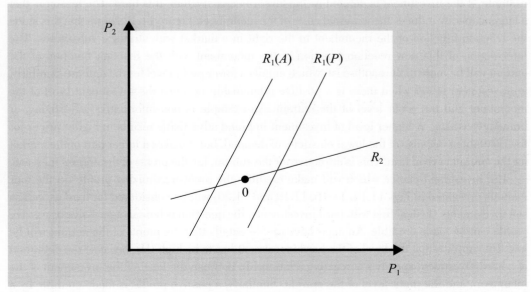

Figure 11.19: A market with strategic complements in which entry can be deterred

Figure 11.20 summarizes how the profit-maximizing profile of the incumbent is to be aggressive in a market with strategic complements in which entry can be deterred.

323

Entry inevitable?	Nature of competition	Profile
Yes	Strategic substitutes	
Yes	Strategic complements	
No	Strategic substitutes	
No	Stratetgic complements	Aggressive

Figure 11.20: Subgame perfect equilibrium profile in a market with strategic complements when entry can be deterred

The profit-maximizing profile of the incumbent in the third stage of the game has to be made credible. This is done by the incumbent in the first stage by its choice of investment. An investment makes a certain profile credible because the costs of the investment are often to a certain extent sunk, i.e. the investment generates revenues for a substantial period of time in a specific relationship, but is less valuable when it is used for something else. This provides a commitment to a certain course of action, and therefore establishes the credibility of the profile.

Two types of investment are distinguished. An investment is *hard* when there is a negative relationship between the investment level of the incumbent and the profit level of the entrant. For example, if the investment is defined as the level of capacity, then it is hard. The reason is that a larger capacity reduces the marginal costs of the incumbent. Figure 11.12 shows that this shifts the reaction function of the incumbent to the right in a market with strategic substitutes. The intersection of this new reaction function of the incumbent with the reaction function of the entrant will be more to the south-east, which entails a lower profit level for the entrant. Similarly, an investment is *soft* when there is a positive relationship between the investment level of the incumbent and the profit level of the entrant. An example is non-informative advertising, or brand advertising. A higher level of investment in brand advertising results in higher prices for the incumbent because of the lower elasticity of demand, but it leaves a larger part of the market for the entrant or rival firm. This is attractive for the entrant, i.e. the profits of the entrant increase.

The investment choice which will make credible the profit-maximizing profile (in the four markets presented in Figs 11.14, 11.16, 11.18 and 11.20) will be considered for hard as well as soft investments. To deal first with hard investments, the question is how an aggressive or passive profile can be made credible. An aggressive profile entails that the profits of the entrant will be low. This implies that the level of the hard investment has to be high (H), because the definition of a hard investment specifies a negative relationship between the level of the investment of the incumbent and the profit level of the entrant. Similarly, a passive profile is made credible by a low (L) level of the hard investment. Figure 11.21 summarizes the subgame perfect equilibrium investment level in the four possible types of markets when the investment is hard.

In the case of soft investments, an aggressive profile means again that the profits of the entrant will be low. This implies that the level of the soft investment has to be low (L), because the

Type of investment	Entry?	Nature of competition	Profile	SPE investment
Hard	Yes	Strategic substitutes	Aggressive	H
		Strategic complements	Passive	L
	No	Strategic substitutes	Aggressive	H
		Strategic complements	Aggressive	H
Soft	Yes	Strategic substitutes	Aggressive	
		Strategic complements	Passive	
	No	Strategic substitutes	Aggressive	
		Strategic complements	Aggressive	

Figure 11.21: Subgame perfect equilibrium investment strategies when the investment is hard

definition of a soft investment specifies a positive relationship between the level of the investment of the incumbent and the profit level of the entrant. Similarly, a passive profile is made credible by a high (H) level of the soft investment. Figure 11.21 summarizes the subgame perfect equilibrium investment level in the four possible types of markets when the investment is soft.

Type of investment	Entry?	Nature of competition	Profile	SPE investment
Hard	Yes	Strategic substitutes	Aggressive	H
		Strategic complements	Passive	L
	No	Strategic substitutes	Aggressive	H
		Strategic complements	Aggressive	H
Soft	Yes	Strategic substitutes	Aggressive	L
		Strategic complements	Passive	H
	No	Strategic substitutes	Aggressive	L
		Strategic complements	Aggressive	L

Figure 11.22: Subgame perfect equilibrium investment strategies for both types of investment

The various combinations of aggressive or passive profile and low or high investment have been given fancy labels by Fudenberg and Tirole (1984), where a high level of investment is associated with overinvestment and a low level of investment with underinvestment, as follows:

Top Dog: overinvestment in order to create an aggressive profile.
Lean and Hungry: underinvestment in order to create an aggressive profile.
Fat Cat: overinvestment in order to create a passive profile.
Puppy Dog: underinvestment in order to create a passive profile.

Figure 11.23 adds these labels to Fig. 11.22, and is called the strategy typology.

Type of investment	Entry?	Nature of competition	Profile	SPE investment
Hard	Yes	Strategic substitutes	Aggressive	Top Dog
		Strategic complements	Passive	Puppy Dog
	No	Strategic substitutes	Aggressive	Top Dog
		Strategic complements	Aggressive	Top Dog
Soft	Yes	Strategic substitutes	Aggressive	Lean and Hungry
		Strategic complements	Passive	Fat Cat
	No	Strategic substitutes	Aggressive	Lean and Hungry
		Strategic complements	Aggressive	Lean and Hungry

Figure 11.23: Strategy typology

11.6 Applications

The above typology implies that only three variables have to be specified in order to determine the profit-maximizing organizational choice or investment in a strategic setting. First, the *investment has to be defined*. This determines whether the investment is hard or soft. The definition of the investment usually starts with 'The extent of . . . '. A specific word, like delegation, vertical integration, or limited liability, has to be added in order to complete it. Determining whether it is a hard or soft investment is the most difficult part of applications, because it requires one's general knowledge regarding economics and management to be brought to the forefront. Second, the *condition regarding entry* has to be specified, i.e. the inevitability of entry. Finally, the *nature of the competitive process* has to be determined, i.e. the slope of the reaction function. The strategy typology has been applied to many situations. This section limits itself to applications which relate to the topics of the previous chapters, like delegation, limited liability, vertical integration, licences and royalties, organizational structure and equity participation and joint ventures.

Application: Strategic delegation

Suppose an incumbent firm is confronted with the possibility of entry. It threatens to start a price war when entry actually occurs, which renders entry unprofitable. However, entry will occur anyway because this threat is not credible; the incumbent will make more money by co-operating (C) with the entrant and the entrant is aware of this. The incumbent can make the threat of a price war credible by appointing a manager whose salary is based on market share (M). Such a manager will (credibly) fight an entrant because entry will reduce his salary. The strategic delegation of decision power deters entry (Vickers, 1985).

The situation is depicted in Fig. 11.24. The incentive scheme of the manager can be based on profits (P) or market share (M) by the firm. The entrant decides to enter (Y) or not to enter (N). Finally, the manager either starts a price war (W) or co-operates (C) with the entrant. The payoffs reflect the various market scenarios. If there is no entry, then the incumbent firm is a monopolist. If there is entry and a price war is started, then the entrant looses money. Both firms make money when they co-operate once entry has taken place. Finally, the manager is rewarded for fighting a price war when incentive scheme M is used. The subgame perfect equilibrium is determined in the usual way by backward induction:

Firm: M;
Entrant: (Y,N);
Manager: (C,C,W,C).

Notice that the above means that a firm may establish profit maximization by not rewarding its manager on the basis of profits. Strategic considerations dictate that market share maximization, rather than profit maximization, by the manager results in the highest profits.

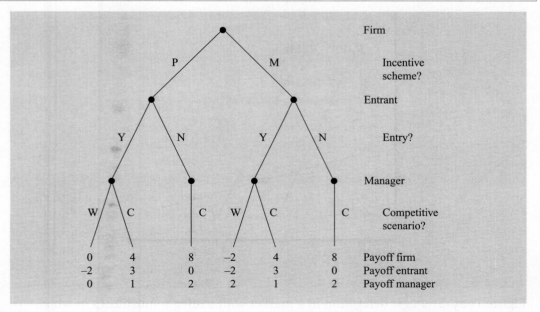

Figure 11.24 Market share maximization as profit-maximizing strategy

The above can also be presented with reaction functions (Lyons, 1987). Define the investment as the extent of market-share-based payments for the manager. This is a hard investment because there is a negative relationship between the level of this investment of the incumbent and the profit level of the entrant. The reason is that a higher degree of market-based payments increases the incentive for the manager to start a price war when entry occurs, which reduces the profit level of the entrant. The level of investment determines the location of the reaction function, where the aggressive investment is presented by M in this application, and the passive investment by P. Entry is not inevitable in the situation presented, so either Fig. 11.17 or Fig. 11.19 applies. The situation with strategic substitutes is considered first. The strategic situation is therefore characterized by

Investment: Extent of market-share-based payment;
Entry: Not inevitable;
Competition: Strategic substitutes.

Figure 11.25 presents the situation. $R_1(M)$ is to the right of $R_1(P)$, which entails that a manager with a market-share-based salary will produce more than a manager with a profit-based salary for every output level q_2 of the entrant. Investment M makes entry unprofitable because the intersection point of $R_1(M)$ with R_2 is to the south-east of 0 on R_2. The investment M is a Top Dog strategy, which gives the incumbent an aggressive profile in order to deter entry. This corresponds with the third case in Fig. 11.23.

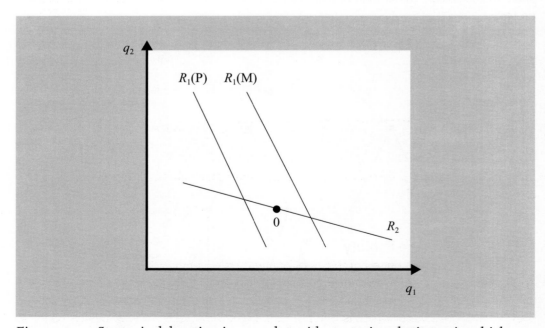

Figure 11.25: Strategic delegation in a market with strategic substitutes in which entry can be deterred

Consider next the situation with strategic complements. The strategic situation is therefore characterized by

Investment: Extent of market-share-based payment;
Entry: Not inevitable;
Competition: Strategic complements.

Figure 11.26 presents the situation. $R_1(M)$ is to the left of $R_1(P)$, which means that a manager with a market-share-based salary will choose a lower price p_1 (on the horizontal axis) than will a manager with a profit-based salary for every price level p_2 (on the vertical axis) of the entrant. Investment M makes entry unprofitable because the intersection point of $R_1(M)$ with R_2 is to the south-west of 0 on R_2. The investment M is therefore again a Top Dog strategy, which gives the incumbent an aggressive profile in order to deter entry. This is in line with the fourth case in Fig. 11.23.

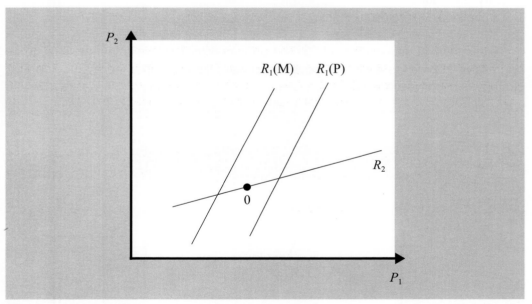

Figure 11.26: Strategic delegation in a market with strategic complements in which entry can be deterred

Application: Limited liability

The strategic consequences of the debt/equity ratio of a firm will be addressed in this application. Equity means that losses as well as gains are borne or made completely by the provider of equity. Debt is different. The provider of debt receives a fixed reward for making funds available, which is independent of the profit level as long as it is above a certain level. If the firm goes bankrupt, then the provider of debt has had bad luck and will not receive his money back. The implication is therefore that all the profits of the debt-financed investment go to the firm, while losses are for the debt-providers. This is the characteristic of limited liability of debt. It encourages risky and/or aggressive investment behaviour, which has already been discussed in Chapter 6.

Define the investment as the extent of limited liability (Brander and Lewis, 1986). This is a hard investment, because a high level of debt induces the firm to choose a risky investment strategy with a high level of output. Either this results in high profits or else the firm will go bankrupt. High profits are nice for the firm, while the costs associated with bankruptcy are at the expense of the providers of debt. The reaction function of the incumbent with a high level of debt, i.e. $R_1(D)$, is associated with higher output levels or lower prices than the reaction function of the incumbent with a high level of equity, i.e. $R_1(E)$. Figure 11.27 depicts a market with strategic substitutes in which entry is inevitable. The strategic situation is therefore characterized by

Investment: Extent of limited liability;
Entry: Inevitable;
Competition: Strategic substitutes.

This is the first case in Fig. 11.23. The profit-maximizing investment profile is to be aggressive in order to elicit a passive response. This is established by the Top Dog strategy of overinvesting in debt financing.

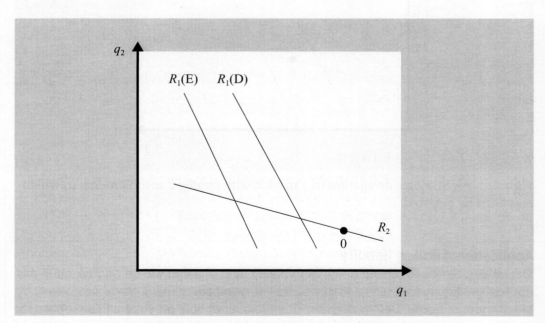

Figure 11.27: Limited liability in a market with strategic substitutes in which entry is inevitable

Figure 11.28 depicts this market with price competition, i.e. the strategic situation is characterized by

Investment: Extent of limited liability;
Entry: Inevitable;
Competition: Strategic complements.

This is the second case in Fig. 11.23. The profit-maximizing investment profile is to be passive in order to elicit a passive response. This is established by the Puppy Dog strategy of underinvesting in debt financing.

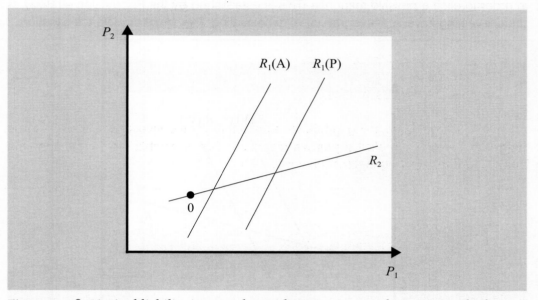

Figure 11.28: Limited liability in a market with strategic complements in which entry is inevitable

Application: Vertical integration

Suppose a processor sells its output to a wholesaler. Usually a profit is made by the wholesaler, i.e. a price is chosen higher than marginal costs. Subsequently the whole-saler makes a profit by selling its output also at a price above its marginal costs. This is called the *double marginalization problem* (Spengler, 1950). Vertical integration reduces this problem to one marginalization problem, because the wholesaler will now receive the output of the processor at marginal costs. The elimination of the double marginalization problem by vertical integration therefore reduces the final product price, i.e. vertical integration intensifies the competitive process. So, vertical integration might not be attractive for the wholesaler because it intensifies competition, i.e. it results in lower prices (Bonanno and Vickers, 1988).

Define the investment as the extent of vertical integration. A low level of vertical integration is wholesaling (W), whereas a high level of vertical integration is vertical integration (VI). It has been argued above that this is a hard investment. Suppose that entry is inevitable and that the competitive process is characterized by price competition. The strategic situation is therefore summarized by

Investment: Extent of wholesaling;
Entry: Inevitable;
Competition: Strategic complements.

Like the previous application, the profit-maximizing investment profile is to be passive in order to elicit a passive response. This is established by the Puppy Dog strategy of underinvesting in vertical integration, i.e. wholesaling. Fig. 11.29 depicts the situation.

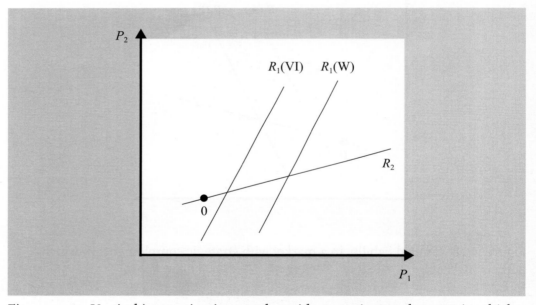

Figure 11.29: Vertical integration in a market with strategic complements in which entry is inevitable

Application: Licences and royalties

An inventor wishes to make as much money as possible with his technological break-through. The new technology lowers the marginal costs of production. The innovation can be sold either by asking a fixed fee, i.e. by licence, or by asking a royalty for each unit sold. The choice of sales method depends on the nature of the market (Bulow *et al.*, 1985).

Firms in a market with strategic substitutes are willing to pay more than the direct savings of the new technology when they can also gain a strategic advantage. This is possible because the lower marginal costs result in less aggressive behaviour of the rival firms. The sale of the new technology by licence ensures that the costs are made in the first period, i.e. the costs of the licence are sunk in the second period. This establishes an aggressive profile and a high level of profits, which implies that firms are willing to pay a substantial amount of money for a licence.

Define the investment as the extent to which royalties are used by the inventor. This investment is soft because a higher level of the investment, i.e. a royalty, is used, increasing the marginal costs in the second period. It results in a lower quantity produced, which is attractive for the rival firm. The profit-maximizing sales method is a Lean and Hungry strategy of underinvestment in royalties in order to create a credible aggressive profile. This is the licence. Figure 11.30 presents the relationship between the sales method and the location of the reaction function, where L indicates licence and R stands for royalty. The strategic situation is summarized by

Investment: Extent of royalties;
Entry: Inevitable or not inevitable;
Competition: Strategic substitutes.

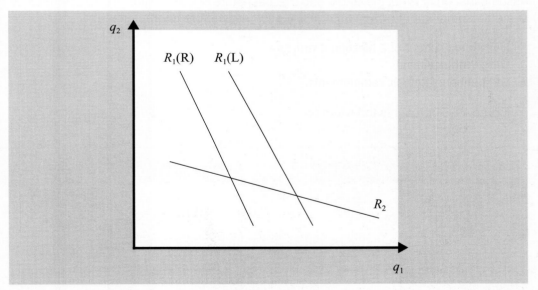

Figure 11.30: Sales method and strategic substitutes

A licence is not a profit-maximizing sales method for the inventor in a market with strategic complements. Lower marginal costs due to a licence result in aggressive actions, and therefore in an aggressive response in this market with strategic complements. The firms will therefore bid less for the licence than the direct cost savings. This disadvantageous strategic effect of the sale of the technology by a licence can be prevented by asking a royalty per unit sold. The marginal costs will stay unchanged in the second period. The Fat Cat strategy of overinvestment in royalties, i.e. the sales method royalty, is therefore advised for the inventor.

Application: Organizational structure

Suppose that an organization considers the choice between a functional and a divisional structure. A functional structure is chosen when the advantages of scale are more important than the co-ordination problems associated with this structure. A divisional structure is chosen when the co-ordination problems are most important. There are also strategic considerations to be taken into account in the choice of organizational structure (Hendrikse, 1991).

Decisions regarding product specifications are taken by the divisional unit in a divisional structure (D), whereas these decisions are taken at a more centralized level in a functional structure (F). A divisional structure is more aggressive in its pricing policy than a functional structure. The reason is that the local decision-making in a divisional structure entails negative externalities, i.e. they compete with each other in order to increase the divisional profits at the expense of the company profits. This makes the market less attractive for potential entrants. Define the investment as the extent of a functional structure. This is a soft investment, because more of a functional structure makes the incumbent less aggressive and therefore increases the profits of the entrant. Assume that entry is not inevitable and that the nature of competition is characterized by strategic complements. The strategic situation is therefore characterized by

Investment: Extent of a functional structure;
Entry: Not inevitable;
Competition: Strategic complements.

Figure 11.31 presents the situation.

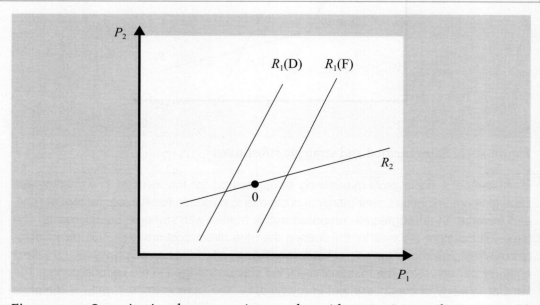

Figure 11.31: Organizational structure in a market with strategic complements in which entry can be deterred

The profit-maximizing investment strategy of the incumbent is to choose an aggressive profile in order to deter entry. This profile is made credible by an underinvestment in a functional structure. This is the Lean and Hungry strategy in terms of the strategy typology of Fig. 11.23, i.e. the eighth case is actual. Notice that the investment of the incumbent could as well have been defined as the extent of a divisional structure. This definition of the investment makes the investment hard, and the subgame perfect equilibrium strategy of the incumbent is overinvestment in a divisional structure. This is the Top Dog strategy in terms of the strategy typology of Fig. 11.23, i.e. actually the fourth case of this typology. Notice that this opposite definition of the investment does not change the choice of organizational structure of the incumbent. The divisional structure is chosen in order to make the aggressive profile credible, which deters entry.

Application: Equity participation and joint ventures

Joint equity participations and joint ventures establish a positive relationship between the profits of the separate firms, because they have a stake in each others' well-being (Reynolds and Snapp, 1986). This reduces the intensity of competition between firms, which results in a lower quantity being produced and higher prices. Define the investment as the extent of equity participations, where H represents a high level of equity participations and L a low level of equity participations. It is obvious that this is a soft investment. Assume that entry is inevitable and that the nature of competition is characterized by strategic complements. The strategic situation is therefore characterized by

Investment: Extent of joint equity participations;
Entry: Inevitable;
Competition: Strategic complements.

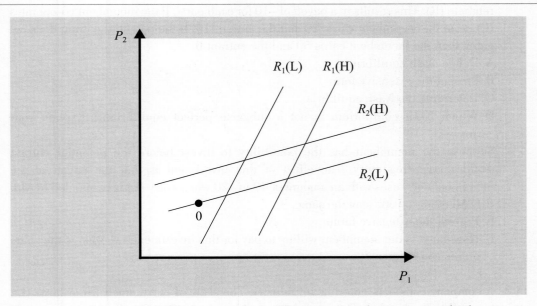

Figure 11.32: Limited liability in a market with strategic substitutes in which entry is inevitable

Figure 11.32 shows the effect of the investment on the location of the reaction functions. The reaction function of the incumbent as well as the reaction function of the rival firm will shift. A higher level of joint equity participations results in a shift of the reaction function R_1 of the incumbent to the east, and a shift in the reaction function R_1 of the rival firm to the north. A passive profile in order to elicit a passive response is made credible by an overinvestment in joint equity participations. This is the Fat Cat strategy in terms of the strategy typology, i.e. the sixth case in the strategy typology of Fig. 11.23.

11.7 Conclusion

Organizational choices are driven by efficiency as well as strategic considerations. Strategic considerations are highlighted in this chapter. A simple framework has been developed to address a large variety of strategic situations in a systematic way. Three variables turn out to determine the choice of investment: the nature of investment, the entry condition and the nature of competition.

11.8 Exercises

11.1   Draw the reaction function of a firm in a market with quantity competition and
     A   Homogenous products.
     B   Independent products.
     C   Substitute products.
     D   Complementary products.

11.2   If a potential entrant actually enters (E) the industry, then the incumbent may start to retaliate (R). This results in a payoff of −10 for each party. If the incumbent co-operates (C), then the incumbent earns 20 and the entrant 10. If the potential entrant does not enter, then the incumbent earns 50 and the entrant 0.
     A   Define Nash equilibrium.
     B   Present the extensive form.
     C   Determine the Nash equilibria
     D   Which Nash equilibrium is not a subgame perfect equilibrium? Explain your answer.
     Suppose the incumbent has the possibility to invest before the potential entrant decides regarding entry. The effect of this investment is that the payoff of the incumbent decreases with an amount of 40 to −20 when entry (E) is responded to with (C). All other payoffs stay the same.
     E   Present the extensive form.
     F   How much is the incumbent willing to pay for this investment, i.e. what is the value of this commitment?

11.3   A company considers entering an industry. The scale of entry, small (S) or large (L), has still to be decided. The incumbent decides after entry regarding starting a price war (P) or to co-operate (C). If the entrant chooses S, and the incumbent chooses P (C), then the entrant earns −1 (1) and the incumbent 2 (3). The choice L of the entrant results in a payoff of −2 (0) for the entrant and 1 (0) of the incumbent when P (C) is chosen.

A Present the extensive form.
B Determine the subgame perfect equilibrium.
C Depict the above situation with reaction functions in a market with price competition.
D Define an investment in order to investigate the strategic consequences of entry.
E Is this investment hard or soft? Explain your answer.
F How is the profit-maximizing investment strategy of the entrant characterized in the strategy typology? Explain your answer.

11.4 Many products consist of several components. For example, a computer consists of hardware and software, photographic equipment of a camera body and a lens. There is product differentiation not only regarding the complete product, but also regarding the separate components. Preferences of consumers differ substantially. Some consumers prefer all components of one brand above another, while there are also consumers whose ideal product consists of one brand regarding the first component and another brand regarding the second component. The availability of this latter product is not clear and is the focus of attention in this application. The company has to decide regarding the compatibility of its components with the components of the rival firm. Assume that Modak and Kinolta are active in the market for photographic equipment, where the components consist of a camera and a lens. The competitive process is characterized by price competition.

A Does the decision regarding compatibility affect the demand or the costs of the company? Explain your answer
B Is the slope of the reaction function positive or negative? Explain your answer.
C Define the investment.
D Is the investment hard or soft?
E Determine the profit-maximizing investment strategy of Modak in the situation where Kinolta cannot be pushed out of the market. Explain your answer with a diagram.
F Determine the profit-maximizing investment strategy of Modak in the situation where Kinolta can be pushed out of the market. Explain your answer with a figure.

Part VI:
Limited cognition

In Parts II and III human cognitive capacities are assumed to be sufficient to comprehend problems in their entirety The assumption of complete rationality has been very productive for the development of various important insights. However, the practical relevance for managers of results like the welfare theorem, the Coase theorem and the Modigliani–Miller theorem seems to be limited. For example, the Coase theorem (Coase, 1960) specifies the circumstances where organizations add no value, i.e. where organizations do not matter. Similarly, Modigliani and Miller specified the conditions in which the way a company is financed has no impact on the value of the firm; i.e. where capital structure does not matter. Finally, the formulation of the welfare theorem in the theory of general equilibrium by Debreu (1959) specifies the circumstances in which markets work well; again, organizations do not matter. Many years later the value of these results has now been shown, for theoretical as well as managerial purposes. Their value derives from the specification of the assumptions needed to formulate them. Subsequent developments investigate which new results can be formulated by relaxing these assumptions in order to achieve a better fit between theory and practice.

Another approach to organizations consists of the systematic description of behaviour in organizations without using the above theorems as a reference point. Fields like behavioural accounting, behavioural finance, economic psychology, organizational behaviour and strategic decision-making are doing this. The investigation and solution of complex problems is at the centre of analysis, which means that problems are analysed where people are unable to comprehend them. The assumption made in Parts I to V of perfect, logical, deductive rationality is therefore abandoned and replaced by bounded or even procedural rationality. It is assumed that humans are only moderately good at deductive logic, and make only moderate use of it. Bernstein (1996) summarizes the criticism of models with complete rationality by saying: 'The failure of the rational model is not in its logic but in the brain it requires.'

The behavioural assumptions of this part are presented in Fig. VI.1. The most important is that rationality is assumed to be limited or even procedural, while various situations regarding the behavioural hypothesis are distinguished. An example of a situation with opportunistic, procedural rational decision-makers occurs when a flock of birds are searching for food. One bird among them wants a particular item of food on the ground just for itself. It therefore imitates the sound of a threatening bird of prey, so causing its companions to flee and to suspend their search for food. A self-interested behavioural hypothesis means that one cares about oneself, but refrains from strategic behaviour in order to manipulate the environment of others. Finally, an idealistic behavioural assumption means that self-interest is moved to the background and common interest receives most attention. Examples are the taking of positions in a beehive

		Behavioural hypothesis		
		Opportunistic	Self-interested	Idealistic
Rationality	Complete			
	Limited		X	
	Procedural	X	X	X

Figure VI.1: Positioning of evolutionary approaches

(queen bee, worker bee) and in a team of racing cyclists (leader, assistants).

An important reason for the descriptive approach in the above behavioural fields is probably a lack of workable concepts or tools of bounded rationality. Limited cognition is in many situations a more realistic assumption than complete rationality. Miller (1956) observed in his well-known article 'The Magical Number Seven; Plus or Minus Two' regarding the empirical research with respect to limited cognition in the 1950s that

> There seem to be some limitations built into us either by learning or by the design of our nervous system, a limit that keeps our channel capacities in this general range.

The view of the firm in evolutionary approaches can be compared to a tree (Fig. VI.2). The organization develops over time in such a way that certain tasks are executed well, just as a tree develops certain capacities. However, the aspect of limited cognition implies that the organization cannot handle all possible tasks perfectly, or that certain changes are hard to make. Efficient organizations take this into account in the choice of their activities. This part addresses this topic.

Figure VI.2: The firm from an evolutionary perspective

12 Limited cognition and organization

Contents

12.1 Introduction

A crucial ingredient in the development of organization theories is bounded rationality. Simon (1961) is outspoken about this:

> If there were no limits to human rationality administrative theory would be barren. It would consist of a single precept: Always select the alternative, among those available, which would lead to the most complete achievement of your goals. The need of an administrative theory resides in the fact that there are limits to human rationality.

Almost thirty years later the same writer (1990) states:

> Human rational behavior is shaped by a pair of scissors whose two blades are the structure of the task environments and the computational abilities of the actor.

This chapter highlights bounded rationality. Section 12.2 addresses the question why it is necessary to explicitly incorporate bounded rationality in organization theories. Section 12.3 treats deductive bounded rationality, while Sec. 12.4 focuses on inductive bounded rationality. The tradeoff between type I and type II errors is addressed in Sec. 12.5. Evolutionary approaches are outlined in Sec. 12.6. Section 12.7 concludes.

12.2 Why make bounded rationality explicit?

Traditional economic theories usually assign complete, logical, deductive rationality to decision-makers. It is important for the estimation of the value of the assumption of complete, deductive rationality to make a distinction between the success of the assumption of complete rationality in predicting behaviour and the formulation of rationality. Some economists choose complete rationality as their point of departure because they do not consider it important to know the way people take decisions, as long as their models predict as well as do models with bounded rationality. The power and success of the behavioural assumption of complete rationality is that many events can be explained by assuming that individuals behave 'as if' complete rationality is guiding their behaviour (Friedman, 1953). One reason for complete rationality is therefore that it works. This is the usual way in science. The philosopher of science Lakatos wrote: 'there is no theory rejection without a better theory' (Smith, 1989). However, while almost everybody agrees that this characterization of humans is not realistic, people continue to work with it because a good alternative is not available, or would not add much.

The 'as if' position means that other decision processes regarding behaviour result in the same outcome as the behaviour of completely rational decision-makers. An extreme example is a canonball. The canonball doesn't have the intellectual ability to solve a differential equation, but its trajectory can be perfectly described by such an equation. The assumption of complete rationality regarding a canonball is therefore no problem. A similar tension between the ingredients of a model and realism applies to models with other behavioural assumptions. The 'garbage can' model of a company (Cohen *et al.*, 1972) is based on ambiguous, inconsistent and vague decision processes. This is no problem as long as the model predicts well, despite the fact that the people involved do not consider the assumptions descriptive. However, models with complete rationality become problematic when they are no longer informative about the decisions taken.

Limited cognition can be defined in various ways and each definition will therefore be ad hoc to a certain extent. The reason for this variety is that there is only one way to be completely rational, while there are many possibilities of being boundedly rational. One way to model bounded rationality is to extend the approach of complete, logical, *deductive* rationality to complex situations, where the cognitive capacities of the decision-makers are insufficient to grasp the complexity of a problem in its entirety. This is done in Sec. 12.3. Psychologists take another approach. They argue that humans are good at seeing, recognizing or matching patterns. Humans use *inductive* reasoning: we use as needed a sequence running from pattern recognition to hypothesis formation, then finally, via deduction using currently held working hypotheses, to hypothesis replacement (Arthur, 1994). As further evidence from our surroundings comes in, it may strengthen or weaken our beliefs in our current hypotheses, discarding some when they cease to perform, so that we replace them as needed with new ones. In other words, when we cannot reason fully or else lack full definition of the problem, we use simple models to fill the gap between our cognitive capacities and the complexity of the situation. Simplified deductions may be carried out regarding such a simplified model or pattern when some guidance for action is sought. This reasoning process is both evolutionary and complex. Sections 12.4 and 12.5 are dedicated to inductive bounded cognition and evolutionary approaches. Section 12.6 presents a statistical approach to bounded cognition.

12.3 Deductive bounded cognition

The degree of rationality is defined in Chapter 2 as the ratio between the cognitive capacities of a decision-maker and the complexity of the problem. However, the numerator and the denominator have not been specified. One way to do this is to use the extent of partitioning of the set of states or situations; other words used for partitioning are 'chunks' (Miller, 1956) and 'bracketing' (Weick, 1979). The number of partitions needed to establish the finest partition is defined as the complexity of the problem. The notion of partitioning will now be illustrated with a colour recognition problem. Suppose there are four possible states: Red (R), Green (G), White (W) and Dark (D). The complexity of this colour recognition problem is three, because each element of the set of states can be distinguished after three partitions. This can be seen as follows. First, divide the set of states into Red and non-Red. Subsequently, divide non-Red into Green and non-Green. Finally, split non-Green into White and non-White, i.e. Dark. Therefore, the set of states has reached its finest partition after three partitions. (There are other sequences of dividing the set of states, but the finest partition is reached always after three partitions in the colour recognition problem.)

The level of cognitive capacities and therefore the degree of rationality both depend on the nature of the decision-maker. Four decision-makers are distinguished. A human is able to distinguish all states in the colour recognition problem. The level of the cognitive capacities of a human is therefore three. A cat is not able to distinguish the colours Red and Green. It is not able to partition the set (R,G) into the sets (R) and (G). Therefore, the cat recognizes the colour White, and the state Dark is distinguished, as well as the situation where either Red or Green prevails. The level of the cognitive capacities of the cat is therefore two. A mole can only distinguish the sets (R, G, W) and (D), i.e. light and dark. The cognitive capacities are therefore one. Finally, a spoon has cognitive capacities zero, because it can recognize none of the states. Figure 12.1 summarizes the colour recognition problem.

Decision-maker	Partitioning of set of states	Cognitive capacities
Human	{(R),(G),(W),(D)}	1
Cat	{(R,G),(W),(D)}	$\frac{2}{3}$
Mole	{(R,G,W),(D)}	$\frac{1}{3}$
Spoon	{(R,G,W,D)}	0

Figure 12.1: Colour recognition capacities of different decision-makers

The human is the decision-maker with the highest cognitive capacities in the colour recognition problem. However, this does not always hold. For example, compared with various animals humans show spoon-like behaviour with regard to recognizing high-frequency sounds. Next to investigating the cognitive capacities of humans compared with other decision makers in various problems, is it also possible to compare different humans. Information or data does often not offer the same interpretation for everybody. Everybody shades the available information in his or her own way. For example, a marketing expert behaves like a spoon regarding the technical aspects of a product, whereas somebody with a technical background is often said to have little feeling for marketing aspects.

Similarly, every approach or slicing of a problem creates and destroys information. This is inevitable given our limited cognition. It is therefore unproductive to dismiss other views. There is also no prospect of agreement because limited cognitive capacities will always be allocated in different ways. The hope is that different slices or approaches generate different insights, and that organizations are structured in such a way that the different perspectives complement each other. For example, the scientific paradigm 'logical empiricism' focuses on different layers of organization (elementary particle, atom, molecule, cell, living organism, social group) and formulates certain (horizontal) insights, while system theory (von Berta-lanffy, 1968; Kaufmann, 1993) is focused on (vertical) results applying to specific aspects of all layers.

Notions like forgetfulness, absentmindedness and making mistakes are closely related to the above. For example, suppose in a multiple-choice exam the possible solutions to 3 − 1 are presented as 0, 1 and 2 and that the cognitive capacity or knowledge of the person answering the question is limited. The numbers 3 and 1 are distinguished and the meaning of 0 is known, but the mathematical operation subtraction is not known. The set $(0,1,2)$ may therefore be partitioned into the sets (0) and $(1,2)$. It is often optimal in such a situation to determine the choice of a number in the set $(1,2)$ randomly (Rubinstein, 1998), which may result in $3 - 1 = 1$.

Using the partitioning method in the subsequent applications will show that the above is an example of deductive rationality. A problem is first characterized in a mathematical way, then subsequently the decision-makers are assumed to allocate their limited cognitive capacities in an optimal way to solving the problem at hand.

Application: Diversification

Managers often execute different tasks, like formulating and evaluating investment projects, evaluating market developments and determining the strategy of the enterprise. Limited cognitive capacities will show up in these policy decisions.

Fershtman and Kalai (1993) investigate the relationship between the degree of diversification of a company and the intensity of competition in different markets. The complexity of the problem of the boundedly rational manager is determined by the number of markets the company is in and the number of competitors in each market. The optimal number of markets is limited, because every new market takes at least one cognitive unit. Adding an additional market to the portfolio of markets must be at the expense of the company's current market. It entails having to take away from the current portfolio of markets at least one cognitive unit in order to allocate it to the new market. This implies that there are at least two markets in the new portfolio of markets which receive only superficial attention, i.e. the new market receives only one cognitive unit of attention and there is one old market which receives one cognitive unit of attention less.

A manager will respond less, i.e. allocate fewer cognitive units, to the strategic moves of the rival when he or she is more concerned about the specific local market circumstances. This may result in divesting activities from markets where entry occurs. It is also possible that where the manager has limited cognitive capacities this will result in less entry than where his or her cognitive capacities are unlimited. Co-operation with an entrant requires more cognitive capacities than does a non-cooperative strategy. The limited rationality of the established company may deter entry, because the less complex non-cooperative strategy makes entry less attractive.

Application: Price recognition

Differences between consumers are conceptualized usually as differences in preferences or availability of information. There may also be differences in cognitive capacities, which may show up in variations in the time needed to take a good decision or the time needed to process information (by way of the number of partitions which can be made.) This may play a role in the purchase decisions of consumers. Take for example the purchase of a stereo tower (Rubinstein, 1993). There is usually not one price for the entire tower, but a separate price for each part, like the tuner, amplifier and so on.

If these prices are based on the quality of the parts, then the consumer can infer something about the underlying quality from the price. Assume that a type 1 consumer has only one cognitive unit available, while a type 2 consumer is endowed with two cognitive units. The seller considers this difference between buyers in the design of his price policy. The price of low quality takes one of two possible values: the reservation price of low quality or the average price of the reservation prices of low and high quality. The price of high quality is the reservation price of high quality.

The level of the cognitive capacities of the customer determines his or her purchase decision. A type 1 consumer is able to partition the set of prices only once, i.e. low prices and high prices can be distinguished. The optimal purchase decision of this consumer is to buy the entire stereo tower only when the price is below a certain level. Only low quality is bought. Nothing is bought at an intermediate price level, i.e. the average of the low-quality and high-quality reservation prices. A type 1 consumer will not buy at an intermediate price because occasionally too much will be paid for low quality. High quality is therefore never bought by this consumer. A type 2 consumer is endowed with two cognitive units to partition the set of prices: low, intermediate and high. The optimal purchase decision of a type 2 consumer consists of not buying when the price is within a certain price range. (A range or interval has two borders, which a type 2 consumer with the capacities to make two partitions is just able to handle.) This decision rule prevents too much being paid for a certain part of the entire stereo tower. A low or a high price is therefore paid, according to the quality level.

A company facing customers with different cognitive capacities may choose the complexity and design of the price list in such a way that the additional costs of the customers with low cognitive capacities are prevented. The price list is intentionally made complex by including many possibilities. Some of these possibilities contain a trap by offering the customer an unattractive combination of price and quality. The customer with low cognitive capacities is occupied with preventing the trap to such an extent that other attractive possibilities are not recognized. The complexity of the price list can therefore be used strategically by the company.

A question regarding type 1 customers is how they are able to choose the most attractive strategy out of all possible strategies with their limited cognitive capacities. (The same question can of course be asked regarding type 2 customers.) A possible (inductive) answer is formulated in the next section.

Application: Management accounting systems

Management accounting entails the collection, classification, processing, analysis and reporting of information to managers (Kaplan and Atkinson, 1979). A management accounting system provides information for managers to support their planning and control activities. The importance of a management accounting system is that the large and complex amount of information is reduced to a manageable amount of data. This occurs in two ways. First, the information is classified or partitioned. Figure 12.2 assumes that there are three possible states, s_1, s_2 and s_3. Five management information systems are possible (Demski, 1980). The first system does not partition at all. Three systems can be distinguished when one partition is made. The fifth system partitions twice. Examples of partitioning methods are input-based (for example an inventory method), process-based (for example an activity-based costing and production unit method) and output-based (for example a division calculation method) systems. The information is aggregated once it is partitioned. This usually entails taking some average regarding the set of states which is not yet partitioned. An example is proportional sharing costs (Fig. 12.2). Notice that h_1 involves complete aggregation of information, while h_5 involves no aggregation of information.

Information system	Partitioning
h_1	$\{(s_1, s_2, s_3)\}$
h_2	$\{(s_1), (s_2, s_3)\}$
h_3	$\{(s_2), (s_1, s_3)\}$
h_4	$\{(s_3), (s_1, s_2)\}$
h_5	$\{(s_1), (s_2), (s_3)\}$

Figure 12.2: Possible partitions of the set of states (Demski, 1980)

Application: Agenda control

Problems in organizations are frequently related to information. There may be asymmetric information, a lack of information or wrong information. This application will focus on the relationship between the way organizations are structured and the generation of wrong information.

There are usually several ways in which information can be channelled from employees to the boss. The channelling of information is important because no one person alone can process all the available information. Information is compressed in the decision-making process in such a way that it can be comprehended by the decision-maker. An important insight is that every structure of information channels, or every slicing of the incredible amount of information, leads inevitably to certain bias in the provision of information (Hammond, 1994). This inevitability implies that the choice of organization is a choice between different kinds of biases.

The McKelvey theorem of Chapter 2 is used for analysing the channelling of information. Suppose that an organization consists of two divisions and that each division consists of two managers. The CEO uses the advice of each division in his or her decision-making, while the divisions base their advice on the information of the local managers. Production manager 1 (2) indicates always (never) that there are possibilities for cost reductions, while marketing manager 1 (2) is always optimistic (pessimistic) regarding additional sales in the future. The information of the local managers is aggregated as follows. A division reports positively only when both local managers are positive. If one manager is positive and the other negative, then the division reports to the CEO that the information is doubtful. Finally, two negative reports by local managers results in a negative report to the CEO regarding possible additional profits of the division.

Different organizational structures aggregate the same local information in different ways. The CEO in a functional structure, i.e. where one division consists of the two production managers and the other division of the two marketing managers, will decide to do nothing. This is depicted in Fig. 12.3. Both divisions will supply doubtful information regarding the possibilities for additional profits.

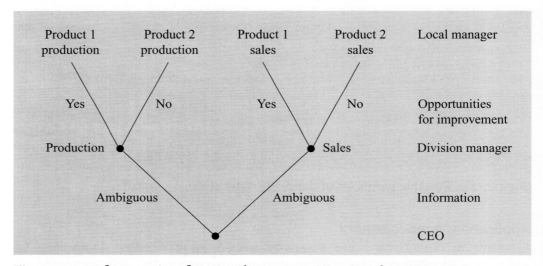

Figure 12.3: Inferences in a functional structure (Hammond, 1994, p. 114)

A divisional structure, i.e. product manager 1 and marketing manager 1 in one division and product manager 2 and marketing manager 2 in the other, will supply different information. Division 1 is positive regarding the possibilities for additional profits, while division 2 is negative. The CEO will, on this information, allocate as many means as possible to division 1 in the future. Figure 12.4 depicts the aggregation of information in a divisional structure.

The conclusion is that the decisions of the CEO are (partly) determined by the way the local information is channelled by the organizational structure, despite the fact that the entire organization possesses the same (local) information. A specific organizational structure is sensitive only to certain kinds of information. Information is lost in the hierarchical processing of advice, where the type of information lost depends on the structure of the organization. A functional structure creates an aggregation bias towards the generation of product-related data, while a divisional structure means an aggregation bias regarding the generation of functionally related data. Therefore, the structure of the learning environment seems to be at least as important as the meaning of things.

The result that the behaviour exhibited by the organization is to a certain extent determined by its structure can be applied directly to a number of other aspects of organizations. First, the advice received by the CEO depends on the organizational structure. Every structure will present a different menu of choices to the top, which will probably have an impact on decision-making. Second, the organizational structure has an impact on the emergence of conflicts and the level at which they are solved.

The idea of agenda control can also be extended to the various current models of *learning.* For example, the nature of the learning process affects the influence of brands on product evaluations (Van Osselaer and Alba, 2000). A human associative model and an adaptive model are distinguished. The former is focused on retrieval, looking at the past and co-occurrence of cues by storing information configurally. These consumers rely on brand cues, and will ignore the underlying attributes. They may differentiate incorrectly between physically identical products. The latter learning model is focused on prediction, looking forwards and storing information more elementally. These consumers will differentiate among brands which possess different attributes.

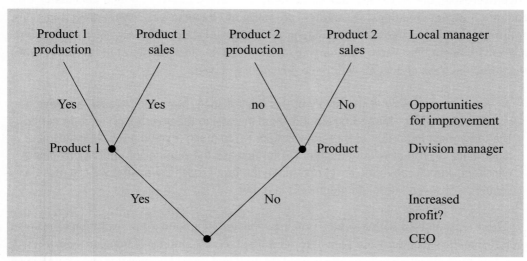

Figure 12.4 Inferences in a divisional structure (Hammond, 1994, p. 115)

12.4 Inductive bounded cognition

Behaviour in many simple situations is well described by the predictions of a theory based on completely rational individuals. However, people are not able to apply analytical methods in more complex environments. Parts of a problem may be addressed in a logical, deductive way, but an inductive way is often required for the entire problem. Decisions are based frequently on limited, local information. The gap between the cognitive capabilities of the decision-maker and the complexity of the problem is bridged by constructing plausible, simpler models which we can cope with. Such behaviour is inductive.

Traditional theorizing regarding the behaviour of completely rational individuals is usually done in a deductive way. A number of axioms or assumptions are formulated and subsequently various hypotheses are logically derived (with mathematical methods). This approach can in principle also be followed when decision-makers have limited cognitive capacities. However, a different approach is usually adopted. *Computer simulations* are used to investigate the interactions between, and the aggregate outcome of, boundedly rational decision-makers. These boundedly rational decision-makers are endowed with a limited number of decision rules in this approach. Another aspect of this approach is that the reductionist approach is abandoned. Problems are no longer divided into smaller problems for which analytical solutions can be formulated. Certain universal rules or laws are still deemed to guide behaviour, but that does not imply that it is sufficient to study isolated problems. Everything depends on everything else, which makes the connections between the various elements, and therefore a higher level of aggregation, an important research topic. Aggregate behaviour of these agent-based simulations emerges in an inductive, bottom-up way. Section 12.4.1 addresses modularity, while Sec. 12.4.2 focuses on how certain behavioural patterns emerge inductively.

12.4.1 Modularity

Humans can usually distinguish only a limited number of aspects of a problem. Our limited cognitive capacities have therefore to be used effectively in order to deal successful with complex, vague situations. Examples are forming hypotheses, formulating analogies, splitting up problems into smaller problems and using rules of thumb based on feedback from our environment. An early summary of the vast psychological literature (Miller, 1956) regarding the ways of dealing with limited cognition states:

> We are not completely at the mercy of this limited span, however, because we have a variety of techniques for getting around it and increasing the accuracy of our judgments. The three most important of these devices are (a) to make relative rather than absolute judgments; or, if that is not possible, (b) to increase the number of dimensions along which the stimuli can differ, or (c) to arrange the task in such a way that we can make a sequence of several absolute judgments in a row.

These ways to deal with complex problems emerge in a bottom-up, evolutionary way. In order to handle such problems, plausible, simplified representations of them are constructed. A certain representation or heuristic is used (by trial and error) because it is successful, even when it is not understood why it works. It is abandoned when a better one comes around. Successful local rules are able to adapt themselves in such a way that they survive in the process of natural selection. They form a balance between exploration and exploitation (March, 1991) of the local environment by simple transition rules.

Another aspect of the evolution of the various ways of dealing with complex problems is the nature of skills which will emerge. General skills are developed to address many different problems, while specific skills are geared towards specific problems. It is for a number of reasons unlikely for global rationality with a few general skills to emerge out of an evolutionary process. First, adaptive or optimal behaviour is dependent largely on the specific situation. Second, the number of combinatorial possibilities explodes on the addition of further dimensions. This prevents general systems functioning. Finally, general systems perform poorly in specific situations because crucial details are not taken into account. So, specific skills are expected to emerge, geared towards the specific context.

Evolution progresses rapidly considering the tremendous number of possibilities which exist. There seems to be a focus on finding good building blocks or modules to serve in the composition of a complicated structure, rather than on constructing a complicated structure directly. Examples of this tendency are *modularity*, hierarchy and parallelism. The hierarchical, modular design of systems is everywhere to be seen. Examples are cells, organs, humans, families, organizations and societies. Computer simulations show that relatively simple mechanisms may explain complex aggregate behaviour. Neither biological life nor the functioning of an organization is embodied in the parts, but in the organization of the parts.

Application: British India

One way to handle complex situations adequately is by an appropriate organization. Such an organization may be complex, but is often the result of bottom-up mechanisms of much simpler systems. Kay (1996) formulates this as follows in the context of India:

> Organisational knowledge may take the form of organisational systems and routines ... It was the power of routines which lay behind the ability of British India to turn inexperienced youths into administrators of large tracts of territories.

The rule of such an immense country as India under the British empire even indicates that an appropriate organization may be more important than the level of education of the people in the organization (Kay, 1996):

> The men who ran British India were, in the main, of mediocre talent. The achievement of the Raj was to create a system within which a small number of these undistinguished people could administer, tolerably well, one of the largest and most diverse nations of the world. Architecture does not create extraordinary organizations by collecting extraordinary people. It does so by enabling very ordinary people to perform in extraordinary ways.

12.4.2 Self-organization

The inductive analysis of problems with procedural rationality, i.e. of high complexity compared with the cognitive capacities of the decision-makers, is usually done with computer simulations. The evolution of a system with many decision-makers or cells is investigated by programming them in a parallel way and allowing them to learn from each other. Each cell is assumed to be in one of several states. Take for simplicity the number of states equal to 2. This can be interpreted in various ways, like 1 or 0, on or off, true or false, alive or dead. The next state of a cell is determined by a simple transition rule, using only the current state of the cell and the local environment. Bounded rationality is responsible for taking only the local environment into account in the computation of the next state of a cell.

Two local environments on the computer screen have attracted a lot of attention. A Von Neuman environment consists of the cells left, right, above and below a particular cell, while a Moore environment includes also the diagonal cells. These two local environments are presented in Fig. 12.5. The number of possible transition rules which can be applied to a cell and its local environment is usually very large. Most transition rules do not result in interesting results due to the interaction between cells, but there are a few simple transition rules which result in surprising aggregate outcomes. The research is geared towards finding these rules. An example of such a transition rule is as follows:

- A living cell also lives in the next period when two or three cells in the Moore environment are alive.
- A living cell dies in all other circumstances (because it is either too crowded, i.e. four or more living neighbours, or it is too lonely, i.e. zero or one living neighbour).
- A dead cell comes alive in the next period when exactly three cells in the Moore neighbourhood are alive.

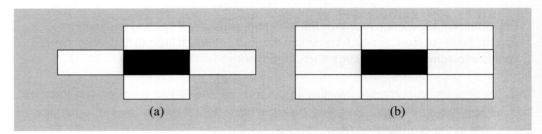

Figure 12.5: (a) Von Neuman environment, (b) Moore environment

The research is geared towards charting the underlying mechanisms (transition rules) which generate complex patterns because of the interaction between cells. The resulting patterns cannot in general be predicted (the 'undecidability theorem'). The starting position of an evolutionary process is to a large extent responsible for the final outcome. This means that only probabilistic outcomes can be formulated. It is possible to trace the evolutionary (historical) process ex post, but not ex ante. The historical process in the form of chance and natural selection therefore receives an important role in the explanation of various phenomena. Complexity of organizational forms is in this approach an emergent property based on a number of simple (transition) rules in interaction with the local environment.

Computer simulations show that locally interacting units *self-organize* in surprisingly complex patterns in a relatively short period of time. This occurs especially when the system is at the edge of order and chaos (Kaufmann, 1993). A result regarding the global dynamics of learning behaviour based on local transition rules is the schema theorem (Holland, 1975). It means that well-functioning, compact clusters or patterns or modules will grow exponentially in number in the population of patterns in evolutionary environments. Applications have been formulated regarding snow avalanches, herd behaviour of animals and humans and financial markets (Lux and Marchesi, 2000).

Application: Segregation

The first computer-based contribution on the phenomenon of self-organization was formulated by Schelling (1971), who investigated the evolution of the composition of the various quarters of cities. His computer simulations show that segregation emerges with the simple transition rule that people move to another part of town when the percentage of neighbours of the same race in their Moore neighbourhood drops below a certain level. Figure 12.6 depicts a starting position, where a square with a 0 is inhabited by somebody from the blue race, and a square with an X is inhabited by somebody from the green race. An empty square is not inhabited.

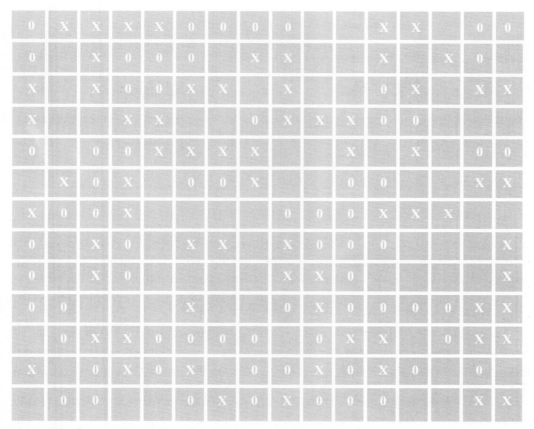

Figure 12.6: Starting position

The transition rule is as follows:

- Do not move to another neighbourhood when at least half the people in your Moore neighbourhood are from the same race.
- Move to the closest square where at least half the people in your new Moore neighbourhood are of the same race when less than half the people in the current Moore neighbourhood are the same colour.

This results in the stationary situation of Fig. 12.7. So, boundedly rational individuals, taking only their local environment into account in their location decision, establish inductively a segregated society. Segregation emerges or self-organizes because of the decisions of boundedly rational agents. There is no central co-ordination by an all-encompassing Walrasian auctioneer. It would be very difficult to detect the micro motives of individuals which have resulted in this behaviour were only aggregate or macro behaviour to be considered.

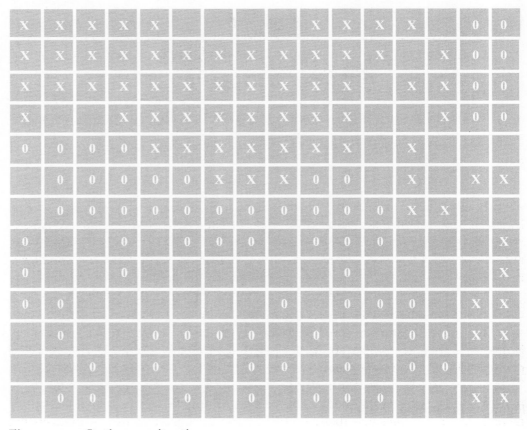

Figure 12.7: Stationary situation

Application: The Game of Life

A well-known computer program is the 'Game of Life'. The computer screen is divided into squares and each square is either black or white. Transition rules determine whether the colour of a square stays the same or switches to the other colour in the next period. The computer shows the transition of all squares on the screen. Interesting patterns emerge already after a few transitions.

Figure 12.8 depicts a pattern, called glider. Applying the same life–death transition rules to this pattern as were applied to Fig. 12.5 distorts the glider, but the glider emerges again after four transitions, while the whole glider has moved to the south-east. (Try this for yourself.) Various relatively simple patterns have been given exotic names, like Beacon, Eater, Snake, Acorn, Canoe, Beehive, r-Pentomino (Sigmund, 1993). The interaction between these diverse patterns is interesting to observe. Computer simulations show that such interaction can result in situations which resemble the complex behaviour of living creatures in organizations. Exercises 12.3 and 12.4 at the end of this chapter are illustrations.

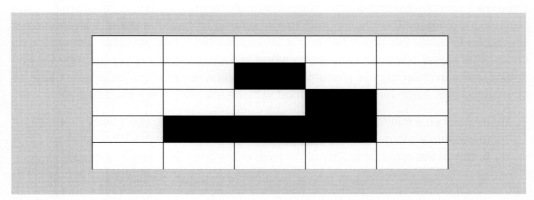

Figure 12.8: Glider

Application: A flock of birds

It is characteristic with a flock of birds, a school of fish, a herd of sheep and pedestrians on a busy sidewalk for many decision-makers to move close together without bumping into each other all the time. One way to describe this behaviour of each decision-maker is to use the mathematics of differential equations. The behaviour of each decision-maker is in this approach the (deductive) solution to a set of differential equations. This solution indicates a position or location at each instant of time. The behaviour of the population is subsequently the solution to a set of sets of differential equations. However, a relatively simple set of differential equations is already not solvable for humans with our current knowledge, let alone for birds.

Inductive limited rationality is a drastically different approach for describing the behaviour of a flock of birds. The flight of a bird is the outcome of the interplay of a limited number of simple transition rules. Different birds (or sheep or fish or pedestrians)

Figure 12.9: A flock of birds

organize themselves subsequently according to these rules such that collective flocking behaviour emerges. The challenge is to formulate a limited number of transition rules which can simulate this group behaviour. Reynolds (1987) has developed spectacular, three-dimensional computer simulations where a flock of birds dives under high-tension cables, splits in order to pass a church and regroups when the flock disperses because of an aeroplane. Each bird is programmed with the following three transition rules:

- Try to maintain a minimal distance from other objects, including other birds.
- Try to keep up the same pace as the birds in the immediate neighbourhood.
- Try to stay in the centre of gravity of the birds in the immediate neighbourhood.

Application: $3x + 1$ problem

Figure 12.10 presents a fluctuating pattern between two variables. One way to discover some systematic pattern in these data is to apply advanced statistical methods. A certain relationship between the two variables is posed, for example a linear relationship, and possible deviations are put in the error term. It is often possible to formulate a regression equation which fits the pattern reasonably well.

A statistical approach turns out not to be appropriate for understanding the above data. There is a completely deterministic procedure which has generated the data. The number x on the horizontal axis is a positive number. The vertical axis depicts the number of steps or transitions needed to turn the number x into 1 on the basis of one (contingent) transition rule. The transition rule means that when x is an even number it has to be divided by 2, while when it is an odd number it has to be multiplied by 3 with 1 added. Every positive, natural number subjected to this transition rule will turn ultimately into the number 1. The number of transitions needed to reach 1 differs substantially from number to number. Figure 12.11 provides the calculation of the number of transitions for the first 10 positive numbers, and Fig. 12.10 depicts this.

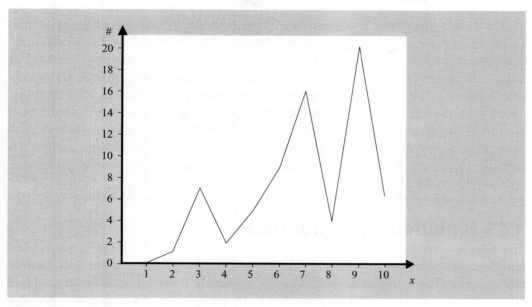

Figure 12.10: The $3x + 1$ problem

X	Transitions	Steps
1	.	0
2	1.	1
3	10, 5, 16, 8, 4, 2, 1.	7
4	2, 1.	2
5	16, 8, 4, 2, 1.	5
6	3, 10, 5, 16, 8, 4, 2, 1.	8
7	22, 11, 34, 17, 52, 26, 13, 40, 20, 10, 5, 16, 8, 4, 2, 1.	16
8	4, 2, 1.	3
9	28, 14, 7, 22, 11, 34, 17, 52, 26, 13, 40, 20, 10, 5, 16, 8, 4, 2, 1.	19
10	5, 16, 8, 4, 2, 1.	6

Figure 12.11: Transitions in the $3x + 1$ problem

The $3x + 1$ problem is presented in order to illustrate two aspects of the result that simple, deterministic rules may result in complex, seemingly unpredictable behaviour. The transition rules in the Game of Life are simple and deterministic, but it is hard to detect any pattern in the behaviour which results. Ex post it can be explained exactly why something happened, but it is hard to formulate a prediction ex ante (Kalman, 1993). An unlimited decimal number can be calculated for numbers like =, exponential e and $\sqrt{2}$, but an underlying structure for subsequent decimals is as yet unknown. The $3x + 1$ problem has the same character. Besides, these examples warn us that the tendency to formulate a stochastic process for observed behaviour may serve as a cover-up for a lack of insight.

12.5 Evolutionary approaches

The ideas presented in the previous parts concerned mainly issues regarding incentives and how they are resolved in equilibrium, while process or development issues received hardly any attention. This is not surprising, because completely rational people understand and foresee the most difficult problems immediately. However, issues of learning, and therefore processes and development over time, are important when people are boundedly rational. Learning by feedback and adapting rules of thumb based on natural selection serve as important ingredients in the development of theory regarding the behaviour in complex environments (Roth and Erev, 1995). A dynamic perspective is required.

Evolutionary approaches regarding human and organizational behaviour take the position that statements regarding aspects of limited cognition have to be based in evolutionary biology. The various evolutionary approaches highlighted in this section originated in biology with the work of Darwin. The bottom line is survival, where evolution and natural selection are the crucial concepts. The next subsections address evolutionary psychology (12.5.1), evolutionary economics (12.5.2) and population ecology (12.5.3).

12.5.1 Evolutionary psychology

Models of bounded rationality are often based only on the plausible notion of limited processing capacity. Although bounded rationality is a necessary ingredient in the analysis of organizations, it is not sufficient for understanding the behaviour of organizations. Also, the organization of the limited processing capacities is of crucial importance for understanding organizations. Evolutionary psychology addresses this topic.

The comparison of the brain with the various designs of computers may illustrate the difference between bounded rationality in general, and the allocation of limited cognitive capacities in a specific direction (Cosmides and Tooby, 1994). The brain was for a long time conceptualized as a computer with general hardware only. Nowadays, however, it is viewed as a heterogeneous network of functionally specialized, sometimes very advanced, computational devices. The appropriate analogy is therefore with a computer which is able to handle only a limited number of software packages. The available devices are geared towards situations which have occurred frequently in the past. This approach means that biases and anomalies will be observed in behaviour, because the limited software has to deal with situations for which it is not designed.

The application of insights from evolutionary biology to problems of cognition is based on a simple idea: *form follows function* (Cosmides and Tooby, 1994). The properties of a mechanism or system reflect the structure of the problem it has to deal with. The nature of the problem indicates the direction of the design of solutions, which may result in empirically testable hypotheses. A well-known example of the idea that form follows function is the claim of Chandler (1962) that 'structure follows strategy'.

Application: Calculating Bayesian probabilities

Models of limited cognition have often been based solely on the plausible notion of limited processing capacity. This seems sensible in light of the experimental consensus regarding the inability of humans to perform (statistical) Bayesian arguments. A well-known example is the problem with the three doors. The winner of a quiz will receive a prize, the size of which depends on the door chosen. A minor prize is behind two of the three doors, the major prize behind the third. The winner is asked to choose a door. Subsequently, the host doesn't open this door, but one of the other doors with a minor prize behind it. Subsequently the winner is asked whether he or she wants to stick with the first choice. Players usually do, while it is twice as likely that the major prize is behind the unopened door which is not chosen the first time.

Humans may be bad at calculating the probability of an event occurring, i.e. Bayesian statistics, but these biases disappear when probabilities are presented as frequencies. The evolutionary explanation is that our hunting-oriented ancestors absorbed a lot of information regarding events in terms of frequencies. The probability of a certain event occurring is not observable, because an event either occurs or does not. Natural selection results in routines or mechanisms geared towards using information in the way it is presented. Evolutionary selection processes can therefore result in complex skills or competencies when this is crucial for the species involved, while biases or anomalies in behaviour occur when the situation or the problem is not important or occurs only once in a while.

Application: Logic versus social interaction

Humans are in general not good at solving logical problems. However, if these problems are formulated in terms of social interactions, then people are much better at finding solutions. The human brain has evolved in order to solve specific problems rather than solving general logical problems.

The *causality* between organizations and human behaviour is not obvious when an evolutionary perspective is taken. Organizations have an effect on human behaviour, and human behaviour shapes organizations. Part IV took the view that institutions are completely determined by human behaviour. The behavioural assumptions of opportunism and bounded rationality explained the allocation of property rights. However, if the preferences of humans are to a certain extent determined by the (local) situation, then it may be that humans behave less opportunistically in organizations than in markets. The situation-dependent allocation of limited cognitive capacities may be responsible for this.

> Similarly, institutions influence the way in which information is presented, which information is communicated and how the information is interpreted. Customs and routines of organizational members are based on this information. Organizations can therefore also channel human behaviour to a certain extent, which reverses the causality of Part IV.

12.5.2 Evolutionary economics

Nelson and Winter (1982 and 2002) present a *routine*-based perspective on organizations. Boundedly rational agents and organizations are assumed to be guided by a set of routines rather than by deliberate choice, where routines refer to all regular and predictable behaviour patterns. Routines determine largely how an organization functions. Nelson and Winter (1982, p. 134) write: 'As a first approximation, therefore, firms may be expected to behave in the future according to the routines they have employed in the past.'

Bounded rationality of agents means that notions like learning, imitation and conscious adaptation through search feature prominently. Evolutionary economics focuses on the role of learning and practice. Skills and routines can be learned and perfected through practice. Firm-specific capabilities are accumulated in the course of time, which have usually a tacit component. This *cumulative learning* has a large trial-and-error component, i.e. it is associated with randomness, chance variations, trial and error, good timing and luck in the emergence of new organizations and routines, rather than with genius and leadership. Most new ideas are wrong or flawed and lead to failure. Individual skills, organizational routines, advanced technologies and modern institutions have evolved.

The emphasis in evolutionary economics is on issues of change, development, innovation and progress in organizations, rather than equilibrium outcomes in markets. Changes in the environment are dealt with by changing the routines. Old organizations may learn new routines, or old organizations go bankrupt and be replaced by new ones. Change is often slow, or does not occur at all, which is explained by the importance of routines. Notice that cumulative learning and change do not necessarily result in optimal outcomes. A 'bad' change is built upon and may be hard to reverse or alter; i.e. path dependence is often involved.

Evolutionary economics models always contain two ingredients in order to analyse evolution: a reproduction function and mutation. The reproduction function takes care of the blossoming of well-functioning practices or routines in the next generation of the population, while the number of badly performing routines will decrease over time. An example of a reproduction function is the difference between the profits of a specific company and the industry average. The practices of the highly profitable companies will spread in the future, while the others will (slowly) disappear in the next generations. Mutation takes care of the emergence of new routines in the population. This may result in new, superior practices.

12.5.3 Population ecology

The focus of organizational ecology is on the evolution and composition of organizations and industries. It applies therefore primarily to populations of organizations rather than to individual ones.

Organizational ecologists take the position that organizations can hardly change their behaviour. They emphasize the structural *inertia* of organizations. Hannan and Freeman

(1977) mention a large number of constraints upon change in organizations, such as limitations on an organization's investment in capital equipment and trained personnel, constraints on the transfer and processing of information, the costs of upsetting the internal political equilibrium, the conservative forces of history and tradition and the legal, political and fiscal barriers to change. Illustrative of their position is the remark that 'Failing churches do not become retail stores; nor do firms transform themselves into churches.'

Structural inertia is an important cause of environmental selection because the inertia in organizational change implies that organizations fail when the environment changes. Change will occur outside the organization by the erection of new organizational forms. Population ecologists therefore emphasize competition and *selection* rather than adaptation processes. Organizations survive on the fit between the organizational form and the environmental characteristics. Positively selected variations survive and reproduce similar others, which then form the starting-point for a new round of selection as mutants appear.

Population ecology is best suited to explain changes in the distribution of organizational forms over the long run – over a period of decades or centuries. Because structural inertia is presumed to be pervasive, founding conditions will stay with the organization, even when environmental conditions change significantly. It is argued that selection favours organizations which can reliably reproduce their actions over time, which inadvertently also favours organizational forms whose core structures are resistant to change. This accounts for much of the *diversity* in organizational forms and implies a strong form of *path dependence* in organizational evolution.

Population ecologists have identified a general pattern which characterizes the *evolution* of populations. A period of gradually increasing growth is followed by gradual decline. Growth of a population starts slowly because it is hard to gain legitimacy and to obtain the relevant experience. As the form becomes more widely accepted, the rate of growth increases. But proliferation triggers competition among the organizations for relevant resources. This will end the period of growth and will result in a period of decline, as consolidation occurs and weaker forms are eliminated.

Notice the difference between the approaches presented in Parts III and IV, and the current ecological perspective. Part IV assumed that organizational structures can be modified. Decision-makers are present who survey the situation, confront alternatives as well as constraints, and select a course of action. This is challenged by ecologists studying organizations at the population level of analysis. They argue that much of the variation in structural forms is due to environmental selection rather than adaptation. In the population ecology approach, organizations are viewed as rather passive, because many fail to modify their structures as quickly as their environments change.

12.6 Type I versus type II errors

In a world with perfect information, organizational design does not matter. In practice, it is of central concern to businesses. The treatment of tournaments in Chapter 6 is an example of organizational design where alternative units performing comparable tasks enable the firm to glean information on the basis of which better incentive systems can be based. Another aspect of organizational design is that individuals with limited information make mistakes, even if they are well-intentioned. Most units in an organization have only limited information at their disposal. Time, means for information processing, and the communication between departments are costly, limited and incomplete. Another important aspect of information processing is determined by the limited cognitive capacities of humans to collect information, absorb and process it. No individual is able to perfectly transfer what he knows to somebody else. Human imperfection results in making errors. Therefore decision-making, like communication, is always imperfect.

The consequence of these observations is that the way individuals are organized to collect information, communicate it and take decisions influences the functioning of an organization. This section examines how the structure of decision-making influences the costs of decision-making. This is analysed by concentrating on the relationship between a *decision procedure* and the probability that good projects are rejected and bad ones accepted.

Decision-making in organizations usually develops through various levels and in various ways. Many departments and persons are asked for their opinion and eventually a decision is being made. Two different decision procedures for aggregating different evaluations of the same project into an organizational decision will be addressed. A decision procedure which combines or aggregates local decisions into an organizational decision is called an *architecture*. There are many examples of architectures. Every member of the Security Council of the United Nations evaluates a specific proposal individually and votes. Every permanent member has the veto. Members of national parliaments vote on many different subjects. Accepting a new law requires a majority of votes, but changing the constitution usually requires a two-thirds majority. A company has to decide whether a local department can start an innovation project, or if permission is needed from a higher level as well. A legal system has to make certain decisions concerning the possibilities of appeal. Doctors have to decide how many tests should be made before an operation is initiated. Firms of accountants examine the annual accounts of their clients. They have to decide internally whether a disapproval by one of the accountants should be checked again by another. Some aspects of such decision procedures will now be further addressed.

Assume that everyone aims for the same objectives, i.e. there are no conflicts of interests. Limited rationality is involved by allowing errors in the evaluation of projects. (Completely rational humans do not make systematic errors.) In such a context it is important in what way individual decisions are aggregated into one decision of the organization as a whole. Suppose an organization has to evaluate a project. Sah and Stiglitz (1986) examine how different evaluations of the same project in an organization can be best aggregated into an organizational decision, given that the evaluations may contain errors. An organization is defined as a collection of (identical) bureaus, which is depicted in the familiar way in Fig. 12.12.

Each bureau evaluates projects and decides for each project to accept (Yes) or not (No). Projects are either good or bad. A good project generates a positive yield, a bad one results in a loss. Often one doesn't know what kind of projects are evaluated. Individuals (bureaus) are assumed to evaluate the same project and to do this independently. Assume that a bureau accepts a project with probability p and therefore rejects a project with probability $1 - p$.

Four kinds of decisions are distinguished: a good project can be accepted, a good project can be rejected, a bad project can be accepted and a bad project can be rejected. Good decisions are accepting a good project and rejecting a bad project. Bad decisions are rejecting a good project, and accepting a bad project. Rejecting a good project is called a *type I error*, whereas accepting a bad project is a *type II error*. Figure 12.13 shows the four decisions.

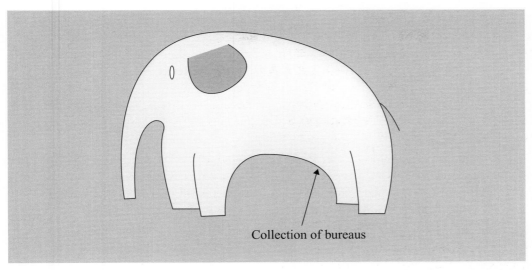

Figure 12.12: The firm as a collection of bureaus

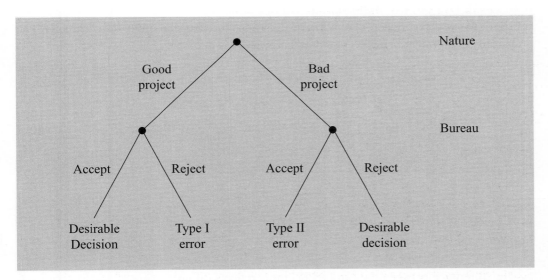

Figure 12.13: Type I versus type II errors

The way the individual evaluations are aggregated in an organizational decision procedure determines the quality of the organizational decision. Two architectures can be distinguished: the hierarchy and the polyarchy. A *hierarchy* accepts a project only when all evaluations are positive. Acceptance therefore requires unanimity, i.e. each bureau or decision-maker or member has vetoing power. Figure 12.14 represents this for an organization consisting of two bureaus. This hierarchical decision-making procedure is used in the European commission and among the permanent members of the United Nations Security Council. The probability of a project in a hierarchy consisting of two bureaus being accepted is p^2.

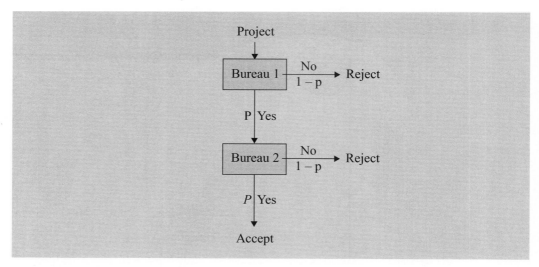

Figure 12.14: Hierarchy

A polyarchy rejects a project only when all evaluations are negative, otherwise the project is accepted. One positive evaluation in a series of negative decisions is therefore already sufficient to start the project. Figure 12.15 illustrates the decision order schematically. The probability of a project being accepted in a polyarchy is $p(2 - p)$.

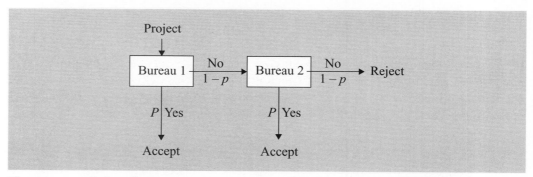

Figure 12.15: Polyarchy

The difference between the two architectures reflects different ways of aggregating local decisions. In a hierarchy, the rule is that more information has to be collected when a bureau accepts a project, whereas a rejection by this bureau means that the project is rejected definitely. The rule in a polyarchy is that a project is accepted when one member accepts, whereas someone can review it again when the project is rejected by another bureau.

A polyarchy always accepts more projects than a hierarchy because $p(2 - p) > p^2$. This applies to good as well as bad projects. Therefore a polyarchy is relatively good in accepting projects, and therefore good in preventing type I errors. The opposite holds for a hierarchy. A hierarchical decision procedure is relatively good in rejecting projects, and therefore good in preventing type II errors. Concluding, a hierarchy makes more type I errors and a polyarchy more type II errors. However, the choice of architecture will be *second-best*, i.e. errors will always be made. This is inevitable because of the lack of information.

It is assumed that there is some screening, i.e. the probability that a given bureau judges a project to be good is a function of its quality. A good project has therefore a higher probability of acceptance than a bad project. A good project is assumed to yield a revenue profit (P), and a bad project loss ($-L$). The probability of accepting a good project is $p(P)$, while the probability of accepting a bad project is $p(-L)$. Screening entails that $p(P) > p(-L)$. If a project is rejected, then the payoff is 0. The fraction of good projects is assumed to be α. Figure 12.16, which is an extension of Fig. 12.13, presents the situation.

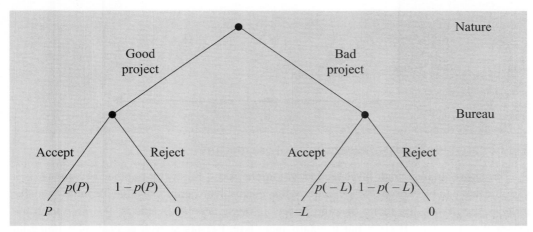

Figure 12.16: Problem of investment selection

The costs associated with type I and II errors determine which architecture is chosen. If the costs associated with accepting a bad project are relatively high (low) compared with the foregone revenues of rejecting a good project, a hierarchy (polyarchy) is preferred. Another result of the comparative statics analysis is that the presence of more good projects in the set of possible projects, i.e. a higher level of α, makes it more desirable to choose a polyarchy. The probability of a bad project decreases, which makes it more desirable to accept projects. A polyarchy is the most suitable architecture for doing this.

Figure 12.17 illustrates these results. Define F_p as the probability that a polyarchy accepts a good project and F_H as the probability that a hierarchy accepts a good project. Similarly, define G_p as the probability that a polyarchy accepts a bad project and G_H as the probability that a hierarchy accepts a bad project. The profit of a polyarchy is therefore $\alpha F_p P - (1-\alpha)G_p L$, where $F_p = [1-(1-p(P)]^2$ and $G_p = 1-[1-p(-L)]^2$. Similarly, the profit of a hierarchy is $\alpha F_H P - (1-\alpha)G_H L$, where $F_H = p(P)^2$ and $G_H = p(-L)^2$. A polyarchy makes more profit than a hierarchy when

$$\alpha F_p P - (1-\alpha)G_p L > \alpha F_H P - (1-\alpha)G_H L$$

$$\Leftrightarrow F_p - F_H > \frac{(G_p - G_H)(1-\alpha)P}{\alpha L}.$$

The horizontal axis represents the (probability) difference between the two architectures regarding accepting a bad project, i.e. $1-[1-p(-L)]^2-p(-L)^2$, whereas the vertical axis shows the (probability) difference regarding accepting a good project, i.e. $1-[1-p(P)]^2-p(P)^2$.

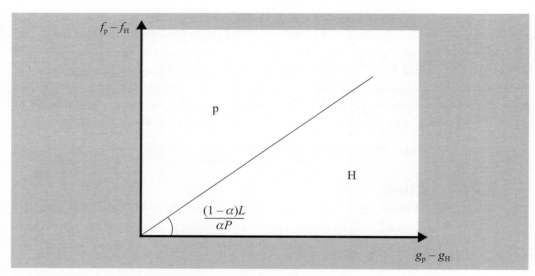

Figure 12.17: Profit-maximizing choice of architecture

The above analysis can be extended in various ways. First, the number of bureaus is a variable that can be chosen. For a hierarchy, this means, for example, that having more agencies reduces the probability that a specific project is being accepted. This is desirable from the perspective of a type II error, but it entails more type I errors as well as costs of running an additional bureau. These considerations together determine the optimal number of agencies.

Another aspect taken for granted in the above analysis is that the probability p of a project being accepted is exogenously given. However, organizations often require a minimal return on investment for new investment projects in order to be accepted. One can choose, for instance, a return on investment of 10, 15 or 20 per cent. The probability p is therefore often an endogenous variable. The choice of p can even be made dependent on the choice of architecture. It has been shown already that a hierarchy always accepts fewer projects than a polyarchy. The disadvantages of a hierarchy can be reduced by changing the probability p in such a way that more projects are accepted. This is done by increasing the probability p, i.e. by lowering the required return on investment.

Finally, the two architectures considered are the two extreme decision procedures. The important question is how large the majority should be in order to take a desirable organizational decision. The hierarchy corresponds with unanimity, or veto power for each evaluator. It is clear that a less stringent majority may be optimal. These intermediate architectures are known as *committees* (Sah and Stiglitz, 1988).

Application: Promotion policy

An example of architecture choice is the promotion policy regarding senior positions in bureaucracies. These functions are usually associated with high salaries and it is often difficult, especially in continental Europe, to fire someone once he or she is appointed. The costs associated with a type II error are therefore high. The observation that decision procedures in bureaucratic institutions often consist of many layers corresponds with the above considerations.

Application: Innovation

If the costs of starting risky and uncertain innovation projects are minor, and the possible future benefits may be large, then the costs related to a type I error are high (which means that high profits are forgone), but the consequences related to a type II error are small (which means that the project doesn't cost much and yields nothing). Therefore, it is to be expected that, when type I errors are more serious in their consequences than are type II errors, decision-making will be decentralized as far as possible to divisions or units. In such a situation a polyarchy is predicted.

12.7 Conclusion

Limited cognition is characteristic of living creatures. Taking this seriously raises questions regarding the cognitive side of people and the question of affect (Tirole, 2002). The cognitive side concerns the way people learn, like understanding memory and awareness, categorizing matters and developing heuristics. This chapter has shown how the cognitive side operates in a deductive, an inductive and a statistical way, and has outlined the implications of this for organizations. The affect side is concerned with the implications of limited cognition for the possible motivations for and biases in behaviour. This is the topic of the next chapter, which addresses the possibilities for organizations to deal effectively with the cognitive as well as the affect side of their members.

12.8 Exercises

12.1 A professor provides his class with an enormous amount of information. First, many of the items shown as projections contain text which duplicates the required literature to a certain extent (D), as well as providing various additional insights (A). Second, there is the oral commentary on the projections. This further duplicates the literature (C) and provides additional insights (I). All this information is too much for students to handle. The class contains two types of students. P-students are prepared, so they recognize immediately what is and is not in the literature. The unprepared U-students are not able to do so.

A Define bounded rationality.

B Explain in words in what way advance preparation decreases the above problem for a P-student.

C Characterize the difference between the two types of students by using the partitioning method of Sec. 12.3.

12.2 Assume the board of directors of a company consists of two people. One of them comes from a marketing background, the other from engineering. Is it important how the board of directors is composed? Formulate your answer along the lines of deductive bounded rationality.

12.3 Use the following life–death transition rules with respect to Moore environments:

– A living cell remains alive when 2 or 3 cells are living.

– A dead cell comes alive when exactly 3 cells are living.

A Show that after four transitions the glider of Fig. 12.8 will have the same shape and has moved to the south-east.

B Show that none of the cells is alive after the crash of the two gliders in Fig. 12.18.

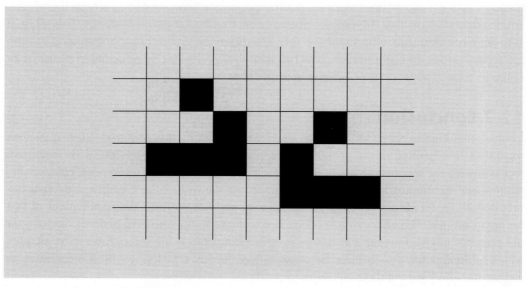

Figure 12.18: Two gliders vanish

C Show that the crash between the two gliders in Fig. 12.19 will result in a block of size 2 by 2 after three transitions.

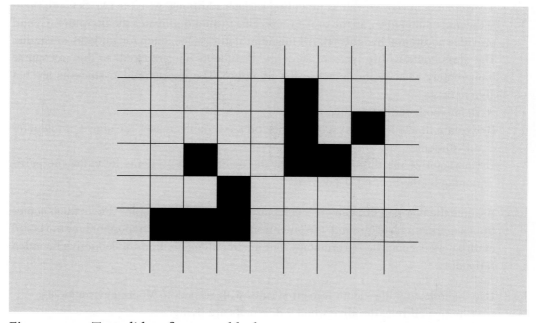

Figure 12.19: Two gliders form one block

D The shape of the two gliders after thirteen transitions in Fig. 12.20 is called an eater. What is the shape of an eater?

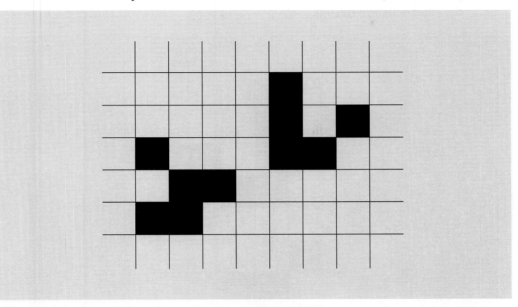

Figure 12.20: Two gliders form an eater

E Show that the eater will have eaten the glider after four periods.

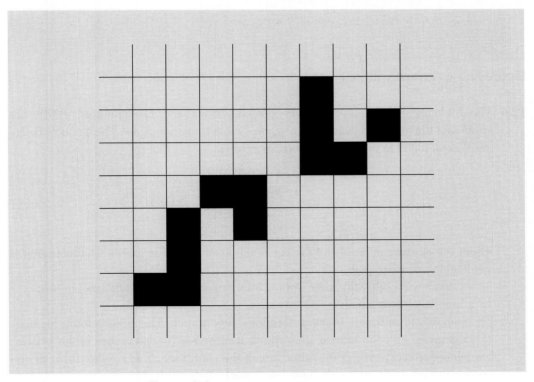

Figure 12.21: Eater swallows glider

F The gliders in Fig. 12.22 move to the south-east and the south-west. Show that after six transitions only one glider remains, that it is moving to the north-east and that the other cells will die out.

Figure 12.22: A crash with one survivor

12.4 The biologist Aristid Lindenmayer (Prusinkiewicz and Lindenmayer, 1990) has simulated the growth of plants using some simple transition rules. The symbols 0, 1, [and] are subject to the following transition rules:

$$
\begin{aligned}
0 &\rightarrow & 1[0]1[0]0 \\
1 &\rightarrow & 11 \\
[&\rightarrow & [\\
] &\rightarrow &]
\end{aligned}
$$

where the starting point of the system is the symbol 0. The graphical illustration is spectacular, consisting of:

0: a branch without (with) a leaf at the end when other branches do (not) follow;

1: a branch without a leaf;

[ ]: symbols within square brackets forming a new branch. This branch forms an angle of 45 degrees with the branch from which it emerges. New branches on an existing branch occur every time at the other side of the main branch where the previous new branch has emerged, where the first new branch starts on the left.

A Depict the starting position, with a vertical direction of the branch.

B Formulate the row of symbols and the graphical presentation after one transition.

C Formulate the row of symbols and the graphical presentation after two transitions.

12.5 The aggregation of local decisions into an organization decision has been analysed by Sah and Stiglitz. Local bureaus decide regarding the acceptance of a project. The probability of acceptance of a good (bad) project is .6 (.5), there are two bureaus and the fraction of good projects is .3. The acceptance of a good project yields a profit of 400, while acceptance of a bad project results in a loss of 200. The polyarchy and the hierarchy are distinguished as possible architecture choices.

A Define a polyarchy.

B What is the probability that a polyarchy rejects a bad project?

C What is the disadvantage of a polyarchy compared with a hierarchy?

D Which choice of architecture maximizes profits?

E How much is a profit-maximizing organization willing to pay for a second bureau?

F How does the attractiveness of a polyarchy compared with a hierarchy change because of

– An improvement of the portfolio;

– An increase in the profit of a good project;

– An increase in the loss of a bad project?

G In what way can the disadvantage of a polyarchy be reduced by endogenizing the probability of acceptance?

12.6 What are the values of $p(P)$ and $p(-L)$ in Sec. 12.5 when there is perfect screening?

12.7 Accountancy firms are nowadays regularly summoned to court because of questionable approvals of annual accounts.

A Define an architecture.

B How is a firm conceptualized by Sah and Stiglitz?

C Which parameter changes in the model of Sah and Stiglitz because of the above development?

D Use Fig. 12.15 to show which organizations change their choice of architecture as a result of the above development.

13 Biases in decision-making

LEARNING OBJECTIVES

After completing this chapter, you should understand:

- Organizational responses to the tendency of people to look only at the near future.

- How organizations deal with shortsightedness

- The asymmetry between gains and losses and its organizational implications.

Contents

13.1 Introduction

Topics in accounting, finance, marketing and organization can be approached from many different angles. Price discrimination was the dominant approach in the 1960s and 1970s, while asymmetric information and conflicts of interests have been the primary perspective since the beginning of the 1980s. The perspective of limited cognition is able to address issues regarding categorization and heuristics from the cognitive side, and motivational aspects from the affect side. The resulting biases in decision-making are hard to address from the traditional approaches in accounting, finance, marketing and organization. However, they are relevant, as witnessed by blossoming fields like behavioural accounting, behavioural finance, economic psychology and organizational behaviour.

Humans with their limited cognitive capacities have to deal with the complex world surrounding them. They look for pattern in a complex problem and simplify the problem to construct temporary internal models, hypotheses or schemata to work with (Arthur, 1994). These working models serve to fill the gap between our bounded cognitive capacities and the complexity of the problem. People learn which of their working models do well, and from time to time they may discard poorly performing hypotheses and generate new 'ideas' to put in their place. However, humans cling to their current working model. They only drop it in favour of a better one when it no longer functions well. This causes a built-in hysteresis, i.e. a working model is clung to not because it is 'correct', but rather because it has worked in the past and must accumulate a record of failure before it is worth discarding.

Many sociologists and psychologists do research with respect to individual and group behaviour that shows a systematic bias with the predictions of models with complete rationality. This has to result in the formulation of other ingredients or concepts in theories regarding organizations. For example, in the theory of general equilibrium uncertainty means that each possible situation occurs with a certain probability, where the probability numbers are known to everybody. Knight (1921) considers this as unrealistic and distinguishes therefore between two kinds of uncertainty: 'risk' and 'uncertainty'. Risk applies to decision-making in situations where it is known how often each situation occurs. This was assumed in Parts III and IV. Uncertainty means that it is impossible to determine the frequency with which each situation occurs.

This chapter starts by summarizing a number of frequently recurring observations regarding behaviour which might be explained from the perspective of the limited cognition of people. Three biases in decision-making are identified in Sec. 13.2. The way organizations deal with these biases is addressed in Sec. 13.3 by identifying their costs and formulating possible solutions. The next three sections treat the organizational implications of the three biases in decision-making processes in more detail. Section 13.7 concludes.

13.2 Biases in decision-making

This section addresses biases in decision-making processes. A bias is always formulated with respect to something. Our yardstick is the way standard economic theory models decision processes. An actual decision which differs from the decision predicted by standard economic theory is called a bias. A bias in behaviour does not imply that something is wrong with the decisions taken by people, but instead that

> the problem is with the model of rationality rather than with us human beings (Bernstein, 1996).

13.2.1 Economic theory versus daily practice

Figure 13.1 depicts the differences between a few dimensions of decision-making processes in standard economic theory and daily practice. The most salient difference is the view regarding the nature of decision processes. According to standard economic theory, behaviour is guided by explicit choices based on logical, deductive inference. However, actual behaviour often seems to differ substantially from *rational choice*. It seems to be based rather on simple, inflexible rules which have little to do with logical inference. An example is that in making a choice a person is often guided by the decision of someone else (Simon, 1993). An explanation for the emergence and selection of rules has often an evolutionary character, i.e. simple rules are tried and then are maintained if they work. (The previous chapter addressed this subject more extensively.)

Decision-making dimension	Emphasis in theory	
	Too much	**Too little**
Process	Rational choice	Rule based
Level of analysis	Autonomous actor	System
Criterion	Clarity, consistency	Ambiguity, inconsistency
Goal	instrumental	Sense making

Figure 13.1: Decision making in economic theory

The decision-maker as *autonomous actor* is highlighted in many theories regarding strategic decision-making. The interaction of the decision-maker with others has not received much attention, a fact which has suppressed the conflict of interests between individuals in decision-making processes. This has now changed because of the development both of game theory and also of evolutionary approaches.

In normative analyses of decision-making processes, *clarity and consistency* are often overemphasized. This is convenient from an analytical perspective and makes it easy to communicate results. However, ambiguity and inconsistency seem to be around in a dominant way. Evolution is not affected by problems being well formulated or not, but by whether things work. Ambiguity and inconsistency may actually be desirable when a balance has to be determined between exploration and exploitation in complex environments.

The *instrumental* character of decision processes is the focus of economic theory. The importance of these processes is, according to this approach, to determine the most desirable course of action. Interpretative approaches view the final outcome only as a by-product of decision processes. Making sense is the overriding concern. According to this view, creating understanding and justifying your own course of action, and determining your role in the local environment, are the most important roles served by a decision process.

13.2.2 Tendencies in decision-making

The difference between the predictions or advice of the standard economic model and actual behaviour illustrates the difference between theory and practice. The difference can be understood by noticing that people, because of their limited cognitive capacities, rely on rules of thumb in order to simplify complex tasks like estimating probabilities and formulating predictions. Many heuristics in decision-making processes have come out of experimental research (Sherman and Corty, 1984). Here, three empirically observed tendencies in learning behaviour will be addressed.

Figure 13.2 presents a number of observations regarding human decision-making processes compared with what is according to of standard economic theory. The classifications of the observations are based on the dimensions of products in general equilibrium theory (Debreu, 1959). Products are distinguished based on time (a Christmas tree at the end of the year is a different product from a Christmas tree in summer), location (a boat in the Netherlands is a different product from one in Austria), and state or uncertainty (ice-cream on a warm day is perceived differently from ice-cream on a cold one). These empirical observations are highlighted by March (1988), and will be contrasted as far as possible with the way they are treated in standard economic theory.

Decision-making dimension	Emphasis in actual decision-making	
	Too much	**Too little**
Time	Near future	Distant future
Distance	Small	large
Result	Success	Failure

Figure 13.2: Tendencies in human decision-making

The emphasis in decision-making in daily life does not usually take into account the consequences the decisions may have in the distant future, for example excessive obedience to authority or the postponement of the initiation or termination of projects. Current costs and benefits seem often more conspicuous than future ones (Akerlof, 1991). This is at odds with the standard behavioural assumption in economic theory of a completely rational, future-perfectly-anticipating, utility-maximizing individual.

The dimension of distance may relate to three different aspects: the number of kilometres, the difference in interest or background and the probability of certain events occurring. It turns out that learning processes give too much weight to local events, especially those events which already occur frequently in the world of experience of the learner. For example, developments in Germany and the United States of America have more impact on decisions in the Netherlands than on developments in China. Similarly, an economist will pay more attention to the economic aspects of a decision than to its judicial aspects. Rare events are even ignored, which is at odds with expected utility theory. For example, people do not insure themselves against the danger of flooding, despite the fact that the premium is much lower than the expected gain (Heiner, 1983).

Decision processes seem also to put too much weight on success. For example, empirical results showing new variables having significant positive or negative effects are easier to get published in scientific journals than results showing the same variables having no statistical effect. Another example is that in many organizations success is rewarded with promotion, when in fact it may have been achieved by over-risky behaviour. The probability of failure is therefore underestimated.

13.3 **Organizational responses**

The above implies that people allocate their cognitive capacities to only a few areas of interest, while other areas of interest receive hardly any attention. The scantiness of the attention spent on these other fields will result in biases in decision-making, and will have consequences for the design of organizations. This section addresses the way in which organizations deal with these tendencies at the level of individuals.

An efficient organization takes the limited cognitive capacities of its members into account, and structures itself in such a way that the cognitive capacities of individuals are channelled in a productive way. The costs of bounded rationality for an organization can be classified as follows:

- Non-productive use of resources (time, energy);
- Bad or suboptimal decisions;
- Organizational adaptations.

The first category means cognitive capacities are allocated in the wrong direction. Thus for example an organization may be focused on making technologically superior products, while the market does not want them. The second category – bad, suboptimal decisions – can be the outcome of the first, in this case for instance the allocation of the budget to R&D instead of the marketing department. The third category – organizational adaptations – entails that each (organizational) choice implies opportunity costs. The choice of focus implies automatically that less attention is paid to other valuable aspects.

The measures an organization can take in order to deal with these costs are based on the following three categories and are classified as follows:

- Changing the costs and or benefits of the choice possibilities;
- Changing the choice possibilities;
- Structuring the amount and nature of information.

The first category entails changing the payoffs, through salaries or budgets, in order to indicate which activities have a high priority for the organization. The freedom of choice of individuals does not change. The second class of measures affects the freedom of choice of individuals. The third category concerns measures which do not affect the freedom of choice of the persons involved, but it does affect the way in which different choice possibilities are perceived. (Notice that these three categories are based on the ingredients of a non-cooperative game, such as was outlined in Chapter 2.)

13.4 **Short-term focus**

A short-term focus applies to situations where the current benefits and costs receive disproportional attention from individuals in decision-making processes. It would actually be desirable to take today some painful, costly decisions which are beneficial in the long run, but these investments are postponed until tomorrow in favour of activities which seem more important today. Such decisions are called *dynamically inconsistent*. There is a dynamic inconsistency because people do not realize that postponement until tomorrow will tomorrow again result in postponement.

The dynamic inconsistency lies in the fact that every current choice which differs only in a minor way from the efficient decision in the long run, and therefore causes only limited costs today, may have major consequences in the long run when such choices are made over and over again. This may result in procrastination over certain actions (Sec. 13.4.1), impulsive behaviour (Sec. 13.4.2), or undue obedience to authority (Sec. 13.4.3).

13.4.1 **Procrastination**

There are many examples of decisions where the person involved is able to take immediate action which would be best for him, but it is postponed time and time again. Examples are quitting smoking, eating a healthy diet, starting to study for an exam and repairing broken objects. This behaviour can be modelled by a very low discount factor, i.e. extreme impatience, which gives the current situation much more weight than the future. Akerlof (1991) gives credit to Irving Fisher for this conceptualization by citing his observation:

> This is illustrated by the story of the farmer who would never mind a leaking roof. When it rained he could not stop the leak, and when it did not rain there was no leak to be stopped. Among such persons, the preference for present gratification is powerful because their anticipation of the future is weak.

Procrastination also occurs in organizations. Examples are waiting too long to start a new project or persisting with a bad one for too long. The task of management is to prevent this behaviour, for example by setting deadlines and checking results frequently. Such behaviour is made worse if information is ignored or eliminated which indicates that procrastination is even worse than already thought. Efficient organizations prepare for such behaviour and exercise various means of dealing with it. Specific rules regarding procrastination can be formulated, like requiring a written statement to explain it, which discourages it. The same effect is produced when a mistake which a responsible person admits making is not punished too harshly. Mistakes will be known earlier and appropriate measures taken sooner.

Excuses may be tolerated by allowing employees to claim that losses are due to uncontrollable, bad circumstances. Procrastination is also less attractive when results are clear and obvious. A project may also be finished with less delay when it is organized step by step. Results of the project will be visible in the near future for those people who are executing it, and management is able to signal problems early on. Other measures for reducing or even preventing procrastination are having different people in charge of the starting and termination decisions of projects, and taking the costs and procedures of finishing projects into account right at the beginning. Finally, job rotation may limit too large a commitment to a specific project.

13.4.2 Impulses and routines

Postrel and Rumelt (1992) focus attention on the importance of impulsive behaviour in organizations. Organizations take this into account in their reward structures, their way of control and the design of their routines. The relationship between impulses and routines will now be addressed.

A *routine* entails activating certain behaviour by habits or customs when certain situations occur. The advantage of routines is that they put a limited claim on the scarce cognitive capacities of the organizational members in a large number of situations. This frees up cognitive capacities for situations with a higher degree of difficulty. Focus can then be placed on solving problems with few standard characteristics. However, a routine entails also a certain rigidity in behaviour. This can be attractive in the sense that dysfunctional impulses in behaviour are easier to suppress. However, it may also be undesirable, because certain functional changes are harder to establish. The value of a routine depends therefore on the relative importance of suppressing impulses as opposed applying it to the specific characteristics of the situation.

13.4.3 Obedience

Akerlof (1991) models obedience, like procrastination, as a dynamic inconsistency in decision-making. If an employee has a hard time saying no to the boss, then the latter can create obedience by eliciting a series of small, escalating concessions by the employee. Experiments with random persons administering substantial electric shocks to others (Milgram, 1975) shows in a bewildering way that the dictum associated particularly with Germans that '*Befehl ist Befehl*' ('Orders is orders') is a universal phenomenon.

This behaviour may also occur in a bureaucratic organization where an employee may turn into a specialist in a certain field by being associated with the same unit for an extensive period. This generates the traditional advantages of specialization. However, it is also possible for a very specific, unproductive culture to emerge. One way to prevent this development is to recognize that non-specialists have the advantage of a broader experience. They are therefore less willing to engage in non-productive group decision processes. It should be noted that a strong local culture need not be bad. Examples are the common practices of highly dedicated scientists (who often project or suffer from a 'mad scientist' image) or disciplined marines.

13.5 **Shortsightedness**

Shortsightedness may concern three different aspects: the actual distance in terms of the number of kilometres, the difference in interest or background and the probability of certain events occurring. A number of applications will illustrate this bias.

Application: Entrepreneurs versus managers

The empirical work of Busenitz and Barney (1994) is focused on biases in the decision-making of starting entrepreneurs and managers of large firms. A starting entrepreneur is the owner-manager of a small company. Entrepreneurship requires that many diverse problems are addressed. It turns out that decisions exhibit two types of biases. First,

---

entrepreneurs are significantly more optimistic or self-assured in their judgments than managers. This holds particularly for unknown problems and problems surrounded with substantial uncertainty. Second, entrepreneurs are less sensitive regarding the representativeness of their data. They overestimate the importance of a small sample. On top of that, new information does not usually result in policy changes, because data are simplified by associating them with known knowledge and with routines developed from previous experiences.

The implications of these observations for advice regarding entrepreneurship are not clear. The biases may be crucial or fatal. Shortsightedness may be necessary in order to start new activities. Were every aspect of a new investment project to be considered first, the attractiveness of the project might evaporate before it could be begun. Besides, blinkers may be necessary in reviewing a project in order not to be overwhelmed by all the problems which could occur. The above biases may of course be an explanation for the large number of bankruptcies of starting entrepreneurs.

Application: Law of small numbers

People often exaggerate the representativeness of a small sample. Conspicuous information often receives too much weight in decision-making. The following passage (Akerlof, 1991) illustrates this:

> Let us suppose that you wish to buy a new car and have decided that on grounds of economy and longevity you want to purchase one of those stalwart, middle-class Swedish cars – either a Volvo or a Saab. As a prudent and sensible buyer, you go to Consumer Reports, which informs you that the consensus of their experts is that the Volvo is mechanically superior, and that the consensus of the readership is that the Volvo has the better repair record. Armed with information, you decide to go and strike a bargain with the Volvo dealer before the week is out. In the interim, however, you go to a cocktail party where you announce your intention to an acquaintance. He reacts with disbelief and alarm: 'A Volvo! You've got to be kidding. My brother-in-law had a Volvo. First, that fancy fuel injection computer thing went out. 250 bucks. Next he started having trouble with the rear end. Had to replace it. Then the transmission and the clutch. Finally sold it in three years for junk.

It will occur frequently in such cases that the Saab is purchased. The importance of the additional information is that the size of the sample of the Consumer Report increases by one. The average repair and maintenance costs will hardly change. However, psychologists say that most people do not treat this new information in this way in their purchasing process regarding a new car. Apparently people sometimes give their private signals more weight than the information regarding the population.

Another example of using the representativeness of a small sample in the wrong way are deviations from the average. Suppose that the average number of daily births in a large hospital is 45, whereas in a small hospital this number is 15. The exact number of births varies from day to day. Each hospital records during a year the number of days that the percentage of boys was larger than 60 per cent. A survey asks which hospital has most days with more than 60 per cent boys. Of those asked, 22 per cent indicate the large hospital, 56 per cent answer that it would make no difference, and 22 per cent give the small hospital as the right answer. The statistical explanation for the right answer, i.e. the small hospital, is the law of large numbers, but it turns out that humans have difficulties with the representativeness of samples. It seems that often a law of small or conspicuous numbers applies (Rabin, 1998).

Application: Financial markets

The departure of most macroeconomic and financial theories in the 1970s was the assumption of rational expectations. This is that people hold the (statistically) correct view regarding the future and incorporate the associated estimations in their choices. The rational expectations view does not mean that the expectation regarding the future is always right. However, the view is that these expectations are on average right. Deviations are random and unpredictable. Sometimes people are too optimistic, sometimes they are too pessimistic. People are therefore on average right and so markets work perfectly. This assumption has been productive in all kinds of settings, but there are also a number of empirical observations which are hard to understand from this perspective.

An example is that people do not give enough weight to rare events. Lettau (1993) explains this with boundedly rational decision-makers in an investment model. Agents decide regarding the percentage of risky investments in their portfolio, investing more (less) in risky investments when returns have been positive (negative) in the recent past. This transition rule implies that funds with temporarily negative returns are underestimated when attractive investment opportunities abound. Investments show therefore a systematic bias in terms of over-risky portfolio composition. An implication regarding the behaviour of markets is that stock prices increase gradually over a long period of time, once in a while disrupted by substantial decreases in stock prices. (Lee (1995) formulates a game-theoretic model with transaction costs that exhibits the same behaviour in equilibrium. His argument is that only those with favourable information are in the market, while those with bad information do not know from each other that they have bad information. However, some people will enter the market when the news is sufficiently bad at a certain moment, and will be followed by others.)

Application: Information cascading

People have two sources of knowledge for learning about their environment: private information and public information. Private information is obtained from your own experience or investigations, while public information is provided by the actions or signals of others. An example of private information is when you go to a restaurant and investigate the quality of the food by ordering a meal. Public information regarding the quality of the food in the restaurant is provided by the length of the queue of people waiting to go in. Similarly, an employer might turn down a job applicant on the basis of an interview, or just because the applicant is known to have been rejected for several similar jobs in the past.

People often combine private information with public information, because direct analysis of alternatives can be costly and time-consuming. Observing the behaviour of others can therefore influence your own processing of information. This is called *observational learning* or *social learning*. Taking observational learning into account implies that the public information may outweigh your own assessment. A pattern of conformity can arise if initial predictions coincide and the inferred information dominates the private information of subsequent decision-makers. The followers go along with the consensus prediction, even if it would not be the 'correct' prediction made only on the basis of their own sample. The choices of a few early individuals determine the choices of all the successors. This is known as an *information cascade*. An information cascade is defined by a sequence of individuals whose decisions do not depend on their private information. Once a cascade starts, public information stops accumulating, because your choice of action no longer depends on your private information. Followers ignore their private signals.

It turns out that the emergence of either a 'correct' or an 'incorrect' cascade is determined by the first time that two identical subsequent actions are observed (Bikhchandani *et al.*, 1998). Two bad actions in the beginning are fatal to the correctness of the cascade. The type of cascade depends therefore not just on how many good and bad signals arrive, but also on the order in which they come. There is *path dependency*. Figure 13.3 illustrates that a cascade, either correct or incorrect, will eventually occur in the long run (Bikhchandani, 1992, p. 998), because the probability that two identical subsequent actions will not occur in the long run is almost zero.

The horizontal axis shows the probability that the signal is correct. The vertical axis shows the probability that a correct cascade or an incorrect cascade occurs eventually. Thus, if the probability that the signal is correct increases, then so does the probability of an eventual correct cascade, and the probability of an eventual incorrect cascade is decreasing. However, an incorrect cascade may always occur because there is a chance that two subsequent wrong actions occur and are observed early in the process.

The above has implications for the desirability of misfits and reputation management. When an individual takes an action which is informative to others, this provides a positive externality. Misfits therefore have an important role in organizations according to Bikhchandani *et al.* (1998, pp. 156–7). They observe:

> If an individual was expected to make the error of following the private signal instead of obeying the cascade, the actions of that individual would add to the public pool of knowledge, to the benefit of the followers. Such altruistic behavior by a number of individuals would ultimately lead to almost perfectly accurate decisions in the long run. Instead, individuals, acting in their own self-interest, rationally take uninformative imitative actions. Bernardo and Welch (1997) point out that irrationally overconfident

entrepreneurs, who place heavy weight on their own signals relative to those of others, may be exceptionally useful citizens. More generally, the theory of informational cascades suggests that social misfits of various sorts – such as newcomers who have not observed the past history, or prophets with special information sources – may disproportionally benefit society.

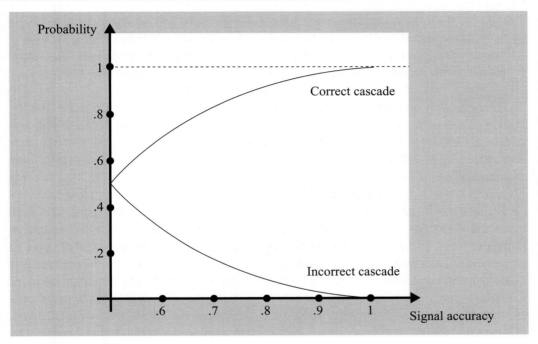

Figure 13.3: Information cascading
Birkchandani *et al.* (1992) 'A Theory of Fools, Fashion, Custom and Cultural Change as Informational Cascades', *Journal of Political Economy*, 100(5), pp. 992–1026, University of Chicago

Public information complements private information, or may even dominate it. Reports of the actions or endorsements of one group of decision-makers often influence the actions of others. This implies that the management of one's *reputation* may use opportunities to manipulate the process by which individuals learn from their predecessors. Bikhchandani *et al.*. (1998, p. 151) provide the following example:

In 1995, management gurus Michael Treacy and Fred Wiersema secretly purchased 50 000 copies of their business strategy book *The Discipline of Market Leaders* from stores across the nation. The stores they purchased from just happened to be the ones whose sales are monitored to select books for the *New York Times* bestseller list. Despite mediocre reviews, their book made the bestseller list. Subsequently their book sold well enough to continue as a bestseller without further demand intervention by the authors. Presumably, being on a bestseller list helps a book sell more because consumers and reviewers learn from the actions of others.'

Application: Diversity of teams

Globalization offers many business opportunities. For example, the merger of people or firms with different backgrounds or skills may be attractive when substantial synergies or complementarities are involved. However, the complementarities between the workers have to be sufficiently important to overcome the costs of communication. Lazear (1999a, p. C15) observes:

> Three factors determine the gains from putting together diverse teams. The gains from diversity are greatest when groups have information sets that are disjoint, that are relevant to one another, and that can be learned by the other group at low costs.

First, diversity gains are greatest when individuals have different information. If information or skill sets are completely *disjoint*, then person A can benefit from working with person B, and vice versa, because neither contributes much to the other's knowledge. Second, skills or information possessed by the other person must be *relevant*. Team members have to have not only different skills or knowledge, but also skills which are complementary. Relevance is interpreted as gains from synergy or complementarity.

Disjointness is important when complementarities are important. Figure 13.4 illustrates the distinction between disjointness and relevance. Consider three individuals, A, B and C. Their individual knowledge is represented by the rectangles, A, B and C, respectively. Suppose a firm would like to put together a two-person team. On the basis of the disjointness alone, it would seem best to put A and C or B and C together, because C has information disjoint from that of either A or B. A team of A and B has considerable overlap of information, so there is more potential for gain in an AC team or a BC team. But relevance matters. Suppose that the skills required to perform the tasks needed by

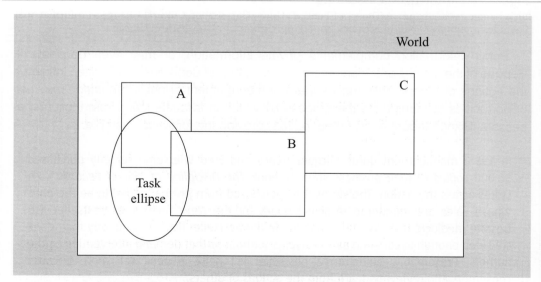

Figure 13.4: Disjointness and relevance (Lazear, 1999a, p. 17)
Lazear, E.P., 'Globalisation and the Market for Team Mates', *The Economic Journal*, Blackwell Publishers

the firm are represented by the oval marked 'Task ellipse'. The task ellipse implies that the best team consists of A and B and excludes C. Although C knows many things that neither A nor B knows, C's information is irrelevant for performing the tasks. The team consisting of A and B has almost all the knowledge necessary to perform the tasks needed by the firm.

Third, communication is necessary. It is important that A and B be able to communicate with each other in order to perform the relevant tasks. Disjointness and relevance of knowledge are useless unless the groups can understand each other. If it were prohibitively costly for one group to learn the language used by the other or obtain the information it possessed, then disjointness and relevance would have no value. The primary reason for employing intercultural teams is that the value gained by putting together disjoint and relevant information by far outweighs the communication costs incurred. Such teams create the most added value when cultures are less positively correlated with one another.

13.6 Loss aversion

One of the core building blocks of economic theory is expected utility theory with regard to consumer behaviour. An implicit assumption in expected utility theory is that a reference point or frame does not play a role in decision-making. The announcement that 'season ticket holders pay 10 euros less' is evaluated the same as 'non-season ticket holders pay an additional 10 euros'. The only thing which matters from the perspective of expected utility theory is the size of the endowment of a person and the preferences. This implies that no distinction is made between profits and losses. An increase in loss by 10 euros is treated the same as a decrease in profit by 10 euros.

Tversky and Kahneman (1992) have formulated *cumulative prospect theory* based on a large amount of experimental evidence. Reference points, and therefore the difference between gains and losses, play a prominent role in this approach. Figure 13.5 summarizes their theory. The utility function shows a kink at the origin (the reference point), i.e. a loss is not perceived as exactly the opposite of a gain. Loss aversion entails that one money unit gain is not sufficient to compensate one money unit loss. Empirical research shows that two money units of gain are needed to compensate one money unit of loss. The kink in Fig. 13.5 depicts the difference between gain and loss. An increase in the loss results in a larger drop in utility than a similar decrease in gain.

A second implication of cumulative prospect theory concerns the response to uncertain outcomes. This depends on the position of the reference point. If there are uncertain profit opportunities, then cumulative prospect theory predicts risk-averse behaviour. Figure 13.6 shows this. A gain of 50 with certainty (probability 1) is valued higher than a project with a gain of 0 with probability 0.5 and a gain of 100 with probability 0.5.

If there are uncertain loss opportunities, then cumulative prospect theory predicts risk-loving behaviour. Figure 13.7 illustrates this. A loss of 50 with certainty (probability 1) is valued less than a project with a loss of 0 with probability 0.5 and a loss of 100 with probability 0.5. The project with the highest uncertainty is chosen according cumulative prospect theory when losses are involved.

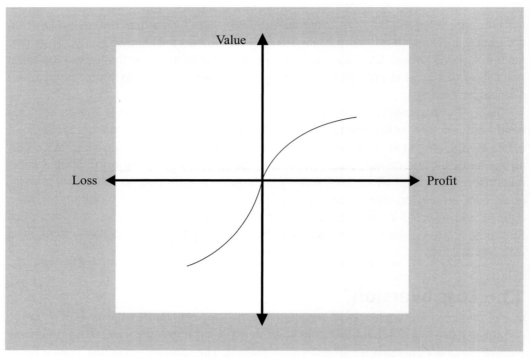

Figure 13.5: Cumulative prospect theory (Tversky and Kahneman, 1985, p. 29)

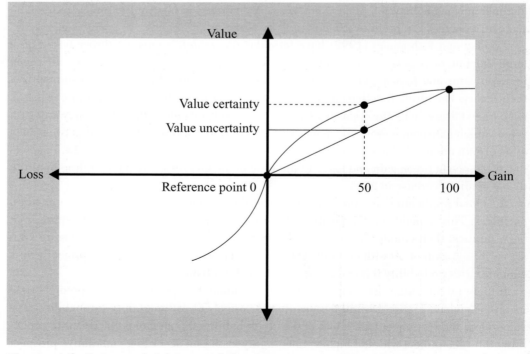

Figure 13.6: Gains and risk-averse behaviour

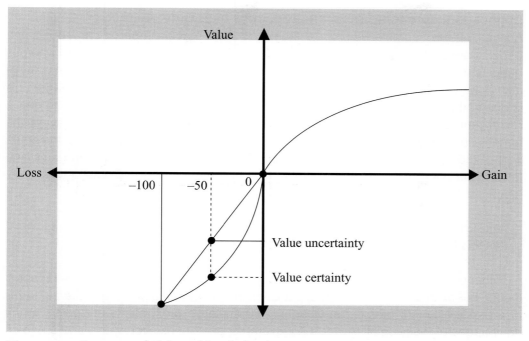

Figure 13.7: Losses and risk-seeking behaviour

Another implication of cumulative prospect theory is that there is diminishing sensitivity. If the same loss or profit is further away from the reference point, then the change in utility will be less. This implies that the choice of reference point is more attractive when losses are perceived as smaller. Money illusion may illustrate this implication. Money illusion means that people make a distinction between nominal and real changes. People prefer a nominal salary increase of 5 per cent during a period of 12 per cent inflation to no payrise in a period of 7 per cent inflation. Figure 13.8 illustrates the effect of diminishing sensitivity when the distance to the reference point increases.

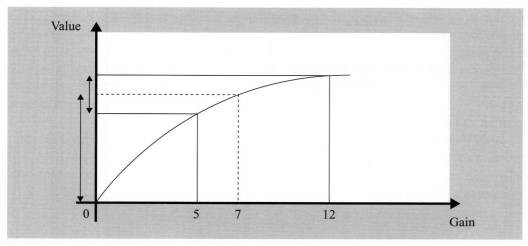

Figure 13.8: Gains far away from the reference point are less attractive

Application: Spreading costs and revenues over time

An implication of cumulative prospect theory is that it may be important how costs and benefits are spread over time. The advice is that all costs are made together, whereas benefits have to be spread over time. Figure 13.3 implies that the decrease in utility of taking the whole loss at once is lower than when the loss is taken in small parts. This is due to the diminishing marginal utility of loss. The same tendency applies to gains. An organization escapes the law of diminishing marginal benefits by paying the benefits in small parts. This establishes that the organization is repeatedly in the steep part of the utility function. This insight regarding the asymmetry between gains and losses has been axiomatized only recently, but it has been applied for a long time; Machiavelli (1513) advised long ago that

> unjustices have to be committed all at once, then they are experienced less: and benefits have to be given little by little, then they taste better.

Other practices can also be understood from the perspective of cumulative prospect theory. For example, the standard explanation of seniority wages is formulated in terms of a principal–agent problem in Chapter 7. Cumulative prospect theory points at the advantages of many small rewards (for example, one bonus every year) and a one-off large loss (for instance, a low starting salary).

Application: Presenting unattractive alternatives

The attention of people can be directed to different aspects of a problem by the way alternatives and policy decisions are presented. This is due to bounded rationality. The way of presentation has an effect on the perception of what is presented because a choice of reference point is involved. The non-robustness of people regarding the way decisions or alternatives are presented can be (mis)used. This will be illustrated with a number of examples.

Supermarkets and filling stations are well aware that the presentation of choice possibilities has an impact on how these choices are perceived, and take the loss aversion of people into account in announcing their price policy. For example, the way price differentiation is presented entails a choice of reference point. Is the lowest price presented as a discount, or the highest price as an additional charge? It is common practice to advertise with the discount aimed at frequent buyers rather than with an additional charge for infrequent buyers.

Another example of the choice of reference point and loss aversion is money illusion. We saw above how a nominal salary increase of 5 per cent during a period of 12 per cent inflation is usually preferred to no payrise in a period of 7 per cent inflation. Figure 13.9 depicts this situation.

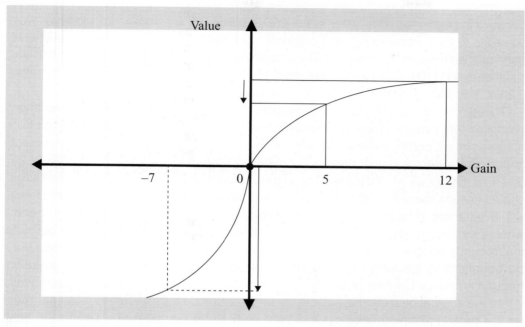

Figure 13.9: Emphasizing the costs of an alternative makes it less attractive

Application: Equity premium puzzle

The annual net return on stocks was 4 to 5 per cent higher than the return on government bonds during the previous century. This is hard to explain for expected utility theory. Benartzi and Thaler (1995) pose loss aversion and infrequent evaluations as an explanation. The idea is that shares are unattractive for persons with loss aversion, because share values usually fluctuate. Some days show a profit, others a loss. However, on average there is a profit. The problem is that for a person with loss aversion a loss weighs much more than a profit. Low-yield bonds are chosen instead of high-yield shares in order to prevent a loss on one of the many trading days. The same holds for an employee having to report frequently to his or her boss. Even though the activities of the employee are high-yield in the long run, he or she still faces the risk of having to take a loss once in a while. This is unattractive when you have to report frequently. The implication is that too much emphasis will be put on preventing losses. This will result in overly cautious behaviour and therefore weaker performance.

The following example illustrates the line of thought. Suppose there is a piece-wise linear utility function, where the utility is $U(x) = x$ when x is positive, i.e. represents profits, and $U(x) = 2.5x$ when x is negative, i.e. represents losses. The loss of 1 euro is therefore 2.5 times as high as the gain of 1 euro. This specification implies that a proposal will be rejected that consists of winning 200 euros with probability 0.5 and losing 100 euros with probability 0.5, because the expected utility is $0.5 \times 1 \times 200 + 0.5 \times 2.5 \times (-100) = -25$. However, were someone to be confronted with this proposal repeatedly and to evaluate it only every two periods, then it would be accepted. The probability distribution of the outcomes in this new situation is 400 (100, −200) with probability 0.25 (0.5, 0.25). The expected utility is therefore $0.25 \times 1 \times 400 + 0.5 \times 1 \times 100 + 0.25 \times 2.5 \times (-200) = 25$.

These considerations have consequences for the composition of investment portfolios. An investor characterized by the above utility function and evaluating his or her investment portfolio every day will not consider shares very attractive. The reason is that share prices almost always fluctuate and the investor values a decrease 2.5 times as highly as an increase. The organizational implication is that shareholders should not ask management to render account too often. Managers of investment funds will invest more in higher-yield, risky investments than in low-yield government bonds when they have to report less. A similar recommendation regarding portfolio policy is that recently bought shares are not allowed to be sold, i.e. a short-run restriction may be beneficial in the long run. A general insight is that someone with loss aversion frequently chooses higher-yield activities when the frequency of evaluations decreases. When the evaluation period is sufficiently large, a unique loss becomes less important for the person involved because it is very likely to be compensated before the next evaluation.

Finally, a word of caution. There is no general agreement about the above findings and results. Fama (1998) argues that these biases in behaviour are not systematic, i.e. overreaction to information is as frequent as underreaction, which is consistent with the traditional market efficiency hypothesis that the anomalies are chance results.

Application: Entry

The difference between an incumbent firm and a potential entrant is that the former makes a profit already and the latter does not (Fershtman, 1995). This entails different reference points according to cumulative prospect theory, and therefore different behaviour. Figure 13.3 implies that this poses an additional barrier to entry. The incumbent firm will respond more aggressively towards an entrant in order to prevent a decrease in profit than an entrant will behave in order to obtain a small profit. This aggressive behaviour may be sufficient to deter the entrant from entry. A similar inertia occurs in the composition of an industry regarding the exit of incumbent firms.

Cumulative prospect theory may have implications for the 'bygones are bygones' aspect of sunk costs. The notion of sunk costs implies that costs made in the past have no impact on current decision-making processes. However, if recent losses do play a role along the lines of cumulative prospect theory, then this will have implications for behaviour. The reference point will not adjust completely with respect to recent losses. This has behavioural implications, but the effect is not clear. It depends on the size of the loss. If profits have decreased and remain positive, then this results in more risk-averse behaviour by the manager. However, if the decrease in profits turns into a loss, then the management engage in more risk-seeking behaviour in order to erase the blame of a loss. ('Desperate needs lead to desperate deeds.')

Management changes can be considered from the same perspective. Replacing one manager with another, even when both are equally qualified, may have important consequences. Replacing a manager involves a different reference point. A manager who has experienced a recent loss may still have the same reference point as in the past. The attractiveness of replacement depends on the difference in reference point and what behaviour the shareholders desire. It is possible that replacement is not desired because the recent loss may result in a less risk-averse manager or a manager choosing a more aggressive strategy.

13.7 Conclusion

The analysis of decision-making is complex because various dimensions are involved, and quite different perspectives can be taken regarding each dimension. For example, the decision-making process can be approached from either a rational choice perspective or a rule-based perspective. Similarly, the level of analysis can be geared towards the autonomous actor or the system, the criterion can be either clarity and consistency or ambiguity and inconsistency and the goal can be either instrumental or sense-making. This chapter has taken a rule-based perspective towards the decision-making process, which results in a number of biases in decision-making when viewed from the rational choice perspective. Prominent examples are short-term focus, shortsightedness and loss aversion. The implication of these three biases in decision-making at the individual level for behaviour at the organization level have been highlighted. Organizational solutions for these tendencies in decision-making have been formulated and illustrated with examples from various behavioural fields of inquiry, such as behavioural accounting, behavioural finance, organizational behaviour and economic psychology.

13.8 Exercises

13.1 A long queue has formed in front of the ticket office to see the new play performed by the theatre company, *The Mosquito With The Golden Tooth*. A new TV station tries to establish itself by giving away tickets to every third person in the queue. The weather turns out to be very bad on the day of the performance.

    A What does expected utility theory predict regarding the fraction of people who stay at home in each of the two groups of ticket-holders?

    B What does the cumulative prospect theory predict regarding the fraction of people who stay at home in each of the two groups of ticket-holders?

13.2 Is the observation that there are multimillionaires who get very aroused when they lose 1 euro in a game of cards more consistent with the expected benefit theory than with the cumulative prospect theory? Explain your answer.

13.3 Taxi cab drivers in New York City pay a fixed fee to rent their cabs for twelve hours and then keep all their revenues. They must decide how long to drive each day (Camerer, *et al.* 2000). There are good days (days with high earnings per hour such as rainy days or days with a big convention in town) and bad days.

A Does the payoff-maximizing strategy entail a difference in the number of hours worked on good and bad days?

B Suppose cabbies set a target earnings level for each day, and treat shortfalls relative to that target as a loss. How long will they drive each day from the perspective of prospect theory?

Part VII:
Alignment

The opportunistic behavioural assumption, as discussed in Parts III and IV, has been a fertile starting-point of analysis for many problems. However, there are also numerous situations where opportunism does not seem to be a good description of the motives guiding behaviour. For example, employees have some emotional binding with their organization and are often very devoted to their company. Simon (1991) observes that

> organizational motivation becomes a major motivation for employees to work actively for organizational goals, quite apart from the mechanisms of reward or the ease with which authority can be policed.

This means in the terminology of Chapter 2 that the *idealistic behavioural assumption* is actual, i.e. all members of the organization share the same objectives. The co-ordination problem is the challenge of aligning the various attributes of an organization when everyone in the organization fully internalizes its goals and puts self-interest aside in order to pursue them. The theories developed with respect to co-ordination problems are characterized by either *complete* or *limited rationality*. The behavioural assumptions of this part are presented in Fig. VII.1 in the familiar classification scheme.

		Hypothesis of behaviour		
		Opportunistic	Self-interested	Idealistic
Degree of rationality	Complete rationality			Co-ordination
	Limited rationality			
	Procedural rationality			

Figure VII.1: Positioning

Chapter 14 characterizes the co-ordination problem and formulates various solutions. In Chapter 15 organizations are characterized as systems of attributes (based on the structure of the co-ordination problem). This view of the firm is shown with the familiar picture of the elephant in Fig. VII.2.

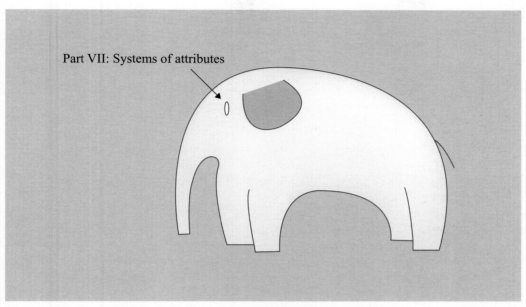

Part VII: Systems of attributes

Figure VII.2: View of the firm from an alignment perspective

14

Co-ordination

Contents

14.1 Introduction

Using the law of comparative advantages, Chapter 1 showed that specialization can result in large increases in productivity. People take specific courses of action in order to do specialized work and use tools geared towards their task. However, specialization also involves problems, like providing the right incentives and establishing co-ordination. Part II indicated the circumstances in which the market handles these problems well by means of prices. However, often the circumstances required for such an ideal world are not met. Other ways of organizing may do better in providing the right incentives and establishing co-ordination.

Division of labour results in specialized entities, like functions, departments, offices and divisions. Specialization has to be accompanied by co-ordination in order to establish alignment, synergy or complementarity between activities. People are regularly confronted with exceptional or unclear situations in which the desirable course of action is not clear from the perspective of the whole organization. *Co-ordination problems* are situations in which one does not know which decision matches best with other decisions in the organization. Various methods of alignment are highlighted in this chapter.

The co-ordination problem is characterized in Sec. 14.2 and the possible solutions induced by this characterization are indicated. Four types of solutions are identified. One section is dedicated to each of these four solutions. Section 14.7 concludes.

14.2 The co-ordination problem

Co-ordination problems are characterized by the fact that the parties aim for the common interest, but that they don't know what the other party will decide. A *co-ordination problem* is defined as a situation with more than one Nash equilibrium. Several equilibria are desirable to all parties, but the problem is that no one knows which equilibrium the other party will choose. If someone takes a decision which is associated with one equilibrium, and the other player makes a choice which belongs to another equilibrium, then the total result is probably bad. The next two subsections address the multiplicity of equilibria (Sec. 14.2.1) and possible solutions (Sec. 14.2.2).

14.2.1 More than one equilibrium

A classical co-ordination problem occurs in a symphony orchestra. Several simplifying assumptions are made to illustrate the problem. First, the symphony orchestra consists of only wind players and string players. Second, each player chooses independently his or her own tempo and cannot communicate with the others. Finally, every member of the orchestra can choose between either a slow or a fast tempo. This results in four possible combinations of decisions. Two of these possibilities are undesirable, because the tempos of the two types of players are not aligned. In these situations, the wind players play fast and the string players play slow, or the other way around. It is desirable that both play at the same tempo, which is represented by the situations A and B in Fig. 14.1. As long as everyone chooses the same tempo it hardly matters for the joint outcome whether they all play slow or fast.

Figure 14.2 presents Fig. 14.1 in strategic form. The two parties decide simultaneously, and therefore independently, regarding the tempo. The payoffs are presented in the familiar

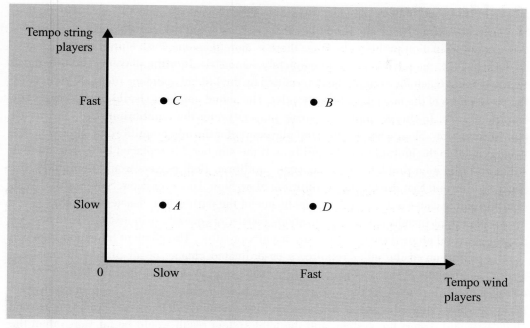

Figure 14.1: Possible combinations of decisions in an orchestra

Wind players String players	Slow	Fast
Slow	(4,4)	(–1,–1)
Fast	(–1,–1)	(6,3)

Figure 14.2: The orchestra

way, with the first number in (x,y) the payoff for the string players and the second number the payoff for the wind players. For example, (6,3) means that the string players earn 6 and the wind players earn 3 when both parties choose the fast tempo.

There are two bad outcomes and two aligned or co-ordinated outcomes. The bad outcomes consist of one party choosing a slow tempo and the other party choosing a fast one. None of these outcomes is a Nash equilibrium, because each player wants to change his choice, given the decision of the other party. The good outcomes are the choices Slow, Slow and the choices Fast, Fast. There is a co-ordination problem because Slow, Slow like Fast, Fast is a Nash equilibrium. The combination of decisions Slow, Slow is a Nash equilibrium because when the string players play at a slow tempo, then the wind players earn most by playing a slow tempo. The same applies to the string players. They receive the highest payment by playing slow, as long as the players of wind instruments play slow. No individual has any reason to play slow when the other plays fast. Similarly, Fast, Fast is an equilibrium as well. If the wind players play fast, then the string players earn most by also playing fast. Similarly, it is attractive for the wind players to play fast when the string players play fast. So, this is a co-ordination problem, because there is more than one Nash equilibrium.

In Fig. 14.2, the payoffs are not completely symmetrical for the players. The difference between 4 and 6 can for example be determined by the kind of audience (demand side) or by the preferences of the musicians (supply side). The actual numbers should be determined by empirical work. In this example, the string players prefer the equilibrium Fast, Fast to the equilibrium Slow, Slow, whereas the wind players prefer the other equilibrium. However, this is not crucial to the multiplicity of equilibria. If the number 3 is replaced by 6, then there is still a co-ordination problem, with the same equilibria. Both players would then prefer the Nash equilibrium Fast, Fast to the equilibrium Slow, Slow. However, Slow, Slow is still a Nash equilibrium, because a unilateral change by one of the parties is a disaster for both.

An important insight is that organizations consist of several attributes which have to be aligned. Several aligned compositions are usually possible. The efficient transition from one Nash equilibrium to the other requires a co-ordinated change of all players/dimensions/attributes/elements of the organization at the same time in order to reap the benefits of the complementarities between the attributes. It is therefore desirable to keep the transition period as short as possible, i.e. a 'big bang' or 'all-or-nothing' change is advised. One-by-one changes would distort the system, and the total system result would be far worse than the equilibrium which is abandoned.

Application: Crossing an intersection

A well-known co-ordination problem is crossing intersections. Two cars arrive at an intersection at the same time. They cannot cross at the same time without causing a crash. This would result in considerable damage, e.g. −10, for each driver. If both drivers stop, this only results in delay without anyone crossing the intersection. Both drivers lose an amount of 1. The situation in which one car goes (G) and the other stops (S) yields a payoff of 5 and 0. Figure 14.3 presents the situation at the intersection.

Car 1 \ Car 2	S	G
S	(−1,−1)	(0,5)
G	(5,0)	(−10,−10)

Figure 14.3: An intersection

Two of these four combinations of decisions are not equilibria. If both drivers stop, it is clear that a driver can change this situation to his advantage by going. The payment for this driver increases from −1 to 5. The other non-equilibrium outcome is that both go. If a driver knows for sure that the other will go, a choice S remains with payment 0 or a choice G with payment –10. The choice will therefore be to stop, so that the situation in which both go is not an equilibrium.

The problem in this traffic situation is that there are two equilibria, i.e. there is a co-ordination problem. An equilibrium entails that one car stops and the other car goes. However, if one arrives at an intersection, then it is not clear which equilibrium each driver has in mind. Driver 1 may think that the equilibrium in which he chooses G and the other chooses S is relevant, whereas driver 2 can focus on the other equilibrium. The result is a crash.

Application: Production and Marketing

Suppose a car company has a production- and marketing department. The production department focuses on the technological aspects of products, whereas the marketing department is oriented primarily towards the wishes of the customers. Assume the production department can choose between a rigid technology and a flexible one. A technology with low (L) flexibility can produce only one product. The advantage of this technology is that economies of scale can be realized when large amounts are produced. A technology with high (H) flexibility entails higher costs, but it is able to tailor the products to specific wishes of consumers. This results in higher product prices. The marketing department has two options as well. It can focus on the development of a marketing policy which offers no (N) variety, i.e. highlighting low prices, or a marketing policy which stresses product variety (V).

The decision V of the marketing department and L of the production department reflect the situation in which the marketing department chooses the policy which is based on a large range of products, whereas the production department is focused on realizing economies of scale by investing in a technology which can produce only one product. The promises made to the customers cannot therefore be fulfilled. The combination of decisions N,H represents the opposite. The marketing department focuses on emphasizing low customer prices, whereas the production department uses an expensive technology geared to produce many different products. This flexible production technology results in higher costs per product, which conflicts with the policy N of the marketing department. Angry customers are again the result. Figure 14.4 presents payoffs in line with these insights. The other two combinations of decisions, i.e. N, L and V, H, are attractive outcomes.

The strategy pairs N,L and V,H are Nash equilibria, whereas V,L and N,H are not. The attractiveness of each Nash equilibrium depends on the specific market of the company. Figure 14.4 represents the situation in the car industry in the 1960s. Realizing economies of scale was important, because the demand of customers was rather homogeneous. Companies achieved the best results by focusing on mass production, i.e. decision L of the production department, and an advertising campaign with an emphasis on price, i.e. decision N of the marketing department. In the course of time, the demand of the customer has become more differentiated. The difference between the payoffs belonging to N,L and V,H became smaller in the 1970s. This can be expressed in Fig. 14.4 by replacing the

Production Marketing	L	H
N	(7,7)	(–1,–1)
V	(–1,–1)	(5,5)

Figure 14.4: Car industry

payment (5,5) with (6,6). The trend towards more product differentiation continued. The difference between the payoffs belonging to N,L and V,H was no longer clear in the 1980s, which can be expressed by replacing (6,6) with (7,7). The company now had two equally attractive policies available. However, it is still of crucial importance that the decisions of both departments are co-ordinated. In the 1990s a wide range of products seemed essential. This situation can be represented in Fig. 14.4 by replacing (5,5) with (8,8).

Many markets have developed in such a way that V,H has become less undesirable, or even more desirable, than N,L. However, a problem may arise in the transition to V,H. Although both parties know that V,H is more desirable than N,L, both departments should switch at the same time from equilibrium N,L to equilibrium V,H. If only one department switches, then everybody suffers. However, switching simultaneously is difficult, because there are no instruments available to establish co-ordination. No department has an incentive to switch, as long as the other department does not. It is better to stick with N,L than to end up in N,H or V,L. This transition is of course even more difficult when more departments are involved.

This application highlights again the tension between the decisions taken in equilibrium and efficiency. It is sometimes claimed that everything which happens in reality is efficient. The above example is a counterexample to that statement. Chapter 2 regarded an equilibrium as a prediction of what will happen, and efficiency was formulated as an evaluation criterion. In Fig. 14.4, N, L as well as V,H are equilibria, but only N,L is efficient. Often, however, the switch from N,L to V,H will not occur without any problems. It is therefore possible that an inefficient equilibrium occurs.

14.2.2 Solutions for the co-ordination problem

A co-ordination problem is characterized by a multiplicity of equilibria. The solution to this problem involves reducing the number of equilibria to one. Guidance on the nature of solutions is again obtained by the various elements or ingredients in the formulation of the co-ordination problem. The game-theoretic formulation points towards the ingredients of a non-cooperative game for possible solutions. Four types of solutions are distinguished: generate additional information (Sec. 14.3), change the payoffs (Sec. 14.4), change the number of players (Sec. 14.5) and decrease the possibilities of choice (Sec. 14.6). They all boil down to changing the game in such a way that the new game has only one Nash equilibrium. Each type of solution will be illustrated with stylized examples and may seem sometimes abstract or even absurd. Examples are informing every member of an orchestra by way of prices about the desired tempo of playing and negotiating the right to pass an intersection. However, the attractiveness of these examples is that they show the variety of solutions which may be considered and how to discriminate between them on the basis of a few criteria. Chapter 15 applies these ideas to many company and market settings.

14.3 Generate additional information

The co-ordination problem is characterized by a lack of information, i.e. the two players decide simultaneously without either knowing the decision of the other. It seems obvious therefore to solve the co-ordination problem by generating additional information. This can be established in many ways. Examples are creating a common background, appointing a co-ordinator, establishing communication channels between various parties and so on.

14.3.1 Common background

Chapter 12 focused on processing and communicating information by specific departments or individuals. Problems arise here because of limited cognitive capacities compared with the complexity of the problem. Choices have to be co-ordinated not only between persons, but also between departments at the level of the organization. An organization cannot afford to store all possible information, nor to formulate a scenario for all possible situations. That would cost too much. Solutions consist of a limited number of rules and procedures which indicate roughly a desirable way of responding to a multitude of possible unforeseen circumstances. Creating a *common background* is an example of a possible solution.

Application: Driving on the left or right side of the road

Traffic situations are often characterized as a co-ordination problem. Consider the choice of side of the road. On the European continent, everyone drives on the right side, whereas in the United Kingdom and Ireland people drive on the left. It doesn't matter which side of the road one takes, as long as all other drivers do the same. The payoffs for all possible combinations of decisions are shown in Fig. 14.5. If either everyone drives on the left or everyone drives on the right, then everyone receives a payoff of 5. A crash yields everyone −10. This is a co-ordination problem because there is more than one equilibrium. The different drivers have no idea what the others will choose. Co-ordination on one specific equilibrium is established by the traffic regulations of a country.

Car 1 \ Car 2	L	H
L	(5,5)	(−10,−10)
R	(−10,−10)	(5,5)

Figure 14.15: Traffic co-ordination

Application: Quiz

Assume two Dutch people and two Australians participate in a quiz. They are given the names of six cities in the Netherlands: Assen (A), Breda (B), Eindhoven (E), Groningen (G), Leeuwarden (L) and Tilburg (T). The two Dutch persons are asked separately to divide these six cities in two groups of three. The Australians have to do the same. If two compatriots make the same division, then they win a prize. The situation is presented in Fig. 14.6. There are 10 possibilities of dividing 6 cities in 2 groups of 3. If both persons make the same division, then they both win a prize. In all other cases, they do not gain anything. This is a co-ordination problem because there is more than one equilibrium. (There are 10 equilibria in this example.) However, co-ordination on one equilibrium often occurs, despite the multiplicity of equilibria. Specific *common knowledge* of the persons involved frequently results in co-ordination on a specific equilibrium. For example, the common geographical knowledge of the Dutch participants will probably result in the grouping of Breda, Eindhoven and Tilburg in the south of the Netherlands and Assen, Groningen and Leeuwarden in the north. The probability of both Australians establishing co-ordination is lower, because they don't share the same geographical knowledge. The first Australian may choose an alphabetical order, whereas the second may choose a division based on the length of the names of the cities.

Person 1 \ Person 2	ABE	ABG	ABL	ABT	AEG	AEL	AET	AGL	AGT	ALT
ABE	(1,1)	(0,0)	(0,0)	(0,0)	(0,0)	(0,0)	(0,0)	(0,0)	(0,0)	(0,0)
ABG	(0,0)	(1,1)	(0,0)	(0,0)	(0,0)	(0,0)	(0,0)	(0,0)	(0,0)	(0,0)
ABL	(0,0)	(0,0)	(1,1)	(0,0)	(0,0)	(0,0)	(0,0)	(0,0)	(0,0)	(0,0)
ABT	(0,0)	(0,0)	(0,0)	(1,1)	(0,0)	(0,0)	(0,0)	(0,0)	(0,0)	(0,0)
AEG	(0,0)	(0,0)	(0,0)	(0,0)	(1,1)	(0,0)	(0,0)	(0,0)	(0,0)	(0,0)
AEL	(0,0)	(0,0)	(0,0)	(0,0)	(0,0)	(1,1)	(0,0)	(0,0)	(0,0)	(0,0)
AET	(0,0)	(0,0)	(0,0)	(0,0)	(0,0)	(0,0)	(1,1)	(0,0)	(0,0)	(0,0)
AGL	(0,0)	(0,0)	(0,0)	(0,0)	(0,0)	(0,0)	(0,0)	(1,1)	(0,0)	(0,0)
AGT	(0,0)	(0,0)	(0,0)	(0,0)	(0,0)	(0,0)	(0,0)	(0,0)	(1,1)	(0,0)
ALT	(0,0)	(0,0)	(0,0)	(0,0)	(0,0)	(0,0)	(0,0)	(0,0)	(0,0)	(1,1)

Figure 14.6: Co-ordination game

Application: Organizational culture and labour contracts

An example concerning the internal organization of enterprises is organizational culture. It is defined as a collection of common values, norms and practices of an organization. Employees of a company are often willing to make decisions in the interest of the company, but sometimes they just don't know what is the most desirable course of action. There is just not enough information to make the right decision. Schelling (1960) observes for such co-ordination problems that:

> What is necessary to coordinate predictions, to read the same message in the common situation, to identify the one course of action that their expectations of each other converge upon. They must 'mutually recognize' some unique signal that coordinates their expectations of each other. We cannot be sure they will meet, nor would all couples read the same signal, but the chances are certainly a great deal better than if they pursued a random course of search.

Organizational culture may play an important role in this context. One of the equilibria becomes special and stands out. It provides a

> clue for coordinating behaviour, some focal point for each person's expectation of what the other expects him to expect to be expected to do.

Organizational culture can serve as a guide for choice in unexpected circumstances. It creates a *focal point* and expresses the priorities of the organization. The members of the organization can use this knowledge in circumstances in which they do not know what is the best decision for the organization. The same considerations apply to the above quiz.

The relationship between a company and its employees can be described in terms of an incomplete contract. The specific rights are described in a labour contract, like the working hours and the type of work. However, it is too complicated to determine for each instance of time what has to be done. Work-to-rule actions use or misuse this contractual incompleteness. The company has the other rights, i.e. it decides in every unforeseen situation what should be done. This is desirable because explicit incentives by the employer can indicate which activities are desirable. However, it is too costly to intervene in each situation which differs from the specific rules. Employees might voluntarily take actions in the interest of the company. A company can try to establish co-ordination through an implicit direction of activities. One way to do so is to create an organizational culture which directs the activities of the employees in a desirable direction in situations where specific directions are not given (Kreps, 1990b). The company is viewed as a set of conventions, practices and norms, which co-ordinates the decisions of the members of the organization in circumstances with incomplete information.

Application: Organizational structure

The formal structure of an organization allocates the decision rights, but an informal structure always develops next to the formal one. An example is the choice of organizational structure. A *functional organizational structure* is set up round functions like marketing, financing and production. The power of this way of organizing lies in exploiting economies of scale. In such organizations one usually sees a culture dominated by engineers. A *divisional organizational structure* is oriented towards products, and is especially suitable to respond to changes in the market. The organizational culture is usually more influenced by the marketing professionals than by the engineers.

The number and nature of unexpected circumstances with which these two organizational structures are confronted differs significantly, and they will be responded to differently. This can be illustrated by the following example. Assume that unexpected circumstances are either technically or market-oriented. A functional organizational structure will hardly be confronted with technical surprises, but there will be many market uncertainties. The unexpected circumstances for a functional organization are therefore related mainly to market demand. The opposite holds for a divisional organizational structure. With this, unexpected circumstances are mainly of a technical nature, because it is focused on market demand. The formal organizational structure shapes the informal structure, and therefore determines the nature of the unexpected circumstances one is confronted with (Hammond, 1994).

Application: Strategic plan

An example of developing an organizational culture is formulating a strategic plan (Hendrikse, 1993). Such a plan formulates the objectives of an organization and some strategies to realize these objectives. Its formulation usually requires a lot of time and effort, yet the result often disappears into some archive without being implemented. One often wonders what has been the value of all the exertion. However, the strategic plan has played its role in the process of formulating the objectives and the ways in which they can be realized. Behaviour of the employees is to a certain extent directed by it and it serves as a guide for decisions in uncertain circumstances.

The above has emphasized the benefits of having a specific culture in solving co-ordination problems. However, an established culture has the disadvantage that it is hard to change. This may result in undesirable *rigidity* or inertia in situations subject to change.

14.3.2 Co-ordination mechanisms

The fundamental welfare theorem indicates that a system based on prices establishes a desirable allocation of goods and services in certain environments. Co-ordination based on prices gives every person individually the right incentives to achieve a good outcome. There is no contract planning involved. The need for information to take the right decisions is limited and local, i.e. knowledge of the preferences and the production technology of others is not necessary. All relevant information is reflected in the market prices.

Such a system of prices is in principle applicable to companies as well. However, a system of transfer prices is not often used to direct the allocation of means in organizations. Prices turn out to be rather sensitive to the local availability of information. A small change in the circumstances of one person has consequences for everyone. It is therefore unlikely that prices will serve their co-ordinating role well. Other possibilities have to be considered in order to establish co-ordination. The best way to induce the separate departments to take good decisions is to generate additional information by a co-ordination mechanism and use it locally. Management has to play an important role in this context. It is the integration or co-ordination of choices which makes a certain policy a coherent strategy.

There is no general theory which indicates which way of generating information is best in a specific situation. To be able to compare the various co-ordination mechanisms, a number of criteria have been established for the evaluation of co-ordination mechanisms. Milgrom and Roberts (1992) formulate the following:

1 The degree in which the co-ordination mechanism selects the efficient solution when information is complete.
2 The degree of simplicity of the co-ordination mechanism.
3 The degree of robustness of the co-ordination mechanism with respect to bad information.

Application: Orchestra

The co-ordination problem in an orchestra occurs because everyone has to decide individually regarding the tempo of playing, without the possibility of communication in order to establish co-ordination. The string players don't know what the players of wind instruments will do. The payoffs in Fig. 14.2 provide no indication for the string players regarding the tempo of the wind players. The same holds for the wind players. It is therefore possible that the string players think that the wind players will go for the equilibrium Slow, Slow, and will therefore choose a slow tempo themselves, whereas the wind players will in fact opt for the equilibrium Fast, Fast. This results in the payoffs (–1,–1). A *co-ordination mechanism* is needed to avoid such undesirable outcomes.

There are various co-ordination mechanisms. In Part II, the *price mechanism* was discussed in the context of markets. In principle, prices can be applied in an orchestra as well. However, establishing the right prices is not easy. One should take into account not only factors like the capabilities of the players, and the mental and physical health of every member of the orchestra, but also the impact of the prices for each member for the entire orchestra. In the terminology of Chapter 3, this entails every member of the orchestra informing the Walrasian auctioneer continuously regarding his preferences and capabilities. All these pieces of information are collected and co-ordinated by him. Subsequently, the conductor sends everyone a separate signal back by way of a price. This can be done by continuously posting for everyone on a large screen a list of prices regarding the tempo for every instance of the entire performance. Every member of the orchestra chooses his tempo based on these prices, where these prices might change frequently. Each player takes into account his capabilities and possibilities at every instant of time, and the information about the others being transmitted through prices. However, the tempo is not the only important variable. Variables like dynamics and colour of sound should also be priced for each member. Using the price mechanism in an orchestra is therefore cumbersome and complex.

Prices sometimes work well in markets in order to establish a desirable allocation, and could therefore also work well in an orchestra. The advantage of the price mechanism is that all the relevant information of each player is being processed when there is complete information. Therefore the price mechanism in an orchestra meets the first criterion of selecting the efficient solution when all the information is available. If there is complete information, then the price mechanism will establish co-ordination in the orchestra. However, the price mechanism doesn't meet the second criterion of simplicity. In a large orchestra, many prices are necessary for every relevant aspect at each instant of time. On top of that, during the play everything should be co-ordinated continuously by prices. The price mechanism is therefore rather complex in an orchestra.

Nor does the price mechanism meet the third criterion of robustness. It is not robust regarding wrong signals. It is difficult to continuously process changing information in prices without making mistakes. Small mistakes in the choice of the prices can disrupt the rhythm of the orchestra and have disastrous consequences. All these problems with the price mechanism entail such high costs, compared with the advantages of the price mechanism, that prices will not be chosen as an instrument to establish co-ordination in an orchestra.

In practice, a *conductor*, instead of the price mechanism, is used as the co-ordination mechanism. A conductor in an orchestra meets all three criteria. In a situation in which everything is clear, he or she does nothing. Besides, a good conductor can communicate a large number of different signals in a simple way by baton movement, hand gesture and facial expression. Finally, a conductor can handle changing circumstances in a flexible way. If we compare the price mechanism and the conductor, the latter is a better co-ordination mechanism. (Notice that a conductor is not always an efficient co-ordination mechanism. Central planning in Eastern European countries often created more problems than the price mechanism.)

Application: Rowing boat

A comparable problem occurs in a rowing boat. If the separate oars are moved at different stroke rates, they will clash and the boat will lose speed. Besides, the stroke rate for both starboard and port oars should be the same. If one side continuously rows faster, the boat will travel in a circle (or hit the bank). Here again one can try to establish co-ordination by means of prices, but the problems associated with this are so large that a (lightweight) coxswain is taken along to set the stroke rate. The choice of co-ordination mechanism is the same as in the previous example. Someone is appointed to determine the tempo or stroke rate directly, because co-ordination by price is too vulnerable. Besides, it is less complicated to report one variable to everyone at the same time than to make a price known to everyone individually.

Application: Prices versus quantities

It often occurs that the information regarding the optimal decision is ex ante not available to the persons involved. For example, various departments in a company do not know exactly how the consumer values a new product, what are the development problems of a new market or which possibilities a new technology embodies. The lack of all relevant information can result in decisions which are not aligned.

Weitzman (1974) compares planning based on prices with a system in which quantities are chosen. It is assumed that there is a two-stage decision process. First, the head office co-ordinates the activities of the operational department with those of other departments by either prices or quantities. Second, the operational department chooses a quantity which maximizes the departmental profits based on the instruction of the head office regarding price or quantity The situations of complete and incorrect information are considered.

Complete information

Planning based on *prices* is considered first. The head office determines a price which maximizes profits based on the available information. Equating marginal revenue (*MR*) with marginal costs (*MC*) determines the profit-maximizing *transfer price choice p** of the head office and results in a production level *E* by the operational department. This situation is presented in Fig. 14.7. The quantity *E* maximizes the producer surplus of the department, i.e. the difference between revenues and costs, which equals *p*BEO – CBEO = p*BC*. The consumer surplus, i.e. the difference between the willingness to pay and what is paid, equals *ABEO – p*BEO = ABp**. The result for the entire company equals the sum of the consumer and producer surplus (*ABC*).

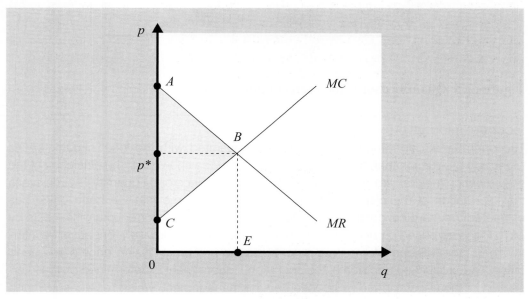

Figure 14.7: Transfer price choice and correct information

Planning based on *quantities* results in the same outcome when information is complete. From *MR* and *MC*, the head office instructs the operational department to produce *q**, and the department subsequently executes this order. Figure 14.8

illustrates this. (The difference between Figure 14.7 and Figure 14.8 is that p^* is replaced by D, i.e. there is no price determined by the head office when planning is based on quantities.) In a situation where the head office has the correct information at its disposal, it does not matter which planning tool – price or quantity – is used. Both instruments result in the same consumer and producer surplus, and therefore perform equally well on the first criterion for evaluating co-ordination mechanisms. Therefore, prices are not essential for co-ordination purposes in establishing an optimal allocation when there is complete information.

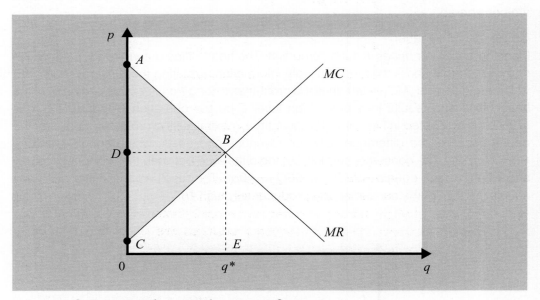

Figure 14.8: Quantity choice and correct information

Incorrect information

The operational department is often better acquainted with the local circumstances regarding production than the head office. It will now be shown that the efficiency of the co-ordination mechanism, whether co-ordination is by price or by quantity, is sensitive to the information at the disposal of the head office. Assume that the head office has estimated the marginal costs too low. Represent the wrong, incorrect marginal costs by MC'. Planning based on *prices* results in a price which is too low (p'), because the intersection of the MR and MC' curves determines the profit-maximizing price of the head office. The production decision of the operational department is determined by the intersection of the transfer price (p') chosen by the management, which replaces MR, and the *real* costs. This results in a production level which is too low.

The evaluation of the price instrument in the situation with incorrect information is again based on the sum of the consumer and producer surplus. This is based on the true marginal costs MC and MR, and equals $AKLC$ in Fig. 14.9. Compared with the situation with complete information, an amount of (consumer and producer surplus) $BC - AKLC = BKL$ is lost.

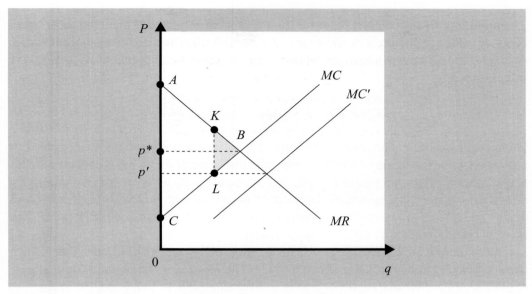

Figure 14.9: Transfer price choice and incorrect information

Planning based on *quantities* also results almost always in inefficient decisions in situations with incorrect information. Too low an estimate of the marginal costs results in a quantity instruction of the head office which is too high (q'). Figure 14.10 presents this situation. The head office chooses q' based on the point of intersection of MR and MC', and the operational department subsequently executes this order. The sum of the consumer and producer surplus equals (surplus) ABC reduced with (loss) BMN. Compared with the situation with complete information, the quantity tool in the situation with incomplete information entails a loss of the consumer and producer surplus equal to BMN.

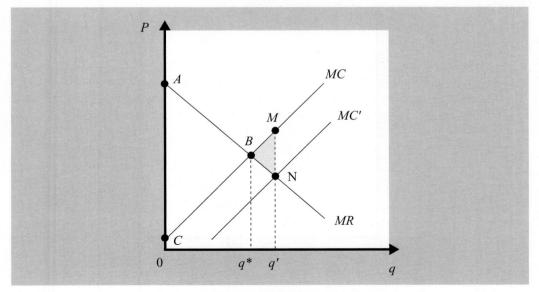

Figure 14.10: Quantity choice and incorrect information

Regarding the robustness criterion, the conclusion is that both planning tools entail costs. An efficient choice of co-ordination mechanism will minimize the loss of consumer and producer surplus. It can be shown that, *in case of uncertainty regarding the marginal costs*,

$$\frac{\text{Loss of price control}}{\text{Loss of quantity control}} = \left(\frac{\text{Slope } MR}{\text{Slope } MC}\right)^2.$$

Therefore, a co-ordination mechanism based on prices is preferred above quantity co-ordination when the slope of *MR* is smaller than the slope of *MC*. (Some caution with the use of this formula is required. First, the reverse holds when there is uncertainty regarding the marginal revenues. Second, in situations with increasing economies of scale, i.e. an *MC*-curve with a negative slope, it is of course inefficient to let the production be handled by different departments.)

The *fundamental welfare theorem* is associated with a system of prices. This follows directly from Fig. 14.11 and the above formula. The *MR* curve in a perfectly competitive market is horizontal because no one is individually able to influence the price, i.e. decision-makers are price-takers. Co-ordination based on prices results via the price p^*, determined by the intersection of the *MR* and the *MC'* curve, in the correct quantity (q^*), regardless of the uncertainty about *MC*. The loss of consumer and producer surplus equals zero. (The formula shows the same result because the slope of the *MR* curve equals zero.) Price information is sufficient for local departments or divisions to take the right decisions (in a decentralized way). The price instrument is therefore very robust regarding incorrect information in a perfectly competitive market. A co-ordination mechanism based on quantities results in the welfare loss *BMN*.

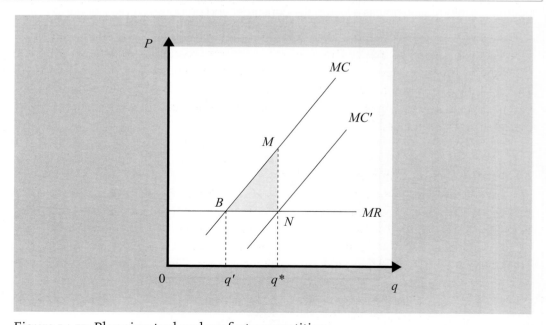

Figure 14.11: Planning tool and perfect competition

The above analysis shows a major difference between the situation with correct information and that with incorrect. If the head office has correct information, then an efficient outcome is established, regardless of the choice of co-ordination mechanism. The entire consumer and producer surplus is realized. In the situation with incorrect information, however, less than the whole surplus is usually realized. The best possible result in a situation with incomplete information has therefore often a *second-best* character. The observation that in situations with incomplete information the maximal surplus is often not possible, has been shown already several times in Parts III and IV. Besides, in situations with incomplete information, it appears to be important which co-ordination mechanism is chosen. The way in which this choice is determined depends on the specific situation, which is illustrated above.

Another aspect of this application is that the head office is assumed to formulate certain restrictions for the local departments. However, crucial information for good decision-making by management often resides with subordinates. One may wonder why management doesn't just ask for such information from the persons involved, so that they subsequently provide it; Parts III and IV formulated various reasons why this is problematic.

The issue of *optimal centralization* has been addressed in this application, because the (central) head office has to choose between a price and a quantity for the (decentralized) department. Part II specified the circumstances in the *fundamental welfare theorem* as well as in the *Coase theorem* in which decentralization results in a Pareto-efficient allocation. The result in this application regarding complete information indicates that decentralization is not necessarily preferred to centralization. Pareto efficiency can also be realized through centralization. It doesn't even matter whether prices or quantities are being used in the situation with complete information, i.e. they are equally good. There is no difference between decentralization and centralization in this representation. This is unsatisfactory, because one would rather see that the theory offers a clear prediction. Some elements are apparently lacking in the current setup such that a distinction can be made. The observations of Hayek (1945) mentioned in Chapter 3 should be seen in this context. Part IV focused on the difference between centralization and decentralization. It is repeatedly emphasized that it is not the difference between prices and quantities which is crucial for the decentralization decision, but the local availability of information.

Application: Hierarchies versus polyarchies

The choice between hierarchy and polyarchy discussed in Sec. 12.5 can also be evaluated with the three criteria. Both architectures score equally well on the criterion of efficiency when information is complete. If it is known which project is good and which project is bad, i.e. $p(P) = 1$ and $p(-L) = 0$, then both decision procedures result in the same outcomes. The decision procedures also cannot be distinguished on the criterion of simplicity. Both bureaus in each architecture have to evaluate an equal amount of projects. Finally, the third criterion of robustness regarding bad information turned out to be decisive in the choice of the decision procedure.

14.4 Change the payoffs

Nash equilibrium is determined by comparing the payoffs associated with the various strategies. If the payoffs are such that there is more than one Nash equilibrium, then there may be possibilities of restructuring the payoffs in such a way that exactly one equilibrium remains.

Application: Collective health insurance

An employer considers buying collective health insurance for his employees. Everyone is currently privately insured. The attractive feature of collective insurance is that the employer and the employee can expect a large premium discount when everyone participates. However, the problem is that any one employee doesn't know the participation decision of the others. Figure 14.12 presents the situation. There is a co-ordination problem because there is more than one Nash equilibrium: everyone insures collectively or everyone insures privately.

Employee 2 Employee 1	Collective	Private
Collective	(10,10)	(−1,1)
Private	(−1,−1)	(1,1)

Figure 14.12: Collective health insurance

In this example, it is possible to change the payoffs in a budget-neutral way such that the only Nash equilibrium entails the unanimous choice for the collective insurance contract. For example, privately insured employee 2 pays a bonus of 3 to employee 1 when employee 1 switches from private to collective insurance. Figure 14.13 presents this proposal, i.e. the payoffs 10 and −1 of player 1 change in 13 and 2 and the payoffs 10 and 1 of player 2 change in 7 and −2.

Employee 2 Employee 1	Collective	Private
Collective	(13,7)	(−2,−2)
Private	(1,−1)	(1,1)

Figure 14.13: Changed payoffs in the insurance problem

Application: Standardization

For several goods and services, *standardization* of certain parts is important to the persons concerned. If everyone handles parts in the same way, important benefits are realized. Think of light bulb fittings, the size of records and CDs, the composition of word processing packages, the voltages of power supplies (110 or 220 V), the layouts of the keyboard of a typewriter or personal computer (qwerty or Dvorak), organizational cultures (technical or marketing-oriented) and economic systems (market- or central-planning-oriented). In this application some aspects of co-ordination regarding standards will be addressed..

Assume that for each person a benefit function can be formulated which indicates on the one hand the individual desirability of a certain standard, and on the other how the number of other persons preferring the same standard is valued. This last aspect, i.e. the size of the network, makes choices interdependent. An important assumption is that, regardless of which standard is chosen, a standard is valued more highly as more people choose the same one. This is called a *positive network externality*. The telephone system is an example. Buying a telephone is more attractive when more people have a connection. If such considerations of *compatibility*, or in another context social pressure, are important in choosing, then the choice of early adopters can influence the decision of others. If person 1 adopts a new standard, it becomes more attractive for person 2 to change than had person 1 not switched. A *critical mass* (Schelling, 1978) emerges that continuously reinforces a process of change once it has been initiated.

As has been shown already with the prisoners dilemma, choices by individuals do not necessarily have to lead to a desirable outcome. The interdependency of choices may result in an inefficient standard. If everyone can anticipate perfectly how everyone else will respond to a certain choice, then there will never be an inferior standard if a better alternative is available. The efficient standard is chosen because everyone knows that it is the best and that it can be realized. However, such information is not usually available. Important network externalities regarding the current standard may cause too much *inertia*. One can be stuck with an inferior standard, while a better alternative is available. The problem is that no one can be sure that if they switch to a new standard others will follow. Incomplete information may result in co-ordination problems, i.e. a new standard may not be adopted, even though everyone prefers it to the current one. Such situations occur when everyone prefers the new standard a little bit more than the old one but not enough to provide anyone with the incentive to be the first to switch. People follow only when enough others have paved the way. Farrell and Saloner (1985) characterize this situation as follows:

> All persons are fencesitters, happy to jump on the bandwagon if it gets rolling but insufficiently keen to set it rolling themselves.

Making an undesirable standard disappear can be speeded up by *replacing* a person who supports a change only reluctantly with a fierce proponent. A strong proponent will support the new standard, regardless of the decisions of others. The old standard then becomes less desirable to everyone adhering to it, which may be sufficient to get them all to switch to the new one. Examples of this comparative statics result are firing some current employees, hiring new personnel and imprisoning or even executing key figures in revolutions. Another way to reduce the co-ordination problem is of course to improve the *communication* between the different parties. Communication changes everyone's personal perception or estimation of the response of others to a change. This may solve the problem to a certain extent, but will not solve it completely.

The time needed to establish a change from one standard to the other has not been discussed so far. The presence of an established standard may result in *inertia*, even with complete information. Arrow (1974) observes that:

> Even if experience has shown the unexpectedly undesirable consequences of a commitment, the past may continue to rule the present.

If a new standard has to be developed with new persons or organizations, delays occur because of the time needed for enough new followers to arrive. A new critical mass of people adhering to the new standard has to develop. These observations imply that the history of an organization is important in the development of a standard. The choices made by the founders influence the behaviour of those who follow. On the other hand, it is also possible that there is too much *momentum*, i.e. too strong an inclination to the new standard (Farrell and Saloner, 1986).

The appearance of people who adopt a new culture or standard entails two externalities. First, it has consequences for those adhering to the old standard. Their standard is no longer spreading and becomes relatively less attractive. Second, an early adopter of the new standard makes this standard more attractive for those who decide later. If the new standard has to be nourished mainly by adopters of the old standard, delays are caused by the time it takes to stimulate them to switch.

Application: Team theory

In every company, many decisions have to be made, which requires a lot of information collection and processing. The limited cognitive capacities of individuals make it impossible to comprehend every piece of relevant information. However, many people are employed in a organization, which offers possibilities for organizing information beneficially. The *law of comparative advantages* indicates that the information processing capacity of a group of managers can be used best by having managers specialize in different tasks. These different tasks, however, are the main cause of failures of co-ordination between managers. The choice of an organization therefore entails a tradeoff between the specialized use of information and the necessity to co-ordinate the activities of the managers.

Companies collect tremendous amounts of data every day, but most decisions are based only on a small part of this information. It is not necessary for all available information to be taken into account in every decision. For most problems, a limited amount of information is already sufficient for a reasonably good decision. On the other hand, different decisions usually require different information. *Team theory* (Marschak and Radner, 1972) analyses the efficient decentralization of information (and information processing) to different managers and the way in which co-ordination between individuals with different information is established. A team consists of a number of decision-makers (managers, divisions) who have a common goal and are continuously in touch with the head office. They have to handle different problems and use different information. Solving a specific problem with team theory entails establishing an organization structure based on two steps. First, the main office divides the tasks (problems, decision variables) and the required information among the team members. Second, the main office determines the efficient decision rules (planning) for the divisions, based on this allocation of tasks and information.

The standard backward induction procedure of solving a problem is to start with the second decision, i.e. the characterization of the efficient decision rule. Therefore, assume a certain allocation of tasks and information has been made. Every manager takes a decision based on this information and within the setting of his or her task. The organization indicates the way this should be done in order to co-ordinate the different activities. This implies that, on the basis of the *efficient decision rule* chosen by the organization, the manager takes a decision which depends on the signals (information) he or she receives. It can be shown that for concave payment or utility functions a decision rule exists which is optimal both for the manager and for the organization or team.

The application of 'prices versus quantities' in the previous section is an illustration. A central planner and only one operational department have been considered, where the main office can choose (only) between prices and quantities (Arrow, 1985). Subsequently the operational department has to take a decision, based on the decision rule of the main office and the local information. Normally, there are of course many operational departments and the problem is to formulate decision rules which co-ordinate the different departments. The result mentioned above simplifies this problem considerably, because it indicates that it is sufficient for the optimal solution that this problem is solved for each department.

This solution of the second stage means that the response to each possible allocation of tasks and information is known. (The efficient decision rule has been determined for each possible allocation.) The optimal allocation of tasks and information will now be determined in the first stage. A general result regarding the first stage in team theory concerns the comparison of information systems. An information system x is more valuable than information system y if x is more informative than y. Being more *informative* means that the information generated by the system is less uncertain than that generated by the other system.

An example of the optimal allocation of tasks and information is 'management by exception', where the value of a specific variable, or a certain pattern, is reported to a higher level in the organization only in exceptional cases. For example, the state of equipment or machines in a certain unit is reported to the manager only when there is a massive breakdown with major consequences for the entire production. 'Management by exception' is a way of organizing which may result in considerable benefits regarding collecting, communicating, storing and processing information. Team theory is an interesting conceptualization of various informational problems, but its use in actual situations has been limited. Take for example the important accounting problem regarding the aggregation of information. An important task of a *reporting or information system* is compressing the available information. The above result indicates that no information is lost as long as the reporting system is a sufficient statistic, i.e. a number summarizing all the relevant information. However, it is clear that reporting systems do much more in reality than compressing information. Relevant information is lost because of the costs associated with processing and transferring information, which are often due to *limited rationality*. In practice, this has two implications at the level of the individual. First, the relevant information needs to be selected. Because of time pressure, this is often a problem in situations with too much as well as too little information. Here reporting systems may play a key role. They aggregate information in such a way that decision-makers have only to focus on a limited number of variables. The second aspect concerns taking a decision, which may consume a lot of time. The game of chess is an example of a decision problem with a simple structure which requires a lot of time. Both aspects imply that the decision-maker has to make a tradeoff between the quality of the information and the process of decision-making on the one hand and the costs of improvements on the other (Simon, 1976).

Application: Bounded cognition and information processing

It is impossible for one person to consider all the decisions and the associated information in an organization. The previous application showed how different decisions can be decentralized on the basis of different information. In team theory, the organization of the execution of decisions is highlighted. However, managers not only spend time on the execution of decisions, but also devote considerable amounts of it to processing and interpreting information. Hardly any attention is paid to the costs associated with processing and collecting large amounts of information in team theory, i.e. complete rationality is assumed. In situations with limited rationality, the costs of information processing have to be addressed.

According to Radner (1992), the costs of processing information are related to the observation of the data, the capacities and numbers of the information processors, the communication network which transfers the data and the delay between the observation of the data and the implementation of the decision or decisions. Besides, the process of information processing is so elaborate that the participation of many individuals is inevitable. This raises the question of the optimal organization of information processing. Geanakoplos and Milgrom (1991) explicitly take into account not only the costs but also the benefits of information processing. In the sense that they cannot process all information well, managers possess only limited rationality. It turns out to be desirable in such situations to focus the attention of managers on only a limited number of tasks. *Specialization* means that a full-time manager is much more productive than two part-time ones. The full-timer has more information at his disposal when a decision has to be taken, avoids duplication in collecting and processing information, and aligns a larger number of activities without needing other people. Although the benefits of specialization are realized by focusing the attention of the management, a *co-ordination problem* arises as well. This can be solved by allocating a co-ordinating task to higher-level managers. Besides some characteristics of the activities of individual managers in a specific position in the hierarchy, the allocation of managers to the different positions is considered as well. Managers differ regarding their capacities to process information. It turns out that situations with serial decision-making are the most suitable in which to place the most qualified manager at the top. In a hierarchy the costs of management rise exponentially, because more decisions are slowed down by an additional layer in the organization, and eventually the benefits of adding additional management layers in the organization decrease to zero. This approach means therefore that the optimal size of a hierarchy is limited. Finally, managers with more talent do better in situations which are more uncertain and difficult to comprehend. This will often be the case in relatively new industries.

14.5 Create one decision-maker

Problems of co-ordination occur when several parties are involved in the decision-making process. Such problems can be eliminated by somehow reducing the number of persons involved.

Application: Part-time working

A classic example of a co-ordination problem is part-time working. The introduction of part-time work means that a job which until now has been done by one person will henceforth be performed by two. This creates issues like dividing the work between the two parties during the week, and the communication of information. However, all the relevant information cannot be transmitted perfectly. Transmission will result inevitably in duplication or delay.

Figure 14.14 presents the stylized situation where employees are asked separately which part of the week they want to work. This causes a problem when both employees choose the same part of the week. This is represented by the payoffs (−1,−1) in the upper left and lower right cells. The attractive outcomes are Nash equilibria. They consist of the choice 'First half' by one player and 'Second half' by the other. Working part-time is characterized as a co-ordination problem because there is more than one Nash equilibrium.

Employee 2 Employee 1	First half	Second half
First half	(−1,−1)	(1,1)
Second half	(1,1)	(−1,−1)

Figure 14.14: Working part-time

> One solution for the problem of co-ordination in working part-time is obvious. When working part-time is prohibited co-ordination by the part-time workers is not needed. A full-time employee takes care of the activities which are otherwise done by two people working half a week. Figure 14.15 presents the situation in which working part-time is not allowed.

| Full-time employee 1 | 2 |

Figure 14.15: Part-time work prohibited

14.6 Reduce the number of choices

The fourth solution to the co-ordination problem deals with the number of choices available to the various players. If fewer choices are available, then the co-ordination problem is less severe. This can be done by eliminating choices (Sec. 14.6.1) or by imposing certain choices (Sec. 14.6.2).

14.6.1 Eliminate choice possibilities

One drastic way of solving the co-ordination problem is by allowing the various parties just one option, i.e. reduce the number of choice possibilities to one. There remains only one possible combination of decisions for the players, which is also the unique Nash equilibrium.

Application: Working part-time

In the application of working part-time, the employer can decide in advance that there is a vacancy for someone during the first half of the week and a vacancy for someone during the second half of the week. There is no co-ordination problem when the employees are not allowed to choose when to work. Figure 14.16 presents this situation.

Employee 1 \ Employee 2	Second half
First half	(1,1)

Figure 14.16: No choice regarding working part-time

14.6.2 Imposing choices

A second possible way to reduce the number of equilibria to one is to impose a choice on each player.

Application: Dispatching taxis

The problem of assigning a taxi to a passenger is that on the one hand the passenger has to be served as soon as possible, i.e. *delay* has to be prevented, and on the other hand there is a need to prevent unnecessary *duplication* of taxi rides. In principle, one can determine which taxi is most appropriate for a specific passenger on the basis of a system of *prices*. However, the problem is that wrong prices may result in unnecessary delay or duplication, as shown in Fig. 14.17. Too low a price results in both drivers staying away (A), so that the passenger has to wait. Unnecessary duplication is the result of a price which is too high. Both drivers go for the ride (G), while there is only one passenger. It will be obvious that these situations cannot be an equilibrium. The other two possibilities, taxi 1 chooses G and taxi 2 chooses A, and taxi 1 chooses A and taxi 2 chooses G, are Nash equilibria.

Taxi 1 \ Taxi 2	G	A
G	(−1,−1)	(3,1)
A	(0,3)	(−1,−1)

Figure 14.17: Duplication versus delay

The problem consists again of reducing the number of equilibria to one. Prices are rather sensitive to wrong information and do not seem appropriate as a co-ordination mechanism in such a situation. They are not sufficiently robust when faced with wrong information and require too much communication, i.e. a price for each taxi, to function well. Thus more direct ways of allocating taxis to passengers, like a taxi dispatcher, are often chosen. For example, taxi 1 is assigned to the ride (Fig. 14.18). The dispatcher is usually continuously in touch with the drivers, but still doesn't always know all relevant circumstances. Examples are local traffic jams, the state of the taxi and the type of passenger.

Taxi 1 \ Taxi 2	A
G	(3,0)

Figure 14.18: Allocation of taxis

Application: Democratic versus dictatorial decision-making

Decentralized systems often have difficulties in handling huge new challenges or problems. Centralization becomes more attractive when local information is less important and co-ordination more so (Bolton and Farrell 1990). Compare this with market systems in times of peace and war. Decentralization is advocated in peacetime, whereas the army is in control, i.e. there is centralization, during wartime. Besides, decentralized systems are often not capable of handling urgent situations adequately. Centralization is a better way to prevent *delay* or *duplication*.

Application: Organization of research and development

Van Cayseele (1987) analyses the internal organization of the research and development (R&D) department. The costs of *duplication* of research efforts and the speed with which new products are developed are considered. In American companies, R&D activities are supervised at a high level in the organization. This has the advantage that there is no duplication. However, the disadvantage is that *delay* occurs. Such an organization doesn't minimize the costs when rapid innovations are required. In Japanese companies, innovations are supervised at the level of the business units. Although there is duplication of activities between business units, the R&D activities are executed faster and more flexibly as a result of the mutual communication.

Application: Traffic lights

The organizational problem in the application of crossing the intersection (Sec. 14.2.1 above) consists of establishing co-ordination, which means that both drivers focus on the same equilibrium. The aim is to reduce the number of equilibria to exactly one. Traffic on an intersection can be co-ordinated in many ways. One can sell the right to cross the intersection first. This can be done by an auction or by *negotiation*. An advantage of such systems is that those in a hurry will probably pass the intersection first, and the others will receive a compensation for waiting. However, this co-ordination mechanism imposes many practical and organizational problems. First, a lot of time is consumed by these co-ordination mechanisms. Besides, implementing the auction, or negotiation, outcome may entail problems. The winner can cross first and leave without paying, or the other can collect the compensation and then pass the intersection. The traffic co-ordination problem is usually solved with *traffic rules*. Generally, the rigid rule of 'Traffic from the right has priority' applies. If one road is much the busier, it can be given the status of 'major road' or 'priority road'. Another possible way to resolve traffic problems is to deploy a *traffic agent* to decide, according to the traffic density on the various access roads, who can pass the intersection first. This can reduce the average waiting time per car considerably. However, it also entails a number of important objections. The safety of the agent can be threatened and it is costly to install one at each intersection. Besides, there is always the danger of nepotism. A solution to some of these problems is to install *traffic lights*, where some priority is assigned to the fire brigade, police and ambulance service. An advantage of this rigid method is its simplicity.

14.7 Conclusion

The co-ordination problem is characterized as a situation with two or more Nash equilibria. Reducing the number of equilibria to one solves the co-ordination problem. Four solutions have been formulated for solving the co-ordination problem: generating additional information, changing the payoffs, decreasing the number of choice possibilities and reducing the number of players. The concept of co-ordination will be used in the next chapter to characterize organizations as system of attributes.

14.8 Exercises

14.1 A Is there a co-ordination problem in Exercise 5.1?
      B Formulate a solution for this problem.

14.2 Two students arrive at the coffee machine at the same time. Each wants of a cup of coffee. Like many coffee machines, this one can only serve one person at a time.
      A What type of problem is presented here: a hidden characteristics problem, a hidden action problem or a co-ordination problem?
      B With which three criteria could a possible solution be evaluated?
      C Illustrate these criteria with two possible co-ordination mechanisms for the coffee machine problem.

14.3 The application 'prices versus quantities' in Sec. 14.3.2 addresses the situation with incorrect information regarding marginal costs. Illustrate with a figure (or prove mathematically) that

$$\frac{\text{Loss } p - \text{instrument}}{\text{Loss } q - \text{instrument}} = \left(\frac{\text{Slope } MC}{\text{Slope } MR}\right)^2,$$

when there is uncertainty regarding the MR (Milgrom and Roberts, 1992).

14.4 The head office of a company co-ordinates the input decisions of its divisions by using either a price instrument or a quantity instrument. Assume the MC curve of a division has a slope of 3 and the MR curve has a slope curve of -1. The head office has complete information about the MC curve of the division, but has made too optimistic an estimate of the MR curve. Divisions have complete information regarding their MC and MR curves. They choose a quantity that maximizes profits, taking into account the choice of instruments of the head office.
      A Which three criteria are used to evaluate the price and quantity instruments?
      B Which instrument is least sensitive with respect to the wrong information? Illustrate your answer with figures.
      C Which instrument is best according to the three criteria?

14.5 Decentralized profit centres of banks handle credit loans. The board of directors co-ordinates the local decision-making either by the interest rate of credit or by setting a credit limit per person. The level of the MC is constant and known centrally. However, a good understanding of the demand for credit is lacking because this is determined partly by the bargaining capabilities of the specific division.

  A Is there an incentive problem between the board of directors and the profit centres? Explain your answer.

  B Present the above situation graphically.

  C Would you advise the head office to co-ordinate by setting a credit limit? Explain your answer graphically.

14.6 A company has decided to co-ordinate its activities centrally. The only decision left to be made by the head office is directing local units on the basis of prices or quantities.

  A Which instrument is most robust against mistakes if the head office has complete information regarding the circumstances of the local company units? Explain your answer with a figure.

A local unit often has better information at its disposal than the head office. Assume that the costs are estimated too high by the head office, that the company uses a technology with constant returns to scale and that there are no competitors in the market.

  B Show in one figure the marginal revenues, marginal costs and the incorrect marginal costs.

  C Is it best to co-ordinate on the basis of prices or quantities? Explain your answer and illustrate it with a figure.

14.7 Is the price mechanism an optimal instrument of co-ordination in the (Arrow–Debreu) model of Chapter 3 which is the basis of the fundamental welfare theorem, given that there is uncertainty regarding the *MC*? Illustrate your answer with a figure.

14.8 The software company GCM develops software for various attributes of a firm, like marketing, production and human resources policies. The development of new software for each separate attribute is based on 'best practice', i.e. the it starts with software which has performed well somewhere else in the past.

  A Define the co-ordination problem and formulate four possible solutions.

  B How is a company conceptualized from a co-ordination perspective?

  C Is the development policy of GCM on the basis of 'best practice' to be recommended from a co-ordination perspective? Explain your answer.

  D Would you advise that the new software be implemented for the various aspects one after another? Explain your answer.

15 Complementarity

LEARNING OBJECTIVES

After completing this chapter, you should understand:

- The concept of the firm in this chapter and its managerial implications.

- A number of principles driving coherence in organizations.

- The problems with gradual change of organizations, and 'best practice' in them.

Contents

427

15.1 Introduction

Firms are complex mechanisms for co-ordinating and motivating the activities of individuals. They have to deal with a much richer variety of attributes and problems than simply the provision of investment incentives and the resolution of hold-ups discussed in Part IV.

An organization consists of many attributes (activities). Examples of attributes are production technology, marketing, logistics, organization, supply systems, communication networks, personnel, accounting, relationships with suppliers, financing and reward systems. This way of viewing organizations implies that the organization is conceptualized as a system of attributes (Fig. VII.2), which can be made precise by using the concept of the co-ordination problem. Attributes are related to each other and have to be aligned with each other. The alignment of the various attributes is an important managerial task, as was already indicated by Fayol (1916):

> To manage is to forecast and plan, to organize, to command, to co-ordinate and to control.

Many ideas and examples in this part have in common the idea that the different parts of an organization make each other more productive. There is synergy between the different parts and everything is connected. Nowadays, synergy is referred to as *complementarity* (Milgrom and Roberts, 1990c). Complementarity means that doing more of one activity increases the return from doing more of the other activity. If only a few activities are aligned, then not all benefits of change are realized. In other words, changes are complementary if the sum of the benefits of doing each separately is less than the benefit of doing both together. Therefore, changes in complementary activities have their desired effects only when both activities are changed. The notion of complementarity applies to activities as well as to incentive instruments.

Sound organizational design requires *organizational consistency or coherence*, i.e. the firm must ensure that each attribute complements the others and that there are no contradictions among them. Notice that there is no single 'best' best design, i.e. there are multiple equilibria, because the optimal design depends on the alignment between strategy and organization. Coherence or co-ordination is regarded as important because it captures that the entire design hangs together. These theoretical insights are backed by empirical studies (Holmström and Milgrom, 1994; Athey and Stern, 1996; Ichniowski *et al.*, 1997; Bresnahan *et al.*, 2002).

Various principles of alignment are highlighted in this chapter, like the contractual externalities in the equal compensation principle (15.2), the law of large numbers (15.3), orthogonality (15.4) and influence costs (15.5). The switch from one coherent system of attributes to another system of attributes is driven by exogenous technological or demand forces, like repeated interaction considerations (15.6), the costs of trade expansion (15.7) and stability of the environment (15.8). Some of the difficulties in changing from one system of attributes to another, as well as the desirability of simultaneous change of all attributes, are addressed in Sec. 15.9. Section 15.10 concludes.

15.2 The equal compensation principle

An organization has to make choices regarding its various attributes, like its organization structure, communication channels, number of layers and so on. Jobs and/or functions can also be interpreted as a system of attributes. Assume for simplicity that the job of a physiotherapist has only three attributes: task freedom, degree of piece-rate wages and ownership of assets. Assume also that these three attributes can only take two values: small versus large, low versus high, no versus complete. This results in eight possible organizational forms, or types of jobs, of a physical therapist. Figure 15.1 illustrates this.

	A	B	C	D	E	F	G	H
Task freedom	S	S	S	S	L	L	L	L
Piece rate	L	L	H	H	L	L	H	H
Ownership	N	C	N	C	N	C	N	C

Figure 15.1: Possible organizational forms regarding the physical therapist

The viability of each of these eight possible compositions of the system of attributes of a physiotherapist will now be addressed. The composition of the system of attributes of a physiotherapist working in a hospital differs substantially from that of an independent physical therapist, i.e. the rights and duties of a physiotherapist differ substantially between these two systems of attributes (Simon, 1951; Hart, 1995). A *physiotherapist in a hospital* is an employee, i.e. the employer determines the working methods and hours, owns the equipment and pays a wage which is hardly related to the number of treatments. This composition of the system of attributes is represented by SLN in Fig. 15.1. An *independent physiotherapist* is his or her own employer. It means that he or she owns the equipment, chooses the working methods and schedule, and earns money on the basis of the number of treatments. This composition is represented by LHC in Fig. 15.1. These two compositions of the system of attributes regarding a physiotherapist are the only two stable clusters of attributes, i.e. only compositions SLN and LHC are Nash equilibria.

The value of a choice regarding an attribute in a cluster or system depends on the choice regarding the other attributes. Many compositions are not Nash equilibria. If a certain composition is not a Nash equilibrium, then the complementarities in the system are not brought to value. One or more attributes must be changed in order to generate more value. The motivation for the change can be based on the *equal compensation principle* (Sec. 6.3). For example, it is not sensible to base the wage of a hospital physiotherapist on the number of treatments, while the hospital owns the equipment. The equal compensation principal indicates that such a composition of the system of attributes goes at the expense of hard-to-measure activities, like good maintenance and sensible handling of equipment. This is problematic because not the physiotherapist but the hospital owns the equipment. This is different for the independent physiotherapist. Payment based on the number of treatments is no problem for the maintenance of the equipment in this composition of the system of attributes, because the physiotherapist owns the equipment. The owner will take care of his or her equipment. A fixed salary for an independent physiotherapist is not desirable, because too much attention would be paid to maintenance of equipment and too little to treatment of patients. Stronger incentives seem appropriate in this situation. Regarding the attribute of task freedom, it is not sensible to give a hospital physiotherapist freedom regarding his or her presence. This will go at the expense of important but-hard-to-measure activities for the organization.

This section concludes with three observations. First, the example of the physiotherapist illustrates the claim that 'There is no one best way to organize.' However, this does not mean that everything can and will be stable. Only 2 of the 8 compositions turn out to be stable. They are known as 'make' for the hospital hiring physiotherapists and 'buy' for the hospital using outside or independent physiotherapists. This is shown in Fig. 15.2. The governance structure 'make' is the hierarchical employer–employee relationship, where the employer owns the assets, pays a fixed wage and determines the task assignments and working hours. This is the physiotherapist employed by the hospital, i.e. composition SLN. The governance structure 'buy' is associated with outsourcing, like an independent physiotherapist. This is composition LHC in Fig. 15.1. The physiotherapist owns the equipment, receives a piecerate wage and determines his or her own tasks and working hours. The specific situation determines which composition is most desirable.

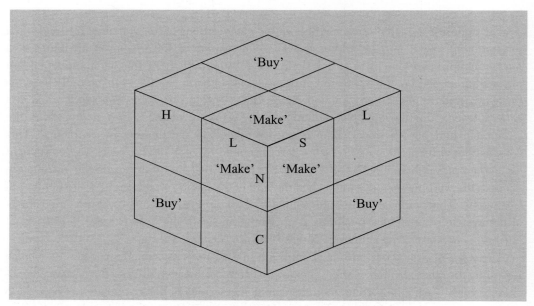

Figure 15.2: A system with three attributes

Second, the precise labels of the attributes in the system are not always straightforward, and often depend on the perspective taken. For example, an alternative way to formulate the attributes of a governance structures is by the following attributes: incentive intensity (High or Low), administrative controls (None or Many) and contract law regime (Legalistic or Forbearance/Fiat). Williamson (2003) characterizes the market with HNL and the hierarchy with LMF. Third, the driving force behind coherence in the system of attributes in this section is the uniform compensation principle. It integrates the agency model of Part III with the theory of property rights allocation of Part IV.

Application: The role of the head office

Just as functions can be viewed as systems of tasks, organizations can be viewed as a system of attributes. The head office of an organization has to make a choice regarding its management structure (centralized versus decentralized), the evaluation criteria for the business units (strategic versus financial) and the diversification strategy (low versus high). Empirical research, based on a large number of Dutch companies (van Oijen, 1997), demonstrates that there are two successful compositions of this cluster. A central management structure, strategic criteria and limited diversification turn out to be an aligned entity. Strategic management fits with limited diversification of activities, because the head office will interfere extensively in the divisions in order to establish the intended synergy between the different business units. In short, concentrating on the core activities argues for a larger head office in order to realize the complementarities in the small portfolio of activities.

Companies engaged in many activities, i.e. which are highly diversified, should hardly be managed by the head office. A small head office with a financial management style, i.e. formulating a limited number of criteria regarding return on investment, turns out to do best in this situation. The number of possible synergies is so large that extensive central management would entail too costly an expansion of the head office.

15.3 Law of large numbers

Companies have to take decisions regarding their delivery policy as well as their assortment. A problem is that demand is often not known exactly. The uncertainty regarding demand can be dealt with by two delivery policies. *Make to order* means that a buyer has indicated what he or she wants and has placed an order. Higher prices can be asked because the specific wishes of consumers are addressed. Another possibility is *make to stock*. Production occurs without additional information regarding demand, and deliveries are made as long as they are in stock. The advantage of the first method is that demand is known and size of production batches can be based on it. However, collecting this information is costly. Producing to stock doesn't entail these costs, but has as a disadvantage that either too much or too little is produced.

A company has also to take decisions regarding its product range. A small or a large range can be chosen. The advantage of a small one is that economies of scale can be exploited by adopting a rigid production technology geared towards a few products. The rigidity of the production technology entails that sometimes too much, sometimes too little is produced. Delivery will be to stock. A large assortment requires a different production technology. In a large assortment, regular production switches make a flexible production technology necessary. This technology is usually expensive, but it has the advantage that specific consumer wishes can be honoured. This usually results in higher prices. Production is to order because the flexible production technology makes it possible to respond to specific consumer wishes. Figure 15.3 shows these two aligned clusters of attributes in the usual way.

Assortment / Delivery	To stock	To order
Small	Rigid technology	
Large		Flexible technology

Figure 15.3: Choice of assortment and delivery policy

Milgrom and Roberts (1988b) show that the profit-maximizing planning of production is never a combination of production to order and production to stock. The profit-maximizing strategy is to produce either completely to order or completely to stock. The reason is that pooling the uncertain demand of customers offers advantages. The well-known *law of large numbers* says that the uncertainty regarding the mean of a sample decreases when the size of the sample increases, i.e. uncertainty regarding the quantity demanded decreases when the market is larger. Production to stock becomes advantageous because it is accompanied by scale economies regarding uncertainty. This implies that when it is already beneficial to deliver partly out of stock and partly to order, then it is even more attractive to deliver either more out of stock and less to order, or the reverse. Repeating this line of thought implies that the most advantageous policy is to produce either completely to order or completely to stock.

The comparative statics analysis demonstrates that production to stock is more attractive when

- The costs of production, like costs of interest and storage, decrease;
- Prices are lower;
- The market is larger;
- The costs of market research are higher;
- Demand is less uncertain.

The optimal product range or assortment is linked with the way production responds to market information. A large set of products is associated with high prices because the specific wishes of customers need to be fulfilled, but the fixed costs increase as a result of setting up many different product lines, or regularly readjusting the more expensive flexible production technology. Besides, effects of pooling are not realized because of the smaller market for each product separately.

This section has characterized organizations by two attributes: inventory and assortment policy. Real organizations have of course many attributes, but some of these are more important in one market than in others. The choice of these attributes drives the choice of others. A more elaborate specification of attributes when mass production is compared with lean production is presented in Fig. 15.4 (Milgrom and Roberts, 1995, p. 234).

Dimensions	Mass production *Transfer lines, specialization, and economies of scale*	Lean manufacturing *Flexibility, rapid responses, and economies of scope*
Capital equipment	Specialized	Flexible (low setup costs)
Production runs	Long runs, large lot sizes	Short runs, small lot sizes
Product changes	Infrequent	Frequent
Markets	Mass markets	Targeted markets
Worker skills	Low or specialized	High, with cross training
Decision-making	Central expertise and hierarchic planning	Local information and self-regulation
Communications	Primarily vertical	Primarily horizontal
Product development	Sequential	Cross-functional teams
Operational focus	Static optimization	Continuous improvement
Day-to-day emphasis	Accent on volume	Accent on quality
Inventories	High	Low
Managing uncertainty	Supply management	Demand management
Customer relations	Make-to-stock, limited communications	Make-to-order, extensive communications
Supplier relations	Short-term, price-based	Long-term, competency based
Vertical integration	High	Low
Employee relations: factory workers	Low commitment, confrontational	High commitment, cooperative

Figure 15.4: Mass production versus lean manufacturing

Application: Publishers

The publishing industry of the eighteenth and nineteenth centuries was characterized by the delivery of books to order. The number of orders of potential customers was estimated first by travelling around, and production would only start when there was sufficient interest. Increasing incomes and a growing population resulted in a larger market, while improved printing techniques, cheaper paper and the mechanization of binding resulted in lower costs. These changes have made it attractive to switch to production to stock by making a rough estimate of the number of copies regarding the first edition before demand is exactly known, and incoming orders are fulfilled out of stock.

Application: Flexible production technology

Flexible production technologies are able to quickly change people, machines and facilities for the production of constantly changing products. This technology is often accompanied by production based on specific wishes regarding the product or delivery time. Delivery does not take place out of stock. Examples are the famous *kanban system* where information about the demand is exchanged between different production processes, and the '*just-in-time*' methods. Important causes of the emergence of such technologies are the changes in exogenous variables, like improved communication possibilities, more precise statistical techniques to formulate improved predictions, higher educated employees and more flexible work agreements.

Application: Restaurants

High prices make it attractive to produce to order. The prediction is that expensive restaurants will address the specific wishes of customers by offering an extensive menu. Less expensive eating places, e.g. fast food outlets, have a smaller assortment and keep large stocks of prepared meals. Company food services and university restaurants tailor their policy to the eaters. If there are hardly any customers around, then meals are not prepared to stock in order to prevent them from getting cold. If somebody shows up, then supply is tailored to the customer. If it is crowded, then as many meals as possible are made without asking every customer for his or her preference.

15.4 Orthogonality

Problems in organizations are often related to information. These problems may be due to asymmetric information, to wrong information or to a lack of information. The way organizations can be structured to prevent the generation of wrong information as much as possible is addressed in Sec. 15.4.1. The degree to which attributes of an organization can be centralized or decentralized is highlighted in Sec. 15.4.2.

15.4.1 Orthogonal information channels

The fact that no organizational structure is neutral in processing information has already been established in Sec. 13.5. Every structure of information processing entails inevitably a certain distortion of information. Dividing and combining information (inevitably) causes loss of information. Institutional design has to anticipate possible distortion(s) of information and incorporate measures to deal with them. The common practice of using several control systems at the same time (Arrow, 1997) can be seen in this light. The shortsightedness entailed by the choice of one attribute is compensated for by the shortsightedness of the choice of the other attribute.

A leader who wants to be informed about the critical factors in his environment should not choose an organizational structure which is designed the same way as the environment (Hammond, 1994). For example, the leader in a product division knows the profitability of a product, but cannot extract the reason out of the information provided by an accounting system based on products. The reason is that discussions about the characteristics of the products of the company will take place inside divisions, rather than between divisions. Similarly, a functional organizational structure generates most information when it is complemented with an accounting system which has a product orientation. Figure 15.5 summarizes the complementarity between the choice of organizational structure and the choice of accounting system in the usual way.

Accounting system Organizational structure	Product orientation	Functional orientation
Divisional		X
Functional	X	

Figure 15.5: Organizational structure and accounting system

Orthogonal slicing of the organization provides most information. This result corresponds with the insight in Part III regarding the relationship between the equal compensation principle (financial incentives) and the role of management (subjective evaluations), despite the fact that the behavioural assumptions differ considerably between Parts III and VII.

15.4.2 Centralization and decentralization

Japanese companies are known for their flexible and swift way of anticipating unforeseen problems in the company. They achieve this by incorporating information of the local operational units in the decision-making process. Aoki (1990) defines a *Japanese way* ('J-way') of organizing as horizontal or decentralized co-ordination based on ex-post available information. The ex-ante planning formulates some global rules within which activities should be developed, while specific details are addressed based on the locally available information and knowledge. For example, every employee is allowed to stop the assembly line if necessary.

One-sided attention for a certain task is not desirable in a J-way of organizing, because the exchange of information and co-operation are important. This is expressed in the famous *quality circles*. Six or seven people from different backgrounds work together in a quality circle in order to solve problems which can emerge in different stages in the production process. This exchange of information is encouraged by a system of task rotation, which exposes employees to several aspects of the production process. A positive side-effect of job rotation is less focus on the goals of a local unit. Altogether, horizontal co-ordination in such a system is relatively intense and rather informal. This is reflected in the labour contracts. They are not very specific and therefore highly incomplete. This calls for a familiarity with various aspects of the work, but entails that it is more difficult to measure performance. Performance measurement is done by a hierarchical system of incentives, which is accomplished by installing a centralized personnel department with substantial discretion regarding hiring and evaluating employees, promotion decisions and determining the rotation of employees over positions. Employees compete to qualify for a more attractive position, while they are rewarded for effectively using a lot of different local information. Rewards are based not on absolute performances, but on relative ones, like a better position, i.e. a promotion, of which there are only a few are available.

Usually a consortium of banks administers a large part of the outstanding equity and the debt percentage is usually high compared with companies in other countries. Despite their large financial stake, banks stay away from the affairs or policy of the company as long as everything goes well. They exchange information regarding the functioning of company regularly, and limit themselves to the role of investor. This minimal interference during good times is also necessary for the accomplishment of an effective horizontal co-ordination of activities. Not only should information be exchanged at every level in the organization, but intensive co-operation is also necessary between the different layers. One-sided directives from the top, including financial decisions, frustrate such a process. The J-way of organizing is therefore characterized by decentralized operational activities and financial decisions. Banks use their financial power to direct company decisions only during bad times. However, if things seem to be going wrong, then this is recognized in time because of the intensive mutual contacts and the necessary adjustments are made. As long as everything works well, the banks stay away and the residual rights are exercised by the company, while these rights switch to the consortium of banks during bad times. There is *contingent control*. (Japanese banks are nowadays in trouble because they hold too much bad debt. Perhaps the lack of decentralized incentives for bank employees led to cosy relationships between banks and firms, at the expense of vital monitoring functions.)

The continuous exchange of information between banks in Japan enables them to evaluate the decisions of managers better than the many small stockholders of companies in the United States ever can. (Berglöf (1989) classifies economic systems as bank- or market-orientated.) This provides an explanation for the relatively intensive use of debt, limited internal financing and restricted use of the stock market by Japanese companies compared with American ones. Imai and Itami (1984) observe that Japanese companies rely more on market finance than their American counterparts. This holds also for their inputs. American companies rely more on internal finance and internal procurement of inputs.

The J-way of organizing is one possible composition of the system of attributes. Another way of organizing emphasizes economies of scale by specialization instead of the exchange of information. For convenience, these organizations will be associated with American companies. Two important aspects of the *American way* ('A-way') of organizing are the hierarchical separation of planning and operational decisions, and the emphasis on economies of scale associated with specialization. Everyone has his own task in the assembly line. If something is wrong, then the technical service is called in. Product development, production planning and control of processes is decided by the top of the separate departments, because they are expected to have certain professional knowledge about the market or the state of technology. They are responsible for, and have knowledge of, the allocation of (financial) means and the operational activities. These latter decisions are further delegated to managers at a lower level. The plan is implemented by specialized operational units.

The A-way of organizing requires a decentralized system of incentives. It entails detailed task specifications and function evaluations. An A-way of organizing defines specific operational activities, and the organization provides incentives to execute them well by specific function rewards and rewarding individual performance. Unforeseen circumstances are handled on the basis of previous agreements, like using inventories and hiring specialists temporarily. New information can therefore not be used at will. It can only be used by the top in the next planning round. Operational and financial decisions are relatively centralized in an A-way of organizing. The advantage of such an organization is that economies of scale are used efficiently, because no time needs to be spent on collecting and communicating information and co-ordinating activities.

The co-ordination and incentive aspects of these two aligned labour contract systems are depicted in Fig. 15.6. Typical American contracts join decentralized (market-orientated) incentives with centralized (hierarchical) processing of information, while typical Japanese companies do the opposite (Aoki, 1990). An effective organization centralizes either co-ordination or incentives, but not both. As in the previous sections, the importance of realizing complementarities (synergies) between the various aspects of an organization is illustrated (Milgrom and Roberts, 1990a).

Incentives Information processing	Decentralized	Centralized
Decentralized		J-way
Centralized	A-way	

Figure 15.6: American and Japanese labour contracts

It is important to realize the complementarities between the various attributes of an organization and its environment, like suppliers, capital market, labour market, communication channels and incentives (Aoki, 1990). This implies that it is not a good idea to try to imitate parts of different systems in one organization. For example, the functioning of the labour market in various Western countries may make the imitation of the Japanese way of organizing undesirable. On top of that, industries are often so different that sometimes an A-way of organizing is advised in Japanese companies, whereas the opposite holds for other industries.

The choice of a specific way of organizing depends on factors like the availability of competent personnel, communication possibilities between the various departments and *uncertainty* regarding the market (Itoh, 1987). Stable environments are suitable for an A-way of organizing because learning effects regarding the operational level contribute little to what has been planned. Well-known examples are the American steel and car industries in the 1960s and 1970s. The J-way of organizing is probably best able to handle moderately changing environments. The increasing differentiation in cars seems to reflect this situation since the 1970s. The success of the J-way regarding process innovations is widely known. The information locally available is so valuable that it outweighs the economies of scale which are lost as the result of job rotation. Very unstable environments work against the J-way of organizing, because in these situations decentralized adjustments result in behaviour which is hard to predict. Examples are highly specialized activities (space travel, chemistry) and the development of totally new concepts. Figure 15.7 summarizes these results.

Degree of uncertainty	Organization
Low	A-way
Moderate	J-way
High	A-way

Figure 15.7: Innovation, uncertainty and organization

15.6 Influence costs

The internal organization of American and Japanese companies shows some remarkable differences. Japanese companies differ from American ones in having employees who stay their entire career with one company, much smaller salary differences between different positions and more participation in decision-making processes. These three features are complementary (Milgrom and Roberts, 1988a) and can be explained by the Japanese labour market. Labour markets in Japan are, compared with the United States of America, characterized by lower labour mobility, fewer entry possibilities for new employees in companies and less pronounced labour unions than in the United States. The possibilities for Japanese employees to get promoted in the external labour market are limited, which makes it unnecessary for the company to worry about turnover in important positions.

Japanese companies will hardly gather information about the outside opportunities of employees because of the malfunctioning labour market, while employees have a reduced incentive to manipulate information to further their own interests because alternatives elsewhere will not be taken into account. These reduced incentives to manipulate information result in an increased willingness of Japanese employers to allow employees to provide information and to participate in the decision-making process. In addition, the less unequal distribution of incomes in Japanese companies gives rise to fewer influencing activities because any payrise associated with a promotion is relatively small. An implication of the Japanese labour market is that within companies the more intense use of information by employees leads to better decisions, which should show in better company results in Japan than in the United States.

The connectedness of the three attributes also holds for *American* companies. The American labour market functions well. An example is a newspaper report (NRC Handelsblad, 1998) stating that '300,000 Americans loose their jobs each year, but the unemployment rate is the lowest in 28 years'. The flexible (F) labour market in the United States forces companies to pay larger (L) salary differentials, because otherwise they would be confronted with serious hidden characteristics problems in terms of the departure of valuable employees. American companies are less (N) inclined to enable employees to participate in decision-making than Japanese companies, because individual employees can benefit more from manipulating information owing to the larger salary increases associated with a promotion. The rigid (R) labour market in Japan allows smaller (S) salary differentials in organizations and entails a more participative (P) decision-making process. The attributes labour market, decision-making process and salary policy are complementary. Figure 15.8 shows the A-way of organizing in composition A of the system of attributes and the J-way of organizing in composition H of the system of attributes.

	A	B	C	D	E	F	G	H
Labour market	F	F	F	F	R	R	R	R
Salary differentials	L	L	S	S	L	L	S	S
Decision-making	N	P	N	P	N	P	N	P

Figure 15.8: Labour market, salary differentials and decision-making

15.6 Repeated interaction considerations

The governance of the vertical relationship between production processes is regularly an issue of debate. Periods of owning many subsequent stages of production are followed by periods with substantial outsourcing, and vice versa. A system of attributes perspective can account for this by arguing that attributes are affected by different developments, like technological developments and the intensity of competition. In this section the impact of these developments on the 'make-or-buy' decision is addressed from a repeated interactions perspective (McMillan, 1995). A stable long-term relationship is possible only when the benefits of short-run opportunistic behaviour are not high enough to forgo the (future) benefits of adhering to the relationship, which was made precise with the Folk theorem in Sec. 10.2.

Outsourcing important parts of the production process is usually accompanied by careful selection of a limited number of suppliers, where aspects other than price are important. The reduced reliance on competitive bidding to select suppliers (in the 'buy' system of attributes) implies a more intense, long-term relationship with a limited number of suppliers. This has implications for the other attributes as well. Input providers receive design responsibilities, are intensely monitored, receive technical assistance and are expected to deliver just in time. Figure 15.9 depicts the 'make' and 'buy' composition of the system of attributes.

	'Make'	'Buy'
Outsourcing?	Limited	Extensive
Number of inside suppliers?	Limited	Extensive
Long-term relations?	No	Yes
Suppliers selected based on price?	Yes	No
Giving suppliers design responsibilities?	No	Yes
Check suppliers?	No	Yes
Provide suppliers with advice?	No	Yes
Just-in-time inventory management by suppliers?	No	Yes

Figure 15.9: Two coherent systems of the vertical relation

Outsourcing is attractive because certain functions can be performed better by specialists who have the advantages of economies of focus and scale. However, these advantages may be swamped by the contracting, monitoring and implementation costs of having a second party provide the service. Because of external forces like technological developments and the intensity of competition, these costs and benefits of outsourcing do not usually change symmetrically. A change in the costs of one of the attributes may result in another composition of the entire system of attributes becoming efficient owing to the complementarities between the attributes.

For example, information and communication technology has undergone a 10-billion-times cost reduction since the middle of the twentieth century. The decrease in these costs has impacted primarily on the transaction costs associated with complexity in communication, i.e. the contracting, monitoring and implementation costs of outsourcing. It enhances the stability of long-term contracts because defections are easier to detect, which makes the switch to the 'buy' system of attributes, i.e. outsourcing, more attractive. It is accompanied by number of other changes for suppliers, like receiving design responsibilities, more intense monitoring, receiving advice and just-in-time inventory management. (Notice that the effect of the developments in information and communication technology is ambiguous, however. The costs of internal control were also lowered, but this was apparently a smaller effect than the lowering of the market transaction costs.)

The development of computer-aided design and manufacturing systems has had the same effect. The general-purpose, flexible nature of these technologies decreases the transaction costs of subcontracting by reducing the specificity of investments. Finally, an increase in the competitiveness of supplier markets favours outsourcing.

Notice that eight attributes are specified in Fig. 15.9. In order to illustrate that there are $2 \times 2 \times 2 \times 2 \times 2 \times 2 \times 2 \times 2 = 256$ possible compositions of this system of attributes and only two stable compositions, it may be illuminating to depict these 8 attributes with an 8-dimensional cube. However, this is not possible. One way to present an n-dimensional cube, with $n \geq 3$, in a 2-dimensional figure is to flatten it into 2 dimensions. (A system with 2 attributes can be presented by a figure with 2 axes, like Fig. 14.1.) Figure 15.10 provides an example of the flattening of the 2-dimensional cube of Fig. 15.2 into a figure with 3 axes. The 3 attributes are defined as

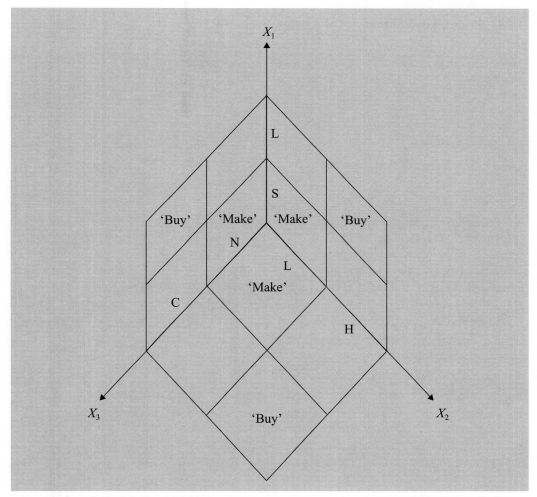

Figure 15.10: A system with three attributes

X_1: degree of task freedom;
X_2: extent of piece-rate wages;
X_3: extent of asset ownership of the physiotherapist.

The same can be done with a system consisting of 8 attributes. Figure 15.11 presents the flattening of the 8-dimensional representation of Fig. 15.9. The attributes have to be formulated carefully in order to have the 'make' choices in the centre and the 'buy' choices at the edge. An example of such a formulation of the attributes on the various axes is

X_1: degree of outsourcing;
X_2: degree of internal procurement;
X_3: extent of long-term relationships;
X_4: extent of other than price criteria;
X_5: extent of design responsibilities;
X_6: degree of monitoring suppliers;
X_7: extent of technical advice;
X_8: degree of just-in-time inventories.

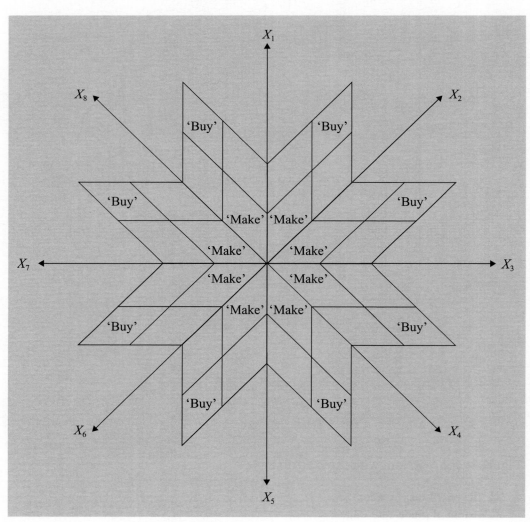

Figure 15.11: A system with eight attributes

The attractiveness of outsourcing implies that the discovery of cost-reducing and quality-improving innovations is left to the input providers, and that this is supported by technical advice. However, innovative efforts by the input provider are hard to cover by a contract. One incentive for innovation is that the status of most preferred suppliers can be granted in the procurement process regarding new projects. Additional outsourcing necessitates long-term relationships. The prospect of a long-term relationship gives input suppliers the confidence that specific investments, for example with respect to just-in-time inventory management, are attractive.

Awarding the status of preferred supplier to well-performing input providers entails that the competition for new projects is based less on price. The production process of the input provider is monitored, and bills are checked, in order to receive some information regarding the costs of the input provider. This is costly, but inevitable in a long-term relationship. These costs are reduced by reducing the number of input providers.

15.7 The costs of trade expansion

Chapter 1 showed that exchange is attractive because resources will go in the direction of highest value added, specialization increases and innovation occurs. A requirement for efficiency-enhancing exchange is that the involved parties have to commit themselves ex ante to contractual agreements which will be honoured ex post. Formal institutions like the judicial system, and private institutions which have emerged within the judicial system, are often helpful. However, Part IV has shown that there are also various limitations associated with formal institutions, and this brings the value of informal institutions to the attention. This application focuses on two different, but aligned, ways of choosing the monitoring and enforcement technologies in a society.

Before the ascent of modern judicial systems and institutions, the relationship between wholesalers and their representatives abroad was endangered in various ways. The wholesaler supplied the merchandise for the exchange abroad. He could travel abroad himself or else hire a local representative. The latter arrangement was efficient because it saved time and prevented the dangers associated with travel, made diversification across different trade centres possible and so on.

The relationship between a wholesaler and a local representative does not usually blossom without supporting institutions, because the representative may behave opportunistically by embezzling the merchandise of the wholesaler. The wholesaler who anticipates this behaviour will therefore not hire the local representative, which results in the loss of valuable trade. There was thus a demand for an institution which enabled the local representative to commit himself to honouring contractual agreements ex post.

Greif (1993, 1994) compares a relation-based trading system with a rule-based trading system in the twelfth century around the Mediterranean. There were two trading areas: Northern Africa and a region with Genoa as its centre. The Maghribi traders were descendants of Jewish merchants who left the politically unstable Baghdad of the tenth century for Northern Africa, where the Maghrib was the westernmost part of the Muslim world. The Maghribi traders used relation-based governance. It is based on the multilateral reputation mechanism, i.e. all traders collectively punish someone who doesn't abide by the rules. For example, a cheater will not be hired as a representative by someone else in the world of the Maghribi. The prospect of losing all future exchange activities induced the Maghribi traders to honour agreements. The social and commercial network took care of generating the required information to detect fraud and to spread the news. This choice of the enforcement and communication technology entailed that new traders were recruited only from the local community. It was a closed community with a horizontal social structure. Every Maghribi trader was a wholesaler as well as a representative. Trade could therefore be very informal, a handshake being enough to seal an exchange.

The relation-based trading system was based on unco-ordinated decisions of traders in various locations. In order to build countervailing power against swindlers, consensus was needed on cheating. This could in principle also be established with a complete (contingent) contract, but in practice was impossible given the slow communication and the complexity of trade. There are two substitutes for a complete (contingent) contract. One is hierarchy, i.e. an authority relationship, which works as a substitute for an ex-ante complete (contingent) contract by allocating the ex-post decision rights to the wholesaler. The other substitute for a complete (contingent) contract is culture, which works by specifying ex-ante codes of behaviour. These two substitutes differ substantially. The commercial codes of a culture have to be mastered ex ante, while ex post there is no communication necessary between the parties. The opposite holds for a hierarchy. Nothing has to be learned ex ante, while communication between the parties is necessary ex post.

It is not surprising that the Maghribi traders used culture as a substitute for complete (contingent) contracts, given the slow communication and transport technologies. This culture expressed itself in a system of trade rules which was treated as a commercial standard or code of conduct. The tradition of joint punishments serves as a focal point in the trade system of the Maghribi and is in line with their collectivistic Islamic culture. It is a specific institution which efficiently handles problems with honouring contracts and establishes co-ordination in situations characterized by asymmetric information, slow communication technology, incompleteness of contracts and limited enforceability of judicial agreements.

Traders from Genoa were also active in the Mediterranean. They used rule-based governance, which was based on the bilateral reputation mechanism and was supported formally by the government. The traders from Genoa had a culture with an individualistic orientation. They were part of the feudal world where bilateral patronage relationships were common. The focus on the individual was in line with Christianity, which placed the individual instead of the group at the centre of the theology. This created a society with the individual as starting-point. Individual punishments were the focal point in the cultural world of Genoa.

In this system a representative honoured agreements with the wholesaler because the relationship would otherwise not be continued. The judicial system ensured also that agreements were written down, that badly treated parties were refunded and that cheaters were punished. This individualistic orientation generated a vertical social structure with two groups: wholesalers and representatives. There was an open community in the sense that people from outside the Genoan system were easily absorbed in this trading system. To secure success, outsiders had only to function well in the bilateral relation within the formal judicial framework. Figure 15.12 summarizes the composition of the attributes of these two trading systems.

Li (1999) discusses the costs of running these two governance systems. The costs of a governance system consist of the costs of the observation technology, i.e. the costs of the detection of cheating and of communicating this information to others, and the costs of the enforcement technology, i.e. the costs of imposing sanctions on cheaters. Relation-based governance like the Maghribi trading system has low fixed costs because the relationship exists when one has been raised in the community and no system-wide investment is necessary to sustain it. However, the marginal costs of relation-based governance are high and rising. Marginal costs are high

System Attribute	Trade system Maghribi	Trade system Genoa
Orientation	Collectivistic	Individualistic
Reputation mechanism	Multilateral	Bilateral
Agreements	Informal	Formal
Society	Closed	Open
Social structure	Horizontal	Vertical
Functions	Homogeneous	Differentiated

Figure 15.12: Two aligned trading systems in the twelfth century

because each additional relationship requires a reputational investment. Marginal costs are rising because new trading partners are less and less known, i.e. larger initial investments in building and enforcing the relationship are needed and there is a greater risk of collapse. Rule-based governance like that of the Genoese trading system has high fixed costs, e.g. the costs of setting up legislative and judicial institutions and the costs of establishing credibility. However, the marginal costs of trade expansion are low and almost constant, i.e. additional parties can be dealt with easily once the system is established. The prediction is therefore that small communities will have self-governance, whereas large communities will have official governance.

This book started with the law of comparative advantages and the fundamental welfare theorem. The tendency of general equilibrium theory is that a large part of the institutional framework of the state which is focused on channelling economic activities can be replaced by the 'invisible hand'. Efficiency results from the unco-ordinated interactions between self-interested individuals. The above discussion shows an alternative. A society is a web of complementary economic, judicial, political, social and moral attributes, which blossom in either an individualistic or a collectivistic society. The efficiency of a specific orientation depends on the circumstances. For example, a collectivistic system is relatively good at supporting agency relations in the system and requires less expensive formal organizations, like courts, but it limits the agency relationships with other societies. The opposite holds for an individualistic society. This society has more specialization, where economic growth is enhanced by the formal institutions supporting anonymous exchange. Entrepreneurial activities and innovation seem to blossom in this system because there is less social pressure to abide by certain behavioural rules. Finally, notice that this application is close to the level of social theory in Fig. 1.5, i.e. the frequency of change of orientation is between 100 and 1000 years.

15.8 Stability of the environment

Strategy and organization have to be aligned for the well-being of the company. Well-known examples of strategy are cost leadership, differentiation and focus (Porter, 1980). The successful execution of a strategy requires an organizational design which is aligned with it.

Two organizational designs are distinguished by Saloner *et al.* (2001). The 'exploiter' is geared towards creating continuous, incremental change in order to maintain its existing competitive advantage. It is particularly suitable for a low-cost strategy. The 'explorer' attempts to create a new competitive advantage by continuously creating new capabilities or positions. Saloner *et al.* (2001, p. 104) illustrate the distinction between exploitation and exploration, which is due to March (1991), by the metaphor of a mountain climber:

> [T]hink of the firm as a mountain climber whose goal is to climb as high as it can. Broadly speaking, the firm has a couple of options. One is to devote its energy to climbing as high as it can up the mountain it is on now. This would involve climbing as efficiently as possible and, to the extent that the firm spends time planning and scouting, to direct that effort toward finding the best possible route up the mountain it is on. Another approach is to spend some energy and resources climbing the current mountain, but to focus on scouting other mountains in case there are higher and/or more easily climbed mountains. Clearly, the former is an exploiter and the latter an explorer.

Saloner *et al.* (2001) distinguish three attributes of organizations: the degree of interdependence among the organization's activities, the share of resources the firm devotes to activities outside its core domain, and the extent to which the process of change is centrally controlled. These attributes of organizational design have to be aligned with the strategy of the organization. For example, the strategy production to order is characterized by tight coupling, i.e. a high degree of interdependence among the subunits of an organization. Tight coupling among units is required in order to establish just-in-time production with a flexible production technology. Substantial costs are prevented by correcting defects swiftly, and rescheduling production in the interdependent production process by the flexible production technology. Loose coupling is associated with explorer firms. From a cost perspective the uncertainty surrounding particular explorations makes it undesirable to have tight coupling.

The amount of discretion allowed to subunits, i.e. the share of resources of the firm devoted to activities outside its core domain, is the second attribute. Exploiters hardly allocate resources outside their core domain. They require that all units fully commit their resources to reaching current operational objectives. This is most likely to enable incremental learning. An explorer system of attributes allocates resources to unit managers to give employees the time and resources to experiment, which may eventually benefit the firm. This investment in innovation and change is referred to as 'organizational slack', because it does not refer immediately to the unit's current performance. Non-routine or non-incremental innovations require this slack. Notice that the nature of this type of innovation, and therefore slack, implies some loose coupling with the other activities in the company.

Finally, the third attribute is the degree of central direction and co-ordination of change. Exploiter firms are characterized by centrally directed change. This is especially desirable when changes in certain parts of the organization require changes in other parts, i.e. tight coupling benefits from central co-ordination. Exploration does not blossom with central direction. The direction of change is less certain and independent research paths should be allowed. Figure 15.13 presents the exploiter and explorer (aligned) system of attributes in the familiar way.

Profile Attributes	Exploiters	Explorers
Interdependency among units	Tightly coupled	Loosely coupled
Discretionary resources	No organizational slack	Substantial organisational slack
Direction of change activities	Centralized	Decentralized
Learning mode	Incremental within the defined domain	Outside the defined domain

Figure 15.13: Exploiter and explorer profiles (Saloner *et al.*, 2001, p. 112)

The efficiency of each of these two profiles depends on the nature of the environment. The exploiter system of attributes is efficient in stable environments for example mature industries. Competition is usually fierce in such environments, which forces the firm to continuously improve its current products in order to stay ahead of the competition. The explorer system of attributes is efficient in rapidly changing environments. Examples are emerging market opportunities and leveraging the resources of the company in completely new ways. Rather than doing better in a given domain, these firms try to change domains.

15.9 Organizational change

Chapters 14 and 15 have highlighted that organizations consist of many attributes which have to be aligned. Several aligned compositions are usually possible. Section 14.2 has argued that a co-ordinated change of all attributes at the same time is necessary in order to reap the benefits of the complementarities between the attributes, i.e. a 'big bang' or 'all-or-nothing' change is advised. However, the transition from one equilibrium to another equilibrium is often cumbersome.

Application: Information technology and organizational transformation
Computers are often perceived as number-crunchers, but their fundamental role is quite different when one thinks about organizations and markets as information processors. Information technology, defined as computers plus related digital communication technology, has the broad power to reduce the costs of co-ordination, communications and information processing. It is therefore a general-purpose technology rather than a specific technology used by the organization. Figure 15.14 presents the impact of information technology on the choice of the attributes of a large medical products manufacturer (Brynjolfsson and Hitt, 2000).

'Old' factory	'New' factory
Designated equipment	Flexible computer-based equipment
Large inventories	Low inventories
Pay tied to amount produced	All operators paid same flat rate
Keep line running no matter what	Stop line if not running at speed
Thorough final inspection by quality assurance	Operators responsible for quality
Raw materials made in-house	All materials outsourced
Narrow job functions	Flexible job responsibilities
Areas separated by machine type	Areas organized in work cells
Salaried employees make decisions	All employees contribute ideas
Hourly workers carry them out	Supervisors can fill in on line
Functional group working independently	Concurrent engineering
Vertical information flow	Line rationalization
Several management layers (6)	Few management layers (3–4)

Figure 15.14: Attribute choices in the 'old' and the 'new' factory (Brynjolfsson and Hitt, 2000, p. 27)

Switching to the 'new' factory may be attractive because the costs of information technology have dropped by 99.9 per cent in a few decades. However, the switch from the 'old' to the 'new' factory may take several years, because an important part of the value of information technology is in facilitating *complementary* organizational investments such as business processes and work practices. The successful implementation of the new technology requires the invention of new processes, procedures and organizational structures which leverage this ability. However, most of our work practices and institutions emerged in an era of relatively high communications costs and limited computational capability. This makes adjustment hard, especially because information technology is heavily associated with intangible assets like the costs of developing new software, populating a database, implementing a new business process, acquiring a more highly skilled staff, changing organizational practices or undergoing a major system transformation.

'Big bang', or 'all-or-nothing', change has been advocated in order to make the complementarities between the attributes blossom. However, gradual processes of change also occur. These may be desirable to start reform early and to prevent too much pressure being put on investment levels (Dewatripont and Roland, 1995). The information generated by gradual change may be sufficiently valuable to compensate for the temporary loss of synergy in the system (Dewatripont and Roland, 1997).

15.10 Conclusion

Functions as systems of tasks, and organizations as systems of attributes, can be conceptualized as a co-ordination problem. In general it is a bad idea for an attractive choice of one attribute of one system composition to be combined with an attractive choice of another attribute belonging to another system composition. Changing one attribute in a well-functioning organization, without changing the choice of the other attributes, will result in a worse performance of the entire organization because of the complementarities between the attributes. For example, the best of Japan and the best of the United States will not lead to a superior system, but to a disaster, owing to the destruction of the alignment in the entire system (Aoki, 1990; Taylor and Wiggins, 1997). Many other examples are illustrative, like the transition of the former communistic countries in Eastern Europe (Gates *et al.*, 1996); companies considering the introduction of market incentives in their internal organization; governments considering functioning like a company; organizations switching to new information technologies (Brynjolfsson and Hitt, 2000); companies with financial performance criteria and decentralized units considering concentrating on some core activities (van Oijen, 1997); agricultural and horticultural co-operatives considering switching some of their attributes to the cluster of stock exchange listed companies, while maintaining the co-operative choice for other attributes (Hendrikse and Veerman, 1997). Similarly, various human resource policy compositions are possible, but an efficient composition will hang together in order to bring the complementarities between the attributes to value (Ichniowski *et al.*, 1997)

15.11 Exercises

15.1 Some years ago, it was reported that the world's biggest aeroplane company Boeing was in trouble. Owing to the very successful efforts of the marketing department, Boeing was confronted with so many orders that the production department was unable to meet its contractual deadlines. The fines turned out to be substantial.

A Is this a hidden action problem or a co-ordination problem?

B Formulate a numerical example which represents the above situation. Indicate the situation of Boeing in this example.

C Formulate two solutions for the above problem.

15.2 Outline, from the system of attributes perspective, for the following statement:
- The problem;
- Why the statement is wrong;
- The right formulation of the statement.

'The advantages of market-oriented systems (United Kingdom, United States of America) and network-oriented systems (Germany, Japan) should be combined, while their disadvantages should be repressed.'

Glossary

Adverse selection
Pre-contractual opportunism arising when one party to a bargain has private information about something affecting the other party's net benefit from the contract, and when only those whose private information implies that the contract will be especially disadvantageous for the other party accept a contract.

Agency costs
A general name given to the contract costs involved in disciplining the behaviour of some party acting on your behalf.

Agency relationship
A relationship in which one person (the agent) acts on behalf of another (the principal).

Agent
A person acting on behalf of another.

Alienable property rights
Private property rights which can be transferred (sold or given) to other individuals.

Allocation
A complete specification of how resources are to be used.

Allocative efficiency
The economy's ability to produce the quantities of the goods and services consumers desire to buy.

Architecture
A decision procedure aggregating individual decisions into an organization decision.

Asset
An investment giving rise to a potential future cash flow.

Asset specificity
The degree to which a resource is committed to a specific task and thus cannot be redeployed to alternative uses without a substantial reduction in its value.

Asymmetric information
The position where one party to a transaction has superior information compared with another party.

Authority relation
A situation in which one party (the superior) has the right to direct the behaviour of the other (the subordinate), at least within bounds, and to supervise, monitor and punish or reward the subordinate.

Backward integration
Bringing the supply of an input under the ownership and management of the input purchaser. Also called upstream integration.

Bankruptcy
A set of legal provisions designed to come into effect when a firm or individual is unable to meet debt obligations.

Bargaining costs
The transaction costs involved in negotiations between or among different parties. These include the time spent on bargaining, resources expended during bargaining or in trying to improve bargaining position, and any losses incurred as a result of failure or delay in reaching otherwise efficient agreements.

Barriers to entry
Anything, either physical, institutional or the result of some decision process making it prohibitive for new firms to enter a market.

Behavioural finance
An approach incorporating psychological aspects in the analysis of financial markets.

Bertrand competition
Position when the competition between two or more firms is characterized by each firm assuming that its rival or rivals' price or prices are fixed and then deciding how to set its own.

Board of directors
Shareholder-elected officials who act in the interest of the owners in a corporation's internal control mechanism.

Bounded rationality
The ratio of the cognitive capacities of the decision-maker to the complexity of the problem.

Brand name capital
A firm's reputation for quality products or living up to its end of a contract; the firm can receive more favourable terms from contracting parties because it is a more desirable partner.

Brand name capital specificity
A form of asset specificity whereby a firm becomes linked to a well-known brand name and thus less free to pursue other opportunities.

Business strategy
Strategy at the business unit level.

Capital structure
The mix of debt and equity financing chosen by a firm.

Cash flow
Accounting net income plus any allowances for depreciation.

Certainty equivalent
Certain income an individual considers equivalent to an activity with risky payoffs.

CEO
Chief executive officer, the highest-ranking officer in a corporation.

Coase theorem
A proposition that if there are no wealth effects and no significant transaction costs, then the outcome of bargaining or contracting is independent of the initial assignment of ownership, wealth and property rights and is determined solely by efficiency.

Coefficient of absolute risk aversion
A measure of the risk attitude of an individual.

Collateral
Tangible assets pledged by a borrower as security in case of default or inability to repay a loan.

Commitment
Determination or promise to follow a particular course of action.

Comparative advantage
Position where one party can produce a good relatively more efficiently (in terms of the opportunity cost) than other parties.

Comparative performance evaluation
The practice of evaluating an individual's performance by comparing it with the performance of others doing similar work.

Comparative statics
The comparison of two different equilibrium points.

Competitive market
Market structure in which no buyer or seller has market power.

Complementarity
Position where doing more of one activity increases the return to doing more of the other activity.

Complements
A set of activities with the property that doing more of any subgroup of the activities raises the marginal return to the other activities.

Complete contract
A contract specifying exactly what is expected of each party under all observable possible future contingencies.

Complete contingent contract
A contract specifying exactly what is expected of each party under all possible future contingencies.

Complete market
A hypothetical set of markets, one for each possible commodity at each future date and for each possible realization of the uncertainty in the world.

Complete rationality
Position where the cognitive capacities of a decision-maker are sufficient to grasp all aspects of a problem.

Consumer surplus
The difference between what final users are willing to pay for a good and what they actually pay.

Contract
Formally, contracts are legally enforceable promises. They may be oral or written, and they typically must involve obligations on each party.

Contract curve
The locus of points in a production Edgeworth box which represent tangencies of each firm's isoquants at the prevailing input price ratio.

Contracting costs
The out-of-pocket and opportunity costs of negotiating, drafting and enforcing contracts; they include search and information costs, and the efficiency losses which result because incentive conflicts are not completely resolved.

Co-ordination costs
A broad category of costs entailing the determination of prices, the costs of acquiring information concerning the location, quality, reputation and availability of different parties, and other costs associated with allocating workers to specific tasks and with bringing transaction participants together.

Co-ordination problem
A situation with more than one Nash equilibrium.

Core competencies
A form of economy of scope which arises out of a firm's ability to carry out some types of activities as well. Typically, this refers to the firm's ability to design, make, sell or distribute a certain kind of product.

Corporate culture
The set of explicit and implicit expectation of behaviour within the firm; it usually encompasses the ways work and authority are organized, the ways people are rewarded and controlled, as well as organizational features such as customs, taboos, company slogans, heroes and social rituals.

Corporate governance
The allocation of decision and income rights regarding assets.

Corporate strategy
Strategy at the firm level, i.e. the determination of which business activities the firm will undertake.

Corporation
An organizational form which allows the enterprise to act as a legal entity separate from its owners, who enjoy limited liability for the corporation's debts.

Cost-plus pricing
Pricing policy where firms set prices by marking up average total cost by an amount designed to yield a target rate of return.

Cournot competition
A situation where the competition between two or more firms is characterized by each firm assuming that the quantity produced by each of its rivals is fixed and then deciding how to set its price.

Covariance
A measure of the extent to which the realizations of two random variables are linked. Calculated as the expected value of the product of the deviations of the variables from their means.

Credibility
The plausibility of claims or promises.

Deadweight loss
The area of consumer and producer surplus lost because of the presence of monopoly power.

Debt
A form of finance requiring regular payments, where control by the providers of the loan is contingent on the honouring of the regular payments.

Decision right
The authority to decide how assets will be used.

Dedicated assets
Assets whose purchase is necessitated by the requirements of one or only a few buyers.

Deductive rationality
Logical, top-down approach to modelling bounded rationality.

Delegation
The shifting of control rights to local decision units.

Diamond–water paradox
The observation that the price of diamonds is much higher than the price of water, while water is essential for life whereas diamonds are not.

Diminishing marginal productivity
A generally accepted theory in economics stating that the marginal product of an input to the production process eventually declines as more units of that input are added to the production process.

Diversification
For an individual investor, the division of invested wealth among a variety of different assets. For a firm, the operation in several different lines of business.

Division of labour
The separation of tasks into a large number of different component activities.

Double marginalization
Increments in the product's price above marginal costs first by the manufacturer and then by the distributor when decentralized pricing decisions are made. The combined profits increase when the intermediate product price is lowered.

Downstream
An activity following the reference activity in the sequence of steps from producing raw materials to delivering a finished product to the customer.

Economic rent
The benefit from an activity going to a resource in excess of what is needed to attract that resource to that activity.

Economies of scale
The reduction in average cost achievable when a single product is made in large quantities.

Economies of scope
The reduction in total cost achievable when a group of products are all made by a single firm, rather than being made in the same amounts by a set of independent firms.

Edgeworth box
A graphical depiction of the total amount of two factors of production going into the production of two outputs.

Efficiency wage
A wage higher than is required to attract and hold workers to a particular employment, the higher pay being designed to induce higher productivity.

Efficiency wage model
A working hypothesis attempting to explain compensation patterns in labour markets; especially useful because it addresses measurement costs and predicts that managers will reward good behaviour by workers with economic rents.

Efficient
An allocation, contract or organization is efficient if there is no feasible alternative one which everyone finds to be at least as good and which at least one person strictly prefers.

Efficient markets hypothesis
The hypothesis that prices in securities markets, and particularly stock markets, fully and accurately reflect all information relevant to forecasting future returns.

Employee-owned firm
A firm in which the providers of labour services hold a controlling interest.

Endowment
The amounts of various goods owned initially, before trade opens.

Entry barrier
Some device keeping other sellers from freely entering a market, including economies of scale and scope, control of a key resource or location, or a patent or copyright.

Equal compensation principle
The principle in incentive contracting that if an agent is to allocate effort among different activities, then each must bring the same marginal return to effort. Otherwise, the agent will focus exclusively on the one yielding the greatest impact on his or her income.

Equilibrium
A stable situation where no party has a reason to change its strategy.

Equity
Securities issued by a firm which represent ownership rights (such as stocks) or are convertible into such securities (such as warrants).

Equity premium puzzle
The empirical observation that the return on equity has been significantly higher than the return on bonds.

Evolutionary economics
A theory of economic organization and industrial structure which focuses on change. The primary assumptions are that (1) firms satisfy rather than maximize, relying on routines and decision rules in doing so, (2) the competitive environment rewards success and (3) any industry is not likely to be in equilibrium at any point in time.

Ex ante
A Latin phrase meaning roughly 'before the fact'.

Exit
A firm leaving the industry.

Exploitation
Doing better in the same domain.

Exploration
Striving to find completely novel ways of doing things.

Ex post
A Latin phrase meaning roughly 'after the fact'.

Extensive form
The representation of a non-cooperative game by a tree diagram, where the nodes represent the players and the sequence of decisions, the branches their available actions, ovals the information structure and the payoffs each player stands to earn from each possible combination of actions.

Externalities
The costs or benefits from the actions of one party which affect the utility or production possibilities of another party.

Fat Cat strategy
Overinvestment in order to create a passive profile.

Firm-specific assets
Assets significantly more valuable in their current use within the firm than in their next best alternative use outside the firm.

Firm-specific human capital
An employee's acquired skills and knowledge which have greater value in their current employing organization.

First-mover advantage
Expected benefits gained by the party deciding first.

Formal authority
The power coming from explicitly assigned decision rights within the organization.

Forward integration
Bringing a downstream activity, such as distributing or selling a firm's product, under the ownership and management of the firm. Also called downstream integration.

Franchise agreement
Contract between the franchiser (parent) and the franchisee granting the use of the parent's name.

Free cash flow
The amount of a firm's cash flow in excess of what can be profitably invested in the firm.

Free rider problem
A situation where each member of a team has an incentive to shirk because each receives the full benefit from shirking, but only bears a part of the costs.

Fringe benefits
Components of the compensation package other than salary and incentive compensation. They are either in-kind or deferred (such as medical insurance and pensions).

Functionally organized firm
A firm in which the traditional functions, such as accounting, sales, manufacturing, and so on, are each controlled by a separate department.

Fundamental welfare theorem
The proposition that the allocation associated with a competitive equilibrium is efficient.

Game theory
A mathematical tool for modelling multi-person decision situations.

General equilibrium analysis
A method of enquiry which simultaneously determines the prices and quantities in all markets.

General knowledge
Knowledge relatively inexpensive to transfer.

Governance structure
The rules by which an exchange is administered. These rules are usually distinguished in decision rights and income rights.

Group incentive pay
Reward scheme basing employee compensation on group performance.

Hard investment
Investment characterized by a negative relationship between the level of investment of the incumbent and the profit level of the entrant.

Hierarchy
Architecture in which a proposal is accepted only when everybody accepts it.

Holding company
A company which owns several other companies but exercises little or no management control over them.

Hold-up
Ex-post opportunism with respect to contractual agreements regarding assets.

Hold-up problem
Inefficient investment due to the anticipation of hold-up.

Horizon problem
A potential mismatch between the planning horizon of the decision-maker and those affected by his or her decision.

Human asset specificity
A situation obtaining where individuals develop skills with narrow applications.

Human capital
The acquired skills and knowledge which make an individual more productive.

Hysteresis
Past behaviour determining future behaviour to a large extent.

Imperfect commitment
Parties' limited abilities to bind themselves to future courses of action.

Imperfect information
The less than complete or accurate data held by at least one buyer or seller.

Implicit contracts
An agreement consisting of promises and shared understandings which are not expressed by formal legal documents but which the parties consider to be binding on one another's conduct.

Inalienability problem
A difficulty occurring in organizations where the net benefits from a business relationship cannot be sold by those currently holding the rights to those benefits.

Incentive compatibility constraint
Limitations on the set of contracts which can be implemented, arising from the necessity of giving individuals appropriate incentives to induce them to adopt the desired course of action.

Incentive intensity principle
The principle in incentive contracting that the intensity of incentives should increase with the marginal productivity of effort and with the agent's ability to respond to incentives, and should decrease with the agent's risk aversion and the variance with which performance is measured.

Incentive problem
A situation where the parties have conflicting interests.

Income right
The way revenues and costs of the deployment of an asset are distributed.

Incomplete contracts
Agreements which fail fully to specify actions under every course of events.

Indifference curve
A depiction of all combinations of goods or services which yield the same utility.

Inductive rationality
Bottom-up approach to modelling bounded rationality.

Influence activities
Activities aimed at changing organizational decisions to allow interested parties to capture organizational rents.

Influence costs
The costs associated with influence activities.

Informal authority
Formal authority delegated to a local decision unit.

Informational asymmetry
A situation where the amount and/or quality of data held by parties to an exchange differs, or is believed to differ.

Informational rent
A return in excess of opportunity costs which accrues by virtue of an individual having private information.

Information cascade
The choices of a few early individuals determining the choices of all successors.

Informativeness principle

The principle of incentive contracting which holds that payments under a contract should depend on the value of a variable if and only if accounting for that variable allows a reduction in the error with which performance is measured.

Intensity of incentives

The rate at which expected income changes with improved performance under an incentive contract.

Internal labour markets

A complex of administrative procedures and rules governing the allocation of labour, investments in it and its compensation within an organization.

Investment

An expenditure of resources which creates an asset.

Irreversible investment

Investment with no alternative use or resale value.

Joint venture

Enterprise owned by two or more independent firms.

Just-in-time manufacturing

A production system in which inventories of goods in process are minimized because the required inputs to each stage of manufacturing are delivered to each work station just as they are needed.

Keiretsu

A network organization employed in Japan. It consists of an affiliation of quasi-independent firms with ongoing, fluid relationships, where the firms typically have cross-holdings in each other's common stock.

Law of comparative advantages

The rule that the total output (production) of a group (persons, companies, countries) is largest when each good or service is produced by the person with the lowest opportunity costs (the comparative advantage).

Law of demand

The rule that the quantity demanded varies inversely with price.

Law of diminishing returns

The rule that the marginal product of a variable factor will eventually decline as the use of the factor is increased.

Law of large numbers

The statistical tendency that the uncertainty regarding the average of a sample reduces when the sample becomes larger.

Law of small numbers

A phrase referring to the representativeness of a small sample being used in the wrong way.

Lean and hungry strategy

Underinvestment in order to create an aggressive profile.

Learning curve

The path of declining unit cost for new products as a manufacturer learns to overcome initial problems.

Licence
A fixed amount of money paid for renting an asset.

Limited liability
The condition of a person whose liability for the debts of a partnership or other organization is limited to the amount of capital he or she has invested.

Limited partner
A partner in a limited partnership who supplies financing and enjoys a share of the partnership profits but who exercises no control of partnership decisions and who has limited liability for partnership debts.

Limited partnerships
A partnership consisting of both general partners and limited partners.

Limited rationality
A situation when the cognitive capacities of a decision-maker are insufficient to grasp all aspects of a problem.

Loss aversion
The asymmetric valuation of gains and losses by a person, where the negative impact on the level of utility of a loss is larger than the positive impact of a gain.

Make-or-buy decision
The choice a firm must make about whether it should make an intermediate good in-house or secure it in some market.

Marginal analysis
An approach considering only the incremental costs and benefits in making a decision.

Marginal cost
The increase in the total costs of production resulting from raising output by one unit.

Marginal product
The change in total product, or output, resulting from the use of one more unit of a variable factor, other things being equal.

Marginal revenue
The change in total revenue resulting from the sale of one more unit of output.

Market
The interaction of one or more independent buyers with one or more independent sellers.

Market clearing price
Price at which the quantity supplied of a product is equal to the quantity demanded.

Market discipline
Market punishment for 'bad' behaviour, i.e. when enough buyers (sellers) having learnt of a particular seller's (buyer's) poor behaviour act together to curtail that seller's (buyer's) activities.

Market failure
The inability of markets to achieve efficient allocations when economies of scale, externalities or missing markets are involved.

Market power

The ability of a buyer or a seller to influence the market price by his or her actions.

Market structure

The basic characteristics of the market environment, including (1) the number and size of buyers, sellers and potential entrants, (2) the degree of product differentiation, (3) the amount and cost of information about product price and quality, and (4) the conditions for entry and exit.

Marketing co-operative

Forward integration by many small farmers into the next stage of production.

Measurement costs

The costs involved in determining the quality of a good or service which a party incurs to improve its bargaining position.

Menu of contracts

A system for compensation in which individual employees may choose which of several different formulas will be used to compute their pay.

Modigliani–Miller theorem

The proposition that the total market value of a firm is independent of how the firm is financed in terms of debt and equity.

Monitoring

An activity aimed at determining whether the contractual obligations of another party have been met.

Monitoring intensity principle

The principle of incentive contracting that indicates that more resources should be used to reduce the errors in measuring performance when stronger performance incentives are being given.

Monopoly

A market structure in which there is a single seller.

Moore environment

The neighbourhood of a unit in a grid consisting of the horizontal and vertical neighbours.

Moral hazard

The post-contractual opportunism arising when actions required or desired under the contract are not observable.

Multidivisional form

The organization of the firm into a collection of business units based on factors such as product or geographic area with autonomy to make day-to-day operating decisions and with control over their own functional departments (accounting, marketing, etc.).

Nash equilibrium

A specification of a payoff-maximizing strategy for each player, given the strategies of the other players.

Nexus of contracts

The identification of the firm as a connected group of (explicit or implicit) contractual relationships among suppliers, customers and workers.

Non-cooperative game theory

A branch of game theory in which agreements are not binding.

Non-specific assets
Assets which are equally useful when employed in combination with any of various other assets or in any of several different relationships.

No wealth effects
The condition on preferences which means that choices among non-monetary alternatives are unaffected by the individual's wealth or income.

Oligopoly
Market with a few (large) competitors who take each other's reactions into account.

Opportunism
The policy of taking advantage of a situation in the pursuit of self-interest.

Opportunistic behaviour
Self-interested behaviour with guile.

Opportunity cost
The value of any resource in its next-best alternative use.

Outsourcing
Moving an activity outside the firm which formerly was done within the firm.

Ownership
The right to decide by whom, how, when, for how long and under what conditions an asset will be used.

Pareto efficiency
A position where there is no feasible alternative which keeps all individuals at least as well off but makes at least one person better off.

Participation constraints
Limitations on contracts or other organizational arrangements arising from the fact that participation is voluntary and so individuals must expect to do at least as well as under their next-best alternatives or they will refuse to participate.

Partnership
A form of organization in which some or all of the multiple owners, the general partners, accept unlimited liability for the organization's debts and exercise management control.

Path dependency
Where past behaviour determines future behaviour to a large extent.

Perfect capital markets
A theoretical ideal in which all individuals can borrow and save on the same terms, the terms being unaffected by the amounts involved.

Perfect competition
An arrangement of buyers and sellers in which there is perfect information, a homogeneous product, similar firms and free entry and exit.

Perfect information
A situation where every participant (and potential participant) in a market becomes aware of every price, product specification and buyer and seller location at no cost.

Physical asset specificity
A particular investment in machinery or equipment which has one narrowly defined purpose.

Piece-rate rewards
A reward system which compensates people in proportion to the amounts they produce.

Polyarchy
Architecture in which a proposal is rejected only when everybody rejects it.

Pooling equilibrium
A situation where agents with different characteristics (utility functions, preferences, payoffs) choose the same contract.

Postcontractual opportunism
Opportunistic behaviour by a party after a contract is signed.

Procedural rationality
A situation where the cognitive capacities of a decision-maker are hardly able to grasp any aspect of a problem.

Puppy Dog strategy
Underinvestment in order to create a passive profile.

Precontractual opportunism
Opportunistic behaviour by a party before a contract is signed.

Preferred shares (stock)
Shares with priority dividend claims but no voting rights.

Price discrimination
Charging different prices for highly similar goods.

Principal–agent model
A model employed to examine incentive problems among contracting parties.

Principal–agent problem
A problem created by the separation of ownership and control in various transactions.

Prisoners dilemma game
A classic example of the tension between group interest and individual self-interest, where individual (selfish) interest leads to the worst possible outcome for all.

Produces surplus
The difference between the minimum amount the seller will accept for any given unit sold and its actual price.

Product attributes
The various characteristics of a product buyers value.

Product life cycle
The pattern introduction, growth, maturity and decline in the demand for products over their life cycles.

Production function
Specification of the maximum feasible output which can be produced for given quantities of inputs.

Production possibilities frontier
The combination of goods an economy can produce by fully utilizing all of its resources including technology.

Profit centres
Business units whose managers are given decision rights for input mix, product mix and selling prices (or output quantities) and are asked to maximize profits given a fixed capital budget.

Property right
An enforceable right to select the uses of a good.

Public corporation
A corporation whose shares are bought and sold through an organized exchange and so may be held by any investor.

Quality circles
Voluntary work groups meeting regularly to discuss how to improve the quality of products and work processes.

Quasi-surplus
The value of an investment minus its recoverable costs.

Ratchet effect
The tendency of performance standards in an incentive system to be adjusted upwards after a particularly good performance, thereby penalizing good current performance by making it harder to earn future incentive bonuses.

Rationality
The principle that individuals and firms act in a consistent manner.

Reaction function
Specification of a payoff-maximizing strategy of a firm for each possible choice of the other firm(s).

Relational contract
A contract which specifies only the general terms and objectives of a relationship and specifies mechanisms for decision-making and dispute resolution.

Relative performance evaluation
Measurement of employees' performances relative to those of their peers.

Renege
Deliberately choose not to carry out a promise or contract to the detriment of the other party.

Renegotiate
Bargain to determine new terms to replace those of an existing contract. If no new agreement is reached, the previous one remains in force.

Rent
Return from an activity above the minimum required to attract resources to that activity.

Rent-seeking behaviour
An attempt by some interested party to alter the allocation of rents in a contractual agreement.

Repeated relationship
A situation where two parties expect to interact with each other over time.

Reputation
The view formed of an individual or organization by another based on past experience, especially as a basis for forecasting future behaviour.

Reservation price
The maximum price the buyer is willing to pay, or the minimum the seller is willing to accept.

Reservation utility
The utility the employee can obtain in the next best alternative.

Residual claimants
Persons who have the legal rights to the profits of the enterprise once the fixed claimants of the firm (for example, bondholders and employees) are paid.

Residual return
The income from an asset or business which remains after all fixed obligations are met.

Residual right
The right to make any decision concerning an asset's use which is not explicitly assigned by law or contract to another party.

Revelation principle
The principle holding that any outcome which can be achieved by some mechanism under the self-interested strategic behaviour which is induced by the mechanism can also be achieved by a mechanism employing a mediator to whom the parties willingly report truthfully and who then implements the outcome which would have resulted from the original mechanism.

Risk-averse individual
An individual preferring the deal with the lower level of uncertainty or risk-holding when both deals have equal expected value.

Risk neutrality
The characteristic of a person who is indifferent between receiving a fixed sum of money or a risky prospect with an expected value equal to the fixed sum.

Risk-neutral individual
An individual caring only about expected value and indifferent to the level of risk.

Risk premium
The difference between the expected value of a risky income stream and its certainty equivalent.

Royalty
A fixed amount of money received or paid for each unit sold.

Routines
Standardized rules for decision and action that, although they may vary to a limited degree with the particular circumstances, are applied across a period of time without further fine-tuning.

Schema theorem
A theorem stating that well-functioning compact clusters, patterns or modules will grow exponentially in number in the population of patterns in evolutionaryenvironments.

Screening
A potential solution to adverse selection which occurs when the uninformed parties to a contract undertake activities to cause the informed parties to distinguish between themselves with respect to some unobservable characteristics.

Segregation
Situation where the population of a neighbourhood is homogeneous.

Selective intervention
The management practice of allowing divisions or businesses to operate with nearly complete independence, intervening only to correct particular problems.

Self-organization
The tendency in computer simulations for locally interacting units to form surprisingly complex patterns in a relatively short period of time.

Self-selection
A situation where people with different personal characteristics identify themselves to outsiders by choosing contracts which best fit with their private information.

Separating equilibrium
A situation where agents with different characteristics (utility functions, preferences, payoffs) choose different contracts.

Separation of ownership and control
A property of publicly held corporations that one group of shareholders owns the firm and a second group of managers runs the firm, i.e. the residual returns and residual rights of control belong to different parties.

Shirking
A form of ex-post opportunistic behaviour arising because of imperfect monitoring, i.e. where one party puts in less effort than it otherwise might if its actions were perfectly observable.

Short run
The operating period during which at least one input (frequently capital) is fixed in supply.

Signalling
A potential solution to adverse selection occurring when the informed parties to a contract undertake activities to distinguish between themselves with respect to some unobservable characteristics.

Site specificity
A situation where an asset is located in a particular place such that it is useful only to a small number of buyers or suppliers and it cannot be moved easily.

Soft investment
Investment characterized by a positive relationship between the level of investment of the incumbent and the profit level of the entrant.

Specialization
The process of narrowing (and, presumably, deepening) the range of tasks a particular individual or machine can perform.

Specific asset
An asset worth more in its current use than in alternative uses.

Specific human capital
Skills acquired by an individual and expected to be useful only within a specific contractual relationship.

Specific investment
An investment creating a specific asset.

Specific knowledge
Knowledge relatively expensive to transfer.

Specific rights
Delineation of the rights and duties in circumstances which are verifiable.

Specific skills
Skills relevant only in some particular job or organization.

Specificity
The extent to which assets are specific.

Spot market
A market in which exchange is made immediately at the current market price with no long-term commitment between buyer and seller.

Spot market contract
A contract for the immediate exchange of goods or services at current prices.

Stakeholder
Any individual or group with a direct interest in a firm's continuing profitable operations (including stockholders, lenders, employees, customers, suppliers, communities where the firm employs workers, and so on).

Strategic behaviour
One party's choices not only affects other parties, but these choices also affect the choices made by the other parties.

Strategic complement
A strategic variable with a negatively sloping reaction function.

Strategic form
The representation of a non-cooperative game by a matrix with the strategies of the players as horizontal and vertical entries, and the payoffs which each player stands to earn from each possible combination of strategies.

Strategic misrepresentation
A situation in which one party may try to benefit by reporting which is less than truthful.

Strategic substitute
A strategic variable with a positively sloping reaction function.

Strategic variable
Where one party's choices affect not only other parties, but also the choices made by the other parties.

Strategy
Specification of an action for each observable history of the game.

Subjective performance evaluation
An evaluation based on the personal opinion of the supervisor rather than on some objective measure (such as the quantity of output).

Substitute product
A good competing with another good, i.e. if the price of one good is increased, the consumer will tend to shift purchases to the other one.

Sunk costs
Non-recoverable costs already incurred, the resources having no alternative use.

Supply curve
A line on a graph displaying the quantity producers are willing to sell at each price, holding all other factors affecting producer behaviour constant.

Survival of the fittest
Principle of economic Darwinism stating that companies have the greatest chance of survival if they are organized efficiently given their particular environment.

Synergy
A situation where the combined effect of two activities is greater than their sum taken separately.

Tacit collusion
Collusion without explicit communication or agreement.

Team production
A production process in which the individual outputs cannot be separately identified.

Tenure
The condition of being protected from termination of employment in a job, regardless of general performance, subject only to meeting certain minimal standards of acceptable behaviour.

Time inconsistency
Short-run behaviour which is not compatible with the long-term interest.

Top Dog strategy
Overinvestment in order to create an aggressive profile.

Total revenue
Price times quantity.

Tournament
A contest in which the prices received depend only on ordinal ranking (first, second, third, etc.) and not on absolute performance.

Transaction
The largest unit of economic activity which cannot be subdivided and performed by several different people.

Transaction costs
The costs of carrying out a transaction, or the opportunity costs incurred when an efficiency-enhancing transaction is not realized.

Transfer prices
The prices used for transactions among departments or divisions within a firm.

Transition rule
A rule describing the transition from one state to another state.

Trust
The belief in a partner's honesty or goodwill.

Type I error
The probability of rejecting a good project.

Type II error
The probability of accepting a bad project.

Unlimited liability
The condition of a person whose liability for the debts of a partnership or other organization is not limited to the amount of capital that person has invested.

Upstream
An activity preceding the reference activity in the sequence of steps from producing raw materials from natural resources to delivering a finished product to the customer.

Utility
An index of personal well-being.

Utility function
A numerical representation of an individual's preferences over different possible choices or situations.

Vertical chain of production
The series of steps in the production process.

Vertical integration
Bringing either one of the input sources or one of the output buyers of the firm under common ownership and management.

Von Neuman environment
The neighbourhood of a unit in a grid, consisting of the horizontally, vertically and diagonally adjacent cells.

Wealth effects
The variation in the amount a consumer is willing to pay for some object or in the quantity which the consumer may wish to buy at a particular price as a result of a change in his or her wealth.

Short answers to exercises

1.1   A The market price is the result of the interaction between demand and supply; the opportunity costs represent the value of the best alternative.

       B A better education raises the reservation wage because better alternatives become available.

1.2   The degree of specialization will increase if B increases, K increases or C decreases.

       A C decreases.

       B K increases.

       C B increases.

       D C decreases.

2.1   B No; this procedure will result in investment in biotechnological markets, which is not the first choice of the CEO.

2.2   B Agent: Not accept.
         Principal: W(hole surplus).

       C No; together the players earn 40, whereas 100 is possible. Part IV will formulate solutions for this (hold-up) problem.

3.1   A A demand curve is a function which specifies the quantity demanded for each price. If the price is more than 2 currency units, the demand will be zero; between 2 and 1 currency units it will be one; between 1 and 0.5 currency unit it will be 2; with the price equal to or less than 0.5, the demand will be 3 units.

       B A supply curve is a function which specifies the supplied quantity for each price. If the price is less than 0.25 currency unit, the supply will be zero; between 0.25 and 0.75 currency unit, the supply will be 1; between 0.75 and 1.5 currency unit, the supply will be two; prices equal to or more than 1.5 currency units entail a supply of 3.

       C A price between 0.75 and 1 currency unit, for which two units are exchanged. (The buyer with a reservation wage of 0.5 currency unit is not willing to pay enough, while the seller with a reservation wage of 1.5 is too expensive.)

       D The sum of the consumer and producer surplus is $(2 + 1) - (0.25 + 0.75) = 2$ currency units.

       E Yes.

       F No; only the reservation wage is relevant.

       G Yes; the buyer with a reservation wage of 2 and the seller with a reservation wage of 1.5 can exchange at a price of for instance 1.75; the buyer with a reservation wage of 1 and the seller with a reservation wage of 0.75 can be connected and can exchange at a price of for instance 0.85; the buyer with a reservation wage of 0.5 and the seller with a reservation wage of 0.25 can be connected and can set a price of for instance 0.40.

H The sum of the consumer and producer surplus is $(2 - 1.5) + (1 - 0.75) + (0.5 - 0.25) = 1$.

I The buyer with a reservation wage of 2 and the seller with a reservation wage of 0.25 will both profit by trading with each other and establishing a price of for instance 1 currency unit.

J The price will tend to 0.75 currency unit, because the buyers have all the power in the negotiations.

K Yes; if the reservation wages are unknown to others, people will try to appropriate a larger part of the surplus by faking the real reservation wage. This may cause there to be no exchange at all, despite the fact that a surplus can be generated.

3.2   A Section 3.2.
    B Figure 3.3.
    C Figure 8.13.

3.3   A Eliminate barriers or constraints which frustrate the functioning of markets. Subsequently, do nothing.
    B Production function.
    C Price ceilings, monopoly power, high unemployment benefits.

4.1   B Yes; allocate the pollution rights to the chemical company.
    C No; the equilibrium will not be efficient if the camping has the rights of pollution at its disposal.
    D Two-sided asymmetric information.

4.2   A According to the Coase theorem, crucial factors for economic (and cultural) development are the allocation of, obedience to and enforcement of ownership rights. If a house is squatted without subsequent intervention by the police, there is no enforcement. This will decrease investment in house building.
    B The Coase theorem focuses on the importance of efficient bargaining and the absence of income effects in the realization of a Pareto-efficient allocation. Houseowners who create vacancies in order to drive up the prices of houses frustrate efficient bargaining, because of the delay in the realization of a profitable exchange. The squatting students increase efficiency because they make it more expensive for houseowners to create vacancies. Houseowners may react to this squatter threat by coming to an agreement regarding selling or renting with less delay.

4.3   A According to the Coase theorem crucial factors for the economic development are the allocation, obedience and enforcement of ownership rights.
    B There will be less investment (in surplus-generating projects).

4.4   A 4.
    B Create a market for pollution rights.
    C 1.

D 1.

E Efficient bargaining, no income effects.

4.5 A Efficient bargaining, no financial restrictions, allocation of the right to determine the date of the exam.

B Yes; student 2 has been awarded these rights according to the course manual.

C Probably not, because there will be asymmetric information regarding the reservation wages and there will probably be many other students.

D Probably, because student 1 will not be able to compensate student 2 financially.

4.6 B Seller: (5,6,7).

Buyer 1: Y.

Buyer 2: Y.

Buyer 3: Y.

C 0.

D 2.

E 2.

G Seller: 6.

Buyer 1: N.

Buyer 2: Y.

Buyer 3: Y.

H 1/3.

I 4/3.

J $1/3 + 4/3 = 5/3$.

K Overbidding of the seller.

L $1/3 - 0 = 1/3$.

4.7 A The project should be terminated because the loss of 200 exceeds the private benefit 100. (Total surplus is represented by the sum of these.)

B Yes; the investor puts no weight on private benefits.

C No; the entrepreneur will continue the project because terminating it results in a gain of only 20 from avoiding losses due to his stake of 0.1, while his full private benefit of 100 is lost.

D The entrepreneur requires at least $100 - 20 = 80$ for terminating the project, while the investor is prepared to offer up to $0.9 \times 200 = 180$. The expectation is that something will be agreed upon in this range.

E Continue the project.

F No.

G Yes.

H The entrepreneur is willing to pay $100 - 0.1 \times 80 = 92$ for continuing the project. The investor wants to receive at least $0.9 \times 80 = 72$ for not closing down the firm. The entrepreneur, if he has the money, could pay the investor an amount between 72 and 92 to persuade her not to close the firm down.

I The entrepreneur is probably wealth-constrained because this is presumably why the entrepreneur approached the investor in the first place. An entrepreneur who was not wealth-constrained would have financed the project him or herself.

5.1 A

Player 2 / Player 1	0	1	2
0	(0,0)	(0,1)	(0,2)
1	(1,0)	(1,1)	(0,0)
2	(2,0)	(0,0)	(0,0)

B No; an increase in the claim of one party, given the claim of the other, will not at the same time lead to an increase in the payment of one party and a decrease in the payment of the other. (Part VII characterizes this situation as a co-ordination problem.)

5.2 A The bike shop.

B No; it is not possible to generate a surplus because the lowest costs are higher than the amount the student is willing to pay. (A Pareto improvement is not possible.)

C Yes; a higher price or smaller effort is profitable for the bike shop, but harmful to the student.

D Yes; the student is not aware of the real costs of repair.

E No; the three conditions of an interesting principal–agent problem are not fulfilled.

6.1 A Complete rationality and opportunistic behaviour.

B The incentive and insurance aspect.

C The (risk-neutral) principal will usually offer the (risk-averse) agent a salary structure consisting of a variable part depending on the observable result. However, a risk premium has to be paid to the agent for bearing the risk, which is not necessary when there is complete information. The unobservability of the action of the agent and the associated hidden action problem causes a loss of efficiency (because of the inefficient allocation of risk due to the variable part of the wage structure).

6.2 B The expected utility is $0.3\sqrt{0} + 0.7\sqrt{400} = 14$.

The certain equivalent income is $\sqrt{I} = 14$, so $I = 196$.

C Certain equivalent assist $\geq$ certain equivalent attempt to score $0.8U(0) + 0.2\sqrt{x}$ $\geq 0.9U(0) + 0.1U(400)$, so $x \geq 100$.

6.3 A A risk-averse (risk-seeking) agent accepts a lower (higher) fixed amount than the expected income associated with uncertainty, in order to receive the same level of utility.

B A higher (lower) fixed reward is associated with a more (less) risk-averse agent regarding an uncertain project. The fixed reward will therefore increase as the agent becomes more risk-averse.

6.4 A Contracts can be based only on observable variables.

B Reduction.

C Yes; such an agent requires a lower risk premium and will therefore obtain stronger incentives.

D A situation in which extremely good outcomes can have resulted only from luck.

6.5 A Debt (i.e. financing with outside capital) will involve incentives which result in too many risky projects. Failure will be at the expense of the providers of debt, whereas success will go to the manager. Jensen and Meckling predict that relatively less debt will be used in company A than in company B in order to minimize the total costs associated with the various forms of finance.

B No. The management of restaurants offers various possibilities for stealing, for privileging friends and relatives, and for free riding. These will increase when a part of these costs can be transferred to external stockholders. They anticipate this behaviour and are not inclined to provide capital. Equity will therefore be mainly in the hands of the manager when the circumstances provide various possibilities of cheating.

6.6 A There is incomplete information regarding the effort of the agent and the external circumstances; the payments are made dependent on the outcome and not on the effort (e) of the agent.

B Participation and incentive compatibility constraints.

C Incentive compatibility constraint: $\sqrt{n} \geq 2 + \sqrt{m}$.
Participation constraint: $\sqrt{m} + 3\sqrt{n} \geq 8$.

6.7 B $w(H) - 2 \geq w(L) - 1$.

C $w(H) - 2 \geq 0$.

D $\{w(L), w(H)\} = \{1,2\}$.

F $[w(9), w(16)]$.

G $w(16) \geq w(9) + 5$.

H $w(16) \geq 10/3 - 2w(9)/3$.

I $[0,5]$.

6.8 A Section 6.2.

B $\beta = 40/(1 + 0.4 \times 300 \times 10)$.

C Risk premium $= 0.5 \times 0.4 \times (40/1201)^2 \times 300$.
$25 =$ risk-free payment $+$ risk premium.

D $0.5 \times 0.4 \times (40/1201)^2 \times 300 - 0.5 \times 0.4 (40/(1 + 0.4 \times 200 \times 10))^2 \times 200$.

6.9 A Yes; $P'(e) = M > 0$, $C'(e) = 2\underline{e} > 0$ and $C''(e) = 2 > 0$.

B $e = \beta/2$.

C The agent takes only the intensity of the incentives (β) into account, when a certain contract has been accepted. (The principal does take the degree of risk aversion (r) of the agent into account. A higher β results in a higher e, but also in a higher risk premium $1/2r\beta^2V$.)

D This salary equals his reservation wage together with a compensation for the risk he has to bear, i.e. $A + 1/2r\beta^2V$.

E The principal will choose β such that the expression $Me - e^2 - A - 1/2r\beta^2V$ will be maximized. Substitute $e = \beta/2$ in this equation. The profit-maximizing β will be $M/(1 + 2rV)$ for the principal. (This corresponds to the incentive intensity principle.) The contractual parameter α is defined by $\alpha + \beta e = A + \frac{1}{2}r\beta^2V$, in which $e = \beta/2$ and $\beta = M/(1 + 2rV)$.

F The principal does not start the project when it is unprofitable. The circumstances in the labour market are summarized by A. (A is the amount the agent can earn somewhere else.) The project is unprofitable when $Me - A - \frac{1}{2}r\beta^2V < 0$, where $e = \beta/2$ and $\beta = M/(1 + 2rV)$. Solving this equation results in $A > (M/1 + 2rV)^2(1 + rV)/2$.

G The entire surplus can be realized in a situation of complete information, because the principal can bear the risk completely (efficient allocation of risk) and is at the same time able to determine the conditions of the contract such that the agent will accept the contract and will provide the maximum effort (efficient incentives). Because the salary is made completely dependent on the effort supplied, the first-best effort level is induced, i.e. the entire surplus will be realized.

In a situation with incomplete information and a risk-averse agent, the risk-neutral principal cannot allocate risk efficiently as well as give the optimal incentives. From the viewpoint of the efficient allocation of risk, the agent has to receive a fixed salary. However, this will frustrate every incentive regarding the provision of effort. A salary structure based completely on the produced quantity is not attractive to the principal either, because in that case the agent will bear a lot of risk and will demand a high risk premium. The optimal reward structure consists partly of a fixed salary and partly of an amount which depends on the produced quantity. The agent will react by providing a smaller effort than in the situation with complete information and the produced quantity will be less. The surplus allocated to the principal will therefore be smaller than in the situation of complete information. This second-best character of the equilibrium is usually unavoidable in an environment of incomplete information.

6.10 A Advantages of a reward structure based on the quantity produced:
- A greater effort becomes more attractive;
- There is less need for control;
- It is an objective evaluation method.

Disadvantages:
- It is inefficient when team production is involved;
- The aspect of quality is neglected;

- There is a ratchet effect;
- The variance between production and effort of all of the employees together is smaller than the remaining variance associated with their own effort.

B Advantages of a reward structure based on skills:
- It provides incentives for employees to invest in human capital, like company-specific skills;
- It increases the flexibility of the employees.

Disadvantages:
- It is not important when there is hardly any relationship between skills and profit;
- An increasing specialization can come at the expense of flexibility.

C If employees perform various tasks at the same time, a reward structure based on skills will encourage them. However, such a structure will no longer provide incentives once the skills are acquired. Rewarding the quantity produced will encourage employees to provide higher levels of effort in that case.

If an increasing efficiency of an employee has little or no influence on the productivity and profitability, as on an assembly line, a salary structure based on results of production will generate little effect.

Conclusion: reward structures based on skills for an assembly line and rewards based on performances for parallel production.

6.11 A Hidden action problem. The agent A takes an investment decision after he has accepted a labour contract with the principal (Coffeng & Co).

B Bad, extremely risky investment behaviour of the agent and bad luck.

C The reward structure encourages risky behaviour of the agent.

D Decrease the conflict of interest by punishing extremely high profits in the reward structure and try to gather extra information regarding (i.e., monitor) the behaviour of the dealer.

7.1 A The decision of a (naive) company may be guided by the thought that the average costs will be 600 euros, and therefore a profit of 100 euros will be made. However, the families with outlays of 200, 400 and 600 euros will not buy insurance. The insurance company will therefore loose on average $(800 + 1000)/2 - 700 = 200$ euros.

B 1000 euros.

C The families with dental outlays of 1000 euros.

7.2 B $q = 0, w < 7$;
$q = 4, 7 \leq w < 10$;
$q = 8, w \geq 10$.

C $w = 10, \theta = 8$.

D $w = 7, \theta = 4$.
$w = 10, \theta = 10$.

E Employees with a low productivity.

7.3 A Information regarding the decisions of the specific manager and the decisions of the others.

    B Yes; herd behaviour.

    C Bottom-up; the ones with the largest career interests are usually young and information about them is less known. They are employed low in the hierarchy of the company. Asked for advice first, they cannot limit themselves to imitating the advice of others.

7.4 Application 'Seniority wages' in Sec. 7.3.

7.5 A Hidden characteristics.

    B The client.

    C Trader or bank employee.

    D Nexus of contracts.

    E Self-selection.

    F Signalling, reputation building.

7.6 A Yes; the three conditions are met.

    B No; a hidden characteristics problem.

    C Time of preparation on the horizontal axis, additions and comments on the literature on the vertical axis.

7.7 A Complete rationality, opportunistic behaviour; the surplus is available, conflict of interests, asymmetric information.

    B Hidden characteristics problem.

    C Yes.

7.8 A 0.5.

    B Piece-rate wages have no incentive effects in this model. Employees decide only where they work, not how hard. Piece-rate wages here serve only a selection purpose.

    C The marginal employee q^* is in equilibrium indifferent between a fixed and a variable wage, i.e. $q^*/2 = q^* - \theta$, which is equivalent to $q^* = 2\theta$.

    D The least-productive employees work for Fixedwage, the most-productive for Piecerate.

    The reason is that $q/2 <(>) q - 2$ when $q >(<) 2\theta$.

    E $\theta \epsilon (0, 0.5)$.

    F 0.25.

    G The socialistic proposal. One aspect of piece-rate wages is that they entail waste. Each person paid by piece rate requires a certification or measurement cost θ. This is required because the amount of output has to be determined. (The costs θ only redistribute income.) These costs are prevented when piece-rate wages are forbidden.

	Fixedwage	Piecerate	q/n
Without law	(0.5)25	(0.5)50	37.5
Forbid Fixedwage	0	50 – 25	25
Forbid Piecerate	50	0	50

8.1 A In case of small numbers opportunistic behaviour can hardly be punished by choosing another market party next time, because there are hardly any other parties.

B Higher transaction costs can arise from:
   – More detailed contracts having to be written, for instance by integrating various competencies;
   – The agreement having to be monitored.

8.2 A $C = 0$. (Quasi-surplus $= A + C + 1000$.) The office has many alternative uses. The value of the best alternative (scrap value) is therefore 4000.

B Finance completely with debt capital.

8.3 A The numbers –1000 and 2000 change; the inventor will earn at least 500 and the downstream party will earn the rest of the surplus of 1000.

8.4 The bargaining position of TCE will not become worse. TCE can pay the same price or even less, because the costs of KPAA have decreased and those of other accountant organizations have remained the same. The price to be established will depend on the bargaining process. An important aspect in this is who can pose the final bid. If KPAA does, the price will be the same as in the last period. A lower price can be expected, however, if TCE finds itself in the position to make an all-or-nothing bid. In that case TCE can even appropriate all savings of KPAA.

8.5 A In case of static markets it doesn't matter whether a company integrates vertically or concludes a 'once-and-for-all' contract. In the first case negotiations are needed about the valuation or appreciation of the assets, in the second case about the price of delivery.

B A standard example refers to the production of iron and steel. Integration of these activities leads to savings in (energy) costs.

C No. The savings could also have been realized by a contract. Vertical integration is necessary only when concluding such a contract would generate high transaction costs.

D Vertical integration can prevent buyers from bargaining jointly, which would make price discrimination ineffective. For an individual company, price discrimination can therefore be a good reason to integrate vertically. For the entire organization, price discrimination can be undesirable.

8.6 A Assume the costs of purchase equal X:
  – Continuing to sell generates a result of 2 000 000 minus (X + 500 000 (rent) + 400 000 (investment costs)) = 1 100 000 – X;
  – Quitting generates a result of –400 000 (only the costs of investment will continue).
  An agent will stop when 1 100 000 – X < –400 000 → X > 1 500 000, which means at a price higher than \$150 000 per Butterfly.
  This problem can also be solved by assuming the costs of investment are irrelevant to the decision. In this case an agent will stop when 2 000 000 – 500 000 – X < 0, so when X > 1 500 000, which also produces an amount of \$150 000. (The reservation price is assumed to be 0.)

  B The value of an asset in the current relation minus the value of the asset in its best alternative use.

  C The quasi-surplus amounts to \$500 000. This amount can be determined in various ways:
  – In this example Butterfly earns 1 000 000 per agent; the agents will only leave at an amount more than 1 500 000;
  – Both the investments (in the special furnishing and training) produce 400 000 + 100 000 (which means the costs of investment are compensated and a profit of 100 000 made); without the relationship with Butterfly the investments will probably have a value;
  – The current yield is 100 000; an agent will leave when the yield equals –400 000.

  D This is unlikely. If Ekeveg detects such behaviour by Butterfly, it can likewise take future behaviour into account and anticipate by for example claiming valuable guarantees of Butterfly or by ending investments in the relationship with Butterfly. (In other words, Butterfly should be concerned for its reputation.)

  E The quasi-surplus will definitely not increase. It can decrease, because the specific investments are made already by the agents and have a positive value for Ekeveg. (The final prices depend of course on the negotiations.)

8.7 A The quasi-surplus equals the value of an asset in the current relationship minus the value of the asset in its best alternative use.
  Two more applied descriptions:
  – In a employer–employee relationship: the earnings which exceed the minimal amount necessary to prevent an employee from quitting his job;
  – In a branch of industry: the earnings which exceed the minimal amount necessary to prevent a company from leaving the industry.

  B The quasi-surplus of the installation equals 3 000 000 euros, i.e. 8000 euros (value in the current relationship) minus 5 000 000 (value in the best alternative use).

  C Degree of specificity = {8 000 000 minus 5 000 000} divided by 8 000 000 = 37 per cent.
  (The degree of asset specificity is the percentage of the value lost if the asset is used out of the specific situation or relationship.)

  D Types of asset specificity are:
  – Specificity of location;

- Physical asset specificity;
- Human asset specificity (know-how);
- Assets tied to a relationship;
- Brand name.

This example matches mainly physical asset specificity. Specificity of location can also be true.

E DSM. The investing party risks the devaluation of its assets. This party owns the quasi-surplus. The other party, Ultegra, can try to appropriate these quasi-rents by behaving opportunistically, for example by raising the prices of raw material. In this case a hold-up is raised.

F The separation can result in insufficient maintenance of the installation:.
- DSM can save costs by decreasing the maintenance too much;.
- The associated disadvantages of the decrease in value of the installation are to the account of Ultegra.

However, DSM will not allow such a decrease, which would threaten its own production.

8.8 A Investment costs minus the value in the best alternative use.

B The Railway company.

C No.

D The new trucking company will face the most fierce competition in the market with the railrway company, because the costs of investment of the railway company are to a large extent sunk. These costs will not be taken into account by the railway company in the decision regarding the continuation of its activities.

8.9 A Influencing activities are efforts to influence the distribution of the benefits of organizational decisions.

B Resources spent on these activities; suboptimal decisions; organizational adjustments anticipating influencing activities.

C Employees in a unit with relatively bad perspectives experience a higher probability of being fired than employees in other units. They will develop influencing activities to keep their jobs.

D Selling the department is a way to prevent influencing activities in situations where managers are threatened with resignation.

E A general education simplifies transferring people from one training to another and therefore decreases the chance of resignation.

8.10 A Mechanisms to reduce influencing costs:
- Reduce the communication between the general board and the faculties:
- Ignore or prohibit political games by the faculties;
- Withhold information the faculties need to play political games effectively;
- Take 'once-and-for-all decisions' regarding the allocation of financial resources;
- Create bureaucracies which are insensitive to the influencing activities of the faculties.
- Reduce the results on the division of welfare of decisions regarding the allocation of financial resources (e.g. the salaries members of a faculty receive);

- Decentralize and separate the faculties (e.g. separate the faculty of economics from the other faculties);
- Structure decision-making processes so that the influencing activities of the faculties are reduced (e.g. introduce strict rules for the allocation of financial resources);
- Remove the general board (i.e. split up the university into several autonomous faculties).

B The decision whether to allow a student to take an oral instead of a written exam should be centralized. This reduces the costs students incur in their efforts to influence professors. The costs they incur in influencing the student counsellor are probably less, because the student counsellor applies a collection of rigid rules. Besides, the student counsellor probably takes better decisions because he or she has more relevant information at his or her disposal (e.g. the progress a student has made in his or her education).

8.11 The structure of this question is analogous to the structure of the questions in Chapter 6.

9.1 A Inefficient bargaining and income effects.
B Selective intervention. Reduce influencing activities by decreasing differences in salary.
C Both.

9.2 Training for idiosyncratic tasks occurs on the job (teaching by doing, learning by doing). This involves the risk of employees who already perform these tasks keeping their knowledge to themselves and using it to their own advantage.

9.3 Problem: the difference between human and physical assets. Human assets, like talent and experience, are inalienable from the owner. Physical assets, like money and machines, can be allocated to people by the board of directors.

In order to strive for horizontal synergy, the board of directors has to position itself explicitly as the 'owner' of all physical assets and to allocate these so as to make the employees use their talent, knowledge and experience as productive as possible.

9.4 The percentage of specific investments by Heineken has increased. In order to make sure Heineken continues to make efficient investment decisions, the bargaining power of Heineken regarding the quasi-surplus should increase.

9.5 A A hold-up problem exists when no surplus-generating specific investment is made at all because the other party is suspected of neglecting its agreements because of opportunistic behaviour.
B Incomplete contracts.
C The size of the (quasi-) surplus, the size of the specificity of the investment and the division of bargaining power.

9.6   The first column changes in 1,0,0 and the second column in ½, ½, 0.

9.7   A Average marginal value added over all possible sequences of the grand coalition.
      B and C

Investor	Governance structure	$v(\theta)$	$v(1)$	$v(2)$	$v(12)$
Farmer	Farmer integration	0	$2r$	0	$2r$
Farmer	Market exchange	0	r	0	$2r$
Processor	Farmer integration	0	0	0	$2s$
Processor	Market exchange	0	0	s	$2s$

      D $1.5r < K =< 2r$ and $L =< s$.

10.1 A Negatively; it becomes more attractive to deviate.
      B Negatively; it becomes more attractive to deviate.
      C Negatively; deviations are more difficult to detect.
      D Negatively; deviations are more difficult to detect.
      E Positively; because deviations are easier to detect.

11.1 A Negative slope.
      B Vertical.
      C Negative slope.
      D Positive slope.

11.2 C Entrant: E.
         Incumbent: C.
         and:
         Entrant: N.
         Incumbent: R.
      D The second equilibrium.
      F The difference in payment to the incumbent in the SPE between the parts E and B
         is $50 - 20 = 30$.

11.3 B Entrant: S.
         Incumbent: (C,P).
      D The scale of entry.
      E Hard.
      F Puppy Dog.

11.4 A The demand for Modak as well as that for Kinolta will increase because when there is compatibility the consumers can choose between more products.

B The reaction function has a positive slope in a market with substitute products and price competition.

C The extent of compatibility.

D Soft. More compatibility results in more demand for the rival, which increases the profits of the rival.

E The Fat Cat strategy of overinvesting in compatibility. (The reaction function of Modak shifts to the right, the reaction function of Kinolta upward.)

F The Lean and Hungry strategy of underinvestment in compatibility.

12.1 A The ratio of the cognitive capacities of the decision-maker and the complexity of the problem.

B The level of complexity of the problem is reduced.

C {(D), (A), (C), (I)} applies to the P-students, while a U-student starts the lecture with partitioning {(D,A),(C,I)}.

12.2 Suppose the engineer is sensitive to the engineering aspects i_1 and i_2, but does not distinguish the sociological aspects s_1 and s_2. The opposite holds for the sociologist. This results in the following partitioning for the two board members: .

Engineer: $\{((i_1,s_1),(i_1,s_2)),((i_2,s_1),(i_2,s_2))\}$.

Sociologist: $\{((s_1,i_1),(s_1,i_2)),((s_2,i_1),(s_2,i_2))\}$.

12.4 A.

B 1[0]1[0]0.

1.

C 11[1[0]1[0]0]11[1[0]1[0]0]1[0]1[0]0.

2.

12.5 A An organization which rejects a project only when everyone rejects it.

B 0.25.

C A polyarchy makes a lot of type II mistakes.

D Hierarchy (13.2 > 10.8).

E 13.2 – 12 = 1.2.

F Yes; yes; no.

G Decrease the probability of acceptance.

12.6 1,0.

12.7 A A decision-making procedure which aggregates local decisions into an organization decision.
B A set of bureaus.
C Loss accompanied by the acceptance of a bad project.

13.1 A It predicts the same. Expenses made in the past are sunk, which means they don't matter in the present behaviour.
B It predicts more for those who received a free ticket. Expenses made in the past determine the point of reference.

13.2 No. In the expected benefit theory changes in the financial position result in a change of behaviour. A quarter has no effect in this view. In the cumulative prospect theory, profit or loss compared with the starting position is the force of behaviour.

13.3 A A maximizing strategy is to work longer hours on good days and to quit early on bad days.
B They will end up quitting early on good days and working longer on bad days, precisely the opposite of the rational strategy.

14.1 A Yes; the requirement of two or more Nash equilibria is met.
B A solution entails reducing the number of equilibria to one. For example, create a culture which would indicate in these situations that they will split 50–50.

14.2 A Co-ordination problem.
B Efficiency of the solution, i.e. does the co-ordination mechanism result in an efficient solution when all of the information is available? Complexity of the mechanism, i.e. is the mechanism simple regarding the cognitive capacity of the participants? Robustness of the mechanism, i.e. how sensitive is the mechanism to wrong information?.
C Arriving first: not always efficient, simple, not robust.
Claiming urgency: efficient, simple, not robust.

14.4 A Efficiency, robustness, complexity.
B Quantity instrument.
C Both instruments select the efficient solution in case of complete information and have the same complexity. The criterion of robustness is therefore decisive, which results in the answer to question B.

14.5 A No.
C No.

14.6 A Both instruments perform equally well.
C Quantity instrument.

14.7 Yes.

14.8 A A situation with several (Nash) equilibria. Decrease the possibilities of choice, create one decision-maker, generate extra information and change the payments.
    B A system of attributes.
    C No; a 'best system practice' is advised instead of a 'best aspect practice'.
    D No; all attributes have to be changed simultaneously in order to generate synergies or complementarities.

15.1 A A co-ordination problem.
    B The marketing department will choose between low and high sales, whereas the production department will choose between low or high capacity.
    C Appoint a co-ordinator, change the payments, decrease the possibilities of choice, merge two departments into one.

15.2 A co-ordination problem. The economic system is perceived as a cluster of attributes, with synergies or complementarities between the attributes. The attractive aspects of two different systems cannot be combined. They cannot form an equilibrium, which causes a reversion to one of the two systems.
    The attractiveness of a system is determined by the circumstances. As a society a choice has to be made for one system of organization. (The system or package of attributes chosen will contain both attractive and unattractive values of the aspects or attributes. However, this is unavoidable.)

References

Admati, A.R. and M. Perry (1991) 'Joint Projects without Commitment', *Review of Economic Studies*, 58, 259–276.

Aghion, P. and P. Bolton (1989) 'The Financial Structure of the Firm and the Problem of Control', *European Economic Review*, 33(2), 286–293.

Aghion, P. and P. Bolton (1992) 'An Incomplete Contracts Approach to Financial Contracting', *Review of Economic Studies*, 59, 473–494

Aghion, P. and J. Tirole (1997) 'Formal and Real Authority in Organizations', *Journal of Political Economy*, 105(1), 1–29

Akerlof, G.A. (1970) 'The Market for Lemons: Qualitative Uncertainty and the Market Mechanism', *Quarterly Journal of Economics*, 84(3), 488–500.

Akerlof, G.A. (1976) 'The Economics of Caste and of the Rat Race and other Woeful Tales', *Quarterly Journal of Economics*, 90(4), 599–617.

Akerlof, G.A. (1991) 'Procrastination and Obedience', *American Economic Review*, 81(2), 1–19.

Alchian, A. and H. Demsetz (1972) 'Production, Information Costs, and Economic Organization', *American Economic Review*, 62(5), 777–795.

Anderson, E. and D.C. Schmittlein (1984) 'Integration of the Sales Force: An Empirical Examination', *Rand Journal of Economics*, 15(3), 385–395.

Aoki, M. (1989) 'The Nature of the Japanese Firm as a Nexus of Employment and Financial Contracts: An Overview', *Journal of the Japanese and International Economies*, 3(3), 345–366.

Aoki, M. (1990) 'Toward an Economic Model of the Japanese Firm', *Journal of Economic Literature*, 28(1), 1–27.

Arrow, K.J. (1974) *The Limits of Organization*, Norton, New York.

Arrow, K.J. (1985a) 'Informational Structure of the Firm', *American Economic Review*, 75(2), 303–307.

Arrow, K.J. (1985b) 'The Economics of Agency', in Pratt, J.W. and R.J. Zeckhauser (eds), *Principals and Agents: The Structure of Business*, Harvard Business School Press, Cambridge, Massachusetts, pp. 37–51.

Arrow, K.J. (1994) 'Methodological Individualism and Social Knowledge', *American Economic Review*, 84(2), 1–9.

Arrow, K.J. (1997) 'Invaluable Goods', *Journal of Economic Literature*, 35(2), 757–765.

Arrow, K.J. and G. Debreu (1954) 'Existence of an Equilibrium for a Competitive Economy', *Econometrica*, 22(3), 265–290.

Arthur, W.B. (1994) 'Inductive Reasoning and Bounded Rationality', *American Economic Review*, 84(2), 406–411.

Asanuma, B. (1989) 'Manufacturer–Supplier Relationships in Japan and the Concept of Relation-Specific Capital', *Journal of the Japanese and International Economies*, 3, 1–30.

Athey, S. and S. Stern (1996) *An Empirical Framework for Testing Theories about Complementarities in Organizational Design*, working paper, MIT, Cambridge, Massachusetts.

Aumann, R. (1987) 'Game Theory', in Eatwell, J., M. Milgate and P. Newman (eds), *The New Palgrave: A Dictionary of Economics*, Macmillan, London, pp. 460–482.

Axelrod, R. (1984) *The Evolution of Cooperation*, Basic Books, New York.

Bajari, P. and S. Tadelis (2001) 'Incentives versus Transaction Costs: A Theory of Procurement Contracts', *RAND Journal of Economics*, 32(3), 387–407.

Baker, G.P. (1992) 'Incentive Contracts and Performance Measurement', *Journal of Political Economy*, 100(3), 598–614.

Baker, G. (2000) 'The Use of Performance Measures in Incentive Contracting', *American Economic Review*, 90(2), 415–420.

Baker, G., R. Gibbons and K.J. Murphy (1999) 'Informal Authority in Organizations', *Journal of Law, Economics, and Organization*, 15(1), 56–73.

Baker, G., R. Gibbons and K.J. Murphy (2002) 'Relational Contracts and the Theory of the Firm', *Quarterly Journal of Economics*, 117(1), 39–84.

Baker, G.P. and T.N. Hubbard (2001) 'Empirical Strategies in Contract Economics: Information and the Boundary of the Firm', *American Economic Review*, 91(2), 189–194.

Baron, J.N. and M.T. Hannan (1994) 'The Impact of Economics on Contemporary Sociology', *Journal of Economic Literature*, 32(3), 1111–1146.

Barzel, Y. (1982) 'Measurement Cost and the Organization of Markets', *Journal of Law and Economics*, 25(1), 27–48.

Baumol, W.J. (1959) *Business Behavior, Value, and Growth*, Macmillan, New York.

Becker, G. and K.J. Murphy (1992) 'The Division of Labor, Coordination Costs, and Knowledge', *Quarterly Journal of Economics*, 107(4), 1137–1160.

Benartzi, S. and R.H. Thaler (1995) 'Myopic Loss Aversion and the Equity Premium Puzzle', *Quarterly Journal of Economics*, 111(1), 73–92.

Berglof, E. (1989) 'Capital Structure as a Mechanism of Control – A Comparison of Financial Systems', in Aoki, M., B. Gustafsson, and O.E. Williamson, Sage, London, 237–262.

Berle, A.A. and G.C. Means (1932) *The Modern Corporation and Private Property*, New York, Commerce Clearing House.

Bernstein, P.L. (1996) *Against the Odds; the Remarkable Story of Risk*, Wiley, New York.

Bester, H. (1985) 'Screening vs. Rationing in Credit Markets with Imperfect Information', *American Economic Review*, 75(4), 850–855.

Bhattacharya, S. (1979) 'Imperfect Information, Dividend Policy, and the "Bird in the Hand Fallacy"', *Bell Journal of Economics*, 10, 259–270.

Bijl, P. de (1996) *Essays in Industrial Organization and Management Strategy*, Tilburg University Press, Tilburg.

Bikhchandani, S., D. Hirshleifer and I. Welch (1992) 'A Theory of Fads, Fashion, Custom, and Cultural Change as Informational Cascades', *Journal of Political Economy*, 100(5), 992–1026.

Bikhchandani, S., D. Hirshleifer and I. Welch(1998) 'Learning from the Behavior of Others: Conformity, Fads, and Informational Cascades', *Journal of Economic Perspectives*, 12(3), 151–170.

Bolton, P. and J. Farrell (1990) 'Decentralization, Duplication, and Delay', *Journal of Political Economy*, 98(4), 803–826.

Bolton, P. and D.S. Scharfstein (1998) 'Corporate Finance, the Theory of the Firm, and Organizations', *Journal of Economic Perspectives*, 12(4), 95–114.

Bonanno, G. and J. Vickers (1988) 'Vertical Separation', *Journal of Industrial Economics*, 36(3), 257–265.

Boycko, M., A. Shleifer and R. Vishny (1995) *Privatising Russia*, MIT Press, Cambridge, Massachusetts.

Brander, J.A. and T.R. Lewis (1986) 'Oligopoly and Financial Structure: The Limited Liability Effect', *American Economic Review*, 76(5), 956–970.

Bresnahan, T.F., E. Brynjolfsson and L.M. Hitt (2002) 'Information Technology, Workplace Organization, and the Demand for Skilled Labor: Firm – Level Evidence', *Quarterly Journal of Economics*, 117(1), 339–376.

Brynjolfsson, E. and L.M. Hitt (2000) 'Beyond Computation: Information Technology, Organizational Transformation and Business Performance', *Journal of Economic Perspectives*, 14(4), 23–48.

Bulow, J., J. Geanakoplos and P. Klemperer (1985) Multimarket Oligopoly: Strategic Substitutes and Complements', *Journal of Political Economy*, 93(3), 488–511.

Busenitz, L.W. and J.B. Barney (1994) 'Biases and Heuristics in Strategic Decision Making: Differences between Entrepreneurs and Managers in Large Organizations', *Academy of Management Proceedings*, 85–89.

Califano, J.A. (1986) 'A Revolution Looms in American Health', *New York Times*, 25 March.

Camerer, C.F., L. Babcock, G. Loewenstein and R.H. Thaler (2000) 'Labor Supply of New York City Cab Drivers', in Kahneman, D. and A. Tversky (eds), *Choices, Values, and Frames*, Cambridge University Press, Cambridge.

Cheung, S.N.S. (1973) 'The Fable of the Bees: An Economic Investigation', *Journal of Law and Economics*, 16(1), 11–34.

Chandler, A.D. (1962) Strategy *and Structure*, MIT Press, Cambridge, Massachusetts.

Chandler, A.D. (1966) Strategy *and Structure*, Anchor Books, New York.

Coase, R.H. (1937) 'The Nature of the Firm', *Economica*, 4(6), 386–405.

Coase, R.H. (1960) 'The Problem of Social Cost', *Journal of Law and Economics*, 3(1), 1–44.

Coase, R.H. (1992) 'The Institutional Structure of Production', *American Economic Review*, 82(4), 713–719.

Cohen, M.D., J.M. March and J.P. Olsen (1972) 'A Garbage Can Model of Organizational Choice', *Administrative Science Quarterly*, 17(1), 1–25.

Coleman, J.S. (1990) *Foundations of Social Theory*, Harvard University Press, Cambridge, Massachusetts.

Cosmides, L. and J. Tooby (1994) 'Better than Rational: Evolutionary Psychology and the Invisible Hand', *American Economic Review*, 84(2), 327–332.

De Sitter, L.U. (1994) *Synergetisch Produceren*, Van Gorcum, Assen.

Debreu, G. (1959) *The Theory of Value*, Wiley, New York.

Demski, J.S. (1980) *Information Analysis*, Addison-Wesley, Reading, Massachusetts.

Demski, J. and D.E.M. Sappington (1984) 'Optimal Incentive Contracts with Multiple Agents', *Journal of Economic Theory*, 33(1), 152–171.

Dewatripont, M. and G. Roland(1995) 'The Design of Reform Packages under Uncertainty', *American Economic Review*, 85(5), 1207–1223.

Dewatripont, M. and G. Roland (1997) 'Transition as a Process of Large-Scale Institutional Change', in Kreps, D.M. and K.F. Wallace (eds), *Advances in Economics and Econometrics*, vol. 2, Cambridge University Press, Cambridge.

Diamond, D.W. (1989) 'Reputation Acquisition in Debt Markets', *Journal of Political Economy*, 97(4), 828–862.

Dixit, A.K. (1996) *The Making of Economic Policy*, MIT Press, Cambridge, Massachusetts.

Dixit, A. and B. Nalebuff (1991) 'Making Strategies Credible', in Zeckhauser, R.J. (ed.), *Strategy and Choice*, MIT Press, Cambridge, Massachusetts, 161–184.

Doeringer, P.B. and M.J. Piore (1971) *Internal Labor Markets and Manpower Analysis*, Lexington Press, New York.

Douma, S.W. (1988) 'Innoveren, Organiseren en Concurreren', *Maandblad voor Accountancy en Bedrijf-shuishoudkunde*, 62, 227–242.

Elster, J. (1991) 'Local Justice', *European Economic Review*, 35(2), 273–291.

Evans, D.S. and S.J. Grossman (1983) 'Integration', in Evans, D.S. (ed.), *Breaking up Bell: Essays on Industrial Organization and Regulation*, North Holland, New York, 95–126.

Fama, E.F. (1998) 'Market Efficiency, Long-Term Returns, and Behavioral Finance', *Journal of Financial Economics*, 49, 283–306.

Farrell, J. and N.T. Gallini (1988) 'Second-Sourcing as a Commitment: Monopoly Incentives to Attract Competition', *Quarterly Journal of Economics*, 103(4), 673–694.

Farrell, J. and G. Saloner (1985) 'Standardization, Compatibility, and Innovation', *Rand Journal of Economics*, 16(1), 70–83.

Farrell, J. and G. Saloner (1986) 'Installed Base and Compatibility: Innovation, Product Preannouncements, and Predation', *American Economic Review*, 76(5), 940–955.

Fayol, H. (1949 [1916]) *General and Industrial Management*, Pitman, London.

Fershtman, C. (1996) 'On the Value of Incumbency: Managerial Reference Point and Loss Aversion', *Journal of Economic Psychology*, 17(2), 245–257.

Fershtman, C. and E. Kalai (1993) 'Complexity Considerations and Market Behavior', *Rand Journal of Economics*, 24(2), 224–235.

Ford, H. (1922) My *Life and Work*, Doubleday, London.

Frank, R.H. (1985) *Choosing the Right Pond*, Oxford University Press, New York.

Freeman, R.E. (1984) *Strategic Management, a Stakeholder Approach*, Pitman, London.

Frey, B.S. and F. Oberholzer-Gee (1997) 'The Costs of Price Incentives: An Empirical Analysis of Motivation Crowding-Out', *American Economic Review*, 87(4), 746–755.

Friedman, M. (1953) Essays *in Positive Economics*, University of Chicago Press, Chicago, Illinois.

Fudenberg, D. and E. Maskin (1986) 'The Folk Theorem in Repeated Games with Discounting or with Incomplete Information', *Econometrica*, 54(3), 533–554. ,

Fudenberg, D. and J. Tirole (1984) 'The Fat-Cat Effect, the Puppy-Dog Ploy, and the Lean and Hungry Look', *American Economic Review*, 74(2), 361–366. ,

Garicano, L. (2000) 'Hierarchies and the Organization of Knowledge in Production', *Journal of Political Economy*, 2000, 108(5), 874–904.

Gates, S., P. Milgrom and J. Roberts (1996) 'Complementarities in the Transition from Socialism: A Firm-Level Analysis', in McMillan, J. and B. Naughton (eds), *Reforming Asian Socialism: The Growth of Market Institutions*, University of Michigan Press, Ann Arbor.

Geanakoplos, J. and P. Milgrom (1991) 'A Theory of Hierarchies Based on Limited Managerial Attention', *Journal of the Japanese and International Economies*, 5, 205–225.

Gibbard, A. (1973) 'Manipulation of Voting Schemes: A General Result', *Econometrica*, 41(4), 587–601.

Gibbons, R. (1999) 'Taking Coase Seriously', *Administrative Science Quarterly*, 44, 145–157.

Gibbons, R. and K.J. Murphy (1990) 'Relative Performance Evaluation for Chief Executive Officers', *Industrial and Labor Relations Review*, 43, 30–51.

Green, J.R. and N.L. Stokey (1983) 'A Comparison of Tournaments and Contracts', *Journal of Political Economy*, 9(13), 349–364.

Greif, A. (1993) 'Contract Enforceability and Economic Institutions in Early Trade: The Maghribi Traders' Coalition', *American Economic review*, 83(3), 525–548.

Greif, A. (1994) 'Cultural Beliefs and the Organization of Society: A Historical and Theoretical Reflection on Collectivist and Individualist Societies', *Journal of Political Economy*, 102(5), 912–950.

Greif, A., P. Milgrom and B.R. Weingast (1994) 'Coordination, Commitment, and Enforcement: The Case of the Merchant Gild', *Journal of Political Economy*, 102(4), 745–776.

Grossman, S.J. (1981) 'The Informational Role of Warranties and Private Disclosure about Product Quality', *Journal of Law and Economics*, 24(2), 461–483.

Grossman, S.J. and O.D. Hart (1982) 'Corporate Financial Structure and Managerial Incentives', in McCall, J. (ed.), *The Economics of Information and Uncertainty*, University of Chicago Press, Chicago, Illinois, 107–140.

Grossman, S.J. and O.D. Hart (1986) 'The Cost and Benefits of Ownership: A Theory of Vertical and Lateral Integration', *Journal of Political Economy*, 94(4), 691–719.

Groves, T. (1973) 'Incentives in Teams', *Econometrica*, 41(4), 617–631.

Hammond, T.H. (1994) 'Structure, Strategy, and the Agenda of the Firm', in Rumelt, R.P., D.E. Schendel and D.J. Teece (eds), *Fundamental Issues in Strategy*, Harvard Business School Press, Boston, Massachusetts, 97–154.

Hannan, M.J. and J. Freeman (1977) 'The Population Ecology of Organizations', *American Journal of Sociology*, 82, 929–64.

Harris, M. and A. Raviv (1991) 'The Theory of Capital Structure', *Journal of Finance*, 46(1), 297–355.

Hart, O. (1995) *Firms, Contracts, and Financial Structure*, Clarendon Press, Oxford.

Hart, O. (2001) 'Financial Contracting', *Journal of Economic Literature*, 39(4), 1079–1100.

Hart, O. (forthcoming) 'Norms and the Theory of the Firm', in Brousseau, E. and J. Glachant (eds), *The Economics of Contract in Prospect and Retrospect*, Cambridge University Press, Cambridge.

Hart, O. and J. Moore (1990) 'Property Rights and the Nature of the Firm', *Journal of Political Economy*, 98(6), 1119–1158.

Hart, O. and J. Moore (1996) 'The Governance of Exchanges: Members' Cooperatives Versus Outside Ownership', *Oxford Review of Economic Policy*, 12(4), 53–69.

Hayek, F. (1945) 'The Use of Knowledge in Society', *American Economic Review*, 35(4), 519–530.

Heiner, R.A. (1983) 'The Origin of Predictable Behavior', *American Economic Review*, 73(4), 560–595.

Hellwig, M. (1989) 'Asymmetric Information, Financial Markets, and Financial Institutions', *European Economic Review*, 33, 277–285.

Hendel, I. and A. Lizzeri (1999) 'Adverse Selection in Durable Goods Markets', *American Economic Review*, 89(5), 1097–1115.

Hendrikse, G.W.J. (1991) 'Organizational Choice and Product Differentiation', *Managerial and Decisions Economics*, 12, 361–366.

Hendrikse, G.W.J. (1993) 'Individual and Group Aspects of Corporate Culture' *Tijdschrift voor Economie en Management*, 38(1), 7–22.

Hendrikse, G.W.J. and C.P. Veerman (1997) 'Marketing Cooperatives as a System of Attributes', in van Dijk, G. and J. Nilsson (eds), *Strategies and Structures in the Agro-Food Industries*, Van Gorcum, Assen.

Hendrikse G.W.J. and C.P. Veerman (2001a) 'Marketing Co-operatives: An Incomplete Contracting Perspective', *Journal of Agricultural Economics*, 52(1), 53–64.

Hendrikse G.W.J. and C.P. Veerman (2001b) 'Marketing Cooperatives and Financial Structure: A Transaction Costs Analysis', *Agricultural Economics*, 26, 205–216.

Hermalin, B.E. (1998) 'Toward an Economic Theory of Leadership, Leading by Example', *American Economic Review*, 88(5), 1188–1206.

Holland, J.H. (1975) 'Adaptation *in Natural and Artificial Systems*', University of Michigan Press, Ann Arbor.

Holmström, B.R. (1979) 'Moral Hazard and Observability', *Bell Journal of Economics*, 10(1), 74–91.

Holmström, B.R. (1982) 'Moral Hazard in Teams', *Bell Journal of Economics*, 13(2), 324–340.

Holmström, B.R. (1989) 'Agency Costs and Innovation', *Journal of Economic Behavior and Organization*, 12, 305–327.

Holmström, B.R. and P. Milgrom (1991) 'Multitask Principal–Agent Analysis: Incentive Contracts, Asset Ownership, and Job Design', *Journal of Law, Economics, and Organization*, 7, S24–52.

Holmström, B.R. and P. Milgrom (1994) 'The Firm as an Incentive System', *American Economic Review*, 84(4), 972–991.

Holmström, B.R. and J. Tirole (1989) 'The Theory of the Firm', in Schmalensee, R. and R.D. Willig (eds), *Handbook of Industrial Organization*, North Holland, Amsterdam.

Hulst, W.G.H. van and J.G.L.M. Willems (1992) *Externe Organisatie*, Stenfert Kroese, Leiden.

Hurwicz, L. (1973) 'The Design of Mechanisms for Resource Allocation', *American Economic Review*, 63(2), 1–30.

Ichiniowski, C., K. Shaw and G. Prennushi (1997) 'The Effects of Human Resource Practices on Productivity: A Study of Steel Finishing Lines', *American Economic Review*, 87(3), 291–313.

Ickes, B.W. and L. Samuelson (1987) 'Job Transfers and Incentives in Complex Organizations: Thwarting the Ratchet Effect', *Rand Journal of Economics*, 18(2), 275–286.

Imai, K. and H. Itami (1984) 'Interpenetration of Organization and Market: Japan's Firm and Market in Comparison with the U.S.', *International Journal of Industrial Organization*, 2(4), 285–310.

Itoh, H. (1987) 'Information Processing Capacities of the Firm', *Journal of the Japanese and International Economies*, 1(3), 299–326.

Itoh, H. (1991) 'Incentives to Help in Multi-Agent Situations', *Econometrica*, 59(3), 611–636.

Jensen, M.C. (1986) 'Agency Costs of Free Cash Flow, Corporate Finance, and Takeovers', *American Economic Review*, 76(2), 323–329.

Jensen, M. and W. Meckling (1976) 'Theory of the Firm: Managerial Behavior, Agency Costs and Capital Structure', *Journal of Financial Economics*, 3, 305–360.

Joskow, P.L. (1987) 'Contract Duration and Relationship-Specific Investments: Empirical Evidence from Coal Markets', *American Economic Review*, 77(1), 168–185.

Joskow, P.L. (1998) R. Schmalensee, and E.M. Bailey, 'The Market for Sulfur Dioxide Emissions', *American Economic Review*, 88(4), 669–685.

Kalman, R.E. (1993) 'Probability and Science', *Nieuw Archief voor Wiskunde*, 11(1), 51–66.

Kaplan, R.S. and A.A. Atkinson (1989) *Advanced Management Accounting*, Prentice-Hall, Englewood Cliffs, New Jersey.

Kaplan, S.N. and P. Stromberg (2001) *Financial Contracting Theory Meets the Real World: An Empirical Analysis of Venture Capital Contracts*, University of Chicago Press, Chicago, Illinois.

Kauffman, S.A. (1993) The *Origins of Order*, Oxford University Press, Oxford.

Kawasaki, S. and J. McMillan (1987) 'The Design of Contracts: Evidence from Japanese Subcontracting', *Journal of the Japanese and International Economies*, 1(3), 327–349.

Kay, J. (1996) *The Business of Economics*, Oxford University Press, Oxford.

Kenney, R. and B. Klein (1983) 'The Economics of Block Bookings', *Journal of Law and Economics*, 26(2), 497–540.

Kim, H.M. and G.R. Parker (1995) 'When Meritocracies Fail', *Journal of Economic Behavior and Organization*, 28(1), 1–10.

Klein, B., R.G. Crawford and A.A. Alchian (1978) 'Vertical Integration, Appropriable Rents and the Competitive Contracting Process', *Journal of Law and Economics*, 21(2), 297–326.

Klitgaard, R. (1985) *Controlling Corruption*, University of California Press, Berkeley.

Knight, F. (1921) *Risk, Uncertainty and Profit*, Houghton Mifflin, Boston, Massachusetts.

Kreps, D.M. (1990a) *A Course in Microeconomic Theory*, Harvester Wheatsheaf, New York.

Kreps, D.M. (1990b) 'Corporate Culture and Economic Theory', in Alt, J.E. and K.A. Shepsle (eds), *Perspectives on Positive Political Economy*, Cambridge University Press, 90–143.

Kreps, D.M. (1997) 'Intrinsic Motivation and Extrinsic Incentives', *American Economic Review*, 87(2), 359–364.

Lafontaine, F. (1992) 'Agency Theory and Franchising: Some Empirical Results', *Rand Journal of Economics*, 23(2), 263–283.

Lazear, E.P. (1979) 'Why Is There Mandatory Retirement?', *Journal of Political Economy*, 87(6), 1261–1284.

Lazear, E.P. (1999a) 'Globalisation and the Market for Team Mates', *Economic Journal*, 109(454), C15–C40.

Lazear, E.P. (1999b) 'Personnel Economics: Past Lessons and Future Directions', *Journal of Labour Economics*, 17(2), 199–236.

Lazear, E.P. and S. Rosen (1981) 'Rank-Order Tournaments as Optimum Labor Contracts', *Journal of Political Economy*, 89(5), 841–864.

Lee, I.H. (1995) *Market Crashes and Informational Avalanches*, University of Southampton, Southampton.

Lettau, M. (1993) Risk-*Taking Bias in a Financial Market with Adaptive Agents*, Princeton University Press, Princeton, New Jersey.

Li, S. (1999) *The Benefits and Costs of Relation-based Governance: An Explanation of the East Asian Miracle and Crisis*, City University of Hong Kong, Hong Kong.

Lux, T. and M. Marchesi (2000) 'Volatility Clustering in Financial Markets: A Micro-Simulation of Interacting Agents', *International Journal of Theoretical and Applied Finance*, 3, 675–702.

Lyons, B. (1987) 'Strategic Behaviour by Firms', in Clarke, R. and T. McGuinness (eds), *The Economics of the Firm*, Basil Blackwell.

McAfee, R.P. and J. McMillan (1987) 'Auctions and Bidding', *Journal of Economic Literature*, 25, 699–754.

McAfee, P. and J. McMillan (1991) 'Optimal Contracts for Teams', *International Economic Review*, 32, 561–577.

Machiavelli, N. (1981 [1513]) *The Prince*, Bantam, New York.

McKelvey, R.D. (1976) 'Intransitivities in Multidimensional Voting Models and Some Implications for Agenda Control', *Journal of Economic Theory*, 12(3), 472–482.

McKelvey, R.D. and T. Page (1999) 'Taking the Coase Theorem Seriously', *Economics and Philosophy*, 15(2), 235–247.

MacLeod, W.B. and J.M. Malcomson (1988) 'Reputation and Hierarchy in Dynamic Models of Employment', *Journal of Political Economy*, 96(4), 832–854.

McMillan, J. (1995) 'Reorganizing Vertical Supply Chains', in Siebert, H. (ed.), *Trends in Business Organization: Do Participation and Cooperation Increase Competitiveness?*, J.C.B. Mohr (Paul Siebeck), Tubingen, 203–222.

McMillan, J. and C. Woodruff (1999a) 'Interfirm Relationships and Informal Credit in Vietnam', *Quarterly Journal of Economics*, 114(4), 1285–1320.

McMillan, J. and C. Woodruff (1999b) 'Dispute Prevention without the Courts', *Journal of Law, Economics, and Organization*, 15(3), 637–660.

Maki, U. (2001) 'The Way the World Works (www): Towards an Ontology of Theory Choice', in Maki, U. (ed.), *The Economic World View, Studies in the Ontology of Economics*, Cambridge University Press, Cambridge, 369–389.

Malcomson, J.M. (1984) 'Work Incentives, Hierarchy, and Internal Labor Markets', *Journal of Political Economy*, 92(3), 486–507.

March, J.G. (1988) *Decisions and Organizations*, Basil Blackwell, Oxford.

March, J.G. (1991) 'Exploration *and Exploitation in Organizational Learning*', *Organizational Science* , 2(1), 71–87.

March, J.G. and H.A. Simon (1958) *Organizations*, Wiley, New York.

March, J.G. and H.A. Simon (1993) 'Organizations Revisited', *Industrial and Corporate Change*, 2(3), 299–316.

Marschak, J. and R. Radner (1972) *Economic Theory of Teams*, Yale University Press, New Haven, Connecticut.

Marshall, A. (1890) *Principles of Economics*, Macmillan, London.

Marx, K. (1966 [1863]) *Capital*, Progress Publishers, Moscow.

Maskin, E. and J. Tirole (1992) 'The Principal–Agent Relationship with an Informed Principal, II: Common Values', *Econometrica*, 60(1), 1–42.

Masten, S.E. (1984) 'The Organization of Production: Evidence from the Aerospace Industry', *Journal of Law and Economics*, 27(2), 403–417. Copyright 1984 by The University of Chicago, All rights reserved.

Masten, S.E., J.W. Meehan and E.A. Snyder (1989) Vertical Integration in the U.S. Auto Industry, *Journal of Economic Behavior and Organization*, 12(2), 265–273.

Mathewson, F. and R. Winter (1989) Incomplete *Contracts as Incentive Devices*, Department of Economics, University of Toronto.

Melumad, N., D. Mookerjee, and S. Reichelstein (1992) 'A Theory of Responsibility Centers', *Journal of Accounting and Economics*, 5(4), 445–464.

Meyer, M., P. Milgrom and J. Roberts (1992) 'Organizational Prospects, Influence Costs, and Ownership Changes', *Journal of Economics and Management Strategy*, 1(1), 9–35.

Milgram, S. (1975) *Obedience to Authority: An Experimental View*, Harper & Row, New York.

Milgrom, P. (1988) 'Employment Contracts, Influence Activities and Efficient Organization Design', *Journal of Political Economy*, 96(1), 42–60.

Milgrom, P. and J. Roberts (1987) 'Informational Asymmetries, Strategic Behavior, and Industrial Organization', *American Economic Review*, 77(2), 184–193.

Milgrom, P. and J. Roberts (1988a) 'An Economic Approach to Influence Activities in Organizations', *Supplement to the American Journal of Sociology*, 94, 154–179.

Milgrom, P. and J. Roberts (1988b) 'Communication and Inventory as Substitutes in Organizing Production', *Scandinavian Journal of Economics*, 90(3), 275–289.

Milgrom, P. and J. Roberts (1990a) 'Bargaining Costs, Influence Costs, and the Organization of Economic Activity', in Alt, J.E. and K.A. Shepsle (eds), *Perspectives on Positive Political Economy*, Cambridge University Press, Cambridge, 57–89.

Milgrom, P. and J. Roberts (1990b) 'Rationalizability, Learning, and Equilibrium in Games with Strategic Complementarities', *Econometrica*, 58(6), 1255–1277.

Milgrom, P. and J. Roberts (1990c) 'The Economics of Modern Manufacturing: Technology, Strategy, and Organization', *American Economic Review*, 80(3), 511–528.

Milgrom, P. and J. Roberts (1990d) 'The Efficiency and Equity in Organizational Decision Processes', *American Economic Review*, 80(2), 154–159.

Milgrom, P. and J. Roberts (1992) *Economics, Organization and Management*, Prentice-Hall, Englewood Cliffs, New Jersey.

Milgrom, P. and J. Roberts (1995) Continuous Adjustment and Fundamental Changes in Business Strategy and Organization, in Siebert, H. (ed.), *Trends in Business Organization: Do Particapation and Cooperation Increase Competitiveness?*, J.C.B. Mohr (Paul Siebeck) ,Tubingen.

Miller, G.A. (1956) 'The Magical Number Seven; Plus or Minus Two: Some Limits on our Capacity for Processing Information', *Psychological Review*, 63(2), 81–97.

Modigliani, F. and M. Miller (1958) 'The Cost of Capital, Corporate Finance, and the Theory of Investment', *American Economic Review*, 48(3), 261–297.

Monks, R.A.G. and N. Minow (1995) *Corporate Governance*, Blackwell, New York.

Monteverde, K. and D.J. Teece (1982) 'Supplier Switching Costs and Vertical Integration in the Automobile Industry', *Bell Journal of Economics*, 13(1), 206–213.

Myers, S.C. (2001) 'Capital Structure', *Journal of Economic Perspectives*, 15(2), 81–102.

Myerson, R. (1979) 'Incentive Compatibility and the Bargaining Problem', *Econometrica*, 47(1), 61–73.

Myerson, R.B. (1999) 'Nash Equilibrium and the History of Economic Theory', *Journal of Economic Literature*, 37(3), 1067–1082.

Nelson, P. (1974) 'Advertising as Information', *Journal of Political Economy*, 81(4), 729–754.

Nelson, R. and S. Winter (1982) An *Evolutionary Theory of Economic Change*, Harvard University Press, Cambridge, Massachusetts.

Noldeke, G. and K.M. Schmidt (1995) 'Option Contracts and Renegotiation: A Solution to the Hold-Up Problem', *RAND Journal of Economics*, 26(2), 163–179.

North, D.C. (1991) 'Institutions', *Journal of Economic Perspectives*, 5(1), 97–112.

North, D.C. and R.P. Thomas (1973) *The Rise of the Western World*, Cambridge University Press, Cambridge.

Panzar, J.C. and J.N. Rosse (1984) *Structure, Conduct, and Comparative Statics*, Stanford University, Stanford, California.

Pareto, V. (1971 [1909]) *Manual of Political Economy*, Macmillan, London.

Peter, L.J. (1970) *The Peter Principle*, Morrow, London.

Porter, M.E. (1980) *Competitive Strategy*, Free Press, New York.

Porter, M.E. (1990) The *Competitive Advantage of Nations*, Free Press, New York.

Postrel, S. and R.P. Rumelt (1992) 'Incentives, Routines, and Self-Command', *Industrial and Corporate Change*, 1(3), 397–425.

Prusinkiewicz, P. and A. Lindenmayer (1990) The *Algorithmic Beauty of Plants*, Springer, Berlin.

Rabin, M. (1998) 'Psychology and Economics', *Journal of Economic Literature*, 36(1), 11–46.

Radner, R. (1991) 'Dynamic Games in Organization Theory', *Journal of Economic Behavior and Organization*, 16, 217–260.

Radner, R. (1992) 'Hierarchy: The Economics of Managing', *Journal of Economic Literature*, 30(3), 1382–1415.

Rajan, R. and L. Zingales (1998) 'Power in a Theory of the Firm', *Quarterly Journal of Economics*, 113(2), 387–432.

Remonola, E.M. (1990) 'Understanding International Differences in Leverage Trends', *Federal Reserve Bank of New York Quarterly Review*,15(1), 31–42.

Reynolds, C.W. (1987) 'Flocks, Herds, and Schools: A Distributed Behavioral Model', *Computer Graphics*, 21(4), 25–34.

Reynolds, R.J. and B.R. Snapp (1986) 'The Competitive Effects of Partial Equity Interests and Joint Ventures', *International Journal of Industrial Organizations*, 4, 141–153.

Ricardo, D. (1951 [1821]) *Principles of Political Economy and Taxation*, Cambridge University Press, Cambridge.

Riordan, M.H. (1990) 'What is Vertical Integration? ', in Aoki, M., Gustafsson, B. and O.E. William-son (eds), *The Firm as a Nexus of Treaties*, Sage, London.

Riordan, M.H. and D.E.M. Sappington (1987) 'Information, Incentives, and Organizational Mode', *Quarterly Journal of Economics*, 52(2), 243–263.

Roberts, K.W.S. (1977) 'Voting over Income Tax Schedules', *Journal of Public Economics*, 8, 329–340.

Rose-Ackerman, S. (1978) *Corruption; A Study in Political Economy*, Academic Press, New York.

Rotemberg, J.J. and G. Saloner (1993) 'Leadership Styles and Incentives', *Management Science*, 39(11), 1299–1318.

Rotemberg, J.J. and G. Saloner (1994) 'Benefits of Narrow Business Strategies', *American Economic Review*, 84(5), 1330–1349.

Rotemberg, J.J. and G. Saloner (1995) 'Overt Interfunctional Conflict (and Its Reduction Through Business Strategy)', *Rand Journal of Economics*, 26(4), 630–653.

Roth, A.E. and I. Erev (1995) 'Learning in Extensive Form Games: Experimental Data and Simple Dynamic Models in the Intermediate Term', *Games and Economic Behavior*, 8(1), 164–212.

Rubinstein, A. (1993) 'On Price Recognition and Computational Complexity in a Monopolistic Model', *Journal of Political Economy*, 101(3), 473–484.

Rubinstein, A. (1998) *Modelling Bounded Rationality*, MIT Press, Cambridge, Massachusetts.

Sah, R.K. (1987) 'Queues, Rations, and Markets', *American Economic Review*, 77(1), 69–77.

Sah, R.K. and J.E. Stiglitz (1986) 'The Architecture of Economic Systems: Hierarchies and Polyarchies', *American Economic Review*, 76(4), 716–727.

Sah, R.K. and J.E. Stiglitz (1988) 'Committees, Hierarchies and Polyarchies', *Economic Journal*, 98, 451–470.

Saloner, G., A. Shephard, and J. Podolny (2001) *Strategic Management*, Wiley, New York.

Salop, J and S. Salop (1976) 'Self-selection and Turnover in the Labor Market', *Quarterly Journal of Economics*, 90(4), 619–628.

Scharfstein, D.S. and J.C. Stein (1990) 'Herd Behavior and Investment', *American Economic Review*, 80(3), 465–479.

Schelling, T. (1960) *The Strategy of Conflict*, Oxford University Press, Oxford.

Schelling, T. (1971) 'Dynamic Modes of Segregation', *Journal of Mathematical Sociology*, 1, 143–186.

Schelling, T. (1978) *Micro Motives and Macro Behavior*, Norton, New York.

Scherer, F.M. (1980) *Industrial Market Structure and Economic Performance*, Houghton Mifflin, Boston, Massachusetts.

Schotter, A.R. (1997) *Micro-economics: A Modern Approach*, Addison-Wesley, Reading, Massachusetts.

Schumpeter, J.A. (1942) *Capitalism, Socialism and Democracy*, Harper, New York.

Selten, R. (1965) 'Spieltheoretische Behandlung eines Oligopolmodells mit Nachfragetragheit', *Zeitschrift fur die Gesamte Staatswissenschaft*, 12(2), 301–324.

Sen, A.K. (1987) 'Rational Behaviour', in Eatwell, J., M. Milgate and P. Newman (eds), *The New Palgrave: A Dictionary of Economics*, Macmillan, London, vol. 4, pp. 68–76.

Shapiro, C. and J.E. Stiglitz (1984) 'Equilibrium Unemployment as a Worker Disciplining Device', *American Economic Review*, 74(3), 433–444.

Shapley, L. (1953) 'A Value for n-Person Games, Contributions to the Theory of Games', *Annals of Mathematical Studies*, 28, 307–317.

Shepard, A. (1987) 'Licensing to Enhance Demand for New Technologies', *Rand Journal of Ecomomics*, 18(3), 360–368.

Sherman, S.J. and E. Corty (1984) 'Cognitive Heuristics', in Wyer, R.S. and T.K. Srull (eds), *Handbook of Social Cognition I*, Erlbaum, Hillsdale, New Jersey.

Sigmund, K. (1993) *Games of Life*, Oxford University Press, Oxford.

Simon, H.A. (1951) 'A Formal Theory of the Employment Relation', *Econometrica*, 19(3), 293–305.

Simon, H.A. (1961) *Administrative Behavior*, Free Press, New York.

Simon, H.A. (1976) *Administrative Behavior*, Free Press, New York.

Simon, H.A. (1990) 'Invariants of Human Behavior', *Annual Review of Psychology*, 41, 1–19.

Simon, H.A. (1991) 'Organizations and Markets', *Journal of Economic Perspectives*, 5(2), 25–44.

Simon, H.A. (1993) 'Altruism and Economics', *American Economic Review*, 83(2), 156–161.

Sinclair-Desgagné, B. (1999) 'How to Restore Higher-Powered Incentives in Multitask Agencies', *Journal of Law, Economics, and Organization*, 15(2), 418–433.

Smith, A. (1976 [1776]) *An Inquiry into the Nature and Causes of the Wealth of Nations*, Clarendon Press, Oxford.

Smith, V. (1989) 'Theory, Experiment and Economics', *Journal of Economic Perspectives*, 3(1), 151–169.

Spence, A.M. (1974) *Market Signaling*, Harvard University Press, Cambridge, Massachusetts.

Spence, A.M. (1977) 'Consumer Misperceptions, Product Failure and Producer Liability', *Review of Economic Studies*, 44(3), 561–572.

Spengler, J.J. (1950) 'Vertical Integration and Antitrust Policy', *Journal of Political Economy*, 58(4), 347–352.

Stiglitz, J.E. and A. Weiss (1981) 'Credit Rationing in Markets with Imperfect Information', *American Economic Review*, 71(3), 393–410.

Sutton, J. (1991) *Sunk Costs and Market Structure*, MIT Press, Cambridge, Massachusetts.

Tadelis, S. (2002) 'Complexity, Flexibility, and the Make-or-Buy Decision', *American Economic Review*, 92(2), 433–437. ,

Tapon, F. (1989) 'A Transaction Costs Analysis of Innovations in the Organization of Pharmaceuti-cal R&D', *Journal of Economic Behavior and Organization*, 12, 197–213.

Taylor, F.M. (1911) *Principles of Scientific Management*, Harper, New York.

Taylor, C.R. and S.N. Wiggins (1997) 'Competition and Compensation: Supplier Incentives under the American and Japanese Subcontracting Systems', *American Economic Review*, 87(4), 598–618.

Teece, D. (1998) 'Capturing Value from Knowledge Assets', *California Management Review*, 40(3), 62–78.

Tirole, J. (1986) 'Hierarchies and Bureaucracies: On the Role of Collusion in Organisations', *Journal of Law, Economics and Organization*, 2(2), 181–214.

Tirole, J. (1989) *The Theory of Industrial Organization*, MIT Press, Cambridge, Masschusetts.

Tirole, J. (1994) 'Incomplete *Contracts*: Where Do We Stand?', *Econometrica*, 67(4), 741–781.

Tirole, J. (2002) 'Rational Irrationality', *European Economic Review*, 46, 633–655.

Tversky, A. and D. Kahneman (1985) 'The Framing of Decisions and the Psychology of Choice', in Wright, G. (ed.), *Behavioral Decision Making*, Plenum Press, New York, 25–41.

Tversky, A. and D. Kahneman (1992) 'Advances in Prospect Theory: Cumulative Representation of Uncertainty', *Journal of Risk and Uncertainty*, 5, 297–323.

Van Cayseele, P.J.G. (1987) 'Economies of Scope in Research and Development', *Journal of Economics*, 47(3), 273–285.

Van Oijen, A.A.C.J. (1997) *Besturing door het Hoofdkantoor en Diversificatie*, Van Oijen, Heusden.

Van Osselaer, S.M.J. and J.W. Alba (2000) 'Consumer Learning and Brand Equity', *Journal of Consumer Research*, 27(1), 1–16.

Varian, H.R. (1978) *Microeconomic Analysis*, Norton, New York.

Vickers, J. (1985) 'Delegation and the Theory of the Firm, Conference Papers', Supplement to *the Economic Journal*, 95, 138s–147s.

Vickrey, W. (*1961*) 'Counterspeculation, Auctions, and Competitive Sealed Tenders, *Journal of Finance*, 16(1), 8–37.

Von Bertalanffy, L. (1968) *General Systems Theory*, George Braziller, New York.

Walras, L. (1954 [1874]) *Elements of Pure Economics*, Allen & Unwin, London.

Weick, K. (1979) *The Social Psychology of Organizing*, Addison-Wesley, Reading, Massachusetts.

Weingast, B.R. (1994) *The Economic Role of Political Institutions: Federalism, Markets, and Economic Development*, working paper, Stanford University.

Weitzman, M.L. (1974) 'Prices vs. Quantities', *Review of Economic Studies*, 41, 477–91.

Williamson, O.E. (1975) *Markets and Hierarchies: Analysis and Antitrust Implications*, Free Press, New York.

Williamson, O.E. (1983) 'Credible Commitments: Using Hostages to Support Exchange', *American Economic Review*, 73(4), 519–540.

Williamson, O.E. (1985) *The Economic Institutions of Capitalism*, Free Press, New York.

Williamson, O.E. (1988) 'Corporate Finance and Corporate Governance', *Journal of Finance*, 43(3), 567–586.

Williamson, O.E. (1991) 'Comparative Economic Organisation: The Analysis of Discrete Structural Alternatives', *Administrative Science Quarterly*, 36, 269–296. © Johnson Graduate School of Management, Cornell University.

Williamson, O.E. (1994) 'Strategizing, Economizing, and Economic Organization', in Rumelt, R.P., D.E. Schendel and D.J. Teece (eds), *Fundamental Issues in Strategy*, Harvard Business School Press, 361–401.

Williamson, O.E. (2000) 'The New Institutional Economics: Taking Stock, Looking Ahead', *Journal of Economic Literature*, 38(3), 595–613.

Williamson, O.E. (2002) 'The Lens of Contract: Private Ordering', *American Economic Review*, 92(2), 438–443.

Williamson, O.E. (forthcoming) 'Transaction Costs Economics', in Menard, C. and M. Shirley (eds), *Handbook of New Institutional Economics*, Kluwer Academic Press, Boston, Massachusetts.

Windsperger, J. (2001) 'The Fee Structure in Franchising: A Property Rights View', *Economic Letters*, 73, 219–226.

Wruck, K.H. and M.C. Jensen (1994) 'Science, Specific Knowledge, and Total Quality Management', *Journal of Accounting and Economics*, 18(2), 247–287.

Zingales, L. (1998) 'Corporate Governance', in Eatwell, J. (ed.), *The New Palgrave of Law and Economics*, Macmillan, London, pp. 497–503.

Zweibel, J. (1996) 'Dynamic Capital Structure and Managerial Entrenchment', *American Economic Review*, 86(5), 1197–1215.

Index